Minority Status, Oppositional Culture, and Schooling

DATE DUE

This book is t   cultural
ecological mo   d during
the past decad   scholarship, which so   hypothesis," is fully p   on of his
new writings   n chap-
ters present   culture
developed. Re   ts of his
cultural ecolog   etween
John Ogbu an   ardent
critics; Ogbu's   cs have
their say.

Minority Status   ontent,
methodology, a   chieve-
ment, school en   ther in
one volume, fo   these
issues as well as   n addition to African   among
Native America   ng for
anyone intereste

Sociocultural, Political, and Historical Studies in Education
Joel Spring, Editor

For additional information on titles in the Studies in Sociocultural, Political and Historical Studies in Education series visit www.routledge.com

Minority Status, Oppositional Culture, and Schooling

Edited by
John U. Ogbu

Routledge
Taylor & Francis Group
NEW YORK AND LONDON

First published 2008
by Routledge
270 Madison Ave, New York, NY 10016

Simultaneously published in the UK
by Routledge
2 Park Square, Milton Park, Abingdon, Oxon OX14 4RN

*Routledge is an imprint of the Taylor & Francis Group, an informa
business*

© 2008 Taylor & Francis Group

Typeset in Sabon by RefineCatch Limited, Bungay, Suffolk
Printed and bound in the United States of America on acid-free
paper by Sheridan Books, Inc.

Library of Congress Cataloging in Publication Data
Ogbu, John U.
Minority status, oppositional culture and academic engagement /
John U. Ogbu.
   p. cm.
Includes bibliographical references and index.
ISBN 978–0–805–85103–8 (hardback : alk. paper) – ISBN 978–0–805–85104–5
(pbk. : alk. paper) 1. Minorities–Education–United States. 2. Children of
immigrants–Education–United States. 3. African Americans–Education–
Social aspects. 4. Academic achievement–United States. 5. Educational
equalization–United States. I. Title.
LC3731.O355 2008
371.829073–dc22

                                                                2007032301

ISBN10: 0–805–85103–8 (hbk)
ISBN10: 0–805–85104–6 (pbk)
ISBN10: 0–203–93196–3 (ebk)

ISBN13: 978–0–805–85103–8 (hbk)
ISBN13: 978–0–805–85104–5 (pbk)
ISBN13: 978–0–203–93196–7 (ebk)

Contents

PART I
History and Framework

Tables and Figures

Tables

Figures

Foreword

Go into any inner city neighborhood, and folks will tell you that government alone can't teach kids to learn. They know that parents have to parent, that children can't achieve unless we raise their expectations and turn off the television sets and eradicate the slander that says a black youth with a book is acting white.

(Barack Obama, Keynote address to the Democratic National Convention, July 27, 2004)

But my hunch is that Brother Obama—as magnificent as he is—still, of course, has his own vision. And his vision is more that of a voluntary immigrant, whereas Black people in America who are descended of slaves are descendants of involuntary immigrants. So there is a sense in which, as brilliant as he is and as wonderful as he is, he tends to lack a certain kind of rage connected to what is meant to be an involuntary immigrant as opposed to a voluntary one.

(Cornel West's analysis of Obama's reference to America as a "magical place" during his Democratic Convention Speech, *Tavis Smiley Show* on National Public Radio, August 4, 2004)

As the quotations above indicate, within the space of eight days surrounding the 2004 Democratic Party's convention, John Ogbu's contributions to understanding the race gap in academic achievement took center stage in the public remarks of two highly visible African Americans, then-Illinois State Senator Barack Obama (and current US Senator and candidate to be the Democratic Party's presidential nominee) and Professor Cornel West. Putting aside the lack of nuance in Obama's analytic use of the concept of "acting White," it remains remarkable that such a prominent U.S. politician invoked a facet of John's work (one small element of his oppositional cultural framework) and that a leading American intellectual contextualized the former's remarks by drawing upon another aspect of John's *oeuvre* (the distinction between immigrant and involuntary minorities). The two comments are emblematic of the profound effect

John Ogbu has on American thought and discourse both in and out of the academy. John's seminal contributions to how pundits, parents, politicians, and the public think about the processes and outcomes of minority students' education cannot be overstated.

Obama and West are only two of the public figures who have drawn from John's work. According to Erin Horvat and Carla O'Connor (2006), between 1986 and 2004 as many as 158 popular press articles made reference to the "acting White" hypothesis. John was mentioned in the *New York Times*'s compilation of the 4th Annual Year in Ideas—which the magazine modestly described as a digest of the most noteworthy ideas of the past 12 months—albeit through Sandy Darity, Karolyn Tyson, and Domini Castellini's research that refuted and refined several aspects of his oppositional cultural framework model (Robinson, 2004).

The debates captured in the chapters of this volume reflect the gift and tragedy of John Ogbu's intellectual career, to borrow Amanda Lewis's (2005) poignant insight. The gift of John's career is obvious: 30 years of provocative scholarship that stimulated popular and academic debates about minority achievement in plural societies. In the academy, John's cultural-ecological model of minority achievement has defined one strand of educational anthropology for decades (Foster, this volume). It also has informed research about minority schooling processes and outcomes conducted by scholars in several social science disciplines, including sociology, psychology, education, and economics. Virtually every serious scholarly monograph or article on the race gap and minority education published in the last 20 years has cited John.

The tragedy of John's scholarly career is apparent as well. Despite the undisputed importance of his foundational contributions to the social science of minority achievement in plural societies, his scholarship has been engulfed by controversies that, at times, threatened to overshadow the impact of the scholarship itself. While serious scholars have engaged, extended, refuted, and refined John's ideas, there also have been unrestrained and harsh criticisms leveled at his work and, at times, at John himself. Less serious interpretations of his theories—too often simplifications that distorted what John actually wrote—occasionally have appeared in scholarly venues, but more commonly have been found in popular outlets, such as newspaper columns and speeches of politicians and celebrities.

To be sure, his work required rigorous criticism, some of which appears in this volume. In my view, the tragedy of John's career springs from some commentators who critiqued his work seemingly without actually having read it carefully—if at all! Other problematic criticisms came from those who ignored John's complicated, nuanced, and elegant arguments—especially what he called his "overall perspective on the problem"—the system (the structural factors of racism, unequal educational opportunities) *and* community factors (cultural values, collective identity, and normative behaviors). Critics who charged that John downplayed the role of racism and unequal schooling appear to have ignored the fact that John argued that compared to the role of peer pressures associated with acting White, "even more important contributors to [involuntary minorities'] low performance are societal, school, and other community forces that discourage academic engagement" (Ogbu, 2004 and Chapter 2 this volume).

The least sophisticated critics reduced the entire corpus of his scholarship to the 1986 article he coauthored with Fordham. This error frustrated him tremendously. He explained to a colleague:

> I jointly wrote the now famous paper—"Black students' school success: Coping with the burden of acting white"—in 1986, partly to help Dr. Fordham put her findings into some "theoretical framework." But drawing from my "theory" to present her "ethnographic findings" did not mean that her ethnographic findings represented all of my theory or that my theory stood or fell because of her findings. Nevertheless, I have long tried to distinguish Dr. Fordham's work from my "theory." This is because of the tendency of readers and researchers to confuse Dr. Fordham's ethnographic findings with my "theory".
>
> (Ogbu, 1994)

Signithia Fordham recalled how John "seethed at being identified with research he had not done and with an explanation with which he did not fully agree" (2004, p. 153).

Fordham, too, found the public perception of their intellectual collaboration frustrating at times. Researchers and journalists repeatedly reversed their names, making it Ogbu and Fordham. She explained:

> His theoretical model . . . emphasized social-structural and historical factors. My approach emphasized expressive as well as adaptive responses to those determinants. I proposed my theory as an addition to his, balancing its structuralism and extending its reach into a dynamics of African American adolescents' cultural repertoire. I am not sure that Ogbu was ever convinced of the validity of my point of view (2004, pp. 152–153 and Chapter 6, this volume).

John's dedication to this book was driven by the expectation that it would set the record straight. His profound frustrations with the misperceptions of his work help explain why he worked on this book's manuscript late into the night prior to entering the hospital for back surgery in the summer of 2003. He took binders filled with chapter manuscripts and computer disks with him to the hospital in anticipation of working on this book during his recuperation. But he never recovered from this back surgery. Between the heart attack he suffered during his first back surgery and the heart attack that took his life during his second back surgery two weeks later, John was on a ventilator.

That this book represents John's last words on his life's work is one of the reasons I agreed to assist Dr. Marcellina Ada Ogbu complete the tasks required to bring this volume to print. I also agreed to her request simply because she asked me to assist her. John's own five chapters were in drafts when he died. They all needed extensive editorial work by someone familiar with his scholarship and the literature in the field. Except for the few that were previously published, all the other chapters in the book also required editorial scrutiny by someone familiar with the substantive and theoretical aspects of the cultural-ecological model, debates over its interpretations, and the various methodological issues involved in these chapters. Although Ada Ogbu is intimately familiar with her husband's work, her training was in public health. When I asked why she asked me to take this role, Ada replied, "You haven't always agreed with John, but you understand him."

I believe Ada sees me in this way because from roughly 1980 through 2003 when he died, her husband was a mentor who became a friend. The first time I met John, I was a graduate student at UCLA, and I had just finished reading his 1978 book, *Minority Education and Caste*. He had presented a paper based on his book at a meeting of the Sociology of Education Association, a small scholarly society that meets at the Asilomar Conference Center in Pacific Grove, California every February. As soon as the applause and questions ended, I approached to ask if he would read a paper I had written, and he agreed. From that day forward, he never refused a request from me: to serve on my dissertation committee, to provide me with feedback on an idea or what I had written, to write letters—many letters—of recommendation for jobs,[1] to provide career advice, to share his lecture notes with me, to suggest readings for a graduate methods course, to speak at my university, or to share a meal at a professional meeting.

As I transitioned from graduate student to colleague, our relationship became more reciprocal. I read and commented on his work, listened to his concerns about how his scholarship was interpreted or used in ways he felt were inappropriate or simply wrong. He described the stinging frustrations of his departmental struggles. He also shared with me his many successes, honors, invitations, and awards. Whenever I was in the San Francisco Bay area for a conference, he and Ada would invite me for dinner at their house or meet me at a conference hotel for lunch. John regaled me with tales of his extended family "back home," often in the form of long, typed personal letters. We also shared diet success and failure stories—alas, many more of the latter than the former.

During the mid 1990s, attending some professional meetings increasingly became an ambivalent experience for John. On the one hand, he had scores of enthusiasts. But John's vocal public critics grew in number and became more vociferous and, frankly, at times vicious. I witnessed several incidents where members of an American Educational Research Association (AERA) audience crossed the boundaries of appropriate professional norms of critical discourse. I recall sitting in audiences where people launched *ad hominem* attacks on John because he was a Nigerian immigrant. In other settings, I observed scholars mockingly deride his evolving typologies of minority statuses. Listening to the arguments of some critics, at times I wondered if they had even read his work. The shallowness of their remarks suggested that they merely had picked up a decontextualized, disembodied phrase like "acting White" and neither knew nor understood what John had argued. In fact, John also suspected that a small number—certainly not all—of his critics had never read his individual publications and relied exclusively on the joint article (Fordham & Ogbu, 1986) or an interpretation of his work by others for their understanding of his scholarly contributions to the field (Ogbu, 2003).

After observing various versions of these interactions for several years at professional meetings of several disciplines, I realized that John's public critics were more likely to be African Americans or Latinos, while Whites, members of voluntary minority groups, and scholars from abroad were more likely to find his theoretical work highly insightful and compelling. I began to think of the dynamics of this public drama as a sort of Rorschach test, whereby individuals' personal histories intersected with their collective experiences with U.S. society to become the prism through which they refracted their own reading of John's scholarship. Why involuntary minority academics' interpretations of the intellectual, political, and practical merits of the cultural-ecological model differed from those of immigrant and White academics is suggested, perhaps, by Cornel West's observation about Barack Obama, who as an immigrant (actually, he's the son of an immigrant) "lacks the rage" of involuntary immigrants.

Once I agreed to work with Ada Ogbu to finish this book, I encountered a number of difficulties. First and foremost, John's chapters were very rough drafts (the exception is Chapter 2, which appeared posthumously in *The Urban Review* in 2004). The challenge was to free his ideas and reorganize them into coherent arguments, without translating them into my words. Ada Ogbu served as an authenticity check on all of my work on John's chapters. As a result of the multiple drafts and the skillful editing of Donna Maurer, the four new chapters (Chapters 1, 3, 4, 5) are John's ideas and words. The sole exception to this generalization is the final section of Chapter 1. I wrote the road map of the book in John's voice so that a switch from the first to the third person would not interrupt the chapter's flow. Any mischaracterization of the contributors' chapters are my error, not his.

The final reason I agreed to help Ada Ogbu prepare this book for publication is that John designed it as a dialogue about the cultural-ecological model and empirical data between himself and the scholarly community—and that most certainly included his serious critics. John's own chapters appear first in this volume so that readers can wrestle with his ideas before they read the chapters written by some of his most articulate critics and supporters. I hope those who never read John, those who read him carefully and honestly disagreed with his arguments, as well as those who innocently misunderstood him, those who snarled their derisive comments, and those who mocked and ridiculed his new ideas, will take advantage of this final opportunity to encounter his theoretical and empirical work.

My final hope is that this volume will stimulate scholars, pundits, policy makers, educators, and all those who care about educating students to move beyond the bitter debates that, as Kevin Foster (Chapter 24) persuasively argues, "dishonor and undermine our ultimate goals." The persistence of race gaps in achievement and attainment means that even several years after his death, John Ogbu's cultural-ecological model and the scholarship in this volume remain both timely and vital.

Roslyn Arlin Mickelson
August 2006

NOTE

1   I once applied for a job and asked John to write a letter of recommendation on my behalf. He agreed, but awkwardly alerted me to the fact that he had also written letters of recommendation for three other candidates for that same job.

REFERENCES

Fordham, S. (2004). "Signithia, you can do better than that": John Ogbu (and me) and the nine lives peoples. *Anthropology and Education Quarterly*, *35*(1), 149–161.

Fordham, S., & Ogbu, J. U. (1986). "Black Students' School Success: Coping with the Burden of 'Acting White'," *The Urban Review, 18*(3), 176–206.

Horvat, E. M., & O'Connor, C. (2006). *Beyond acting white: Reassessments and new directions in research on black students and school success.* New York: Teachers College Press.

Lewis, A. (2005). Personal communication.

Ogbu, J. U. (1978). *Minority education and caste*. New York: Academic Press.

Ogbu, J. U. (1994). Letter to Dr. Sheree Marshall. May 7.

Ogbu, J. U. (2003). *The anthropologist and native scholars: Epistemologies in conflict*. Unpublished research note.

Ogbu, J. U. (2004). Collective identity and the burden of "acting white" in black history, community, and education. *The Urban Review*, 36(1), 1–35.

Robinson, C. (2004). The fourth annual year in ideas. *New York Times Magazine* (December 12), 57–106.

Preface

John U. Ogbu

After many years of studying minority education in the United States and elsewhere, I concluded that minority school performance is influenced by two sets of factors: (a) those arising from societal and school treatment of minorities, and (b) those arising from the dynamics of minority communities. For example, in 1986 Signithia Fordham and I introduced the notion of opposition to "acting White" as one of those factors arising from the dynamics of minority communities. At issue was the relationship between the collective identity of a minority group and the school experience of its members.

The concept, now known as the Fordham-Ogbu thesis, has become the focus of both scholarly and political debate. Prior to the 97th annual meeting of the American Sociological Association held in Chicago in 2002, I reviewed and read many published and unpublished works examining the validity of the thesis in order to prepare for a special ASA session devoted to examining the concept. The debate was lively and stimulating, and a multitude of ideas were advanced. I felt the special session was a good start towards engaging in an intellectual dialogue on the thesis, as well as on the relationship between Black (minority) identity and academic engagement. While I had been thinking about editing a book on collective identity and schooling, the Chicago session reinforced my belief in the need for such a book. Soon after the session, I began the process of organizing this volume and inviting scholars to contribute to it.

This book revisits the Fordham-Ogbu thesis, first explored in the article "Black Students' School Success: Coping with the Burden of 'Acting White'," published in *The Urban Review* in 1986. That publication continues to generate debates and research, but, as readers might deduce from this volume, the major points of contention remain unresolved. This is not surprising. In 1974, I characterized the debates in the field of education as often marred by theoretical confusion, methodological shortcomings, politics, and a lack of emotional detachment. I further noted that policies and programs developed within this context would not succeed in reducing the school performance gap between Blacks and Whites. Thirty years later, it seems that my evaluation of the state of the educational debate still holds true. Unfortunately, the gap in achievement between Black and White students also persists.

The reactions from scholars, researchers, policy makers, Black organizations, and lay persons to the 1986 article have been varied. I valued many of the criticisms because they have influenced my continued research on the topic, revisions of my ideas, and further articulation of the framework. However, several criticisms have been based on a misinterpretation of the 1986 thesis, arrogating concepts that are not mine to me. Some criticisms appeared to me as attempts at advancing personal agendas, political correctness, or misplaced anger. As much as I understood the topic's sensitivity, it was very frustrating to me because many researchers and commentators have focused on one behavior, "Acting White," as the explanation for Black students' poor school performance.

Further, many of these critics have reduced *my own* explanation, in fact the entire body of my work, to oppositional culture/acting White. My entire work is not based on oppositional culture or acting White; rather, the central focus has been to explain minority students' school performance. I defined the performance of minority students to include how students do in all situations involving academic achievement. Moreover, there are two features that are important to consider when evaluating my work. One is that it is comparative in nature—not just comparing minorities and the dominant group in society, but also comparing minorities among themselves. The second feature is that minority education or performance is influenced not only by what goes on inside the school and the family, but also what is happening in the wider society, including minorities' historical experiences. These factors, when brought together, form what I called the cultural-ecological model (CEM).

I view the CEM as a framework for studying and understanding the various factors that influence minority students' school performance. The CEM consists of a wide range of interlocking factors, each of which may independently influence the school performance of all or just a few students in a given minority group. "Acting White" is only one very small component of the community forces, and it is not central to my thesis, as many critiques have tried to situate it. In an attempt to clarify my position, given the continued debate and the flurry of books and articles on the subject, in this volume I tried to revisit the 1986 "acting White" thesis. Therefore, the purpose of this book is to bring together in one volume some of the different perspectives on the thesis, as well as to further articulate the concept of collective identity and schooling and to more fully articulate the CEM. To accomplish this objective, I invited authors who have researched or written on the "acting White" /oppositional culture thesis to contribute their work to this volume. The book is structured as a dialogue, and I hope that it will stimulate much more substantive debate on the topic.

A Note from Marcellina Ada Ogbu

My husband, John Ogbu, died in August 2003. As I collected his belong-
ings from the intensive care unit, I went first for the backpack containing
the draft copies of this book that he had taken to the hospital with the
hope of beginning the revisions during his recuperation. In my shock over
his death, I simply promised to complete the book. But as I later reflected
on my promise, I realized that the book had to be completed for a number
of reasons. First, it would be John's last book. Second, the book already
had been accepted for publication. Third, and even more importantly,
I knew that John wanted the book to be published. I recalled him working
tirelessly the night before his surgery, assembling the draft articles,
contributors' contacts, publisher's contract, disks, and other relevant
materials into a red binder. Although his surgery was scheduled for seven
the next morning, he worked past midnight. As I reflect back on that
night, I am not sure whether he knew the task would fall on someone else
or it was just John's penchant for organization. Regardless of his motivation to work that night, finishing the book did fall on me, our family,
and some great colleagues.

Without reading the binder's contents, I contacted the publisher to
make sure that they still wanted to publish the book. Fortunately,
they were willing to go forward with the project. That out of the way,
I began reading the chapters in the draft binder. They were not what
I expected. In my raw state, I was taken aback by what I considered
vicious attacks on John and his work. I wondered to myself, why did John
want this book published? What was he thinking when he embarked on
the project? Had he not had enough of the attacks? Why would *he*
assemble the attacks into one accessible volume? I tried hard to understand and to come up with an explanation. One night, I thought that I
had found the answer: perhaps the horrible back pain he was experiencing had affected his thinking. When I got up the next morning,
though, I realized that my theory made no sense. Despite lying in the
intensive care ward, John was alert, lucid, and logical.

As I tried to grasp his reasoning, I began wondering aloud to his friends, colleagues, and mentors, but they did not understand my surprise or why I was taking the attacks so hard. They explained that criticisms had followed John throughout his career. Then I remembered the criticisms of *The Next Generation* and *Minority Education and Caste.* Although numerous scholars hailed the research and publications as pioneering in the field, John had his detractors.

John's last book, *Black American Students in an Affluent Suburb*, generated wide acclaim and won the Critic's Choice Award. However, some scholars and laypersons, as well as a number of Black organizations, disagreed with the findings and, in fact, the thesis of John's work in general. The attacks were personal, vicious, and relentless. The book's findings were condemned even before anyone had read the book or it had even been published. John was labeled a conservative,[1] accused of enabling political conservatives and blaming victims, with some even calling him the Clarence Thomas of the education community. He was threatened and told to go back to where he came from. With this in mind, I was not sure why I was surprised by the contents of this book's draft.

I had suggested to John more than once to abandon this line of research and do something on Africa. I argued that there were many important issues facing Africa that required his expertise and indigenous knowledge. Although the nature of the personal attacks had been uncomfortable, he always reminded me that it came with the territory. Even still, I wondered about American society. What kind of society helps build one up and then does everything to pull him down, waiting to see how fast he can fall? As if he could read my thoughts, John would always say to me, "I know how you feel, but I am very lucky. You know, very few people get to do what I am doing, enjoying my work and raising questions about how the society educates its children, particularly those who are disenfranchised." He often would follow this with a Nigerian proverb, "If the town crier sounds his *ogene*,[2] and the village square remains empty, something must be wrong. Either the villagers do not care or they have dismissed his call as unimportant. But if, on the sound of the *ogene*, the villagers come to inquire, he has gained their attention regardless of the response to his message." John's only wish was that the attacks be substantive because those types of attack challenged him to look deeper. They pushed him to articulate his thesis better and motivated him to try and understand the achievement gap.

It took courage for John to be a researcher in this pioneering field for almost 30 years, and his effort to bring together these divergent opinions is further evidence of his willingness to let people come to their own conclusions. This is not to say that John was not protective of the Cultural-Ecological Model. He was opinionated about the thesis, but not close-minded.

Finally, one of John's mentors helped me transcend the feeling that I needed to protect his memory. She wrote:

> He was passionate about what he did. He believed in its importance and that it was important because it dealt with contemporary issues vital to contemporary society and to those who must struggle with its inequities. . . . What he wrote was controversial because people knew what he was saying and often countered established ways of thinking and a variety of vested interests among scholars and policy makers. But he was prepared to defend himself against those who queried the validity of what he had to say about his research findings. . . .

Upon reflection, my instinct to protect was silly: John wrote extensively and his words are out there; I could not protect him regardless of whether this book was published or not, and, above all, there was nothing to protect him from. Such disagreements are part and parcel of academia.

My apprehension having subsided, I moved forward with the book. I contacted Roslyn Mickelson, a colleague and friend, to help me navigate the book through publication. I needed to work with someone who knew and understood John in and outside his work. Although close to the family, she still could be more detached from the book than I. She provided the balance, thoughtfulness, scholarship, and the push the book needed.

Although John wrote all his chapters (which are reassembled at the beginning of the book), and collected all the invited chapters, he was able to write only a few paragraphs for the concluding chapter. The concluding chapter he started suggests that he did not intend it to be a summary of or rebuttal to his critics; instead, it was to be an invitation to readers and scholars to draw their own conclusions. He also asked researchers to not lose sight of what is at stake: the need to bridge the achievement gap and to enhance minority academic engagement, regardless of students' country of origin, wealth, or station. With that in mind, we invited Professor Kevin Foster to write the concluding chapter. I believe that his piece carries some of the intended spirit of John's final chapter, conveys an understanding of the diversity of opinions reflected in the book, and provides some future directions for John's work.

John's road to Minority Education was serendipitous. He was unable to go to Africa to do field work for his dissertation and found himself in Stockton, California. As a graduate student studying schools in the central valley, he could hardly imagine that this research would be the beginning of a career. More importantly, it would become a personal mission. As a poor student from Africa, he was unwilling to accept the explanation that minorities do poorly in school because of inferior genes or a cultural deficiency, both theories that dominated education research at the time of his study. He had to refute these theories time and again despite his research to the contrary. As Professor Elizabeth Colson of the University of California, Berkeley wrote[3]:

> John Ogbu's research reflected his own deep-seated faith that people, that humans by their inherent nature can be expected to do their best to overcome obstacles to achieve desired ends and that everybody wants to get ahead in this world. Obstacles to him were something to be overcome, not excuses for failure. His research on minorities and their response to education carried out over more than thirty years was a response to his amazement that others did not treat obstacles in the same way that he did.

This belief is not to be confused with the American clichés of "pulling oneself up by the bootstraps" or "going from the log cabin to the White House"; rather, it was predicated on the idea that people have an innate desire to overcome hurdles. He believed that it was irresponsible to not see people in general, and minorities in particular, as thinking, creative, intelligent people who can overcome adversity and succeed. As Colson noted, "He believed in human intelligence and courage and valued their ability to win against all odds."

In the end, it is best that his final book ends with a number of questions. In so doing, it keeps the issue of minority education, academic engagement, and the achievement gap at the front and center, so that we do not forget.

NOTES

1   Interestingly, after John's first two books were published, he was labeled as a communist by some and a structuralist by others.
2   An instrument that is used as part of music ensemble or to summon the community to a regular or emergency meeting.
3   Professor Elizabeth Colson, personal communication, Sept. 7, 2003.

Acknowledgments

My husband, John Ogbu, passed away in August 2003 before completing this book. Although he reviewed the first draft (with the exception of the conclusion), he was not able to navigate the book through the publication process. Thus the task of completing the book fell on a number of individuals. I am greatly indebted to Professor Roslyn Arlin Mickelson, who worked tirelessly on the book as if it were her own. I thank Donna Maurer, from academic-editor.com, for her superb editorial work and for providing a third set of eyes in addition to Roz's and mine. My appreciation also goes to Emily Ostendorf and Astrid Davis for the very first round of edits, literature searches, and copyright requests and Fidez Bituin for typing several of the manuscripts.

To my children (Elizabeth Ijeoma, Cecilia Chinyere, Nnanna Francis, and Christina Ndidi), I extend a big thank you for editorial help, support, and encouragement. I am grateful to Professor Elizabeth Colson and countless other individuals who provided a needed push, encouragement, and strength during a particularly difficult time in my family's life.

Thank you to Routledge for wanting to continue with the publication and for their support and patience. Special thanks to Naomi Silverman, editor at Routledge, for all her editorial help and support and, above all, for being patient and understanding, to Mary Hillemeier, editorial assistant for help through the publication process and thanks also to the copy-editor, Sue Dickinson.

Finally and not the least, I extend my deepest gratitude to the individual authors for their contributions and patience over the past several years while this volume was being prepared for publication.

Part I

History and Framework

Chapter I

The History and Status of a Theoretical Debate

John U. Ogbu

In a joint 1986 publication, Professor Signithia Fordham and I first argued that cultural frame of reference and collective identity should be included among the widely recognized, interlocking societal, school, and community factors known to influence minority students' school performance. A cultural frame of reference reflects an ethnic group's shared sense of how people should behave, and a collective identity expresses a minority group's cultural frame of reference. In some situations, an ethnic minority group's collective identity may oppose what its members perceive as the dominant group's view of how people should act (Ogbu, 1982a, 2000; Ogbu & Simons, 1998). When the cultural frame of reference is oppositional, it can adversely affect an ethnic minority group's schooling. Students may not engage in certain behaviors that are conducive to doing well academically to avoid having their peers identify them with the dominant group.[1]

Based on Fordham's research at Capital High School in Washington, DC, we reported in our joint article that efforts to steer clear of such identification led some minority students to avoid certain attitudes and behaviors that their cultural frame of reference associated with Whites. Such avoidance contributed to the minorities' low school performance. We called the students' attempts to resolve the tension between the school's demands to behave in ways that result in academic achievement and their peer groups' demands not to do so "the burden of 'acting White'."

The thesis of this joint article was that (a) discrimination by society (e.g., denial of minorities' adequate rewards for their educational accomplishments through employment barriers and lower wages), (b) discrimination in the education system (e.g., school segregation, inferior curriculum, low teacher expectations), and (c) Black American responses to the mistreatment by society and school (e.g., disillusionment, lowered academic effort, mistrust of the schools) all result in low school performance; however, (d) an oppositional collective identity and an oppositional culture frame of reference also contribute to low school performance because minority students avoid (so-called) White attitudes and behaviors conducive to academic success.

The purpose of this book is to further broaden our understanding of the current debate on the achievement gap between Black and White students and bring together various perspectives on it. My research and studies by others have shown that oppositional collective identity and oppositional cultural frames of reference influence minority students' school performance. These two factors need to be examined to better understand school performance and variability within given minority groups, as well as among minority groups in multiethnic societies.

There have been many criticisms of the 1986 article, even though it has been very influential. Although the intent of this volume is to explain my position in the persistent debate on the achievement gap, I would be remiss if I did not acknowledge some of the criticisms of the Fordham-Ogbu article as well as those of my own cultural-ecological model (CEM), which is often confused with the 1986 thesis.

Critics have argued that the Fordham-Ogbu thesis has many limitations. Unfortunately, many critics have lumped together my CEM and the 1986 thesis and treated them as one and the same. Hence, my entire body of work, as well as my theoretical formulations, has been mislabeled or referred to as oppositional culture theory or "acting White" theory. Some have argued that the theory does not explain within-group differences; that it neither adequately addresses the impact of societal racism and discrimination, nor takes into account the daily school experiences of Black students; that it fails to distinguish between cultural and instrumental assimilation; and that its treatment of culture is too structural and static, and not sufficiently dynamic. Other critics have labeled the theory as a deficiency model that does not explain variability among groups, or have argued that it focuses too much on less successful blacks. Also, critics have claimed that the theory does not adequately address racial identity and successful academic outcomes.

Some groups have criticized the theory for being too historical or structural, while others have argued that the theory does not understand Black history and education. Yet, another group of critics, particularly quantitative researchers, have contended that there are actually no differences between Blacks and Whites on a number of key indicators. They have reported no evidence of discrepancies between Black students' verbal responses and their actual performance and, in fact, found no evidence of oppositional culture.

The above list of criticisms is not exhaustive. I have tried in many of my publications to respond to or clarify some of the issues (1974, 1989, 1992, 1994, 1997, 2003; Ogbu & Simons, 1998). In reviewing the criticisms on opposition culture and schooling, a pattern became evident to me. First, many critics failed to distinguish among my cultural-ecological model, the

Fordham-Ogbu thesis, and Fordham's perspective, and second, they constructed or replaced the thesis of the 1986 article or CEM with their own interpretations (see Figure 1.1). Their criticisms have rested on flawed interpretations of my work—the lumped formulation that is the amalgam of my cultural ecological model and the Fordham-Ogbu thesis.

To enhance the contributions of oppositional culture scholarship to understanding the patterns of minority school performance, I will briefly describe the evolution of collective identity and cultural frames of reference as conceptual tools in the study of minority education. Next, I will explain how the three perspectives on collective identity and schooling (my cultural-ecological model, the Fordham-Ogbu thesis, and Fordham's theory) differ from each other. The chapter then concludes with an overview of the remaining chapters in this volume.

A BRIEF HISTORY OF CONCEPTUAL TOOLS

The concepts of collective identity and cultural frame of reference came from several sources. The first was my fieldwork in Stockton, California between 1968 and 1970. While conducting that study, I found that some Black and Mexican American students did not want to do their school-work or speak Standard English because they considered these behaviors "White" or "Anglo." One African American parent reported a discussion she had with a Black student about behaving like White people. The student accused her of "thinking like a White person" because she advised him to go back to school and graduate. My informant went on to say:

> This is what that young boy told me. . . . He said, "You're thinking like the White man. Because what is an education?" He said, "I can go out right now and come back with 100 suits or diamond rings." I said, "Oh yeah! You probably could, but you got to know how. You got to be smart, you know?" He said, "You don't have to have the White man's education to get to be rich or to get what you want." . . . This is the way he seemed to think. I was telling him, I said, "Well!" It was two of us and we had a big long discussion and . . . I had to stop. And I was saying to him, "Don't you think that you ought to go back to school?"

Other Black school personnel also reported on how they often advised Black students that even though Standard English is the White man's language, they should master and speak it in order to do well in school and to get a good job after they graduate. One Black school administrator in Stockton used the following slogan to drive home this message: "Do your Black thing, but know the White thing, too." During an interview in

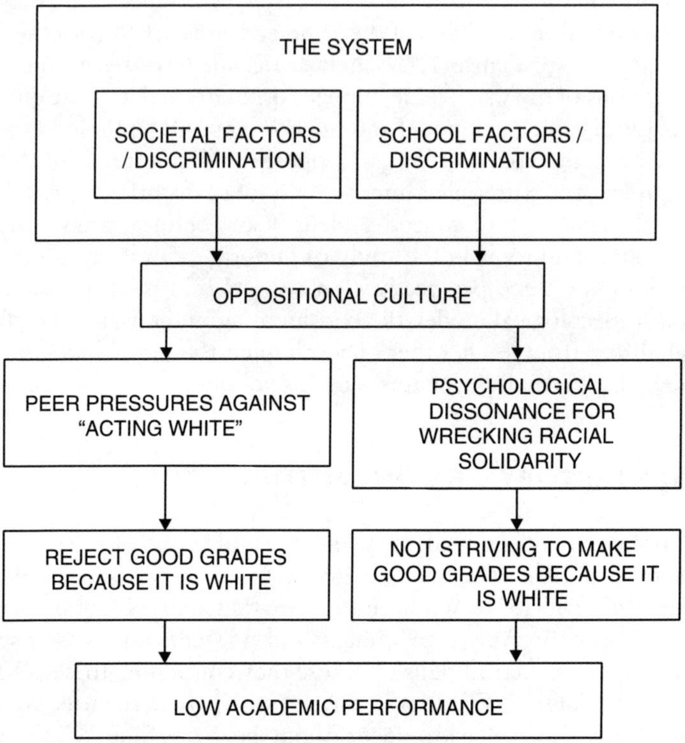

Figure 1.1 Critics' construction of the cultural-ecological model.

1970, this informant went on to explain why it is important for Black Americans to master Standard English. In his words,

> You hear a lot of people say, "Well, why should I speak the White man's language?" Well, [the Black man has to because] he's living in the White man's world. And the White man controls the resources. He controls the finances. He controls all of these things. And you know, I've often said, "By Jimmy! I want to speak his language [i.e., Standard English] better than him. I want to be able to do the things he's [the White man's] doing better than him." And the thing is, this is his [the White man's] world. Now if I'm living in Africa, I'd learn the African thing. But now that we're living in America in a White racist society, we have to learn his language if we're going to do it [succeed] because— you know, you can make it on Black people's [resources]—but not many of them do. And I believe that in this American society a Black man can use all these White man's resources. And you don't have to degrade yourself. I don't feel that I'm degrading myself a heck of a lot in

my lifetime to learn the White man's way. You can still maintain your dignity. But I think that many of the kids . . . this is where a lot of the kids get sort of mixed up, you know . . . they say, "Well, we want to do a Black thing." Well, fine, I believe in the Black thing. But you've got to learn that White thing, too. *"Do your Black thing, but know that White thing, too."*

Black adults and students expressed their opposition to "the White man's ways" in other contexts, too. For example, during my research in Stockton, they organized rallies and conferences at which some speakers condemned "the system" and objected to "doing the White man's things" required by that system. I was invited to speak at one of these conferences, but the day before my presentation I was uninvited because, as I was told, *I was too White!* I found out later that because of my university education at Berkeley, I was perceived as behaving like White people.[2]

Another factor contributing to the development of the concepts of collective identity and cultural frame of reference was my review of ethnographic studies of U.S. minority students' experiences as compared to the experiences of children attending Western-type schools in developing countries. Educational anthropologists and other researchers in the 1970s emphasized the underlying role of cultural differences or cultural conflicts in minority students' school adjustment problems and their academic failure (Burger, 1968; Erickson & Mohatt, 1986; Gallimore, Boggs, & Jordan, 1974; La Belle, 1976; Lewis, 1979; Philips, 1976). They recommended culturally compatible teaching and learning as remedies for minority groups' educational problems. Similar remedies were recommended for solving the educational problems of children in developing countries (Gay & Cole, 1967; Inkeles, 1968; Spindler, 1974). However, based on my research on minority education in the United States (Ogbu, 1974) and my review of data on the cultural experiences of school children in Africa, I did not think that the cultural problems of minority students in the United States were similar to those of students in the developing countries (Heyneman, 1979; Imoagene, 1981; Malinowski, 1939; Musgrove, 1953).

An additional key source in my development of the concepts of collective identity and cultural frame of reference consisted of the ethnographic studies of U.S. minority school experience conducted by educational anthropologists and other social scientists in the United States. These studies compared the experiences of U.S. minorities to those of children in developing countries attending Western-type schools. Another valuable source of insights was the literature on revitalization movements among colonized and oppressed people (Lanteracnni, 1967; Penfold, 1981; Sundkler, 1961; Thrup, 1962).

Searching for Concepts to Capture Observations

As a result of my observations in Stockton and the insights I gained from the literature cited above, I began to think that some minorities in the United States and elsewhere perceived and interpreted their cultural practices as alternatives to those of the dominant group; they viewed theirs as a kind of *alternative culture*. The minorities seemed to prefer behaving in ways they considered *different* or opposite from the ways of the dominant group, which they considered their oppressor.

I first presented this perspective on cultural differences and schooling in 1979 during an invited address at the First Jerusalem International Conference on Education at the Hebrew University. In that address, I distinguished alternative cultures from non-alternative cultures in minority groups' responses to the cultures of dominant groups. I later presented a revised version of the paper in 1980 at the annual meeting of the American Anthropological Association. In that paper, which was eventually published (1982a), I introduced a typology of cultural differences, consisting of universal cultural differences, primary cultural differences, and secondary cultural differences.

I defined universal cultural differences as those differences between home culture (and language) and school culture (and language) that every child encounters upon entering school. Regardless of their cultural background, all children make a transition from home culture to school culture and thus confront these differences.

Primary cultural (language) differences exist before two populations come together, for example, before members of a population (e.g., immigrants) became a minority group in the United States. Bearers of primary cultural differences experience problems in teaching and learning, as well as social adjustment, because they bring to school their customary behaviors, as well as the assumptions underlying those customary behaviors, that are different from those of the public school, as well as the dominant group members who control the school (Musgrove, 1953; Ogbu, 1982a).

Secondary cultural differences are what I previously designated as alternative cultures (Ogbu, 1979). These differences usually come about after group members have been forced into an oppressed minority status. Secondary cultural differences also characterize the cultural responses of some colonized and dominated peoples throughout the world. A careful examination of these cultural differences suggests that they are usually oppositional.

A Conceptual Clue to a Paradox

One of the most challenging research problems I faced in the early 1980s was explaining the paradox of high educational aspirations and simultaneously low school performance among Black Americans and similar minorities, not only in the United States, but also in other societies (Ogbu, 1978a, 1978b, 1978c, 1982b, 1982c). A clue to the paradox came from reviewing the works of Castile and Kushner (1981), DeVos (1984), Green (1981), Holt (1972), and Spicer (1966, 1971), as well as the writings of some Black critics of the public school curriculum (e.g., Clark, 1971). This corpus of literature directed my attention to the interconnection between the collective identity and cultural frame of reference among subordinate peoples and how they were represented and treated in public school textbooks. Until that point, I had been treating collective identity and cultural frame of reference separately. Some of these authors, however, described the processes of opposition in the majority–minority group relationship as sustaining and reinforcing minorities' separate identity systems (DeVos, 1984; Green, 1981; Holt, 1972; Spicer, 1966, 1971).

This literature also provided examples of persistent or enduring peoples: people who have remained unassimilated for centuries despite changes in their societies. Examples are the Basques, Catalans, Cherokee, Irish, Maya, Navajo, Seneca, Welsh, and Yaqui (Spicer, 1966, 1971); the Buraku and Koreans in Japan (DeVos, 1967, 1984); the Tewa, Pueblo, and Hopi in the U.S. Southwest (Dozier, 1951); and Black Americans (Green, 1981). Different authors offered various reasons for the persistence of these minorities' separate identities. Spicer gave three reasons: (a) individuals' beliefs in their personal affiliation with the meaning of certain symbols; (b) the people's continued beliefs about unique historical events that forged their separate collective identity; and (c) the group's definition of its historical destiny (Spicer, 1971, p. 786).

DeVos (1967) suggested how collective identity is formed under oppression. According to him, when people are oppressed, they respond subjectively with a type of "ethnic consolidation" or a collective sense of peoplehood. This subjective or expressive feeling leads them to use cultural symbols (materials, ideas, behaviors, etc.) "to differentiate themselves from other groups" (DeVos, 1995, p. 25). The cultural materials and ideas then become emblems or symbols for the collective identity. The symbols show others one's identity, or "who one is and to which group one's loyalty belongs." DeVos's classic examples are Christians wearing the cross and Jews wearing the Star of David. According to DeVos, individuals experience a group's collective identity subjectively as a sense of social belonging, ultimate loyalty, and continuity.

The Origins of Black Collective Identity

Both Green (1981) and Holt (1972) directly addressed how Black Americans became an enduring people with a collective identity and cultural frame of reference. Green (1981) described the development of a sense of collective identity among Black Americans, despite their heterogeneity (regional, class, gender, and so on). Collective identity developed because all segments of the Black population historically have felt the pressures of racial attitudes and mistreatment by the majority White Americans as encompassing. That is, regardless of the region in which they reside, or their education, socioeconomic status, and physical appearance, Blacks learned and came to believe during the course of their history that they could not escape their blackness or birth-ascribed status. They realized that White Americans did not wish to assimilate them and that they could not expect to be assimilated like various White immigrant groups for whom the door of assimilation was open (see Myrdal, 1944, p. 100); nor could they return to a "homeland" as some other non-White immigrants could and did. Only a few had the option to assimilate through passing (Warner, 1965; Wirth & Goldhammer, 1939). But even among those who could pass, only a few did so successfully because of the social and psychological costs. This led some to give up trying to pass and to accept their blackness in the 1960s. Furthermore, Black Americans recognized that their demeaning experiences, their lack of opportunities for advancement, and their generally unsatisfactory life situation were due to White people's exploitation and not because of anything inherently wrong with them. Green concluded with these words: "[I]t appears that racism and the trinity of prejudice, discrimination, and segregation, by their persistence have in essence given birth to the Black Americans as an enduring people" (Green, 1981, p. 77).

Holt (1972) introduced the term "inversion" to explain the evolution of Black English dialect; it suggested the process through which Black Americans developed their oppositional cultural frame of reference. Cultural inversion is the practice whereby members of an oppressed group redefine their indigenous way of talking or behaving, and it occurs when they adopt a new way of talking or behaving in opposition to the ways of the dominant group, their oppressors. This form of oppositional culture is often associated with a group's sense of collective identity and is laden with emotion. As a result, members of the minority group define certain ways of talking, behaving, and self-expression as more appropriate for them, in opposition to other ways of talking, behaving, and self-expression, which they consider appropriate for their oppressors. From the minorities' point of view, there co-exist two opposing cultural frames of reference or ideal ways to behave: one appropriate for minorities and the other appropriate for their oppressors. Holt's concepts are important because they illustrate that the "burden of 'acting White'" among Black students is not just the product of their encounter with the public schools.

THREE PERSPECTIVES ON COLLECTIVE IDENTITY AND SCHOOLING

A serious limitation of the current discourse in the field of oppositional culture and schooling is critics' failure to distinguish three separate perspectives on the relationship between oppositional culture identity and schooling. In preparing this volume, I reviewed more than 33 works on oppositional culture and schooling written between 1996 and 2003. To my surprise, all of them explicitly or implicitly regarded me as an oppositional culturalist and changed the cultural-ecological model (CEM) into an oppositional culture theory. More than a third of the authors labeled me as an oppositional culturalist without citing anything that I have written on achievement gap besides the joint article with Professor Fordham. In fact, some had not read anything that I have written, including the 1986 article, but based their criticism or labeling on others' critiques. At the same time, most researchers seemed to assume that my CEM, Fordham's work, and the Fordham-Ogbu thesis are the same and could be correctly labeled oppositional culture theory. But distinctions among them are necessary and important.

Ogbu's Cultural-Ecological Model

My cultural-ecological model or cultural-ecological framework postulates that there are two separate parts to the problem of minority education and school performance (see Figure 1.1): (a) societal and school factors, called the "system" and (b) minority community factors, called "community forces" (Ogbu & Simons, 1998). The model is intended to help study and understand the various factors that influence minority school performance. It is not a thesis or hypothesis based on a single factor (such as oppositional culture) that can predict the school performance of any particular minority group. Rather the model includes a wide range of interlocking factors, each of which may independently influence the school performance of all, many, or just a few students in a given minority group. Indeed, there are so many of these interlocking factors in the model that it may be difficult to study all of them or to determine their total influence in a single research project. It is a framework for studying how different factors (societal, school, and community) affect minority education, including academic performance.

Part one of the model, the system, consists of three sets of factors, namely, (a) the educational policies of local, state, and national educational agencies (e.g., segregation, school funding, and staffing) (Ogbu 1974, 1978a, 1979, 1986); (b) treatment of minority children within the school and classroom, including teacher expectations, the breadth and depth of curriculum, assessment tools and practices, and tracking

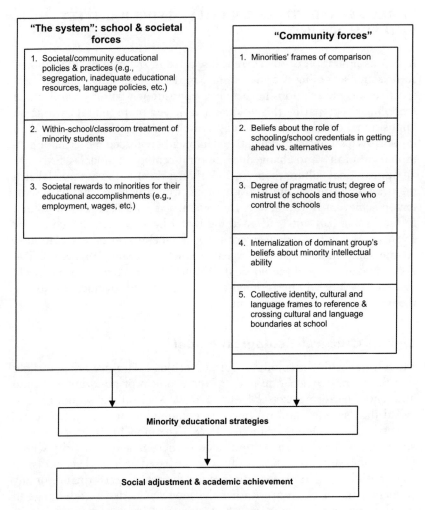

Figure 1.2 A two-part problem requiring a two-part solution.

(Leacock, 1985; Low, 1982; Lucas, 1999; Ogbu, 2003; Persell, 1977; Reed, 1988; Rist, 1970); and (c) the rewards that society gives or does not give to minorities for their educational accomplishments, such as employment and wages. These societal and school factors are a part of the historical, discriminatory treatment of minorities in society at large. I have argued in several publications that these societal and school factors influence minority students' school performance (Ogbu, 1974, 1978c, 1982a, 2003; Ogbu & Simons, 1998).

However, from a comparative perspective, discrimination alone is not enough to fully explain why minority children fail or succeed in school.

For example, in the early part of the 20th century, Chinese immigrants in Oakland, Stockton, and San Francisco were poorly rewarded for their school success, yet they continued to do well academically (Litherland, 1978; Low, 1982; Ma & Ma, 1982; Ogbu, 1982a, 1982b). To explain the variability in minority school performance in spite of discrimination, we turn to Part Two of the model, community forces, or the dynamics within the minority community. Community forces are the dominant patterns of attitudes, beliefs, and behaviors in the domain of education that are found in minority communities (see Figure 1.2). The four major components of community forces are:

(1) The frame of reference for comparisons that minorities use to evaluate their treatment or situation in society and school: to shed more light on the contributions of the dynamics of minority communities, I compare immigrant minorities and non-immigrant minorities because the two types differ in their community dynamics and the educational consequences of the latter. Immigrant minorities compare their situations in the United States with what they would have been "back home," or their place of origin. The immigrants think that they have more and better educational opportunities in the United States, especially opportunities for higher education and professional status. After all, many of them came to the United States to give their children a better future through education. The non-immigrants compare their situation with that of the White middle class and often conclude that they are worse off for no other reason than that they are minorities. Note that in the earlier versions of the cultural-ecological model, I compared the two types of minorities along this instrumental opportunity structure without reference to oppositional culture.

(2) Instrumental beliefs about schooling: these beliefs include the minorities' folk theory of getting ahead through education. Another factor under instrumental beliefs is the nature of alternative strategies for getting ahead adopted by the minorities and the role of education in those strategies. A third part of the instrumental beliefs is the influence of education in shaping a minority group's role models.

(3) The relational domain. This includes several factors that affect minority education: (a) perennial conflicts, such as collective struggles to achieve equal educational opportunities; (b) the degree of trust or mistrust toward school, teachers, and other school personnel; (c) the degree of pragmatic trust or lack of it; and (d) a belief about the role of schooling in the group's subordination or oppression.

(4) Expressive factors, including: (a) collective identity, and (b) cultural and language frames of reference. This is where the issue of oppositional collective identity and oppositional culture arises. That is, for some minorities, usually non-immigrants, their collective identity and cultural frame of reference may be oppositional to what the minorities

perceive as White American collective identity and cultural frame of reference. This fourth part is an oppositional culture adaptation or response.

To conclude, the cultural-ecological theory is not a theory or a hypothesis to be tested with a single factor like oppositional culture. Rather, it is a framework for studying and understanding various factors that influence minority students' school orientation and performance. Oppositional culture is just one of several community factors in the framework. (For more details about the theory, see Ogbu & Simons, 1998.)

The Fordham-Ogbu Thesis

The Fordham-Ogbu thesis, published in 1986 in *The Urban Review*, is only a part of Ogbu's cultural-ecological model, not the entire theory. That said, the Fordham-Ogbu thesis (1986) rests on three factors: (a) societal and school discrimination; (b) some instrumental community factors (e.g., Black people's perceptions of and responses to lack of job opportunities and inferior education); and (c) Black oppositional culture. Together, the three dynamics contributed to Black students' low academic performance at Capital High.

After the American Anthropological Association's annual meeting in 1980, Signithia Fordham informed me that while conducting ethnographic research at Capital High, she had observed the phenomenon of "acting White" among Black high-school students and in their Black community. She had recorded about 17 attitudes and behaviors that some Black students there labeled "White" and avoided. Four of the 17 "White" attitudes and behaviors were about schooling: speaking Standard English, spending a lot of time in the library studying, working hard to get good grades in school, and getting good grades in school.

In our subsequent joint article based on her research, "Black Students' School Success: Coping with the Burden of 'Acting White' " (Fordham & Ogbu, 1986), we stated that instrumental discrimination by society and school, as well as Black responses to the instrumental discrimination, were not enough to explain the school performance pattern. Instrumental discrimination was not enough because it did not explain "why some Black students are academically successful even though as a group Black students face a limited adult opportunity structure or a job ceiling and are given substandard education" (Fordham & Ogbu, 1986, p. 180). Furthermore, instrumental discrimination did not explain why other minority groups, such as immigrants, who faced similar school and societal discrimination, do better than Blacks in school (p. 181). We argued that two additional factors, oppositional collective identity and oppositional cultural frame of reference, must be considered as well (pp. 178–179).

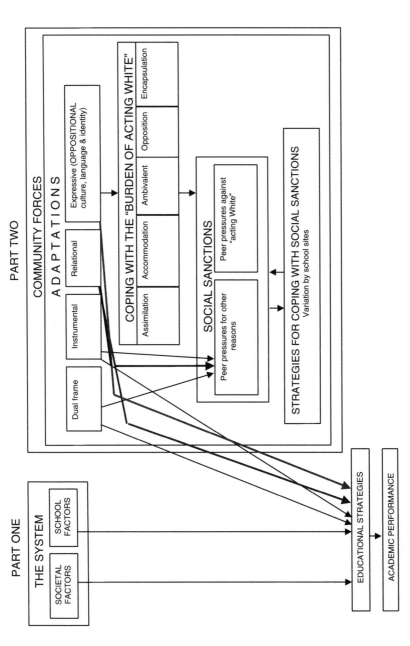

Figure 1.3 A cultural-ecological framework.

We analyzed the data from some of the 33 students whom Fordham had studied, some of whom were successful, while others were not (Fordham & Ogbu, 1986, p. 186). Our analysis showed that there was some tension between the language (Standard English) and certain attitudes and behaviors conducive to making good grades, on the one hand, and, on the other hand, the demands by Black peer groups to speak and behave in accordance with the norms of Black fictive kinship or collective identity. Black students responded to these tensions in one of three ways: by assimilating, by accommodating without assimilating, or by resisting the tensions. Each of the three responses sought to "reclaim" Black identity in its own way.

We interpreted the burden of "acting White" to mean that Black students at Capital High expended extra effort to resolve the dilemma of whether to "act White" or to not "act White" and avoid peer sanctions for "acting White." This resulted in a conscious or subconscious choice between making good grades by "acting White" and not making good grades by refusing to "act White." Put differently, the situation placed extra responsibility on Black students to resolve the conflicting demands at school to "act White" and their peer group's demands to act Black. (However, I have discovered over the years that this dichotomy of either "act White" or "act Black" is not so distinct; rather, Black students make many more choices.) The situation also placed an extra responsibility on Black students to deal with the academic, social, and psychological stresses they faced, no matter how they resolved the tension between school and peer demands. Based on our analysis of the students' "fictive kinship" (collective identity) and acceptable attitudes and behaviors (cultural frame of reference) in the school context, we concluded that "one major reason Black students at Capital High did poorly in school was because they experienced inordinate ambivalence and affective dissonance in regard to academic effort and success" (p. 177).

The thesis of the joint article, then, is not that Black students do not want to and are not striving to succeed in school because of oppositional culture. It is, rather, that two additional factors—oppositional collective identity and cultural frame of reference—played a significant role in the students' low academic performance (Fordham & Ogbu, 1986, p. 201). The thesis holds that *one* reason for Black students' low school performance is that some students reject certain attitudes and behaviors conducive to making good grades rather than engage in them because they regard making good grades as "acting White." But we did not conclude, as some critics have charged, that all or the majority of the Black students at Capital High did not want or did not make good grades because making good grades would be "acting White."

Fordham's Theory

Fordham's thesis, articulated in her book *Blacked Out* (1996), is closer to the Fordham-Ogbu thesis than to my cultural-ecological model. It shares with the cultural-ecological model three conceptual tools, but with different emphases: (a) collective identity (cultural-ecological model) or fictive kinship (Fordham's theory); (b) cultural frame of reference; and (c) peer pressures. In the cultural-ecological model, these concepts apply mainly to community dynamics (Part Four), but they constitute almost the entire basis of Fordham's theory. Fordham's theory does not explicitly treat as separate, causal factors (a) the system or societal and school factors and (b) the following factors in the community dynamics: frame of reference, instrumental adaptation, and relational adaptation issues. Moreover, the two perspectives differ on the issue of peer pressures. Fordham's theory assumes that most peer pressures arise from the demands of fictive kinship against "acting White." The cultural-ecological model distinguishes peer pressures due to collective identity from peer pressures due to other factors (see Chapter 4, this volume; Ogbu, 2003).

Several other distinctions between Fordham's theory and my cultural-ecological model are worth mentioning. Fordham's work focuses on the intersection between race and education, especially the effect of Black–White relations on Black school performance (Fordham 1984, 1988, 1991, 1996). The cultural-ecological model is about the intersection between minority status and education, regardless of race. For example, minority status affects academic performance in societies where there are racial differences, such as in the United States, New Zealand, Canada, and Britain, and in societies where there are no racial differences, such as India, Israel, Japan, and Singapore (Ogbu, 1978a, 1991; Ogbu & Simons, 1998; Ogbu & Stern, 2001).

Also, Fordham's work is not comparative. For example, she has not sought to explain why other non-White minorities do better than Black Americans in school, even though they also are expected to "act White," for example, by speaking "proper English." The cultural-ecological model, with its comparative approach, does do this. Fordham (1988) employed some conceptual categories, such as racelessness, that I did not encounter at the various sites where I studied Black students' school experience. On the contrary, some Black students in Stockton (CA), Oakland (CA), and Shaker Heights (OH) emphasized the importance of their race in striving to succeed in school. They want to make good grades to show the White man that the Black man is smart. They also believe that well-educated Blacks are a credit to their race (Ogbu, 1974, 2003).

Perhaps the most important difference between our theoretical models is that Fordham attributed the pattern of Black students' school performance more or less to a single factor, coping with the burden of "acting

White" or oppositional culture. In contrast, the cultural-ecological model postulates two sets of factors: (a) societal and school discrimination and (b) a host of community forces, one of which is coping with "acting White."

OVERVIEW OF THE BOOK

The remainder of this chapter offers readers an overview of the book and brief summaries of the chapters in it. I invited scholars working within the disciplines of anthropology, sociology, psychology, education, and social work to contribute chapters to this volume. Some of the contributions are previously published journal articles, while others were specifically written for this volume. Quite a few of the authors I invited are critics of my work. As a result, the book offers a rich mix of research methodologies and paradigmatic approaches to exploring, testing, and elaborating the cultural-ecological model of minority achievement.

Part I: History and Framework

The first five chapters (of six) in Part I lay out the intellectual history and theoretical foundations of my cultural-ecological model of minority achievement. As I pointed out earlier in this chapter, a number of my critics have misinterpreted the cultural-ecological model, or reduced it to the 1986 Fordham-Ogbu article, a small portion of which is the "burden of 'acting White'." Based on their interpretations of my work, some scholars have constructed and tested a thesis about Black students' school performance that is quite different from either the Fordham-Ogbu (1986) article's thesis or the more comprehensive, multi-faceted cultural-ecological model I developed subsequent to 1986. Some critics have reduced oppositional culture to the phrase "acting White" and have failed to distinguish my own scholarship from the joint work I did with Fordham and also Fordham's own research. To assess the contribution of the scholarship that purports to challenge, extend, support, clarify or refute the cultural-ecological model, oppositional culture, or "acting White," it is necessary for readers first to understand what I previously have written, and then to compare it to what critics and supporters contend I have written. Finally, readers can assess the contribution of the research on minority achievement written by other scholars in the field.

To that end, in this present chapter I have traced the history and development of the concepts of collective identity and cultural frame of reference over two decades. I clarified the differences in the theoretical approaches to minority achievement among my cultural-ecological model, the Fordham-Ogbu thesis, and Fordham's theory.

In Chapter 2, I elaborate upon the concept of collective identity and how it evolved among Black Americans in historical context, distinguishing it from other concepts of identity. I trace the evolution of the concepts of oppositional collective identity and cultural frame of references, connecting them to the Black experience with "the burden of 'acting White'." Finally, I suggest the continuities between the historical and contemporary experiences of "the burden of 'acting White'."

I draw upon my ethnographic fieldwork in Stockton, CA, Oakland, CA, and Shaker Heights, OH to develop and support the arguments that I present in the next four chapters (2 through 5). In Chapter 3, I make the case that the epistemological elements of ethnographic research are the most appropriate for investigating the questions regarding minority academic achievement about which I am concerned. I identify why ethnographic research is the appropriate research design, describe the elements of ethnographic research that distinguish it from other forms of qualitative inquiry, and argue that neither nonethnographic, qualitative strategies nor survey research can produce the rich, textured, nuanced understanding of the informants' lives necessary to examine the questions that motivate my research agenda. These distinctions are crucial because my critics frequently base their challenges on the results of survey research or qualitative interviews, not ethnographic research they have conducted.

Chapter 4, draws upon findings from my ethnographic studies of peer pressures among Black students in Shaker Heights, OH and Oakland, CA. I found that not all peer pressures exerted by Black students are negative. However, the chapter focuses on two kinds of peer pressures that adversely affect students' academic engagement: one arising from students' interpretation of certain school requirements as "White"; the other pressures are related to nonacademic priorities.

Chapter 5, describes more fully the historical and cultural dynamics of collective identity as they affect schooling in an African American community. I use findings from a comparative investigation of community forces and collective identity in Oakland, CA to illustrate (1) that "acting White" is not merely a result of students' interactions with the school, but rather, it reflects historical patterns and transactions in the larger community contexts outside the school walls, and (2) Blacks reject certain "White" attitudes and behaviors conducive to school success, but not because achievement is "White." Most Black students want both school success (good grades) *and* to be accepted by peers, and thus they face demands for contradictory conduct—to achieve academic success, but not to engage in behaviors that are both conducive to making good grades and to challenging their identity as an authentic Black person (e.g., by speaking Standard English).

In Chapter 6, Signithia Fordham provides a rare insight into the conceptualization of the influential 1986 article, "Coping with the burden of 'acting White'," her professional relationship with me, and her own struggles as a scholar. Fordham discusses the differences between her theoretical formulation and mine. She argues that unlike the cultural-ecological model, which emphasizes social-structural and historical factors, hers stresses expressive as well as adaptive responses to those determinants. She notes that although her theory was built upon mine, she "was not sure if Ogbu was ever fully convinced of the validity of my point of view." This chapter is important for many reasons, not the least of which is because the author reinforces the claim that critics who do not distinguish between the cultural-ecological model, the Fordham-Ogbu thesis, and Fordham's own work fail to make crucial distinctions, and thereby weaken their critique of the work.

Part II: Collective Identity, Black Americans, and Schooling

Part II presents five ethnographic studies and one empirical investigation of the effects of achievement ideologies, peer group effects, and racial identities on academic behavior among Black American youth. David A. Bergin and Helen C. Cooks, in Chapter 7, investigate 38 relatively high-achieving African American and Mexican American students in various high schools, public and private, in a Midwestern city. The respondents do not report shunning academic achievement in order to avoid accusations of "acting White." Most of the good students interviewed reported no loss of ethnic identity. Good students reported feeling strong resentment toward peers who accused them of "acting White," but they denied being intimidated by the accusations.

In Chapter 8, Linwood Cousins draws upon findings from his ethnography of Community High in Newark, where students have ethnic pride while embracing education. Cousins argues that there is significant variability in responses to education among Black youth. Some African Americans are pro-Black and pro-education, while others are pro-Black and anti-education. Cousins challenges the narrowness of the concept of "acting White" by noting its failure to consider the dimensions of time and place in the formulation of student identities vis-à-vis education and achievement.

Much of the prior scholarship on oppositional cultural frameworks has depicted involuntary minority cultures as internally uniform. In Chapter 9, A. A. Akom challenges the oppositional cultural explanation: (1) by demonstrating that through the religious tenets and practices of the Nation of Islam (NOI), young female members develop a Black achievement ideology, resulting in their adoption of the kind of studious orientation to school that is usually demonstrated by voluntary immigrant groups; and

(2) by demonstrating the ways in which Black people differentially make sense of and enact what it means to be "Black."

In Chapter 10, Margaret Beale Spencer and Vinay Harpalani employ Cross's Nigrescence model and Spencer's Phenomenological Variant of Ecological Systems theory as frameworks to argue that the Fordham-Ogbu thesis misinterprets the meaning of "acting White." Spencer and Harpalani suggest that racial identity, sociohistorical context, and cultural socialization are important to discussing achievement orientation. Rather than have the African American community reevaluate its attitude toward education, Spencer and Harpalani suggest that changes must occur in American society that foster more equitable and supportive education. In addition, the authors call for Afrocentrism and the necessary material and cultural resources to improve education for African American youth.

Lois Weis makes the case in Chapter 11, that student cultures play a mediating role in the production of school outcomes. Weis maintains that student cultures are semi-autonomous and are linked to the structural conditions of the larger society. She draws on her own ethnographic study of Black students' community college culture, as well as ethnographies conducted by other scholars, to show how the structural tensions reflected in student cultures are recreated in school. Given that students recreate their own cultures within schools and that peer culture affects academic outcomes, she argues that educational reform also must target social institutions beyond the schools.

Karen McCurtis Witherspoon, Anita Jones Thomas, and Suzette L. Speight investigate the influence of African Americans' racial identity and peer relations on academic achievement in Chapter 12. Using survey data from Upward Bound students at one university, they find that within-group differences in racial identity attitudes are related to student performance. Contrary to the "acting White" argument, the authors find that a positive self-identity as a Black American is linked to academic success for many students.

Part III: Reassessment and Methodological Issues

The five chapters in Part III illustrate an ongoing debate among scholars who employ quantitative data to explore various aspects of the oppositional cultural framework. Phillip J. Cook and Jens Ludwig (Chapter 13) and Douglas B. Downey (Chapter 14) test oppositional culture theory using large national survey data. Neither finds support for it. George Farkas (Chapter 15), in contrast, argues that Downey's analyses are flawed and that, in fact, survey data support the model's tenets. Roslyn Arlin Mickelson (Chapter 16) uses data from a single school district and finds support for the notion that an oppositional cultural framework impedes achievement for some Black students. Collectively, the chapters highlight the strengths and methodological challenges of quantitative approaches for investigating the cultural-ecological model of minority achievement.

In Chapter 13, Philip J. Cook and Jens Ludwig test the "acting White" hypothesis using data collected from the National Educational Longitudinal Study (NELS). The authors are concerned with whether African American students report feeling alienated from school, and whether school success leads to greater peer ostracism than it does for Whites. Cook and Ludwig find no race difference in levels of alienation or ostracism among successful students. They argue that differences in peer group attitudes do not account for the Black–White achievement gap.

Chapter 14 summarizes earlier research that Douglas B. Downey conducted with James Ainsworth using nationally representative survey data. The authors expected to confirm oppositional culture theory, but instead found evidence that Blacks reported more pro-schooling values than Whites, contrary to what oppositional culture theory predicts. In this chapter, Downey notes that current disputes surrounding oppositional culture theory depend, in part, on what kind of evidence is accepted as reliable indicators of Black students' attitudes and values. Although Blacks exhibit poorer classroom behavior than Whites, their consistently pro-school attitudes suggest that lower performance cannot be due to an oppositional culture that devalues education. Downey makes the case for trusting that Blacks mean what they say about school.

George Farkas's chapter continues his ongoing exchange with Downey (and Ainsworth) about the existence and effects of oppositional culture on the achievement gap. In Chapter 15, he highlights the qualitative/quantitative methodology debate of which he has been a part, summarizes and critiques the published work of Downey and Ainsworth, and then offers new evidence in support of the oppositional culture model's effects on achievement. Farkas reports that, as predicted, oppositional culture is stronger among ethnic minority and low-income students than among White and middle-class children. However, he finds that oppositional culture explains only a modest proportion of the achievement gap between these groups. He speculates that it may be a consequence of poor achievement rather than a cause of it.

In Chapter 16, Roslyn Arlin Mickelson extends her earlier research on the attitude-achievement paradox among Black adolescents. She uses survey data from the Charlotte-Mecklenburg Schools (NC) to test the relationships among students' oppositional, abstract, and concrete attitudes and academic performance. She reports that oppositional attitudes vary by race, class, and gender and that they affect adolescents' achievement in predictable ways. Notably, oppositional attitudes have a negative effect on achievement while concrete attitudes have a positive effect.

Mickelson explores the implications of her findings for the cultural-ecological model and the minority achievement gap.

In Chapter 17, Miles Anthony Irving and Cynthia Hundley investigate achievement motivation among African American males. The authors operationalize oppositional identity by measuring cultural mistrust, academic outcome expectations, outcome value, resistant cultural attitudes, and ethnic identity affirmation. They employ structural equation modeling to show that oppositional identity had a negative influence on the academic achievement of 115 African American male high-school students.

Part IV: Cross-Cultural Studies of Identity

Ethnic identity is a central element of the cultural-ecological model, and the chapters in Part IV explore identity and achievement cross-culturally. One value of cross-cultural studies is their ability to demonstrate the utility of a theoretical model across multiple sites. The chapters in this section illustrate the value of the cultural-ecological model for understanding the educational performance of Latinos and Navajo youth, as well as African Americans.

Maria Eugenia Matute-Bianchi discusses situational ethnicity and patterns of school performance among immigrant and nonimmigrant Mexican-descent students in Chapter 18. Matute-Bianchi explores the relationship of ethnic identity and consciousness among various groups of Mexican-descent students to their patterns of school performance. She demonstrates how a specific ethnic label serves as a cognitive resource that is strategically exploited and manipulated within given contexts of structured inequality.

Donna Deyhle presents the results of a decade-long ethnographic study of the lives of Navajo youth in a border reservation community in Chapter 19. She describes manifestations of the racial and cultural struggle between Navajos and Anglos in schools and the workplace. While differences in culture play a role in the divisions between Anglos and Navajos, Deyhle asserts that these differences intertwine with power relations in the larger community and that Navajo students' school successes and failures are best understood as part of this larger racial conflict.

In Chapter 20, April Taylor presents findings from a study of middle-school students' ethnic identity and achievement. She finds ethnic differences between Latino and African American students' reports of perceived discrimination, cultural mistrust, unfair school rules, immobility, and strong ethnic identity. Taylor's findings offer support for the model of oppositional identity used in her research, but they suggest that oppositional identity may be composed of different dimensions for different ethnic groups. Results are discussed in terms of their implications for the cultural-ecological model.

Angela Valenzuela uses the cultural-ecological model as a lens to examine the dissatisfaction and frustration with schooling among Mexican-Americans at Sequin High School (TX). In Chapter 21, Valenzuela discusses how Mexican-American student resistance is grounded in widespread feelings of resentment toward subtractive schooling, that is, the kind of schooling that fails to reflect or honor Mexican-American students' cultural heritage. She shows how and why students demand a respectful, trusting relationship between themselves and educators, as well as a curriculum inclusive of their Mexican culture and identity.

Part V: Model Programs and Applications

A number of school reformers have incorporated insights from research on the cultural-ecological model into systematic programs designed to narrow the race gaps. The two chapters in this section of the book offer examples of this type of research-based intervention. The first chapter examines an intervention designed to narrow the higher education enrollment and retention gap. Hugh Mehan, Lea Hubbard, and Irene Villanueva describe the positive effects of AVID, a detracking and college preparatory program for Latino and African American high-school students from San Diego, CA. Chapter 22 discusses how by adopting a strategy of "accommodation without assimilating"—a strategy for academic success previously associated with voluntary minority ethnic groups—these students from involuntary minority ethnic groups affirmed their ethnic identity and developed an academic identity that contributed to their school success.

The second chapter in this section describes a grassroots program to enhance academic performance among Blacks in Shaker Heights, Ohio. In Chapter 23, Mary Lynn McGovern, Astrid Davis, and John U. Ogbu present the historical roots, philosophy, organization, precepts, activities, and early outcomes of the Minority Achievement Committee (MAC), a student-run program for underachieving Black males. Although the academic outcomes of MAC Scholars compared to non-MAC scholars are only suggestive of positive program effects, the data offer some evidence that grassroots initiatives can be effective agents for change, especially if they target the collective identity of Black students.

Part VI: Conclusion[3]

Kevin Michael Foster begins the final chapter in this book, Chapter 24, by asking readers rhetorically how many scholars have produced grand assessments that have remained relevant and worthy of discussion

30 years after their initial formulation. After duly noting that very few have done so, he observes that regardless whether one agrees or disagrees with the cultural-ecological model, one must acknowledge its power, resonance, and influence over the past 30 years. Foster's chapter situates my contributions in the field of educational anthropology, summarizes the criticisms of my work, and lays out an agenda for future scholarship that can clarify, correct, and strengthen the contributions of the cultural-ecological model. Foster argues that by forthrightly laying out this model and then allowing other scholars to engage and critique it, this volume also will encourage further research on my ideas. In doing so, Foster suggests this volume makes an important and lasting contribution to ongoing and vitally important discussions of the core problematics and theoretical debates in educational anthropology.

The final contribution to this book is the original 1986 *Urban Review* article, "The Burden of 'Acting White'," which appears in the appendix. It is included in the volume so that readers can either familiarize or reacquaint themselves with this influential piece of scholarship.

NOTES

1   Among African Americans, these behaviors are labeled as "White"; they are called "Chinese" by Malays in Singapore; "Ippan" by Buraku outcasts and Koreans in Japan; and "Pakeha" by Maoris in New Zealand.
2   Editors' note: For readers who never met him, it may be useful to know that John U. Ogbu was a Nigerian scholar educated at the University of California, Berkeley.
3   Marcellina Ogbu invited Kevin Foster to write a conclusion for the volume after John U. Ogbu's death.

REFERENCES

Burger, H. C. (1968). *Ethnic pedagogy: A manual in sensitivity, with techniques for promoting cross-cultural teaching by fitting ethnic patterns.* Albuquerque, NM: Southwestern Cooperative Educational Laboratory, Inc.

Castile, G. P., & Kushner, G. (1981). *Persistent peoples: Cultural enclaves in perspective.* Tucson: University of Arizona Press.

Clark, E. M. (1971). *A syllabus for an interdisciplinary curriculum in African-American studies.* Oakland, CA: Merritt College & Berkeley Unified School District, Mimeo.

DeVos, G. A. (1967). *Japan's invisible race.* Berkeley: University of California Press.

DeVos, G. A. (1984). *Ethnic persistence and role degradation: An illustration from Japan.* Unpublished manuscript presented at the American-Soviet Symposium on Contemporary Ethnic Processes in the USA and the USSR. New Orleans, LA.

DeVos, G. A. (1995). Ethnic pluralism: Conflicts and accommodation. In L. Romanucci-Ross & G. A. DeVos (Eds.), *Ethnic identity: Creation, conflict, and accommodation* (pp. 15–41). Walnut Creek, CA: Altimira Press.

Dozier, E. P. (1951). Resistance to acculturation and assimilation in an Indian pueblo. *American Anthropologist, 53*, 56–66.

Erickson, F., & Mohatt, J. (1986). The social organization of participant structure in two classrooms of Indian students. In G. D. Spindler (Ed.), *Doing the ethnography of schooling: Educational anthropology in action* (pp. 132–174). New York: Holt.

Fordham, S. (1984). *Ethnography in a high school: Learning not to be a native.* A paper presented at the 83rd Annual Meeting of the American Anthropological Association, Denver, CO, November 14–18.

Fordham, S. (1988). Racelessness as a factor in Black students' success: pragmatic strategy or pyrrhic victory? *Harvard Educational Review, 58*(1), 54–84.

Fordham, S. (1991). Peer-proofing academic competition among Black adolescents: "Acting white" Black American style. In C. E. Sleeter (Ed.), *Empowerment through multicultural education.* Albany: State University of New York Press.

Fordham, S. (1996). *Blacked out: Dilemmas of race, identity, and success at Capital High.* Chicago: University of Chicago Press.

Fordham, S., & Ogbu, J. U. (1986). Black students' school success: Coping with the burden of "acting White." *The Urban Review, 18*(3), 176–206.

Gallimore, R., Boggs, J. W., & Jordan, C. (1974). *Culture, behavior, and education: A study of Hawaiian-Americans.* Beverly Hills, CA: Sage.

Gay, J., & Cole, M. (1967). *The new mathematics and an old culture: A study of learning among the Kpelle of Liberia.* New York: Harcourt.

Green, V. M. (1981). Blacks in the United States: The creation of an enduring people. In G. Castile and G. Kushner (Eds.), *Persistent peoples: Cultural enclaves in perspective* (pp. 69–77). Tucson: University of Arizona.

Heyneman, S. P. (1979). Why impoverished children do well in Ugandan schools. *Cooperative Education, 15*(2), 175–185.

Holt, G. S. (1972). Inversion in Black communication. In T. Kochman (Ed.), *Rappin' and stylin' out* (pp. 152–159). Chicago: The University of Illinois Press.

Imoagene, O. (1981). Personal communication. Department of Sociology, University of Ibadan, Nigeria.

Inkeles, A. (1968). Social structure and the socialization of competence. In *Harvard Educational Review, Socialization and Schools* (pp. 50–68). Cambridge, MA: Harvard University Press.

La Belle, T. J. (1976). An anthropological framework for studying education. In J. I. Roberts & S. K. Akinsanya (Eds.), *Educational patterns and cultural configurations: The anthropology of education* (pp. 67–82). New York: David McKay Company.

Lanteracnni, V. (1967). *The religion of the oppressed: A study of modern messianic movements.* New York: Mentor.

Leacock, E. (1985). The influence of teacher attitudes on children's classroom performance: Case studies. In K. Borman (Ed.), *The social life of children in a changing society* (pp. 47–64). Norwood, NJ: ABLEX.

Lewis, D. K. (1979). *Schooling, literacy and sense modality.* Unpublished manuscript, Department of Anthropology, University of California, Santa Cruz.

Litherland, R. H. (1978). *The role of the Church in educational change: A case history of a feasible strategy.* Unpublished doctoral dissertation, Department of Advanced Pastoral Studies, San Francisco Theological Seminary.

Low, V. (1982). *The unimpressive race: A century of educational struggle by the Chinese in San Francisco.* San Francisco: East-West Publishing Co., Inc.

Lucas, S. R. (1999). *Tracking inequality: Stratification and mobility in American high schools.* New York: Teachers College Press.

Ma, E. A., & Ma, J. H. (1982). *The Chinese of Oakland: Unsung builders.* Oakland, CA: Oakland Chinese History Research Committee.

Malinowski, B. (1939). Native education and culture contact. *International Review of Missions, 25,* 480–515.

Musgrove, F. (1953). Education and the culture concept. *Africa, 23,* 110–126.

Myrdal, G. (1944). *An American dilemma: The Negro problem and modern democracy.* New York: Harper.

Ogbu, J. U. (1974). *The next generation: An ethnography of education in an urban neighborhood.* New York: Academic Press.

Ogbu, J. U. (1978a). *Minority education and caste: The American system in cross-cultural perspective.* New York: Academic Press.

Ogbu, J. U. (1978b). *The paradox of high aspirations and low school performance among Black students: A structural explanation.* University of Illinois, College of Educational Psychology, Urbana, Illinois, April 28.

Ogbu, J. U. (1978c). *The paradox of high aspirations and low school performance among Black students: A structural explanation.* Stanford University, School of Education, May 25.

Ogbu, J. U. (1979). *The paradox of high aspirations and low school performance among Black students: A structural explanation.* A paper presented at Stanford University, School of Education, May 25.

Ogbu, J. U. (1982a). Cultural discontinuities and schooling. *Anthropology and Education Quarterly, 13*(4), 290–307.

Ogbu, J. U. (1982b). *The paradox of high aspirations and low school performance among low income Blacks in Stockton, California.* A paper presented at the University of California, Berkeley, Department of Physics, April 26.

Ogbu, J. U. (1982c). *The paradox of high educational aspirations and low school performance among low-income Blacks.* A paper presented at Northwestern University, Evanston, IL, March 18.

Ogbu, J. U. (1986). *Identity, cultural frame and schooling among subordinate minorities.* Working Paper #6. Unpublished manuscript, University of California, Berkeley.

Ogbu, J. U. (1989). The individual in collective adaptation: A framework for focusing on academic under-performance and dropping out among involuntary minorities. In L. Weis, E. Farrar, & H. G. Petrie (Eds.), *Dropouts from schools: Issues, dilemmas and solutions* (pp. 181–204). Buffalo: State University of New York Press.

Ogbu, J. U. (1991). Immigrant and involuntary minorities in comparative perspective. In M. A. Gibson & J. U. Ogbu (Eds.), *Minority status and schooling* (pp. 3–33). New York: Garland.

Ogbu, J. U. (1992). Understanding cultural diversity and learning. *Educational Researcher*, 21(8), 5–14.

Ogbu J. U. (1994). Racial stratification and education in the U.S.: Why inequality persists. *Teachers College Record*, 96(2), 264–298.

Ogbu, J. U. (1997). Racial stratification in the United States: Why inequality persists. In A. H. Halsey, H. Lauder, P. Brown, & A. S. Wells (Eds.), *Education: Culture, economy, and society* (pp. 765–778). Oxford: Oxford University Press. (A modified version of 1994 publication.)

Ogbu, J. U. (2000). Collective identity and schooling. (English version.) In K. Shimizu (Ed.), *Education, knowledge and power* (pp. 410–449). Tokyo: Shinyosha Ltd.

Ogbu, J. U. (2003). *Black students in an affluent suburb: A study of academic disengagement*. Mahwah, NJ: Lawrence Erlbaum.

Ogbu, J. U., & Simons, H. D. (1998). Voluntary and involuntary minorities: A cultural-ecological theory of school performance with some implications for education. *Anthropology and Education Quarterly*, 29(2), 155–188.

Ogbu, J. U., & Stern, P. (2001). Caste and intellectual development. In J. Sternberg & E. Grigorenko (Eds.), *Environmental effects on cognitive abilities* (pp. 3–37). Mahwah, NJ. Lawrence Erlbaum.

Penfold, B. (1981). Personal communication. Education Officer, Maori and Island Education, Department of Education, Wellington, New Zealand.

Persell, C. H. (1977). The genesis of teachers' expectations. In B. N. Pavan (Ed.), *Education and inequality: The roots and results of stratification in American schools* (pp. 101–121). New York: The Free Press.

Philips, S. U. (1976). Commentary: Access to power and maintenance of ethnic identity as goals of multi-cultural education. *Anthropology and Education Quarterly*, 7(4), 10–12.

Reed, R. J. (1988). Expectations and student performance. In *Ethnicity, gender, school practice and the communication of expectations* (vol. 1). Sacramento: California State Department of Education.

Rist, R. (1970). Student social class and teacher expectations: The self-fulfilling prophecy in ghetto education. *Harvard Educational Review*, 40, 411–451.

Spicer, E. H. (1966). The process of cultural enslavement in middle America. 36th Congress of International de Amerianistas, *Seville*, 3, 267–279.

Spicer, E. H. (1971). Persistent cultural systems: A comparative study of identity systems that can adapt to contrasting environments. *Science*, 174, 795–800.

Spindler, G. D. (1974). The transmission of culture. In G. D. Spindler (Ed.), *Education and culture: Toward an anthropology of education* (pp. 279–310). New York: Holt.

Sundkler, B. (1961). *Bantu prophets*. New York: Oxford University Press.

Thrup, S. (1962). *Millenarian dreams in action: Essays in comparative study*. The Hague: Mouton.

Warner, W. L. (1965). Introduction. In A. Davis, B. B. Gardner, & M. R. Gardner (Eds.), *Deep South: A social anthropological study of caste and class* (pp. 3–14). Chicago: University of Chicago Press.

Wirth, L., & Goldhamer, H. (1939). The hybrid and the problem of miscegenation. In O. Klineberg (Ed.), *Characteristics of the American Negro* (pp. 249–270). New York: Harper.

Chapter 2

Collective Identity and the Burden of "Acting White" in Black History, Community, and Education

John U. Ogbu

Introduction

Having conducted comparative research on minority education for more than 15 years, I came to the conclusion that discrimination in society and school as well as minority responses to the discrimination, though significant, are not enough to explain why there are differences in school performance among minority groups. My comparative study suggested that two additional factors from the dynamics in minority communities also contributed to school performance differences. In a joint publication with Dr. Signithia Fordham in 1986, we stated that the two additional factors were *collective identity* or *fictive kinship* and *cultural frame of reference* (Fordham & Ogbu, 1986). We also reported a study of Capital High students in Washington, DC where we found that the two factors played a major role in school performance of Black adolescents.

The joint article has generated responses from the academic community beyond what we anticipated. It is the subject of dissertation studies (Carter, 1999; O'Connor, 1996; Taylor, 2001), several publications (Ainsworth-Darnell & Downey, 1998; Bergin & Cooks, 2002; Cook & Ludwig, 1997) and organized sessions at professional meetings (Epstein, 2003; Horvat & O'Connor, 2001). During the past two years, I have reviewed more than a dozen books and journal manuscripts on oppositional culture and schooling for publishers. Although it is gratifying to see the impact of the joint article on the academic community, the potential contributions of these activities to scholarship are limited by misinterpretations of the problem, replacing the thesis and making a different conclusion.

One of the shortcomings of current scholarship is the failure to distinguish among three different perspectives on collective identity, cultural frame of reference, and the schooling of Black adolescents. This has resulted in the translating of my cultural-ecological framework into a single-factor hypothesis of *oppositional culture*. In effect, critics construct and study a different problem than the one we laid out in the joint article.

An equally serious problem is that there is no evidence that authors are aware that throughout their history Black Americans have experienced the "burden of 'acting White' " because of their oppositional collective identity and cultural frame of reference. Lacking this knowledge, critics ignore the historical and community contexts of Black students' behavior and focus almost exclusively on the transactions between the students and their school. Basing their analysis on data collected at the level of student-school transactions, it is not surprising that some critics accuse Fordham and myself of assigning a race label ("acting White") to a common ridicule, namely, teasing and harassment, endured by academically achieving adolescents or "nerds." They also believe that we have read too much into a "concept that they themselves manufactured."

The purpose of this chapter is to correct these misinterpretations. I will start with the meaning of collective identity and how it differs from other identity concepts used in discussing Black students' experiences. This will be followed by a brief account of the evolution of Black American collective identity, a presentation of my study of Black American experience with the "burden of 'acting White' " in contemporary United States, and conclude with an exploration of a possible continuity between Black historical and community experiences with the "burden of 'acting White' " and the experience of Black students that I and my students have studied in Stockton (1968–70), Oakland (1989–93), San Francisco (1991–92), and Shaker Heights (1997).

PERSPECTIVES ON IDENTITY AND STATUS PROBLEMS

Psychologists have examined the development and school experience of minority children from a number of interesting perspectives as they relate to identity. Among them are: (a) the *Ericksonian ego identity* (Hauser, 1972); (b) *ethnic identity* based on Erickson's theory (Phinney & Rosenthal, 1992; Phinney & Rotheram, 1987); (c) *racial identity* as measured by racial attitudes (Branch, 1999); and (d) *underclass oppositional identity* (Cross, Strauss, & Fhagen-Smith, 1999, pp. 29–30). Among non-psychologists some have proposed (a) *negotiated identity* (Yon, 2000), and (b) *circumstantial/marketable identity or politics of recognition* (Cornell & Hartman, 1998). These are useful and interesting ways of looking at identity and minority status, but they have to be distinguished from collective identity as used in this chapter.

What is Collective Identity?

Collective identity refers to people's sense of who they are, their "we-feeling" or "belonging." People express their collective identity with emblems or cultural symbols that reflect their attitudes, beliefs, feelings, behaviors, and language or dialect. The persistence of a group's collective identity depends on the continuity of the external (historical and structural) forces that contributed to its formation. It also depends on the continuity of responses of the group (Castile & Kushner, 1981; DeVos, 1992, 1995; Spicer, 1966, 1971).

Collective identity usually develops because of people's collective experience or series of collective experiences. Warfare, conquest, colonization, forced labor, mass emigration, imposition of an outcast status, and enslavement are examples of the collective experience that leads to the formation of collective identity (Castile & Kushner, 1981; DeVos, 1995; Spicer, 1967). Usually, the collective identity of an oppressed minority group is created and maintained by two sets of factors: status problems and minority response to status problems.

Status Problems

Status problems are external forces that mark a group of people as a distinct segment from the rest of the population. A group so created is usually bounded and named. For example, the Emperor of Japan, by proclamation, created the Burakumin as an outcast group from the Japanese people when Japan established a four-tiered, rigid, caste-like stratification system during the Edo era in the 17th century. Before the establishment of the status groups, the people in the outcast category, the Burakumin, had been, like other Japanese, warriors, peasants, and artisans. Designated as outcasts, the Burakumin (people of special hamlet or residential area) were assigned the role of slaughtering animals and executing criminals, functions that the general public perceived as "polluting functions" under Buddhist and Shintoist beliefs. Their social ostracism and discrimination have continued even since they were emancipated in 1871 (DeVos, 1967; Hirasawa & Nabeshima, 1995). Similarly, White Americans created Black Americans as a separate and an enduring segment of the United States society through enslavement. Status problems are collective problems that members of the subordinate group find difficult if not impossible to solve within the existing system of majority–minority relations. They include the following:

1   *Involuntary incorporation into society*: Usually these minorities do not become minorities by choice. Rather they are forced into minority status against their will by conquest, colonization, enslavement

(e.g., Black Americans) or arbitrary subjection to the status of a pariah caste (e.g., the Burakumin of Japan).

2   *Instrumental discrimination*: for example, denial of equal access to good jobs, education, political participation and housing.

3   *Social subordination*: for example, residential and social segregation, hostility and violence; prohibition of intermarriage; requirement of the offsprings of intergroup mating to affiliate with one group with no choice. In some cases oppressed minorities are forced against their will to assimilate into the dominant group, although this assimilation usually results in marginalization.

4   *Expressive mistreatment*: for example, cultural, language, and intellectual denigration.

Dominant group members stigmatize minorities' food, clothing, music, values, behaviors, and language or dialect as bad and inferior to theirs. These four mechanisms are used by the dominant group to create and maintain the collective identity of the minorities; in other words, to "carve them out" and maintain them as a separate segment of society with a distinct identity. The existence of the minorities with a distinct collective identity remains as long as these mechanisms or mistreatment of the minorities remain (Ogbu, 2000).

The Response of Minorities to Status Problems

Minorities, both as a group and as individuals, feel the impact of status problems. Minorities experience their mistreatment regardless of their individual differences in education and ability, status, physical appearance, or place of residence. They know full well that they do not have the option of membership in the dominant group; they also know that they cannot easily escape from their more or less ascribed membership in a subordinate and disparaged group. Individuals who "pass" physically or culturally often find that the social and psychological costs are very high. Oppressed minorities are bitter for being forced into minority status and subjected to oppression. They usually hold the dominant group responsible for their "troubles" (e.g., their inferior economic and political status, demeaning social positions, poor health and housing, and stigmatized cultures and languages or dialects). Under this circumstance, involuntary minorities respond collectively as a group and they also respond as individuals in ways that reinforce their separate existence and collective identity. Furthermore, their response often makes their oppositional collective identity vis-à-vis their perceptions of the collective identity of the dominant group. That is, their very attempts to solve their status problem lead them to develop a new sense of who they are, which is in opposition to their understanding of who the dominant group members are.

Cultural and Language Frames of Reference

Closely related to their sense of collective identity is the way minorities interpret the cultural and language or dialect differences between them and the dominant group. We use the term "cultural frame of reference" to refer to the correct way of behaving and "language or dialect frame of reference" to refer to the correct way of talking from the point of view of the minorities. Cultural and language frames of reference are closely tied to collective identity, so that we can speak of them as the cultural identity and the language identity of the minorities. Where the latter is oppositional, the former is usually oppositional. Furthermore, where that is the case, we can regard the situation as one of oppositional culture and oppositional language or dialect. The relationship—oppositional or non-oppositional—between the cultural and language frames of reference of the minorities and that of the dominant group, determines to some degree the difficulty individual members of the minority group have in crossing cultural and language boundaries or learning to behave and talk like White people. However, this does not mean that all members of the minority group respond to the culture and language of the dominant group in opposition. As we shall see, minorities usually develop some strategies to deal with the demands that they behave and talk like dominant group members in order to achieve self-betterment in situations controlled by members of the dominant group.

THE CASE OF BLACK AMERICANS

Black American oppositional collective identity began to form before emancipation and has remained to the present. We have more information on the subject for more recent than earlier periods.

Pre-Emancipation Period

Status Problems

Enslavement and Mistreatment under Slavery

Black Americans became involuntary minorities when they were enslaved by White Americans. For more than 200 years they were denied basic human rights and exploited economically, politically, socially and expressively. They were tightly controlled by White slave owners, who forced them to behave like slaves. They were forbidden to behave in certain ways considered White prerogatives and were punished if they disobeyed. For example, they were punished for learning to read and write, where slaves were forbidden these activities (Haley, 1976). Punishment was sometimes extended to all slaves on the plantation, not just limited to the slave who committed the offence. This collective punishment was important in the creation of Black collective identity.

The treatment of Blacks following Nat Turner's "insurrection" is a good example of the collective blame and punishment that increased their sense of being a separate people with a collective identity. A slave, Nat Turner, led an "insurrection" in Southampton, Virginia in 1831. Following this incident, the movement of *all* Black people throughout the United States was restricted. Blacks were forbidden to assemble among themselves. The restriction even applied to children. For example, Black children in Washington, DC were no longer allowed to attend Sunday School with White children, as they did previously, for no other reason than that they were Black (Fordham, 1984; Styron, 1966).

Instrumental Discrimination

During slavery, Blacks were excluded by law and custom from economic, political and other opportunities open to Whites.

Social Discrimination

Non-reciprocal social interaction between Blacks and Whites was instituted during slavery. According to Starker (1971, p. 6), the ritual of social interaction required Blacks and Whites to behave toward each other in certain prescribed ways. For example, they had to use certain prescribed forms of address that expressed the "ritual." Blacks addressed White slave owners as master (*massa*), mistress (*mistis*), miss (*missy*), *boss* or *buckra*, with or without given names. Slave owners addressed Blacks as aunt, uncle, mammy, and sometimes daddy, boy (Starker, 1971, p. 6). The etiquette also required slaves to behave in a certain manner when he or she was spoken to by Whites. For example, the slave had to "stand attentively, respond politely, bow servilely to the extent, at times, of extreme evasion and deceit" (Starker, 1971, p. 7).

Expressive Discrimination

Expressive discrimination refers to White Americans' beliefs that Black slaves were culturally, linguistically, and intellectually inferior to them; it also refers to the treatment of Blacks based on such beliefs. Historically, the overarching ideology of White Americans was that Black Americans belonged to a race that was inferior to the White race biologically, culturally, and socially.

White denigration of Black culture began during slavery, with the myth that the slaves came from the "dark continent" of Africa that had not produced civilizations like other continents (Becknell, 1987). They forced the slaves to give up their African cultures and to adopt superior White culture. White cultural values, behaviors, and speech were presented as correct or proper; in contrast, Black cultural values, behaviors, and speech were presented as incorrect and improper.

In the case of language, slave owners took deliberate steps to rid the slaves of their indigenous African languages. There appeared to be a policy not to have several slaves speaking the same language on a plantation for fear that they would teach others their language, and that speaking the same language would make it easy for slaves to plan an escape or a slave revolt. To avoid such incidents, the slaves were forced to speak English. The language situation during slavery, especially the evolution of Black English dialects, contributed to the creation of Blacks as a separate and enduring people with a distinct collective identity.

Intellectual Denigration

This was (and is) an expressive exploitation because it makes White people feel good to think that they are more intelligent than Blacks.

Black Response to Status Problems during Slavery

Black Americans began to develop their sense of collective identity and of belonging together during slavery. Collective experience of oppression and exploitation caused them to develop the sense of a Black community that embodied their collective racial identity. It has been suggested that racial identity was more important than class or gender identity for the slaves because they knew only too well that all of them, regardless of class or gender, could be punished for an offence of one slave; and they could also be rewarded because of the good deed of one (Green, 1981; Rawick, 1972; Bethel, 1997). The racial identity formed during slavery has continued to influence Black perceptions of and responses to White treatment to this day. In my ethnographic research in Black communities, I have often found that, regardless of social class and gender, Black Americans tend to code their experiences with White Americans and with social institutions in terms of race, and not class or gender.

The expressive response of Blacks was particularly important in their construction and maintenance of oppositional collective identity. As noted earlier, White people forced Blacks to give up their African cultures and languages. Under oppression, Blacks developed a new culture and an English dialect different from and oppositional to the White way of behaving and talking (Green, 1981). Another area of expressing opposition was religion. Black religion evolved to satisfy slave masters' expectations that this would make it easier to control Blacks, but it turned out to be the opposite of those expectations. Reverend Calvin Marshall described this paradox as follows:

> [T]he [White] man systematically killed your [i.e., Black] language, killed your culture, tried to kill your soul, tried to blot you out—but somewhere along the way he gave us Christianity and gave it to use to enslave us. But it freed us because we understood things about it and we made it work for us in ways that it never worked for him.
>
> (Holt, 1972)

Black music was yet another aspect of cultural evolution for expressing difference and opposition to White domination and White ways. Blacks used their music not only to entertain, and to lighten the burden of their labor and other sufferings, but also as a means of communication, especially the transmission of messages they did not want White people to understand. For example, when Harriet Tubman sang "Steal Away, Steal Away, Steal Away to Jesus," she was not pleading for Blacks to convert to Christianity. Rather, she was telling them to run away through the Underground Railroad to the North of the United States or to Canada (Baer, 1984; Becknell, 1987, pp. 45–49).

The development of the Black English dialect was yet another means of expressing differences toward collective identity. Blacks developed their dialect because, as noted earlier, slave owners forbade them to speak indigenous African languages and required them to speak the English dialect. The slaves developed an English dialect that the slave masters did not and could not understand (Becknell, 1987; Holt, 1972).

Black American English dialect differs from White American Standard English in phonology, morphology, and syntax. But these differences are not as important for oppositional collective identity as are differences due to secondary meanings. The secondary meanings arose from dialect inversions. The inversion was that Blacks assigned to words, phrases, or statements reverse meanings or changed their functions from what they mean to White people. Thus, the same words appearing in both White English and Black English may have different and, often, opposite meanings. For example, the word "bad," which always means "bad" in White peoples' English, sometimes means "good" in Black English.

According to Holt (1972), Black slaves developed their linguistic opposition because they recognized that to use English like their White masters would mean submitting to an identity defeat. That is, it would mean that they accepted definitions of their slave or caste status built into the White semantic system. Language inversion "emerged during slavery to fight both linguistic and psychological entrapment" (Holt, 1972, p. 154).

The Burden of Acting White during Slavery

Black Americans became bi-cultural and bi-dialectical during slavery because they lived and worked in two different worlds that expected them to think, act, and react in a particular way, depending on where they found themselves. In the Black community and among themselves, most Blacks felt at ease to talk and do things they would never attempt in a White environment. Conversely, in a White environment, Blacks talked and behaved as White people expected, which would be inappropriate among the Black community (Becknell, 1987, p. 30).

As noted earlier, the ritual of social interaction between Blacks and Whites established during slavery required the two groups to behave toward each other in certain prescribed ways. Blacks were expected to act and react the way Whites wanted them to; otherwise, they would be punished or even put to death. As survival was the name of the game for Blacks, they talked and behaved the way Whites wanted.

Note, however, that Whites did not require Blacks to talk and behave the same way that White people actually talked and behaved; in other words, White slave owners did not require Blacks to "act White." In fact, Blacks were forbidden to talk like Whites; for example, they were forbidden to learn to read and write. What the Whites wanted was for Blacks to talk and behave according to White people's construction of Black speech and cultural behavior. When in front of White people, Blacks tried to talk and behave out of compliance to what White people were demanding. But when they were among themselves, they acted according to their cultural ways that White people hardly observed.

The same situation existed with regard to speech. White English dialect was portrayed by Whites and Blacks as proper, correct, good, and standard. Black English dialect, by contrast, was stigmatized as improper, incorrect, flat, country, slangish, and bad. Although White people required Blacks to speak in a particular way, the requirement was not for Blacks to talk like White people actually talked; in other words, White people did not require Black slaves to speak "correct" or "Standard English." Rather, they wanted Blacks to talk according to the White construction of Black speech based on Black "improper English." Blacks talked the way Whites wanted them to talk when with Whites out of compliance, but talked "Black" among themselves.

The burden of "acting White" before emancipation was how to comply with the White demand that Blacks should behave and talk like Blacks the way Whites thought that Blacks talked and behaved. It was not that Blacks should choose between behaving and talking the way White people actually behaved and talked and the way they themselves preferred to behave and talk.

There was no uniformity in Black response to this conflicting demand before emancipation. Rather, they evolved several strategies of coping with the "burden of 'acting White'." This is evident in the variety of stock characters played in novels, plays, drama, short stories, and films of and about that era (Bogle, 1989; Nestby, 1982; Starker, 1971). The characters included accommodative slaves, rebellious slaves, clowns, tragic mulattoes, Black mammies, and coons. These characters represented different responses to the "burden of 'acting White'." The accommodative slave (tom, servile Negro), for example, accepted his place as defined by Whites; and behaved and talked according to the White definition. The rebellious slave or "bad Negro" defied the law and the ritual of non-reciprocal social interaction. Black mammies were the nurturers of White offspring.

Black Collective Identity after Emancipation

Status Problems

Blacks continued to face status problems after emancipation. Instrumentally, they were subjected to extreme economic exploitation. They were denied free and fair competition with Whites in employment, wages, promotion, and entrepreneurship (Moore, 1981; Norgren & Hill, 1964; Novak, 1978). Before 1960, about the only places where Blacks could get jobs based on formal education and ability were segregated educational and health institutions serving the Black community (Frazier, 1957; Marshall, 1967; Ross, 1967). Although school credentials were a requirement for employment in the wider society, White employers used a job ceiling to deny them access to jobs, promotion and wages commensurate with their qualifications.

In the social domain, residential, sexual, social, and school segregation continued. Black people were residentially segregated by statute, regulatory authorities, and custom (Ogbu & Margold, 1986). School segregation followed suit. In many states sexual relationships between White women and Black men were forbidden and severely punished when the taboo was violated (Johnson, 1943, p. 220; Myrdal, 1944). Until the year 2000, there was a culturally sanctioned rule backed by statutes in many states, namely, that biracial children should be defined as Black and should affiliate with Blacks (Rockquemore & Brunsma, 2002; Wright, 2001).

Ritual non-reciprocal social interaction continued. White people continued to believe that Blacks were inferior to them. These beliefs were expressed in their treatment of Blacks' jokes, novels, short stories, drama, and movies (Johnson, 1931, p. 100). The beliefs aroused White aversion to Blacks and this, in turn, led to another White belief, namely, that Black Americans were not assimilable. Whites did not mean by this that Blacks were not capable of acquiring the education, economic status, and life-style of the White middle class. Rather, what they meant was that it was not desirable or acceptable to assimilate Blacks into White society to share their collective identity because they were colored and inferior (Myrdal, 1944, pp. 54, 100).

Whites continued to make Blacks collectively responsible for the offense of a single Black person. For example, in Rosewood, Florida in January 1923, about 1,500 White men from Rosewood and surrounding communities went to the Black neighborhood in Rosewood and killed 40 Black men, women, and children in retaliation for an alleged rape of a White woman by a Black man (CBS Television Network, 60 *Minutes*, 1984).

The threats of violence and punishment and the prevalence of lynching led Blacks to petition the United Nations in 1951 to intervene on their behalf (Patterson, 1951). Blacks suffered because Whites used them as scapegoats in times of economic hardships and political crisis (Frazier, 1957, pp. 155–156; Shapiro, 1988). They were denied political power through disenfranchisement in the Southern states and through gerry-mandering in the North.

Black Response to Status Problems after Emancipation

Blacks tried both as a group and as individuals to solve their status problems after emancipation. Blacks firmly believed that they were treated differently and badly because of their race and history. This interpretation of their social reality further motivated them to forge collective solutions to their collective status problems that reinforced their oppositional identity. Their collective solutions included the following:

Instrumental Solutions

Blacks accepted the criteria of getting good jobs, decent wages, and upward social mobility through education and hard work like Whites. But they soon realized that there was a job ceiling that prevented them from achieving these goals by merely meeting the criteria or rules that worked for White people. For this reason they developed folk theories of getting ahead in spite of the job ceiling. As a group, they came to believe that they had to meet additional requirements, which included collective struggle at a group level and clientship or uncle tomming as individuals. The various forms of collective struggle up to the 1960s constituted modes of coping with the instrumental aspect of their status problems. They included the following.

First, Booker T. Washington's idea of accommodation under the caste-like system of the old South was advocated. He believed that Black Americans could achieve economic self-sufficiency through industrial education and vocational training for the Black masses and through independent business enterprise for the higher classes. He emphasized working within mutually separate collective identities for Blacks and Whites (Hall, 1979).

W. E. B. DuBois and the National Association for the Advancement of Colored People (NAACP) disagreed with Washington's view. By contrast, they demanded equality of opportunity with Whites and full acceptance by White people, the second strategy. Actually, some version of this strategy was initiated during slavery by free Blacks like Delany and Douglas. In the 1930s its advocates picketed and boycotted White businesses in Black communities that discriminated against Blacks (Drake & Cayton, 1970; Hall, 1979, p. 99). This strategy increased the tension and mistrust between Blacks and Whites. More importantly, however, it increased Black Americans' sense of oppositional collective identity (Becknell, 1987).

The third strategy was separatism. The separatists did not believe that it was possible to achieve a satisfactory solution to Black status problems within the American social and economic system. They believed that the solution was for Blacks to leave the United States society both physically and spiritually, while heading for places like Africa, Mexico, Latin America, or a part of the United States set aside for Blacks. The best-known separatist movement was led by Marcus Garvey. It appealed to many Blacks, whether or not they formally belonged to it, because the movement promoted Black pride and collective identity (Hall, 1979; Redkey, 1969; Sygnnerstvedt, 1972, p. 133). Another influential separatist movement, especially in its early phase, was the Black Muslim Movement.

Social Response

It took about 50 years for the social response to the post-emancipation status problems to crystallize. Locke (1925, p. 631) reported that during the first 50 years "the minds of Blacks were burrowed in trenches of the Civil War and Reconstruction." But underneath this was a psychological development that eventually enabled Blacks to liberate themselves from "the tyranny of intimidation and implied inferiority" (Locke, 1925, p. 631). The new era arrived in the mid 1920s when Blacks began to demand changes in their representation in the White minds or social image. Until then, the prevailing social image was expressed in the ritual-ized non-reciprocal interaction and forms of addresses carried over from slavery, as well as other renditions created by the Civil War (Locke, 1925, pp. 631–632). By the 1920s, for example, "Tom and Sambo" were no longer acceptable. Locke (1925, p. 632) noted that "The Negro today wishes to be known for what he is, even in his faults and shortcomings;

[he] scorns a craven and even precarious survival at the price of seeming to be what he is not." Locke quoted an apt passage from a poem by Claude MacKay about the outlook of the *New Negro*:

Mine is the future, grinding down today
Like a great landship moving to the sea,
Where the green hungry waters restlessly
Heap mammoth pyramids and bark and roar
Their eerie challenge to the crumbling shore.

(Locke, 1925; p. 633)

Collective struggle against social discrimination went beyond ending non-reciprocal social interaction. Black Americans demanded social justice and acceptance by White Americans as social equals. Their strategies for achieving these goals included boycotts, protests, riots, civil disobedience, law suits, and lobbying for legislation (Berry, 1971; Weisbrodt, 1991). White Americans, of course, resisted the Black collective struggle for social justice and inclusion. This resistance, in turn, made Blacks more disappointed and mistrustful of White people, a situation that further increased their sense of oppositional collective identity.

Black fear and experience of physical violence also promoted their sense of oppositional collective identity and group loyalty. Group loyalty was necessary because White violence was often indiscriminate (Fordham, 1985). The Rosewood incident described earlier was an example of White indiscriminate violence after the emancipation period.

Expressive Responses

The emergence of the Harlem Renaissance and *The New Negro* also brought changes in the post-emancipation expressive adaptations of Black Americans. New interpretation of the *Negro Spirituals* is a case in point. Before the first quarter of the 20th century, *Negro Spirituals* were not accepted as original creations of folk hymns by Blacks. Instead, they were regarded as imitations of White Wesleyan hymns. Blacks were ashamed of this interpretation, but by the 1920s they were courageous enough to reject the White interpretation that their hymns were not original. Equally important is that Blacks began to express their collective identity at this time in poetry, jazz, art, and culture (Hayes, 1925; pp. 666–677).

The Burden of "Acting White" after Emancipation

The burden of "acting White" after emancipation was different from the burden of "acting White" before emancipation. Recall that before emancipation "acting White" was that out of compliance Blacks had to behave and talk in the manner defined for them by the Whites to satisfy White people's expectations. Again, White people did not require that Blacks should behave and talk the way White people themselves actually behaved and talked.

However, after emancipation, Blacks were required to behave and talk the way White people actually behaved and talked: (a) in situations requiring the mastery of certain White knowledge, behaviors, and speech, such as for formal education, upward social mobility, and participation in societal institutions controlled by White people, while (b) Blacks were also now required to behave and to talk like White people to gain social acceptance and to be treated as social equals by White people. Blacks, therefore, now had to master two sets of cultural and dialect frames of reference: (a) Black ways of behaving and talking among themselves; and (b) White ways of behaving and talking in White-controlled situations. The co-existence of Black and White frames of reference, of course, has had a dynamic relationship and changed over time. What was not required of Blacks was to assume White people's collective identity.

But there was one additional problem: Blacks were often not rewarded or accepted as equal by Whites when they successfully learned to behave and talk like Whites or had obtained stipulated educational qualifications.

Coping with the Burden of "Acting White" after Emancipation

After emancipation, Black Americans did not abandon their oppositional cultural and dialect frames of reference to embrace the White cultural frame of reference for education and upward social mobility. However, they accepted the need to behave and talk like White people (to "act White") for education, upward social mobility, equality, and acceptance by White people. This was a dilemma for Black people. How they responded to this dilemma, in other words, how they resolved the tension between the demands that they act according to White frames of reference, rather than the Black frames of reference in situations controlled by White people, constituted their coping with the "burden of acting White." They developed five identifiable coping strategies.

Cultural and Linguistic Assimilation

Some Black people, after emancipation, chose to assimilate in culture and language. They tried very hard to emulate White people in behavior, speech, and thought because they believed that their chances of success in education, employment in the corporate economy, and in being socially accepted by White people would be better if they abandoned Black frames of reference and emulated White people. Becknell (1987) has described some techniques such as Blacks used to assimilate: They straightened their hair with scalp-brushing chemicals because Black people's hair was stigmatized as "bad"; bleached their skin to look more White (some even stopped drinking coffee because coffee made a person "black"); pinched their nose to make it more pointed instead of flat; learned to talk like White people, including going for special coaching to talk more "properly"; distanced themselves socially from other Black people; and joined White churches.

Accommodation without Assimilation

Another coping strategy for some was to more or less live in two worlds at different times: Black and White. Within the Black community they behaved and talked according to the Black frames of reference. In the White world, like school, work, and among White people, they behaved and talked like White people required. This category of Blacks could "go home again," according to Becknell (1987).

Ambivalence

The third coping strategy was ambivalence. Ambivalent Blacks knew, for instance, that "proper English" was necessary for school success and for getting good jobs. However, they also knew that no matter how hard a Black person tried to talk like White people, he or she would still sound Black. So, for them, trying to "talk proper" was only "puttin' on" or pretending to be White (Ogbu, 1999). Similarly, some ambivalents believed that the obstacles facing Blacks in employment, wages, promotion, and education were racial; the fact that they were Black, not because they did not behave or talk like White people, was the key (Ogbu, 1999). I will give a concrete example later in the chapter.

Resistance or Opposition

Some Blacks opposed adopting White cultural and language frames of reference or "acting White" anywhere because they believed or feared that this would mean giving up their Black ways. It would also mean accepting White people's interpretation of the cultural and dialect differences between the two races. From their point of view, White people defined White ways as good and defined Black ways as bad. One informant in Oakland, California, gave a historical explanation of this resistance to "acting White" in the Black community. He said that, since slavery, White Americans have tried to get Black people to replace their inferior culture and dialect with superior White culture and language before White people would accept them. It began with teaching house slaves to imitate their White masters to make them different and superior over field hands. After emancipation, White people established "finishing schools" and "special education" to improve Black speech, manners, and behaviors. These programs assumed that Black speech, manners, and behaviors were bad and should be replaced with good White speech, manners, and behaviors. A similar reason was given by some Black parents during ethnographic interviews in San Francisco for not wanting to speak Standard English (Luster, 1992).

Encapsulation

Finally, some Blacks were more or less encapsulated in Black cultural and dialect frames of reference. They did not behave or talk like White people because they did not know how to rather than because they were opposed to doing so.

I have limited data on social sanctions or peer pressures against Blacks who chose any of these coping strategies to resolve the conflicting demands. Nor do we have data on how people handled or coped with the social sanctions. But there must have been consequences. More research is needed in this area.

Post-Civil Rights Era Black Responses to "Acting White"

Status Problems

Significant changes have occurred in the status problems of Blacks since the civil rights movement of the 1960s. These changes were most evident in the economic and political sectors. The factors that raised the job ceiling for Blacks included (a) executive orders (e.g., President Kennedy's Committee on Equal Employment Opportunity in 1961); (b) federal legislation (e.g., Title VIII of the Civil Rights Act of 1964); (c) the war on poverty; and (d) pressures from civil-rights organizations (Burkey, 1971; Ferman, Kornbluh, & Miller, 1968). Although the changes have benefited mainly college-educated Blacks, not the Black masses, college-educated Blacks in the White establishments have complained of a glass ceiling. They say that they lag behind their White peers in promotion because of their race (Benjamin, 1991; Case, 1995).

Social Discrimination

This has decreased but has not been entirely eliminated. Hostility and violence are still directed against Blacks and other minorities in times of economic recession, such as during the 1980s (State of California, 1982). The definition of inter-racial children as Black and their affiliation with Blacks continued until the census of 2000. Children can now choose their affiliation. Residential and school integration is now more or less a matter of economic status, but segregation remains because of "White flight."

Expressive Discrimination

Many Whites probably no longer believe that Blacks are inferior to Whites but the residue of this belief remains. A poll conducted by *Newsweek* magazine in 1978 found that about one quarter of the Whites (25 percent) still believed that Blacks had less intelligence than Whites, and about 15 percent thought that Blacks were inferior to White people (*Newsweek*, 1979, p. 48). The publication of *The Bell Curve* by Herrnstein and Murray (1994) is a reminder that the Whites' belief in the inferiority of Blacks still exists even in White "scientific" circles. After a recent report in the *San Francisco Chronicle* about my research on Black academic performance, one reader sent me statistics on standardized test performance along with a lengthy letter on the genetic basis of the low score of Blacks. The debate goes on about Black genetic endowment for intelligence (The Gene Media Forum, 2002). As this goes to press, Black culture and language are still stigmatized.

Black Response to Status Problems in Post-Civil Rights Era

The civil rights mobilization of the 1960s reinforced Black collective identity, especially with the emergence of the Black Power Movement. For Blacks, the ideology and strategies of the movement removed the stigma attached to being Black, increased race pride and provided a shared slogan that "Black is Beautiful." Thus, their response to the status problems complemented their collective identity as we find it today.

OPPOSITIONAL COLLECTIVE IDENTITY IN THE CONTEMPORARY BLACK COMMUNITY

Black Americans have always aspired to succeed like White Americans, but they have always been aware of the obstacles facing them because of their status or race (Ferman, Kornbluh, & Miller, 1968; Myrdal, 1944; Ogbu, 1978; Rowan, 1967; Sochen, 1972). Another obstacle is the "burden of 'acting White'." Before and after emancipation, as well as after the civil rights movement, they responded to this obstacle with one of the five culturally patterned strategies or coping responses described earlier: assimilation, accommodation without assimilation, ambivalence, resistance or opposition, and encapsulation. Clearly, resistance or opposition has always been just one of the coping responses. It is probably by no means the most prevalent coping strategy during any of the periods.

Even though it is just one of the strategies for coping with the "burden of 'acting White' " I focus on it in this section to show that oppositional collective identity or oppositional culture exists in the contemporary Black community or post-civil rights movement and provides the context for understanding why Black students label and avoid some attitudes and behaviors as "White."

In the 1980s, I studied the collective identity and frames of reference in the Black community by reviewing ethnographic and other literature (Ogbu & Margold, 1986). The latter included more than 50 Black American autobiographies (Ogbu & Simons, H. D., 1998). I discovered in this research six recurring identity themes: (a) oppositional collective identity, (b) oppositional cultural frame of reference, (c) strategies for coping with the burden of "acting White," (d) interpretations of the coping strategies, (e) social sanctions or peer pressures against some coping strategies, and (f) coping strategies against the social sanctions. I will revisit each of these now.

Oppositional Collective Identity

One indicator of a sense of collective identity among contemporary Black Americans is the frequency that Black authors cite the passage about "double consciousness" from DuBois' (1982/1903) *Souls of Black Folks*. In the second half of the 20th century, a number of events have reinforced this double consciousness. Among them are the civil rights mobilization, the Black Power Movement and the Black Muslim Movement. As noted earlier, the Black Power Movement was particularly important in reinforcing the oppositional collective identity. Its ideology and tactics removed the stigma attached to being Black and increased race pride and provided an appealing slogan, "Black is Beautiful." These practices removed the fear, shame, and stigma as well as the social costs of being Black for those who wanted to express the outward symbols of Black collective identity. They began to display openly what they had always felt covertly, namely, that they were proud to be Black. The new public and psychological acknowledgement and the expression of Black collective identity have not been limited to activists or poor Blacks. They have reached every segment of Black America. They have permeated the works of Black artists, performers and scholars (Becknell, 1987). They have been embraced by Black professionals and the Black middle class in general.

This development was taking place during my ethnographic research in Stockton, California in 1968 and 1970, the heyday of the movement. Thus, I had a chance to observe identity transformations among both poor and middle-class Blacks first-hand. The transformation included shifts in identity labels from "Negro" to "Colored" to "Black"; changes in identity symbols, such as from processed to natural hair styles; and changes in organizational membership, such as Black teachers in Stockton who refused to join the Black Teachers' Alliance in 1969 (because the term Black was bad and militant) to 100 percent membership by the same teachers in the Black Teachers' Alliance in 1972. The changes continued. During my research in Oakland in the early 1990s, a conference was organized in New Orleans by Blacks to change their collective identity label to African Americans. We also studied the response to this label change by Blacks in Oakland.

The strongest evidence of oppositional collective identity among contemporary Black Americans is linguistic. For example, Blacks use positive labels among themselves, such as "soul" (implying eternity, spirituality, and transcendence); "brother and sister" (implying some of the closest of kin), and "bloods" (referring to the very stuff of life). In contrast, they label White people, particularly White men, "Ofays" (i.e., enemies, foes). According to Johnson (1972, p. 172), Blacks have only one positive label for White men, namely, "blue-eyed soul brother" which was usually reserved for "hippies" in the 1960s.

Oppositional Frames of Reference

The literature review provided evidence that Black and White cultural and dialect frames of reference are different and oppositional. For example, both Smitherman (1977, p. 75) and Boykin (1986, p. 63) described Black culture as characterized by spirituality, harmony with nature, and being "in time" rather than "on time." Boykin (1986, p. 63) added other areas in which Black and White cultures are also oppositional. For example, Blacks use more organized metaphors, have more preference for expressive movement, place more emphasis on inter-connectedness, and have a richer oral tradition. The two cultures differ in cognitive modes and non-verbal discourse (Shade, 1984); styles of walking, talking, and gesturing (Folb, 1980, p. 45); and attitudes (Davis and Watson, 1985, p. 113; Folb, 1980, p. 45; Weis, 1985, p. 35). The strongest evidence of oppositional frame is in language use or communication (Boykin, 1986, p. 58; Daiby, 1972; Folb, 1980, pp. 227–260; Holt, 1972; Smitherman, 1977). According to Daiby (1972, p. 175), Black Americans believe that they have to be "one jump ahead" of White people in verbal communication. He goes on to say that the function of Black vernacular English has been to "strengthen the in-group solidarity of Black Americans to the exclusion of Whites, and to deceive, confuse and conceal information from White people in general" (Daiby, 1972, p. 172).

Interpretations of Adoption of "White" Culture and Dialect Frames

An important clue as to how Black Americans interpret the adoption of White cultural and language frames of reference or "acting White" for professional success comes from a description in *Black Rage* of the dilemma of successful Black professionals in White business. As the authors put it:

> The only way out, if indeed it can be so considered, is a poor one at best and the price paid for success is terribly high. We speak of those Negroes who make it by emulating the White man. They accept as a fact that Negroes are not so smart as White people and decided to reject their blackness and, insofar as possible, embrace whiteness. They identify with White men in every way and add to that contempt for black people. In the process they gain some of the "White man's magic." They acquire some of the superior qualities they attribute to him. They may as a result feel more competent, but it is a direct function of the feeling that "other Negroes" are incompetent. In this way they develop a contempt for themselves, because, however much they avoid it, they remain black, and there are things about themselves that will yet remind them of their blackness and those reminders will evoke feeling of self-hatred and self-depreciation.
>
> (Grier and Cobbs, 1968; emphasis added)

Many authors state explicitly that they themselves and/or Black Americans in general see successful participation in White institutions (e.g., school, the corporate economy) as an assimilation, a one-way acculturation or a subtractive process, that takes away their Black identity (Baker, 1987; Campbell, 1982; Davis & Watson, 1985; Mitchell, 1982; Steele, 1992; Taylor, 1973). Based on her ethnographic findings in a community college, Weis (1985) suggested that the students more or less interpreted mastering academic work as a one-way acculturation. A Black professor told the researcher that "a lot of Black students see [the academic world] as a White world. . . . [If I] tell students, "you're going to be excellent . . ." often times excellence means being . . . White . . . [and] that kind of excellence is negative here" (Weis, 1985, pp. 100–101). Labov (1972, p. 135) asserted that it is apparent to some Black youth "that accepting . . . school values [is] equivalent to giving up self-respect."

Some Black professionals in corporations, according to Taylor (1973, p. 13), find that it is in their best interest to embrace overtly the behaviors of Whites. He went on to say that "the flight into the White role behavior is . . . at a high cost." This is because for a minority person to be accepted into the top echelons of the corporations, he or she (the minority professional) must "think, manage, behave like a majority group member and be White except in external appearance" (Taylor, 1973, pp. 16–17). Campbell concluded from her study of Black female executives that they are forced to pull away from their Black cultural identity, and to consciously modify their speech, their laughter, their walk, their mode of dress and their choice of car to conform to mainstream requirements. Thus, as Black executive women move up, they become isolated from those in their old world (Campbell, 1982, pp. 68–69, 70). Davis and Watson (1985) repeatedly mentioned the "phenomenal estrangement of corporate Blacks" from Black cultural traditions, from their own families and communities, and even from their own pre-corporate life styles, ways of dressing, and sense of humor (see also Baker, 1987; Mitchell, 1982).

Coping Today with the "Burden of Acting White"

In the context of oppositional collective identity and cultural frame of reference as well as negative interpretation of "acting White," contemporary Blacks adopt definite strategies to cope with the demand that they adopt certain "White" attitudes and behaviors in White institutions and establishments. The strategies they use to resolve the tension between meeting the demands of the White-controlled situations and the demands to conform to the Black ways are similar to the coping strategies of Blacks after emancipation. They include the following.

Assimilation or Emulation of Whites

Contemporary Black professionals in this category choose to abandon Black cultural and dialect frames of reference to behave and talk primarily according to White frames of reference. Like their predecessors, they believe that their choice is more likely to help them succeed in education, upward social mobility in the wider society and acceptance by White people. Some other Blacks think that the assimilating Blacks not only reject Black dialect, but also appear to have a kind of linguistic self-hatred. Assimilationists try very hard to talk like White people. Some go for special coaching to "talk better" in order to keep their job or get promoted. Some send their children to private school where they will learn to "talk better" or to ensure that they learn to "speak White" when they have to, such as at school, on the job, and in the company of a "better class of people."

Strong evidence of the assimilation strategy can be found in studies based on William Cross's (1991) theory of negrescence. Before being influenced by the Black Power Movement (1968–75) these professionals and well-educated Blacks had developed a negative self-image of themselves as Black people. However, when they became involved in the Black Power Movement, they underwent a transformation from their pre-involvement identity (a non-Afrocentric identity) to a new identity that is Afrocentric (Cross, 1991, p. 190).

Accommodation without Assimilation

Another strategy is accommodation without assimilation. Blacks in this category adopt White cultural and language frames of reference where they have to in order to succeed in school or in other White-controlled institutions that are evaluated by White criteria. They do not, however, give up their Black identity or cultural and language frames of reference. They learn and follow the standard practices for success in White Americans in their institutions, without giving up their racial identity and ways of behaving or talking (Haynes, 1985; Sowell, 1974). Marva Collins (CBS Broadcasting, 1979) will serve as a good example of accommodation without assimilation. She is a Black educator who realizes that Black colloquial language is "not considered good enough" when applying for a job. Her solution was to teach Black children to master and use Standard English.

Some Black autobiographers have mentioned two important functions of accommodation: (a) it helps Blacks to maintain their sanity in a racist society, and (b) it helps get them ahead in White establishments. It is in this vein that Wiederman (1985) wrote of the "seventh sense" that Blacks need in order to stay sane in America:

> It was a trick I learned early on. A survival mechanism as old as slavery. If you're born Black in America you must quickly teach yourself to recognize the invisible barriers disciplining the space in which you may move. This seventh sense you must activate is imperative for survival and sanity. Nothing is what it seems. You must always take second readings, decode appearances, pick out the abstractions erected to keep you in your place. Then work around them. What begins as a pragmatic reaction to race prejudice gradually acquires the force of an instinctive response.
>
> (Wiederman, 1985, p. 222)

Edwards (1980, p. 120) saw the need to learn Standard English and code-switch for upward mobility:

My father always had a way of changing his voice when he was talking to White folks. We used to say that he could sound more like them than they could sound like themselves. He was just a regular every day "Blood" right up until a White person came on the scene. And then you never heard so many "gushes" and "golly, gee whizzes" in your life.

Ambivalence

I noted earlier that, after emancipation, some Blacks were ambivalent about adopting White behavior and talk in order to achieve success because they did not believe that the reason Black people are not as successful as White people was because they did not know how to behave or talk like White people. This was brought home to me in 1969 when I was attending a workshop on Black history and culture at the University of California, Los Angeles. One of my teachers narrated a story about a Black applicant enrolled in a program for training minority technicians in the Hollywood movie industry. The applicant was turned down because she did not speak "correct English." My teacher offered a different explanation; she said that until the late 1960s, Blacks could not work, rent, or buy homes in Westwood or Hollywood even when they spoke perfect English. She said that the applicant was turned down because of racism.

Resistance or Opposition

Some are afraid that mastering proper English will cause them to lose their Black dialect identity. They do think that they should not give up their dialect because their collective identity requires them to talk like Black people, not like White people. Several Black women in San Francisco considered "talking proper" an attempt to dissociate oneself from the Black race, to show that one is superior to other Blacks and an act of betrayal (Luster, 1992). The women "consciously resisted learning and using Standard English because they believed that it is a White imposition on Blacks."

Encapsulation

Some are encapsulated in Black cultural and dialect frames of reference and do not behave or talk like White people anywhere. The reason may be that they have not learned to behave or speak proper English.

Social Sanctions (Peer Pressures) against "Acting White" Today

The belief that adopting White attitudes, behaviors, and communication style as a one-way assimilation or abandonment of Black identity and frames of reference leads to social sanctions against potential assimilation. Accommodators without assimilation are also potential targets of sanctions. Other Blacks are opposed to individuals in these categories who are perceived as trying to behave or talk like Whites in certain situations because such individuals are seen not merely as "acting White" but also as trying to betray the cause of Black people or trying to "join the enemy." The sanctions are both psychological and social.

Some individuals trying to "act White" may experience psychological stress or what DeVos (1967) called affective dissonance. That is, because individual Blacks share the group's sense of oppositional racial identity, the would-be assimilationists may feel that by behaving or talking like White people they are, indeed, abandoning, or betraying their own people.

There was evidence in the literature of both psychological and social sanctions against "acting White." Some Black professionals not only fear that they are being co-opted by the White world, but also experience social pressures from the Black community. Take the case of Mitchell (1983, pp. 22–23). Reflecting on her position as a Black professor at a major research university, she described the dilemma for Black academics: "The Black community rates service to the community high and research low . . . also the type of research that the community regards as worthwhile is that which advocates change, helps to get money and speaks in plain language." In contrast, the university regards this type of research as particularistic and subjective.

The sanctions experienced most commonly by Blacks striving for academic and professional success are: (a) accusation of uncle tomism or disloyalty to the Black cause or Black community (Petroni, 1970, p. 263); (b) threat of personal embarrassment and humiliation (Mitchell, 1983, pp. 22–23); and (c) fear of losing friends and/or a sense of community (Abdul-Jabbar & Knobles, 1983; Labov, 1972; Weis, 1985). The individual also feels the need to perform a social cost–benefit analysis of his or her chances for making it (Davis & Watson, 1985, p. 51; Mitchell, 1982, p. 35). He or she may experience intense frustration and the perception of a closing down of options (Davis & Watson, 1985, p. 74). In some cases, the latter has led to suicide, while some individuals suffer from self-doubts, guilt, alienation, and paranoia (Luster, 1992).

Reports by Becknell (1987), Kochman (1987, 1981), and Luster (1992), as well as my own study in Oakland, California (Ogbu, 1999), provide evidence of contemporary community pressures against "acting White," especially against "talking proper in the community" because it would mean denying and ultimately losing one's Black identity. Becknell (1987, p. 36) talked about the pressure this way:

> When I encounter a group of Blacks on the street in my home community, I can't go up to them and say "Good afternoon, gentlemen. How are you dong today?" [i.e., greet them in Standard English]. They would laugh at me and then feel sorry for me. They'd think, "Poor Charles, when he left here for college, he was OK. [That is, he talked appropriately like us and maintained his Black identity]. But now, look what they've done [i.e., White people or White educational institutions] to him!" [i.e., he has learned to "talk proper" or "act White"].

According to Kochman (1987, p. 228):

> Black intonation patterns function as an inside [ethnic] boundary marker; those who do not manifest the distinctive Black intonation in their speech regularly acknowledge the adverse criticism they receive from other Blacks, the substance of which characterizes them as being "assimilation-oriented" or "acting White." I have observed often the nonverbal criticisms directed at these Blacks by other Blacks who do manifest such intonations (criticisms also often verbalized about them later on, when the person is no longer present). The accused are often called upon to demonstrate the extent of their group affiliation in other ways, and may be further tested for their "Blackness" before the final judgment is rendered.
>
> (See also Ogbu, 1999)

Luster tells us that among Black women (and many were parents) who were attending a community school in San Francisco to get their GED, the biggest opposition was against speaking Standard English:

> There is a continual delineation and reinforcement of behaviors, practices, and attitudes that are "Black" (and appropriate) versus those that are "White" (and inappropriate). . . . "Acting White" is an acknowledged and identifiable practice within the community. The women who were both observed for more than a year and then interviewed consider "speaking proper" or using the Standard English is an attempt to disassociate oneself from the race; an attempt to demonstrate superiority, an act of betrayal. It angered and disgusted the community. The women consciously resisted learning and using the Standard English because it would mean accepting what the

White society defines as "right" or "White" to replace what the same White society defines as "wrong" or "Black".

(Luster, 1992, p. 202)

I also found that talking proper was a strong signifier of "acting White" in Oakland, California. The parents I studied believed that talking proper in the community was pretentious because no Black person could really talk like a White person. Talking proper was not natural for Blacks. There was yet another reason for the opposition: talking proper signified adopting White people's attitude of superiority toward Blacks. Here is how the community would treat a person trying to talk proper, according to my informants:

PARENT 1: You know, talkin' all—you know, talkin' like White people.

INTERVIEWER: Oh, talking—so people would not be interested in that. . . .

PARENT 1: No.

INTERVIEWER: Ok. Well, how would they treat them?

PARENT 1: Probably standoffish . . . Ignore them. . . . Because they're trying to [show that they are] better than they are. . . . Maybe that type of attitude.

PARENT 2: People in the community will say, "He thinks he's smarter than everyone else, or he thinks he's White." We don't want to listen to this. I don't want to listen to this thing or that.

PARENT 3: They [other Lafayette Blacks] would probably tend to be somewhat prejudicial of someone speaking very proper English, and they would probably make an assessment on that person's character as being "uppity" or . . . she is trying to be White, or something like that, you know.

Coping with Social Sanctions against "Acting White" Today

Contemporary Blacks who must "act White" for whatever reason know full well that their behavior is not endorsed by the community. There are cultural ways of handling or shielding them from the social sanctions. The strategies found in both the literature and my ethnographic studies include the following.

Camouflaging: Involvement in the Black Struggle

This requires activities that give other Blacks the impression that one is for Black people, not for White people. Active participation in the civil rights struggle is a good way to camouflage. Middle-class Blacks are expected to be involved in the collective struggle against White oppression. They have to demonstrate their concern for and loyalty to the "race" through "the struggle" to be accepted as good role models for Black youth. Some Black professionals I interviewed reported that they were accused on many occasions of not being for the race because they were "not involved." This is how one Oakland parent described the attitude of the community toward a professional suspected of abandoning the community, followed by a Stockton school administrator's description of the dilemma of Black professionals:

PARENT 5L: By now they've [i.e., successful Black professionals] gone somewhere else to live in a totally different neighborhood. So, you know, it's really hard to. . . .

INTERVIEWER: That's right. So, they've moved away from the community?

PARENT 5L: That's right.

SCHOOL ADMINISTRATOR: Let me tell you something else about this community, about the Black people, that they don't have a lot of trust in each other, either you know. . . . The Black people who live in north Stockton, [professionals] . . . if they came to the Black Community Council they would be literally attacked by the people from south Stockton [Black ghetto residents]. They [from south Stockton Blacks] feel that they [north Stockton Blacks] have abandoned them for having moved up there. So, once you become a professional, and successful, and others who are not, sort of cast dispersion on you because of it. It's a difficult thing to go back and serve, to help when people are challenging you every step of the way, you know.

Accommodation without Assimilation

Convincing others that one is able to behave and talk like White people in White-controlled environments and yet behave and talk like Black people in the Black community is another way to handle social sanction. Some Blacks learn to live alternately in the Black world and in the White world (Becknell, 1987). Some Black parents in Oakland recognized the importance of code-switching behavior. One mother said that she mastered proper English to disguise her racial identity, minimize racial discrimination and increase her chances of getting a good job.

PARENT: [Talking proper] is not a problem for me because I can change my tone of voice and speak in a different [way]. Well, I appear to speak in a different—with an accent. Certain [White] people don't really know who they're talking to.

INTERVIEWER: Okay.

PARENT: Whereas if they were to see me, they would not [have agreed to what I said or wanted] . . . because of the Afro.

Support Group or Mentorship

Black professional organizations or associations function to provide needed support to Blacks. Getting a mentor helps Black professionals succeed in the mainstream. One function of the mentor is to serve as a stabilizing force against peer pressures and self-doubt. Mentors are very important even in professional sports, as can be seen in the experience of Abdul-Jabbar. Early in his professional sports career, a mentor provided him with tips on how to play. One of two other mentors who gave him emotional support was a Muslim. His Muslin mentor admonished him to both take his religion seriously and affirm his U.S. citizenship and get all his rights as a citizen (Abdul-Jabbar & Knobles, 1983). However, the literature indicates that mentorship is not frequently available to Black achievers. According to Davis and Watson (1985, p. 89), mentoring is limited by a lack of structural opportunity. They noted that, "In the early 60s . . . Blacks always had a 'godfather' or corporate mentor who would look out for them. But that did not mean that the mentor would help Black employees rise through the ranks" (Davis & Watson, 1985, pp. 29–30).

COPING WITH THE BURDEN OF "ACTING WHITE" AT SCHOOL

I have discussed at length the collective identity and frames of reference among Blacks in contemporary United States because critics of the Fordham-Ogbu thesis focus almost exclusively and atomistically on Black students' attitudes and behaviors in the school context, divorced from Black history and community. But Black students are products of Black history and members of the contemporary Black community. They face the same dilemma, due to the same oppositional collective identity and frames of reference characteristics as members of their community. Therefore, in examining the students' conduct, I will not repeat the above discussions of the dilemma of "acting White" among contemporary Black Americans. Suffice it to say that at school, students responded to required attitudes and behaviors labeled "White" like adult Blacks in White institutions and corporate America. Among the students, as among adults, there are assimilationists, accommodators without assimilation, ambivalents, resisters, and the encapsulated. It is important to bear in mind that although Black collective identity and cultural frame of reference are oppositional, only one of the five categories of Blacks among both adults and students is explicitly opposed to adopting White attitudes, behaviors, and speech. In my own study, I have generally found that there are relatively few students who reject good grades because it is "White." On the contrary, they want to make good grades and many report that they are well received by their close friends when they get good grades, such as when they get an A (Ogbu & Simons, 1994, p. 95).

What the students reject that hurt their academic performance are "White" attitudes and behaviors conducive to making good grades (Ogbu & Simons, H. D., 1998). In Shaker Heights, for example, they include speaking Standard English, enrollment in Honors and AP classes, being smart during lessons, and having too many White friends. In Oakland, they include talking proper, studying a lot or doing homework every day, having mostly White friends, taking hard/advanced placement courses, acting like a nerd, taking mathematics and science classes, spending a lot of time in the library, and reading a lot. Black students experience peer pressures from other Black students to discourage them from adopting such White attitudes and behaviors. Black students also experience peer pressures for other reasons than "acting White." In Shaker Heights, these include nonacademic priorities like pressure to work too many hours on part-time jobs to pay off credit card debts, as well as maintaining a certain lifestyle. Oakland students are pressured to sell drugs, smoke weed, cut classes, hang out with friends, and believe that school does not matter. It is important to note that all peer pressures that hurt students' grades are not for preventing students from "acting White."

Coping with Social Sanctions against Peer Pressures at School

Like the adults, Black students have strategies for coping with peer pressures. It is difficult to separate strategies for handling pressures against "acting White" from strategies for handling peer pressures for other reasons. Shaker Heights students reported three major ways they handled peer pressures. One was family upbringing and continued parental supervision, including screening their friends and monitoring their schoolwork. The second was a student's own initiative, whereby he or she carefully chooses Black friends who are serious about school and about making good grades. Finally, some students interpret peer pressures as distractions from their goal of school success and take necessary steps to avoid them.

In Shaker Heights, the school made a significant indent into the peer pressures by establishing an academic identity program for achieving Black students, called The Minority Achievement Committee (MAC) Scholars. Academically promising students are invited to join the program. The scholars meet periodically to discuss how they can handle peer pressures and improve their school performance. They also have an annual award ceremony for academic improvement. Equally important is that they wear special symbols identifying them as MAC Scholars and greet one another in a special way. Both of these express their pride in academic achievement. The MAC Scholars are generally admired as good role models by other Black students (Ogbu, 2003, pp. 125–126).

The most common strategy in Oakland is camouflaging. A good example of this is to be highly involved or to excel in Black activities and avoid "White" activities. Another common strategy is to help friends with their homework or let them copy one's assignments. Some students act dumb in class or as class clowns. Some study in secret and their good grades, achieved "without studying", are attributed to the fact that they are "naturally smart." A few students get "bullies" to protect them in exchange for helping the latter with assignments. There seem to be more students in Oakland than in Shaker Heights, however, who "give in" to friends or yield to peer pressures and "let their grades suffer."

There are several things to be stressed as a conclusion. First, Black students face the same burden of "acting White" that Black Americans have faced throughout their history and still face in contemporary United States. Under this circumstance, they have developed culturally patterned ways of coping with the dilemma or the burden of "acting White" which one finds both in the contemporary Black community and among the students. Second, in the course of their history, Black Americans have had to cope with peer or community pressures against "acting White," and they have also developed strategies to handle such pressures. The social sanctions or pressures and the coping strategies still exist in the contemporary Black community and are shared by Black students. Third, Black students experience peer pressures for other reasons than for "acting White." The peer pressures unrelated to the burden of "acting White" also contribute to their low school performance. Lastly, other and even more important contributors to their low school performance are societal, school, and other community forces that discourage academic engagement (Ogbu, 2002, 2003; Ogbu & Simons, H. D., 1998).

NOTE

REFERENCES

Abdul-Jabbar, K., & Knobles, P. (1983). *Giant steps: The autobiography of Kareem Abdul-Jabbar*. New York: Bantam Books.

Ainsworth-Darnell, J. W., & Downey, D. B. (1998). Assessing the oppositional culture explanation for racial/ethnic differences in school performance. *American Sociological Review, 63,* 536–553.

Baer, H. A. (1984). *The Black spiritual movement: A religious response to racism.* Knoxville: The University of Tennessee Press.

Baker, H. A., Jr. (1987). *Modernism and the Harlem renaissance.* Chicago: University of Chicago Press.

Becknell, C. F. (1987). *Blacks in the work-force: A Black manager's perspective.* Albuquerque, NM: Horizon Communications.

Benjamin, L. (1991). *The Black elite: Facing the color line in the twilight of the twentieth century.* Chicago: Nelson-Hail.

Bergin, D. A., & Cooks, H. C. (2002). High school students of color talk about accusations of "acting white." *The Urban Review, 34*(2), 113–134.

Berry, M. F. (1971). *Black resistance/White law: A history of constitutional racism in America.* New York: Appleton-Century-Crofts.

Bethel, E. R. (1997). *The roots of African American identity: Memory and history in the antebellum free communities.* New York: St. Martin's.

Bogle, D. (1989). *Toms, coons, mulattoes, mammies, & bucks: An interpretive history of Blacks in American films.* New York: Continuum.

Boykin, A. W. (1986). *The triple quandary and the schooling of Afro-American children.* In U. Neisser (Ed.). *The school achievement of minority children: New perspectives* (pp. 57–92). Hillsdale, NJ: Lawrence Erlbaum.

Branch, C. W. (1999). Race and human development. In R. H. Sheets & E. R. Hollins (Eds.), *Racial and ethnic identity in school practices: Aspects of human development* (pp. 7–28). Mahwah, NJ: Lawrence Erlbaum.

Burkey, R. M. (1971). *Racial discrimination and public policy in the United States.* Cambridge, MA: D. C. Heath.

Campbell, F. (1982). Black executive and corporate stress. *The New York Times Magazine, 12,* 1–42.

Carter, P. (1999). *Balance "acts": Issues of identity and cultural resistance in the social and educational behaviors of minority youth.* Ph.D. Dissertation, Department of Sociology, Columbia University, New York, NY.

Case, E. (1995). *The Rage of the Privileged Class: Why are Middle-class Blacks Angry? Why Should America Care?* New York: Harper Collins.

Castile, G. P., & Kushner, G. (1981). *Persistent peoples: Cultural enclaves in perspective.* Tucson, AZ: University of Arizona Press.

CBS Television Network (1984). The Rosewood massacre. *60 Minutes XVI* (47), 16–22.

Cook, P. J. and Ludwig, J. (1997). Weighing the "burden of acting white": Are there differences in attitudes toward education? *Journal of Policy Analysis and Management, 16*(2), 256–278.

Cornell, S. E., & Hartman, D. (1998). *Ethnicity and race: Making identities in a changing world.* Thousand Oaks, CA: Pine Forge Press.

Cross, W. E., Jr. (1991). *Shades of Black: Diversity in African American identity.* Philadelphia: Temple University Press.

Cross, W. E., Strauss, L., & Fhagen-Smith, P. (1999). African American identity development across the life span: educational implications. In R. H. Sheets & E. R. Hollins (Eds.), *Racial and Ethnic Identity in School*

Practices: Aspects of Human Development (pp. 29–47). Mahwah, NJ: Lawrence Erlbaum.

Daiby, D. (1972). The African element in American English. In T. Kochman (Ed.), *Rappin' and "stylin" out: Communication in urban Black America* (pp. 170–188). Urbana: University of Illinois Press.

Davis, G., & Watson, C. (1985). *Black life in corporate America: Swimming in the mainstream.* Garden City, NY: Anchor Books.

DeVos, G. A. (1967). *Japan's Invisible Race.* Berkeley: University of California Press.

DeVos, G. A. (1992). *Ethnic persistence and role degradation: Koreans in Japan.* Boulder, CO: West View Press.

DeVos, G. A. (1995). Ethnic pluralism: conflicts and accommodation. In L. Romanucci-Ross & G. A. DeVos (Eds.), *Ethnic identity: Creation, conflict, and accommodation* (pp. 15–41). Walnut Creek, CA: Altimira Press.

Drake, St. C., & Cayton, H. R. (1970). *Black metropolis: A study of Negro life in a northern city,* Vols. 1 and 2. New York: Harcourt.

DuBois, W. B. (1982, originally 1903). *The Souls of Black Folks.* New York: The New American Library.

Edwards, H. (1980). *The struggle that must be: An autobiography.* New York: Macmillan.

Epstein, T. (2003). *Adolescent racial/ethnic identity and academic achievement revisited.* Paper presented at the AREA Annual Meeting, Chicago, April 21–24.

Ferman, L. A., Kornbluh, J. L., & Miller, J. A. (Eds.). (1968). *Negroes and jobs: A book of readings.* Ann Arbor, MI: The University of Michigan Press.

Folb, E. A. (1980). *Runnin' down some lines: The language and culture of Black teenagers.* Cambridge, MA: Harvard University Press.

Fordham, S. (1985). *Black students' school success as related to fictive kinship.* Final Report to the National Institute of Education, Washington, DC.

Fordham, S. (1984). *Ethnography in a high school: Learning not to be a native.* A paper presented at the 83rd Annual Meeting of the American Anthropological Association, Denver, CO, November 14–18.

Fordham, S., & Ogbu, J. (1986). Black students' school success: coping with the burden of "acting White." *The Urban Review, 18*(3), 176–206.

Frazier, E. F. (1957). *The Negro in the United States* (Rev. Ed.). New York: Macmillan.

The Gene Media Forum. (2002). *Race, genes and intelligence.* New York: Author.

Green, V. M. (1981). Blacks in the United States: The creation of an enduring people. In G. P. Castile & G. Kusher (Eds.), *Persistence peoples: Cultural enclaves in perspective* (pp. 69–77). Tucson: University of Arizona Press.

Grier, W. H., & Cobbs, P. M. (1968). *Black rage.* New York: Basic Books.

Haley, A. (1976). *Roots: The saga of an American family.* New York: Dell.

Hall, R. L. (1979). *Black separatism in the United States.* Hanover, NH: The New England University Press.

Hauser, S. T. (1972). Black and White identity development: Aspects and perspectives. *Journal of Youth and Adolescence, 1*(2), 113–130.

Hayes, R. (1925). *Harlem, mecca of the New Negro, March 1925* (pp. 631–635). Baltimore: Black Classic Press.

Haynes, R. L. (1985). *Minority strategies for success*. Unpublished Manuscript, Department of Anthropology, University of California, Berkeley. Special Project.

Herrnstein, R. J., & Murray, C. (1994). *The bell curve: Intelligence and class structure in American life*. New York: The Free Press.

CBS Broadcasting (1979). *60 Minutes*, November 11. *60 Minutes* [Television Broadcast]. New York: CBS Broadcasting Inc.

Hirasawa, Y., & Nabeshima, Y. (1995). *Dowa education: Educational challenge toward a discrimination-free Japan*. Osaka, Japan: Buraku Liberation Research Institute.

Holt, G. S. (1972). Inversion in Black communication. In T. Kochnan (Ed.), *Rappin' and stylin' out: Communication in urban Black America* (pp. 152–159). Chicago: University of Illinois Press.

Horvat, E. Mc., & O'Connor, C. (2001). *The Black-White achievement gap and Black cultural opposition to acting White: Where do we go from here?* American Sociological Association, 97th Annual Meeting, Chicago.

Johnson, C. S. (1931). *The Negro in American civilization*. London, England: Constable and Co.

Johnson, C. S. (1943). *Backgrounds to patterns of Negro segregation*. New York: Crowell-Collier.

Johnson, K. (1972). The vocabulary of race. In T. Kochman (Ed.), *Rappin' and styling' out: Communication in urban Black America* (pp. 140–151). Urbana: University of Illinois Press.

Kochman, T. (1981). *Black and White styles in conflict*. Chicago: University of Chicago Press.

Kochman, T. (1987). The ethnic component in Black language and culture. In J. S. Phinney & M. J. Rotheram (Eds.), *Children's ethnic socialization: Pluralism and development* (pp. 117–133). Beverly Hills, CA: Sage.

Labov, W. (1972). *Language in the inner city: Studies in the Black English vernacular*. Philadelphia: University of Pennsylvania Press.

Locke, A. (1925). Enter the new Negro. In R. Hayes (Ed.), *Harlem, mecca of the New Negro, March 1925* (pp. 631–635). Baltimore: Black Classic Press.

Luster, L. (1992). *Schooling, survival, and struggles, Black women and the GED*. Unpublished Doctoral Dissertation, School of Education, Stanford University.

Marshall, R. (1967). *The Negro workers*. New York: Random House.

Mitchell, J. (1982). Reflections of a Black social scientist: Some struggles, some doubts, some hopes. *Harvard Educational Review, 52*(1), 27–44.

Mitchell, J. (1983). Visible, vulnerable, and viable: Emerging perspectives of a minority professor. In J. H. Cones, J. F. Noonan, & D. Janha (Eds.), *Teaching minority students: New directions for teaching and learning*, No. 16. (pp. 17–28). San Francisco, CA: Jossey-Bass.

Moore, J. T., Jr. (1981). *A search for equality: The National Urban League, 1910–1961*. University Park: The University of Pennsylvania Press.

Myrdal, G. (1944). *An American dilemma: The Negro problem and modern democracy*, Vol. 1. New York: Harper.

Nestby, J. P. (1982). *Black images in American films, 1896–1954: The interplay between civil rights and film culture*. New York: State University of New York Press.

Newsweek Magazine (1979). February 26, p. 48.

Norgren, P. H., & Hill, S. E. (1964). *Toward fair employment.* New York: Columbia University Press.

Novak, D. A. (1978). *The wheel of servitude: Black forced labor after slavery.* Lexington: The University of Kentucky Press.

O'Connor, C. (1996). *Optimism despite limited opportunity: Schooling orientation and agency beliefs amongst low-income African American students.* Unpublished Dissertation, University of Chicago, Chicago, IL.

Ogbu, J. (1978). *Minority education and caste: The American system in cross-cultural perspective.* New York: Academic Press.

Ogbu, J. (1999). Beyond language: Ebonics, proper English, and identity in a Black-American speech community. *American Educational Research Journal, 36*(2).

Ogbu, J. (2000). Collective identity and schooling. (English version.) In H. Fujita & K. Shimizu (Eds.), *Education, knowledge and power* (pp. 410–449). Tokyo: Shinyosha Ltd.

Ogbu, J. (2002). Black-American students and the academic achievement gap: What else you need to know. *Journal of Thought, 37*(4), 9–33.

Ogbu, J. (2003). *Black students in an affluent suburb: A study of academic disengagement.* Hillsdale, NJ: Lawrence Erlbaum.

Ogbu, J., & Margold, J. (1986). *A summary of literature review on Black oppositional identity and cultural frame of reference.* Unpublished Manuscript, Survey Research Center, University of California, Berkeley.

Ogbu, J. & Simons, F. (1998). *Community forces and minority educational strategies: The second part of the problem.* Berkeley: Department of Anthropology, University of California.

Ogbu, J., & Simons, H. D. (1994). *Cultural models of school achievement: A quantitative test of Ogbu's theory. Final report.* Graduate School of Education, National Center for the Study of Writing, University of California, Berkeley.

Ogbu, J., & Simons, H. D. (1998). Voluntary and involuntary minorities: A cultural-ecological theory of school performance with some implications for education. *Anthropology and Education Quarterly, 29*(2), 155–188.

Patterson, W. L. (1951). *We charge genocide.* New York: International Publishers.

Petroni, F. A. (1970). "Uncle toms": White stereotypes in the Black movement. *Human Organization, 29*(4), 260–266.

Phinney, J. S., & Rotheram, M. J. (1987). Children's ethnic socialization: Themes and implications. In J. S. Phinney & M. J. Rotheram (Eds.), *Children's ethnic socialization: Pluralism and development.* Newbury Park, CA: Sage Publications.

Phinney, J. S., & Rosenthal, D. A. (1992). Ethnic identity in adolescents: Process, context and outcome. In G. R. Adams, R. P. Gullotta, & R. Montemayor (Eds.), *Adolescent identity formation* (pp. 145–172). Newbury Park, CA: Sage Publications.

Rawick, G. P. (1972). *From sundown to sunup: The making of the Black community.* Westport, CT: Greenwood.

Redkey, E. S. (1969). *Black exodus: Black nationalist and back-to-Africa movements, 1890–1910.* New Haven, CT: Yale University Press.

Rockquemore, K. A., & Brunsma, D. L. (2002). *Beyond black: Biracial identity in America*. Thousand Oaks, CA: Sage.

Ross, A. M. (1967). The Negro in the American economy. In A. M. Ross & H. Hill (Eds.), *Employment, race and poverty: A critical study of the advantaged status of Negro workers from 1865 to 1965* (pp. 3–48). New York: Harcourt.

Rowan, C. T. (1967). The Negro's place in the American Dream. In J. D. Harrison and A. B. Shaw (Eds.), *The American dream: Vision and reality*. San Francisco: Canfield Press.

Shade, B. (1984). Personal traits of educationally successful Black children. *Negro Educational Review, 32*(2), 6–11.

Shapiro, H. (1988). *White violence and Black response: From reconstruction to Montgomery*. Amherst: University of Massachusetts Press.

Smitherman, G. (1977). *Talkin' and testifyin': The language of Black Americans*. Detroit, MI: Wayne State University Press.

Sochen, J. (1972). *The unbridgeable gap: Blacks and their quest for the American dream*. Chicago: Rand McNally.

Sowell, T. (1974). Black excellence: The case of Dunbar High School. *The Public Interest* (Spring), 5–7, 10–11, 12.

Spicer, E. H. (1966). *The process of cultural enclavement in middle America.* 36th Congress of International de Amerianistas, Seville, *3*, 267–279.

Spicer, E. H. (1967). *Cycles of conquest*. Tucson: University of Arizona Press.

Spicer, E. H. (1971). Persistent cultural systems: A comparative study of identity systems that can adapt to contrasting environments. *Science, 174*, 795–800.

Starker, C. J. (1971). *Black portraiture in American fiction: Stock characters, archetypes, and individuals*. New York: Basic Books.

Steele, C. (1992, April). Race and the schooling of Black Americans. *The Atlantic Monthly*, 68–73.

Styron, W. (1966). *The confessions of Nat Turner*. New York: Random House.

Sygnnerstvedt, S. (1972). *The White response to Black emancipation: Second-class citizenship in the United States since reconstruction*. New York: Macmillan.

Taylor, S. A. (1973). Some funny things happened on the way up. *Contact, 5*(1), 12–17.

Taylor, B. L. (2001). *Navigating knowing/complicating truth: African American learners experiencing oral history as real education*. Unpublished Dissertation, Louisiana State University and Agricultural Mechanical College.

Weis, L. (1985). *Between two worlds: Black students in an urban community college*. London: Routledge.

Weisbrodt, R. (1991). *Freedom bound: A history of America's civil rights movement*. New York: A Plumer Book.

Wiederman, J. E. (1985). *Brothers and keepers*. New York: Penguin Books.

Wright, M. A. (2001). *I'm chocolate, you're vanilla: Raising healthy Black and biracial children in a race-conscious world*. San Francisco: Jossey-Bass.

Yon, D. A. (2000). *Elusive culture: Schooling, race, and identity in global times*. Albany: State University of New York Press.

Chapter 3

Ways of Knowing

The Ethnographic Approach to the Study of Collective Identity and Schooling

John U. Ogbu

Some scholars have rejected the Fordham-Ogbu thesis on the ground that the ethnographic research method is not scientific.[1] Therefore, in this chapter, I want to address two methodological issues. First, I will argue that the ethnographic approach or way of knowing is as scientific as any other methodological paradigm. Second, I will show that the ethnographic method is more appropriate for the study of collective identity and schooling than the statistical and nonethnographic qualitative methods that critics of the Fordham-Ogbu thesis have employed. Through ethnography, we can learn about how Black students' attitudes and behaviors are a part of the oppositional attitudes and behaviors in their communities, something that cannot be known or explored fully through the use of other research methods that critics of the Fordham-Ogbu thesis have employed.

CONTEMPORARY METHODOLOGICAL APPROACHES

Three research methods have been used to study the influence of oppositional culture on Black students' school performance: statistical/ "scientific" (primarily survey research), nonethnographic qualitative, and ethnographic. Each method, on its own, falls short of what is needed methodologically to understand or explain the influence of oppositional culture on Black students' school performance. Figure 3.1 presents a schematic model of the three methodological approaches.

The Statistical or "Scientific" Approach

The statistical or "scientific" approach to research is grounded in logical positivism. Those who subscribe to the positivistic paradigm think that social scientists should produce the kinds of explanations about the social world or social phenomena that natural scientists (e.g., physicists,

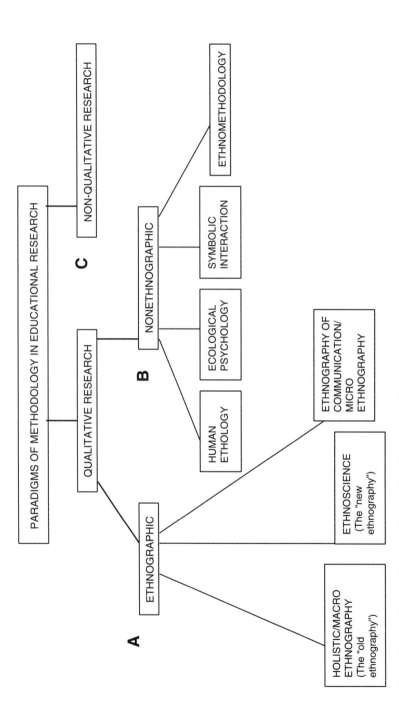

Figure 3.1 Paradigms of methodology in educational research.

chemists, biologists, etc.) produce about the natural world. This view holds, for example, that social scientists should make law-like statements, such as A causes B. Social scientists should, in their view, make such statements when they are talking about relationships between social phenomena or events.

In terms of methodology, positivists hold the view that social scientists should imitate the methodologies of the physical sciences or natural sciences. This means that researchers should consider social phenomena as naturally occurring events, and they should use the methods of the natural sciences to construct and test their explanations/hypotheses. Common research techniques followed or used by positivists include: (a) survey/statistical research for correlations and/or causality, and (b) experimentation to establish causality. Formulations of rigorous hypotheses for testing and quantitative techniques are two characteristics of positivistic research.

James Spradley (1980) explained the process of doing ethnographic research and how this process is different from those used in other social science methods. He called the process used in ethnography *a cyclical process* and the nonethnographic approach *a linear process* or sequence. The nonethnographic process or the linear sequence in other social science methods is represented by Figure 3.2. According to Spradley, the sequence described in Figure 3.2 indicates that the researcher knows ahead of time almost all the major features of the field and that the investigator also knows *exactly* what he or she is looking for and will go out and get it. This is precisely *not* what happens in ethnography.

Researchers in the logical-positivist tradition who analyze their survey or experimental data employing inferential statistics claim that their approach is more systematic and scientific for assessing the oppositional culture hypothesis than is ethnography (Ainsworth-Darnell & Downey, 1998; Cook & Ludwig, 1997; Downey, this volume).

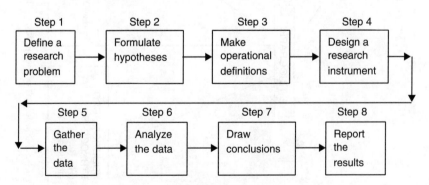

Figure 3.2 The linear sequence in social science research.

Source: J. P. Spradley (1980). *Participant Observation* (New York: Holt), p. 27.

In their paper, "Weighing the Burden of 'Acting White'," Cook and Ludwig (1997) argued that the "acting White" hypothesis had been played up in the mass media as a "fact," but had not been demonstrated as such. They also said that although ethnographers (e.g., Ogbu) had provided evidence of anti-achievement norms, they had yet to provide scientific data to support or refute the hypotheses that Black students were "burdened" by having to balance their pursuit of academic achievement with their social relations (peer pressures); and that the Black students' "burden" was greater than that of other high-achieving students, namely, White students. Their evidence was data from the National Educational Longitudinal Study (NELS: 88 and 90). Based on their analysis of this data set, Cook and Ludwig concluded that they found no support for the Fordham-Ogbu thesis because: (a) Black youth were not more alienated from school than white students; (b) Blacks and Whites had virtually the same expectations as to how far they expected to go in school; (c) there was no evidence that Black students accumulated more absences than White students; (d) Black and White students reported spending the same number of hours per week on homework; and (e) Black parents were as involved with their children's education as White parents of similar socioeconomic backgrounds. They defined parent involvement as making at least one phone call to the teacher per semester, attending one school meeting, attending one school event, and sometimes checking on their child's homework. It is important to ask whether these are adequate or valid indicators for measuring school engagement.

Another serious problem with the "scientific" method that critics of the oppositional culture thesis have used is their uncritical acceptance as "scientific facts" students' verbalization of their own and their families' academic orientations and behaviors (see Ainsworth-Darnell & Downey [1998, p. 540], as well as Downey, Farkas, and Mickelson, this volume). Even Cook and Ludwig acknowledged that researchers have established that all students'—particularly Black students'—self-reported grades tend to be higher than their actual grades. I found this to be the case in my study in Oakland, California.[2]

A similar discrepancy exists between Black students' reports of their own and their families' educational orientations and behaviors. I have found this discrepancy everywhere I have studied Black students' schooling, including Stockton (Ogbu, 1974), Oakland (Ogbu, 1998), and Shaker Heights (Ogbu, 2003). In every one of these studies, I began by asking the students about the relation between effort and academic achievement: "What does it take to make good grades in your school?" Their answer was usually that it required hard work, including studying a lot, doing class work, and doing homework almost every day. However, that was not what the students in Stockton, Oakland, and Shaker Heights did. For example, we observed more than 100 classroom sessions in Shaker

Heights, and many classrooms in Oakland, and concluded that the students did not study as much as they claimed, and they did not do their class work or homework. Although some of the parents participated in their children's education at school and at home, they were not involved to the extent that one might have expected on the basis of the students' verbalization in survey studies, such as that used by Cook and Ludwig (see Ogbu, 1974, 1998, 2003).

In every community in which I have conducted ethnographic research, I have documented the "norms of minimum effort" or "getting by" (as well as some "norms of maximum effort"). In Oakland, even students who were doing well academically were ambivalent toward studying because they felt that they were doing a lot of work; they thereby negated the necessity of having to work strenuously. Ethnographic data revealed discrepancies between what students knew they should do and what they did. It was as if students recognized the connection between good grades and hard work, but tried to see how they could rise above that connection, either by being "naturally smart" or by refuting the actual importance of studying. As a result, some successful students went back and forth between working hard and "getting by" in their attitudes and behaviors concerning homework and studying. Thus, Black students may not have differed from White students in their self-reported educational aspirations, study habits, time spent on homework, or beliefs about the larger society's opportunity structure. However, their actual behaviors belied these self-reports (Ogbu, 1998, 2003). Discrepancies existed in the reports on their parents' attitudes and their behaviors in educational contexts.

Nonethnographic Qualitative Approaches to the Study of Education

Although some people include human ethnology and ecological psychology/sociology among the qualitative approaches used in the study of education, I will not discuss them here because they are rarely used. Instead, I will focus on the following: symbolic interactionism, ethnomethodology, "participant observation," and school ethnographies.

Symbolic Interactionism

Symbolic interactionism is an approach to the study of human behavior that developed from the works of George H. Mead, Charles H. Cooley, John Dewey, and W. I. Thomas. One main assumption of symbolic interactionism is that people's experiences are mediated by their own interpretations of those experiences. Individuals create their interpretations of those experiences through interaction with others, *and* they use the interpretations to achieve specific goals. In their research, symbolic inter-actionists want to understand how people develop the interpretations of their experiences and how they use such interpretations in specific situations (e.g., in school contexts).

Symbolic interactionists do not begin their research with an explicit theory or a well-formulated, testable hypothesis. Rather, their research designs are emergent. That is, data collection and analysis are done sequentially, guiding future data collection and analysis. Participant observation is one of the principal techniques for collecting data; symbolic interactionists also collect data through life histories, autobiographies, case studies, and open-ended interviews (see Glaser & Strauss, 1967).

Ethnomethodology

Ethnomethodology, like symbolic interactionism, developed out of criti-cisms of the positivistic orientation of conventional sociological research. It is concerned with the study of the commonsense knowledge of every-day life.

Like symbolic interactionists, ethnomethodologists tend to view the world and social reality as interpretations of the people they are studying. Thus, ethnomethodologists focus their research on language, persons, and social encounters. Ethnomethodologists deal mostly with the explicit practices found in people's talk and actions, together with implicit prac-tices, such as "background assumptions," which function as a tacit con-text for the objective sense of social reality. Most ethnomethodological studies have been conducted in settings where the construction of social reality is carried out explicitly.

Participant Observation

The term "participant observation" is often used in educational research to describe a variety of research techniques that are not quantitative or experimental in nature. (Please see Ogbu, 1981, for my view of such studies that claim to be ethnographic.)

School Ethnographies

Most studies on the burden of "acting White" have used a nonethno-graphic, qualitative approach like school ethnography. This usually means collecting observational and interview data at school sites with some observations and interviews in the home, where parents may be asked about their children's school experiences and educational expectations. Often such studies were not designed initially to study the phenomenon of "acting White" or "oppositional culture." Rather, researchers became interested in the topic as an afterthought. For example, Bergin and Cooks (2002, p. 119, and in this volume) were almost halfway through their research when they began to ask students about "acting White." As a result, they interviewed only 17 of the 38 students in their study.

Bergin and Cooks's study also illustrates three other problems commonly shared among studies using the nonethnographic, qualitative research approach. The first is the use of an unrepresentative sample of Black students. The second is an assumption that "oppositional culture" is totally responsible for Black students' low school performance. The third problem is the frequent use of samples that have undergone or are undergoing an intervention. For example, in their study, Bergin and Cooks sampled Black and Puerto Rican students in a special program grooming them for college. The program, based at a university, provided the participants with tutoring; sent them on field trips to Ghana, Texas, and Mexico; and held a summer institute for them (2002, p. 117, this volume). The authors did not provide information to readers about the students' histories and cultural backgrounds. Similar problems have plagued many other nonethnographic, qualitative studies. For example, many of the studies "debunking" the 1986 Fordham-Ogbu "burden of acting White" research used samples that consisted of only highly successful African American students or only Black females. It is well known that Black females are more academically successful than Black males and may be less affected by the problem of "acting White."[3] Clearly, this begs the question of whether the lack of academic success among those not included in the survey is due to the burden of "acting White."

Another shortcoming of studies using a nonethnographic, qualitative methodology is that they tend to treat Black students as if they were divorced from their community. Many of these studies have failed to examine the historical, structural, and cultural contexts of Black students' academic attitudes (see also, Horvat, 2001; O'Connor, 1997). In studies of "oppositional culture" and schooling, both quantitative (statistical or "scientific") and nonethnographic, qualitative approaches have suffered from a lack of recognition that their subjects are not just atomistic individuals. Black students belong to a minority group, with a unique history, culture, language, and identity. This uniqueness may influence their perceptions of social reality and their behaviors in society and school. Finally, some qualitative researchers may recognize cultural differences, but, using a revised version of Pierre Bourdieu's theory of practice, constructed their own oppositional culture hypothesis based on the assumption that cultural differences are due to transactions between Black students and the public schools (Carter, 1999).

Anthropological Ethnography

Anthropological ethnography differs from the research approaches of other social scientists. There is a link between the ethnographic approach and the nonethnographic, qualitative approaches to anthropological research. In the sections below, I describe some of the characteristics of the holistic ethnography that I practice. My main task is to suggest some of the ways in which ethnographic research approaches in anthropology, including its "cyclical" processes, differ from other research approaches employed in social sciences.

In contrast to the positivist researcher who knows ahead of time almost all the major features of the field and knows *exactly* what he or she is looking for, the ethnographer has some ideas, some hunches, or some hypotheses, to be sure, but he or she is prepared for surprises and to change those ideas, hypotheses, or hunches based on what he or she will learn in the course of fieldwork.

Figure 3.3 represents the ethnographic process, which is cyclical. According to Spradley (1980), the cyclical sequence of ethnographic research assumes that the ethnographer is like an explorer who has some

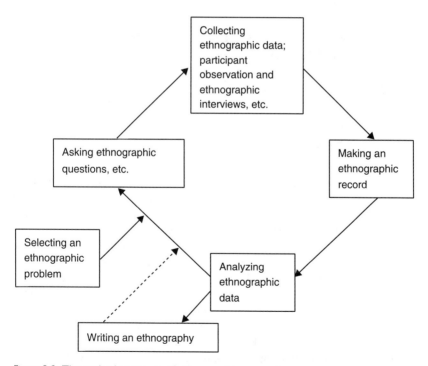

Figure 3.3 The cyclical sequence of ethnographic research.

Source: J. P. Spradley (1980). *Participant Observation* (New York: Holt), p. 27.

idea of what he or she wants to discover, but does not have all or the full knowledge of the field and is therefore prepared to make modifications and to accept unanticipated discoveries.

The cyclical sequence can by roughly summarized as follows:

1   Select an ethnographic research problem.
2   Design an ethnographic research, especially, decide what techniques to use.
3   Collect ethnographic data through participant observation and other appropriate techniques.
4   Record and organize your field data.
5   Analyze your ethnographic data in the course of the research; i.e., do not wait until completion of research to begin preliminary analysis of the data you have collected.
6   Discover new questions to ask, fill gaps in your knowledge; new, unanticipated knowledge usually arises in the course of fieldwork.
7   Go back to the "field" to collect more ethnographic data. REPEAT THIS PROCESS as often as necessary to do a good ethnographic study and as long as time and resources permit.

THE ETHNOGRAPHIC RESEARCH APPROACH AS I HAVE PRACTICED IT

The cyclical nature of ethnography requires the researcher to engage in certain standard procedures and practices. These include the following.

A Long Period of Residence

The ethnographer needs to live or be with the people he or she is studying for a relatively long period of time for several reasons: (a) the ethnographer needs to collect data on people's behavior or events in their natural setting; (b) the ethnographer requires a long period of residence because this helps him/her establish the kind of rapport that makes it possible to obtain certain kinds of information that he or she would not otherwise be privileged to get; (c) the long period of residence helps the ethnographer obtain more reliable information through repeated participation, observation, questioning, and gossip; (d) a long period of residence helps the ethnographer become fluent in the local language, whether this local language is a professional jargon (e.g., in educational research), an ethnic dialect (e.g., Black English), or a street talk or tribal language.

The ethnographer lives in the community and more or less becomes a member for a relatively long period of time. He or she interacts informally and formally with community members. This enables him or her (a) to elicit the "insider" view of the people's history, socio-cultural adaptations, and educational beliefs and behaviors, and (b) to discern the discrepancies between what the people say they do (the ideal) and what they actually do (the real). The ethnographer can attain these goals by becoming immersed in the community's culture and being in the community and interacting with the people in everyday life, usually for one year or longer. This allows the ethnographer to form some impressions about the people and learn about their own categories of knowledge. The ethnographer should listen to the community members' "talk" in both formal and informal interviews, in discussions, in public debates, and at private meetings and read relevant documents produced by group members. The ethnographer should observe how people behave or avoid behaving in the areas of the study as they occur, such as at school, in the family, and in the community; furthermore, the ethnographer should try to elicit individuals' explanations of their beliefs, attitudes, and behaviors.

Competence in Native Language

Competence in the local language helps the ethnographer gain more trust, acceptance, and rapport; it also enables him or her to collect data coded in the language. Some data are not easy to translate and must be learned as the ethnographer becomes socialized into the native theory of speaking. The need to learn the local language applies even when one is doing research in American society because various groups and professions have their own language or argot.

My research experience in Stockton, California may serve as a good example. During my research, I discovered that school personnel were not just speaking middle-class or Standard English; but often they used peculiar vocabularies and expressions, which I had to learn in order to understand various memos from the central and branch offices of the school district; the reports of state-mandated tests; proposals for various remedial programs and their evaluation reports; and periodic and annual reports of school principals and other officials. I also had to learn the language of the school psychologists and counselors, as well as the language of the students and their parents. My taped interviews and transcripts of these interviews sometimes required translating the interviews with school personnel into Standard English, which was much like translating the interviews with parents and children into the same Standard English. Sometimes school personnel had to "translate" their English for middle-class members of the Stockton community who attended Board of Education meetings.

Establishing and Maintaining Rapport

In order to collect valid or reliable data, an ethnographer must establish and maintain good rapport with the people being studied. This is not an easy task and may take several months. Gaining entry or access to the populations that one is studying is just a first step. But having permission to participate and observe is not very useful until one establishes a good rapport. To begin with, the ethnographer must avoid being identified with a particular faction in the population or with some unpopular members of it. The ethnographer needs to discover how best to get along with nearly everyone. Then he or she must discover some members of the population who are reliable informants with whom he or she can establish special relations. To such people the ethnographer can return from time to time for clarification of his or her findings.

How does the ethnographer go about establishing these relationships or this rapport? Traditionally, anthropologists have relied on reciprocity as the tool for doing this. In general, the ethnographer feels a deep sense of obligation to return favors to those from whom he or she demands so much in terms of time and information. The ethnographer may reciprocate by providing the informants with material things, including money, and/or by rendering services to them. But giving informants or local people material things like money is not the same as paying them. While most anthropologists have not paid informants, today some do.

My experience in Stockton, California may serve as an example of the problems and benefits of establishing rapport with the people one studies. In Stockton, California, I spent the first three months of my research trying to gain acceptance by the community and within its local schools. I did this by going to various churches and to neighborhood centers, where I usually explained to people what I was doing. I rode bicycles and played with the children after school and on weekends. I interacted with teachers and other school personnel in the schools and at various community meetings. I did some volunteer work, including tutoring, baby-sitting, and taking people to hospitals and doing grocery shopping. I invited people to dinner and prepared Nigerian dishes for them, and went to their homes to prepare Nigerian meals when invited to do so. Because my notes seemed more complete and I was frequently in attendance, I was more or less forced to become the official secretary of a number of neighborhood organizations.

My aim in performing all these activities was to establish the kind of relationship with people in the schools and community that would enable me to visit with them outside official hours and enable them to visit me without invitation. In addition, I established special close relationships with some reliable informants, which in some cases involved entire families; I consulted with these people from time to time, and I reciprocated with them in many ways. I never really left the community at the end of my research because I was made a life member of the neighborhood association during the send-off party organized by the neighborhood people I studied. Some additional qualities are useful to conducting ethnographic fieldwork, as follows.

Empathy

An ethnographer should have empathy. In other words, he or she should be able to experience the world of his or her informants as the people being studied experience it.

An Ethnographic Imagination

The fieldworker should be able to seek and find interrelationships among his or her observed data, see relationships between his or her observed data and other facts and ideas with which he or she is familiar, evaluate their relevance, and weigh their importance, according to Berreman (1968). To do all of this well, the ethnographer should have a reasonable theory of how society or culture works; that is, an ethnographer should have an understanding of the nature of social structure, and social interaction from a theoretical and practical perspective. That is, the researcher needs to have some theory to guide the research, and a theory about the particular phenomenon will probably be enhanced by the research findings.

A Holistic Viewpoint

The ethnographer should maintain a holistic point of view in his or her research. An ethnographic study is "holistic" in the sense that the ethnographer endeavors to show the interrelationships between the institution he or she is studying and other institutions in society, or the relationships between the behavior being studied and other aspects of the culture. For example, the ethnographer may try to discover how education or schooling, say in Stockton or Philadelphia, is related to the city's economy or political organization. Or, the ethnographer may try to show how the school behavior of the people being studied is related to their beliefs about education or examine the relationship between schooling and adult economic opportunity.

Flexibility in Research Techniques

Finally, although participant-observation is the principal technique for collecting ethnographic data, methodological flexibility is the mark of a good ethnographer. The ethnographer can and should employ a host of other techniques, including life histories, interviews, questionnaires, projective tests, documentary study, and video-taping, where appropriate.

AN ETHNOGRAPHY OF COLLECTIVE IDENTITY AND SCHOOLING IN HOWARD COMMUNITY

In this next section, I will describe the ethnographic research approach as I have practiced it and explain how I have used its findings to conclude that oppositional collective identity and oppositional cultural frame of reference are additional factors that contribute to the pattern of Black students' school performance. In what follows, I will show that: (a) the ethnographic way of knowing is systematic and scientific; (b) it produces more reliable "scientific" data because it allows researchers to compare verbalized attitudes and behaviors with actual attitudes and behaviors; and (c) it does not divorce students from their community's history and culture; indeed, it examines the extent to which the attitudes and behaviors manifested by Black students in school are similar or different from the attitudes and behaviors prevailing in their community. Thus the ethnographic method assumes that one cannot truly understand the school attitudes and behaviors of Black or any other minority group students without knowledge of the same attitudes and behaviors in their community.

It is necessary to clarify key terminological differences between my work and the work of researchers who have not employed ethnographic methods. Most authors in this volume and elsewhere have centered their work on oppositional culture. In this chapter, volume, and everywhere else, my central concern is with collective identity. Collective identity is people's sense of who they are or a sense of belonging or "we-ness," which results from collective historical experience. Collective identity can be oppositional or nonoppositional. Collective identity is tied to people's culture and language. Thus, where collective identity is oppositional *vis-à-vis* the collective identity of the dominant group, the minorities' cultural frame of reference (the code of conduct or the correct way to behave, to act among themselves) is also oppositional; likewise, the minorities' language frame of reference (the correct way to talk or speak among themselves) is oppositional. Focusing on collective identity rather than oppositional culture, I have tried to address the oppositional cultural identity issue separately (Ogbu, 1995) from the issue of oppositional language identity (Ogbu, 1997, 1999). As will be explained in the present chapter, I asked different or separate questions about culture, language, and identity and how they are linked to school orientations and educational strategies.

From 1988 to 1991 I conducted an ethnographic study in Oakland, California. This large-scale study of collective identity and schooling explored how community forces—oppositional collective identity and cultural frame of reference—influenced students' school attitudes and behaviors.

Over the years I had developed an explanation of the school performance of minority groups, namely, a cultural-ecological model (see Chapter 1). This explanation posits that there are two sets of factors influencing minority school performance: how society at large and the school treat minorities (the system) and how minority groups respond to those treatments and to schooling (community forces). The model further posits that differences in school performance between immigrant and non-immigrant minorities are partly due to differences in their community forces.

For these reasons, the Oakland study was comparative. It examined the community forces of immigrant Chinese-Americans, non-immigrant Black Americans, and semi-immigrant Mexican Americans in Oakland and Union City, California. My research assistants and I used ethnography to understand how these minorities perceived and responded to their histories, treatments, and schooling. The rest of this chapter presents the research method used in that study.

The Cultural Context of a Complex Problem

The comparative study was designed to investigate a complex set of interlocking factors. Furthermore, I had learned over decades of studying minorities that they live in what can be described as a set of "dual cultural worlds." The "outer cultural worlds" of different minorities are sometimes similar, and in some respects, similar to the "outer world" of mainstream White Americans. Because of the similarities in their "outer cultural worlds," immigrant minorities (e.g., Chinese), non-immigrant minorities (e.g., Blacks), and White Americans sometimes give similar answers to the same questions (see Mickelson, 1990). However, from the perspective of their "inner cultural worlds," which we call cultural models of social realities, immigrants, non-immigrants, and White Americans do not necessarily mean the same thing. One good example is the response of immigrants and non-immigrants to a question about speaking Standard English. Both groups described speaking Standard English as "acting White." To the immigrants, this is good because it is a sign that one is overcoming language barriers and has a good chance of succeeding in school or getting a good job. In contrast, some non-immigrant minorities are ambivalent about speaking Standard English: it could be a sign that the minority person thinks he or she is better than other members of the group.

The Ethnographic Method

Given the nature of the knowledge I wanted to gain and the context in which it would be acquired, I believed that ethnography was the most appropriate method. Several authorities in the field have discussed the requirements of this approach (Berreman, 1968; Spradley, 1979; Stewart, 1997; Wolcott, 1999).

In most of my research, I have employed ethnography. This meant that I lived in the community and interacted on a daily basis with students, their families, and other community members, as well as the students' teachers and school personnel. Participation in the daily community and school activities enabled me to establish good rapport with the students, school personnel, and people in the Black community. The goal of this rapport and daily interaction was twofold: (a) to understand the people's own ideas about schooling and (b) to observe how students actually go about getting their education and how their parents and their community implement their educational expectations at school and in the community. In other words, gaining rapport and interacting with the students, parents, and community members make it possible to both "get inside the heads of the natives" to discover their beliefs about schooling and evaluate their behaviors regarding their verbalized expectations. The actual techniques of collecting data included group and individual discussions, individual interviews, participant observations, and reviewing existing documents.

The Setting: Why Oakland?

I chose Oakland, California as the site for the study because of its large Black population with a long history. Black students constituted over 50 percent of the public school population. I also selected Oakland because of its large Chinese population, the second largest in northern California. Thus, it was an appropriate site for a comparative study of collective identity and schooling among immigrant and non-immigrant minorities.[4]

The portion of the city designated as a Black or Chinese community was the attendance area of an elementary school extending to the junior and senior high schools attended by children from the elementary school. Most of the participant observation and formal interviews were done within this boundary. This chapter focuses on Oakland's Howard community. Howard community is somewhat representative of Blacks in Oakland. Their beliefs and attitudes reflect those of many Blacks living in Oakland. Further, the people in Howard community are sometimes influenced by educational ideas and events initiated by Blacks living elsewhere in the city (see Ogbu, 1999).

Recruitment and Training of Research Assistants

I recruited and trained three assistants in the ethnographic research method: a senior researcher with a doctoral degree and two junior researchers with bachelor's degrees. My senior assistant served as the associate director of the Howard study. She was responsible for studying parents and other adult members of the community and supervised the junior assistants. The male junior ethnographer studied male students, and the female junior ethnographer focused on female students. All three assistants were Black Americans who had either grown up or lived in Oakland for many years. I deliberately selected individuals with this background as research assistants because I believed that their background would enhance the study. For example, they brought to the study "indigenous knowledge" of the research problem, and they used their networks of social relations to recruit participants into the study.

The researchers received a three-month intensive training in ethnographic research. The training was divided into four parts: (a) a study of the "research problems," involving reading and discussion; (b) several months of a two-hour weekly workshop on how to do an ethnographic research study, during which the trainees read and discussed past ethnographic research accounts; (c) a weekly "practice" fieldwork under the associate director; and (d) a one-hour weekly feedback session with me or the associate director to discuss the "practice fieldwork."

Study Participants

We (hereafter, my research assistants and I will be referred to as "we" or "the researchers") observed many people in various cultural- and identity-negotiating situations, but we formally interviewed 33 parents and grandparents, as well as some other adults in the community. The adults we interviewed were people we had met at various events during the study's participant observation phase. We also interviewed 72 students: 12 elementary, 24 junior high, and 36 senior high students, with equal numbers of males and females.

Research Questions

The research questions were based on several background studies: a literature review (Ogbu & Margold, 1986), a study of Black American autobiographies (Ogbu & Simons, 1988), and previous fieldwork in Stockton (Ogbu, 1974) and Capital High (Fordham, 1985; Fordham & Ogbu, 1986); and discussions during the participant observation phase of the research. Table 3.1 shows examples of the formal interview questions

Table 3.1 Interview questions

Culture and identity	Some people say that the culture of Black people is different from the culture of the school; they say, moreover, that the culture of the school is White culture. They explain that the differences in the school culture cause learning problems for Black children. What do you think? Please explain with examples.
	In general, how do you feel about White people's culture?
	Some Black people accuse other Blacks of "acting White." Does it mean that the Black person: —is acting in a way that is unacceptable to other Black people? —is working to be successful? —is trying not to appear Black? —is trying to behave in a way that is more acceptable to White people than to Black people?
	How are Black people who behave like White people treated by other Black people?
Language and identity	Some people say that there are language differences between Black people and the schools and schools use White people's speech or language. —Have you observed such speech or language differences? —Do the language differences cause problems for Black people? —Do the language differences cause problems for you as a parent (student) at meetings with teachers and other school personnel? If so, what kind of problems?
	Do well-educated Blacks speak differently than White people or do they tend to talk like White people?
	How do you feel about the English courses your children (you) are taking?
Collective identity	What do you and your friends prefer to be called? Why? —Black; Black Americans; Afro-Americans; African Americans; Colored; Negro; Other (specify)
	Does it matter if a person is Black or White in life? Some say that Blacks have a difficult life and that they have had to survive in America. Given that difficulty, if you had a choice, would you rather be White than Black? Why or why not? You have probably heard it said that Black persons are "acting White." When and where did you first hear it? Please explain what it means that a Black person is "acting White." Do you know of any Black people who fit this description?
	How are Black people who go to college perceived? Why? Also, do they act differently from other Black people? If so, how?
School/academic orientation and strategies	How important is it for you that you (your child) get good grades in school? Explain why it is important or not important.

Tell me why some Black students do well in school. Give examples.

Tell me why some Black students don't do well in school. Give some examples.

What about Advanced Placement Courses? Who takes them? Who avoids them? Why? (Interviewer: Some parents may not know what these courses are and you may have to explain.)

Are there courses that Black students avoid taking because they think the courses are "White", "too hard", or "not for Blacks"?

What kinds of pressures do your friends (your children's friends) put on you (them) that hurt your (their) schoolwork and grades? Explain with examples.

How many Black students get good grades but don't act like White students? What do you and your friends think of such students who make good grades, but do not act like White students?

---

focusing on collective identity, cultural and language frames of reference, and schooling. The study also addressed other community forces; therefore, questions that were more about other community forces, but with implications for collective identity, have been included. Likewise, some of the questions listed in Table 3.1 address issues other than collective identity and schooling. We added to and amended some of these questions because of what we learned through participant observation.

As the principal investigator, I drafted the initial interview questions and asked my assistants to review them. The final set of questions resulted from team discussions, testing, and revisions. Adults and students were asked the same questions, but the questions were tailored to elicit adult or student perspectives. The questions were open-ended, and informants' responses were audio-taped. We encouraged our informants to elaborate on their answers to questions.

Procedures and Data Collection

We spent about two years (1988–90) collecting ethnographic data in the community. The long period of fieldwork enabled us to become "members" of Howard community through both informal and formal interactions with the people. We attended community events, including religious services, meetings on special issues, informal gatherings, weddings, and funeral services; we hung out in barber shops and beauty salons and visited families. These participant observations helped us learn about community forces, including attitudes and behaviors, from the residents' actual expressions, and to learn what additional questions to ask besides the ones we started with and what to emphasize in the ethnographic interviews. Furthermore, conducting participant observations enabled us to compare what people told us in interviews with what we saw them actually do.

Interviews were scheduled at the informants' convenience. Most interviews took place in the informants' homes. Before each interview began, the researcher explained the purpose of the study and answered the informant's questions about the study. After the interview, the researcher might continue talking with the informant, asking for clarification or elaboration of some points made in the interview.

We obtained permission from parents and school officials to interview students. We also conducted the research in school. During the participant observation phase, researchers served as teacher aides, assisted with school plays and other programs, and supervised children's activities on the school grounds and during field trips, school sports, etc. We attended school board meetings, and collected documents and statistics on school attendance, disciplines, academic performance, and participation in extracurricular activities. For classroom observations, we made charts of students' seating arrangements and observed and recorded students' interactions with one another and with teachers. We interviewed some teachers, counselors, and other school personnel. Only the student interviews are discussed in this chapter.

During the data collection phase, we met once a week for two to three hours. At each meeting, we discussed some of our major findings and the general impressions that were emerging in the field about the research problems. The discussions were audio-taped and transcribed. I reviewed each transcript before the next meeting to make suggestions for changes or new emphases.

Transcription and Coding of Interviews

The audio-taped interviews were transcribed by trained transcribers, who were fluent in Cantonese-English and Spanish-English. The transcribers received specific instructions on how to transcribe the interviews, and when and how to make insertions in the transcripts. They met weekly with their supervisor to discuss specific or general problems encountered in the transcription.

I developed a coding system for the ethnographic interviews, participant observational descriptions, and other qualitative data. My coding categories were derived from both the concepts in the study's conceptual framework and the new categories that emerged during the fieldwork. The associate director for the comparative study received special training in computer coding of ethnographic data. She then trained and supervised five coders using the Textbase Alpha program (Tesch, 1990). The coders had an inter-rater reliability of over 80 percent.

The analyst and coders met weekly for one to two hours. At these meetings, coders raised questions that emerged during the coding. The analyst also asked the coders to report on the interviews they had been reading. First, the coders mentioned any interviews they had read that they felt were particularly important. A record of such interviews was kept in a file folder labeled, "Notes for Analysis." Second, the coders noted any trends they saw in the interviews. The analyst typed up these trends and put them in a folder labeled, "Trends."

Analysis and Interpretation

Each topic was assigned a unique code. For example, "Cultural differences and frame of reference" was assigned the code "0." This was further divided into several sub-codes. Thus, 0 01 was "Black-White cultural differences," as reported by informants; 0 03 was "The meaning of "acting White"; and 0 05 was "Treatment of or thoughts about Blacks who are 'acting White'." Adults and students were assigned separate files with their own codes. For example, Howard parents were identified as File 11, Code 0 for cultural differences and Howard Students as File 21, Code 0 for the same topic (see Table 3.2). Black collective identity was coded File 11, Code N for parents and File 21, Code N for students (see Table 3.3). Sub-code N 01 was, "preferred group label," sub-code N 02 "The significance of color" and sub-code N 04 "Acting White." The strategies that Howard individuals used for coping with demands to behave or

Table 3.2 O codes: cultural differences/frames of reference

Sub-code	Item	Parents	Students
O 01	Black-White cultural difference		
O 02	What to do about cultural difference		
O 03	Meaning of "acting White"		
O 04	Black view of white culture		
O 05	Treatment of or thought about Blacks who identify with or "Act White"		
O 07	Cultural inversion		
O 09	No recognition of cultural differences		
O 11	Little awareness of "acting White"		
O 13	Black and White differences in food		
O 14	Black and White differences in dress		
O 15	Black and White differences in art		
O 16	Black and White differences in religion		
O 17	Black and White differences in hair style		
O 18	Black and White differences in manner		
O 19	Black and White differences in thinking		
O 20	Black and White differences in family life		

Table 3.3 N codes: Black collective identity

Sub-code	Item	Parents	Students
N 01			
N 02	The significance of color		
N 03	Passing		
N 04	Acting White		
N 05	Identification with Whites		
N 06	Educated Blacks and Black identity		
N 07	Labels for Whites		
N 08	Labels for other minorities		
N 09	Being a minority in America		
N 10	Identification with Whites		
N 11	Identification with other minorities		
N 13	Pride in Black identity		
N 14	Identification with ancestral heritage		
N 15	No preferred label		
N 16	Ambivalence about identification with Blacks of being Black		
N 17	Ambivalence about "acting White"		
N 18	Little or no knowledge of the term "acting White"		
N 19	Economic identification with Whites		
N 20	Self compared to members of other groups		
N 21	Personal history		

talk according to school and work requirements ("acting White") and demands to act and talk according to a Black frame of reference was designated as File 11, Code T for parents and File 21, code I for students (see Table 3.3), and dealing with conflicting demands by society and school to "act White and by the community or peer groups to conform to the Black ways of conduct" was assigned File 21, code T (Table 3.4). Sub-code T.01 was "Assimilation or emulation of Whites"; 1.12 was "Self-determination."

The procedure for data analysis was "trend analysis." Thus, the analysis of Code 0 for Howard parents and adults began by summarizing the entry for each sub-code; then all the entries for the entire 0 code were summarized. During the summary of a sub-code or the entire code, the dominant patterns of beliefs, attitudes, or behaviors in the data were noted. The research framework guided the search for trends or patterns. The same procedure was followed in the analysis of the students' code. The trends for the two sub-populations (e.g., parents and students) were subsequently compared.

Comparing the trends allowed us to reach some conclusions about collective identity and cultural frames of reference and how they affected adults' and children's beliefs, attitudes, and behaviors toward schooling.

Table 3.4 T codes: individual coping strategies

Sub-code	Item	Parents	Students
T 01	Assimilation or emulation of Whites; disaffiliation with Blacks		
T 02	Alternation or accommodation without assimilation		
T 03	Encapsulation in Black culture or community		
T 05	Mentorship		
T 07	Racelessness		
T 08	Bi-culturation		
T 10	Acting dumb in front of White people		
T 12	Self-determination		
T 13	Clientship/uncle tomming		
T 14	Maintaining Black culture and identity		
T 15	Seeing oneself as good or better than Whites		
T 16	Other		
T 17	Self-doubt		

Conclusions also were based on the researchers' impressions about the people's attitudes and behaviors over the period of participant observation and interviews. The researchers' understandings of the Howard people's beliefs, attitudes, and behaviors came from paying attention to the cognitive distinctions that Howard people themselves made about their own and White people's attitudes, beliefs, and behaviors. Some of the findings of the Howard study are included in Chapter 5 in this volume, where I present my understanding of the community forces and schooling among Howard adults and students.

Conclusion

In this chapter, I have tried to show that ethnography is rigorous, scientific and a more appropriate methodology for studying school engagement and community forces than other approaches. Some attitudes and behaviors simply cannot be captured through surveys or interviews. The ethnographic methodology as described here allows the researcher to understand the "lived" experiences of the people they are studying and the nuances of everyday living, to compare verbalized attitudes and actual behaviors, and to see community dynamics in action.

NOTES

1   *Editor's note:* The epistemological issues that Ogbu addresses in this chapter have been central to social science and educational research for decades. The passage of the Educational Science Reform Act of 2002 intensified the

importance of the debate regarding research on the minority achievement gap. The Act declared that scientifically based research designs—randomized, controlled trials—would become the gold standard for federal policy and funded research support. The Act defined scientifically based research as that which employs rigorous, systematic, and objective methodology to obtain reliable and valid knowledge; that employs empirical methods that draw on observations or experiments; and that makes claims of causal relationships only in random assignment experiments (Department of Education 2003; P.L. 107–279). Ogbu's treatment of the epistemological debate about ways of knowing is both timely and illuminating *vis-à-vis* the questions about collective identity, oppositional culture, and the minority achievement gaps.

Professor Ogbu created verbatim lecture notes, which he passed out to his students. He also provided students with hand-drawn (in the era prior to PowerPoint) figures to illustrate his arguments. Occasionally he sent me copies of these lectures. I saved his *Lecture 11: What Makes Educational Ethnography Ethnographic?* from his Education and Culture (Anthropology 153) course. His distinctions between ethnographic and nonethnographic, qualitative research are quite helpful for appreciating why he considers some of his critics' nonethnographic, qualitative research flawed, and why their conclusions are of questionable validity or reliability. His descriptions of positivist research methods illustrate why he felt survey research (including my own survey research reported in Chapter 16) missed the mark so widely, and why it was largely inappropriate for investigating collective identity, oppositional culture, and ethnic variations in school achievement. Therefore, I inserted passages from Ogbu's Lecture 11 wherever I felt they would elaborate the arguments in the original draft of his chapter.
—R.A.M.

2   In that study, 40 percent of the Black students reported that they made a grade point average (GPA) of 3.0 or higher. However, the school records showed that only 9 percent of them had a 3.0 GPA or higher (Ogbu, 1998). Students from all groups tend to report higher grades than their actual grades, but the discrepancy is wider for African American students. For example, in our Oakland study, 71 percent of Chinese students reported getting As and Bs, while school records showed that 51 percent had actually earned such grades.

3   Data from my Shaker Heights study support this gender difference. In that study, conducted from 1992 to 1995, 22 Blacks were among 310 students in the top 20 percent of the graduating class; 4 of the 22 were males and 18 were females. However, there were 295 students who made up the bottom 20 percent; 195 of these students were Black males and 100 were females (Ogbu & Davis, 2003).

4   I added a second site, Union City, because of its large Mexican American population, but I do not include that site in this chapter's discussion.

REFERENCES

Ainsworth-Darnell, J. W., & Downey, D. B. (1998). Assessing the oppositional culture explanation for racial/ethnic differences in school performance. *American Sociological Review, 63,* 536–553.

Bergin, D. A., & Cooks, H. C. (2002). High school students of color talk about accusations of "acting White." *The Urban Review*, *34*(2), 113–134.

Berreman, G. (1968). Ethnography: Method and product. In J. A. Clifton (Ed.), *Introduction to cultural anthropology* (pp. 336–373). Boston: Houghton Mifflin.

Carter, P. (1999). *Balancing "acts": Issues of identity and cultural resistance in the social and educational behaviors of minority youth*. Ph.D. Dissertation, Department of Sociology, Columbia University, New York.

Cook, P., & Ludwig, J. (1997). Weighing the burden of "acting White": Are there race differences in attitudes toward education?" *Journal of Policy Analysis and Management*, *16*, 256–278.

Fordham, S. (1985). *Black students' school success as related to fictive kinship*. Final Report to the National Institute of Education. Washington, DC.

Fordham, S., & Ogbu, J. U. (1986). Black students' school success: Coping with the burden of "acting White." *The Urban Review*, *18*(3), 176–206.

Glaser, N., & Strauss, A. (1967). *The discovery of grounded theory: Strategies for qualitative research*. New York: Aldine.

Horvat, E. Mc. (2001). *The Black-White achievement gap and Black cultural opposition to acting White: Where do we go from here?* ASA 2002 Session Proposal Draft.

Mickelson, R. (1990). The attitude-achievement paradox among Black adolescents, *Sociology of Education*, *63*: 44–61.

NELS (1988). *National Education Longitudinal Study 88 and 90*. Institute of Educational Science, US Department of Education, National Center for Education Statistics.

O'Connor, C. (1997). Dispositions toward (collective) struggle and educational resilience in the inner-city: A case analysis of six African American high school students. *American Educational Research Journal*, *34*, 593–629.

Ogbu, J. U. (1974). *The next generation: An ethnography of education in an urban neighborhood*. New York: Academic Press.

Ogbu, J. U. (1981). School ethnography: A multilevel approach. *Anthropology and Education Quarterly*, *12*(1), 3–10.

Ogbu, J. U. (1995). Cultural problems in minority education: Their interpretations and consequences—Part one: Theoretical background. *The Urban Review*, *27*(3), 187–203.

Ogbu, J. U. (1997). Racial stratification in the United States: Why inequality persists. In A. H. Halsey, H. Lauder, P. Brown, & A. S. Wells (Eds.), *Education: Culture, economy, and society* (pp. 765–778). Oxford: Oxford University Press.

Ogbu, J. U. (1998). *Community forces and minority educational strategies: The second part of the problem*. Unpublished manuscript. Department of Anthropology, University of California, Berkeley.

Ogbu, J. U. (1999). Beyond language: Ebonics, proper English, and identity in a Black-American speech community. *American Educational Research Journal*, *36*(2), 147–184.

Ogbu, J. U. (2003). *Black students in an affluent suburb: A study of academic disengagement*. Mahwah, NJ: Erlbaum Associates.

Ogbu, J. U., & Margold, J. (1986). *A summary of literature reviews on Black oppositional identity and cultural frame of reference.* Unpublished manuscript. Survey Research Center, University of California, Berkeley.

Ogbu, J. U., & Simons, E. (1988). *Black autobiographies: A search for cultural models of minority status and American society.* Unpublished manuscript. Survey Research Center, University of California, Berkeley.

Spradley, J. P. (1979). *The ethnographic interview.* San Diego: Harcourt Brace Jovanovich.

Spradley, J. P. (1980). *Participant observation.* New York: Holt.

Stewart, A. (1997). *The ethnographer's method.* Quantitative Research Method Series 46. Thousand Oaks, CA: Sage Publications.

Tesch, R. (1990). *Qualitative research: Analysis types and software tools.* New York: Farmer.

Wolcott, H. F. (1999). *Ethnography: A way of seeing.* Walnut Creek, CA: Alta Mira Press.

Chapter 4

Multiple Sources of Peer Pressures among African American Students

John U. Ogbu

In all of the ethnographic studies of Black students that I have conducted, I have found that peer pressures leading to academic disengagement and poor school performance are due to a number of factors in addition to the phenomenon of "acting White." In this chapter I will report the findings from my studies of peer pressures in two settings: Shaker Heights, Ohio and Oakland, California. My studies show that negative peer pressures are widespread among African American students and that these pressures contribute significantly to the students' academic disengagement.

I found that not all peer pressures exerted by Black students are negative. As one student noted, "The picture is not so dichotomous." While there are some positive peer pressures to do well in school among Black students, in this chapter I focus on the two types of peer pressures that adversely affect students' academic engagement. One arises from students' interpretations of certain school requirements as "White"; the other pressures are not related to this interpretation, but to non-academic priorities. Students in Oakland and Shaker Heights did not reject making good grades because doing so would be regarded as "acting White." Getting good grades and being an academic success were not the problem. Rather, some students rejected *certain attitudes and behaviors* conducive to making good grades because they interpreted them as "White." These attitudes and behaviors included speaking Standard English, enrolling in Honors and Advanced Placement classes, being "smart" during lessons, and "hanging around" too many White students.

I have examined the school performance of low-income and middle-class Blacks in different parts of the United States and have found that at every social-class level, Black students perform less well than their White peers (Ogbu & Simons, 1998). Peer pressures against "acting White" exist in both affluent suburban communities and urban communities. This chapter will discuss the types of peer pressures and conclude with a brief illustration of how students in one school handled peer pressures in order to increase their academic engagement and performance. I present findings from two recent ethnographic studies of comparative community forces to illustrate the ways that academic and nonacademic peer pressures influence academic disengagement.

PEER PRESSURES IN AN AFFLUENT SUBURB—BEYOND THE INNER CITY

My study of academic disengagement in Shaker Heights illustrates how peer pressures to disengage from academics arise from many sources. Shaker Heights, an affluent, upper-middle-class, Midwestern suburb with a population of about 30,000, was voluntarily integrated during the civil-rights period of the 1960s. At the time of the study, about one-third of the community was African American. According to the 1990 census, about 32.6 percent of the Black households and 58 percent of the White households had average annual income of $50,000 to over $100,000 (Stupay, 1993, p. 8). The median family income was $66,000. The community was highly educated, with about 61 percent of the residents over 25 years old holding at least a bachelor's degree, three times the national average. Many Black and White residents were professionals and corporate executives (Singham, 1997).

My study of Shaker Heights began with an invitation from the Black parents and leaders, who were concerned with their children's academic performance. For example, the average GPA of Black students at the time was less than 2.00, in contrast to the average 3.45 GPA of their White peers. Eventually, Black leaders and the local school district jointly sponsored my investigation.

The school system was (and still is) one of the best in the state and nation. The community is proud of its excellence in education, and this resonates in its motto: A community is known by the schools it keeps. About 85 percent of its high-school graduates go to college, a rate higher than that of similar suburban school districts; many of its graduates are National Merit Scholarship finalists or semi-finalists.

But there is a problem: a wide gap in academic achievement exists between White and Black students. The deep concern of Blacks and Whites over the academic achievement gap was succinctly expressed in a question that an African American parent asked during a public presentation to a mixed-race audience. She asked:

> In this community we have large numbers of Black families which are stable and in which both parents are well-to-do, educated professionals, upholding all the virtues that are assumed to be the prerequisites of educational success. And yet, the children of these

families still seem to under-perform when compared with similar White families. What is going on?

(Singham, 1997, p. 5)

In the eight-month ethnographic research study that followed, my assistants and I sought to discover the factors that led to Black students' academic disengagement in this affluent community. Guided by the framework of the cultural ecological model, my research assistant and I attempted to discover (a) the societal and school factors and (b) the community forces that contributed to the disengagement. Peer pressures are manifestations of community forces. In the following pages, I report only on peer pressures.

In the study, I sought to examine the extent to which peer pressures contributed to academic disengagement. I also explored whether students avoided certain attitudes and behaviors because they regarded them as "White," and if they perceived that adopting the White ways would be detrimental to their collective racial identity and solidarity. I also examined the extent to which peer pressures caused academic disengagement by forcing students to adopt other attitudes and engage in activities not conducive to academic achievement.

Peer Pressures and Academic Disengagement

Shaker Heights school personnel described Black peer groups as more cohesive than White peer groups. Our observation throughout the fieldwork confirmed the two worlds of Black and White students. Black students also reported that Black and White peer groups had different norms and different degrees of involvement with schoolwork. According to students in the Shaker Heights study, Black friends did not study together; instead, some actually influenced others to do poorly in school. In contrast, White friends encouraged one another to do well in school. One female participant described White peer pressures as encouraging enrollment in Honors and Advanced Placement classes and hard work. She believed that among Whites "all their friends work[ed] hard" and all the people around them worked hard. For that reason, "they're gonna work harder." In contrast, most Black students took less difficult Skills and College Prep classes. Even so, they still did not make good grades because they and their friends did not work hard. None of their friends were doing well. "So, they're not gonna do well."

Black students explained that they formed separate peer groups partly because they did not feel welcomed in White peer groups. A second reason offered by Black students is that tracking segregated Black and White students, thereby limiting opportunities for the two races to interact informally. A third reason is that in social activities and conversations,

White students did not include their few Black classmates. As a result Black students did not feel that they belonged socially. Among some students this contributed to their reluctance to enroll in Honors and Advanced Placement Classes.

Shaker Heights students had high educational aspirations. They and their families had moved to this suburban community because of its academic reputation as the best school system in the state. The students wanted to make good grades. When asked what it took to succeed or make good grades in their school system, the consensus reply was that it required more effort than elsewhere. By "effort," they meant that a student must work hard, do classwork, do a lot of homework, and spend much time studying. In other words, the student must be academically engaged (Ogbu, 2003, p. 12). However, they were disengaged from academic work partly because of peer pressures.

The Use of Standard English

Speaking Standard English could be seen as requiring Black students to cross dialect boundaries and potentially diminish their dialect identity. Perhaps for this reason, some Black students resisted speaking Standard English. This, no doubt, adversely affected their school performance. However, I did not come across many students who did not want to use Standard English, and Black students in Shaker Heights recognized its importance. They were socialized in the two English dialects, with Black English as their primary dialect. Some parents and grandparents spoke mostly Black English, which was all that the children heard and learned before starting pre-school or regular school. Many students seemed to follow a definite rule for using Standard English in their schoolwork and with school authorities, while speaking their own dialect at home and among friends. Those who did not speak Standard English in appropriate settings were criticized by other Black students.

The students, like adults in their community, did not want to give up their dialect in exchange for the Standard English required for school success because their dialect was a part of their collective identity. Some students solved the language problem by choosing to speak Standard English most of the time and in appropriate situations; some chose to switch between their own dialect in the community and Standard English at school.

Enrollment in Honors and AP Classes

Students repeatedly pointed out that Blacks avoided taking Honors and Advanced Placement classes because they were "hard"; another reason was that those who took them were mostly White. Peer pressures to avoid "difficult classes" (i.e., Honors and Advanced Placement), along with various dynamics of schooling, resulted in few Blacks taking these rigorous classes. At the same time, Blacks constituted the majority in the easier classes. The few Black students in the Honors and Advanced Placement classes did not always fit in socially with their majority White classmates. In addition, Blacks in these classes often were subjected to criticisms by other Black students, who accused them of trying to be White. Since students wanted to fit in, they avoided enrolling in the Honors and Advanced Placement classes and striving for the high grades that would qualify them for those classes. Janelle,[1] a female high-school student, explained how this happened:

> JANELLE: Oh, okay. Um, what I'm saying is that you got to think about [your friends] influencing you. . . .I think that has a lot to do with it. I mean, if Black kids see a lot of the [other Black] kids not doing well, they can do it. Nobody wants to be an outcast and then like, they do label people as acting White. I see one Black student who does do well and, of course, they say they're acting White, because the majority of Black students aren't achieving like that. They see that the White students are the ones doing well, so they label it as acting White. I mean, basically, that's what the problem is. You want [to do well but you don't because your friends don't].

Some students do rise above the peer pressure, however. As Janelle noted:

> But I think it's an individual thing. It's like your personal mentality. You have to, if you want something bad enough, you have to try for it. I mean, you don't [depend on others]. It's basically your own personality. I mean you can't let all these people influence you: And you'll say, "I'm not gonna do this, because everybody else isn't doing it." You have to go for it and get it yourself. You can't worry about what other people are gonna say.

Several students mentioned their concern about fitting in socially in the Honors and Advanced Placement classes during formal interviews. The social integration of Black and White students in these classes appeared to be a problem. Although when we observed the classes, Black and White students participated more or less equally in discussing the subject matter and in interaction with teachers, there was not much interaction between the two groups of students. According to students, the social relationship between the two groups in the classroom was uncomfortable. In less rigorous classes, Blacks "fit in" socially, but their work often suffered from the norms of minimum effort and discipline problems more often found in lower tracks.

Being "Smart" During Lessons

Peer pressures can prevent "smart students" from performing according to their ability. Those who refuse to conform might make good grades, but they suffer for them socially. Andre, a male student, described the smart student's dilemma in this way:

> I think when kids choose their friends, a lot of times they're your friends. You think they're you're friends. [Later you realize that they, in fact, will be the first ones to discourage you. They'll] say, "Man, look, I ain't takin' the test." And then you'll say, "Man, you ain't gonna take that test, man." "What man?" You know what I'm saying? And they do that. And then when they don't pass, they're like he said, they got that attitude.... And they gonna bring you down with them, 'cause you know . . . they don't want you to be different from them. Also, we might say, "Every Black kid in Shaker, they want to be good students." They want to be good, man. I don't care. They want to be good students. It's just that, you know, maybe they're not gettin' it from home or whatever; that it's probably they really, you know, they don't want to embarrass themselves by goin' to all of their classes and makin' A's. 'Cause like uh we said, they don't want to get picked at by their friends. You know, nobody wants to get picked on, you know.

That the accusation of "acting White" was about "fitting in" and not about "making good grades" is further illustrated by the treatment of "smart students" in and outside school. Smart students were defined as those who paid attention during lessons, "raised their hands" to answer questions, "always" got the answers right, and did their schoolwork and homework. These students experienced pressures against "acting White" by answering teachers' questions during lessons or behaving in other "smart" ways in class. We heard from several students who had been subjected to these kinds of peer pressures. Mrs. Bernard, a school counselor, described a "very bright" student who never volunteered to answer questions during lessons:

> MRS. BERNARD: He was very bright. And I go and evaluate classes all the time. He sat in front of me in one of our science classes. The teacher asked a question. He didn't put his hand up. I heard him mutter under his breath the right answer. I poked him, and said, "Hey. What's going on here? Why don't you put your hand up?" "Oh, duh duh, I don't know, duh duh." The class was over. He's walking out, and I said, "Come to my office. I know you're smart. I've seen you in the office. I've seen you in class. Why didn't you answer any questions? He said to me, "You don't understand." I said,

"You're right. I don't. That's why I'm asking you, so I, so I could understand."

OGBU: You're an anthropologist. [Laughs; general laughter by other school personnel.]

MRS. BERNARD: He said, *"You don't have to ride home on the bus like I do."* I said, "You're right. I don't." *"You don't have to play in the neighborhood with all the other kids."* I said, "You're right. I don't understand." He said, *"I don't want 'em to know I'm smart. They'll make fun of me. I won't have any friends."* I said, "So you'd rather sit there and pretend that you don't know than face kids who might say you're smart." And he even said, *"Worse than that."* I said, "Well, what's worse than that in your world?" He said, *"Where I live, they're gonna say I'm White."* I said, "Oh!" I said, "Now I think I understand. I don't agree with you, but I, now I hear what you're saying: I don't want 'em to call me names. I want 'em to think I'm just like everybody else, and if that means sitting in class and not raising my hand, and not doing better in school, I have to live here. And that's my world. So don't think that you can say, 'Oh, you should be proud of being smart.' " He says, *"I am, but I can't let anybody know that."* And that's coming from one of the, one of the 14-year-old youngsters.

Hanging Out with too many White Students

Good grades themselves were not at issue, but "hanging out with Whites or behaving like White students who got good grades" was. Black students also were accused of "acting White" for hanging out with Whites in nonacademic settings, such as playing lacrosse, going skiing or swimming, and playing tennis.

It was not acceptable for Shaker Heights high-school students to "hang around" or have "too many White friends," although it should be noted that these were not problems for elementary school-aged students.[2] By middle school, however, the notion that certain behaviors and attitudes were "white" and that those making good grades were "acting White," and "hanging around too many White students and behaving like White students" were not acceptable. These accusations most likely came from the fact that Black students who were "hanging out" with White friends often were the ones in Honors and Advanced Placement classes where most students were White and where Black students were making good grades like White students. LaTanya explained how she understood the impact of hanging out with White friends.

[Y]ou'll see some, I mean very few Black kids with White [students], you know, acting like [the] White group. And they be like the only Black kid in the White group. Those [Blacks] are the ones who be

gettin' good grades with them. 'Cause, you know, White people like . . .
to learn and stuff like that. You know what I'm sayin'? So, like if they
[Black kids] hang around with them, then they be gettin', you know, the
education they need. . . .

Why Do Students Label these Attitudes and Behaviors "Acting White"?

I asked middle- and high-school students why they labeled certain
behaviors, such as working hard, doing homework, speaking Standard
English, enrolling in honors class, and participating in class (behaviors
assumed to be conducive to making good grades), as "acting White."
These students made an explicit distinction between "White" and "Black"
attitudes and behaviors. Their explanations included the following.

Success in White Establishments and bona fide Black Identity

Students believed that it was not appropriate or normal for a Black person
to behave like a White person because it implied renouncing Black identity. Yet when Blacks did just that (behaved like a White person), other
Blacks used some pressures to keep peers behaving like Blacks and not like
Whites. Since the students had in mind academically successful students in
the school district and professionally successful Blacks in the White establishment, I asked if the successful student and professional did, indeed,
abandon their Black identity. And how did that happen? If they did
not abandon their Black identity, why were they accused of abandoning
their racial identity? Did Black students who made good grades and took
Honors and Advanced Placement classes reject their Black identity? I
explained that giving up their racial identity meant not only adopting
White attitudes and behaviors that enabled them to succeed academically,
but also adopting other White attitudes and behaviors that were not
related to the academic or school context. Did such students, for example,
take up White extra-curricular activities, like skiing and tennis, have
White hair-styles, and hang around mostly White students?

Most middle-school students I talked with did not believe that Blacks
abandoned their cultural or racial identity when they became successful
students. But several high-school students suspected that some Black students who made good grades and some adults who had higher education,
or were successful as professionals in White establishments, did, indeed,
give up their Black culture and identity. The majority was not sure about
this; however, only two students downplayed the issue, explaining why it
was not important. Some high-school students knew other Black students
and adults who believed that school success had a negative influence on

Black collective identity. However, the informants denied believing this themselves.

Nearly half of the high-school students I interviewed believed that some highly educated and successful Black professionals who worked in White institutions had abandoned their culture and racial identity. They gave two reasons why this might happen. One was the acculturation process that started with schooling. In the school, some very ambitious Black students would take Honors and Advanced Placement courses, hang around too many White students, and learn to think, talk, and behave like White people. When they got to college, they took more hard courses, socialized with more White people, and got into more habits of thinking, talking, and behaving like White people. Through this acculturation process, they lost their racial identity, since they no longer knew how to behave or talk like Black people; furthermore, they no longer interacted with many other Blacks.

The second explanation that students gave was that some Black professionals give up their cultural identity and embrace White cultural identity as a survival strategy. This might happen because Black professionals in a White establishment must learn to "fit in" with highly educated White colleagues. Under this circumstance, Blacks were more or less pressured to adopt White people's attitudes, behaviors, and speech styles.

Ambivalence about Success in White Institutions and Establishments

According to high-school students who were asked why Blacks were under-represented in the Honors and Advanced Placement classes, Black Americans, as a group, are ambivalent toward other Blacks who are successful in White institutions and establishments. This ambivalence results in accusations that Blacks who are successful in White schools or White establishments have abandoned their racial identity. This ambivalent attitude was present among the students. Some admired and praised students who excelled because they were setting good examples and making other Blacks proud. But at the same time, students in the Honors and Advanced Placement classes and those who made good grades were criticized and accused of "acting White."

As I already noted, the idea that a Black person would give up his or her identity because of school or professional success was not widespread until high school. A few middle-school students reported that some Black students were accused of giving up their cultural identity or labeled as "acting White" because of their school success. Many middle-school students were not afraid that they themselves would be accused of abandoning their culture if they did well in school. In fact, they felt very comfortable and looked forward to doing well in school. The situation at the high-school level was different and more complicated. High-school students acknowledged the prevailing belief that good grades, higher education, and professional success made some Blacks give up their culture and identity. Although some did not believe that this happened, many informants provided interesting explanations for why some Black people held these beliefs.

Inadequate Knowledge of the Black Struggle for Education

The third explanation was that some students equated making good grades with "White behavior" because they did not understand the history of Black people's struggle for education. The students further suggested that Black students who were not aware of the extent of the Black struggle for access to an equal education mistakenly believed that only White people developed the cultural value of working hard to make good grades in school. These students assumed that making good grades is a part of White, but not Black culture. Furthermore, they may think this way because they are not aware that even during slavery, when Blacks were forbidden by law to learn to read or write, some Blacks defied the law and did so anyway. This showed that Black people, like White people, did develop a cultural value of getting an education and making good grades. In the words of one student,

> It is uninformed students who don't want to make good grades because they think it is White. But uninformed students don't want to because they don't know. They don't know that doing well in school [being a good student] is not a White thing. They don't know that their ancestors, you know, were the part of the struggle. They defied the law and learned to read.

Black Opposition to the White Establishment

The fourth explanation students offered for equating good school performance with "acting White" and rejecting academic and professional success was that Black Americans share a general opposition to White society or held "anti-White establishment" tendencies. This explanation, in the words of a student named Anthony, is worth reproducing in full because of the way he (like other informants) linked Black educational attitudes and behaviors to other features of Black experience in history and society at large. Anthony suggested that because of the marginal position of Blacks in U.S. society and White institutions, Blacks had developed anti-establishment beliefs and behaviors that were partly expressed in peer pressures against the school norm of achievement.

I had a comment that was kind of connected to both questions [asked by the anthropologist]. Um, one thing is [that we] Blacks, it seems like, we always want to go with the anti-establishment. [That is], we [want to] go against society. Traditionally in American society, it has seemed like we have been under oppression. For example, there were laws simply to oppress Black people. . . . So because of this [oppression] Black people came to believe that it was always good, you know, if you could find some way, just somethin' small, you know, just to annoy society. [You do this] . . . just . . . so that you could go against society. That would make you feel good. And so that's why a lot of times even drug dealers will [say], "Well, they [i.e., White people] say it's wrong. So, you know, [I don't feel bad]; I feel like . . . I'm gettin' [at them], you know. . . . The cops are chasin' me and everything. And so that's good." And they [drug dealers] want to do that [i.e., go against society]. And the same thing with education [i.e., in students' attitude toward education]. Because, you see all these White people get up on the stage and talk about education this and education that. And you [as a Black person] just gonna be like [i.e., say to yourself], "Well, I don't care what you [got in mind]." And so you don't cheat [you don't behave like White people to make good grades].

Teasing

A final explanation offered by student informants was that the accusation of "acting White" was a form of joking relationship among students. In the joking relationship, teasing is not necessarily linked to school performance. For instance, a Black student in an Honors class, and therefore, a good student, might accuse another student of "acting White," as in the following cases:

OGBU: Okay, um, have you heard the term "acting White?"

CHERI: Yes, I have. [Raising her voice.]

OGBU: Okay, how does someone get accused of "acting White"?

CHERI: Well, [laughing] I'm not gonna lie. I can't say I haven't used that term myself before, but . . . um—

OGBU: Mmm-hmm, it's okay.

CHERI: Uh, let's see, okay. Um, you want me to actually give you the details and everything like that?

OGBU: Yeah, I mean if you want to.

CHERI: Well, it's all about, it revolves around the question that you asked about a Black person losing their culture depending on who they hang around with. Um, like for instance, it's kinda hard. Um, if okay, well, of course. You've seen, um, the movie Clueless, right?

OGBU: Uh-huh.

CHERI: Well, if you see a Black person, um, or any other person, um, walking around and acting like that, saying "Oh yeah," like you know, like "totally cool, man," you know, and stuff like that. I don't know. It kind of strays from the point, but you know you can tell that they're acting different just in front of their friends instead of the way that they would normally act.

NON-ACADEMIC PRIORITIES AND PEER PRESSURES

My analysis of the other influences that led to academic disengagement found many Black students who sought to be cool, to be popular, and to keep their friends also found it difficult to become engaged with their schoolwork.

Cool Status

Many students believed it was not cool to work hard in school or to be academically engaged. One strategy of achieving the cool status or becoming "a cool guy" was to not do one's schoolwork. Other strategies included avoiding "difficult classes," cutting school, cutting classes, and not doing homework. Being cool was mainly "a male thing." But our best descriptions of the practice of being cool came from two female students. In the following interview excerpt, Kara, a Black female student, noted some of the negative academic effects of being cool.

I think that part of the problem with the Black people in this school is a lack of respect for academic striving, because of being in, trying to be part of the crowd. Trying to be with the cool people [cough drowns out some words]. That is not to say that everybody's like that. But some don't want to be put down [by the crowd]. [They know that] it's hard to sit as minorities in AP and honors classes. So they gonna try to [be in class with] all minorities. We may not be minorities in school any longer, but we are in those [AP & Honors] classes. That's where we are the minorities.

A second student added that although some students believed that making good grades was not cool, this attitude was not entirely free from self-doubt about the ability to succeed like White students. According to Suzanne, Blacks give in to peer pressures to be cool partly "because they don't have the strong foundation laid to want to, um succeed as much as a lot of the White students do."

The Quest for Popularity

Being cool was not the only way to achieve popularity among peers. One also could become popular and admired for wearing nice clothes and expensive shoes, and having other expensive material possessions. Some students were pressured by their peers to acquire these things at the expense of doing their schoolwork and striving to make good grades. Students who reported the pursuit of material goods for peer popularity and admiration at the expense of their schoolwork did not usually describe their own personal experience. Referring to other Black students, Kris observed,

> But most Blacks, they think they um, wanna be popular and stuff like that. And they don't focus on their schoolwork. They just focus on just goin' to school and tryin' to be hard [cool] and stuff like that. . . . They focus on popularity more than their schoolwork. They worry about what people might think of them or stuff like that. And they don't really wanna do bad. I mean some people care about education, but it's the friends, the people they hang around with. That just makes them different.

Keeping Friends

Some students were disengaged from their schoolwork because they wanted to conform to what their friends wanted them to do. Otherwise, they would lose their best friends.

> OGBU: How important do you think people's friends are to how well they do in school?
> HAROLD: I think very important. . . . Because like if you hang out with people that, you know, get straight As and all this and that, I mean, that's gonna motivate, you know. It's gonna help you. I mean it's gonna make you feel like, "Well, they get straight As, I should, you know, apply myself. And, you know, force myself to do good." But like most of them [students] talk probably be about schoolwork and all this stuff, but they don't do as well, you know. They'll be ready to hang out instead of do homework and stuff like that. So it takes away a lot of your time and your study time.

Middle- and high-school students also wanted to be like their friends who took on part-time jobs, often working too many hours, rather than striving to take difficult classes or studying to make good grades, even in "easy" courses.

PEER PRESSURE IN AN URBAN COMMUNITY

This section is based on a part of a large-scale, comparative study of community forces conducted in Black, Chinese, and Mexican neighborhoods in Oakland, California. The area studied is described in depth in Chapter 3, on methodology, in this volume. I used surveys, interviews, and participant observation to collect data in Oakland's Howard Community, which was the focal point of this study. In contrast to Shaker Heights, many of the Howard residents are working- and middle-class. The Oakland school system does not have bussing for desegregation, and students generally go to their neighborhood schools. Although I studied students of African, Mexican, and Chinese descent, I will limit the discussion here to Blacks, while occasionally offering comparisons with other ethnic groups to emphasize a point. Very few Whites attended the school. Hence, the percentage of Black students with White friends was only 1.24 percent. Most students befriended people from their own ethnic group; 95.9 percent of Blacks had only Black friends.

Peer Pressures and School Engagement

Even though Oakland students endorsed making good grades, there were peer pressures against behaving in ways conducive to making good grades. Just as in the Shaker Heights case, Howard students experienced several sources of peer pressures beside those related to "acting White." Since many of the other sources of peer pressure appear to be similar, I will not discuss their non-academic sources.

I began to examine social sanctions against behaviors conducive to making good grades by asking students about their close friends' reactions when they told them that they had received an "A" in a class. My informants reported that their close friends' reactions were generally favorable. About 48.4 percent of the Black students said that their friends were happy for them or proud of them. An insignificant number of Black students, 2.11 percent, reported being accused by their close friends of "acting White" for getting an A. Nonetheless, there were other negative reactions that amounted to sanctions. These included calling the student names, teasing him or her, and getting jealous. A comparison with Chinese students shows that twice as many Black students were likely to sanction a fellow Black student for doing well (Chinese—13.88 percent, Blacks—27.29 percent). Quite a few students reported that their close friends did not care what grades they got (Chinese—14.67 percent, Blacks—17.31 percent).

Outside their circle of close friends, Black students reported receiving fewer compliments and less approval for getting good grades. For example, only 10.44 percent of the Black students said that they received compliments from their peers when they made good grades; 48.01 percent reported that their peers had sanctioned them (name calling, laughing at them, and picking fights) for making good grades; and 6.45 percent had been accused of "acting White."

Academic Success and Group Membership

I also examined the role of group membership and peer response for academically successful students. First, I asked students what they, members of their families, and their communities thought of well-educated members of their group (such as people with college education). The students reported both positive and negative perceptions of the effects of having a college education on minority identity and group membership. On the positive side, the majority of the students (68.15 percent) said that well-educated members of their group proved to White Americans that minorities are "smart" and that well-educated minority individuals are a "credit to their race," proud of their cultural heritage, and want to help their own people. However, more than 16 percent of the students reported negative perceptions of the effects of being well educated, for example, that highly educated Blacks tend to think that they are better than other members of the community (Blacks—16.12 percent, Chinese—7.65 percent), and that they tend to disaffiliate with the community (Blacks—13.3 percent, Chinese—4.89 percent).

Similar negative perceptions of well-educated minority individuals extended to academically successful minority students: 46.91 percent of the Black students did not think well of academically successful students in their groups. These students were said to make other students from their group "look bad." They were viewed as probably being not for their own people, but for White people, as usually being "stuck up," or as thinking that they are better than others. However, about 40.71 percent disagreed with such an assessment of successful students.

Coping with Social Sanctions or Peer Pressures

We have seen that even though most of the students said that they wanted to make good grades and a fairly large number of those who made good grades were complimented by their peers, especially their close friends, others experienced various types and degrees of social sanctions. I next tried to find out how academically successful students coped with the social sanctions of their peers, particularly those outside their circle of friends.

Acting Dumb during Lessons

Ethnographic observations in classrooms and personal interviews revealed that many smart Black students "act dumb" during lessons. Survey data also indicated that 23 percent of the respondents noted that Black students were ridiculed by other students if they *always* raised their hands to answer questions in class, knew the right answers to a teacher's questions, did class assignments, were praised by the teacher for getting good grades, or paid attention in class. When asked why Black students did not always show their smartness during lessons, some respondents indicated that a fear of being accused of "acting White" was not the main reason for playing dumb in class. About 37 percent of the students were called names like "nerd," "wimp," and "lame," compared to 8.95 percent who were accused of "acting White." However, 25 percent of the students feared rejection by other members of their group. Irrespective of the reason, hiding the fact that one is smart in class was one way of coping with peer sanctions.

Coping with Sanctions from Close Friends

My interviews with Howard students further investigated how smart Black students coped with sanctions from their closest friends. Specifically, I wanted to know what they would do if their closest friends did not think it was important to study or make good grades, but they themselves thought otherwise. The most common strategies included convincing their friends to study and make good grades, helping their friends with homework, letting them copy their assignments, camouflaging their smartness, transferring to another school, getting away from discouraging friends, and changing friends. Convincing their friends to study and make good grades was the most common. A very few number of students admitted to giving in to peer pressure and letting their grades suffer.

Coping with Sanctions from Peer Groups in General

In addition to the strategies students developed for dealing with peer pressures from their close friends, students revealed several additional coping strategies they used in order to remain bona fide members of their peer group while continuing to engage in activities needed to make good grades. The coping strategies used with more general peer groups were somewhat different from those for close friends. For peer groups in general, good students relied less on convincing or helping their peers to study and make good grades and more on camouflaging (used by 54 percent of the respondents). Camouflaging included playing dumb in class; pretending that grades are not important; clowning; studying when away from friends and appearing to be naturally smart; and getting involved in what their friends like to do, getting very involved in "Black activities," and avoiding involvement in "White activities." A small number of students said they would transfer to other schools or change their friends. A surprising strategy, though rarely used, was to get a "bully" to protect one from peer hostility in return for helping the bully with his or her schoolwork.

The ethnographic study of Howard students further elaborated the strategies that students used to deal with their peers. Some students who experience the conflicting demands of school and Black codes of conduct develop some surreptitious forms of doing well. They avoid directly or openly using methods that presuppose the utility of generally prescribed forms of behavior that contribute positively to good school performance (i.e., primary educational strategies). Instead, they adopt methods for school achievement that shield them from their peers' negative social sanctions.

Code-switching: A Time and Place for Everything

Although there are many forms of code-switching, one form that students in Oakland used was to be serious in class, but compensate for it when outside class by acting wild or crazy, as expected by peer groups. Marion illustrated this form of coping:

> INTERVIEWER: Do you feel sometimes that your friends would not take you or would not accept you if you try to be serious about your schoolwork or try to make really good grades?
>
> MARION: I don't feel that way, 'cause they know how I am. 'Cause my friends, like today, they tell me, you, they say I'm a nerd because I go to class and I do what I'm supposed to do. But then they don't think of me as a nerd because when I'm outside of class I act crazy. They say, um, you say I don't have it all. [Laughs.] But it just important—I know there's a time and there's always a time and a place for the things—for certain thing to be done. And then, class, that's the time and place for you to learn. Once you outside of the class, then you let go and be yourself. So therefore as long as I'm in that class getting my education and sitting down and being nice. Once I get outside the class, I'm on my own, so therefore none of the teachers can tell anything.

Camouflaging

Camouflaging, or doing schoolwork in secret, was a frequently discussed strategy. A number of the students discussed their own use of this strategy or told stories of other students they knew who used it. The following exchange between the interviewer and two students, Damien and Kevin, illustrates how students continued to be with their crowd, but studied in secret.

> INTERVIEWER: How does a student behave so that his or her friends will not know that he or she is really serious about school or works hard to make good grades?
>
> DAMIEN: Hmm, probably act like their friends, you know. Try to be with the "in crowd": Yeah, Man, I did this, and I did that, but knowin' you didn't. You was at home studyin' you know just to be with them.
>
> INTERVIEWER: How about stuff that they did?
>
> DAMIEN: Yeah. Like their friend's say "I did somethin' " and you'd say "Oh, man, I did that, too." You know lyin' and everything else.
>
> KEVIN: Their friends cutting. Basically, cutting. Um, playing around in class. Just to look, you know, but you know, just to be funny, you know. I don't know. 'Cause I know there's a lot of, um, there's a lot of smart people that—I know this one guy, Frank Valentine. He surprised all, became at the senior's awards; he got a scholarship to, um, UCLA.
>
> INTERVIEWER: Oh, wow!
>
> KEVIN: And it's like, you know, the crowd he hung around with wasn't, you know, wasn't that crowd that, like, went to school every day. And, um, you know, he dressed pretty neat, but now, he was with the latest fads.
>
> INTERVIEWER: How, how was this, how do you think that guy was able to, you know, get good grades even though he had friends who didn't go to school and stuff?
>
> KEVIN: Well, he probably wanted to make something out of his life and probably tried to psych his friends out by, you know, looking like them, talking like them. But not acting, you know, being like that. You know, just so he wouldn't be called a "nerd" or just be, you know, in those cliques or whatever.

Belief that Good Grades Came from Cheating the System

Several students camouflaged by getting their friends to believe that one did not get good grades by studying, but instead by getting around the grading system through cheating, copying their friends' work, changing grades, and teacher favoritism, etc. Here are examples of reports on this form of camouflage:

> JEAN: They say, "What's you do, blood?" [Interviewer laughs.] Then they would think I snuck up behind the teacher and bubble in my

grades. [Interviewer laughs.] They come up with any, they come up with every excuse other than he studied and worked for it.

INTERVIEWER: So, you've seen people who act like they don't care about it, that they got around with their friends, but then they go home and study and don't let their friends know that they study?

JEAN: They, yeah. Friends call: "What you doing?" "Nothing." "Want to go out?" "No." "Why? What you doing?" "Oh, nothing." "Ok. Come on, let's go."

INTERVIEWER: And how do friends explain that that student is getting good grades even though they act like they're not studying?

JEAN: People these days are so stupid they just, but mostly they'll think you cheated. You cheated or this or that. And they'll just let them believe what they want. I know 'cause me myself I wouldn't go and explain to 'em. It ain't none of their business, this is my grade, not theirs. And if I cheated, then I cheated. If I studied, I studied.

INTERVIEWER: Have you seen kids who do that [camouflage]?

JEAN: Uh, huh. 'Cause I even do it some of the time.

INTERVIEWER: What kind of things do you do?

JEAN: I just try to give them the impression that, you know, that can wait, you know. This work can wait, that class can wait. And then, like when I get home, then I just do everything that I shoulda did or whatever.

COPING WITH PEER PRESSURES IN AN AFFLUENT COMMUNITY

At Shaker High, several of the students' accounts indicated that not all students succumbed to negative peer pressures. Despite peer pressures, some students enrolled in Honors and Advanced Placement classes, worked hard, and made good grades. How did these students handle the peer pressures that likely prevented others from doing similarly?

There were several factors that minimized the negative impact of peer pressure on good students; that is, on students taking Honors and Advanced Placement classes and those making good grades. One was family upbringing and support. Some parents instilled in their children the importance of making good grades in school and taking Honors and Advanced Placement classes, and they also supervised their homework. Their parents or guardians monitored their work and screened their peer group membership; thus these parents ensured that their children's friends did not distract them from their schoolwork and homework. Here is how one student explained this type of family educational strategy.

> OGBU: Mmm-hmm. So what gave you the strength then, to resist peer pressures, because that . . . seems to be something that comes up a lot; and that's peer pressure. So, what gave you the strength to avoid that?
>
> CELESTE: I guess it's, I don't know really. It's just something I knew I had to do. . . . I guess it maybe, like traditions and stuff that have been instilled in me by my parents . . . stuff like that.

Students also developed their own strategies. In this case, good students handled the negative peer pressures by carefully choosing other Black students who were also good students as friends. For example, they chose Black students who also enrolled in Honors and Advanced Placement classes.

Another action taken by students was to interpret peer pressures as distractions from the goal of school success and, therefore, they took the necessary steps to avoid them. One student explained this interpretation quite nicely. She said that it depended on individual students. A student who really wanted to succeed in school would strive to do so, take Honors and Advanced Placement courses, and study to make good grades. He or she would not cave in to peer pressures. She concluded, "You can't worry about what other people are gonna say."

Shaker High reduced the impact of the negative peer pressures by establishing the Minority Achievement Committee (MAC) Scholars program, which helped students gain pride in their academic identity and gave them a support group (see McGovern & Davis, this volume). Students with certain grade point averages are considered potential scholars and invited to join the program. The scholars meet periodically to discuss how to handle peer pressures and help improve their school performance, and there is an annual award ceremony during which academic improvement is rewarded. The scholars wear special symbols of MAC Scholars and have special greeting-symbols for one another when they meet. They are proud to be academic achievers and are not intimidated by peer pressures. Moreover, other Black students generally admire the MAC Scholars as good role models (Ogbu, 2003, pp. 125–126).

The prevalence and negative influence of peer pressures were discussed at several middle- and high-school MAC meetings. On one occasion, when a teacher asked students what deterred them from doing well in school, the overwhelming response was distractions—friends and talking with them on the phone. Friends made students forget their homework and shift their priorities from schoolwork to other things. The students said that they understood that schoolwork should come first, but their friends made them reverse their priorities. At another MAC meeting, a student emphasized that everybody wanted to do well in school, but that they might not want to show this openly because their friends might accuse them of being "nerds." The same speaker advised his fellow high-school scholars "to do it for yourself." That is, ignore the distractions from peers and strive to do well in school.

The school staff that initially organized the MAC program believed that one reason the program contributed to academic engagement was that the scholars "learned to invert the meaning of studious behavior among Black students." The high-school scholars learned to attach positive meanings to academic engagement and success. They came to prefer being on the Honor Roll as a result of hard work than to achieve popularity among their peers for nonacademic activities. The high-school scholars eventually began to feel proud of being on the Honor Roll because they worked hard, and when they did not make the Honor Roll, they were openly disappointed. So, for these young Black scholars, working hard to do well became a goal worth pursuing. Eventually, as at the time of our study, MAC Scholars also enjoyed popularity because of their academic success. To reach this point, though, the MAC program had to overcome norms that undermined academic engagement.

Conclusions and Implications

While not all Black students experienced peer pressures, those who were exposed to pressures were not necessarily affected by them, nor were all peer pressures negative. At the same time, evidence presented in this chapter shows that among the many Black students who experienced negative peer pressures, the peer pressures undermined their academic engagement. There was a consensus among the informants that Blacks more than Whites believed that they had to conform to "fit in," even when this meant not doing well in school. In the two settings, affluent Shaker Heights and Oakland's working-class Howard community, teachers, counselors, and the students themselves were fully aware of how negative peer pressures had the potential to affect academic disengagement. It was not merely a matter of "ability," bad teaching, or low teacher expectations (although all these factors were important) that led to academic disengagement. The achievement norm of peer groups played an equally important role in Black students' poor—as well as high—academic performance.

Peer pressures increased as students got older and as they progressed through higher levels of school. At the elementary level, pressures were not noticeable and had limited effects on students' schoolwork. Elementary-school students seemed generally enthusiastic about their classes, and many actively participated during lessons. They also did things to gain teachers' approval. We even found some instances in which Black students competed with one another to do well, for example, when four Black girls were doing a group project. We did not come across any elementary-school students during the study in Oakland or Shaker Heights who were rejected by their friends for doing well in class. But at the high-school level, some students recalled that their peers had rejected them in elementary school because they were good students. Those who remembered being teased in elementary school reported that students who went to remedial classes also were teased. One was teased during the sixth grade when she left the regular class to go to a remedial reading class. In other words, teasing at the elementary school was directed toward both good and poor students.

By middle school, the adverse effects on academic engagement and performance of increased peer pressures and teasing were evident. Several students admitted that peer pressures affected their own schoolwork or that of other students they knew. Friends sometimes supported one another's academic goals, helped each other with homework, and competed among themselves to make good grades. For the most part, however, the students said that negative peer pressures were pervasive and led to disengagement from schoolwork.

Peer pressures reached their peak during high school, where they had a much greater influence on student enrollment in Honors and Advanced Placement classes and academic performance. Students acknowledged that their friends had a strong influence on the classes they chose to take, their attitudes toward school, and their academic performance.

At the high-school level, the older the students were, the more peer pressures they experienced, and generally these pressures were negative. Middle- and high-school students, in particular, felt strongly that they had to "fit in." Overall, then, it appears that elementary-school students did not associate getting good grades with "acting White," nor did they think that it was bad to make good grades. Middle-school students did not criticize Black students for getting good grades, and they did not stigmatize good grades. Instead, they criticized them for hanging out with White students, thereby behaving like them, by "talking proper," for example. The White behaviors they criticized, however, were those conducive to making good grades. It was at the high-school level that behaviors conducive to making good grades were most often equated with "acting White" and thus a source of criticism.

Black students tended to experience high levels of negative peer pressures; however, not all of these pressures came from "acting White." Among Howard students, low academic performance was not due to students' rejection of good grades or their striving to make good grades because it was "White." Instead, the low performance was due more to the fact that they rejected certain attitudes and behaviors. Unfortunately, some of the attitudes and behaviors labeled "White" and avoided by the students were those that enhanced school success. Similarly, in Shaker Heights, students experienced peer pressures against activities labeled as "acting White." But they also experienced peer pressures for other reasons. Both types of pressures were prevalent and contributed to students' academic disengagement.

There are differences in the ways students minimized the effects of peer pressures, some by their family upbringing and continued support and supervision, and others on their own initiative, by carefully choosing their friends and other coping strategies. Equally important was what schools did to limit the adverse impact of peer pressures on students' academic orientation and performance. A good example was the establishment of the MAC Scholars program in Shaker Heights. MAC Scholars acquired an academic identity, of which they were proud; they also were admired by others and received a good deal of peer support. Indeed, the MAC Scholars program generated peer pressures for academic engagement and good performance.

NOTES

1   To protect the study participants' anonymity, all names are pseudonyms.
2   In Oakland, there were too few White students for this dynamic to be an issue.

REFERENCES

Ogbu, J. U. (2003). *Black students in an affluent suburb: A study of academic disengagement*. Mahwah, NJ: Erlbaum Associates.

Ogbu, J. U., & Simons, H. D. (1998). Voluntary and involuntary minorities: A cultural ecological theory of school performance with some implications for education. *Anthropology and Education Quarterly, 29*(2), 155–188.

Singham, M. (1997). *The canary in the mine: closing the academic gap between black and white students*. Unpublished manuscript.

Stupay, D. S. (1993). *The Shaker Heights city schools: An overview*. Shaker Heights, OH: Shaker Heights School District.

Chapter 5

Language and Collective Identity among Adults and Students in a Black Community [1]

John U. Ogbu

In this chapter, I use findings from my research in a Black community called Howard to illustrate two critical aspects of Black students' collective identity and its effects on their academic engagement. The first is that Black students' attitudes and behaviors are rooted within their community, where they are shared among their parents and other adults. Hence, Black students' collective identity is not merely a product of students' interactions with their peers and transactions with their schools. Most current work on oppositional culture and schooling focuses on students' attitudes and behavior in school and assumes that students' attitudes and behaviors are the results of their transactions with the public school. Another assumption of critics of the Fordham-Ogbu thesis is that Black students reject good grades or striving to make good grades because these would be "acting White" (Bergin & Cooks, 2002; Carter, 1999; Horvat, 2001; Horvat, 2003; O'Connor, 1997; Cook & Ludwig, 1997, 1998). The second critical clarification this chapter will address concerns Blacks' poor performance. Black students' poor school performance occurs not because they reject good grades or view striving to make good grades as "acting White"; rather, they reject certain dominant groups' attitudes and behaviors that I believe are conducive to making good grades.

My investigation of community forces and collective identity in Oakland's Howard community is a part of a larger comparative study that examined community forces and educational strategies among Blacks, Chinese Americans, and Mexican Americans in the San Francisco Bay area. My research team and I conducted the study between 1988 and 1991. One component of the study, and the subject of this chapter, was the relationship between these minorities' collective identity, their cultural and language frames of reference, and their educational orientations and strategies.

Howard community, the area of the research, is located in Oakland, California. Oakland, situated west of San Francisco, is the eighth largest city in California. The city population is 41.1 percent African American,

33.9 percent White, and 16.3 percent Asian. The average household income is about $46,000. Howard schools perform poorly on all performance indicators. In the schools studied, Black students make up more than 70 percent of the population.

The research community consisted of an elementary school and extended to the junior and senior high schools to which the elementary school sent its students. Most of the participant observations and formal interviews were conducted within this boundary. In many respects, Howard was somewhat representative of the Black community and schools in Oakland. It shared many educational ideas, attitudes, and behaviors with the rest of the Black community and was similarly influenced by the educational ideas and experiences of Blacks living in other parts of the city.

My three research assistants and I spent 1988 through 1991 in the community and schools observing, interviewing, and collecting and studying documents. My senior research assistant interviewed parents and other adults in the community. A male research assistant interviewed male students and a female research assistant interviewed and observed female students. During the three-year period of study, we became more or less members of the Howard community. We maintained both informal and formal interactions with the residents; attended community events, including religious services, meetings on special issues, informal gatherings, weddings, and funeral services; hung out in barber shops and salons; and visited families. Through participant observations, we learned about Howard's community forces (see Ogbu's Chapter 1 in this volume for a definition of community forces), heard people express their attitudes toward a variety of issues, and witnessed their behaviors and expressions.

BEING BLACK IN HOWARD COMMUNITY: ADULTS

Awareness of Cultural Differences

Shortly after the study began, we noticed that the people of Howard distinguished between their own language and culture and the language and culture of White Americans. As we started paying attention to the distinctions, we found that Howard residents delineated and reinforced attitudes, behaviors, and speech that they considered "Black," and therefore appropriate, and the attitudes, behaviors, and speech that they considered "White," and therefore, inappropriate for them. This was similar to Luster's (1992) findings from a study of a Black community in San Francisco. Many Howard parents said that Blacks and Whites had significantly different cultures. They believed Black and White cultures differed in attitudes, behaviors, cultural orientations, interests, economics, speech styles, lifestyles, life experiences, and family structure. For example, Howard parents said that White people took more risks; spent more money, and spent it differently; were individualistic; and engaged in certain past-time activities (e.g., golf, tennis, etc.).[2] Black people, in contrast, were more inclined to "appear well off" and "to be calculative; they also had 'extended' families." Several Howard parents described the cultural differences between themselves and White people:

> MR. CARTER: Well, it's [White culture] definitely very different from ours, you know.
> INTERVIEWER: Uh-huh.
> MRS. CARTER: The cultures are different.
> MR. CARTER: They also do things very different from [what] I do. Their priorities are different from mine.
> MRS. WITHERS: It's just our culture to be demonstrative, to be emotive, emotional, you know.
> INTERVIEWER: Uh-huh.
> MRS. WITHERS: And with the Whites they can just be quiet and calm.
> MS. SPENCE: I mean, you might have some White kids that are totally out to lunch, but Black kids usually count up the cost before they do something. And they usually be, they're usually very calculative [sic] to find out just how much they [have], because they know just how far to go.

Awareness of Language Differences

An overwhelming majority of the adults believed that Blacks spoke differently than White people. Many noted that they spoke both proper and Standard English and slang or Black English. However, Black English and slang were used frequently, especially at home. Parents acknowledged that some children may have difficulty understanding Standard English as spoken at school. Mr. Grover explained the importance of language differences for African American students:

> They say, you know, that uh, because we are Black people and a lot of time we use a lot of slang; so you know, when a kid goes to school, you know, he may hear the right word, you know, and they [the children] can't associate it with the slang word that they may have been hearing all the time [at home]. You know, that might cause a problem. But you know, that's really not the child's fault because parents don't teach him [the right word], you know.

Adults' Oppositional Frames of Reference

In addition to distinguishing their culture and language from those of White Americans, Howard parents also distinguished their cultural and language frames of reference. A frame of reference is the culturally prescribed, correct way to behave or talk—the approved code of conduct in a community. The approved codes can be inferred from the descriptions of cultural differences, the attitudes and behaviors that a group approves for itself. According to the parents, where the two groups differed most in their frames of reference was in the use of "proper English." Other differences included certain ways of behaving to make money, and surprisingly, certain ways of behaving that were conducive to academic and professional success. It was not that people in Howard did not promote education, or want to achieve academic or professional success; rather they were ambivalent about certain attitudes and behaviors considered essential for succeeding in mainstream American institutions. In many cases, these mainstream attitudes and behaviors were not part of Howard adults' accepted codes of conduct.

Their frames of reference also discouraged participating in "White activities" and "hanging around" with too many White people. They had explicit views and feelings about people in the community who did not conform to the expected codes of conduct, since they interpreted the behaviors of those people as rejecting Black culture, language, and identity. In some cases, they accused others of "kissing up" to White people in order to get ahead.

Howard Black adults' frames of reference were both different and oppositional to those of Whites. But members of the community also knew that they had to behave and talk according to Whites' frames of reference in some situations. Take for example, speaking Standard English. The adults had rules about when to use or talk "proper English," which they call their "public language," and rules about when to use their "slang English," which they call their "private language." Mrs. Ferguson explained this:

MRS. FERGUSON: There is such a thing as a dialect of English—
INTERVIEWER: Yes.
MRS. FERGUSON: —that Black people do use privately, and we all do it. But we also have our public language that we use also.
INTERVIEWER: Very interesting.
MRS. FERGUSON: That I'm using right now.
INTERVIEWER: Now, what about this public language that you're talking about? Is it, how would you describe it?
MRS. FERGUSON: It's correct, uh, it is the correct English language, [in which one says] "this," "that."
INTERVIEWER: Yes, correct grammar and so forth?

MRS. FERGUSON: Yes. Correct grammar.

The expected norm was to use "correct English" at school and work and with outsiders, but not with members of the community. Those who did not make this distinction were generally ostracized, according to several parents. For example, Mrs. Dobson explained that speaking proper English was not looked upon well in the community.

> Like I was tellin' you before, when I first came out here, and I was going to school, and I got teased a lot about talkin' proper. So, I don't think it goes over here too well. [They] think that people who try to talk "real proper" are trying to be like someone else, and not themselves.

The Meaning of "Acting White" among Howard Adults

Language and Speech

In Howard, a person was labeled as "trying to 'act White' " when he or she manifested—within the community, among other Blacks, or in the family—attitudes or behaviors that the community regarded as more appropriate for Whites than for Blacks. Talking proper in private situations was the prime indicator of "acting White." Many people agreed that Blacks who "acted White" tended to talk like a White person; they talked in a more formal manner. Their intonation, pronunciation, and choice of words or vocabulary were described as more similar to "White speech" (which was distinguished from "Black speech"). Ms. Higgins explained it this way:

> I'm hearing you, I'm maybe hearing what—I'm thinking about that if, if, you, if you speaked [sic], if you speak with diction, and you speak with pronunciation, and use correct terms—many people will say you, you, you try to be White. Or, maybe if you, I think, if you walk and talk and act a certain way, you're acting White.

"Talking proper" or deliberately trying to speak "without street accent" was often tied to academic or professional success because, as the parents explained, the person talking proper might have changed as a result of having had an education or a professional career.

Hanging Out with Whites

Hanging out with White people was another indicator of "acting White." Some parents said that being Black meant more than just having the same black skin color; it involved conforming to many Black people's cultural norms. The belief was that when a Black person started hanging around many White people, he or she would start taking on their attitudes, behaviors, speech habits, and so on; simultaneously, the individual would begin to reject Black culture and language. Mr. Carter explained it this way:

> MR. CARTER: Okay. Being Black, we usually have a certain tone to our voice.
> INTERVIEWER: Yeah.
> MR. CARTER: Okay. There are certain words we use, I mean, you know.
> INTERVIEWER: Uh-huh.
> MR. CARTER: In general, there are certain types of food that most Black people like.
> INTERVIEWER: That's right.
> MR. CARTER: And when you say that a certain Black person is acting White, it's like this Black person is trying to divorce himself from all that.

Mr. Carter went on to explain how he thought the rejection of Black cultural identity began: "If you start to hang around with White people, you'll start to sound like a White person." Having a lot of money also might lead some Black people to "act White." He gave the example of Blacks who became wealthy, moved away from the Black community, and then gave up their Black culture and identity.

In essence, anyone who did not seem to conform to a Black cultural frame of reference in behavior, mannerisms, and values—indicators of Black collective identity—was likely to be labeled as "acting White." Other candidates for the label were Blacks with high social status, successful Blacks, Blacks who lived in predominantly White neighborhoods, highly educated Blacks, and those who were professionally successful in the White establishment or institutions. They regarded such people as having been marked by their "White" attitudes, behavior, and speech.

Community Reaction to those Perceived as Rejecting Black Ways

Howard parents expressed definite feelings of animosity toward people in the community who "chose to reject" Black culture. They viewed such people as "not being themselves" because they were forgetting or giving up their own culture. The three parents below were among those who were troubled by this type of attitude and behavior.

> MS. JOHNSTON: They are Black but they want to be superior to Black.

INTERVIEWER: Uh-huh. And how do other, how do other Blacks react to them?

MS. JOHNSTON: [With voice raised.] I'll tell you how I react to 'em.

INTERVIEWER: How do you, how do you react to 'em?

MS. JOHNSTON: Very ugly.

MR. McGEE: They're just trying to act White, and Black[s] don't like to see Blacks acting White. Be yourself, that's the way I see it.

INTERVIEWER: Uh-huh. Okay. So when a Black, some Black people try to only show the White side, and just show, you know, engage themselves in White experiences—

MRS. GREEN: Right, and, and—something else came to my mind when you said that. Where they, they don't express any of their own experiences. They're always talking about White experiences because our experiences as Black people are different.

Loose Ties to the Community

The problem of loose ties between the community and its successful members was brought to my attention as far back as 1969, during an interview with a Black school administrator in Stockton, California, who explained the problem thus:

> The Black community never, never gains. Every time you educate a Black man, you lose him, because once he get that degree, he's got his education. The White man has taught him—and he has been under the White man for all these years—the White man has taught him [that] "If you associate with these people that don't have this degree, you are lowering yourself." The Black man [is like] the White man. We have been trained and we strive for this middle class [with having] that two cars [as a symbol]. When people talk to us, we want to show that we are now middle class. Talk to a Black man and get to know him real well, and in an hour's time he'll start telling you how much he's got in the bank. You can't associate with the south part of Stockton and do this [with this kind of behavior].

Some of the severest criticisms were leveled against those who disaffiliated with or moved out of the community. Howard people believed that professional or economic success in the White establishment made people reject their Black culture and identity because their success in the White establishments and institutions often required them to adopt White ways, an act that Howard Blacks equated with a rejection of Black ways. The feelings and criticisms of the loose ties that professional or successful Blacks had with the community are reflected in the following interview excerpts.

MS. LAWSON: By now they've [successful members] gone somewhere else to live in a totally different neighborhood. So, you know, it's really hard to—

INTERVIEWER: Is that right? So, they're, they've moved away from the community.

MS. LAWSON: Right.

For these reasons, some Howard parents said that they did not personally know any Blacks who had become successful besides teachers and school counselors.

Those who move away are also thought to lack concern for the plight of the Black community. As evidence of their lack of concern, Howard parents pointed out:

MRS. JOHNSTON: They think it's changed 'em, make them better or the—it don't, to me.

INTERVIEWER: Well, how do you know that they could, that they think that way?

MRS. JOHNSTON: Because they talk about it.

INTERVIEWER: Oh! Really? Oh, they say that they have changed?

MRS. JOHNSTON: Sure, they think, they, they—most of 'em say they won't even move back into the neighborhood. They wouldn't want their kids to go to that [Howard] school. Because there are nothing but Blacks there.

Attitudes toward Adults Accused of "Acting White"

We also heard from some Howard Blacks who were accused of "acting White." For example, one parent talked about what it was to be subject to such accusations. She reported that a co-worker did not trust her because she was "too prissy." When we asked her for a possible explanation for her co-worker's feeling, she replied:

MRS. CARTER: Well, you know, Sheila is a typical street person. Although I was raised in Mississippi in the country, I never picked up all this street slang. I went to college and so I learned, I was used to using correct English.

Another parent, Mrs. Anderson, experienced a similar reaction, curiously enough, from her husband. He did not want her to take her children to ice skating or to a play because "that's what White people do." A third parent, who was a teacher, said she was compelled to switch between Black and White mannerisms to cater to the demands of her Black and White students' frames of reference.

We learned from the Howard Black community parents that they saw the White world as different in terms of speech, wealth, values, and familial relationships. These features of the White world required distinct attitudes and behaviors or codes of conduct that differed from those of their own world. Consequently, people from their community who ventured into the world risked being accused of rejecting their own culture. Some community members also felt resentful toward those who were successful and who, they said, were not comfortable living in the community and therefore moved out. These members were accused of forgetting where they came from—their culture and identity.

Most community members did recognize that some of the nonsanctioned behaviors and attitudes could lead to the better opportunities they desired. Thus, some approved of adopting behaviors that may be characterized as "acting White" for self-betterment *outside* the community. But within the community, it elicited negative responses from other Blacks, such as "acting White", or teasing labels, such as "snobs," "squares, "unnatural," and "oreos." Several parents talked about these community perceptions:

> MS. GREENE: I feel they are losing part of their identity when they're trying to act [like White people]. And they, number one, they can't be White. So, I don't see why they would even try to take on this.
>
> MRS. JOHNSTON: I don't want nothin' to do with 'em. Because they're not being themselves. They're not being Black.
>
> MRS. FERGUSON: So, there's a certain degree of ostracism involved. That's how the people who act White [are treated]. If they come into a mainstream, as you said, a mainstream type of community of say, up here [in Oakland Hills]. . . .
>
> INTERVIEWER: By "mainstream," mainstream Black?
>
> MRS. FERGUSON: Yeah, yeah, yeah. Then, sure, there would be a certain degree of ostracism if they weren't able to interact.
>
> MRS. CARTER: I think there is a little bit of stigma. I notice when my kids, they, I make an effort that they speak good English, and they—like, the kids tell them [that] they speak "White" or "she's like, like a White girl" or "you talk proper" which I don't know what's wrong with "talkin' proper." But [the same thing goes on] in the Black community. Here a lot of my friends are tellin' me, "You speak proper." It's an insult [to speak proper in the community].
>
> INTERVIEWER: So speaking Standard English in the community is not always the best?
>
> MRS. CARTER: I don't think they really like them [those who speak proper]. I think they are kind of rejected.
>
> MS. HIGGINS: I think most people think about the person as "acting." [They will] think they are "acting White." People kind of try to

avoid talking about him and, you know, [they will] just dissociate himself with him [ostracize him].

Notice that the demand to follow the rule of language usage applied among the middle class. As Mrs. Ferguson told the interviewer, when a mainstream Black came to visit other mainstream Blacks living up in Oakland Hills, they were expected to talk like Black people, not like Whites.

The criticism was not just about speaking proper, but also about how proper English was spoken. Howard parents made a distinction between the way Whites spoke proper English and the way Black people talked proper, as the next informant explained:

INTERVIEWER: How do they react to Black people who act White?
MS. McGEE: . . . They turn their nose up at 'em and look down on them. It's not the speaking—it's the way they carry their selves. How they act, and the type of car they drive. You might hear a few people say something about the way that person talked, but it's mainly the way that they act, the way they carry themselves, and the type of car they drive.

There were, of course, people in the community with positive opinions of Blacks who "act White." Mrs. Carter said there was nothing wrong with talking proper: "Sometimes I speak Standard English and there is no reaction to it or anything like that."

HOWARD STUDENTS' EXPERIENCES AND PERSPECTIVES

As we moved from the adult community to observe and interview Howard students, it was obvious to us that their experiences and attitudes were somewhat similar to those of the parents. Howard students felt the same conflicting demands as their parents and other adults in the community. Some students did behave and talk in the Black vernacular at home, and behaved and talked in the Standard English at school, where this was required and rewarded. As we will see, students' responses to these demands were similar to those of the adults in their community.

Awareness of Cultural Differences

We began by asking students the same questions we had asked their parents about cultural and language differences. Students identified cultural differences related to wealth, styles of dress, and styles of social interaction. They described social interaction in the White community as "sophisticated" and "formal," and in the Black community as less formal, but "warm." One student described the difference in behavior as follows:

> JAMAL: It's the way they act. They act the same, but it's different. They have a different way of actin'. Like for instance, the White person will seem so jolly, like "Hi! How are you doing," but a Black person say "Whassup! How you doin'?", you know. It's just different, they just more laid back and they shouldn't be laid back like that.

Blacks and Whites had different leisure and other activities, including those associated with education. Gilbert elaborated these differences in activities.

> GILBERT: Bein' White is reading, learning, is getting a good job, is wearing a suit and tie. . . . It's going to the opera . . . [It] is seriously White. It's wearing, uh, readin' books. You [Blacks] do not want to do that. And being Black is wearing Nikes, playing basketball, loving football, you know; speaking, you know, and I mean really broken up English, like "ain't" and stuff like that. But I don't really care. . . . That's just the distinctions they have shown me.

Awareness of Language Differences

Howard students believed that Whites spoke Standard English, as well as a White slang known as "valley"; Blacks spoke a different slang English. The term "slang" can be interpreted to mean the use of not only slang words, but also incorrect grammar. Erik explained the difficulty that White people had in understanding Black slang; someone had to interpret it for them.

> ERIK: We speak a slang. Like we say something to a White person in a slang.
> INTERVIEWER: Do they see anything that they respect at all in slang?
> ERIK: No, They'll be like, "Who you talkin' about?" They'd be lost. Like, if you say "famous," "we goin' to get famous"; like "We'll to the mall and get famous and that's poppin', that's jumpin' off." They'll be like, "What you talkin' about?" We like have to tell 'em what we mean, have to break it down and tell 'em how it means. Well, if we bust out, that's radical, yeah; they understand what we sayin' in a minute. Radical, tough, weird. But if we say somethin' like [unclear] man, they be like—

INTERVIEWER: Like Gee Wow! Man!!

ERIK: Yeah, Gee! Wow, all right.

Cultural and Language Frames of Reference

The cultural and language frames of reference or codes of conduct approved among Black students excluded behaving and talking like White students, participating in White activities, hanging out with many White students, and "talking proper" among Black peers. The differences in the students' frames of reference were best demonstrated in language use. Some Black students acknowledged that they spoke slang among themselves, but spoke Standard English when they were in class at school. They reported that they felt pressured to speak Standard English in school and in the presence of White guests, as in the case of Simone:

> INTERVIEWER: Slang or something? Do you think there's other times right here in this country where you need to know how to use proper language?
>
> SIMONE: Well, yes and no. 'Cause, yes, at school you got to know how to use proper language and then at my mother's house, in company [of White people], I have to know how to speak properly. She'll be like, "You don't talk to them that way." Then I get into trouble for talking to people like bad. Like one day she had company, and she had some White, some, I'm not going to put it like a proper way, White people. And they were very, very proper. They was my mother's friends.
>
> INTERVIEWER: The White people, you said?
>
> SIMONE: I didn't understand and they was talkin' like, "Hello dear, how you doing?" And I was looking at them, I'm like, "What's happening" back. I was like "Momma! You know you don't talk that way." She came in the kitchen and I said, "Mom! You know you don't [talk] that way, why you [ain't] talkin' normal?" She said, "Normal? What's normal?" I said, "Not the way you talkin' like that." And then so like my friend came over, and my mother told her to keep me busy while she [my mother] had company because she knew I was going to watch her talk like that. She knew I was going to say something. So she said to keep me busy. I was mad.

There was also pressure to not speak proper English, especially outside the classroom or to other Black students. Students who did follow this pattern of accepted behavior were accused of "acting White" or acting like a "nerd." Here is how a transfer student from a predominantly White school described her experience of having violated the code of speech in Howard:

ANGELIQUE: And I grew up in a predominantly White environment and that's how you're used to hearing people talk [i.e. Standard English]. And then over here [if] somebody talk proper English. "Hey, you White! Hey, you oreo! You know, you get away from me." And you get to cussin' about it. You know, he's just trying to say he's better than me. But you know he hasn't done anything wrong. All he's done is learn. He learned how to talk. And that's how he talks. He don't talk Black and he don't talk White. You're gonna have to talk cuz that's the only way you gonna make it any way. I don't care what you're doing.

The Meaning of "Acting White"

There were 63 instances in our data in which the students discussed the meaning of "acting White." Most of the students had heard the term and had specific things to say about it. For example, some students believed that a Black student was "acting White" if he or she was more attached to White than to Black culture and identity. Students identified others who were "acting White" with several characteristics, including the following:

Talking Proper

In 16 instances, students used "talking proper" to describe students who were labeled as "acting White." In other words, these students were speaking Standard English. One example that a student described is presented below:

INTERVIEWER: Have you ever heard the term "acting White?" Where do you hear it, or where have you heard it?

CARL: Um, in—well, our friends used to say I "acted White," 'cause I talked, you know—I used to talk kind of proper.

INTERVIEWER: Mm-hmm. [Laughs.] So what do you think they mean by acting White?

CARL: Because I used proper grammar, you know.

INTERVIEWER: Mm-hmm.

CARL: And I wasn't talkin' like them—talkin' a lot of slang, and all that.

Disaffiliation

In addition to speech, another factor that students identified as a marker of collective identity was how people maintained community ties. Some students observed that some Blacks not only disaffiliated from the Black community, but they also forgot to help their own people.

INTERVIEWER: What does it [acting White] mean?

VERONICA: Like what I said before, how some Black people they don't act like they're Black. They act White, as if they had to get up and to that certain position or how they act White they act as if they don't know they own coat, you know, they don't even help you anymore, you know, like they just against Black people when they [are] Black themselves.

INTERVIEWER: What kind of specific behaviors do they do? Like if you saw somebody whose house—

VERONICA: Like if I was a Black person lookin' to get a job. A Black person would probably give it to a White person over me. That's what I mean by they tryin' to act White and you know, they act as if they don't know us anymore. Once they get their money or whatever, they act like they don't know any Black people anymore.

Other students also explained that the right way or wrong way to behave could not be left to individuals to determine.

INTERVIEWER: How's somebody actin' "White" if they're "actin' White?"

NATASHA: Shoot! Um, I think, when we say "you always be actin' White" and stuff like that, they'll say, "Watch you mean?" Why you always act like them White people? You 'spose to act like us. You see, how we always be, all hip and stuff, you be all proper and stuff like that." 'Cause most White people talk real, real proper.

Hanging Out with too Many Whites

About 12 students reported that Howard students were accused of "acting White" if they had many White friends. Like their parents, they believed that those who spent too much time with White people would pick up White speech and behavior and then start "acting White." As the students below explained:

MORGAN: Well, it'd be like, uh huh, but it's like the area they grew up in. They probably grew up around White people. You know. Bein' around White people, went to White schools, I mean you know, pick up they, they talk [sic], and the way they act and dress. Wear their hair and everything.

INTERVIEWER: Okay, so do you think that school makes some Black people less Black and more White when they talk too White or they talk too Black?

RODNEY: Oh, if it's probably around 30 White people in the classroom and 5 Blacks, they'd probably start talking like that because they,

> they surrounded by 'em. They might start, um talking like them and
> acting like them.
>
> DIANA: And then here was this Black girl with all these White girls, you
> know, have their own look, and you say, "Ew, she wishes she was
> White." 'Cause she began to act like them, and—just talk like them,
> and stuff. She would act like, oh gosh! Like that! Like a Valley Girl!
> Like, sayin' stuff like, "Ooh! that's gross!" or something like that.
> Start even dressing like them—just being with them, and then
> —you know, she wanted—I'm not sayin' this is wrong, but then
> —you know, she used to be with the Black boys until, you know,
> she started being with her White friends, and then she just
> stopped being with Black boys and started being with White
> boys.

In general, among Howard students, "acting White" meant behaving in a
manner not acceptable to other Blacks because the behaviors did not fall
within the approved codes of conduct or speech.

Students' expectations that other students should behave according to
their codes of conduct were not always verbalized, but could be inferred
from their statements. Among Howard students, "acting White" was not
primarily about making good grades or about striving to make good
grades. Rather, "acting White" was about adopting various "White" attitudes and behaviors, including some attitudes and behaviors that were
conducive to making good grades or achieving school success.

Treatment of Students Who "Act White"

Some students reported that peer pressure was an instrument used by
both the community and among themselves to make people conform to
acceptable codes of conduct. Because the adult community defined its
collective identity, culture, and language in opposition to the culture and
language of White people, those who failed to conform were seen as not
acting in a manner that promoted Black culture and identity. Marcus
described the effectiveness of peer pressures:

> Peer pressure, that, that, that's you know, that has more effect on a
> person than, I think, than a parent does. You know, 'cause kids they
> gonna—I think in a lot, a majority of 'em will listen to their peers, you
> know, rather than their parents. So it, it does bother me. It's just the
> fact that, you know, I wanta be accepted.

Some Howard students reported that some of them were teased and
treated differently when they failed to exhibit proper Black attitudes and
behaviors. Two students described this way of treating students who did

not conform. One described how he was treated because of his non-conforming behavior:

> JACOB: I have heard it before 'cause people always used to accuse me in the junior high school, 'cause I was the oddball in junior high school. I did my homework. I always did.

Howard students understood the expected codes of behavior and speech. Those who displayed behavior outside the Black cultural norms were seen as deviating from and rejecting Black cultural identity and therefore posing a threat to the group's solidarity. As a result, many of the students interviewed criticized other Blacks who "acted White" in the community and among themselves. However, they did not object to "acting White" and talking proper when the school required it.

Conclusion

The subject of this chapter was the relationships among collective identity, cultural and language frames of reference, and minority students' educational orientations and strategies. The ethnographic data that my team and I collected point to several conclusions. First, they show that Howard students' attitudes and behaviors in school were not simply the result of their school experience. Students were critical of certain attitudes and behaviors in school—behaviors that their parents and other members of their community also oppose (see Chapter 2 for an analysis of the origins of these attitudes in the history of the Black–White experience in America). The second conclusion is that low academic performance of Howard students was not due to their rejection of good grades or the striving to make good grades because it was "acting White." Instead, it is due more to the fact that students rejected certain attitudes and behaviors that are conducive to making good grades. The third conclusion I draw from these data is that Black students tend to experience high levels of negative peer pressures to avoid certain behaviors that can lead to academic success, but, as noted, the pressures do not all emanate from the avoidance of "acting White."

The final conclusion I reach is that, because most of the Howard students I met wanted school success or good grades *and* to be accepted by their peers, they had to deal with conflicting demands for appropriate conduct. Like their parents, the students had several options, albeit not easy ones. Consequently, they developed a number of coping strategies (including surreptitious methods of doing well in school, such as code-switching and camouflaging), which generally permitted them to remain true to their collective identity and to engage academically.

NOTES

1   *Editors' note*: This chapter is the last one written by John Ogbu. It was incomplete at the time of his death and was the least conceptually developed of his five chapters in this book. The editors were uncertain as to whether to include or remove the chapter from the volume. In the end, they decided to include the chapter for several reasons. The first reason is that including the chapter keeps the volume faithful to John's vision of the book. The second reason is that the findings in this chapter have never been published before in any of John's prior books or articles. They are drawn from his unpublished ethnographic study of African American, Asian American, and Chinese American families from Oakland and nearby cities in the San Francisco Bay area of California. John was in the process of writing a book about that study when he put that project aside to complete this volume. This chapter, then, offers an opportunity to publish a portion of his findings.

The editors understand that it is somewhat risky to publish this unfinished chapter, lest it fuel the battles over the meaning and validity of the oppositional cultural framework, and OCF's contribution to his overarching cultural-ecological model. Nevertheless, the editors believe readers will benefit from seeing the new ethnographic data from the Oakland study, how John interpreted these findings, and how he sought to add these findings to his analysis.

2   This research was conducted before Tiger Woods and the Williams sisters added professional golf and tennis to the list of athletic competitions where Blacks excel. Arthur Ashe and Althea Gibson were renowned Black tennis players, but it took Woods' and the Williams' extraordinary achievements to change public perceptions of tennis and golf as White sports.

REFERENCES

Bergin, D. A., & Cooks, H. C. (2002). High school students of color talk about accusations of "acting White." *The Urban Review, 34*(2), 113–134.

Carter, P. (1999). *Balancing "acts": Issues of identity and cultural resistance in the social and educational behaviors of minority youth*. Ph.D. Dissertation, Department of Sociology, Columbia University, New York.

Cook, P. J., & Ludwig, J. (1997). Weighing the burden of "acting White": Are there race differences in attitudes toward education? *Journal of Policy Analysis and Management, 16*, 256–278.

Cook, P. J., & Ludwig, J. (1998). "The burden of 'Acting White: Do Black Adolescents Disparage Academic Achievement?" In C. Jencks & M. Phillips, *The Black-White test score gap* (pp. 375–400). Washington, DC: The Brookings Institute.

Horvat, E. M. (2001). *The Black-White achievement gap and Black cultural opposition to acting White: Where do we go from here?* ASA 2002 Session Proposal Draft.

Horvat, E. M. (2003). Reassessing the "Burden of Acting White": The Importance of Black Peer Groups in Managing Academic Success. *Sociology of Education, 76*, 265–280.

Luster, L. (1992). *Schooling, survival, and struggles: Black women and the GED.* Unpublished doctoral dissertation. School of Education: Stanford University.

O'Connor, C. (1997). Dispositions toward (collective) struggle and educational resilience in the inner-city: A case analysis of six African American high school students. *American Educational Research Journal, 34,* 593–629.

Chapter 6

"Signithia, You Can Do Better Than That"

John Ogbu (and Me) and the Nine Lives Peoples

Signithia Fordham

I remember it as though it were yesterday—or today. On a bright, sunny morning in March, I met John Ogbu's plane at National Airport in Washington, DC and drove him to an important policy meeting in the city. I was then a fledgling graduate student collecting ethnographic data in a high school in Washington, so these monthly meetings of senior scholars were off limits to me. Nonetheless, Ogbu's frequent consulting trips gave me unparalleled opportunities to talk with him about my research project—but only if I sent a written draft for him to read on the plane before he arrived. He was, after all, a very busy man. On this particular day, we agreed to meet later for dinner to talk about my work on "Capital High." That afternoon, as I sat at my assigned desk in the Library of Congress, I wondered how to explain to him why I had not written anything—again. Having a desk of my own at the Library of Congress (courtesy of my Congressional representative) gave me unlimited access to books and validated my standing as a scholar-to-be. Nothing could stand in sharper contrast to my childhood memories of chasing book mobiles and enduring the stern admonitions of wanna-be-librarians who did not believe I could read the books I requested and who viewed my repeated efforts to take more than the allotted number as an attempt to steal or cheat rather than a little girl's insatiable desire to learn. So there I sat, wrestling with how to tell Ogbu that I had not yet begun to write, despite the massive data streams I had collected. I feared telling him that I had failed to do what he expected—again. I had no adequate explanation of my inability to put pen to paper; after all, I could talk about my work fluently enough. Ogbu had years of experience dealing with graduate students, so I knew that what I told him had to be something other than *drylongso* (ordinary). I was trying to invent any explanation to avoid facing the real one: that I was *terrified*, unable to write what I had discovered. I knew that, as soon as the truth came out, he would voice the refrain that he seemed to have invented just for me: "See-nee-shee-ah, you can do better than that."

At dinner that evening, Ogbu and I talked about the lively debates that had taken place at the meeting he had just attended. I hoped that if I could keep him talking about the latest controversy he might forget to ask me about my research project or neglect to interrogate me about the progress of my writing. No such luck. My flight from the inevitable came to a halt in a totally unanticipated way. Instead of asking me the question I expected—"What is the current status of your research project?"—he made an off-hand remark in his heavily accented, flawless English: "See-nee-shee-ah, I have decided to return to Nigeria. I am not sure when—or if—I will be coming back. If you want me to read what you have written for your dissertation research, you should plan to get it to me before I leave at the end of the summer." Leaving? What was going on? Had the meeting he just attended been that confrontational? Using graduate student logic, I wondered if he were seeking to escape some terrible personal problem. My mind skittered back and forth between concern about his welfare and my own selfish interests. The panic was so all-consuming that I had difficulty breathing. I could not eat the delicious dessert we had ordered. I kept asking him why, why he was suddenly leaving. I did not understand his uncharacteristically vague responses. This was puzzling, because he usually communicated with extraordinary clarity. Typically, if he thought I did not quite grasp what he was suggesting, he would take out his pen and make diagrams on whatever was available—newspapers, napkins, receipts—to reinforce his point visually. Tonight, however, the only thing that registered was the idea that he was leaving the United States—soon. I had to get most of the dissertation written before the end of the summer when he would return to Nigeria.

When I returned to my apartment that night, I wrote-nonstop. I wrote virtually every night before his next monthly meeting in Washington. I could not stop. Words tumbled from an interior source I did not recognize, stumbling over each other in their haste to be the first to get on paper. It was as if the words had been dammed up for a lifetime, a flood pushing relentlessly against a gate that had, until this moment, refused to budge. The undamming of my emotions enabled me to write against the grain. I wrote out of my personal and professional pain. I wrote what I had been unable to write for years. I wrote in violation of the belief system that had been drummed into me throughout my entire school career. I wrote that Black students' academic performance was negatively affected by the burden of acting White; that in school they were held hostage to the hegemony of the norms, values, and expectations of the dominant society and so they resisted and rebelled, defiantly but deliberately confirming White society's predictions of their failure; that those Black students who, like me, succeeded on White society's terms did so at a huge psychological and intellectual price, since there was an unbridgeable gap between our life experiences and perspectives and the viewpoint of the dominant culture in academe. Above all, I wrote, we had trouble writing outside our cultural experience.

My longest chapter—more than 300 pages—was the one he jettisoned first. He chided me for not being concerned about my readers and insisted on my slashing it to less than half its length. At the same time, he demanded that I do a better job of integrating the theoretical model I was proposing and the ethnographic data I proffered. I withered in the wake of his critique. But, because I trusted his judgment, I started over, reworking that chapter and all the others to a more manageable length. In doing so, I demonstrated that he was right—again.

Ogbu did not return to Nigeria that fall—he had no intention of doing so—and the written work I gave him that spring and summer was the first of many drafts. He called often, gently prodding me to send him what I had written before his next visit to Washington. Because I had access to the limitless resources at the Library of Congress to buttress my ethnographic data, I supplied him with massive streams of information on Black students' academic achievement. He critiqued my inchoate thoughts and seemed to be constantly telling me: "See-nee-shee-ah, you can do better than that." Initially, I did not believe him. I was not yet persuaded that he was an accurate judge of professional potential. My schooling had taught me to doubt my own abilities, to believe that I was capable of only so much. At this early stage of my career, despite our growing friendship, I was so thin-skinned and so lacking in academic savvy that I often interpreted his comments as personal attacks. That was certainly never his intention. My difficulty in dealing with constructive criticism caused me much anguish, grief, and pain, which I had to overcome alone, without anyone in the discipline knowing. Ultimately it was Ogbu's belief in me rather than my belief in myself that carried the day.

It is no secret that John Ogbu and I often disagreed. We openly acknowledged our differences—even though the public that responded to our coauthored article (Fordham & Ogbu, 1986) and the discipline that named our theory the "Fordham-Ogbu Hypothesis" did not. In the beginning, our divergent views enriched our dialogue about the reasons for Black students' academic underachievement. Later on, we no longer collaborated. At most we worked in parallel, each developing his or her own aspect of a model that we had originally proposed as complementary.

We met as a distinguished scholar, master teacher and a highly motivated but insecure graduate student, and in some ways our relationship never grew past that beginning. We debated the causes, consequences, and remedies for the achievement gap between Black and White students as a superordinate and subordinate might. I recognized that when I was yearning for books that offered compelling explanations for African American students' academic performance, he published works that, with unerring aim and amazing effectiveness, called into question the models of biological inferiority and cultural backwardness that rationalized public schools' continuing failure to educate minority students and the persistence of segregated and inferior education after *Brown* (Ogbu, 1974, 1978, 1981a, 1981b, 1981c, 1982a, 1982b).[1] The cultural-ecological model he proposed highlighted the structural and historical factors that had shaped Black Americans' social position and their responses to secondary status.

So I respectfully opened our discussions by remarking that the typology he proposed to explain minority status achievement, which emphasized the socially imposed limits on Black Americans' occupational horizons, illuminated my own experiences at school, the patterns of behavior I observed among the Black students I was then teaching, and the child-rearing practices of my middle-class, African American friends. But, I tentatively suggested, because the typical research focus—including his own—was so one-sided in its attention to academic failure, the dominant image of students whose ancestors were enslaved in America was monolithic. I argued that there was—and still is—a real need for researchers to explain the academic performance of successful African American adolescents. Their achievements might hold a clue not only to the structural and cultural barriers that all minority students face, but also to the strategies some students use to surmount them. Any reformulation of the question must begin by acknowledging that such students comprise a significant component of the African American student population. Ogbu agreed that Black students are generally represented as total failures in both the academic and the popular press and that the striking success of a few matters theoretically, but he challenged me to offer an explanation that would account for this divergence in Black students' academic performance. His theoretical model, with its emphasis on structural factors such as job ceilings and on Black students' realistic adaptation to limited opportunities, applied equally to all. So I set out to take up his challenge as I analyzed the ethnographic data I had collected at Capital High.

Ironically, when I did what he suggested and proposed an alternative explanation (Fordham, 1985, 1987b, 1998, 1993, 2001; Fordham & Ogbu, 1986), he was not convinced. My dissertation research fueled our disagreement and clarified its grounds (Fordham, 1987a; see also Fordham 1996). I proposed that the hegemony of the norms of the dominant society within the school compels African American students to resist the stigmatized social position allotted to them by resisting the mandate to "act White," leading them to underperform academically and, ironically, to confirm the prevailing view of their capacities. Ogbu's approach emphasized social-structural and historical factors; it inscribed a cultural ecology. My approach emphasized expressive as well as adaptive responses to those determinants; it mapped a terrain of contest within African American culture as well as between it and the dominant culture. I proposed my theory as an addition to his, balancing its structuralism and extending its reach into the dynamics of African American adolescents' cultural repertoire.

I am not sure that Ogbu was ever fully convinced of the validity of my point of view. To be fair, perhaps he recognized more fully than I did that what I had proposed was not a minor addition to his model or even a mid-course correction. He seemed to treat it as an alternative, even incompatible, explanation that led in a different direction. It is doubly ironic that, as he told me years later, our coauthored article was cited more frequently than anything else he had published—or, as he put it, it was his most frequently cited work. To his credit, when reporters called him to talk about the article we wrote together he invariably referred them to me, telling them (as they repeated to me) that it was my work.

We collaborated only on our famous—or infamous—article, "Black Students' School Success: Coping with the Burden of Acting White," published in *The Urban Review* in 1986. I initially presented the paper, which was based on my research at Capital High, at the American Anthropological Association Annual Meeting in Washington, DC in December 1985 (Fordham, 1985). I was surprised by the paper's reception at the meetings. I attributed the intense media interest in the presentation to its being a "local color" story: the research was about a school in Washington, and the conference was in that city. Although the AAA Press Corps had submitted the title of my paper to the media, I declined to speak to the reporters from *The Afro-American*, *The Washington Post*, *The Washington Times*, *Psychology Today*, or any other publication. I was hesitant in part because I was an unpublished graduate student. But my hesitancy had a much deeper source: the fear that was the product of the lies embedded in Black Americans' academic underachievement.

Before my research at Capital High, I—like most people, Black and White—assumed that Black students did not write well, or at all, because they did not understand the process or know the rules of grammar. Although I could have known better from my own experience, I thought that most Black students' problem was merely mechanical. It is not. These high school students' fear, which was their dominant response to writing assignments (Fordham, 1998, 1999), propelled me to a place I did not want to go: back to my past and the emotional difficulty of writing outside my cultural experience.

The smell of fear at Capital High was hauntingly familiar to me. The questions that framed my dissertation research grew out of my own childhood experiences of fear, as well as my observations of the predicament of young Black students in urban school systems. When I was a little girl, what I hated most about my life was the cacophony of lies: the lies that White folks told us, the lies the preachers preached and the church ladies regurgitated, the lies my parents inadvertently and deliberately told me. Most intensely of all, I hated the lies my teachers taught: lies about who were kith and kin; about work, property, and poverty; about democracy, equal opportunity, and social justice; and about the inadequacy of Black folks' intellectual capabilities—my enslaved ancestors', my parents', and, by implication, my own. Teachers lied about the efficacy of schooling and the existence of meritocracy. Most egregious of all, they lied by saying that intellectual ability outweighed every other social or cultural attribute of individuals. Now as I look back on my own childhood, it was not so much the lies and the distorted human relationships those lies created that I abhorred as it was my inability to jam their transmission. Unable to write an alternative narrative, to refute or rebut these lies, my peers and I were compelled to endorse and thus to participate in the (re)production of our own dehumanization. So we did not write. Our unconscious response was to obstruct the hegemonic narrative of life in the Black community by freezing our reactions, by becoming mute, by refusing to write in blackface. As I analyzed the resistant responses of students at Capital High, I also shared these stories of my childhood with Ogbu.

As I struggled to write my dissertation and to communicate to Ogbu how this experience across generations in the African American community was implicated in both our involuntarily minority status and our mute, rebellious response to this stigmatization and degradation, I realized how debilitating were the lies taught in school. I vividly recalled how I stood out, not only because I succeeded in mastering White people's language but also because I attempted to write about life as it was actually lived in the Black community. That desire was repeatedly thwarted. The responses of my teachers and other school officials were predictable to everyone but me. Single-minded, I was blind to much of what trampled the lives of so many of my peers. Yet not surprisingly, because as young Black students we were unable to write in our own voices and tell our unique stories, our academic efforts were subverted. Our performance reflected the evolution of our fear. We came to fear our own writing, to fear that what we wrote would further distort our lived reality. Indeed, given the choice of being misrepresented in blackface or blacked out, most of my generation opted for silence. Nevertheless, the then-dominant blackface constructions stuck to us like ill-fitting garb, barely masking our fury. Because these predatory images of blackness were achieved primarily through claims made by written documents, our fear of writing about ourselves was matched only by our fear of what was written by others about us. This pervasive fear ran like a river through our individual and collective psyches. As school-aged children, we dreaded rather than coveted the power of the pen. The rapacious hegemony of writing, coupled with our total lack of involvement in the construction of our own self-images, blacked out our dreams.

Fearing that this kind of explanation would be dismissed, I did not feel prepared to defend the claims presented in my paper to sophisticated Washington journalists. One journal was not deterred. Shortly after the meetings ended, the editors of *The Urban Review* sent me the following letter of invitation, dated 3 February 1986:

> Dear Dr. [*sic*] Fordham:
>   Please send me a copy of the paper you presented at the recent AAA meetings in Washington, D.C. Also, please indicate if you would be interested in having the paper reviewed for possible publication in *The Urban Review.*
>   Sincerely,
>   William T. Pink, Editor

Again, fear was my primary emotion. Despite my excitement, I sat on the invitation for more than a month. During Ogbu's next visit to Washington, I shared the letter with him. He appeared mildly bemused by my anxiety and a bit disinterested in my argument. Nevertheless, he agreed to edit the essay. Uncertain that I needed his assistance, we agreed that I would be the first author. I came to believe that he would not have agreed to be the second author had he been unequivocally convinced of the accuracy of the analysis. Unfortunately, researchers and journalists repeatedly reversed our names, making the publication authored by Ogbu and Fordham rather than Fordham and Ogbu. This reversal was particularly annoying for me because the article in *The Urban Review* caught the public imagination, surpassing both our expectations. I cringed every time I saw this inaccuracy, while Ogbu appeared nonchalant. But underneath, I believe, he seethed at being identified with research he had not done and an explanation with which he did not fully agree.

One of the many amusing stories Ogbu told me during the early stages of our relationship was how he came to disbelieve the mantra of *The New York Times*: "All the news that's fit to print." He had come to the conclusion after the publication of his critically acclaimed book, *Minority Education and Caste: The American Education System in Cross Cultural Perspective* (Ogbu, 1978). At the invitation of editors at the newspaper, he sat for hours in a room at the *Times* trying to write something fit to print in that august publication. He was not successful. I sensed that this infuriated him and that he joked about it to mask the anger this rejection aroused. Yet this rejection underlined what he postulated in the book that while work is the most salient symbol of status in a human population, the group that controls the definition of work and determines its value can enhance or negate the image of any segment of a population over which it has control. Ironically, not long after our coauthored article was published, a long story about his work in a Washington, DC high school appeared in *The New York Times*. I don't know entirely what to make of this fact. Our minority status made us both interlopers in this context, yet we did not share a conspiratorial glee at capturing the public imagination.

When I learned of Ogbu's untimely death, the incident that opens this essay came immediately to mind. Death and his involuntary return to Nigeria were merged because of his warning that he was going back there when we had dinner together so many years ago. Nigeria was—and is—his homeland, the sacred space of his birth. His experience and understanding of migration, and his comparison of the voluntary and involuntary movements of peoples, formed a critical component of the compelling typology he proposed in his early work on the academic performance of different types of minorities, not only in the American educational system but in most contemporary nation-state contexts. A little village in Nigeria is his final resting place. Yes, he has gone home—almost 20 years after he told me he would.

As I look back at my relationship with John Ogbu, I realize it was multilayered, complex, and riddled with contradictions. This piece is less a discussion of his enormous contributions to the discipline of anthropology and education and more a conversation about our relationship and my academic journey with him. I feel honored to have had the opportunity to be mentored by the most influential anthropologist on Black and minority schooling since the 1954 *Brown* decision. My sadness is multifaceted, beginning with our discipline's loss of such a powerful intellect and ending with the unacknowledged power struggles between Ogbu and me that made us less effective as anthropologists working for social change than we could and should have been. I mourn the intellectual loss to the field of anthropology and the state of our relationship when he died—an alienation that I hoped would not last forever but had as yet found no way to heal. He had so much more to give, and we had so much more work to do together.

I wonder how many of our differences arose from our divergent histories and social locations. Although we both belonged to social categories that are central to his model of minority status, I belong to a caste-like, involuntary minority, while he belonged to an immigrant minority. My African American identity and his African identity did not always mesh. I recall him shifting back and forth between "us"—referring to the entire African Diaspora—and "you"—referring to Black Americans whose collective identity has been forged over centuries on this continent. He sometimes looked to me for knowledge of the inner dynamics of African American culture, but he also occasionally assumed that my view was blinded by belonging.

What he seemed not to see were the gender and generational differences that always made us unequal within the highly stratified world of academe. Our collaboration could not erase, or even substantially modify, the hierarchy of teacher and student, mentor and mentee with which we began. After I defended my dissertation, I hoped that our relationship would metamorphose into a more equal one. Instead, it became more formal and distant. My invitations to him to join me as a discussant or presenter on panels or a participant in symposia were routinely refused. We appeared together at only two professional conferences: the American Psychological Association meeting in San Francisco in 1991 and the American Sociological Association meeting Chicago, Illinois in the summer of 2003. Even then, we did not collaborate. We presented papers we had prepared independently. He never sought my opinion on anything he wrote or any project he proposed to undertake. Episodically, he would send me a copy of his latest published work. The University of California honored him as a distinguished professor. He received numerous grants and awards in the wake of our coauthored article. Everything he submitted for publication was embraced; what he did not want to see in print never appeared. My post-dissertation career is best characterized by migration; indeed, migration could be my middle name. While "Visiting" does not precede the title of my current professorship, which carries the name of the 19th-century equal rights activist, Susan B. Anthony, its term limit suggests lack of stability, even more migration. I am visiting but from nowhere—except, perhaps, the homes of my kinfolk. Like my ancestors, I have moved frequently, not only mentally but also physically, and often involuntarily. I began this professional journey with the unexpected good fortune of publishing an article, and then a book, that captured the public imagination for better and for worse. But I continued to labor in academe in relative obscurity, denied tenure at a second-rate university, inundated with requests from journals to evaluate the submissions they received but having virtually everything I submitted rejected. Despite his analysis of caste as well as class stratification, Ogbu never appeared to fully understand the elementary facts of being Black and female in America.

Over all the years I exchanged sources with Ogbu, I remember him giving me only one book: Castile and Kushner's (1981) *Persistent People's Cultural Enclaves in Perspective*, which I mentally retitled, "The Nine Lives Peoples Book." During one trip to Washington, he pulled it from his baggage, handed it to me, and ordered me to read it. He had already signed it in black ink: "From John Ogbu to Signithia." At the time I did not fully appreciate how important this work was to his emerging ideas regarding the centrality of collective identity in minority status. And, although Ogbu had an uncanny way of passing on things whose significance grew over time, I never anticipated how important it would become to mine.

Ogbu (1997a, 1997b, 2001, 2002) was convinced that, despite his frequent reference to collective identity in much of his later work, his earlier work (e.g., Ogbu, 1974, 1978, 1981a, 1981b, 1981c, 1982a, 1982b) and even his most recent book (2003), as he conveyed to me in our last communications, tended to be cited with reference to the minority typology. This was frustrating for him and he blamed himself for not making a more compelling case for the centrality of a collective identity for the "nine lives peoples." After reading and reflecting on the analyses offered by many of the authors in Castile and Kushner's (1981) book (e.g., Castile, 1981; Green, 1981; Leone, 1981; see also Spicer, 1961, 1971, 1980), Ogbu became convinced that social groups whose collective identities are shaped by the conditions chronicled in these sources are in a special category of what is widely known as minority status. As he indicated to me, collective identity is at the core of the anthology he was compiling prior to his death and that will be published posthumously by Routledge. He assured me that he was committed to making collective identity the central issue in his emerging work.

African Americans are included among these "persistent peoples," of course, since we have constantly had to reinvent ourselves in the face of social death: the soul-murder of the trans-Atlantic passage and enslavement; the sundering of kinship ties so lovingly recreated; the repeated sexual violation of Black women by White men; forced migration from whatever place had become home to raw settlements in the deep South and urban West. Between the First Emancipation and the Second, which was wrought by the late twentieth-century Civil Rights Movement, came generations of stigmatizing segregation, disfranchisement, and deliberately imposed poverty, all enforced by organized terror against "uppity" men and women. Our physical, spiritual, and political survival required strategies both subtle and outrageous: evasion and dissemblance to avert violation and avoid the tyranny of pain; creating and passing on alternative identities to those imposed by the master class; erecting and sustaining autonomous institutions, such as the Black church; organizing to defy the well-defended boundaries that hemmed us in or, at least, to demonstrate that these were not our own limitations. I understood what it meant to persist in the face of such obstacles.

Castile and Kushner's book encompasses many other "persistent peoples," including Jews, Armenians, Native Americans, even Mormons. Concerted efforts to destroy these peoples, repeated over centuries, have proved ineffectual. These peoples, despite involuntary migration and dispersion, have refused to dissolve or disappear. I call them the "nine lives peoples" because, like cats, they have a talent for defying (social) death. Do they have some inner gyroscope so they land feet-first when thrown from great heights? Displaced peoples and involuntary migrants must reinvent themselves constantly, often from positions of systematic subordination or threatened extinction. Persistence is not an individual act but a collective one—although it makes the continued existence of the self possible under conditions that would otherwise extinguish it.

Peoples who are engaged in reconstituting themselves do not seek to disown or liquidate their pasts, however painful or traumatic. Indeed, constructing an acceptable and usable past in the present is central to their definition of who they are (Friedman, 1992, p. 851; Trask, 1991, p. 164). The stories that such peoples tell themselves do not deny their suffering but transmute it. They record, codify, and transmit survival strategies that can be deployed in resent circumstances. Indeed, telling and retelling these histories become acts of persistence. Shared from one generation to the next and across a Diaspora, they constitute and nourish a collective identity that enables a people to flourish even when planted in hostile soil (for a detailed discussion of Black Americans' persistence see Fordham, 1996, pp. 67–101).

Finally, I am saddened that Ogbu and I squandered an unparalleled opportunity to build on the collaboration we began with the publication of our joint article. Perhaps, since we built our own professional personae and imagined our collective identities on the basis of different histories as well as within the peoplehood of Africans in the Diaspora, my conviction that we could have collaborated more closely is naïve. But I was—and remain—convinced that we could have become professional and political allies as we worked to describe both the social conditions undermining minority students' academic performance and thinkable alternatives that were likely to transform cultural practices and alter the difficulties that his work identified and mine elaborated. I mourn his passing and our joint failure to cross the gender, cultural, and ethnic divide that constantly undermined our collaboration. Making use of the rapacious hegemony of the pen, I honor Ogbu's memory and hope to continue our interrupted description of the "nine lives peoples" by repeating the mantra he bestowed on me during the best days of our collaboration: "See-nee-shee-ah, you can do better than that." I will always try to live up to his towering intellect and resist the blackout of our dreams for the "nine lives peoples." John Ogbu's legacy challenges us as a discipline to do no less.

NOTE

1   *Brown v. Board of Education of Topeka* is a 1954 landmark decision of the United States Supreme Court, which overturned earlier rulings going back to *Plessy v. Ferguson* in 1896, by declaring that state laws which established separate public schools for Black and White students denied Black children equal educational opportunities <en.wikipedia.org/wiki >.

REFERENCES

Castile, G. P. (1981). Issues in the analysis of enduring cultural systems. In G. P. Castile & G. Kushner (Eds.), *Persistent peoples: Cultural enclaves in perspective* (pp. xv–xiv). Tucson: University of Arizona Press.

Castile, G. P., & Kushner, G. (Eds) (1981). *Persistent peoples: Cultural enclaves in perspective*. Tucson: University of Arizona Press.

Fordham, S. (1985). *Black students' school success: Coping with the burden of "acting White."* Paper presented at the 84th Annual Meeting of the American Anthropological Association, Washington, DC, December.

Fordham, S. (1987a). *Black student school success as related to fictive kinship: A study in the Washington, D.C. public school system*. Ph.D. dissertation proposal, Department of Anthropology, American University.

Fordham, S. (1987b). Racelessness as a factor in Black students' school success: Pragmatic strategy or pyrrhic victory? *Harvard Educational Review, 58*(1), 54–84.

Fordham, S. (1993). "Those loud Black girls": (Black) women, silence, and gender "passing" in the academy. *Anthropology and Education Quarterly, 24*(1), 3–33.

Fordham, S. (1996). *Blacked out: Dilemmas of race, identity and success at Capital High*. Chicago: University of Chicago Press.

Fordham, S. (1998). "Speaking Standard English from nine to three": Language usage as guerrilla warfare at Capital High. In C. Adgers & L. Hoyt (Eds.), *Language usage and older children* (pp. 205–216). New York: Oxford University Press.

Fordham, S. (1999). Dissin' "the standard": Ebonics as guerrilla warfare at Capital High. *Anthropology and Educational Quarterly, 30*(3), 272–293.

Fordham, S. (2001). "Why can't Sonya (and Kwame) fail math?" W. H. Watkins, J. H. Lewis, & V. Chou (Eds.), *Race and education: The roles of history and society in educating African-American students* (pp. 140–158). Boston: Allyn and Bacon.

Fordham, S., & Ogbu, J. U. (1986). Black students' school success: Coping with the burden of "acting White." *The Urban Review, 18*(3), 176–206.

Friedman, J. (1992). The past in the future: History and the politics of identity. *American Anthropologist, 94*(4), 837–859.

Green, V. M. (1981). Blacks in the United States: The creation of an enduring people? In G. P. Castile & G. Kushner (Eds.), *Persistent peoples: Cultural enclaves in perspective* (pp. 69–77). Tucson: University of Arizona Press.

Leone, M. (1981). Mormon "peculiarity": Recapitulation of subordination. In G. P. Castile & G. Kushner (Eds.), *Persistent peoples: Cultural enclaves in perspective* (pp. 78–85). Tucson: University of Arizona Press.

Ogbu, J. U. (1974). *The next generation: An ethnography of education in an urban neighborhood*. New York: Academic Press.

Ogbu, J. U. (1978). *Minority education and caste: The American system in cross-cultural perspective*. New York: Academic Press.

Ogbu, J. U. (1981a). Education, clientage, and social mobility: Caste and social change in the United States and Nigeria. In G. D. Berreman (Ed.), *Social inequality: Comparative and developmental approaches* (pp. 277–306). New York: Academic Press.

Ogbu, J. U. (1981b). On origins of human competence: A cultural ecological perspective. *Child Development, 52*(2), 413–429.

Ogbu, J. U. (1981c). *Schooling in the ghetto: An ecological perspective on community and home influences.* National Institute of Education Follow Through Planning Conference. Philadelphia: National Institute of Education.

Ogbu, J. U. (1982a). Cultural discontinuities and schooling. *Anthropology and Education Quarterly, 13*(4), 290–307.

Ogbu, J. U. (1982b). Societal forces as a context of ghetto children's school failure. In L. Vernon-Feagans & D. C. Farran (Eds.), *Language of children reared in poverty: Implications for evaluation and intervention* (pp. 117–138). New York: Academic Press.

Ogbu, J. U. (1997a). Racial stratification in the United States: Why inequality persists. In A. H. Halsey, H. Lauder, P. Brown, & A. S. Wells (Eds.), *Education: Culture, economy, and society* (pp. 765–778). Oxford: Oxford University Press.

Ogbu, J. U. (1997b). Understanding the school performance of urban Blacks: Some essential background knowledge. In H. J. Walberg, O. Reyes, & R. P. Weissberg (Eds.), *Children and youth: Interdisciplinary perspectives* (pp. 190–222). Chicago: University of Illinois Press.

Ogbu, J. U. (2001). Collective identity and schooling. In H. Fujita (Ed.), *Education, knowledge, and power* [Japanese] (pp. 409–449). Tokyo: Shinyosha Ltd.

Ogbu, J. U. (2002). Black-American students and the academic achievement gap: What else you need to know. *Journal of Thought, 37*(4), 9–33.

Ogbu, J. U. (2003). *Black students in an affluent suburb: A study of academic disengagement.* Mahwah, NJ: Lawrence Erlbaum.

Spicer, E. H. (1961). Introduction. In E. Spicer (Ed.), *Perspectives in American Indian culture change* (pp. 1–16). Chicago: University of Chicago Press.

Spicer, E. H. (1971). Persistent cultural systems: A comparative study of identity systems that can adapt to contrasting environments. *Science, 174*(4011), 795–800.

Spicer, E. H. (1980). *The Yaqui: A cultural history.* Tucson: University of Arizona Press.

Trask, H.-K. (1991). Natives and anthropologists: The colonial struggle. *Contemporary Pacific, 3*(1), 159–167.

Part II

Collective Identity, Black Americans, and Schooling

Chapter 7

High School Students of Color Talk about Accusations of "Acting White"

David A. Bergin and Helen C. Cooks

Acting White and *fear of acting White* have become common terms among those who investigate the well-being of students of color in the United States. An early published use of the term *acting White* appeared in 1970 in the context of discussion groups that included both White and Black students (McCardle & Young, 1970). The Black students held a goal of achieving equal rights and opportunities without "acting White." For them acting White meant to "become more inhibited, more formal, or to lack 'soul' " (p. 137). Note that academic achievement was not named as a marker of acting White. The students felt that acting White would result in alienation from their peer group. In two 1994 *Wall Street Journal* articles and in a book, journalist Ron Suskind described avoidance of academic achievement and accusations of acting White in a grim Washington, DC high school (Suskind, 1994a, 1994b, 1998). Peshkin and White (1990) also encountered fear of acting White in a northern California high school. For example, one student they interviewed said, "Sometimes, I have to change and act White; sometimes, I have to act Black. Say I go downtown talking like I am now. They will just stare at me, sayin', 'look at the nigger trying to act White. What's wrong with him? I ought to go poke him in his head' " (p. 26). Educators are interested in fear of acting White because of its potential influence on academic achievement. If avoiding acting White means not listening to heavy metal music and not wearing khakis, educators see no problem. If avoiding acting White means not trying hard in school or avoiding good grades in school, educators see a major problem. Some investigators have reported that avoiding acting White does mean avoiding high achievement. For example, Suskind (1998) described an attempt by high school administrators in Washington, DC to induce academic effort by paying $100 for straight-A performance in any of the year's four marking periods. Winners had to collect their checks at school assemblies. After a few such assemblies, "The jeering started. It was thunderous, 'Nerd!' 'Geek!' 'Egghead!' And the harshest, 'Whitey!' . . . The honor students were hazed for months afterward. With each assembly, fewer show up" (p. 3).

Probably the most widely known work on the issue of acting White is by Fordham and Ogbu (1986), who described fear of "acting White" as a significant factor that influenced the attitudes and undermined achievement of African-American students at "Capital High" in Washington, DC. They stated that "*one major reason* Black students do poorly in school is that they experience inordinate ambivalence and affective dissonance in regard to academic effort and success" (p. 177; emphasis in original). According to Fordham and Ogbu's theoretical framework, African-Americans experience a group identity or fictive kinship with other African-Americans. One aspect of this group identity is that members of the group are united in an oppositional social identity that is partly defined as not doing things that are associated with White Americans, who are viewed as their historical oppressors. Ogbu (1987) distinguished castelike, involuntary minorities, who have suffered a long history of oppression and discrimination, from voluntary immigrant minorities, who may suffer current discrimination but who as newcomers lack the history of persecution of castelike minorities. Castelike minorities are most likely to experience fictive kinship, an oppositional social identity, and low achievement. It is they who fear being accused of acting White because it would suggest that they are not "good" members of their group.

Attitudes and behaviors that the students at Capital High identified as acting White included listening to White music, studying, working hard to get good grades, actually getting good grades, going to a Rolling Stones concert, and putting on "airs" (Fordham & Ogbu, 1986). An important marker for acting White is speaking Standard English; Phinney (1990) pointed out that "language has been considered by some as the single most important component of ethnic identity" (p. 505).

The issue of avoidance of acting White can be framed as an issue of resistance. Various writers have documented or analyzed the tendency of students, those of color or not, to resist what they view as an unfair power structure (Alpert, 1991; D'Amato, 1988; Giroux, 1983; Miron & Lauria, 1998; Sanders, 1998; Sun, 1993). Student resistance is usually based upon issues of ethnicity or class or both and occurs when students perceive that they are oppressed or disadvantaged due to their ethnicity or class. In the case of avoidance of acting White, resistance has a strong base in ethnic identity and ethnic relations. Resistance can be described as a desire to reject dominant culture and norms and to embrace subcultural norms and values. For example, Fordham (1996) described middle-income Black children whose parents were frustrated by their children's underachievement: "Their parents perceived their actions as deliberate rejection of academic success, success that they can easily achieve if they are willing to do so. Instead, the daughters perceive success in school-sanctioned learning as physical and mental separation from the black community" (p. 194).

However, some writers have pointed out that youth can construct their resistance through appearing to *embrace* dominant culture and proving that they can excel in it. For example, Fordham (1996) stated, "There appears to be less familiarity with resistance as conformity. Indeed, nominal conformity to school rules is often equated with acceptance and, in some instances, even acquiescence to a dominant ideology. However, as I shall argue throughout this book, at Capital High conformity to school norms and values could be and often is interpreted as resistance" (p. 40). Likewise, Mirón and Lauria (1998) stated that "at City High resistance is more *productive* because students and teachers do not take out their hostilities toward White hegemony on each other. Instead they struggle for a quality education together, thus partly ensuring a better quality of life in the future" (p. 204; emphasis in original). Sanders (1998) found that of 10 students who were highly aware of racism and racial barriers, 6 were high achievers; "however, instead of reducing their motivation and academic effort, this awareness seemed to increase them" (p. 89).

Thus, we can see that some students of color resist White hegemony and the school power structure by avoiding academic achievement and other behaviors that might mean alliance with White culture. Other students of color may seek academic achievement in order to achieve better lives *and* to resist White hegemony.

While there is good documentation that fear of acting White exists, at least two articles have pointed out that in fact White students and Black students may not differ in the rate at which they suffer from peer rejection for academic achievement. Cook and Ludwig (1998) used data from the 1990 National Education Longitudinal Study (NELS), a national sample study, to analyze whether Blacks and non-Hispanic Whites differed on such well-reported variables as low levels of school effort, high levels of school effort, and social standing. They concluded, "While ethnographers observe that Black adolescents sometimes taunt high-achieving Black students for acting White, it appears that either these taunts do not inflict especially grievous social damage or high achievement has offsetting social effects" (p. 391). Likewise, Ainsworth-Darnell and Downey (1998) analyzed NELS data using self-report variables such as value of education, endorsement of cheating and breaking rules, and popularity as well as teacher ratings of classroom effort and disruptiveness. They concluded that their data contradict key claims of the oppositional culture model for explaining racial/ethnic differences in school achievement. Collins-Eaglin and Karabenick (1993) also found little evidence of widespread academic alienation among African-American students. Spencer, Noll, Stoltzfus, and Harpalani (2001) have been particularly critical of the "acting White" assumption. Studying African-American youth in a metropolitan southeastern American city, they found that high self-esteem and achievement goals were related to high Afrocentricity, not high Eurocentricity.

A purpose of the present study was to further investigate the social pressure to avoid acting White. Fordham's (Fordham, 1988, 1996; Fordham & Ogbu, 1986) data came from a single predominantly African-American high school in Washington, DC. We wished to expand understanding of fear of acting White by talking with youth of color in various high schools in a Midwestern city. In the current study, the respondents came from a variety of types of schools: public and private, predominantly Black, predominantly White, and racially balanced, The respondents had applied during eighth grade for a scholarship incentive program targeted at groups underrepresented in higher education. The program required a B grade average, so the students were relatively high achievers. They were interviewed several years later; during the time lag, they could have reduced their achievement if peers accused them of acting White. The respondents included some Mexican-American students; anecdotal evidence and logic suggest that Mexican-American students experience the same social expulsion threat as Black students if they "act Shite." These were the major questions of the present study: (1) Did students report avoiding academic achievement in order to avoid appearing to act White? And (2) did they perceive that they had given up ethnic identity in order to do well at school?

METHOD

Study Participants

Thirty-eight students were interviewed for this study. They had all applied at the end of eighth grade to participate in a program named EXCEL. Twenty-eight were participants in EXCEL, and 10 were in a comparison group. We will briefly describe EXCEL, then the comparison group. Approximately 50 eighth grade students are selected each year to participate in EXCEL, a scholarship incentive program for students from groups underrepresented in higher education. In order to be eligible, at the end of eighth grade they must be at grade level on standardized tests, have a B average, and be nominated by a teacher or counselor. Benefits of the program include summer institutes at the university, field studies (field studies have been conducted, for example, in the civil rights South, Ghana, and Taxco, Mexico), academic tutoring at the university during the school year, and a scholarship to the local university. Admission to the program is not based on income, so family incomes vary widely. Students come from public and private schools throughout a medium-sized, predominantly White (about 70 percent) Midwestern city. Program activities occur mostly at the university. While the schools are supportive of the program and provide data regarding achievement, they do not administer program elements.

For one year of the program, students who qualified for the program were admitted by random assignment (Bergin & Cooks, 1997) because more students qualified than could be admitted. About equal numbers of students were randomly assigned to the EXCEL group (43) and to the comparison group (40). The initial purpose of the control group was to test the effects of the EXCEL program on grades and enrollment in college. We have included the members of the comparison group in the present study because their comments help us know whether the EXCEL students' perspectives are unique to EXCEL students.

Students were selected from interviews from three consecutive EXCEL groups and front the comparison group. They were selected not randomly, but to provide diversity in gender, ethnicity, achievement, and year of graduation. Their mean high-school grade-point average (GPA) was 3.3. Students in honors classes were graded on a 5-point scale, so it was possible to attain a cumulative GPA over 4.0. At the time of the interviews, 10 students were freshmen in college, 21 were high school seniors, and 7 were high school juniors. Thus, we had had extensive experience with the EXCEL students for 5, 4, or 3 years and knew them well. We did not have such extensive background knowledge of the comparison group. Seniors are overrepresented because they include both an EXCEL group and the comparison group. While the EXCEL program includes Asian-American and low-income White students, for the purposes of this study only African-American, Mexican-American, and mixed-race students were included. The EXCEL students were not paid for their participation. The non-EXCEL students were paid $20 for their participation. A related article (Bergin & Cooks, 2000) discusses an overlapping set of students' experiences with academic competition.

Interviews

The 38 students were interviewed regarding high school and family experience; EXCEL students were also asked about EXCEL. Interviews took 1 to 1½ hours and were transcribed. The interview was semistructured; thus, every student was supposed to be asked the same basic questions, but the interviewers were free to follow up on responses as seemed appropriate. All but six of the interviews took place in students' homes; eight of the interviewers were African-American and one was White. The interviewers included one professor, one graduate student, and six parents. Parent interviewers were trained by the researchers and were paid a modest stipend. Follow-up sessions were held with the parent interviewers to assist them in dealing with the interview process. Because our intent was to describe personal, subjective experience, and because the follow-up questions varied by interviewer, the interview responses were not quantified.

We analyzed the transcripts by gathering all comments that related to ethnicity, ethnic identity, and acting White. We gathered the comments by reading all transcripts and by using computer search capabilities. Nearly all relevant comments occurred as a response to the interview question regarding ethnic identity. The comments were then analyzed for recurring patterns. These patterns and exceptions to them are described in the following section.

RESULTS AND DISCUSSION

One of the questions interviewers asked was whether students felt they had to give up their ethnic identity in order to do well in school. Initially, the interview protocol asked about ethnic identity but not specifically about acting White; as the interviews proceeded and feedback arrived, it became apparent that the interviewers should ask about acting White. This delay explains why some students were explicitly asked whether they had been accused of acting White and others were not. Where names are used, they are pseudonyms. In the quotes, we used the following convention: a dash (—) indicates a pause and an ellipsis (. . .) indicates deleted words. In the following descriptions, some details have been changed to protect confidentiality.

Description of Acting White

The students with whom we talked were familiar with the term acting White. This was true of both African-American and Mexican-American students. They provided the following descriptions of acting White:

Speech:
Talk proper
Don't talk slang or curse
Don't use ghettoish talk, with half words, making your own words
Use big words and enunciate
Say your Spanish surname with an English accent
Instead of saying you are going to the movies, say you are going to a flick.

Music:
Listen to White music, classical music, heavy metal, or rock music.

Dress:
Don't wear tennis shoes
Dress like a preppie
Wear a tie
Button your shirt instead of having your chest hang out

Wear penny loafers
Dress White—for a girl, roll up your pants, have the back of your shirt hanging out, tuck the front in, and have big poofy bangs (fringe).

School:
Suck up to the teachers a little bit
Kiss butt
Work up to your potential at school
Get good grades
Always do your work
Be really neat.

Other behaviors:
Date White girls
Act like Carleton (on television show Fresh Prince of Bel Air)
Have lots of White friends, hang around with White people
Act stuck up.

Of the 17 students who were specifically asked whether they had been accused of acting White, 7 said no. One was Nikki Dryden, a Black female who was among the top 10 in her class at a predominantly Black school. Her single mother had wanted her to attend a Catholic school, but she chose the public school. The school serves the city's inner city, where it is an icon of the African-American community. The school is a historic building that is situated on the main street of the city's most historic district of homes and churches. The school seems to have a reputation (some argue undeserved) that leads some parents, African-American or not, to prohibit their children from attending. Nikki was active in student government, band, and science club. She stated that she knew what acting White meant, but:

> 33: No. I've never had that problem. Because it seems like, in high school, everyone knew me. They knew that I always did my best and it was just like they respected me for it. I mean as far as people getting in trouble or whatever, it was like a lot of times people wouldn't treat me as they would everyone else. I mean they respected me more because of my grades and everything. So it was like I got more respect because of that. . . . I understand what you're saying but I've never had that problem. It's just like everyone there, they knew me, they would encourage me. Or if I would get kind of like a low grade or something on my test, they were like, "Why did you get that? You know you could do better than that." I mean that kind of thing. So I've never had that problem.

While Nikki was not accused of acting White, she understood what it meant. Even though some students were not directly accused of acting

White, it is important to recognize that all students understood what the term meant. Nikki was not ostracized because of her good grades; in fact, she was elected to a student government office. It appears that Nikki did some things that could have attracted accusations of acting White, but her style of being allowed her smooth commerce with her fellow students. She was an achiever, but other students did not perceive her to be allied with the Other. In fact, she explicitly states that other students supported and encouraged her high achievement.

Selena Sanders, on the other hand, reported quite a different experience. She was at the same school as Nikki and was also in the top 10 of her class, but she said that she was often accused of acting White:

34:     People tell me I talk White. And then I ask the question, "Well, how do White people talk?" And they say, "You know, proper like." But I—acting White? They tell me I act preppy or something like that. But that sort of got away from that White, acting White type of thing. They go "preppy." They say another word now, "Oh, she's prep-like" or something like that.

INT: Does it still have the same racial overtones?

34:     Um hum, it does. It's just little things like I wear penny loafers. So wearing penny loafers, I have on my shoes, my hair is always done, I talk really proper, my work is always done, I'm really neat, those type of things. So everything together I guess. And then I don't say too much to people. I sort of let them say what they want to say to me and then I'll respond. I'm not the first person to always start a conversation. I like to listen more than I like to talk and—

INT: So people view that as being stuck up or acting White or both?

34:     Stuck up *is* acting White.

Both young women were highly achievement-oriented but they differed in their styles. Nikki, who was not accused even with high achievement, behaved in ways that did not attract accusations of acting White. She was relatively quiet and did not seek the limelight (though she was a prominent student government officer). In contrast, Selena was very socially active and was not afraid of controversy. She was elected to several prominent posts and liked to assert her individuality through her dress and speech. She not only had high grades but also chafed against the high school culture. She said, "High school was not what it was supposed to be—the time between childhood and adulthood where you have all these great experiences." She would be a more likely target for accusations of acting White because her behavior went beyond high academic achievement into areas of dress, speech, and attitude. Note that in her comments she did not mention academic achievement as a reason for being accused of acting White.

Spending Time with White Students Leads to Accusations

A reason that several students who attended racially mixed schools gave for accusations of acting White was that they were perceived as spending too much time with White students. They were enrolled in college preparation or honors courses that tended to be mostly White. Therefore, they spent most of their school time with White students, and the result was that many of their school friends were White. For example, Christi, a Black female at a public mixed-race school, said:

31:   The majority of my classes are honors classes; therefore there's a lot of White people in my honors classes, and there's not too many—I don't have a class that has more than four Black people in it. And if I'm in a class with all the Whites and the Chinese and everything else, all of a sudden Christi's not Black anymore. Maybe I'm just misinterpreting from what they say to me.

INT: What who says?

31:   My Black peers.

INT: Okay. What do they say?

31:   They basically ask me, "Why aren't you true to your color?" And I'm like, "Well, how am I not true?" I'm sorry if I'm smart, you know. I'm not going to sit there and hold myself back just so you can have this feeling that I am being Black. I'm being Black whether I'm smart, dumb, stupid, or whatever.

Christi lived in the catchment area of the same African-American school that Selena and Nicki attended, but Christi's father said that there was no way she was going there. He had heard bad things about that school. She attended a mixed-race public school that she grew to like because she "intermingled with white people and Hispanic people." The school serves working-class Black and White neighborhoods and is located on a large plot of land in a predominantly White neighborhood. African-American students who attend the school travel farther than most of the White students. Christi was active in student government, National Honor Society, a conflict resolutions program, and Leadership Club and was also elected to the homecoming court[1]. Her father said she liked to be in the limelight. The honors classes she attended were predominantly White, so there was a perception that she preferred to spend time with White students. Thus, it was not just achievement that led to accusations of acting White, but also the inaccurate assumption that she preferred White people.

Joe Murphy, a Black male, attended the same school. He was a very successful athlete and a very successful student. He stated:

30: Yes. I've been accused by a lot of people, actually, of doing so. A lot of the Black people that I know, or that think they know me, only see an image of me being around a lot of Whites. Whereas most of the times I hung around my classmates and I was usually the only Black male, so I got to really know my classmates and those are my friends. Outside of school, I didn't really have a lot of friends—. . . my teammates, I had a lot of white teammates. So the people I hung around were the people that I saw in school the most. So a lot of people got an image of me as, oh, he's a sellout.

These quotes from Joe and Christi suggest that affiliation with Whites is a major component of being perceived as acting White. In their interviews, these two students did not mention accusations based on their being in honors classes or earning high grades; rather the accusations appeared to be based on the fact that students of color frequently saw them with White students. Joe Murphy's parents said that they thought he had been accused of acting White and attributed this accusation to the fact that he spent more time with White students than with African-Americans. They said this was not because he preferred White students, but because the students most likely to share his aspirations (to become a physician) and skills (e.g., athlete in a "White" sport) tended to be White. They were careful to state that he knew where his ethnic roots were.

Denials of Giving Up Ethnic Identity

Students generally claimed that they had not given up their ethnic identity in order to do well in school, nor had they allowed accusations of acting White to affect their study habits or effort to achieve. For example, we interviewed three girls from the same Catholic all-girl school. The school is one of the elite Catholic schools in the city and won national recognition for quality soon after the data for this study had been gathered. Two of the girls said they had not given up their ethnic identity:

INT: Do you feel as though you have to give up some of your ethnic identity in order to do well in school?

8: No. That's another reason why I chose to go to the academy, because I did go to public school for junior high and a lot of the kids were pretty well, "You sound like a White girl, you're stuck up, blah-blah-blah," because I was in honors classes. A lot of times I was the only Black in the class. Coming to the academy, everyone wants to succeed. So, it's not really a problem.

This student had frustration in a public junior high school because the students lacked a desire to learn and achieve. The public school that she had attended had a mixed-race student body and mixed levels of achievement. She much preferred the private school because everyone was interested in learning and achieving good grades.

The second student who attended the academy was asked:

INT: Do you feel as if you have to give up any of your ethnic identity or Blackness in order to do well in school?

6:       No. Not at all. It feels good to see other Black students trying to do well at school. And, you know, it seems like that's when we come together the most in school for schoolwork. And there's not much of us in the school. There's only a handful of Black students in the school.

However, the third student, Karen Cook, assumed that every African-American had to give up ethnic identity to do well in the school:

7:       No . . . I feel everybody in the academy is in the category of not totally being themselves, hiding their ethnic identity. Those who aren't able to adjust just leave. Those who are willing to adjust—maybe adjust somewhat—can stay.

INT: So, what would happen if you did not acclimate or adjust?

7:       I wouldn't have been there.

INT: No? Why not?

7:       Because it's almost as though you can't take the atmosphere—the whole atmosphere of the academy; you just can't take it. It's just something you can't deal with on a day-to-day basis.

Thus, Karen implied that she had given up some of her ethnic identity in order to fit into a White world. Karen lived in a relatively upscale suburban White neighborhood. Karen commented with pride that four minority students—including two of her friends—had graduated with honors, yet she also commented regarding African-American high achievers: "Their ethnic background is definitely African-American, but their mental set, or their mind state, is not." While she lived in a White neighborhood and attended a predominantly White school, she was critical of students who were too "White." Karen was one of the few interviewed students who criticized others regarding ethnic identity.

Selena Sanders felt that she had not given up ethnic identity to do well in a predominantly Black public school, though she was accused. She was in the running for valedictorian[2], active in organizations in school and outside school, and had won various university scholarships. She expressed herself as follows:

INT: You ever feel as if you gave up any of your ethnic identity in order to do well in school?

34: What do you mean? I don't understand that question.

INT: Do you have to be less Black. . . .

34: At my high school?

INT: . . . .in order to do well in school?

34: No, not at my high school. I didn't have that problem. I think the most of, let me think, I didn't really have a problem with identity, racial identity or Black identity or anything like that because everyone around me was the same. I think it might have been different if I would've gone to another high school, maybe.

INT: Sometimes it seems like students who do well at a predominantly Black high school have the hardest time, if they do well in school.

34: I don't see myself having a problem. You mean with education-wise or . . .?

INT: No, with other students.

34: OK, I can see that. Yeah. It's just, it's not animosity, but that's the only world I could think of. Sometimes I feel, uncomfortable and it's not, it's like a group of us, that these 13 people over here do well and everyone knows they do well, so they're sort of in the shadows.

INT: What do you mean in the shadows?

34: They consider you nerds or they think that you think you're better than them type thing. Yeah. But you learn to look over that. But yeah.

Selena seemed bothered by accusations of acting White, but not sufficiently enough to change her behavior. She held strong achievement goals that drove her to attain high grades, join clubs, and participate in school politics. She was not about to allow other students' accusations of acting White to affect her life goals.

Samuel Jackson, an African-American male, attended a school that was mixed White and Black and that served both low- and middle-income families. He was also accused of acting White and also denied having given up his ethnic identity.

INT: Do you feel as though you had to give up some of your ethnic identity or "Blackness" in order to do well in school?

21: Not at all. I think in order to do well in school I had to more-or-less identify with myself and of course keep my Afrocentric point of view basically throughout everything. If there was ever a discussion in class, I would voice my African-American opinion whatever it would be—I can never, I don't think I was ever really subjected to having to choose between acting Black or acting White, which is something that I sort of hate.

INT: Were you ever accused of acting White?

21:    Yeah. Plenty of times.

INT: Who accused you?

21:    Black students. Usually other Black students who, in fact, weren't doing as well. I was accused of acting White simply because I got good grades. And I would say, "Is it wrong for Black people to do well?" I would go back and say, would say, "Did W. E. B. Du Bois act White his whole life?" They'll say, "No, that's different."

INT: Now did they know who he was?

21:    No. Often I would have to explain to them. They say, "Well, that's different," and if I say, "Well, was Martin Luther King acting White?" they'll say, "No, that's different." . . . They'll say, "Why are you buttoning? You're supposed to have your chest hanging out." I don't like that. And they would say, "OK, so you're trying to act White." I thought, it got sort of amusing but it was—I don't know, it never bothered me.

Samuel was one of the few students who explicitly named high academic achievement as a key reason for attracting accusations of acting White. Nevertheless, it is not clear that high academic achievement was in fact the primary reason why Samuel was accused. Samuel's style of dress suggested he wanted to stand out as an individual and probably had something to do with the accusations. While Samuel denied being bothered by accusations of acting White, he also said that he did not like the accusations. Most people would feel uncomfortable when accused of rejecting their roots and their people. We did a follow-up interview with Samuel about a year later, after he was well into his college career at a major university. We pointed out that he had stated earlier that accusations of acting White did not bother him. He laughed and said that of course the accusations had bothered him.

Another Black male, Daniel Smothers, claimed that he didn't act White, though he seemed threatened by the question and appeared ambivalent about accusing two other students (including the just-quoted Samuel Jackson) of acting White:

INT: Do you feel as if you had to give up part of your ethnic identity on your Blackness in order to do well in school'?

19:    Hmm. In a way, but in a way not. Not really given up so much, just try to be supersmart, but that's something that other students did more than me. For instance, like Samuel—and Samuel's just like Ervin Brooks—they were more—not they didn't give it up, but they were more uppity, try to be supersmart. And then me, I came off as yeah, I'm smart, but I'm going to be the way I'm going to be.

INT: Would you say that they tried to act White?

19:    No. They didn't try to act White. They just—no, they didn't act White, I'm not saying that they were sellouts or they always tried to act White. They just—no, they weren't a sellout or anything. They didn't try to act White. They were Black on everything. They had Black ways, but it's just they—I don't know. They tried to, I don't know. Sometimes it seemed like they were trying to be so intelligent and they tried to say things more formal—I don't know how to describe it. Samuel talked slang but it's like he really wouldn't really talk it. That's what I mean. They're not, not that they're sellouts. They would act Black. They do everything Black, but they wouldn't talk slang because to them it made them look ignorant, and to me, it's like, well, I have nothing to prove to anybody because if you know you're smart, prove it to yourself, and show everybody, which I have already done, so it's like I already know I'm smart. So what else do I have to show?

Daniel appeared uneasy about accusing Samuel and Ervin of being sellouts because he recognized that they were knowledgeable about Black history and spoke out on Black issues, but he felt that they avoided slang and acted "uppity" to prove their smartness. Daniel then described Joe, who came closer to being a sellout:

19:    There weren't any [sellouts] in EXCEL—Wait a minute. They accuse Joe—I'd say he's not really a sellout. He knew he was Black and he understood that. But sometimes it did bother me when he tends to overindulge in Whiteness. From the standpoint of, not so much listening to White music, just—
INT: How did he overindulge?
19:    Well, dating White girls.

This accusation that a fellow high achiever or EXCEL student was a sellout was unusual. Only two other students volunteered similar comments that a fellow high achiever was a sellout. One was Karen Cook, who has already been quoted, and the other was Dave, who said that some of his friends had given up their ethnic identity by "just completely doing everything that White people do. Not to say that they're White things that they do. But they feel that if White men in this country are successful that they, in order to be successful, have to do the things that White men do, and they completely do everything that White people do."

The Mexican-American students whom we interviewed reported experiences similar to those of African-Americans regarding acting White; they denied having given up their ethnic identity but said that they were sometimes accused of it. Consider Maritza, a Mexican-American female. She lived in the catchment area of a school that served primarily students of color who experienced relatively low achievement. She transferred to a predominantly White school that served different income levels, including some of the city's higher-income neighborhoods. She stated that she was perceived in her neighborhood as having given up her ethnic identity:

> INT: Do you feel as though you have had to give up some of your ethnic identity in order to do well in school?
>
> 25: I think other people see that I have. I've noticed as soon as I started high school, and I went to School X [higher-income, mostly White], and my other friends went to Y [lower-income, multiple ethnicities], or they just quit high school, they kind of said—this is a good one—"Oh, Maritza's changed a lot." Some people just don't recognize me. They may have known me since I was in third grade, and they look at me now, and they just couldn't recognize me. I don't look different. I look the same. I'm the same person. I just study more. I spend more time doing things that they just don't do anymore. They're too busy working, or they have their babies to take care of or something. Most of the kids around here don't speak Spanish, and my parents taught us Spanish. I know Spanish and English. I just know both of them fluently. I could go from English to Spanish in a second, without thinking about it, and I do it a lot. A lot of the kids, they say I speak English funny. I guess I speak properly or something—I don't know. It's just, to them, it sounds funny because I just don't talk the way they do. It kind of makes me mad sometimes because they really shouldn't say anything because they don't speak their own native language, and they don't know about things like I do. I work hard for something that they don't want. I don't see that I've lost anything. I think of myself as more Mexican than they'll ever be. I think they're the ones that have kind of lost a lot and are out of touch with their ethnic group.

Maritza and her family lived in a modest home in a low-income neighborhood. During the interview, the interviewer observed two police officers across the street handcuffing a man and carrying a television out of his house while a matronly woman shook her finger at him. Maritza said that her friends' parents would not let her friends visit because they considered the neighborhood dangerous. When asked why they did not move, the mother said that they had considered moving, but they liked the neighborhood and had decided to stay. Nevertheless, Maritza was accusing of selling out because she did not attend school with her neighbors, did not speak street lingo, and did well in school. So mere academic achievement did not attract accusations. Rather, Maritza's perceived rejection of the neighborhood, evidenced by her rejection of the local high school, and her style of speech were key behaviors that attracted accusations.

The students clearly voiced their frustration against accusations that they acted White or were sellouts and disagreed with the suggestion that they had given up their ethnic identity in order to do well in school. Most pursued a high-achievement path that included honors classes, earning good grades, studying, and using "proper" English in school. In the next section, we discuss their feelings toward their accusers.

Anger toward Accusers: I Know More about My Ethnic Heritage than You Do

Several students whom we interviewed seemed offended that people who appeared to know nothing about their own ethnic heritage would accuse more ethnically knowledgeable people of acting White. For example, Maritza was offended that Mexican-Americans who could not even speak Spanish would dare accuse her of talking funny and acting White when she could speak Spanish and in fact had visited Mexico several times. Joe Murphy, who attended a racially balanced school, felt the same way about being accused of selling out:

> 30: It made me feel bad because I had probably known more Black history and had done more to delve into my history than most of them, and they had the nerve to see me as something that was trying to negate my heritage. So I mean it made me feel pretty bad but I just learned to try to ignore it. I mean I still can't ignore it when I hear that, it pisses me off, but not everyone is going to like you, and they're going to find some way to try to make you angry so I've just tried my best to ignore it.

The EXCEL students were particularly confident about their knowledge of ethnic heritage because most of them had participated in field studies of the civil rights movement (Bettis, Cooks, & Bergin, 1994) or in Mexico. It seemed that one reason the high-achieving students in our study were able to resist the pressure to conform was that they considered the source of the accusations and asked themselves, "Why should I follow the advice of people who don't even know about their own ethnicity and heritage?"

Competition for Grades

If an aspect of acting White is getting good grades and studying hard to get ahead, then *competing* for grades would appear to be a sure indicator of acting White. We were surprised at how many students whom we interviewed were competing for grades. We described the students' competitive attitudes at length in another article (Bergin & Cooks, 2000).

Suffice it to say that both males and females competed for grades and academic honors and, in contrast to some of Fordham's and Suskind's informants (Fordham, 1996; Fordham & Ogbu, 1986; Suskind, 1998) did not report doing things to avoid being perceived publicly as high achievers. Students stated that the competition gave them something to shoot for and improved their performance. While there is evidence that competition may not be good in school settings (Bergin & Cooks, 2000), these students of color endorsed it. It would be highly inaccurate to say that they were avoiding academic achievement.

Mixed Ethnicity

The whole notion of ethnic identity and acting White rests on the assumption that people claim that they are members of an identifiable ethnic group. Three of the students identified themselves as being of mixed race. (We are using the terms *ethnic group* and *race* interchangeably here because that is how the students used them.) On the other hand, two other students had an African-American father and a White mother, yet neither of them mentioned being of mixed race. Thus, students who were of mixed ethnicity varied in whether they identified themselves as being of a single ethnic group or of mixed ethnicity. When asked about giving up ethnic identity in order to do well in school, one student stated:

> 10: No. I don't think so. I might just sit there and be real quiet. It's not that I'm afraid to or anything. It's just I don't think anybody would understand where I'm coming from just because I'm two races. I'm not just African American; I'm mixed. And I don't think anybody would understand. So I might just be there and be quiet other than try to speak up. But if it was something that bothers me, I would let them know.

As intermarriage among ethnic groups continues to increase, the issue of ethnic identity and ethnic affiliation will become increasingly complex. If a child's parents are of mixed race—say, Filipino, Black, White, and Chinese—how does he or she self-label? Is labeling possible where such mixtures are dominant? Can accusations of acting White be leveled? Such issues will become more common in the future and may undermine some of the pressure for ethnic solidarity or may generate new ethnic categories.

Conclusions

At the beginning of this article, the first major question that we posed was "Did students report avoiding academic achievement in order to avoid appearing to act White?" The respondents in this study did not report avoiding academic achievement in order to avoid accusations of acting

White. In fact, their mean GPA was 3.3, and many reported competing for grades. If we had interviewed only EXCEL students, we might have attributed the lack of fear of acting White to the EXCEL program, which included a field study of the civil rights South (Bettis *et al.*, 1994), instruction on multicultural issues, and leaders of color who served as models. However, the statements of comparison students were similar to those of EXCEL students. Keep in mind that the EXCEL and non-EXCEL students had both applied to the program in eighth grade and were interviewed several years later. Thus, there was plenty of time for them to falter in academic achievement and to be affected by peer pressure to achieve or not achieve.

The second question that we posed at the beginning of the article was: "Did students perceive that they had given up ethnic identity in order to do well in school?" Most of the students we interviewed reported no loss of ethnic identity. They made very few comments that could be interpreted as reflecting adoption of fear of a raceless persona (Fordham, 1988). The students felt resentment toward accusations of acting White and, unlike some of Fordham's and Suskind's informants (Fordham, 1988, 1996; Fordham & Ogbu, 1986; Suskind, 1998), did not seem to be intimidated by the accusations, though they were bothered by them. Our informants made comments like feeling "pissed off" and not wanting to hold themselves back in order to fit in. Some seemed to identify more with leaders like Du Bois and Martin Luther King than with low-achieving students.

It would be useful if future research addressed the conditions under which resistance to and avoidance of acting White are most likely to occur. It appears that when students feel affiliated with a group of students who hold similar values and goals, they are not so threatened by accusations of acting White. Being in a demanding sequence of classes with like-minded peers can reduce the pain of accusations of acting White or selling out because of the solidarity that such a group can experience. The students whom we interviewed reported that at each school there were students of color who chose honors classes and high achievement, which provided a peer group of like-minded students. For example, Selena Sanders reported sharing competition for grades with a group of high-achieving African-American students at her predominantly African-American school. In addition, the EXCEL students have had such a group in EXCEL, though the influence of EXCEL may not have been felt on a daily basis because program participants were small in number at individual schools.

Whether a school is predominantly White, predominantly Black, or racially balanced can affect students' ethnic identity and need for racial solidarity. It appears that students of color in predominantly White schools are less likely to be accused of acting White at school because there are so few students of color. The students of color may be in different classes and different lunch periods. They might, however, be accused in their neighborhoods. Students of color in predominantly Black schools seem likely to be harassed about acting White if their behavior goes beyond high achievement and shows "proper speech," or "White dress," or preference for other "White" things. High-achieving students of color in racially balanced schools appear most likely to be accused of acting White because their enrollment in advanced classes puts them in constant contact with White students, and at the same time, there is a large number of students of color who are in a position to notice and comment on the supposed defection. One student, a Black student in a Catholic girls' school, had experienced accusations of acting White in her racially balanced junior high, but not in the private, nearly all-White high school. Students in racially balanced schools seemed to feel more polarization based on race, so they were under more pressure to "choose sides." We say "seemed" because our data were not originally designed to test this point. Our sample depended on who had applied to EXCEL and thus was not randomly or purposefully selected from various types of institutions.

It might be useful to study how different racial balances affect perceptions of ethnic identity and accusations of acting White. For example, Jacob (1995) and Ulichny (1996) found that mixing Black students and bilingual Hispanic students in the same school-within-a-school had some positive effects but also led to racial tensions. Neither author discussed either ethnic identity or accusations of acting White, but the fact that Black students felt threatened in terms of the adequacy of their culture and ethnicity might increase accusations of acting White by heightening the need for ethnic solidarity.

When students reject the school of their catchment area and transfer to another public school or enroll in a private school, they seem especially likely to be accused of acting White. The accusations may be predicated not on the level of achievement, but on the perceived rejections of neighbors, culture, and ethnicity. "Aren't we good enough for you?" might be a common question.

The students we interviewed frequently named academic achievement as one marker of acting White; however, mere academic achievement did not appear to be sufficient to attract accusations of acting White. Most of the students we interviewed could be considered adequate or high achievers, yet in the interviews, they did not dwell on their grades, advanced-placement classes, or honors status as drawing accusations of acting White. The issues pertaining to acting White that they dwelled on in the interviews included dialect, hanging around with White students, acting stuck up, and style of dress. Being in an honors class was not necessarily a problem; the problem was that at some schools, if you were in an honors class, you were with mostly White students. The interviewees seemed to draw the ire of fellow minority students when they went beyond high grades and also dressed out of the norm for their group; or spoke proper English, especially outside of the classroom; or hung around with White students.

Fordham and Ogbu's study (1986) and Suskind's (1998) journalistic treatment show students going out of their way to avoid academic achievement that might elicit accusations of acting White. Our data are more positive about students' goals and behavior. Our data are more congruent with quantitative studies of the goals and achievement of African-American youth (Ainsworth-Darnell & Downey, 1998; Collins-Eaglin & Karabenick, 1993; Cook & Ludwig, 1998; Spencer et al., 2001), which do not find rejection of academic achievement. The differences between our data and Fordham's could be the result of method: she used intensive, lengthy ethnographic observations, while we used relatively brief interviews (though we had broad, experience-based knowledge of the students). Differences could be the result of city setting: the inner city of Washington, DC may be quite different for African-Americans than the inner city or suburban areas of a mid-sized Midwestern city (note that Suskind's Washington, DC observations were congruent with Fordham's). Differences could be the result of school setting: Fordham studied a single school and its students intensively, while we interviewed students from different school of radically different types. Differences could be the result of time frame: Fordham's data were apparently collected during the 1980s, while ours were collected during the 1990s. Note that Suskind's interviews and observations occurred during the 1990s and were congruent with Fordham's. Differences could be the result of participant selection: Fordham selected the students to interview based on her observation of the school, while we selected students in eighth grade based on their achievement and interviewed them several years later.

In conclusion, we did not hear a single comment from students admitting that they had altered their behavior, reduced their effort, or earned poor grades in order to avoid accusations of acting White. However, we are not claiming that no students alter their behavior, reduce their effort, or earn poor grades in order to avoid accusations of acting White. We are claiming that a significant proportion of African-American and Mexican-American students who were earning good grades in eighth grade were still doing so in high school and did not report reducing or hiding their academic effort in order to avoid accusations of acting White. We suspect that students who reject academic achievement and students who embrace academic achievement exist side by side in schools throughout the United States. Further investigation could study what factors affect whether students choose to avoid being accused of acting White. It would also be useful to investigate the perceptions of students who make the accusations. What proportion are genuinely concerned about issues of resistance, racial oppression, and racial solidarity? What specific situations and behaviors trigger their accusations? Further investigations could also study the development of awareness of "acting White," that is, at what age do children begin to be aware of the dangers of appearing to act White and to accuse others? In order to understand the phenomenon of accusations of acting White, we need to understand the accusers as well as the accused.

ACKNOWLEDGMENT

This research was funded by a grant from the U.S. Department of Education (R117E30184-93).

NOTES

1   Homecoming is an annual tradition in United States in several universities, colleges and high schools in which former residents and alumni are welcomed back. It usually includes activities for students and alumni, such as sports, cultural events and a parade through the streets of the city or town. The Homecoming court usually consists of seniors, in high school, 17- or 18-year-old students in their final year. They are generally students who have excelled in academics, involved in campus activities and service to the school community. In some schools members of the Homecoming court are required to attend Serendipity, the Homecoming bonfire, the Homecoming parade and the Homecoming football game. The members of the court are also expected to appear in publicity photographs and may be asked to make public appearances on behalf of the school. Usually the court has a king and a queen.

2   Valedictorian: In the United States and Canada, the title of Valedictorian is given to the student with the highest academic rank of the graduating class. The traditional role of the Valedictorian is to deliver the valedictory at the graduation ceremony.

REFERENCES

Ainsworth-Darnell, J. W., & Downey, D. B. (1998). Assessing the oppositional culture explanation for racial/ethnic differences in school performance. *American Sociological Review, 63,* 536–553.

Alpert, B. (1991). Students' resistance in the classroom. *Anthropology & Education Quarterly, 22,* 350–366.

Bergin, D. A., & Cooks, H. C. (1997, March). *Does the motivational promise of a college scholarship improve academic achievement and other outcomes for aspiring minority youth?* Paper presented at the Annual Meeting of the American Educational Research Association, Chicago.

Bergin, D. A., & Cooks, H. C. (2000). Academic competition among students of color: An interview study. *Urban Education, 35,* 442–472.

Bettis, P. J., Cooks, H. C., & Bergin, D. A. (1994). "It's not steps anymore, but more like shuffling": Student perceptions on the Civil Rights Movement and ethnic identity. *Journal of Negro Education, 63,* 197–211.

Collins-Eaglin, J., & Karabenick, S. A. (1993, April). *Devaluing of academic success by African-American students: On "acting White" and "selling out."* Paper presented at the American Educational Research Association, Atlanta.

Cook, P. J., & Ludwig, J. (1998). The burden of "acting white": Do black adolescents disparage academic achievement? In C. Jencks and M. Philips (Eds.), *The Black-White test score gap* (pp. 375–400). Washington, DC: Brookings Institutional Press.

D'Amato, J. (1988). "Acting": Hawaiian children's resistance to teachers. *Elementary School Journal, 88,* 529–544.

Fordham, S. (1988). Racelessness as a factor in black students' school success: Pragmatic strategy or pyrrhic victory? *Harvard Educational Review, 58,* 54–84.

Fordham, S. (1996). *Blacked out: Dilemmas of race, identity, and success at Capital High.* Chicago: University of Chicago.

Fordham, S., & Ogbu, J. U. (1986). Black students' school success: Coping with the "burden of 'acting white.' " *The Urban Review, 18,* 176–206.

Giroux, H. A. (1983). Theories of reproduction and resistance in the new sociology of education: A critical analysis. *Harvard Educational Review, 53,* 257–293.

Jacob, B. A. (1995). Defining culture in a multicultural environment: An ethnography of Heritage High School. *American Journal of Education, 103,* 339–376.

McCardle, C. G., & Young, N. F. (1970). Classroom discussion of racial identity or how can we make it without "acting white"? *American Journal of Orthopsychiatry, 40,* 135–141.

Mirón, L. F., & Lauria, M. (1998). Student voice as agency: Resistance and accommodation in inner-city schools. *Anthropology & Education Quarterly, 29,* 189–213.

Ogbu, J. U. (1987). Variability in minority school performance: A problem in search of an explanation. *Anthropology & Education Quarterly, 18,* 312–334.

Peshkin, A., & White, C. J. (1990). Four black American students: Coming of age in a multiethnic high school. *Teachers College Record, 92,* 21–38.

Phinney, J. S. (1990). Ethnic identity in adolescents and adults: Review of research. *Psychological Bulletin, 108,* 499–514.

Sanders, M. G. (1998). Overcoming obstacles: Academic achievement as a response to racism and discrimination. *Journal of Negro Education, 66,* 83–93.

Spencer, M. B., Noll, E., Stoltzfus, J., & Harpalani, V. (2001). Identity and school adjustment: Revisiting the "acting white" assumption. *Educational Psychologist, 36,* 21–30.

Sun, A. (1993). *Development of an instrument for measuring high school student resistance to schooling.* Unpublished doctoral dissertation, University of Toledo, Toledo, Ohio.

Suskind, R. (1994a). Against all odds. *Wall Street Journal* (May 26), pp. 1, 8.

Suskind, R. (1994b). Class struggle. *Wall Street Journal* (September 22), pp. 1, 6.

Suskind, R. (1998). *A hope in the unseen.* New York: Broadway.

Ulichny, P. (1996). Cultures in conflict. *Anthropology & Education Quarterly, 27,* 331–364.

Chapter 8

Black Students' Identity and Acting White and Black

Linwood Cousins

This chapter expands the debate on the notion of "acting White" by answering two questions that arise from that debate: is it as pervasive as one might assume, given the attention it has received in the scholarly literature and public media? Should it be used as a dominant explanatory factor of African-American students' participation in schooling?

This inquiry is intended to pose a direct challenge to those who depend heavily upon the notion of "acting White" to inform their understanding of the interplay between Black culture and schooling and to explain Black children's school performance. This chapter also raises the view that research on "acting White" has suffered from a kind of ahistoricity—a limited scope across time and place. Indeed, Fordham and Ogbu (1986) said as much in their article on "acting White" by calling for a comparative perspective (comparisons among African Americans and comparisons between them and other subordinate minority groups in the United States (pp. 198–201).[1]

Equally critical, however, is that individual and collective identities are embedded in the notion of "acting White." On its face, "acting White" is an *identity practice* that is loaded with a variety of social, cultural, and psychological meanings. Thus, given what we know about the complex process of meaning making, especially when taking political and economic factors into account, a notion such as "acting White" must not be allowed to take on a distorted life of its own. It should in fact be difficult, to say the least, for skeptical researchers and observant citizens to accept all of the "hoopla" that "acting White" has received (see Crouch 1999 and McWhorter 2000, both of whom have graced TV news shows and public radio with their opinions on this matter). Public and scholarly attention has helped "acting White" to congeal into a sort of public, taken-for-granted, narrative about Black people's participation in school. As such, it has much potential to misdirect school and community reform and public policy.

In this chapter, I cannot address all of these issues. But having acknowledged them, I want to locate "acting White" as part of the cultural complex of human identity making. Identity will serve as the backdrop for questions about the reach and scope of "acting White" as a Black schooling phenomenon across *time and place*. When and where students attend school are key factors shaping individual and collective identity processes that might produce something such as "acting White." And *identity processes* are part and parcel of the "community forces" that shape African Americans' responses to schooling, according to Ogbu and Simons (1998). Ogbu and others have documented schooling and community life in a way that includes both Black students' school participation and their historical contexts, which implies time and place (Anyon, 1997; Fordham, 1996; MacLeod, 1995; Ogbu, 1974; Weis, 1985). In these instances, however, how practices differ and are similar across time and place have ultimately taken a back seat to time- and place-specific research questions about how students succeed, fail, resist, and otherwise circumvent the system, their parents, and themselves.

With few exceptions, researchers have rightly narrowed their focus to one or more aspects of school success and failure, for a variety of reasons. First, school failure leads to multiple social and economic problems that parents and communities want their children to avoid. Second, the contemporary context of policy issues, and the money and power that drive it, prohibits the long-term efforts that more complete answers would require. That is, researchers have identified economic, social, and political factors that interact with the school participation issues above, and many have addressed issues related to historical contexts (Anyon, 1997; Fordham, 1996; Ogbu, 1974; Patterson, 1997; Rich, 1996). However, we still lack studies that systematize the complex array of Black schooling factors across Black student populations (e.g., class and family structure) *and* across time and place.

Even in my own research (Cousins, 1994, 1997, Cousins & Mabrey, 1998), where I have focused largely on social class and social race/ethnicity as explanatory factors in Black schooling participation and community life, I have not systematized findings comparatively across time and place. For example, why did class culture and Black life in the 1960s in Newark give rise to one set of schooling attitudes and outcomes that differed from those of Black students in, say, Washington, DC, or Richmond, Virginia, or Charlotte, North Carolina, or Boston, Massachusetts, during the same time period? What is similar and different about these cities and their Black communities, and what did the 1960s add to the equation? How can we compare Black student schooling outcomes from the 1960s to outcomes in the same cities in the 1980s, while controlling for time and place factors?

Similar questions apply to "acting White." Did it exist four decades ago? If so, in what time-place contexts? Was it the attitude of a majority of students? Does it begin in elementary or middle school? Is it more a factor among low-income students and communities as compared to middle-income ones? The questions and issues surrounding the "acting White" debate, the public discourse on "acting White" in particular and Black schooling in general proceeds as if these questions and issues have been resolved. One goal of this chapter is to interrupt this discourse. In this chapter, I provide a brief overview of identity, followed by a discussion of Ogbu's notion of community forces and identity. Next, I consider the importance of time and place factors and then discuss my data from an ethnographic study of a Black high school in Newark, New Jersey.

IDENTITY IN (ACTING) BLACK AND WHITE

This discussion of identity is limited to establishing a general understanding of how it might be usefully interpreted for issues related to how Black students participate in schooling. Individual and collective identities and school participation are, and have been, contentious issues for African Americans. Three scholarly and journalistic debates are presented below, each of which highlights both the issue of Black identity and the participation of Blacks in schooling. All three discussions show the importance of identity in African Americans' endeavors, but the latter two debates appeared in relatively polemic, but nonetheless important, essays by scholars who used their interpretation of Black identities to argue how identity plays an essential role in the school problems of Blacks—"acting White and Black" included.

Claude Steele (Steele and Aronson, 1995; see also Steele in Perry et al., 2004) has published important research on the experience of "stereotype threat"—being at risk of confirming, as self-characteristic, a negative stereotype about one's group—showing how it influenced Black college students' underperformance in relation to White students on difficult verbal tests (1995, p. 797). Their findings affirmed the influence of identity—and the interaction between individual and group identity—in how African-American students perceived themselves and others, as well as how their perceptions influenced their practices and participation in school. Their findings indicate that, for better or worse, identity is folded into processes that determine what an individual and group become, and how that shapes members' and non-members' perceptions of a group. Within these processes are issues regarding whether such identities, especially identities espoused within a group, are seen by insiders as authentic or "true" representations of the group (Appiah, 1994)—both a maneuver associated with "acting White" and one that S. Steele and McWhorter give too much explanatory power.

Shelby Steele and John McWhorter also raised important questions about the ways in which, as they saw it, the collective identity of Black people compromises individual identity and success in endeavors such as schooling. In an essay called, "The Age of White Guilt and the Disappearance of the Black Individual," S. Steele (2002) lamented the loss of responsibility, motivation, and initiative among African Americans, which he attributed to racial group identity politics—aided and abetted by White guilt. He said ours is an "America that has moved from its long dark age of racism into an age of white guilt" (p. 38). Accordingly, group politics has stifled African Americans' ability to raise themselves up, transcend the "impotent" remnants of racism, and make affirmative action obsolete. From his own childhood and career trajectory, to Great Society programs, to modern-day affirmative action and academic politics, Steele's narrative indicated a host of enemies of individual Black identity. Steele ended his essay by saying, "Today in black life there is what might be called 'identity grievance'—a certainty of racial grievance that is entirely disconnected from actual grievance. . . . We should help people who need help. There are, in fact, no races that need help; only individuals, citizens" (pp. 40–41).

On the same theme, in *Losing the Race: Self-Sabotage in Black America*, McWhorter (2000) surveyed anti-academic attitudes, including "acting White," that cripple Blacks as part of the group's "cult of victimology." He continued by saying that "the main reason black students lag behind all others starting in kindergarten and continuing through postgraduate school is that a wariness of books and learning for learning's sake as 'white' has become ingrained in black American culture" (p. 125). Where Shelby Steele blamed these individual identity problems partially on social policy driven by White guilt, McWhorter largely blamed Black American culture and its influence on collective identity, and a debilitating collective identity's influence on individual practices.

Shelby Steele and John McWhorter adopted different arguments to reach the same conclusion. No doubt, they raised important questions about identity and Black participation in schooling. Their analyses were too overly simplistic and narrow, however, to explain Black students' participation problems or to make public policy.

K. Anthony Appiah (1994) and Charles Taylor (1994) provide much more refined explanations of individual and collective identities. Especially important here is Taylor's and Appiah's explication of the dialogic nature of individual and collective identity processes:

> We define our identity always in dialogue with, sometimes in struggle against, the things our significant others want to see in us. Even after we outgrow some of these others—our parents, for instance—and they disappear from our lives, the conversation with them continues within us as long as we live.
>
> (Taylor, 1994, p. 33)

Taylor also described the role that a dialogic understanding of identity can play in clarifying some of the almost mystical qualities of "acting White" or "acting Black" in the combined context of Black people's historical subjugation, the contemporary political economy in Black and non-Black communities, and Black students' school participation:

> Identity designates something like a person's understanding of who they are, of their fundamental defining characteristics as a human being. The thesis is that our identity is partly shaped by recognition or its absence, often by *mis*recognition of others, and so a person or group of people can suffer real damage, real distortion, if the people or society around them mirror back to them a confining or demeaning or contemptible picture of themselves.
>
> (Taylor, 1994, p. 25)

Taylor's definition could easily be seen as a justification for Blacks that both constructs a notion like "acting White" and then punishes those who act in terms of it. Later, Appiah speaks directly to this process. However, there is also more to Taylor than that, which exposes some of what Steele and McWhorter missed. Again, Taylor argued that although we might speak of individual identity as one that is particular to you or me, more accurately, identity reflects the fact that human life is fundamentally constructed in interaction with others (1994, pp. 28, 33). Put differently, identities are the "imaginings of self in worlds of action, as social products. . . . [They] are psychohistorical formations that develop over a person's lifetime, populating intimate terrain and motivating social life" (Holland, Lachicotte, Skinner, & Cain, 1998, p. 5). Identity involves, in short, processes that cannot be reduced to the kinds of linear relationships and outcomes that S. Steele and McWhorter have described.

Building on Taylor, Appiah made the direct connection between individual and collective identities. In his view, the self of individual identity is dialogically constituted because it is constructed "from a tool kit of options made available by our culture and society. We do make choices, but we do not determine the options among which we choose" (1994, p. 155). The "tool kit" largely consists of scripts and narratives. *Collective identities* provide scripts and narratives that individuals can use in shaping their life plans and in telling their life stories. Collective identities therefore fit individual identities into a larger narrative—a narrative that tells the what, why, and how of a group's (*race/ethnic*) existence (pp. 160–161).[2]

Especially important is that none of these identity processes, according to Appiah, need wrap an individual or group too tightly into an essential, monological racial or ethnic identity. In accordance with the reciprocal and interactive nature of the identity process, African-American identity is shaped by American society and institutions, as well as life in African-American communities (1994, p. 155; 1996, p. 95). Thus, when C. Steele, S. Steele, and McWhorter talk about Black people as a group and then infer individual identities to that group, how do we know what in these outcomes is due to American culture, class culture, gender culture, and the like? Are Black lives so simple and formulaic? If so, and aside from the complexities inherent in making and implementing policy, why have public and school policy been unable to take advantage of such simply lived lives and identity processes?

African Americans' interpretations of "acting White (or Black)" are embedded in the narratives and maneuvers that signify at least one interpretation, both individual and collective, in response to the shapes and textures of life in their communities and schools. Indeed, in one sense, the positive and negative evaluations associated with "acting White (or Black)" can be what Appiah called a "form of healing," of "constructing a life of dignity" ([1996] p. 161). Ridiculing "acting White" is to praise "acting Black." It is a positive script in the face of the negative ones that have historically demeaned Black humanity and, by extension, Black identity.

In addition to agents' creative maneuvers at both individual and collective levels, I wish to emphasize *communities* in contrast to a monological *community*. For example, racial formations (Omi & Winant, 1994) cover all African Americans like a blanket. However, people react to racial formations in various ways, depending on where and when they live, and their individual and collective economic, social and political means and motivations. Variations in what Black people create and how they live under this proverbial blanket might be slight, but they are variations nonetheless. Thus, some Black communities and individuals have created narratives that are remarkably pro-Black and pro-education, while others have created ones that are pro-Black and anti-education, which is a miniscule piece of "acting White." The ethnography that will be presented later explores these points.

Hence, because of the dialogically constituted nature of identity, Black identity cannot be pulled apart or reconstituted in as simple a way as S. Steele and McWhorter suggested. Both scholars acknowledged individual and collective identities, but they minimized the complexity of the dialogical processes between and among these subject positions. C. Steele argued convincingly one outcome among many—stereotype threat. S. Steele was nearly as convincing in his narrative that included subject positions across time and place. But where C. Steele proceeded cautiously, S. Steele went boldly. C. Steele tested his hypotheses about stereotype threat across groups (e.g., women and Whites; see also Steele in Perry, Steele, & Hilliard, 2003). S. Steele, in contrast, generalized his outcome—that Black individuals lose themselves to the influence of an errant collective, fueled by White guilt—to too many Black people, people who in fact embrace their collective identity and believe in the things that S. Steele said that they had abandoned (Cousins, n.d.; see Perry and Hilliard in Perry et al., 2003).

And then there is McWhorter,[3] who seemed to have missed all of these dialogical nuances. McWhorter largely lamented that African Americans are not collectively or individually who they should be regarding education and upward mobility. But in his characterization, he reduced African Americans' preferences to largely being for or against intellectual things—schooling, reading, and the like. The corrupting influence of Rap music and other hedonistic popular culture productions are trance-like—producing non-reflexive African Americans, who are dominated and guided by structures and forces they should be able to overcome (Bourdieu, 1977; Giddens, 1979; Ortner, 1989, 1996).

Together, in arguing to weaken the Black collective's grasp on Black individuals, S. Steele and McWhorter essentialized the collective. They over-determined the group's influence on individual identity and thereby, inadvertently, I believe, constructed an impotent, too tightly wrapped, individual. This is the same individual that they wanted to resist the group and become all-powerful in building a successful life. No cultural group in the United States has struck the balance they want Blacks to achieve—to be in the group but not of it; to promote and practice only the positive aspects of the group. This is one variation of many ongoing historical debates about group membership (ethnic, race, gender, etc.) and individual identity (D'Andrade & Strauss, 1992; Holland et al., 1998). Striking just the right balance is problematic, in part, because what such a balance should comprise is subject to various interpretations. Also, even where individuals in other cultural groups do excel in the face of their group's "maladaptation" around a particular circumstance, specifically when and where this is the case has yet to be addressed. How long are such individuals able to do this and at what cost to them? What narratives are they constructing to build such a life and how does this narrative relate to those of the group they have resisted (see Scott's *Weapons of the Weak*, for example)?[4]

In the end, S. Steele and McWhorter showed how the processes implicated by the dialogical nature of identity can be minimized or distorted. The community represents just one context in which such identity processes operate, demonstrating why these processes must be explored to adequately explain the schooling participation of African-American students.

OGBU'S COMMUNITY FORCES AND IDENTITY

John Ogbu's ideas regarding why Black students as involuntary minorities perform as they do in school are worth summarizing (Gibson & Ogbu, 1991; Ogbu & Simons, 1998). In short, minorities, whether voluntary or involuntary, make sociocultural adaptations to develop collective solutions to collective problems. These adaptations hinge on interactions among a group's history (the acquisition of minority status and subsequent treatment by White Americans), the predominant cultural model in the United States, and cultural models used in relationship to minority status (e.g., dual frame of reference, instrumental adaptation, relational adaptation, and symbolic adaptation). Cultural models that minority group members employ influence the development of their beliefs and interpretations about schooling. But these cultural models interact with *community forces* (which are social, economic, and political) to shape both the interpretation of schooling and strategies for participating.

Implied above, but generally less emphasized, are interactions that are at every point mutually influential. In broad terms, histories, structures, and human agency are all involved and exert known and unknown influences on one another (Bourdieu, 1977; Ortner, 1989, 1996). Thus, cultural models and adaptations influence responses to schooling, but the outcome of a group's relationship with schooling also can influence a group's self-interpretation of its overall history in a community and society and why the group has adapted as it has. That is, what minority groups consider—historically and contemporarily, to interpret their overall history in the United States—is influenced by their social, economic, and political relationships, inclusive of their experiences in schooling. Paraphrasing Charles Taylor, Smith explained: "The manner in which meanings appear is historically conditioned, hence historically variable" (2002, p. 7). This is the case for both individuals and the groups to which they belong.

To be sure, Ogbu's framework acknowledged within-group variation in his cultural model of Black school performance: "Not all members of the group believe the same thing or behave the same way. Some individuals will always believe or behave differently from the dominant pattern in their group" (Ogbu & Simons, 1998, p. 168). Also, Ogbu rightly argued that structural forces play a key role in how African Americans approach schooling and understand the opportunities that result from educational achievement. However, in the theoretical space that Ogbu leaves open for alternatives and particulars is the opportunity to explore intracultural variations, including variations across cites, states, schools, and time periods. It is to this theoretical space that my research is addressed.

TIME-PLACE FACTORS

Fordham (1996) identified the influence of time-place factors that shaped the worldviews and ethos of Black students who attended the Washington, DC high school she studied in the 1980s. Likewise, Ogbu (1974) described how Stockton, California had its own set of historical characteristics that shaped the lives of the low-income Burghersiders he studied between 1968 and the early 1970s. But why have scholars of Black schooling not emphasized more of this—exploited the depth and breadth of time-place factors, given their significance in cross-cultural research? And where scholars have made such an emphasis, how and why has the policy discourse on Black schooling lacked, at least in media representations, within-group variation?[5]

Of course, one could cite numerous studies of Black schooling that focused on variation and documented differences based on parental or family income, occupation, and education; or family structure, community structure, school characteristics, and more (Ford, 1993; Jencks & Phillips, 1998; Neisser, 1986; Solorzano, 1991; see also footnote 4). But the grounded, mundane, everyday experiences that embody these variables are not well represented in statistics-driven studies. This especially is the case in studies that compare conditions across cites and historical eras, and in social, economic, and political perspective. Consequently, we must understand what we are asking our data to do, recognize their limitations, and generalize accordingly. This admonition doubly applies when our data are used for problem solving, wherein conceptualizations of "trouble" ought to be holistic or systemic and not reified by confusing symptoms with complex disorders (Rappaport, 1993, p. 297; Cousins, 1997, 2001).

Consider two sets of studies that broke important, stubborn ground in exposing the depth, breadth, and inner- and outer-workings of time-place factors for both within-group and between-group processes related to schooling. Two sets of studies are presented: the first set of studies is briefly presented to make my point in general, and the second set addresses my point more specifically.

The first set of studies—Stephen S. Smith's (2004; see also Douglas, 1995) study of the political economy of school desegregation in Charlotte, North Carolina, Formisano's (1991) study of *Boston against Busing*, and Pratt's (1992) study of education and race in Richmond, Virginia between 1954 and 1989—give insight into the interactions among the social, economic, and political transactions that shaped how Black communities defined their schooling experience between the 1950s and the late 1980s. Boston and Richmond were openly hostile toward school desegregation due to relatively hardened attitudes about race and school desegregation, but school desegregation also agitated and reproduced these attitudes.

Even farther south than Richmond, Charlotte took a different track in desegregating its schools in order to preserve and increase a business-friendly environment and grow the city's economy. The push of Black citizens and civil rights activists was key to making this happen. At the same time, bankers and other pro-growth business leaders in the city and region aligned with several influential Black and White citizens, politicians, and school officials. This resulted in relatively more tolerant attitudes about race and school desegregation by Whites and Blacks. If we are ever to understand Black participation in schooling, especially in comparative perspective, we must weigh its meaning and practice in the light of such localized and national characteristics and events as did the studies above and those that follow.[6] That said, we move to the next set of studies, which raise a few more points about time and place in schooling research.

First is a study of Black and Latino Advancement Via Individual Determination (AVID) students in San Diego who became academically successful without losing their ethnic identity or "acting White" (Mehan, Hubbard, & Villanueva, 1994). This was a potent example of the influence of "place"—at the school-program level in this instance—on minority adaptation to schooling. I would suggest that "time" is a factor here as well: the influence of historical and contemporary events on the ethos that evolved for Blacks and Latinos in the aftermath of civil rights and related movements, the focus on cultural diversity and inclusion after that, and, today, in what might be called the backlash against some of the above-mentioned activities.

Introduced to the San Diego school system in 1980 and studied through the 1990s, Black and Latino AVID students learned to put academic achievement and the achievement ideology in a critical perspective that motivated them and preserved their ethnic, social, and cultural selves. The AVID students practiced accommodation without assimilation, a pattern that Gibson (1988) associated with voluntary rather than involuntary minorities. This study showed how "place," as the institutional arrangements in a school, mediates relations between social constraints and educational outcomes related to ethnic and class identity. AVID students did not disavow the history of racism and related barriers in their communities. Instead, they learned to "express a belief in their own efficacy and a belief in the power of schooling to improve their lives and the lives of others" (Mehan et al., 1994, p. 97; Chapter 22, this volume; see Hubbard 1999 for a related study that focused on gendered strategies for low-income African-American high-school students in San Diego).

In an interesting contrast, Hemmings's (1996) study showed how two desegregated high schools "share[d] virtually the same image of the good or 'model' student [b]ut student peer cultures differed significantly between the sites regarding the acceptability of this and other images of

African Americans" (p. 20). Unfortunately, but understandably, the author did not disclose the location of the schools, other than that they were located in a large, midwestern city, with neighborhoods divided along racial and social class lines. However, the high schools of focus were similar in their curricula and other organizational features, while other elements of their cultures were markedly different, due primarily to the students' social-class backgrounds (p. 25). One high school was a college-preparatory magnet school with a reputation for academic excellence, and the other was a comprehensive high school of mostly working-class students.

Focusing on six high-achieving boys and girls with working- or middle-class backgrounds, Hemmings argued that Black students do not form identical identities; Black students differ because they and their schools differ. Identity is an image of self that drives adolescents' behavioral adaptations in interaction with the cultures of their schools (1996, pp. 22–23). Although I would also emphasize "time" factors here (the era in which these students attended school), Hemmings showed how "place," both in terms of school infrastructure and community contexts, interacts with social and personal identities to explain variations in model students' participation in high school. And like the students in Fordham's studies (1986 with Ogbu; 1988, 1993, 1996) who experienced social and interpersonal conflict, such conflict for Hemmings's students was based on varied influences on the students' individual identities (e.g., peers, race, gender, class, family, occupational interests, etc.) *and* where they attended school.

Finally, Flores-Gonzalez (1999) argued on behalf of the "diversity of responses to academic success among involuntary minorities" and used Puerto Rican high achievers to make her case. More radically, and as an explicit challenge to Ogbu's assertions about dominant minority patterns, she said her 1992–93 study of a Chicago high school "shows that there does not seem to be a pattern in how involuntary minorities in general deal with academic success" (1999, p. 358). Most of the students were low-income; 55 percent were Puerto Rican, 12 percent were African American, and the rest were Asian and Latino of various nationalities. Flores-Gonzalez focused on how Puerto Rican high achievers reconciled their ethnicity and academic success.

Included in the overall equation for academic success were minority status, social class and, important for my argument, the school's sociocultural context. The school's sociocultural context shaped students' attitudes toward schooling and how schools use the curriculum to structure students' formal and informal opportunities. Flores-Gonzalez suggested that structural conditions (in and out of school) do not necessarily lead to the development of oppositional student identity (1999, p. 360).

Flores-Gonzalez's findings were as likely to be related to the time-period during which her students attended school as they were to the other factors. My own study was conducted during approximately the same time-period as hers (1992–1994). The students in my study of Community High grew up during a period of rapid social, economic, and political transition. Like other adolescents, they were both inventors and consumers of particular cultural forms, of both the past (in my case, a socially and politically radical, as well as an ethnocentric worldview and ethos) and the present (radical popular culture, such as Rap and Hip Hop, and African Americans' increasing economic and occupational mobility). These factors had as much to do with their approach to schooling as did the influence of their school structure, class status, family life, and gender.

COMMUNITY HIGH

My ethnography of Community High focused most intensively on a sub-population of students in the senior class of 1992–1993 (approximately 50 of 155; Cousins, 1994).[7] It also focused on the school's general characteristics and the milieu created by relationships among the structure and administration of the school, the student body, and the community. Community High was a comprehensive, public high school that served part of Newark's South Ward, but was largely perceived as belonging to Village Park residents. To more fully appreciate the identities and practices of Community High students in a spatial and temporal context, we need to review a few factors in the evolution of Newark, Village Park, and the school.

Robert Coles (1984) said that the politics of adults become the psychology of children—in other words, the meanings and understandings that they use to navigate the world. What the children and adolescents of Newark had as the social cultural material with which to make their worlds was a densely populated city of 275,000 people within less than 23 square miles. Long before I conducted my ethnographic study from 1992 to 1994, Newark was a city with a high poverty rate, a high crime rate, and low-performing schools (Anyon, 1997). Newark was home to Africans at least as early as 1666, but the concentration of Blacks that is familiar to us today came after the two World Wars (Curvin, 1977; Mikell, 1987). In addition to the city's long history with Blacks, other pertinent historical factors about Newark include economic booms and busts, ethnic diversity and competition over jobs and housing, and the early presence of Black freemen, which contributed, by the early 1900s, to the emergence of a Black middle class and Black civic protest organizations that reached into the 1960s (National Association for the Advancement of Colored People (NAACP), Urban League, Black-Jewish-Italian underworld alliances to safeguard working-class jobs).

By the 1980s, there had been a succession of Black mayors and an increase in Black political power. Yet there was persistent poverty, failing schools, and high crime rates. Still, two strands of Black consciousness prevailed from the 1960s and reflect, for better or worse, the ethos and realities I found while I was in the city: "Newark is a black city . . . What we have that we love we made for ourselves, things we value are black things" (Amiri Baraka, quoted in Porambo, 1971, p. 176); versus, "[T]he election of Black officials and the proliferation of Black bureaucrats have altered our conditions very little. Black leaders have represented little more to Black people than the bitter-sweet residue of our ego-trip on 'Black Power' and Black Capitalism' " (Heard, 1978, p. 603). Though dated, the contemporary currency of the sentiments expressed by these statements was affirmed through my interactions with local community politicians, old and young residents in Village Park and Newark at large, and many Sunday morning sermons in the Black churches I visited.

By the 1990s, and with little change in Newark's social and political environment, another legacy from the 1960s had managed to survive, even if in a revised form, along with an evolving economic renaissance in Newark: Islam. Radical forms of Christianity notwithstanding, Islam, in both its nationalist (Nation of Islam) and orthodox (Sunni and Shiite) forms, has had an important history and influence in Newark (Cousins, 1994; El-Amin, 1990; Haddad & Smith, 1994; Howell, 1966; Lincoln, 1961, 1984; Lincoln & Mamiya, 1990; Price, 1975). And, however slightly and gently, Islam was part of the individual and group identities of the generation of students I studied at Community High.

Islam: An Ethnic-ethic

Community High teachers told me how Islam surged into the school milieu in the 1970s and 80s, and I saw its remnants in the 1990s. The Nation of Islam and orthodox Muslims (largely Sunni) varied in dress and adherence to Islamic traditions, customs, and rituals. But they, particularly the Sunni, also offered a "self-determined identity and a tangible effort at reversal" regarding the historical and contemporary class- and race-based conditions of Blacks in Newark and other cities (Lincoln, 1984, p. 164). Students who were attracted to the teachings of the Nation of Islam, but not its nationalist tenets, turned toward the Sunni. In any case, Islam provided many of its Black followers both personal and social rebirth.[8] (See Chapter 9, this volume.)

Whether Muslim or not, and most residents and students were not, a religiously influenced *ethnic ethic* found wide favor among teachers and students in Community High and Village Park. One conspicuous outcome was the numerous students in Community High (and in Newark at large) who had Arabic or Islamic names: Abdul-Hamid, Abdul-Wahid,

Al-Bayyinah, Sajjad, Hazizi, Kamilah, Rashaad, Alfurquan, Rashim, Malik, Shadiki, Hasan, and so on. Popular Hip Hop recording artist Lauryn Hill, who grew up in nearby East Orange, acknowledged this. In a song titled, "Every Ghetto, Every City," about growing up in the Newark area, Hill sang/rapped: ". . . And car thieves got away through Irvington/Hillside brings beef with cops/ Self-Destruction record drops/ And everybody's name was Muslim" (Hill, 1998).

Pam, a senior, grew up going to Masjid with her mother one week and church with her father the next. Bright, articulate, and rather mature for an 18-year-old, Pam worked part-time and had plans to be a child psychologist, but she earned average grades. She told me she could do better and that she had to. By contrast, Carl seemed to have found the answer to his identity in Islam. Carl's school performance was marginal, but his participation was sincere. Carl said that his mother was a Christian and his deceased father was a Muslim. Although not yet fully involved, Carl told me he wanted to get more into Islam, but he did not know what to tell his mother. Among other things, he said he wanted to get into Islam because of his father and because

> A lot of Muslims, they talk deep. They talk real deep. They deep in their religion. I like that. Plus what they say about the white man and stuff like that. Like what Malcolm X said.

The intersection of Islam with everyday life was inescapable in Newark and Village Park. Islam's presence in the students' lives may indicate their acute need for a temporal interpretation of life that generated purpose, direction, continuity, and motivation in the face of the invidious social, economic, and political circumstances they faced as residents of Newark and Village Park. A dismissal of this milieu cannot but distort these students' social and educational lives and the predicaments that we try to understand when we study them and make public policy. However, portraying this milieu relatively accurately means acknowledging its dialogic nature, which is further demonstrated below.

Oasis (or Mirage) in the Desert: Village Park and Community High

Notwithstanding the solidarities and divisions fostered by Islam, it would not be an exaggeration to suggest that the incipient, radical ethos of Black Newark residents (in 1992–93, a city where over half the residents were Black) was based on decades of both ethnic and class tension and solidarity. Paradoxically, tension and solidarity were partially responsible for the influx of Blacks, between the 1950s and the 1970s, from less prosperous parts of Newark to the idyllic, White, and Jewish middle- and working-class Village Park community. By 1994, Village Park had approximately 58,000, residents, over 95 percent of whom were Black.

Briefly, other key factors likely affecting the lives and identities of Community High students included: the inheritance and adoption of a materially and educationally oriented middle-class community; the reinforcement of ethnic pride through academic achievement in school,[9] and the ever-present spirit of radical Christianity and Islam (Sunni and the Nation of Islam). All of these and more contributed to a peculiar outcome: groups of students who embraced education without compromising their ethnic identities as Black people.

In particular, most of the top 25 graduates in the class of 1992–93, and many of their peers who performed less well in that academic year, possessed self-affirming ethnic pride and embraced education. These Community High students saw their achievements as "Black behavior." None said that their peers had accused them of "acting White" or any other negative or pejorative term that signaled a strain between being Black and being educated and smart. These perceptions were consistent with not only my observations, but also the comments of teachers and others in the school and community.

Embracers of Education and Black Identities

According to Rose, a student in a group discussion on the academic performance of Black students in Community High,

> They doubtin' us? Cause the generation we growing up in, they sayin' we don't really wanna learn. [I]t make me strive higher so I can prov'm wrong.

Rose emphasized her desire to achieve academically, although her performance faltered at times. Rose was a 17-year-old senior who grew up in Village Park with her family, which had a relatively marked history in the community and the school. One of her aunts was an alumnus of Community High; when I was there, she was a community and school leader at the forefront of restoring pride in the "ole Orange and Brown" school colors that represented the school spirit. Rose lived with her mother (a real estate broker and executive secretary), her father (a construction worker), and her 14-year-old brother. Rose's 24-year-old sister, a nurse, did not live with the family. Rose grew up Christian but had wanted to become a Muslim for many years. When she turned 18, she began going to the Masjid.

Rose, like many young women in Community High, dressed in professional suits, but accented them with the latest Hip Hop hairstyle, jewelry, and attitude.[10] She represented the students I knew who consciously and unconsciously "acted Black" (or ethnic and class-conscious in dress, verbal and nonverbal interpersonal interactions, and attitudes), but did their schoolwork. School was socially important, but also focused on preparing for the future. Rose told me:

> I believe that education is essential to my life. It's really hard for me because sometimes I really can't stay focused on what I'm trying to do, or I can't put what I want to on paper. But I believe that with education I can go to the limit.

Compelled to achieve by her parents and teachers, Rose explained that her rather limited achievement resulted from being too involved with boys and the social scene at school. Having matured during her last two years in school, however, she did not give up boys, but learned to prioritize. Moreover, Rose was a leader in several student groups and was loved and admired by her peers and teachers.

Like Rose, Bobby was not one of the best students in his class, but he was one of the most sincere, ethnically confident, and academically focused. He was 18 years old and had spent the last 12 years living in Village Park with his paternal grandparents and his divorced father. Bobby's 16-year-old and 14-year-old brothers, and his 15-year-old sister, lived with his mother. Bobby's 43-year-old father grew up in the Newark of the 1960s, graduated from high school a month before the riots of 1967, and dabbled with Islam before returning to Christianity. When I talked with Bobby's father, he was unemployed from full-time work and had a part-time job driving a limousine. Bobby's father attended college, and for about 20 years he worked in management in several corporations and in an insurance company before being laid off. Bobby's mother finished high school and had owned a beauty parlor at least since Bobby was a young child.

Bobby's parents and paternal grandparents pushed education and he internalized their message. He told me that "given the right education, you can go very far with it, I think. . . . Education is something that you have to want. It's not something that has to be given to you, you gotta want it. I think a lot of people take it for granted." I have heard similar words from students in Community High with both high and low performance levels. Yet what stood out about Bobby was confidence in his ethnic and personal identity, combined with his worldliness. He was neither a nerd nor sports jock. And in my observations of him with his peers, he was certainly no "punk!," as the kids put it, which meant he was not a pushover with other males.

Further, it is difficult to fully describe the excitement and surprise I felt upon observing Bobby and several of his friends cussing and fussing over the answers to calculus problems on their own time while waiting for an

English class to begin. I knew and had interviewed each of the boys in the group. Each of them epitomized their version of Black masculinity—being cool with the girls, being in touch with the latest Hip Hop and Rap music and styles, and carrying himself with confidence. This is not to say that all was well with these boys, because it was not. Some of them were unsure of their next move after high school. They were not sure that their education would get them to where they wanted to go, and, at times, their attitudes reflected an almost paralyzing ambivalence.

Certainly there were undercurrents of conflict and outright incompatibilities between fully participating in school and fully participating in life as the students knew it in Village Park. In fact, being involved in the social life of one's adolescent peers after the school day ended often meant that one did not study or do all or most of the assigned homework, which meant that one would fall behind in school or earn a low grade. Still, in such a scenario, students were not explicitly accusing each other of "acting White" or being a "punk," "stuckup," or a "nerd" for doing schoolwork. But participating with peers in the community's social life to the exclusion of doing schoolwork certainly came at a cost, nonetheless. However, the cost did not mean, in most instances, that embracing education and or being relatively successful at it equaled ethnic emasculation or being ambivalent and stripped relative to one's identity as a Black person. One final case example follows.

Stan, a 17-year-old participant, was loved and adored by some of his peers, despised and hated by others; he was the epitome of an academic challenge for teachers and staff. Stan dealt drugs and worked other hustles to make money to buy his motorcycle and stylish clothes, and to keep his car equipped with the latest stereo. By December of his senior year, Stan was living with his pregnant girlfriend. Stan had two younger brothers, and his older brother dropped out of school in the tenth grade. Until he moved in with his girlfriend, Stan had lived with his 40-year-old mother, who was a supervisor in the word-processing department of a federal agency, and his 42-year-old stepfather, who worked in a meat-processing plant. Stan's biological father, who was never married to his mother, sold drugs and lived in various communities in Newark. Stan's mother went to college and his father completed high school.

Stan was precocious and seemed to understand more about life than he should at the age of 17. Toward the end of the school year, one of Stan's acquaintances had been shot and killed in a drug deal. Stan was frequently questioned (he said "harassed") by the police, who thought he knew who did it. I believed then and now that Stan's life circumstances undermined his academic success, but not his interest and motivation, given that he made it to the twelfth grade and nearly met the requirements for graduation. In fact, he said, "Education is something we all need. I know we can mess around and stuff, but we know that's the bottom line.

We gotta get a education to make it." When I asked him why he believed that, he said,

> 'Cause after high school, without a education you're nothin'.... My mother talk about it a lot. She talk about high school all the time. ... She talk about education [during] good times and bad times. So education, that go back a long way.

My observations of Stan's participation in some of his classes and in other school settings confirmed both his interest in school and his academic ability. His lifestyle, however, deterred high academic achievement and may well have reflected his living an undermining definition of what it meant to be a Black man. Yet, based on what I learned about Stan, he simultaneously embraced being Black and the importance of schooling and education. For Stan and some of his peers, their focus on education and success in school was a result of being a senior. By default, they faced the acute reality and push to carve out a life as an emerging adult. They likely fell back on education as one of the clearest avenues of success, even if it was not realizable due to prior personal actions. Such outcomes certainly depict a complicated and uneven process.

Furthermore, being ethnically self-affirming ("acting Black") yet engaged, motivated, and even successful in school is no less powerful an outcome of schooling and culture than its opposite ("acting White"). Disengagement from school that is related to self-doubt and the strain of the guilt associated with betraying one's ethnic group is a more prevalent outcome. This raises the issue of "authenticity" attributed to Appiah earlier and is just the point that S. Steele and McWhorter tried to make. However, neither side of the debate (i.e., weak individuals versus a powerful group, or too tightly wrapped ethnic/racial identities in the context of either pro- or anti-academic attitudes and practices) should stand alone to describe and explain Black schooling or to construct policy. These outcomes exist on a continuum and should be recognized as such in order to paint a more representative portrait of schooling in the context of ethnic culture and identity.

Conclusion

Identity is at the center of the notions of "acting White." However, with its corollary, "acting Black," "acting White" is buried inside questions of culture and meaning in the sense postulated by Clifford Geertz (1973, 1983, 2000) and Roy Rappaport (1979). The most instructive explorations of contemporary education in the United States address education's historical evolution (Tyack & Cuban, 1995). Explorations of Black students' contemporary education could benefit from the same kind of "long view." With a long view, African Americans' school participation is a far richer phenomenon than what it has come to signify in its most common portrayals in the media, school policy practice, and some research. Because of this situation, academics and others must practice a sort of self-conscious doubt about what have come to be seen as acceptable, common-sense realities of human diversity that are represented in such issues as Black schooling. Practicing in this way will generate more instructive questions about Black schooling, but the answers to these and other questions certainly should include issues of *time and place*—when, where, how, and, especially, why does one participate in schooling? If we follow this path, we may indeed find that "the diversity of responses to academic success [and failure] among involuntary minorities" *or* others will not be minimized (Flores-Gonzalez, 1999, p. 346).

NOTES

1 I would think that similar arguments have been raised about the pervasiveness of the anti-educational/ intellectual or socially progressive attitudes—ultimately issues of social class status and how lifestyles are constrained by that subject position—outlined by Du Bois (1899/1996) in his Philadelphia study, Frazier (1939, 1957) in his study of Black Chicago families and communities, Davis, Gardner, and Gardner (1941) in their study of Black southerners, on up to the present. Historian Robin Kelley (1994), among others, has challenged one-sided historical views of Black people and helped develop a more accurate portrait, if that is at all possible.

2 I have glossed over some of the "individual" versus "collective" nuances of Taylor's and Appiah's discussion of identity. But I do not believe that this has distorted the authors' meanings or weakened my overall argument and goal in this chapter.

3 See S. Steele's (1990) earlier work for an interpretation that is strikingly similarity to McWhorter's.

4 In *Weapons of the Weak*, Scott (1983) argued that historically, the weak undermine the position and ideology of dominant elites through subtle techniques that erode the latter's hegemonic power.

5 A struggle for all researchers is that policy makers and pundits grab hold of the most salacious aspects of one's findings; for example, not only of Blacks' low academic performance, but their social problems in school, too. Publicly, this translates into a view that Blacks have widespread social problems in general and education problems in particular. Perhaps this situation justifies Ogbu's and others' focus on general patterns of failure in Black culture.

6 Though addressing primarily non-African Americans, ethnographies by Foley (1990), Eckert (1989), MacLeod (1995), and others have addressed some of the variables I am concerned with here as well. Added to this are varying perspectives on Black life by Kelley (1994), Lewis (1991), Loury (2002), Patterson (1997), and Trotter (1985), to name a few relevant cases.

7 Except for publicly elected officials, I use pseudonyms for the school, the community, and their members.

8 See Dannin (2002) and McCloud (1995) for other takes on the issue of African Americans and Islam.
9 The relatively high achievements of White students in pre-1970 Community High were well known (e.g., a high rate of college acceptance and professional careers; see Anyon, 1997).
10 This is more fully described in Cousins and Mabrey (1998).

REFERENCES

Anyon, J. (1997). *Ghetto schooling: A political economy of urban educational reform*. New York: Teachers College Press.

Appiah, K. A. (1994). Identity, authenticity, survival: Multicultural societies and social reproduction. In A. Gutmann (Ed.), *Multiculturalism: Examining the politics of recognition* (pp. 149–164). Princeton, NJ: Princeton University Press.

Bourdieu, P. (1977). *Outline of a theory of practice* (R. Nice, Trans.). Cambridge: Cambridge University Press.

Coles, R. (1984). *The political life of children*. Boston: Atlantic Monthly Press.

Cousins, L. (n.d.) Acting "Black" and embracing education: Time and place and dominant and non-dominant outcomes in research on Black schooling. Unpublished manuscript.

Cousins, L. (1994). *The complexity of race and class in a Black urban high school*. Unpublished Ph.D. dissertation, The University of Michigan.

Cousins, L. (1997). Toward a sociocultural context for understanding violence and disruption in Black schools and communities. *Journal of Sociology & Social Welfare, 24*, 41–63.

Cousins, L. (2001). Moral markets for troubling youths: A disruption. *Childhood, 8*(2), 193–212.

Cousins, L., & Mabrey, T. (1998). Re-gendering social work practice and education: The case for African American girls. *Journal of Human Behavior in the Social Environment, 1*, 91–104.

Crouch, S. (1999). Being a dummy makes one a real person: the braining down of the education of African Americans. *The Journal of Blacks in Higher Education, 24*, 103–105.

Curvin, R. (1977). Black ghetto politics in Newark after World War II. In J. Schwartz & D. Prosser (Eds.), *Cities of the Garden State* (pp. 145–159). Dubuque, IA: Kendall/Hunt.

D'Andrade, R., & Strauss, C. (Eds.) (1992). *Human motives and cultural models*. New York: Cambridge University Press.

Dannin, R. (2002). *Black pilgrimage to Islam*. New York: Oxford University Press.

Davis, A., Gardner, B., & Gardner, M. (1941). *Deep south: A social anthropological study of caste and class*. Chicago: University of Chicago Press.

Douglas, D. (1995). *Reading, writing, and race: Desegregation of Charlotte schools*. Chapel Hill: University of North Carolina Press.

Du Bois, W.E.B. [1899 (1996)]. *The Philadelphia Negro: A social study*. Philadelphia: University of Pennsylvania Press.

Eckert, P. (1989). *Jocks and burnouts: Social categories and identity in the high school*. New York: Teachers College, Columbia University.

El-Amin, M. (1990). *The religion of Islam and the Nation of Islam: What is the difference?* Newark, NJ: El-Amin Productions.

Flores-Gonzalez, N. (1999). Puerto Rican high achievers: An example of ethnic and academic identity compatibility. *Anthropology & Education Quarterly, 30*(3), 342–362.

Foley, D. (1990). *Learning capitalist culture: Deep in the heart of Texas*. Philadelphia: University of Pennsylvania Press.

Ford, D. Y. (1993). Black Students' Achievement Orientation as a Function of Perceived Family Achievement Orientation and Demographic Variables. *Journal of Negro Education, 62*, 47–66.

Fordham, S. (1988). Racelessness as a factor in Black students' school success: pragmatic strategy or Pyrrhic victory? *Harvard Educational Review, 58*, 54–84.

Fordham, S. (1993). "Those loud Black girls": (Black) women, silence, and gender "passing" in the academy. *Anthropology & Education Quarterly, 24*, 3–32.

Fordham, S. (1996). *Blacked out: Dilemmas of race, identity, and success at Capital High*. Chicago: University of Chicago Press.

Fordham, S., & Ogbu, J. U. (1986). Black students' school success: Coping with the burden of acting White. *The Urban Review 18*(3), 176–206.

Formisano, R. (1991). *Boston against busing: Race, class, and ethnicity in the 1960s and 1970s*. Chapel Hill: The University of North Carolina Press.

Frazier, E. F. (1939). *The Negro family in the United States*. Chicago: University of Chicago Press.

Frazier, E. F. (1957). *Black bourgeoisie*. New York: The Free Press.

Geertz, C. (1973). *The interpretation of cultures*. New York: Basic Books.

Geertz, C. (1983). *Local knowledge: Further essays in interpretive anthropology*. Basic Books.

Geertz, C. (2000). *Available light: Anthropological reflections on philosophical topics*. Princeton, NJ: Princeton University Press.

Gibson, M. (1988). *Accommodation without assimilation: Sikh immigrants in an American high school*. Ithaca, NY: Cornell University Press.

Gibson, M. A., & Ogbu, J. U. (Eds.) (1991). *Minority status and schooling: A comparative study of immigrant and involuntary minorities*. New York: Garland Publishing.

Giddens, A. (1979). *Central problems in social theory: Action, structure, and contradiction in social analysis*. London: Macmillan.

Haddad, Y., & Smith, J. (Eds.) (1994). *Muslim communities in North America*. Albany: SUNY Press.

Heard, N. (1978). Newark: the dying ideal. In S. B. Winters (Ed.), *Newark, an assessment: 1967–1977* (pp. 603–606). Newark, NJ: New Jersey Institute of Technology.

Hemmings, A. (1996). Conflicting images? Being Black and a model high school student. *Anthropology & Education Quarterly, 27*(1), 20–50.

Hill, L. (1998). Every ghetto, every city. *The miseducation of Lauryn Hill* [CD]. New York: Ruffhouse Records.

Holland, D., Lachicotte, W., Jr., Skinner, D., & Cain, C. (1998). *Identity and agency in cultural worlds*. Cambridge, MA: Harvard University Press.

Howell, H. (1966). *Black Muslim Affiliation as Reflected in Attitudes and Behavior of Negro Adolescents with Its Effect on Policies and Administrative Procedures in Schools of Two Eastern Cities, 1961–64*. Ann Arbor, MI: University Microfilms.

Hubbard, L. (1999). College aspirations among low-income African American high school students: general strategies for success. *Anthropology & Education Quarterly, 30*(3), 363–383.

Jencks, C., & Phillips, M. (Eds.) (1998). *The Black-White test score gap*. Washington, DC: Brookings Institution Press.

Kelley, R. (1994). *Race rebels: Culture, politics, and the Black working class*. New York: Free Press.

Lewis, E. (1991). *In their own interests: Race, class, and power in Twentieth-Century Norfolk, Virginia*. Berkeley: University of California Press.

Lincoln, E. C. (1961). *The Black Muslims in America*. Boston: Beacon Press.

Lincoln, E. C. (1984). *Race, religion, and the continuing American dilemma*. New York: Hill and Wang.

Lincoln, E. C., & Mamiya, L. (1990). *The Black Church in the African American experience*. Durham, NC: Duke University Press.

Loury, G. (2002). *The anatomy of racial inequality*. Cambridge, MA: Harvard University Press.

MacLeod, J. (1995). *Ain't no makin' it: Aspirations and attainment in a low-income neighborhood*. Boulder, CO: Westview Press.

McCloud, A. (1995). *African American Islam*. New York: Routledge.

McWhorter, J. (2000). *Losing the race: Self-sabotage in Black America*. New York: Perennial.

Mehan, H., Hubbard, L., & Villanueva, I. (1994). Forming academic identities: accommodation without assimilation among involuntary minorities. *Anthropology & Education Quarterly, 25*(2), 91–117.

Mikell, G. (1987). Class and ethnic political relations in Newark, New Jersey: Blacks and Italians. In L. Mullings (Ed.), *Cities of the United States* (pp. 71–98). New York: Columbia University Press.

Neisser, U. (Ed.) (1986). *The school achievement of minority children: New perspectives*. Hillsdale, NJ: Lawrence Erlbaum Associates Publishers.

Ogbu, J. U. (1974). *The next generation: An ethnography of education in an urban neighborhood*. New York: Academic Press.

Ogbu, J. U., & Simons, H. (1998). Voluntary and involuntary minorities: a cultural-ecological theory of school performance with some implications for education. *Anthropology & Education Quarterly, 29*, 155–188.

Omi, M., & Winant, H. (1994). *Racial formations in the United States*. New York: Routledge.

Ortner, S. (1989). *High religion: A cultural and political history of Sherpa Buddhism*. Princeton, NJ: Princeton University Press.

Ortner, S. (1996). *Making gender: The politics and erotics of culture*. Boston: Beacon Press.

Patterson, O. (1997). *The ordeal of integration: Progress and resentment in America's "racial" crisis*. Washington, DC: Civitas/Counterpoint.

Perry, T., Steele, C., & Hilliard, A. G., III (2003). *Young, gifted, and Black: Promoting high achievement among African-American students*. Boston: Beacon Press.

Porambo, R. (1971). *No cause for indictment: An autopsy of Newark*. New York: Holt, Rinehart and Winston.

Pratt, R. (1992). *The color of their skin: Education and race in Richmond, Virginia: 1954–1989*. Charlottesville: University of Virginia Press.

Price, C. A. (1975). *The Afro-American community of Newark, 1917–1947. A social history*. Unpublished Ph.D. dis., Rutgers University, The State University of New Jersey.

Rappaport, R. (1979). *Ecology, meaning, and religion*. Berkeley, CA: North Atlantic Books.

Rappaport, R. (1993). The anthropology of trouble. *American Anthropologist, 95*, 295–303.

Rich, W. (1996). *Black mayors and school politics: The failure of reform in Detroit, Gary, and Newark*. New York: Garland.

Scott, J. C. (1983). *The weapons of the weak: Everyday forms of peasant resistance*. New Haven, CT: Yale University Press.

Smith, N. (2002). *Charles Taylor: Meaning, morals and modernity*. Malden, MA: Blackwell.

Smith, S. (2004). *Boom for whom? Education, desegregation, and development in Charlotte*. Albany: SUNY Press.

Solorzano, D. (1991). Mobility aspirations among racial minorities, controlling for SES. *Social Services Review, 75*, 182–188.

Steele, C., & Aronson, J. (1995). Stereotype threat and the intellectual test performance of African Americans. *Journal of Personality and Social Psychology, 69*, 797–811.

Steele, S. (1990). *The content of our character: A new vision of race in America*. New York: HarperCollins Publishers.

Steele, S. (2002). The age of white guilt and the disappearance of the Black individual. *Harper's Magazine, 305*(1830), 33–42.

Taylor, C. (1994). The politics of recognition. In A. Gutmann (Ed.), *Multiculturalism: Examining the politics of recognition*. Princeton, NJ: Princeton University Press.

Trotter, J. M., Jr. (1985). *Black Milwaukee: The making of an industrial proletariat, 1915–45*. Urbana: University of Illinois Press.

Tyack, D., & Cuban, L. (1995). *Tinkering toward Utopia: A century of public school reform*. Cambridge, MA: Harvard University Press.

Weis, L. (1985). *Between two worlds: Black students in an urban community college*. London: Routledge.

Chapter 9

Reexamining Resistance as Oppositional Behavior

The Nation of Islam and the Creation of a Black Achievement Ideology (The Remix)

A. A. Akom

THE OPPOSITIONAL CULTURE EXPLANATION

The oppositional culture explanation for racial disparities in educational achievement introduced by Ogbu (1978, 1991) suggests that individuals from historically oppressed groups (involuntary minorities) display their antagonism towards the dominant group by resisting educational goals. According to this line of argument, castelike minorities (including native-born Blacks, Puerto Ricans, Mexicans, and American Indians) withdraw from academic pursuits because they believe that racial discrimination and prejudice limit their access to high-paying jobs. Ironically, however, in their unwillingness to play the "credentializing" game, they reproduce existing class relations, and remain mired in subordinate economic positions (Willis, 1977; Solomon, 1992).

In contrast, individuals from the dominant group and groups who have migrated to the United States of their own accord (voluntary/immigrant minorities) maintain optimistic views of their chances for educational and occupational success. A key component in this explanation is the difference between the migration trajectories of involuntary and voluntary minorities and their children.

Voluntary minorities tend to develop positive attitudes regarding their chances for success and remain optimistic in their outlook towards educational advancement. Involuntary minorities, on the other hand, in response to these unfavorable conditions, tend to behave in four ways: First, they equate schooling with assimilation into the dominant group. Second, they do not try to achieve academically. Third, they pay a unique psychological wage, which Fordham and Ogbu (1986) refer to as the "burden of acting White," if they do try to achieve academically. And finally, they engage in actions of resistance against the school and societal norms.

In the case of the Nation of Islam (NOI), a religious organization primarily composed of African Americans, I did not find patterns of oppositional behavior in the way this construct has been traditionally documented and defined. Although an oppositional cultural frame of reference was evident among the young women whom I studied and observed, this frame of reference was distinct in character from that offered by Ogbu and associates and did not produce the academic outcomes commonly associated with this model (Ogbu & Simons, 1998).[1] Instead I observed an involuntary minority culture of mobility whereby involuntary minority students in the NOI resisted schooling and societal practices that they viewed at odds with their religious tenets and practices, yet drew on the moral, spiritual, and material resources facilitated by their tightly knit community in order to achieve social mobility and academic success.

Previous research that assigns involuntary minorities an oppositional orientation towards educational and social mobility neglects the class and cultural heterogeneity inherent within all minority communities. Even poor minority neighborhoods are culturally diverse, including people who hold to conventional norms of behavior, those who choose a street-oriented or oppositional lifestyle, and those who vacillate in between (Anderson, 1990; Patillo-McCoy, 1999). Other theories of Black educational underachievement remain underdeveloped as well: first, because of their tendency to reduce the relationship between cultural identity and academic engagement into a zero-sum game for involuntary minorities; and second, because of their inability to capture the ways in which African Americans (or other racial/ethnic groups) maintain their own cultural identity and strategies for collective mobility in the context of discrimination and group disadvantage (Flores-Gonzalez, 1999; Foley, 1991; Hemmings, 1996).

This chapter seeks to complicate and extend previous accounts of a uni-dimensional oppositional social identity frequently ascribed to involuntary minority individuals and communities by focusing on the experiences of seven young women in the NOI.[2] More specifically, I demonstrate that involuntary minorities do not have to choose between performing well in school and maintaining their racio-ethnic identities. Instead I show that it is possible to simultaneously be "involuntary," "oppositional," and to a certain degree, a "model" student (Hemmings, 1996).[3]

In an effort to illustrate the ways in which a group of low-income African American students associates school success neither with "acting White" nor as a "middle-class" trait, I invoke the concept of "organizational habitus" (McDonough, 1997).[4] Organizational habitus refers to a set of dispositions, perceptions, and appreciations transmitted to individuals through a common organizational culture (McDonough, 1997). Although Bourdieu (1986) has conceptualized and written about habitus as a function of social class, less attention has been paid to incorporating race into structures that shape habitus, as well as the ways organizations such as the NOI act to shape structures that influence individuals in everyday life.

I use the notion of organizational habitus to better understand the ways in which the NOI as a religious organization transmits racial and religious ideologies to individual actors, which in the school context, work to enhance educational outcomes.[5] Race and religious orientation not only influence individual members in the NOI, but play an important role in shaping how the school acts and reacts to NOI members as well. The interaction of race and religion influences how NOI women construct their academic and social identities as well as the strategies they choose to succeed in school.

This chapter is divided into four sections. The first section explains the historical origins of the NOI's Black achievement ideology—a central component of the NOI's organizational habitus—and its relation to the formation of an oppositional social identity.[6] The second section describes the research setting and methods. The third section presents the research data and suggests that it is the ways involuntary minority group members construct their racio-ethnic identities, internalize and display an achievement ideology, and are guided by community forces that affect their performance in school. The final section illustrates the ways in which Black people differentially make sense of and enact what it means to be "Black" that challenge previous binary or dichotomized accounts of Black oppositional social identity.

THE AFRICAN-AMERICAN EXPERIENCE OF ISLAM, OPPOSITIONAL SOCIAL IDENTITY, AND THE EMERGENCE OF A BLACK ACHIEVEMENT IDEOLOGY

In America, while all Muslims may be called Muslim or refer to their religion as Islam, the experience of African-American Muslims is different from that of Muslims who were born and raised in Muslim countries or in an immigrant Muslim cultural milieu.[7]

The earliest African-American Muslim communities were in fact a reaction to racist practices, evasive actions, and exploitative relationships fostered by segregation during the Jim Crow era (Gardell, 1996). The Black social and cultural institutions and ideologies that emerged out of this social context constructed what George Lipsitz (1988) referred to as a "culture of opposition." According to Lipsitz these cultures of opposition constituted a partial refuge from the humiliation of racism, class pretensions, and low-wage work for African Americans while also allowing them to nurture collectivist values that were markedly different from the prevailing individualistic ideology of the white ruling class (Lipsitz,

1988). Ironically, then, segregation facilitated the creation and development of the NOI.

The expressed goals of the NOI are as follows: first, to gain self-determination in North America—not in Africa as preceding movements such as Garveyism or the Moorish Science temple had proposed; second, to reconstitute the Black nation by embracing blackness as an ideal (according to the NOI, the Black man is the original man and all Black people are members of the NOI whether they are conscious of it or not); third, to gain collective economic independence through individual achievement (Lincoln, 1973). These goals, in conjunction with the belief that a Black man variously named W.D. Fard or W.F. Muhammad was God in the flesh, and that the Honorable Elijah Muhammad was his prophet, are some of the essential elements which constitute the NOI's Black achievement ideology (see Table 9.1).

Utilizing this dialectical understanding of White power and Black resistance suggests that the NOI's Black achievement ideology offers a set of cultural tools that provides strategies for educational and economic mobility in the context of historical discrimination and group disadvantage. The NOI's Black achievement ideology is not a whole culture, but rather a set of cultural elements relevant to the problems of educational and economic mobility in the face of instrumental discrimination (e.g., in employment and wages), relational discrimination (such as social and residential segregation), and symbolic discrimination (e.g., denigration of the minority culture and language) (Massey & Denton, 1993).

Within the NOI, the Black achievement ideology often co-exists with an oppositional social identity. Members of the NOI are often familiar with each, and the relative influence of both is dependent upon social context as well as individual factors such as personality or school or work trajectories. Thus, even though oppositional social identity might seem antithetical to the NOI's Black achievement ideology, historically the two have emerged in tandem, as dual responses to conditions of racism and group discrimination.

In short, rigid morals, self-determination, non-traditional Islam, and Black nationalism are the key elements that constitute what I refer to as the NOI's Black achievement ideology. The Black achievement ideology is a theory about the world, how and why it was created, and how human beings relate to and should act in the world (Gardell 1996). Since the Black achievement ideology (in this context) is essentially a religious construct, it provides adherents with a frame of reference that governs their interpretation and experiences in the world.

Table 9.1 Differences and similarities between achievement ideologies[1]

DIFFERENCES

Nation of Islam's Black achievement ideology	Mainstream achievement ideology
Absolute ethnic difference and race consciousness	Pluralism and color blindness
Institutional discrimination is a pervasive factor that can impede mobility	Institutional discrimination does not exist or is minimal
Visibility: loud or overt cultural nationalism	Invisibility: quiet or crypto-nationalism
Resistance to cultural assimilation via cultural preservation	Cultural assimilation
Collectivist values, community goals, informed by Islamic law and work ethic	Individual achievement, individual goals informed by Protestant work ethic[2]
Non-traditional Islam—belief that a black man variously named W.D. Fard was God in the flesh, and that the Honorable Elijah Muhammad was his prophet	Modernity—belief in Judeo-Christian or secular values

SIMILARITIES
Self-reliance, hard work, sobriety, individual effort and sacrifice

These principles are collectively termed the "achievement ideology" due to the widely shared belief that adherence to such values brings monetary reward, economic advancement, and educational mobility

---

[1] Admittedly, the Black achievement ideology and the mainstream achievement ideology as terms are rather unsatisfactory ways of naming processes of cultural mutation, yet as processes of inclusion and exclusion as well as mobility processes they are integral to identity formation and defining of community boundaries.

[2] Weber (1958) argued that "the Protestant ethic," "the inner-worldly ascetism" rationally expressed in work as a calling, resulted in the creation of "the spirit of capitalism." A similar process can be discerned in the NOI's version of the Protestant work ethic, which because of its ban on wastefulness and demands for hard work, has resulted in the formation of an economic empire with assets estimated to be as much as $80,000,000 (Mamiya, 1983, p. 245).

RESEARCH METHODOLOGY

Despite the fact that Islam is well on its way to surpassing Judaism as the second largest religion in the United States—dwarfing Protestant denominations such as the Episcopal church—qualitative research is rare (Gardell, 1996).[8] Studies on the NOI, with some notable exceptions, have been mainly based on secondary sources, due in part to the unwillingness of the NOI to be the object of inquiry.[9] The present study, which is based on participant observation, field notes, and recorded interviews, began in September 1996 and ended in August 1998.

During that time I—a young Black, non-Muslim, male—conducted an ethnographic study of Eastern High (a pseudonym), an urban high school located in a predominantly African-American neighborhood in West Philadelphia. The social fabric of Eastern High, including demographics (98 percent Black), attendance, suspension rates, drop-out rates, poverty levels, and test scores—parallel other comprehensive high schools suffering from deindustrialization, resegregation, and the transition to a postindustrial economy. For example, in 1995–1996, the Average Daily Attendance at Eastern (total population 1,700) was 76 percent, while 40 percent of the student body was suspended at least once, and roughly 40 percent–50 percent of the ninth-graders who entered in the fall of 1990–1991 failed to graduate four years later. As an indication of students' economic status, 86 percent of the student population attending Eastern did so from low-income families or families on Aid to Family with Dependent Children (AFDC).

When I first began collecting data, the goal was to examine the relationship between Black students' self-perceptions, aspirations, and low academic achievement.[10] However, after two years of fieldwork, extensive participant observation, and intensive interviews with students ($n = 50$), teachers ($n = 10$), administrators ($n = 2$), and community members ($n = 6$), what emerged was not a group of low-achieving Black students. Instead student, teacher, and administrative interviews coupled with participant observation directed my attention to a group of high-achieving Black students with a history of disciplinary problems and resisting school authority.[11] By high-achieving students, I mean those who were in good academic standing with at least a B grade point average, were on schedule to graduate in four years, were college eligible, and were not in danger of dropping out. These students, according to student and staff interviews, had developed an interesting set of strategies for maintaining academic, racial, and cultural identities at school, while simultaneously resisting schooling and societal practices that they viewed at odds with their religious tenets and practices.

Clusters of interviews with these students, all American-born women who had converted to the NOI, became the basis for the utilization of the extended case method, which ascertains a social phenomenon by looking at what is "interesting" and "surprising" in a particular social situation (Burawoy, Burton, Ferguson, & Fox, 1991).[12] Consequently, from an initial group of three 11th-grade female students, snowball sampling based on mutual associations produced three more 11th-grade students and one 10th-grade female student.[13] All seven primary study participants came from low-income families in which no parent held an advanced degree.[14] Additionally, all of the primary informants in the study self-identified as Black.

In order to test whether the general cultural norm of peer sanctioning for high achievement was prevalent among women in the NOI, I conducted intensive, in-depth life history interviews and focus groups with these students. I ended up with an average of three or four interviews per week that became the basis for detailed case studies, whereby every attempt was made to understand the women in terms of their entire network of social relations and socioeconomic circumstances that were possibly influencing their orientation to school and achievement.

As my field notes and interviews began to accumulate, analyses of issues and themes across individuals and groups became increasingly possible. It also became possible to analyze the school as an institution and, finally, to analyze the importance of the relationship between external community forces and academic achievement for the seven primary informants.[15]

The advantage of focusing on a small number of participants lies in the detail and richness of the data gathered. Although the small sample size may limit generalization of the results, my findings are consistent with those of recent related research on school success and ethnic identity cited here. Most interviews took place at school. However, informal discussions and conversations took place in lunchrooms, hallways, or outside of the temple. Most interviews were tape-recorded. School records, school reports, and other school documents complemented the observations, interviews, and focus groups.

Despite the fact that the research described herein focuses on the experiences of seven young Black women, gender is not a major focus of the analysis. To be sure, gender has been shown to influence students' school experience and social identities (Collins, 1990). However in this chapter, gender is addressed only to the extent that the primary participants are all women. As a result, my findings may not reflect similar individual and organizational interactions experienced by boys in similar settings.

The Setting and Establishing Rapport

I attended Eastern High three to five days a week to assess how school culture and climate influenced participants in everyday life. Given my daily presence and constant interaction I established good rapport with the participants. However, like many other qualitative-oriented researchers, I view the research act as one that is far from value free (Denzin & Lincoln, 1994). Part of the research endeavor is the process of making meaning and not just observing but shaping, interpreting, and framing the research process. Like Peshkin (1988), I view my subjectivity as "a garment that cannot be removed" (p. 17). Consequently, rather than ignoring my own subjectivity, I engaged in a formal systematic monitoring of self throughout the course of the data collection which enabled me to monitor my personal and professional growth and evolution in the research process.

To this end, I wrote self-reflective memos, shared the manuscripts of analyzed data with study participants, and discussed emerging themes with colleagues familiar with the project.

Moreover, I believe that my background shaped my role as a researcher. I am a Black male in my late twenties who grew up in Pennsylvania about two hours from the area where this research was conducted. Socioeconomically, I grew up in a single-parent, female-headed household, as did all of the primary participants. Additionally, my adolescent schooling experiences were entirely within public institutions.

Given my background as a young, Black, non-Muslim male, I am often asked how I was able to establish rapport with the young women in this study and how was I certain that I was able to adequately appreciate the standpoint from and context within which they lived. My ability to establish rapport was greatly enhanced by sharing the same race with the primary participants.[16] In other words, despite the fact that in all cases there were gender differences—and to a lesser extent class differences given my mother's advanced education—to overcome in establishing a connection with each student, race was always the same. Consequently, our commonness as "Blacks" committed to community development and nation building provided the bridge that we needed to connect with one another, while other shared experiences (parents' divorce, the universal traits of adolescence, or shared hobbies) served as additional reference points.[17]

Rapport was evidenced by displays of affection from the primary participants (friendly greetings), the sharing of personal confidences, and the open expression of trust (many participants called me to ask about college preparation). Moreover, I was able to interact informally with the primary participants while observing them at the school. Often these informal interactions served as "icebreakers" prior to the interviews.

However, my findings must not be viewed as some objective representation of the "truth" about the social world of the NOI or of Eastern High. Rather, my findings are my most accurate representation of the perspectives that were gathered during this study.

BECOMING A MEMBER OF THE NOI: DEVELOPING A POSITIVE, DUAL FRAME OF REFERENCE

The NOI is an extremely hierarchical organization. In order to transform raw recruits into NOI members, young Muslim brothers visit jails and penitentiaries, pool halls and barbershops, college campuses and street corners. The goal of this proselytizing is to "restore black people in America to their original industrial and commercial greatness so that

African Americans can become self-sufficient in the production of food, clothing, shelter, health care, education, and employment" (Gardell, 1996, p. 319).

The NOI's recruitment efforts have been particularly successful with respect to incarcerated criminals and drug addicts. Their record of rehabilitating former convicts and addicts has been acknowledged by social workers and documented by scholars and journalists alike (Lincoln, 1973, p. 84).[18] Additionally, true to its ideology of "do for self," the NOI rejects the American welfare system. Though not condemning Americans who live on welfare, the present leader of the NOI, Minister Louis Farrakhan Muhammad (1991), warns of the system's consequences: "Welfare if you turn it around means farewell. It means bye to the spirit of self-determination. It means so long to the spirit that God gives to every human being to do something for self. It makes you a slave. Welfare, farewell." (Quoted in Gardell, 1996.)

Discussions with NOI women about their life experiences prior to joining the NOI show how conversion not only introduces new sets of beliefs, but more fundamentally entails the displacement of one universe or discourse by another (Snow & Machalek, 1984).[19] The following interviews with Latasha and Erikka demonstrate the ways in which acculturation into the NOI positively influences racial identity, educational aspirations, and a desire to uplift the Black community:

> LATASHA: Once I joined the NOI I started getting a real education . . . a Black education . . . an education that made me see the truth about me and my history . . . and that made me see who I really was . . . a Black queen . . . Now I love my Black skin . . . not that I didn't before . . . but I don't think I was aware before like I am now of what it means to be Black . . . we have a great history . . . that's way different than the white lies that white people tell . . . and now I feel more responsible and proud to be what I am and I work harder in school because I know I have to put Islam and submission to the Will of Allah first in everything I do . . . and that gives me power . . . lots of power . . . I feel powerful like nothin' can hold me back from gettin' my goal of goin' to college and raisin' a family . . .

These students also assert that not only did their mind set change after joining the NOI, but also their behavior.

> ERIKKA: Before joining the NOI I didn't do well in school . . . I wasn't focused . . . I was unsure of myself . . . but the Messenger teaches us that you have to take responsibility for your own success . . . He teaches us that no individual in the Nation stands alone

because we are one Nation . . . The last independent Nation on earth . . . I mean a real Nation within a nation . . . with our own flag, laws, rules and stuff . . . And with all these strong Black people behind me . . . I feel like I can do whatever it is that needs to get done . . .

AA: But . . . what is it that you're trying to accomplish? What are your personal goals?

ERIKKA: Well . . . I know for sure I want to graduate from high school . . . go to college . . . and get a good job . . .

AA: And has the Nation helped you in accomplishing these goals?

ERIKKA: Yea . . . Like I just said . . . before I joined the Nation I wasn't doing that well in school . . . Studying was hard for me . . . cause no matter how hard I studied I still got bad grades . . . And then when I joined the Nation this sister took me by the hand and taught me how to study . . .

AA: What do you mean how to study?

ERIKKA: You see now when I sit down to read something . . . I got a system . . . I get my notebook out . . . I get my dictionary . . . and sit and really read . . . you know . . . not just memorize the words . . . but really try to understand what their trying to say to me . . . And then I write out questions . . . just so I can really figure out if what they're saying is true . . . and if it really makes sense . . . What I'm saying is . . . not only did sister Muhammad [the sister who pulled her aside] teach me how to study . . . but she made me believe that I was smart . . . I went from studying once or twice a week to five or six hours a day . . .

By marking their members as part of a special group, and providing them with a black achievement ideology as well as a visible means of support, the NOI fosters the development of new social and academic identities. An important component in the conversion process is the development of a dual frame of reference. Women in the NOI, although not voluntary immigrants, acquire a dual frame of reference that works in a similar manner as it does for non-U.S.-born immigrants. That is, instead of correlating being Black with underachievement or with the social pathologies often ascribed to Black American youth and other U.S. minorities, women in the NOI use previous economic and political oppression, as well as religious socialization, as a catalyst to make present sacrifices in the United States more tolerable. Safiya's description of her pre-conversion attitudes and behaviors serves to illustrate this point:

Before I joined the NOI I was all wrong . . . I smoked weed a lot . . . I hung out with the wrong people . . . didn't do well in school . . . basically I was like a lot of these other [Black] students who don't even like themselves or their own people . . . and with me you could tell I was all wrong because I would fight for mines . . . or talk about other people . . . I've even watched fools get killed . . . It's like slaves of the past gonna be slaves of the future unless you make a change . . . but we're taught (at the NOI) the other way around . . . it's foolish not to love yo' self and yo' people . . . especially if you want to get anywhere . . . you have to love yo' self and work hard . . .

Aisha, who before "was about relaxin," reports:

Before I joined two years ago I used to kick it all the time and watch music videos . . . now I organize meetings . . . go to study group . . . I don't even watch t.v . . . . I do fund raisin' . . . bake sales and stuff . . . I speak Arabic . . . I eat right . . . I read more . . . I am more focused . . . I think . . . I think about the world in a different way . . . . I feel more awake . . . more conscious . . . like I'm tryin' to liberate myself and my people . . . I wasn't about that before . . .

A teacher who knew Aisha before she joined the NOI commented:

TEACHER: When I first met her I didn't think she was going to make it at this school . . . knowing where she grew up and the type of neighborhood she comes from and who her friends were . . . but she is a totally different person now . . . and I suppose a lot of students change at this age . . . but you rarely see kids change from bad behavior to good behavior so dramatically . . . Not the way that Aisha did . . .

AA: And what do you think accounted for the change?:

TEACHER: What jumps out at me are her religious beliefs . . . I think they had a lot to do with it . . . It's like she took on a different culture . . . so now she's a different person . . . she dresses different . . . acts totally different . . . hangs out with different people . . . so in my opinion her conversion to Islam had a lot to do with her improvement in school . . . not just educationally . . . but socially and emotionally . . .

To seal the conversion or personal rebirth, women in the NOI first had to cast off their old selves and take on a new identity. This involved changing their names, their religion, their language, style of dress, their moral and cultural values, their very purpose in living. To commemorate their rebirth, converts drop their last name and become known simply by their first name and the last name of Muhammed.[20]

For women in the NOI, changing one's name was important because it signaled a change in social networks, conversion of their identities, as well as collective ownership and formal membership in the organization. Conversion also has a strong effect on the women's educational aspirations and performance in school.

TRANSFORMING THE "BURDEN OF ACTING WHITE" INTO THE "HONOR OF BEING BLACK"

Women in the NOI present a special challenge to the "burden of acting White" thesis proposed by Fordham and Ogbu (1986). More specifically, the organizational habitus of the NOI has inverted the cultural construct of "acting White" so that instead of associating it with positive educational outcomes (i.e., academic achievement) and potentially negative cultural outcomes (disassociation from Black cultural forms), the NOI associates "acting White" with negative attitudes and behaviors that do not conform to uplifting Black individuals or the black community. Conversely, the NOI associates "being Black" with positive educational and cultural outcomes. In this manner, by changing a community's interpretation of both itself and its history, and redefining morality and acceptable social behavior, the NOI has been able to systematically create an organizational habitus which encourages black achievement for its members, resulting in the transformation of the "burden of acting White" into the "honor of being Black."

The following interviews illustrate this point.

> AA: What does acting white mean to you?
> ERIKKA: ... To me actin' white means getting' by the easy way ... like takin' things that don't belong to you ... or cheatin' ... or not workin' hard ... but actin' like you somethin' you're not ... like actin' like you don't want to be black ... that's what actin' white means to me ... actin' fake ...

Safiya expressed a similar view:

> I would say lookin' down on poor people ... or you kno' ... people who ain't doin' too good.... that's what actin' white means to me ... and I see lots of kids in this school actin' a fool ... like white people got a hold of their minds ... and those are the kids who I try to talk to ... so I can shake 'em up ... 'Cause they're ain't nothin' wrong with being poor ...

One member, Rochelle, spoke of elements of Hip Hop music as "acting White." According to Rochelle:

> I think a lot of hip hop music is actin' White . . . I know that sounds funny
> . . . but I think it is . . . A lot of these so-called artists be fillin' our heads
> with garbage and filth . . . and to me . . . that's just another way to keep
> the White man on top . . . just another form of White supremacy . . .
> another way White people got Black people miseducatin' each other.

When I asked Rochelle to describe for me what she thinks of when she
thinks of Black culture, she responded by saying:

> When I think of black culture . . . I think about how great we are . . .
> how we are really the chosen people . . . Black gods in a lost world . . .
> the creators of all science, wisdom, and history. . . . That's what we
> learn at the temple . . . and that's what I think about. . . . I think about
> how just 'cause you see Black people perpetuatin' ignorance . . . don't
> mean you have to act ignorant . . . and just cause you see ignorance
> that ain't Black culture. . . .

The notion of Black greatness and entitlement is central to understanding
the organizational habitus of the NOI. The following field notes from a
local temple the young women regularly attend illustrates how the
NOI combines Black and religious nationalism in a way that prioritizes
the imagined community of the NOI over other racial and ethnic
communities.

> MINISTER: Black people you have been brainwashed into thinking that
> this country doesn't owe you anything . . . But I ask you . . . Have we
> put our blood, sweat, and tears, into this country?
> CONGREGATION: Yes Sir.
> MINISTER: Have our women broken their backs for the white man?
> Cooked his meals . . . raised his children . . . And taken out his trash?
> CONGREGATION: Yes Sir.
> MINISTER (voice strong and proud): White people don't think we deserve
> what we deserve . . . And after all we've done for this country . . .
> They still don't want to treat us right . . . But I say don't let 'em
> brainwash you . . . don't let 'em trick you into not gettin' what
> you deserve. If you're going to college and there is only a handful
> of scholarships for us black folks . . . you are entitled to those
> scholarships . . . If you are going for a job and there are only a
> handful of jobs for us black folks . . . You are entitled to those
> jobs . . . But don't stop there . . . cause you black Kings and
> Queens . . . divine creators of the universe and you don't have to
> beg the white man for anything . . . You have to learn to do for
> yourself . . .
> CONGREGATION (with vigor): Yes sir.

MINISTER: How else are we going to build a better future for our nation and our children . . . How else are we gonna build a nation unless we have a strong black family . . . We need to have our own economic institutions . . . We already have our own companies . . . we've built our own industries . . . We own this building . . . This land that I am standing on . . . We own ourselves . . . And that's why we don't need the white man . . . because we are independent . . . Isn't that right?

CONGREGATION: Yes sir.

In group interviews, all seven women spoke of how these aspects of NOI creed are drilled into them. Kesha explained that once she joined she could no longer "flirt with boys anymore or go out dancin' and actin all crazy." While Tiffany and Latasha discussed how countless times they have been told that, "Black people are supreme," and that "Black people are the original people," or, "How important it is to avoid drugs and alcohol to keep the mind and the body clean." Latasha added that, "Once I really believed this I knew nothin' could stop me from achievin' my goals." The goal of this form of indoctrination is to get converts to adopt a new frame of reference that restructures his or her perception and "sense of ultimate grounding" (Heinrich, 1977, p. 673).

These field notes and interviews illustrate the ways in which the organizational habitus of the NOI has inverted the racial code that equates "acting White" with school success and instead equates the notion with historical, psychological, institutional, and subjective levels of oppression. In this manner, NOI women not only demonstrate the heterogeneity of the African-American experience, but also illustrate the ways in which Black people differentially make sense of and enact what it means to be Black that challenge dichotomized or binary accounts of how Black cultural identity is implicated in the underperformance of African-American youth.

ATTITUDES TOWARDS THE NOI'S RESISTANCE AND ACADEMIC PERFORMANCE

Although the seven women in this study possessed strong opinions about "acting White," there was no animosity toward them for doing well in school. They were not singled out or harassed because of their academic accomplishments. They were not labeled, ostracized, or physically assaulted for doing well in school, as Fordham and Ogbu (1986) reported occurs among African-American high achievers. Yet, the high achievers in the NOI were not simply seen as another group among the few high achievers at the school. Rather, interviews with students and teachers revealed that although women in the NOI enjoyed high social and academic standing, they also had a reputation for being disruptive and argumentative.

NOI Women as Strong Academic Performers

NOI women were seen as high academic achievers. The following excerpts taken from group and individual interviews with non-NOI students demonstrates the extent to which NOI members were viewed as strong academic performers by their peers: "Them Islamic heads are serious people ... I always see them studyin'." Another student said, "They work hard ... that's why I think people respect them ... 'cause they're serious about their buziness ... they're the hardest working students at this school."

In terms of demonstrating help-seeking behavior one student commented:

> They help me out ... I ask them for help because they really know what they're doin ... they help me get better grades because they take studyin' seriously and they're just down for black people ... They ain't afraid to say the truth ... that's what I like about them ... they'll tell anybody to their face what time it is.

Teachers had similar responses to NOI women. They reported that when they saw NOI students arriving to class on time, taking notes in class, and turning assignments in on time, it indicated to them that NOI students had a strong desire to excel in school. In ten interviews with teachers, seven specifically identified NOI women as strong academic performers:

> TEACHER: Sometimes they dominate class discussion ... but that's because they want to be the best they can be ... and I admire that ... I also think that other kids can learn from it ... look at the example they're setting ... come to class on time, study hard, be prepared, and get good grades ... They're almost perfect students ... but I'm not saying I agree with everything they do or stand for .... There are some things about them that I don't respect ...
>
> AA: For instance?
>
> TEACHER: Their religion ...

Another teacher added:

> I think they get more attention than the other kids because of the way they dress ... Both good and bad. ... But overall they complete all of

their assignments on time and bring a critical perspective into the class room . . . In fact, they're frequently the ones who challenge students on topics we're discussing in class or their personal beliefs . . . Sometimes that can become a disruption though . . . Cause they don't know when enough is enough . . . And they kind of have an arrogance about them . . . like a gang mentality . . . maybe it comes from them studying together or just hanging out . . . but if you mess with one you're messing with them all . . . For the most part, though, they're good kids . . . not angels . . . but good kids . . .

Studying Together

NOI women were not solitary learners. Instead they formed academic communities composed of other NOI women who shared a common purpose. The following teacher interview illustrates this point:

> TEACHER: . . . I offer my classroom for anybody to come [after school] . . . and often times it is only the NOI girls who come into the study hall . . . They study hard . . . they ask each other questions and help each other with their homework. . . . They're definitely good at working together . . . and I think that's why they . . . at least the students who attend my study hall . . . do well in school.
> AA: How do you know they do well in school?
> TEACHER: I saw a couple of their names on the honor roll . . .

NOI women participated in formal and informal study groups where they would ask each other questions, critique each other's work, and assist one another with homework problems. Their collaboration was guided by the NOI's formal study group sessions that emphasize a merger rather than a separation of academic and social identities (Treisman, 1985). The following field note illustrates how the NOI's formal study group sessions systematically taught NOI students to form academic communities whereby their social and academic identities could begin to merge:

> One evening . . . around 7 o'clock . . . I went to an NOI study group held at a local temple . . . as I joined the group . . . . brotha Muhammad (the study group instructor) briefly explained to me general tips for note taking . . . he stressed compiling main ideas and generating dissenting views in order to help potential members such as myself ascertain "the truth." He also gave general instructions about how to sit and behave . . . Here he placed emphasis on sitting up right and erect . . . respecting one another . . . and helping each other's moral and spiritual development . . . Lastly . . . before I joined the group . . . he expressed the importance of keeping this notebook and the

accompanying strategies in which he just shared at all times . . . He said
"being consciously reflective would help me grow and develop as a
man." At the end of study group . . . students broke into two small
groups . . . One group practiced vocabulary words and analogies "the
kinds of problems that individuals may encounter in rhetorical
debate," said brotha Muhammad . . . and another group practiced math
. . . In this group one of the members explained that he could teach us
better "math tricks than the white students use in their schools . . .,"
and emphasized that, "it was important for us to study together
so that we can have each other's backs in a world full of white
duplicitousness and deceit . . .".

I attended many other study groups like the one above and each time
a number of supplementary educational activities were emphasized:
writing, inquiry, collaboration, role modeling/mentoring, and career-
exploration.[21] In this manner, by encouraging the utilization of academic
techniques in their religious indoctrination, the NOI is giving explicit
instruction in the invisible culture of the school. In other words, the NOI
teaches explicitly in the temple what middle-income students learn
implicitly at home. Bourdieu (1986) labels the invisible culture the NOI
teaches its pupils as cultural capital. The organizational habitus of the
NOI gives low-income individuals some of the cultural capital in the
temple that is similar to the cultural capital that more economically
advantaged parents give to their children at home (Bourdieu, 1986).

NOI Women as Bearers of High Expectations in the Midst of a Dysfunctional School

At Eastern High, NOI women were strong achievers in the midst of a
dysfunctional school.[22] As evidence I observed teachers not only allowing, but also encouraging, students to watch the Jerry Springer show on a
daily basis. The following field notes highlight the low level of student
expectations and meager instructional delivery and support at Eastern
High, as well as the ways in which NOI women responded to this dysfunctional educational environment:

One morning in October I went to observe a Spanish class . . . Two
students in the NOI were the first people to arrive . . . the teacher
arrived 15 minutes late . . . The two students in the NOI were among
seven students who actually stayed . . . and around 10 more students
actually showed up but left . . . When the regular teacher finally arrived
the teacher promptly put in a Jerry Springer tape in English . . . not as
an educational exercise, but as a way to "kill time and make sure students' behaved." The two students in the NOI were the only students

to ask the teacher for a homework assignment and to sit in the back of the class and complete their work . . . all of the other students either listened to Walkmans, played cards, or left . . . This teacher practices this sort of instructional neglect and blatant disregard for the teaching standards two to three times a week.

In other classrooms I observed similar practices of institutional and instructional neglect:

On a mid morning in November I was observing a health class . . . two NOI women were in the class [a different two students than above] . . . again the teacher as well as the instructional assistants arrived late . . . besides handing out some below grade level handouts . . . the main instructional activity was to turn on a "boom box," place it in front of the classroom, and abandon students to "educate" themselves for the entire period. Again these teachers practice this sort of instructional neglect and blatant disregard for the teaching standards daily. Women in the NOI initially respond by complaining directly to the teacher about the lack of "real education" offered at the school . . . However, by the end of the month NOI members had resorted to skipping the class altogether . . . Instead of going to class . . . they began to go to the library or into the hallway to do their homework and study for other classes . . .

Women in the NOI not only voiced the power of their own agency, their statements about advanced placement courses also displayed a critical awareness of structural inequality:

TIFFANY: We don't even have any Advanced courses at this school . . . And we have been the ones askin' for them . . . Like almost beggin' . . . How do you expect us to go to college if we don't have the same chance to learn . . .

While many students at Eastern acquired "ritual competency," as Goffman (1959) termed it, by putting their heads down, listening to Walkmans, sleeping in class, reading magazines, practical joking, and for many becoming part of the "drop-out rate"—which Michelle Fine (1991) more accurately described as the "push-out" rate—NOI students did not. Instead I encountered a set of institutional arrangements in which NOI women developed a different ideology and adopted a different course of action than has been described by previous research. More specifically, the NOI provided highly valuable forms of academic and social support by connecting these seven women (and other members) to an organizational collectivity committed to helping them achieve.

Resistance as Oppositional Behavior

NOI women expressed a belief in their own efficacy to improve their lives and to uplift the Black community. They translated this belief into action by actively participating in classroom discussions, as well as resisting school practices that they viewed at odds with their religious tenets and practices.

The following field note illustrates one of the ways in which cultural differences between NOI students and school authorities became politically charged and created conflict:

> On a Tuesday morning . . . in mid March . . . around ten o'clock . . . I went to observe an American History class . . . in the midst of distributing a written quiz . . . the teacher made the following statements: "You know I don't trust any of you . . . All students will cheat if they get a chance . . . and I'm paranoid . . . because I don't trust any of you in this classroom . . ."
>
> Immediately three female students in the NOI protested (Tiffany, Safiya, and Latasha) . . . Tiffany led off by saying that she was "very insulted, and unless she received an apology wouldn't take the quiz." Safiya said that "her religion doesn't permit her to cheat . . . cheating is for white people." And Latasha followed by stating succinctly: "You ain't no teacher to me . . . cause you act like a white lady (the teacher was black) . . . You don't teach us nothin' that's gonna make us smart . . . You just give us the same book to read over and over again . . . and then you be actin' all paranoid and everthin' . . . we don't even need to cheat . . . mumble . . . mumble . . . and white people ain't shit."
>
> The teacher responded in a voice full of authority: "I am the teacher . . . and you are not allowed to talk to me like that in this classroom . . . do you understand me young lady . . . I don't care if you think that you are holier than thou . . . wearin' that stuff on your head . . . I don't give a damn . . . you can't talk to me like that." Safiya responded, "But this is a democracy ain't it . . . don't we have freedom of speech . . . don't we?" Teacher: "Well you're right and wrong young lady . . . cause you see . . . I teach about democracy . . . but that doesn't mean I run my class that way." Tiffany chimed in, "but who is runnin' this class . . . cause you sure as hell aren't."
>
> As the quiz continued . . . three students were caught cheating . . . However, none were members of the NOI . . . The overt resistance by the NOI students was acknowledged by the teacher: "I respect those girls . . . everybody does . . . but what I don't like is they think they know everything . . . When really they're the ones who are always causing problems . . . I mean they think cause they dress funny they can

accuse people of not being black enough . . . who do they think they are . . . they don't know what I've been through . . . that's like the pot callin' the kettle black."

Many educational researchers have found that African-American students often protect their pride as Black students by adopting anti-school behaviors (Erickson, 1987). However, NOI students did not respond in this manner. Their actions and belief statements were not conformist, assimilationist, or regressive. Rather, to handle the complexities that they encountered, they adopted an instrumental view of education (as the means to an end), yet were highly critical of their school, teachers, and peers. In other words, unlike Willis's lads' who were blind to the connection between schooling and mobility, or MacLeod's (1987/1991) "Hallway Hangers" or Foley's (1990) "vatos," who withdraw from academic pursuits, act up in class, ignore homework and cut classes—and unlike Ogbu's involuntary minorities who tend to equate schooling with assimilation into the dominant group, and thus do not try to achieve academically—members of the NOI resisted the cultural and linguistic patterns of the majority culture, yet embraced educational achievement.[23]

As a result, NOI women's response to schooling may be considered transformative rather than merely reproductive, because the agency the students display comes from a unique form of religious socialization which produces a social consciousness whereby students are encouraged to politicize their cultural resistance and develop counter-ideologies, while assessing the costs and benefits of not playing the game. In this manner, by utilizing a Black achievement ideology, women in the NOI avoid what Ogbu (1991) referred to as the victim contributing to their own victimization by transforming rather than reproducing educational outcomes commonly associated with oppositional identity and resistance for African Americans.

Another cultural incongruity between NOI women and the school was the lack of opportunity to practice their faith in accordance with Islamic principles. Generally speaking, Black Muslims are required to pray five times a day, an obligation that does not cease on school days. Prayer times vary in accordance with sunrise and sunset, and early and late prayers usually do not conflict with the school day. However, the midday and mid-afternoon prayers did present problems for all seven women interviewed, as did rituals of absolution which are required before each prayer. The following interviews with Safiya and Kesha highlight the ways in which NOI women resisted schooling practices that they viewed at odds with their religious tenets while maintaining a strong orientation to academic achievement.

AA: Is it difficult to find prayer time at school?

SAFIYA: Yes . . . whenever I have to pray I either ask to go to the bath-
room . . . or just skip out of class all together . . .

AA: So does that mean that you skip school everyday?

SAFIYA: Yeah . . . but I make up for it in the study group that we have at
the temple every week . . .

KESHA: This school don't respect our beliefs . . . so sometimes we have
no choice but to break the rules . . . but I ain't gonna let that stop
me from getting to college . . . or from doin' what I'm supposed to
be doin' in school . . . I'll do whatever it takes to keep up . . . I don't
mind workin' hard . . . but I'm a black Muslim first . . . before I'm
anything else . . .

Members of the NOI not only withdrew from classes due to prayer, but
also because of unacceptable or offensive curricula. Tiffany stated this
point succinctly:

All I kno' is in history class all they teach about is White people . . . we
don't learn nothin' about Black history or Black achievements . . . and
even when we do it is like a little tiny bit of class time . . . but when we
learn about white people it goes on and on and on . . . for weeks . . .
That's why other kids listen to me . . . cause they kno' that I kno' about
black history . . .

Tiffany added:

People don't respect our religion around here . . . They don't care
if we pray or where we pray . . . they don't care what we eat . . . and
they don't honor how we dress or our need to fast . . . But I guarantee
you if it's a white holiday they're gonna celebrate it . . . Why do you
think that is? It's cause we don't believe in a white God that's why
. . . that's why they treat us bad even though we're good honest
people . . .

These interviews and field notes illustrate that at Eastern High a simple
dichotomy between "resistance" and "conformity" overlooks the complexity of student behaviors and responses. More specifically, women in
the NOI demonstrate that accommodation is not the only path to success
in school, nor does opposition necessarily lead to failure. Rather, NOI
students resisted what they perceived as acts of oppression within the
school, while at the same time pursuing strategies that enabled them to
be academically successful. By combining strategies attributed to recent
United States immigrants with a black achievement ideology, women in
the NOI displayed a unique mobility strategy usually not expressed by

low-income African-American youth or other involuntary minority groups (Gibson, 1997). Adding these complexities to notions of resistance suggests that we reexamine the relationship linking resistance with failure and accommodation with success (Lee, M., 1996), because in women in the NOI we find both qualities exhibited by the same students.

CONCLUSION: FROM ANALYSIS TO RECONSTRUCTION OF THEORY

This chapter charts a theory of Black educational achievement. It does so by challenging the work of Ogbu (and others) by examining which claims have held up, need to be complicated, or should be reconstructed. I begin by illustrating how a group's original terms of incorporation, while significant, are one of a number of different variables that shape the school-adaptation patterns for an involuntary minority group. Academic engagement depends not only on historical, political, and economic realities facing students, but also on day-to-day experiences in school, in the community, and in what John L. Jackson (2001) referred to as the performative dimension of race, that is, how specific cultural practices are used to constitute racial identity. In the case of the NOI, their Black achievement ideology is intentionally organized in opposition to the ideology of white supremacy, and as such, counters folk theories concerning Black intellectual inferiority—contributing to a culture of academic achievement.

The NOI's ability to create a Black achievement ideology suggests that we reconstruct Ogbu's typology that categorizes separate and distinct ideologies for voluntary and involuntary immigrant groups (see Figure 9.1 in the Appendix). Women in the NOI do not fit this typology. While NOI women describe a system that is not sympathetic toward Blacks in general, and Islamic women in particular, they maintain that it is possible to better themselves, their sub-cultural community, and society at large, by being disciplined, avoiding drugs and other vices, practicing ethical integrity, and working hard.

The NOI's Black achievement ideology, which is simultaneously culturally and academically affirming, further complicates the traditional relationship between academic achievement, socio-economic status, and educational success. Women in the NOI understand the importance of developing culturally appropriate social behavior, academic skills, and achieving academically. At the same time, due to the fact that they practice Islam in a non-Islamic setting, they also represent a challenge to common sense notions of what are (or are not) the culturally appropriate norms, attitudes, and behaviors.

The NOI's Black achievement ideology also problematizes the "burden of acting White" thesis because NOI women have transformed the "burden of acting White" into the "honor of being Black." In this manner, NOI women demonstrate the heterogeneity of the African-American experience.

Previous research has assumed a binary or dichotomous pattern of cultural orientation for low-income students such as those in the NOI—one in which individuals are either accommodating or resisting, succeeding or failing, involuntary or voluntary. However, my research documents how innovation occurs precisely because NOI women simultaneously engaged in: 1. structural assimilation (promoting traditional values such as hard work); 2. separation (affirming their own racial and cultural identities); and 3. resistance (problematizing key tenets of the achievement ideology by not conforming or assimilating to school rules or social etiquette) while, at the same time, understanding the importance of academic achievement.

As a result, NOI women provide fertile ground for reinterpreting popular notions of resistance which suggest that working-class students get working-class jobs because they refuse to develop skills, attitudes, manners, and speech that are necessary for achievement in a capitalist society. My research contradicts key aspects of resistance theory by documenting how resistance for women in the NOI is transformative, rather than merely reproductive of existing patterns of social relations. NOI women's response to schooling may be considered transformative rather than reproductive because they utilize a Black achievement ideology and a dual frame of reference to produce positive educational and social outcomes—and achieve working-class mobility. Paul Willis (1977) in particular, and resistance theory in general, tend to understate the role of race, immigrant status, community forces, and power relations in the production of educational achievement, and as a result, do not adequately account for nuances in variations of achievement among involuntary minority groups.

However, focusing on the NOI does not mean that I am placing the onus of educational success squarely within the minority communities themselves and leaving the educational system exempt from responsibility. Rather, by extending the Bourdieuian theoretical framework I have attempted to reveal how individual actors' lives are influenced by an organizational habitus that is rooted in racial and religious distinctions and how oftentimes the concept of oppositionality originates in and is nurtured by schools themselves.

In sum, this research suggests that *guided* cultural and social resources within an ethnic community, regardless of voluntary or involuntary status, increases the chance for educational success and increases the likelihood that youth will not deviate from paths of mobility. In other words, the best course for many youths is to remain securely anchored in their ethnic communities while pursuing a strategy of selective acculturation or segmented assimilation. However, this research differs from previous research on selective accommodation or segmented assimilation by documenting the ways in which *involuntary* minority students can be academically successful without being conformists and without rejecting their racio-ethnicity.

Consequently, if we extend the case of the NOI we can make the following predictions about the kind of environments that are likely to promote academic achievement among African-American youth: (a) African Americans will achieve in school environments that create cultures of achievement extended to all members with a strong sense of group ownership where high expectations are explicitly and regularly communicated in public and group settings; (b) African Americans can achieve in these environments regardless of class backgrounds and prior levels of preparation; (c) regular and rigorous academic support services must be available to ensure that all students are able to achieve; and (d) deliberate socialization is important so that all students develop practices, beliefs, behaviors, and values that support cultures of achievement (Perry, Steele and Hillard, 2003). Obviously, further research is needed to uncover the extent to which the case of the NOI is generalizable, as well as to determine the extent to which school racial composition, gender, grade level, and other socio-economic factors affect school-related behavior and attitudes among black students in general, and NOI students in particular. Hopefully, this work will stimulate other researchers to address similar questions. I expect that with time some of what is presented here will be superseded by knowledge generated by better research. I theorize that there are other achievement ideologies that exist, and that society, social science, and the media will benefit from the illumination of their complexity.

APPENDIX

Table 9.2 Interview data summary

Name	Grade	Highest parental/ guardian level of education	Mother or grandmother's occupation	Family structure
AISHA	11th	H.S. Dropout	Dishwasher	Single parent Resides with mother No siblings
ERIKKA	11th	H.S. Diploma	Elderly care provider	Parents separated Resides with mother 3 siblings; one older
KESHA	11th	H.S. Diploma	Disabled	Resides with grandmother One younger sibling
LATASHA	11th	H.S. Dropout	Unemployed, living on welfare	Single parent Resides with mother 2 siblings; one older
ROCHELLE	10th	H.S. Dropout	Employed at local fast-food restaurant	Single parent Resides with mother 2 older siblings
SAFIYA	11th	H.S. Diploma	Unemployed, living on welfare	Parents separated Resides with mother One younger sibling
TIFFANY	11th	H.S. Dropout	Unemployed, living on social security	Resides with grandmother No siblings

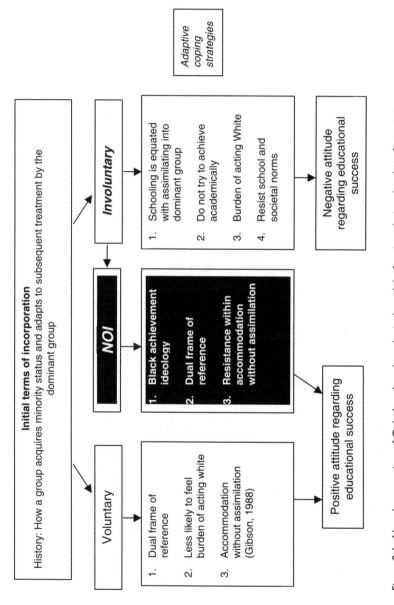

Initial terms of incorporation

History: How a group acquires minority status and adapts to subsequent treatment by the dominant group

Voluntary

1. Dual frame of reference
2. Less likely to feel burden of acting white
3. Accommodation without assimilation (Gibson, 1988)

Positive attitude regarding educational success

NOI

1. **Black achievement ideology**
2. **Dual frame of reference**
3. **Resistance within accommodation without assimilation**

Involuntary

1. Schooling is equated with assimilating into dominant group
2. Do not try to achieve academically
3. Burden of acting White
4. Resist school and societal norms

Negative attitude regarding educational success

Adaptive coping strategies

Figure 9.1 Akom's extension of Ogbu's cultural-ecological model of racio-ethnic school performance.

ACKNOWLEDGMENT

Akom, A. A. Reexamining resistance as oppositional behavior: The nation of Islam and the creation of Black achievement ideology. *Sociology of Education*, 76(4) October 2003. Reproduced by permission of American Sociology Association.

NOTES

1   The oppositional cultural explanation has three main components. The first concerns the way that minorities are treated or mistreated in education in terms of educational policies, pedagogy, and returns for their investment or school credentials. Ogbu and Simons (1998) referred to this as the *system*. The second component is about the way minorities perceive or respond to schooling as a consequence of their mistreatment. The last is how and why a group became a minority in America in the first place. All of these factors, including explaining minority disadvantage in education as a result of a culture that discourages academic effort by branding it as "acting White," constitute the oppositional cultural explanation (Ogbu & Simons, 1998).

2   Authors ranging from Ogbu (1987) to Portes and Zhou (1993) have written about the ways in which voluntary immigrants who wish to be identified as "American" and not foreign, acculturate into an oppositional subculture developed by involuntary youth (i.e., African-American). Portes and Zhou (1993, p. 83) cited the example of Haitian children in Miami, who feel pressured to choose between remaining "Haitian" and being looked down on by their African American peers, or adopting an African-American identity, which generally carries with it counter-school attitudes and behaviors. While these studies have added much to our understanding of the relationship between "community forces" and positive immigrant school performance, few have taken sufficient account of the role of involuntary minority cultures of mobility in shaping student identity, school experience, and academic performance.

3   According to Hemmings (1996) Black high achievers in different school contexts have different definitions of "Blackness." In comparing Black high achievers in two high schools, Hemmings found that the way they reconciled being a "model student" and "being Black" differed. Black high achievers in a predominantly middle-class high school experienced pressure to act middle-class, with no distinction being made between White and Black middle-class behavior. By contrast, Hemmings found that high achievers in a working-class school experienced pressure to conform to peer images of "Blackness," which involved rejection of "Whiteness." Hemmings's findings point to the significance of school context and social class in shaping involuntary perceptions of "model," "resistant," and approaches to academic success.

4   See also Cook and Ludwig (1998); Downey and Ainsworth-Darnell (1998).

5   For this study, I find the concept of organizational habitus more useful than the similar concept of organizational culture because of the former's emphasis on structure (Horvat and Antonio, 1999). While organizational culture concentrates on the meaning conferred by the set of practices, beliefs, and rules of an organization, organizational habitus is more concerned with

how the same set of (in this case) religious-based practices, beliefs, and rules not only provide meaning but also structure social interaction.

6   According to the *American Heritage Dictionary*, third edition, ideology refers to (1) the body of ideas reflecting the social needs and aspirations of an individual, a group, a class, or a culture or (2) a set of doctrines or beliefs that form the basis of political, economic, or other systems.

7   In America, Islam is also a mosaic of many different ethnic, racial, and national groups. The majority are first- or second-generation immigrants or African-American converts (Haddad, Yasbeck & Esposito, 2000).

8   See Lincoln (1973); Essien-Udom (1962); Halasa (1990); Lee, M. (1996); Gardell (1996). However, none of the studies mentioned deals with the relationship between the NOI's religious socialization and enhanced educational aspirations and performance. Previous research that does address religious socialization and its impact on educational outcomes suggests that many of the socialization experiences emanating from religion are conducive to a number of positive outcomes including educational achievement (Hopson & Hopson, 1990). However, most of these studies focus on Protestantism, the Black church, or Catholicism, and fail to illustrate the ways in which processes of religious socialization influence educational achievement for non-conventional faiths (such as Black Muslims).

9   A discussion of how I was able to establish rapport is provided under the sub-heading "the Setting and Establishing Rapport".

10   Within research literature, aspirations are often defined as those life outcomes that are preferred or desired by individuals (MacLeod, 1987/1991).

11   Data on grade improvement were taken mainly from three sources: self-reports, school records provided by the students, and teacher records regarding course examinations. At Eastern, students are divided into what are known as Small Learning Communities (SLCs). SLCs range in size between 165 and 330 students. Seven teachers generally provide basic instruction in various subjects—Math, English, Science, Social Studies (the two largest SLCs, out of 9, have 28 teachers between them). Many of the women whom I interviewed were in different SLCs; however, all spoke of noticeable increases in educational and occupational aspirations, study habits, and skills, since joining the NOI. Five out of seven indicated that their GPAs had increased between .3 and .9 percent since joining the NOI per year. And the other two indicated one year increases of 1.1–1.3. All had joined in the 9th or 10th grade.

12   See Burawoy et al. (1991).

13   Out of a population of 1,700 students it was impossible to measure the exact number of Black Muslim students since this information is not part of school records data. However, the Black Muslim population "appeared" to be significant.

14   Table 9.2 Interview data summary.
Information on occupation of fathers is omitted because none of the participants had significant economic or social ties with them. All of the participants were the first in their immediate families to join the NOI.

15   Ogbu (1983) and Ogbu and Simmons (1998) hypothesized "that the study of community forces would shed light on why immigrant minorities do well in school while non-immigrants do less well" (p. 157). However, to my knowledge neither of these researchers has analyzed or provided empirical data on the role of community forces in the academic achievement of involuntary minorities.

16   Individuals who share the same race as NOI members are often viewed as potential members.
17   I also disagree with the notion that unless individuals have shared a specific experience or background they will be unable to understand and appreciate one another. Indeed, as Collins noted, Black feminist thought challenges the notion of additive oppression and replaces it with a conceptual framework in which "all groups possess varying amounts of penalty and privilege in one historically created system" (1991, p. 225); one need not win the oppression sweepstakes in order to understand and appreciate the pain of exclusion and domination (Horvat & Antonio, 1999).
18   This is important because it rules out the possibility that the association between NOI membership and strong academic habits and aspirations are due to selection into the NOI, rather than effects of NOI membership.
19   The NOI's recruitment efforts have been particularly successful with respect to incarcerated criminals and drug addicts. Their record of rehabilitating former convicts and addicts has been acknowledged by social workers and documented by scholars and journalists alike (Lincoln, 1973, p. 84). This is important because it rules out the possibility that the association between NOI membership and strong academic habits and aspirations are due to selection into the NOI, rather than effects of NOI membership.
20   Muhammad refers to W.D. Muhammad, the founder of the NOI.
21   Similar to AVID (Mehan et al., 1994), the NOI's formal study groups emphasized writing, inquiry, and collaboration, as well as role modeling/ mentoring, and career-exploration. More specifically writing for the NOI is seen as a learning tool. Students are encouraged to take notes and develop questions based on their notes. In addition to note taking, members are encouraged to work through curricular readers on topics of import to the organization. Inquiry for the NOI is viewed as a rhetorical strategy used to help combat white discrimination and prejudice as well as a tool to facilitate self-empowerment. In order to develop inquiry as a rhetorical strategy NOI ministers often use a Socratic method of questioning in their "speeches" that inevitably guides members to a logical conclusion foreseen by the minister (see above dialogue between minister and congregation). The Socratic method is also practiced in study groups by not giving the participants answers, but instead encouraging them to clarify their thoughts through provocative questioning. Collaboration is also a formal instructional strategy employed by the NOI. Collaboration is used by the organization to encourage members to work together for educational or entrepreneurial goals. More specifically, collaborative groups allow members to work together as sources of information and to establish boundaries in order to differentiate between who belongs to the NOI and who does not.
22   Recently, the low expectation and the loss of "state social capital" came to fruition when Philadelphia became the first city in the country to turn over 42 of its public schools to private and non-profit industry (see *New York Times*, April 12, 2002).
23   Mac an Ghaill, M. (1988, pp. 26, 35) termed this strategy "resistance within accommodation." However, women in the NOI complicate this terminology on two counts: first, because a central tenet of their religious indoctrination advocates for 'accommodation leading towards separation, and second, because unlike Mac an Ghaill's "Black sisters" or Gibson's voluntary minorities, NOI women feel that they must (and do) speak out when the school is operating in discriminatory ways. Consequently, the accommodation that

NOI women display is not consistent with the accommodation hypothesis offered by Gibson (1988) or Mac an Ghaill (1988).

REFERENCES

Anderson, E. (1990). *StreetWise*. Chicago: University of Chicago Press.
Bourdieu, P. (1986). The forms of capital. In J. Richardson (Ed.) *Handbook of theory and research for the sociology of education* (pp. 241–258). New York: Greenwood Press.
Burawoy, M., Burton, A., Ferguson, A. A., & Fox, K. J. (1991). *Ethnography Unbound*. Berkeley: University of California Press.
Collins, P. H. (1990). *Black feminist thought: Knowledge, consciousness, and the politics of empowerment*. New York: Routledge.
Cook, P. J., & Ludwig, J. (1998). The burden of "Acting White": Do Black adolescents disparage academic achievement? In Jencks, C. & Phillips, M. (eds.) *The Black and White academic gap*. (pp. 375–400). Washington, DC: The Brooking Institute.
Denzin, N., & Lincoln, Y. (1994). Entering the field of qualitative research. In N. K. Denzin & Y. S. Lincoln (Eds.), *Handbook of qualitative research* (pp. 1–17). Newbury Park, CA: Sage Publications.
Downey, D. B., & Ainsworth-Darnell, J. (1998). Assessing the oppositional culture explanation for racial/ethnic differences in school performance. *American Sociological Review, 63*, 536–553.
Erickson, F. (1987). Transforming school success: the politics and culture of educational achievement. *Anthropology & Education Quarterly, 18*, 335–356.
Essien-Udom, E.U. (1962). *Black nationalism*. Chicago: University of Chicago Press.
Farrakhan. L. (1991). Who is God? Part three. *Final Call* (April 22).
Fordham, S., & Ogbu, J. U. (1986). Black students' school success: Coping with the "burden of acting white." *The Urban Review, 18*(3), 176–206.
Flores-Gonzalez, N. (1999). Puerto Rican high achievers. *Anthropology & Education Quarterly, 30*(1), 343–62.
Foley, D. (1991). *Learning capitalist culture: Deep in the heart of Texas*. Philadelphia: University of Pennsylvania Press.
Fine, M. (1991). *Framing dropouts*. Albany: State University of New York Press.
Gardell, M. (1996). *In the name of Elijah Muhammad: Louis Farrakhan and the Nation of Islam*. Durham, NC: Duke University Press.
Gibson, M. (1988). *Accommodation without assimilation: Sikh immigrants in an American high school*. Ithaca, NY: Cornell University Press.
Gibson, M. (1997). Ethnicity and school performance: Complicating the immigrant/involuntary minority typology. Special issue. *Anthropology and Education Quarterly, 28*(3), 411–430.
Goffman, E. (1959). *The presentation of self in everyday life*. Garden City, NY: Double Day.
Haddad, Y., Yasbeck, Y., & Esposito, J. (2000). *Muslims in the Americanization path*. New York: Oxford University Press.

Halasa, M. (1990). *Elijah Muhammad*. New York and Philadelphia: Chelsea House Publishers.

Hemmings, A. (1996). Conflicting images? Being Black and a model high school student. *Anthropology & Education Quarterly, 27*(1), 20–50.

Heirich [see text p.364], M. (1977). Change of heart: A test of some widely held theories about religious conversion. *American Journal of Sociology, 83,* 653–680.

Hopson, D. P., & Hopson, D. S. (1990). *Different and wonderful: Raising black children in a race-conscious society*. New York: Prentice-Hall.

Horvat, E., & Antonio, A. (1999). Hey, those shoes are out of uniform: African American girls in an elite high school and the importance of habitus. *Anthropology and Education Quarterly, 30*(3), 317–342.

Jackson, J. (2001). *Harlem world: Doing race and class in contemporary Black America*. Chicago: University of Chicago Press.

Lee, M. (1996). *The Nation of Islam: An American millenarian movement*. Syracuse, NY: Syracuse University Press.

Lee, S. (1996). *Unraveling the "model minority" stereotype: Listening to Asian American youth*. New York: Teachers College Press.

Lipsitz, G. (1988). *A life in the struggle: Ivory perry and the culture of opposition*. Philadelphia: Temple University Press.

Lincoln, E. (1973) 1994. *The Black Muslims in America*. Boston: Beacon Press.

MacLeod, J. (1987/1991). *Ain't no makin' it: Leveled aspirations in a low-income neighborhood*. Boulder, CO: Westview Press.

Massey, D., & Denton, N. (1993). *American apartheid: Segregation and the making of the underclass*. Cambridge, MA: Harvard University Press.

Mac, An. Ghaill, M. (1988). *Young, gifted, and Black*. Milton Keynes, England: Open University Press.

Mamiya, L. (1982). From Black Muslim to Bilalian: The evolution of a movement. *Journal for the Scientific Study of Religion, 21*(2), 138–152.

McDonough, P. (1997). *Choosing colleges: How social class and schools structure opportunity*. Albany: State University of New York Press.

Mehan, H., Hubbard, L., & Villanueva, I. (1994). Forming academic identities: Accommodation without assimilation among involuntary minorities. *Anthropology & Education Quarterly, 25*(2), 91–117.

New World Dictionary. (1979). p. 696.

Ogbu, J. U. (1978). *Minority education and caste: The American system in cross-cultural perspective*. New York: Academic Press.

Ogbu, J. U. (1983). Minority status and schooling in plural societies. *Comparative Education Review, 27*(2), 168–190.

Ogbu, J. U. (1987). Variability in minority school performance: A problem in search of an explanation. *Anthropology & Education Quarterly, 18*(4), 312–334.

Ogbu, J. U. (1991). Immigrant and involuntary minorities in comparative perspective. In M. Gibson & J. U. Ogbu (Eds.), *Minority status and schooling*. (pp. 3–37). New York: Garland Publishing.

Ogbu, J., & Simons, H. (1998). Voluntary and involuntary minorities: A cultural-ecological theory of school performance with some implications for education. *Anthropology and Education Quarterly, 29*(2), 155–188.

Patillo-McCoy, M. (1999). *Black picket fences: Privilege and peril among the Black middle class*. Chicago: University of Chicago Press.

Perry, T. (2003). *Young, gifted, and Black: Promoting high achievement among African-American students*. Boston: Beacon Press.

Peshkin, A. (1988). In search of subjectivity—one's own. *Educational Researcher* (October), 17–21.

Portes, A., & Zhou, M. (1993). *City on the edge: The transformation of Miami*. Berkeley: University of California Press.

Solomon, P. (1992). *Black resistance in school: Forging a separatist culture*. Albany: State University of New York Press.

Snow, D., & Machalek, R. (1984). Sociology of conversion. *Annual Review of Sociology, 10*, 167–190.

Treisman, P. (1985). *A study of the mathematics performance of Black Students at the University of California at Berkeley*. Unpublished Doctoral Dissertation, University of California at Berkeley.

Weber, M. (1958). *The Protestant ethic and the spirit of capitalism*. New York: Charles Scribners Sons.

Willis, P. (1977). *Learning to labor: How working class kids get working class jobs*. New York: Columbia University Press.

Chapter 10

What does "Acting White" Actually Mean?

Racial Identity, Adolescent
Development, and Academic
Achievement among African
American Youth

Margaret Beale Spencer and Vinay Harpalani

Introduction

In their widely-noted 1986 article, "Black students' school success: Coping
with the burden of 'acting White,' " Signithia Fordham and the late John
Ogbu contended that one important reason for academic underachievement among African American youth is the overarching, cultural devaluation of educational attainment within Black communities. Fordham and
Ogbu (1986) stated:

> Apparently, Black children's general perception that academic pursuit
> is "acting White" is learned in the Black community. The ideology
> of the community in regard to the cultural meaning of schooling is,
> therefore, implicated and needs to be reexamined.
>
> (p. 203)

Since the publication of this article in the *Urban Review*, the popular media
has focused much attention, often uncritically, on the "acting White"
hypothesis (Gregory, 1992; Pearson, 1994; Suskind, 1994; Lewin, 2000).
Fordham and Ogbu's (1986) work has also been cited, again usually
without criticism, in several well-known academic volumes (e.g., Massey
& Denton, 1993; Hoberman, 1997; McLaren, 1998). Additionally, neo-
conservative authors, seeking to exploit deficit-oriented, cultural deprivation arguments about African American educational attainment, have
also employed the "acting White" hypothesis (e.g., McWhorter, 2000; see
Gunn, Harpalani, & Brooks, 2001 for a critique).

Both Fordham (1988, 1996) and Ogbu (2003) individually expanded
upon and revised their ideas; nevertheless, their core contentions remain
the same, and several key conceptual errors characterize both the original
"acting White" hypothesis and its revisions. In fact, many scholars have

critiqued Fordham and Ogbu's (1986) initial pronouncement and future work by both authors. However, these critics have generally not undertaken a broad reinterpretation of the phenomenon; they have not critically examined what "acting White" actually means to Black youth.

In this chapter, we critique the Fordham and Ogbu (1986) hypothesis and shed light on the question of what "acting White" really means to African American adolescents—as these youths engage normative developmental tasks (Havighurst, 1953), including school achievement. To accomplish this we draw upon our prior work (Spencer, Noll, Stoltzfus, & Harpalani, 2001; Harpalani, 2002; Spencer, Cross, Harpalani, & Goss, 2003) to discuss how racial identity, cultural socialization, and normative developmental tasks, along with intervening processes, interact with vast structural and social inequity to explain the academic achievement and underachievement of African American youth. First, we review Fordham and Ogbu's (1986) article as the basis for the "acting White" hypothesis. We then consider selected recent empirical studies that refute their hypothesis. Subsequently, we examine the conceptual flaws in Fordham and Ogbu's (1986) work, building on several, existing empirical critiques. To accomplish this end, we employ Cross's (1971, 1991) Nigrescence models and Spencer's (1995, 2006) Phenomenological Variant of Ecological Systems Theory as conceptual frameworks to help us answer the question of what "acting White" really means to Black youth, given the vast social inequity that characterizes American race relations. We incorporate empirical studies into our theoretical analysis; this includes a partial examination of Ogbu's (2003) recent data. Our aim is to show how Fordham and Ogbu (1986) misinterpreted the meaning of "acting White" in both their original article and in subsequent work. In the process, we reframe the issue from an identity-focused, cultural-ecological, developmentally-sensitive perspective, and we highlight the need to integrate issues of racial identity, sociohistorical context, and cultural socialization when explaining achievement orientation outcomes for Black youth.

Before continuing, however, it is important for us to recognize explicitly the important contributions of John Ogbu, who passed away suddenly in August 2003. Although we are very critical of some of Ogbu's ideas and remain steadfast in our criticism, there is no doubt that Ogbu's work tremendously advanced understanding of ethnic differences in academic achievement. Our work grew through debate and discussion with Ogbu, and his overall impact on urban education research will be felt for some time to come. Elsewhere, we have paid tribute in more detail to Ogbu's life and work (Harpalani & Gunn, 2003). We will miss the intriguing and insightful dialogues that were sparked by our different perspectives.

THE "ACTING WHITE" HYPOTHESIS

Fordham and Ogbu (1986) contend that one primary reason why Black students often do not perform well in school is that "they experience inordinate ambivalence and affective dissonance in regard to academic efforts and success" (p. 177). According to their hypothesis, the cultural orientation of Black communities equates learning with "acting White." Building on Ogbu's (1978, 1991) framework, the authors classify minorities into three categories: 1) Autonomous minorities, who constitute a distinct numerical minority within the society (e.g., Jews and Mormons in America); 2) Immigrant minorities, who voluntarily came to America with the goal of improving their stakes in life (i.e., many (but not all) Asian American groups); and 3) Castelike, or involuntary minorities (i.e., Blacks, Native Americans, and Chicanos), who arrived in America involuntarily via slave trade, or through conquest (Fordham and Ogbu, 1986; Ogbu, 1991).

Fordham and Ogbu (1986) focus on the "castelike" minority groups, specifically African Americans, and they claim to examine the expressive dimension of the relationship between such groups and the dominant cultural group (i.e., White Americans). Through examining this relationship, Fordham and Ogbu (1986) contend that because of their treatment in America, which includes a history of political and economic oppression, African Americans develop a sense of identity in opposition to the social identity of Whites. With the idea of an "oppositional" frame of reference, the authors denote protective devices aimed at (reactively) promoting Black identity and maintaining boundaries between African Americans and the dominant White culture. Considered together, the twin phenomena of oppositional cultural identity and oppositional frame of reference (see also Ogbu, 1991, 1994) create a unique relationship between Black and White Americans, according to the authors.

Consequently, Fordham and Ogbu (1986) contend that children learn these twin phenomena at an early age. They also develop an associated feeling of identity and belonging known as "fictive kinship"—an intense sense of group membership and loyalty that extends beyond typical family relations. Fordham and Ogbu (1986) claim that the "fictive kinship" began with the exploitation of Blacks during slavery, when Whites often thought of Blacks as a monolithic group. Thus, there is an emphasis on group loyalty in situations involving conflict and competition with the majority group. Elsewhere, Ogbu (1985) also implicates the effect of parenting on youth investment in particular survival strategies (see Bronfenbrenner, 1985 for a critique of this perspective). Fordham and Ogbu (1986) suggest these factors affect children's perceptions of their potential for future success (see also Fordham, 1988, 1996).

By combining these ideas, Fordham and Ogbu (1986) argue that

African American students, especially adolescents, attending both integrated and predominantly Black schools face the burden of "acting White"; they view school success as a White attribute. As a consequence, according to the authors, the academic effort and success of Black students are compromised, leading to underachievement.

The authors have also individually commented further on the "acting White" phenomenon. For example, Fordham (1988; 1996) also contends that Black students who are successful must adopt a "raceless" persona, distancing themselves from Black cultural attributes. Similarly, in his most recent work, Ogbu (2003) stated that "acting White" does not refer to academic achievement itself, but rather behaviors associated with and conducive to high scholastic achievement; he contended that the cultural orientation of Black communities tended to shun such behaviors.

EMPIRICAL REFUTATION OF THE "ACTING WHITE" HYPOTHESIS

Recent studies using large, national data sets have contradicted Fordham and Ogbu (1986). Using data from the 1990 National Education Longitudinal Survey (NELS), a nationally representative sample of 17,544 tenth graders, Cook and Ludwig (1998) report several findings that stand against the "acting White" hypothesis. According to their analysis, before controlling for socioeconomic status, about 60 percent of both Black and White tenth graders in the NELS sample expect to complete a four-year college degree. After adjusting for socioeconomic factors, African Americans actually expect to remain in school longer, and other data suggest that they actually do stay enrolled in school longer than Whites (Haveman & Wolfe, 1994). Also, the NELS data show no racial differences in school absence. After controlling for family characteristics, Blacks miss slightly fewer days than Whites. There were no race differences in reported time spent on homework.

Cook and Ludwig's (1998) analysis also indicated the interest and involvement of Black parents. Black students were more likely than Whites to report that their parents had attended meetings at school or gotten in touch with their teachers. After controlling for socioeconomic status, African American parents were also more likely to check their children's homework and to attend events at school. This contradicts the assumption of Fordham and Obgu (1986) that Black parents and community members do not value education.

Peer popularity data from Cook and Ludwig's (1998) NELS sample also do not show support for the "acting White" hypothesis. There are no reported differences in popularity among Black students according to math grades. Moreover, Black honor society members are significantly more popular than their classmates. Cook and Ludwig (1998) also report that academic success has a more positive impact on social status in predominantly African American schools than in White schools.

Adding to the empirical critique, Ainsworth-Darnell and Downey (1998) refute Obgu's (1991, 1994) oppositional culture framework, noting,

> [the] model's key claims have not received empirical verification . . . and proponents have failed to systematically compare perceptions of occupational opportunity and resistance to school across involuntary, dominant, and immigrant groups.
>
> (p. 537)

Ainsworth-Darnell and Downey (1998) dispute four propositions of the "acting White" hypothesis, also using the 1990 National Educational Longitudinal Study's (NELS) data. Their sample included 2,197 African Americans, 653 Asian Americans, and 13,492 non-Hispanic Whites who were all in the tenth grade.

First, the "acting White" hypothesis would suggest that involuntary minority (African American) students perceive fewer benefits to education and more limited occupational opportunities than do dominant (White) students or immigrant minorities (Asian American) students. Ainsworth-Darnell and Downey's (1998) analysis refuted this suggestion; African American students were significantly more likely than White students to note the importance of education in future employment opportunities, and they also had more positive occupational expectations.

Second, Fordham and Ogbu's (1986) thesis would posit that involuntary minority students resisted school engagement more than do White or immigrant students. This was also refuted by Ainsworth-Darnell and Downey's (1998); African American students "had more positive attitudes towards school than [did] White students" (p. 541).

Also inherent in the "acting White" hypothesis is that high-achieving involuntary minority students are negatively sanctioned by their peers. In contrast to Fordham and Ogbu's (1986) claim that high-achieving students face the burden of being criticized for "acting White," Ainsworth-Darnell and Downey (1998) found that in relation to their White counterparts, African American students were more popular when they were very good students.

Finally, the notion that resistance to school accounts for the racial gap in school performance between involuntary minorities and the other groups of students is also disputed. Ainsworth-Darnell and Downey's (1998) results indicate that after controlling for grades, Black students had more positive attitudes toward school than White students, and when controlling for attitudes toward school, Black students earn lower grades than Whites.

CONCEPTUAL FLAWS IN THE "ACTING WHITE" HYPOTHESIS: ISSUES OF SOCIOHISTORICAL CONTEXT

In order to further understand the relationship between racial identity and academic achievement, it is also helpful to examine the major conceptual flaws which are apparent in the "acting White" hypothesis. Studies on African American youth have often employed ahistorical and decontextualized analyses (Spencer and Harpalani, 2001; Spencer, Harpalani, Cassidy, Jacobs et al., 2006), which ignore youths' unique meaning making process (Spencer, 1990, 1995, 1999, 2006). While Fordham and Ogbu (1986) did draw upon Ogbu's (1978) sociohistorical framework, they do not place this history in proper context. Mere classification of minority groups, while acknowledging situational and historical influences to an extent, fails to capture the meaning-making processes that translate these influences into perceptions and behaviors (Van Oers, 1998). Although the authors acknowledged structural barriers to Black academic success, their analysis is reductionist, as they drew unwarranted psychological inferences from a sociohistorical taxonomy (Trueba, 1988).

Historical evidence also suggests that in spite of their status as involuntary or castelike minorities, African Americans have a long history of valuing education (Spencer et al., 2003). For example, Carter G. Woodson (1919) writes about different phases of Black desire for education during slavery, illustrating the drive of African Americans for educational attainment. Anderson (1988) highlights the esteem bestowed upon Blacks who attained literacy after the Civil War. In *Black Reconstruction*, W.E.B. Du Bois (1935) discusses the motivation of ex-slaves toward education, calling it one of the most amazing stories in Western history—one that was unfortunately often suppressed by White racism. Other accounts, such as that of Vanessa Siddle Walker (1996), describe how Black communities voluntarily increased taxes to keep schools open, and how teachers and school administrators in these communities extended their efforts far beyond schools and classrooms. Thus, Fordham and Ogbu's assumption that Black communities have not valued education seems highly erroneous. Indeed, historical accounts generally highlight the resilience of African Americans in pursuing education.

CONCEPTUAL FLAWS IN THE "ACTING WHITE" HYPOTHESIS: ISSUES OF IDENTITY AND ADOLESCENT DEVELOPMENT IN CONTEXT

Perhaps even more significant than their misapplied sociohistorical analysis is Fordham and Ogbu's (1986) neglect of racial identity and developmental processes. Although they employed the "language of identity" in the 1986 article and in subsequent work (Fordham, 1988, 1996; Ogbu, 2003) the two authors fail to consider identity formation processes, particularly with regard to race. Indeed, while both race and identity are central to the "acting White" hypothesis, it is quite telling that both Fordham and Ogbu did not cite or consider the pioneering work of William E. Cross on Black racial identity, or for that matter any of the subsequent theorizing on Nigrescence (Cross, 1971, 1991; Cross, Parham, & Helms, 1991). Nor did they consider any of the vast body of general theorizing on identity formation (e.g., Erikson, 1968; Marcia, 1980), or literature related to racial socialization (e.g., Stevenson, 1994, 1998).

More generally, the analysis presented by Fordham and Ogbu lacked a normative, developmental perspective; it failed to view African American youth as normal, developing beings who are maturing in a hostile context of racial inequity. Instead, the authors' preconceived assumptions, based on deficit-oriented thinking, dominated their interpretation of African American youth's attitudes and behaviors. They did not acknowledge how African American youth can succeed and still maintain their Black identities; in fact, Fordham (1988, 1996) generally denies this possibility. Ogbu (2003) also began his analysis with the assumption of Black academic disengagement, instead of examining individual variation in engagement. In both their joint and individual works, Fordham and Ogbu employed a deficit-oriented perspective and misunderstood the meaning of "acting White" references.

In order to properly understand the "acting White" phenomenon, it is useful to employ two theoretical frameworks which help us understand racial identity formation and normative human development: Cross's (1971, 1991) Nigrescence framework and Spencer's (1995, 2006) Phenomenological Variant of Ecological Systems Theory (PVEST). After reviewing these models, we will apply them to elucidate the meaning of "acting White" for Black youth.

CROSS'S NIGRESCENCE FRAMEWORK

Racial identity development refers to the "process of defining for oneself the personal significance and social meaning of belonging to a particular racial group" (Tatum, 1997, p. 16). Cross's original Nigrescence model

(Cross, 1971; Cross, Parham, & Helms, 1991) delineates four stages of racial identity for African Americans. During the *pre-encounter* status, individuals view the world from a White, Eurocentric frame of reference, consciously or unconsciously holding pro-White and anti-Black attitudes. With the second status, the *encounter* phase, individuals begin to change these attitudes; this involves an event or series of events that cause individuals to recognize that they cannot fully assimilate into White society and will not be fully accepted in it. *Immersion-emersion* represents a reaction to the encounter phase; individuals become more interested in their Black identity and also show increased awareness of racism. This phase may be characterized by anti-White attitudes. *Internalization* occurs as individuals become secure with their Black racial identities and move toward a more pluralistic perspective. African Americans then represent the primary reference group, but individuals' attitudes are not anti-White.

Initially derived through research on adults, the Nigresence framework has been modified to incorporate a more dynamic and flexible view of racial identity within development. Individuals may recycle through stages at various developmental periods; thus, the stages should not always be viewed as a literal progression. Cross (1991) added a fifth stage to the original four; this stage, known as "Internalization-commitment," represents a more consistent internalization phase. He also denoted different modes of internalization, some of which include bicultural identities (Cross, personal communication, November 20, 2000).

The stages in the Nigresence framework also correspond to the racial attitudes of adolescents (Spencer et al., 2001). The pre-encounter status represents Eurocentrism, the encounter phase characterizes a Transition, immersion-emersion suggests reactive Afrocentrism, and internalization represents proactive Afrocentrism. Depending on previous experiences and socialization history, Black adolescents may show greater or lesser attributes of the different statuses.

PHENOMENOLOGICAL VARIANT OF ECOLOGICAL SYSTEMS THEORY (PVEST): AN IDENTITY-FOCUSED, CULTURAL-ECOLOGICAL PERSPECTIVE

As a synergistic, synthesized formulation, Spencer's (1995, 2006) Phenomenological Variant of Ecological Systems Theory (PVEST) serves as a model to examine normative human development—framed through the interaction of identity, culture, and experience—for individuals of all ethnicities. It allows us to analyze the cognition and socio-emotional dependent meaning-making processes that underlie identity development and outcomes (Spencer, 1995, 1999, 2006; Spencer, Dupree, & Hartmann,

1997; Spencer et al., 2006). PVEST serves as a heuristic device that can account for the differences in experience, perception, and negotiation of stress and dissonance (or lack thereof). As such, PVEST utilizes an *Identity-focused Cultural Ecological* (ICE) perspective, integrating issues of social, political, and cultural context with normative developmental processes.

The PVEST framework consists of five basic components that form a dynamic theoretical system (see Figure 10.1).

The first component, *net vulnerability level* (1), represents the history of prior experiences and coping outcomes that may potentially pose challenges during an individual's development. Accordingly, it denotes a kind of tension between risk contributors and available protective factors. Risk contributors are factors that may predispose individuals for adverse outcomes. The risks, of course, may be offset by protective factors, thus

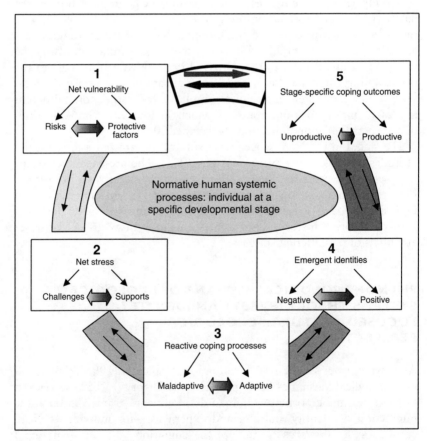

Figure 10.1 Phenomenological variant of ecological systems theory (PVEST).

Source: Spencer (1995, 2004 Rev.)

defining net vulnerability for a given individual. For marginalized youth (many African American and low resource youth), risk contributors include socioeconomic conditions such as living in poverty, imposed expectations such as race and gender stereotypes, and larger historical processes, including racial subordination and discrimination. Self-appraisal, directed by cognition, is key to identity formation; perceptions of the risks one faces and the protective resources available (e.g., cultural socialization experiences) are pertinent in the process. The resulting tension is translated into the socio-emotionally-based experience of stress.

Net stress engagement (2), the second component of PVEST, denotes the actual experiences that challenge an individual's well-being; these are risks that are either actualized or inferred and must be negotiated by the individual. Available social supports, often stage-specific, can help individuals negotiate experiences of stress; thus, supports are actualized or inferred protective factors. Whereas risks and protective factors denote potential entities within the environment, stress and support refer to the actual or translated manifestations of these entities (i.e., experiences in context). In this way, PVEST forges links between environment and experience. These links are dependent upon intrapsychic meaning-making processes (see Spencer, 1986; Spencer and Markstrom-Adams, 1990).

Experiences of racism—both subtle and overt—and related dissonance-producing affect are salient stressors, particularly for African American youth (Chestang, 1972). These serve to compound the normative developmental challenges that all adolescents encounter (e.g., puberty, identity exploration, peer relationships). Adult role models and peer mentors may serve as significant supports to help youth cope with these experiences.

In response to stage-specific challenges and in conjunction with available supports, which together define the net experience of stress, *reactive coping methods* (3) are employed to resolve dissonance-producing situations. Normative cognitive maturation makes awareness of dissonance acute and unavoidable. Reactive coping responses include problem-solving strategies that can lead to either adaptive or maladaptive solutions.

As youth employ various coping strategies, self-appraisal processes continue, and strategies that yield desirable results for the ego are repeated. Accordingly, as exercised repeatedly over time and space, these strategies become stable coping responses, and, coupled together, yield *emergent identities* (4). Emergent identities define how individuals view themselves within and between their various contexts of development (e.g., family, school, neighborhood). The combination of cultural socialization, gender role understanding, and self and peer appraisal all contribute to the definition of one's identity.

Identity processes provide behavioral stability over time and space.

Identity lays the foundation for future perception, self-appraisal and behavior, yielding adverse or productive *life-stage, specific coping outcomes* (5). Productive outcomes include good health, academic achievement, positive relationships, and high self-esteem, while adverse outcomes can include poor health, underachievement, incarceration, and self-destructive behavior.

The PVEST framework represents dynamic processes that continue throughout the lifespan as individuals balance new risks against protective factors (representing particular levels of vulnerability), encounter new challenges that require specific supports (representing levels of stress engagement), establish more expansive coping strategies, and redefine how they view themselves. Thus, PVEST provides a direct, process-oriented delineation of developmental trajectories throughout the lifespan.

WHAT DOES "ACTING WHITE" REALLY MEAN?

By applying the Nigrescence model and PVEST both in our empirical study (Spencer et al., 2001) and to other literature on the "acting White" phenomenon, the meaning of such references can be elucidated. In a study of 562 Black adolescents, aged 11 to 16 from a Southeastern U.S. city, Spencer et al. (2001) found that those with a Eurocentric orientation, as indicated by a high score in Cross's (1971, 1991) Pre-Encounter stage, showed relatively lower academic achievement and self-esteem, as did individuals with a reactive Afrocentric orientation (Immersion-emersion stage). However, African American adolescents who had a proactive Afrocentric orientation—the Internalization stage—performed better than both the Eurocentric and reactive Afrocentric groups, indicating that a strong, proactive sense of Black cultural identity is associated with positive academic achievement for Black youth.

The study by Spencer et al. (2001) also illustrates the importance of considering both adaptive and maladaptive coping outcomes and shows how Black racial identity can be related to both. It also contradicts the claims of Fordham and Ogbu (1986) and Fordham (1988, 1996), who contend that Blacks must distance themselves from Black culture in order to achieve. As part of normative developmental processes, adolescents of all ethnicities engage in identity searching and strive for acceptance and approval. Cross's (1971, 1991) Immersion-Emersion stage may be characterized by anti-White attitudes; while this can be maladaptive, it is not an abnormal preliminary reaction to devaluation, particularly during adolescence, which is a developmental period of high psychological vulnerability. If Black youth perceive a classroom, school, or any other setting as a context where they are devalued, they may reactively cope by defining the expectations of this context as "acting White," particularly as they are normatively exploring and developing their own racial identities. However, this is reflective of context-linked normative identity development processes rather than a cultural devaluation of education.

As Spencer et al. (2001) note, "acting White has so many potential variations based on multiple contextual realities" (p. 28). Depending on the specific circumstances, various behaviors may be labeled as "acting White." For example, in the second author's high school, African American football players who attempted to gain the favor of a particular White coach (who had supposedly rejected other Black players in different ways) were said to be "acting White." Accusations of "acting White" are a manifestation of reactive (i.e., defensive and ego-serving) Afrocentric identity, not a fundamental component of Black culture. While these accusations may be linked to attributes of Black culture (e.g., listening to certain kinds of music), they can also be linked to completely independent behaviors. In fact, Ogbu (2003) even cites one interesting and ironic example in his recent book:

> One man reported that his daughter was accused of acting White because she wore her hair natural . . . to her Black peers this was acting White because, like White people, she did not have to worry about processing her hair.
>
> (quoted in Ogbu, 2003, p. 179)

In this instance, "acting White" actually denoted a feature—natural hair—that is usually associated with an Afrocentric orientation (!).

Ironically, Ogbu's (2003) data also demonstrated the process of racial identity development even though he did not appear to recognize it. He repeatedly notes that Black elementary school students did not equate academic achievement with acting White; in fact, they made fun of students who did not do well in school. According to Ogbu (2003) middle-school students also did not refer to school success as "acting White," although they did begin to make "acting White" references. It is only in high school (when racial identity is often transitioning from pre-encounter to encounter to immersion-emersion stages and youth have access to more mature cognitive processing including inferences about broad political and societal associations) that Ogbu (2003) notes that "acting White" is at times equated with achievement-linked behaviors. Ogbu also gives examples of Black students' increasing awareness of racism, their comparatively greater knowledge of Black history, and their increasing dissonance regarding the way they are viewed in the school setting. As illustrated earlier, an application of the Nigrescence and PVEST frameworks would help clarify how African American youth interpret and react to these phenomena.

In fact, we assert that Ogbu (2003) continued to draw deficit-oriented conclusions because he neglected to recognize developmental processes (components two through four of PVEST). His analysis drew narrow and deterministic links between the more obvious components (i.e., one and five), net vulnerability and life-stage outcomes; accordingly, the perspective ignored the *process components* (i.e., two through four) that bring attention to the different encounters of challenge and support (i.e., net stress experienced), various means of coping, and the emergent identity formation that mediate this process. Thus, the consequent linear and deterministic reasoning did not account for the range of adolescent coping strategies and, in fact, misinterpreted those that he did consider.

Other studies also support a more nuanced and contextualized interpretation of "acting White" assertions. Datnow and Cooper (1996) also show the importance of considering coping processes in context. In their interviews of 42 African American students, grades 10 through 12, who attended elite, predominantly White independent schools in the Baltimore area, the authors concluded that Black peer groups within the schools actually socialized their members towards academic striving, although some Black students reported negative feedback from Black peers outside of the schools. This provides an illustration of adaptive coping within the school context and shows how peers of the same race within different contexts (i.e., perceived levels of support) interpret the same phenomena differently.

Tyson, Darity, and Castellino (2003) examined the "burden of acting White" in 11 North Carolina public schools, which included 3 elementary schools, 2 middle schools, and 6 high schools. In their interviews with 125 students at these schools, the researchers reported that they only encountered the term "acting White" at two schools, one middle school and one high school. In their study, Tyson, Darity, and Castellino (2003) noted that "acting White" only appeared to be linked to high academic achievement in schools where the most academically rigorous courses were characterized by a *disproportionate under-representation* of both students of color and low-income students. They suggest that such school environments breed animosity toward the few students of color who are enrolled in rigorous courses—an assertion consistent with our view of "acting White" as a reactive coping strategy in response to youths' perceptions of a hostile contexts. In fact, in an expanded discussion of their work, Tyson, Darity, and Castellino (2005) discuss how various types of school environments can breed oppositionality, and how factors such as schools' racial and socioeconomic composition affect this phenomenon.

In a similar vein, Ford, Harris, Webb, and Jones (1994) note how Fordham (1988) neglects the phenomenon of "code switching"—demonstrating different modes of cultural communication and style in different settings—and that Black students can become bicultural rather than "raceless" and thus maintain their ethnic identities. Bicultural identity is one of several different modes of the Internalization stage that Cross (personal communication, November 20, 2000) describes in his work. It also represents a particular emergent identity within the PVEST framework; undoubtedly, one that is not represented in Fordham's (1988; 1996) or Fordham and Ogbu's (1986) work.

Overall, the "acting White" phenomena, as it occurs, is not responsible for Black academic underachievement, nor is it reflective of a broad cultural frame of reference, as Fordham and Ogbu (1986) suggest. It is simply one of many possible reactive or "in the moment" (see Stevenson 1998) coping responses; these reactions are most often utilized by Black youth in response to inferred but unacknowledged encounters of academic devaluation, perceived social inequities and rejection. These experiences, given normative developmental processes, occur in varying social contexts as youth broaden their social experiences and represent what Chestang (1972) describes as individual character formation efforts occurring in hostile environments.

Conclusion

It is interesting to note that Fordham and Obgu's (1986) paper was not the first scholarly article to employ the phrase "acting White." Sixteen years earlier, McArdle and Young (1970) published a paper entitled "Classroom Discussion of Racial Identity or How Can We Make It without 'Acting White.' " In reference to the Black youth that they interviewed for this paper, McArdle and Young (1970) note, "Their goal, to have equal rights and opportunities without 'acting White,' strengthened a sense of being 'Black and beautiful' " (p.137)—to be successful and to reach Cross's (1971; Cross et al., 1991) Internalization stage. This suggests that these Black youth were not defining success as "acting White," but rather that they were perceiving that a racist society devalues their cultural heritage. Consequently, they were struggling to cope adaptively —to attain success in this society without assimilating and compromising their racial and cultural identities.

Many Black youth today are struggling with the same issues. Indeed, the very question posed by McArdle and Young (1970) implies that it is possible for African Americans to "make it" without "acting White," a notion generally denied by Fordham (1988) and Fordham and Ogbu (1986). Fordham and Ogbu (1986) assert that the Black community needs to re-examine its attitude toward education. Numerous lines of evidence suggest that their reasoning is flawed, and empirical studies have largely refuted their stereotypic assumptions. A more appropriate assertion is that, from a *human rights* perspective, American society needs to re-examine its attitudes, assumptions, and stereotypes regarding Black communities and provide for a more *equitable and supportive* set of educational experiences and opportunities since normal adolescent cognitive maturation makes the *awareness of social inequities unavoidable*; the awareness requires adolescent coping responses that may be misinterpreted by uninformed social observers. We strongly affirm that this re-examination should include not only the oppression that African Americans have faced, but also the tremendous resilience, driven by proactive Afrocentric attitudes, that Black communities have displayed. Accordingly, rather than changing the "cultural meaning of schooling" (Fordham & Ogbu, 1986, p. 203) in these communities, it is the context of schooling that must change—to promote proactive Afrocentrism and to provide all of the material and cultural resources necessary to improve educational opportunities for African American youth.

REFERENCES

Ainsworth-Darnell, J.W. & Downey, D. B. (1998). Assessing the oppositional cultural explanation for racial/ethnic differences in school performance. *American Sociological Review*, 63, 536–553.

Anderson, J. D. (1988). *The education of Blacks in the south, 1860–1935*. Chapel Hill: University of North Carolina Press.

Bronfenbrenner, U. (1985). Summary. In M. B. Spencer, G. K. Brookins, & W. R. Allen (Eds.), *Beginnings: The social and affective development of Black children* (pp. 67–73). Hillsdale, NJ: Lawrence Erlbaum Associates.

Chestang, L.W. (1972). *Character development in a hostile environment*. Occasional Paper No. 3 (Series) (pp. 1–12). Chicago, IL: University of Chicago Press.

Cook, P. J., & Ludwig, J. (1998). The burden of "acting White": Do Black adolescents disparage academic achievement? In C. Jencks & M. Phillips (Eds.), *The Black-White test score gap* (pp. 375–400). Washington, DC: The Brookings Institution.

Cross, W. E. (1971). The Negro-to-Black conversion experience. *Black World* (July), 13–27.

Cross, W. E. (1991). *Shades of Black: Diversity in African American identity*. Philadelphia: Temple University Press.

Cross, W. E., Parham, T. A., & Helms, J. E. (1991). The stages of Black identity development: Nigrescence models. In R. L. Jones (Ed.), *Black psychology* (pp. 319–338). Berkeley, CA: Cobb & Henry.

Datnow, A., & Cooper, R. (1996). Peer networks of African American students in independent schools: Affirming academic success and racial identity. *Journal of Negro Education*, 65(4), 56–72.

Du Bois, W. E. B. (1935). *Black reconstruction*. New York: S. A. Russell Company.

Erikson, E. (1968). *Identity: Youth and crisis*. New York: Norton.

Ford, D.Y., Harris, J. J., Webb, K. S., & Jones, D. L. (1994). Rejection or confirmation of racial identity: A dilemma for high-achieving Blacks? *The Journal of Educational Thought*, 28(1), 7–33.

Fordham, S. (1988). Racelessness as a strategy in Black students' school success: Pragmatic strategy or pyrrhic victory? *Harvard Educational Review*, 58(1), 54–84.

Fordham, S. (1996). *Blacked out: Dilemmas of race, identity, and success at Capital High*. Chicago, IL: University of Chicago Press.

Fordham, S., & Ogbu, J. U. (1986). Black students' school success: Coping with the "burden of 'acting White.' " *The Urban Review*, 18(3), 176–206.

Gregory, S. S. (1992). The hidden hurdle. *Time* (March 16), 44–46.

Gunn, R., Harpalani, V., & Brooks, S. (2001). Bamboozled at Berkeley: John McWhorter's new millennium minstrel show. *Black Arts Quarterly*, 6(1), 30–32.

Harpalani, V. (2002). What does "acting White" really mean?: Racial identity formation and academic achievement among Black youth. *Penn GSE Perspectives on Urban Education*, 1(1). (ERIC Document Reproduction Service No. EJ654885) Available: <www.urbanedjournal.org/commentaries/c0001.html>

Harpalani, V., & Gunn, R. (2003). Contributions, controversies, and criticisms: In memory of John U. Ogbu (1939–2003). *Penn GSE Perspectives on Urban Education*, 2(2). Available: <www.urbanedjournal.org/ogbu_memorial.html>

Haveman, R., & Wolfe, B. (1994). *Succeeding generations: On the effects of investments in children*. New York: Russell Sage.

Havighurst, R. J. (1953). *Human development and education*. New York: McKay.

Hoberman, J. (1997). *Darwin's athletes: How sport has damaged Black America and preserved the myth of race*. New York: Mariner Books.

Lewin, T. (2000). Growing up, growing apart: Fast friends try to resist the pressure to divide by race. *New York Times* (June 24) [Electronic version]. Retrieved October 21, 2001 from: <www.nytimes.com>.

Marcia, J. E. (1980). Identity in adolescence. In J. Adelson (Ed.), *Handbook of adolescent psychology*. New York: Wiley.

Massey, D. S., & Denton, N. A. (1993). *American Apartheid: Segregation and the making of the underclass*. Cambridge, MA: Harvard University Press.

McArdle, C. G., & Young, N. F. (1970). Classroom discussion of racial identity or how can we make it without "acting White"? *American Journal of Orthopsychiatry*, 40(1), 135–141.

McLaren, P. (1998). *Life in schools: An introduction to critical pedagogy in the foundations of education*. Reading, MA: Addison Wesley Longman, Inc.

McWhorter, J. H. (2000). *Losing the race: Self sabotage in Black America*. New York: The Free Press.

Ogbu, J. U. (1978). *Minority education and caste: The American system in cross-cultural perspective*. New York: Academic Press.

Ogbu, J. U. (1985). A cultural ecology of competence among inner-city Blacks. In M. B. Spencer, G. K. Brookins, & W. R. Allen (Eds.), *Beginnings: The social and affective development of Black children* (pp. 45–66). Hillsdale, NJ: Lawrence Erlbaum Associates.

Ogbu, J. U. (1991). Low performance as an adaptation: The case of Blacks in Stockton, California. In M. A. Gibson & J. U. Ogbu (Eds.), *Minority status and schooling* (pp. 249–285). New York: Grand Publishing.

Ogbu, J.U. (1994). From cultural differences to differences in cultural frame of reference. In P. M. Greenfield & R. R. Cocking (Eds.), *Cross-cultural roots of minority child development* (pp. 365–391). Hillsdale, NJ: Lawrence Erlbaum Associates.

Ogbu, J. U. (2003). *Black students in an affluent suburb: A study of academic disengagement.* Mahwah, NJ: Erlbaum.

Pearson, H. (1994, November 23). The Black academic environment. *Wall Street Journal*, p. A14.

Spencer, M. B. (1986). Risk and resilience: How Black children cope with stress. *Social Science, 71*(1), 22–26.

Spencer, M. B. (1990). Development of minority children: An introduction. *Child Development, 61*(2), 267–269.

Spencer, M. B. (1995). Old issues and new theorizing about African American Youth: A phenomenological variant of ecological systems theory. In R. L. Taylor (Ed.), *Black youth: Perspectives on their status in the United States* (pp. 37–70). Westport, CT: Praeger.

Spencer, M. B. (1999). Social and cultural influences on school adjustment: The application of an identity-focused cultural ecological perspective. *Educational Psychologist, 34*(1), 43–57.

Spencer, M. B. (2006). Phenomenology and Ecological Systems Theory: Development of Diverse Groups. In W. Damon and R. Lerner (Eds.) (6th Edn), *Handbook of Child Psychology*, Vol. 1 (ch. 15, Theory Volume). New York: Wiley Publishers.

Spencer, M. B., Cross, W. E., Harpalani, V., & Goss, T. N. (2003). Historical and developmental perspectives on Black academic achievement: Debunking the "acting White" myth and posing new directions for research. In C. C. Yeakey & R. D. Henderson (Eds.), *Surmounting all odds: Education, opportunity, and society in the new millennium* (pp. 273–304). Greenwich, CT: Information Age Publishers.

Spencer, M. B., & Harpalani, V. (2001). African American adolescents, Research on. In R. M. Lerner & J. V. Lerner (Eds.), *Adolescence in America: An encyclopedia*, Vol. 1 (pp. 30–32). Denver, CO: ABC-CLIO.

Spencer, M. B., Harpalani, V., Cassidy, E., Jacobs, C., Donde, S., Goss, T., Miller, M.-M., Charles, N., & Wilson, S. (2006). Understanding vulnerability and resilience from a normative development perspective: Implications for racially and ethnically diverse youth (ch. 16). In D. Cicchetti & E. Cohen (Eds.), *Developmental Psychopathology*, Vol. 1, pp. 627–672. Hoboken, NJ: Wiley Publishers.

Spencer, M. B., Dupree, D., & Hartmann, T. (1997). A phenomenological variant of ecological systems theory (PVEST): A self-organization perspective in context. *Development and Psychopathology, 9*, 817–833.

Spencer, M. B., & Markstrom-Adams, C. (1990). Identity processes among racial and ethnic minorities in America. *Child Development, 61*, 290–310.

Spencer, M. B., Noll, E., Stoltzfus, J., & Harpalani, V. (2001). Identity and school adjustment: Questioning the "Acting White" assumption. *Educational Psychologist, 36*(1), 21–30.

Stevenson, H. C. (1994). Racial socialization in African American families: The art of balancing intolerance and survival. *The Family Journal: Counseling and Therapy for Couples and Families, 2*(3), 190–198.

Stevenson, H. C. (1998). Raising safe villages: Cultural-ecological factors that influence the emotional adjustment of adolescents. *Journal of Black Psychology, 24*, 44–59.

Suskind, R. (1994, September 22). Poor, Black, and smart, an inner city teen tries to survive MIT. *Wall Street Journal*, p. A1.

Tatum, B. (1997). *Why are all the Black kids sitting together in the cafeteria?: And other conversations about race*. New York: Basic Books.

Trueba, H. T. (1988). Culturally based explanations of minority students' academic achievement. *Anthropology & Education Quarterly, 19*(3), 270–287.

Tyson, K., Darity, W., & Castellino, D. (2003, August). Breeding animosity: The significance of school placement patterns in the development of a "burden of acting White." Paper presented at the Annual Meeting of the American Sociological Association, Atlanta, GA.

Tyson, K., Darity, W., & Castellino, D. (2005). It's not "a Black Thing": Understanding the burden of acting White and other Dilemmas of high achievement. *American Sociological Review, 70*(4), 582–605.

Van Oers, B. (1998). From context to contextualizing. *Learning and Instruction, 8*(6), 473–488.

Walker, V. S. (1996). *Their highest potential*. Chapel Hill: University of North Carolina Press.

Woodson, C. G. (1919). *The education of the Negro prior to 1861: A history of the education of the colored people of the United States from the beginning of slavery to the Civil War*. Washington, DC: The Associated Publishers, Inc.

Chapter 11

"Excellence" and Student Class, Race, and Gender Cultures*

Lois Weis

Just then Jack turned around. "Hey, you guys, my brother says he and some guys from the high school are going to put on a kegger [of beer] next week over in Forest Grove, I'll bet we could get a ride over."

"OK," Steve said emphatically. "Can you get a bag [of marijuana]?" Jack said, looking at Don. "I'll manage." Don smiled on his way into the science room. As we sat down, the four of them—Jack, Don, Steve, and Morris—began a chorus of their favorite song.

" 'And I said no-no-no-no, I don't smoke it no more, I'm tired of waking up on the floor; No thank you, please, it only makes me sneeze, And then it makes it hard to find the door.' "

The bell rang. Mr. Franks barked out, "Class, turn to page 328 in your science books. And stop the singing back there, Don, yesterday you remember . . ., I told you about igneous rocks . . ."

(from Robert Everhart, *Reading, Writing and Resistance*)

Many of the recent reports on "Excellence in Education" tend to assume that student cultures can be manipulated easily. The production of "excellence," for example, has been linked in the various reports to a longer school day, pay increases for teachers, more rigorous teacher training, a "core" curriculum, less federal and/or state control, increased attention to the traditional academic subjects, and increased attention to science and technology. The attempt is to alter certain school-related factors, with the assumption that altering such factors will produce higher achievement scores among students.[1]

The reports which fall under the rubric of "Excellence" do not say the same thing.[2] As Kelly points out, there are striking differences within the current set of proposed reforms, and it is a mistake to view the reports as monolithic. They differ internally in terms of the criteria by which they assess schooling in the first place, the kinds of prescriptive statements made with respect to the curriculum, the extent to which they support teacher autonomy, and the level at which they lay responsibility for implementing proposed reforms.[3]

There is agreement, however, that our educational system needs improvement. There also seems to be tacit agreement that a key level in the system is the secondary school. The American high school is in deep trouble, whether because of low achievement scores, student boredom, or lack of attention paid to the creation of students capable of consuming and especially producing high-level scientific and technological knowledge presumably linked to the maintenance of America's position as a world power. While the criteria through which the schools are assessed and the proposals for reforms themselves are different, there is general consensus that *something* is wrong with the nation's schools.

Although the reports differ in some rather profound ways, they all assume student cultures can be *made* to change. This assumption—that student outcomes are a simple function of certain within-school factors and can be altered if only these factors are manipulated—is incorrect. Student outcomes are tied rather directly to the cultures students themselves produce within the institutions in which they reside. These cultures do not arise in relation to within-school factors alone. While elements of student cultures may represent a response to certain school practices, the practices that might elicit such a response are not pinpointed in the reports.

John Goodlad and Theodore Sizer both acknowledge the importance of student cultures in relation to school outcomes. Goodlad, for example, talks about the intensity of nonacademic interests among students and indicates that "research findings regarding the youth culture lead one to wonder why we have taken so little practical account of them in schools."[4] Sizer is even more straightforward when he discusses the effects of student culture. Whether students go along with the structures of the school or not, he argues, they possess "the autonomous power not to." The fact that most students go along with the system masks the actual power students hold—they can always collectively, whether quietly or not, decide to say no.[5]

Despite the fact that Goodlad and Sizer acknowledge the importance of student culture in relation to school outcomes, neither takes a serious account of these cultures in their proposals for reform; and neither addresses the reasons why student cultures take the shape and form that they do. The remainder of the proposals do not, for the most part, take student cultures into account at all. This lack of attention to these cultures, and the reasons why such cultures arise will, as I argue here, contribute to the almost certain failure of this newest round of reforms.[6]

This chapter challenges the assumption that student outcomes can be altered easily through a change in factors, such as those outlined in the reports. It will be argued that student cultures play a key mediating role in the production of school outcomes, and that such cultures are not a simple response either within or outside the schools. Student cultures are, rather, semi-autonomous and, as such, cannot be controlled easily or directly. They arise in relation to structural conditions in the larger society and the way in which these conditions are mediated by both the experience of schooling and the lived experiences of youth in their own communities. None of the proposals for reform address these issues. Since student cultures are closely linked to school outcomes, such outcomes cannot be altered in any substantial way by manipulating within-school factors, such as those noted in the reports.

This chapter addresses the following questions: what do student cultures look like; what gives rise to them; and to what extent might they respond to school-based alterations such as those proposed in the excellence reports? I will explore these issues through an examination of recent work on class, race, and gender cultures by Paul Willis, Linda Valli, Robert Everhart, Angela McRobbie, John Ogbu, and myself.[7] The overriding question is, to what extent can we alter student outcomes, given the cultures students themselves produce within educational institutions and the reasons why such cultures take the shape and form that they do? I use the organizing categories class, race, and gender since these constitute areas of key structural tension. Such structural tensions are worked on and through at the level of student-lived culture, producing distinct cultural forms. The school provides an arena in which such tensions are lived out, worked upon, and partially created anew.

SOCIAL CLASS

Paul Willis's study of working-class boys in England provides an excellent example of the way in which student outcomes are at least partially created at the cultural level by the students themselves, irrespective of input at the official or pragmatic operating level.

Learning to Labour is an ethnographic account of a group of working-class boys at an all-male comprehensive school in an industrial area of England. Rather than internalize messages distributed through the school, the "lads" self-consciously reject school-based meanings and spend their time "working the system," in order to gain some control over obligatorily spent time: they use school time to "have a laff." The "ear 'oles," in contrast (so named by the lads because they simply sit and listen), comply with educational authority and the notions of qualifications and credentials. The lads actively differentiate themselves from the "ear 'oles" and school culture, generally, categorizing them as effeminate and unrelated to the masculine world of work.

The most obvious dimension of the lads' culture is generalized opposition toward authority and school meanings. The lads engage in behavior designed to show resentment while stopping just short of outright confrontation. They also exhibit extensive absenteeism, signaling their

generally oppositional stance; their "struggle to win symbolic and physical space from the institution and its rules and to defeat its main perceived purpose: to make you 'work'."[8] The core skill here is being able to
get out of any given class, thus preserving personal mobility within the
school. Personal mobility encourages the preservation of the collective—
cutting class means meeting friends elsewhere. This can be seen as a
limited defeat of "individualism."

Willis's ethnography is important in that it demonstrates that we cannot
assume that meanings distributed through schools are internalized by students. Just because schools legitimate certain norms and forms of knowledge does not mean that students necessarily accept these valuations. In
the lads' case, though the school encouraged independence and achievement (as it relates to specific knowledge forms), the lads inverted these
valuations and embraced the opposite. Opposing school-based meanings
was valued at the lived cultural level. It became as important to the lads
not to succeed as it was to school authorities that they *do* succeed.[9] Thus
school "failure" is not necessarily defined as such on the cultural level.

Willis's analysis goes further, however, in important ways. By rejecting
the world of the school and the compliance of the "ear 'oles," the lads
rejected mental labor, cross-valorising, patriarchy, and the distinction
between mental and manual labor. Thus, manual labor became associated with the social superiority of masculinity, and mental labor with
the social inferiority of femininity. Since, as Harry Braverman, Michael
Buroway, and others have argued, hierarchical capitalist social relations
demand the progressive divorce of mental from manual labor, and certainly profit from (if not demand) gender-based distinctions, the lads'
rejection of the world of the school, and the way in which this rejection is
linked to masculinity, reproduces at an even deeper level the social relations of production necessary for the maintenance of a capitalist economy.[10] Although the lads live their rejection of the school as a form of
cultural autonomy and freedom, they help, at the level of their own
culture, to reproduce existing social structures.

It must be clear, however, that cultural production (and the shape and
form that lived cultures take) is not a conscious response nor does it lie
in any individual act. Its logic lies only at the *group* level; the behavior
represents a creative response to a set of lived conditions. It arises out of
definite circumstances in a specific historical relation. While not predetermined and certainly not conscious, it is also not accidental.[11] I will
return to this point later in the chapter.

In highlighting Willis's study, I do not mean to imply that the English
and American cases are identical, nor that working-class students in
Britain are the same as working-class students in the United States. Britain
has had a more overt set of class antagonisms than the United States and a
sense of "working classness" will differ to some extent simply on that

basis. My point here is not to suggest that American students are like Willis's lads; they may or may not be. What is important is the way in which student culture acts to shape school outcomes. It is not the case that the lads are less "intelligent" (as measured by standardized tests) than "successful" students. In fact, a number of the lads had been among the most intelligent students, relinquishing this position only when they decided to become a lad.

A second example of working-class cultural forms comes from Robert Everhart's ethnography of a junior high school in the United States. Unlike Willis, Everhart does not focus on those students who create overtly oppositional forms in school. He focuses, instead, on those who compromise with school culture, giving the bare minimum, taking care to complete necessary assignments without causing undue trouble.

That Everhart's students complete assignments and do not overtly reject school content or form does not mean that they are involved with the process of schooling, nor that their valuation of achievement qua achievement is any different from that of the lads. All it means is that they do not value the specific and overt negation of school meanings in the same way that the lads do. Students view school as a place to meet friends, "goof off," smoke a joint, and pursue other activities that are not related to the official learning process. To students at Harold Spencer Junior High School, it was important "that one should conform to the requirements of the school in sufficient detail so as to 'get by,' all the while creating a separate culture that permitted the maximum elements of self-determination."[12]

Students create their own cultures within schools and these cultures have a great deal to do with the production of academic outcomes—with what students "choose," so to speak, to value. It is not simply within-school factors (teachers, curriculum, etc.) that "create" student "success" as the current reports on the schools suggest. Outcomes are mediated by the culture students produce themselves.

Such cultures are materially grounded. They are, in many ways, sensible responses to existing social structures—structures that are strikingly unequal by class, race, and gender. While Willis and Everhart offer different explanations for the culture students produce, both are, at their root, structural, while at the same time allowing for some creative response to existing conditions. It is not simply that working-class students come from homes where education is not valued (which is not necessarily the case in any event) and that they, in turn, act on this valuation in school. Such students are not necessarily less intelligent than middle-class students either. It is also not true that working-class students become working-class simply because schools prepare them specifically to do so by offering them only course work in vocational areas.[13]

Willis suggests that the basic determinants of cultural form can only be found below the surface of ethnography in a more interpretive mode. He argues that the lads' rejection of so much of the form and content of schooling stems from an unconscious (and correct) realization that while working-class youth can succeed as individuals, schooling will not work for the working class as a whole. Only the destruction of the entire class structure could do the latter.[14] This insight is only partial, however. Paradoxically, insights about schooling that the lads exhibit on the cultural level are "bound back finally into the structure they are uncovering in complex ways by internal and external limitations. There is ultimately a guilty and unrecognized—precisely a partial—relationship of these [insights] to that which they seem to be independent from and see into."[15]

Everhart also stresses the relative autonomy of student cultural form. He draws attention to what he calls reified knowledge—knowledge that while abstract, tenuous, and problematical is treated as if it is concrete and "real."[16]

Such knowledge is treated unequivocally as a fact and as information to be used in the formation of real (empirical) relationships said to exist between these facts. . . . The world of education is that which supplies objective facts, concrete and agreed upon, that are to be learned, manipulated, and applied in an empirical fashion toward predefined ends.[17]

In contrast, regenerative knowledge is that which students themselves produce. It is based on mutuality of communication and "created, maintained, and re-created through the continuing interaction of people in a community setting and because what is known is, in part, dependent upon the historical forces emerging from within the community setting."[18] Regenerative knowledge is *experienced* by students as socially constructed—they feel that they have a hand in its creation. This is not the case with reified knowledge. Student regenerative knowledge is oppositional to school knowledge. While students exert no control over reified knowledge (either its production or the process through which they are supposed to consume it), they exert substantial control over regenerative knowledge. Furthermore, regenerative knowledge and its creation and recreation among students reveals that the deterministic forces of the school, as exemplified by reified knowledge, do not always take root and in fact may scarcely be paid any attention to at all. The student culture and the regenerative knowledge that grows from it may serve to resist that alienative aspect of learning by creating oppositional forms that contradict the mechanistic process of school learning.[19]

Everhart conceptualizes students qua students as a class. In school they learn that they have little control over either the process or product of their own labor. They, in turn, create their own knowledge—their own set of valuations and styles[20] that includes humor, jokes, and "goofing off" rather than, in Robert Dreeben's terms, the norms of independence, achievement (as it relates to school knowledge), universalism, and specificity.[21] Students create a "separate reality"—one that is under their control and not the institution's. (It does, of course, emerge dialectically in relation to the institution.) Within their own culture, students accord little value to official school knowledge and maximum value to humor, "goofing off," and control of their own space and time within the school.

Wills and Everhart make it clear that school outcomes are not under the control of the student culture—a culture that is produced within educational settings and differs by class, race, and gender.

RACE

The issue of race is particularly important. The American population as a whole is aging, but the youth population among Blacks and Hispanics remains large and is proportionately increasing. In 1980, less than one-third of White Americans were 19 years old and under. Forty-three percent of Hispanics and 40 percent of blacks were of comparable age. In 1981, 52 percent of white families had children of school age, whereas 71 percent and 75 percent of Black and Hispanic families, respectively, had children under 18 years old.[22] This has profound significance for schools of the future: the population of minority students is growing and this is precisely the group with which schools have been least "successful."

Both John Ogbu and I explore minority student culture in schools. While Ogbu focuses on the common school and I focus on the community college, our conclusions regarding the elements of minority student culture are rather similar.

Ogbu's study begins with the question, why do some children do so badly in school, especially minority children? The main thesis of his study, which was conducted in Stockton, California, is that the "high proportion of school failures among subordinate minorities is both a reaction to and adaptation to the limited opportunity available to them to benefit from their education."[23]

While it is often argued that minority parents do not care about their children's schooling, thus accounting for the high failure rate among these groups, Ogbu suggests that this is not the case. There is strong indication that the educational goals of "Burgherside" parents and their children are, in general, higher than those of white working-class families and higher than they were some years ago.

It is nevertheless true that the failure rate of minority students is exceptionally high. Ogbu documents this for Burgherside and suggests that this phenomenon must be rooted historically. Blacks and Mexican Americans did not have equal access to the occupational structure. Minorities do not achieve well in school because of adaptations they made in the past, when members of subordinate minority groups were not allowed to receive social and economic benefits from education.

Burghersiders fail to meet their *own* educational goals, not because they try and cannot do the work, but because they do not even try to do the work.[24] Thus a major component of minority "lived culture" in school is the minimization of effort. This minimization must be seen historically; Blacks and other subordinate minorities have not had equal access to valued goods in the society. Ogbu argues as follows:

> It would appear from their tradition of collective struggle in the field of education that caste-like minorities have looked to formal education as a means of improving their social and occupational status, if not for achieving full status with the dominant group. But their expectations have not been met because their education is not designed to help them do so and because of institutional barriers against them in adult life. They have responded to this situation, it appears, in a number of ways that have actually tended to reinforce their educational preparation for marginal economic participation. Some of these responses include conflict with the schools, disillusionment, lowered efforts, and survival strategies.[25]

In my recent ethnography of Black students in the community college, I draw similar conclusions. Like Ogbu, I find that student cultural form is, in itself, contradictory: students embrace and reject schooling at one and the same time. They affirm the process that is education but drop in and out of school, arrive late to class, exert little effort, and engage in extensive drug use that serves to distance them from the process of schooling. As I argue in *Between Two Worlds*, the effects of the culture are twofold: (1) an exceedingly low graduation rate per entering class, and (2) the reproduction of deeply rooted race/class antagonisms in the broader society.

Unlike the case for working-class Whites, the form and content of education is, on one level at least, affirmed by Blacks. At the same time, this affirmation is contradicted at the same lived cultural level.

Given that race has its own dynamic in the United States and that the economic position of White workers and Black workers is different, it is not surprising that the elements of student culture differ by race. Along these same lines, cultural form is also affected by the nature of historic struggle for particular groups. The Black struggle in the United States has, by necessity, taken a different form than the struggle for a better life among working-class Whites. Blacks have, until recently, engaged in what Gramsci calls a "war of maneuver"—a situation in which subordinated groups seek to defend their territory from assault and develop their own society as an alternative to the existing system—a system in which they are relegated to the lowest possible status. Based on the strength gained through a "war of maneuver," Black Americans were able to mount a subsequent "war of position"—a strategy that has sought to

transform the dominant racial ideology in the United States, to rearticu-
late its elements in a more egalitarian and democratic discourse.[26] Both
the fact that Blacks constitute a castelike minority in the United States
and the particular form that struggle had to take in the Black community
exert an impact on the shape and form of student culture.

While working-class White students overtly reject much of the form
and content of schooling and act on this rejection within educational
institutions, Black student opposition will be coded differently, given my
points above. Like working-class Whites, however, Blacks have understood the unequal reality they face. While they do not reject the form and
content of schooling (this must be seen as historically oppositional in and
of itself), their own lived culture reveals these impulses. Students realize
to some extent the "true value" of education for Blacks. Thus the pattern
of exerting little effort that Ogbu uncovers, and the cultural elements that
I describe at the community-college level, must be seen as impulses within
the culture toward a true understanding of the group within the social
whole, despite the current ideology of "equality of opportunity" that
suggests otherwise. Part of this is consciously understood by Blacks.[27]
This can be contrasted to working-class Whites where this process is
largely unconscious.

Black student culture arises in relation to social structure. Black students are, as a group, responding to very real conditions in the society,
both historic and current. As Michael Olneck argues, the rates of return
to schooling for Blacks and Whites are not the same. "The cost of being
Black" in the United States is that Whites get greater rewards for any
given amount of schooling than non-Whites. This is particularly true
for elementary and secondary education; it is only upon completion of
the bachelor's degree that the expected status advantage is larger for
non-Whites than Whites.[28]

While the cultures students produce in schools differ by class and race
and represent a creative response to lived conditions, cultures are, in the
final moment, bound to the social structure. Students do not respond
simply to factors within schools. While such factors cannot be ignored
(especially since certain school factors tend to parallel race/class lines
in the United States), student culture cannot be seen in relation to institutional factors alone. Student cultures are dynamic, produced on-site,
and linked in important ways to economic and social structures.

GENDER

Gender has its own dynamic in classrooms and schools. The very "stuff"
of schooling normalizes the separation of prime responsibility in public
and private domains for males and females. Sexist meanings and practices

are embedded within authority and staffing patterns, subject-matter staff segregation, the formal curriculum, differential treatment within the classroom and school, and counseling.[29] There is no question that the school "acts upon" students to reinforce gender-based meanings.[30]

My purpose here, however, is to focus on the culture females themselves produce. As in the case of class and race cultures, the reproduction of patriarchical relations on the cultural level cannot be seen simply as a response to educational policies and practices *or* broader economic and political arrangements.

Angela McRobbie's research on working-class girls in England is helpful here. While McRobbie's "girls," for the most part, endorse traditional "femininity," they do so as a creative response to their own lived conditions rather than as a passive acceptance of meanings imposed by either school or family. In spite of the fact that they know, for example, that manual work and housework are far from glamorous, they construct a fantasy future in which both realms are glamorous by elaborating what might be called an "ideology of romance." Like Willis's lads, these working-class girls create an anti-school culture, but one that is specifically *female* in that it consists of interjecting sexuality into the classroom, talking loudly about boyfriends, and wearing makeup. As McRobbie argues,

> Marriage, family life, fashion and beauty all contribute massively to this feminine anti-school culture and, in so doing, nicely illustrate the contradictions in so-called oppositional activities. Are the girls in the end not doing exactly what is required of them—and if this is the case, then could it not be convincingly argued that it is their own culture which itself is the most effective agent of social control for the girls, pushing them into compliance with that role which a whole range of institutions in capitalist society also, but less effectively, directs them toward? At the same time, they are experiencing a class relation, albeit in traditionally female terms.[31]

The extent to which working-class girls "achieve" in school is linked to the culture they produce within the institution. This culture, rather than express a valuation of achievement, expresses instead a valuation of the ability to work the school system to their own, specifically female, ends. These ends, like those of working-class males, are largely unconnected to the official culture of the school. The girls' culture is rooted in, but not totally determined by, the material position that they occupy—their social class, future role in production, and present and future role in domestic production.

Linda Valli's study of working-class girls in an American high school extends our understanding of the way in which gender culture and school outcomes are linked and the reasons why gender cultures take the form that they do. Valli studied a group of girls in a cooperative education program, a vocational program in which senior high students go to school part time and work part time in an office. She explored the way in which students construct work and family identities and, more specifically, the way in which ideologies regarding the family and the social and sexual division of labor impact upon the production of cultural forms.

Valli clearly documents the way in which gender culture shapes school-related behavior and choices. Taking the office preparation curriculum is "not the result of either 'office career aspirations' or an oppositional school culture. Instead, it represented a sensible accommodation to their future possibilities and probabilities as the students and their parents saw it. This view of future probabilities resulted not only from a realistic perception of the job market, but also from a notion of what was a good job 'for a woman'."[32]

Taking the office curriculum was perceived as the best of available options. Openings exist in the clerical area and the work was not seen as derogatory to the students' sense of femininity. Once in the program, the training that students received further marginalized their identities as wage laborers. The identity as workers outside the home was presented as secondary to a home/family identity. "While in some minimal ways the women may have rejected the ideology of male supremacy," Valli argues, "at a more fundamental level, they affirmed it, granting superiority and legitimacy to the dominance of men in a way that appeared spontaneous and natural."[33]

The girls' culture must be situated within ongoing social structural arrangements. In many ways, choosing the office work curriculum represents a "sensible" accommodation to sexist structures, in giving them *some* control over their own labor.[34] Unfortunately of course, such "choices" reproduce the very structures that give rise to them to begin with. As Valli states,

> Given the scarcity of professional level or interesting career-type jobs and the difficulty of handling such a job along with home/family responsibilities, the emphasis the co-op students placed on a traditional feminine code exhibited a certain amount of good sense. Reproducing a traditional culture of femininity can be interpreted as a way of escaping the tedious demands of wage labor and of denying it power over the self. It can even be seen as an unconscious resistance to capitalist domination. The irony, of course, is that this culture both reproduces patriarchical domination and fails to alter capitalist exploitation which is quite amenable to a segment of the skilled labor force having a tangential relation to it.[35]

In the final analysis, the girls, at the level of their own culture, opted out of academic areas and placed a low valuation on school knowledge and achievement. Once again then, culture mediates outcomes.

CULTURE AND "EXCELLENCE"

I have argued here that student cultures are tied to the production of academic outcomes. The current reports on the schools suggest that factors such as teacher training, curricular offerings, degree of federal and/or state control of schools, and so forth, "create" student "success." While this may be true to some extent, outcomes are linked to a far greater extent to cultures students themselves produce within schools.

These cultures arise in relation to existing social structures—structures that are strikingly unequal by class, race, and gender. Any proposal for reform that seeks to alter achievement levels but does not take into account these structures is doomed to almost certain failure. Given that cultures do not arise simply in relation to teachers, for example, how can we expect raising teacher salaries to impact on the form that student cultures take? How will changing curricular requirements impact upon student outcomes, given that valued practices and styles among students do not arise solely in relation to curriculum? Can we really affect student cultures through a set of within-school reforms that do not directly address the structures that give rise to them to begin with? I think not.

As I have argued throughout, student cultures must be seen as sensible responses to existing conditions. What students "choose" to value represents a creative response to the material conditions of their lives—to their position, as they experience it, as classed, raced, and gendered persons in a society such as our own. This does not mean that the form of such cultures is totally unrelated to what schools do. The cultures students produce in schools are at least partially a response to school practices themselves. In the case of the lads, for example, their working-class culture would not necessarily have produced in them the kinds of within-school actions that it did had the school not been so ignoring of their culture to begin with. By attempting to impose uncritically a middle-class cultural and reward system on students, the school elicited a stronger collective working-class response than might have been the case if the school had been more sensitive to working-class culture. My point here is that schools *may* be related to student culture in significant ways, but these relationships are tied to the lived experiences of students *outside* schools—to the material conditions of their lives, and the extent to which these material conditions are affirmed, denied, or simply ignored within educational institutions. At present, we possess relatively little knowledge about the ways in which school practices are actually linked to the production of student cultural form. This needs to be a central focus for future research on schools.[36]

It is possible, of course, to argue that the proposed reforms will produce higher test scores among those students whose lived culture reflects a valuation of academic achievement to begin with—in other words, middle-class students. While this is possible, I am uncomfortable with this notion for a number of reasons. To begin with, it is not at all clear to me that middle-class students have not made similar compromises regarding school knowledge and culture. Linda McNeil's excellent study suggests that they have; that middle-class students also give the minimum, what they perceive as necessary to attend college, thus maintaining their position in the class structure.[37] Secondly, the reports themselves tend to emphasize that "excellence" must be accompanied by equity, in which case the points raised here about class, race, and gender cultures are critically important. America is still not interested (at least on the ideological level) in totally abandoning equality of opportunity. This is reflected in the reports.

It is difficult for me to oppose the concept of "excellence." I support a number of the proposed reforms in that I would like to see more academic content in the schools, and I have never been a supporter of tracking.[38] All students should, I believe, be exposed to a solid academic curriculum. Teachers should be paid more, and they should exert more control over their own labor in the classroom. There is too much time wasted in school and there are too many classroom interruptions, often from the office by means of the public address system. Philip Cusick has pointed out that over three hours of a seven-hour school day is spent in procedural and maintenance details. A large part of the students' day is spent in a state of spectatorship, during which time he or she simply watches and waits.[39] Others have made this same comment, most recently Everhart and Goodlad. Surely we have need for improvement simply on that score alone.

Stating that I support some of the proposed reforms does not mean that I believe that any of them will, *in and of themselves*, have the desired effect of raising achievement levels. In order for student cultures to change, there must be change in other sectors of the society. Class, race, and gender conflicts are historic in this country, and cultural creation in schools reflects historically rooted oppression, struggle, and adaptations on the part of different groups. These struggles have been waged and continue to be waged in a system that is highly unequal by class, race, and gender. Unless we address these inequalities and tensions directly in the economic, political, *and* cultural sphere where schools lie, we will not substantially affect school outcomes. Within schools, we need to acknowledge and legitimate the lived experiences of all students. At the same time, we must work toward altering society itself so that opportunity structures are more equal.

Even if such structures change, however, we will not see quick shifts on the cultural level. Culture embeds a people's historic trajectory—as such, it does not change overnight. I support some of the reforms because they are what I value. I also believe that extending a more serious academic curriculum in an across-the-board fashion may enable more individuals to attain the social mobility this country promises. Over time, this may lead to some alteration in the social structure, in that inequality may be more randomly distributed across class, race, and gender lines than it is currently. To think that we can alter school outcomes easily, however, is a mistake. We have much more to learn about *why* students behave in schools as they do before we assume we can control outcomes.

NOTES

*   This chapter was previously published in P. Altbach, G. Kelly and L. Weis, (Eds.), *Excellence in Education* (Buffalo: Prometheus Press, 1985), 217–233. It represents a response to the then recently released corpus of "excellence" reports, specifically the National Commission on Excellence in Education, *A Nation at Risk: The Imperative for Educational Reform* (Washington, DC: Government Printing Office, 1983); Ernest Boyer, *High School: A Report on Secondary Education in America* (New York: Harper and Row, 1983); John Goodlad, *A Place Called School: Prospects for the Future* (New York: McGraw Hill, 1983); Theodore Sizer, *Horace's Compromise: The Dilemma of the American High School* (Boston: Houghton Mifflin, 1984); Mortimer Adler, *The Paideia Proposal: An Educational Manifesto* (New York: Macmillan, 1982); and the National Science Board Commission on Pre-college Education in Mathematics, Science, and Technology, *Educating Americans for the 21st Century*, 2 vols. (Washington, DC: National Science Foundation, 1983). While the author stands behind the general point of her argument, research over the past twenty years necessitates modification of select key points. In particular, not enough attention is paid in this piece to the ways in which the workings of the schools themselves (for example, tracking, nature of "official knowledge", teacher–student interaction patterns, and conceptualized and observed school-community relations) disadvantage certain groups, particularly African Americans.

1   Although couched in different language, this is reminiscent of studies within the Coleman Report genre, where the attempt is to locate within-school factors that predict academic achievement. See, for example, Central Advisory Council for Education, *Children and their Primary Schools*, Vols. 1 and 2. The Plowden Report (London: Her Majesty's Stationery Office, 1967); and James Coleman et al., *Equality of Educational Opportunity* (Washington, DC: U.S. Government Printing Office, 1966).

2   Numerous reports fall under this rubric. The ones I am dealing with specifically include: National Commission on Excellence in Education, *A Nation at Risk: The Imperative for Educational Reform* (Washington, DC: Government Printing Office, 1983); E. Boyer, *High School: A Report on Secondary*

Education in America (New York: Harper and Row, 1983); John Goodlad, *A Place Called School: Prospects for the Future* (New York: McGraw-Hill, 1983); T. Sizer, *Horace's Compromise: The Dilemma of the American High School* (Boston: Houghton Mifflin, 1984); Mortimer Adler, *The Paideia Proposal: An Educational Manifesto* (New York: Macmillan, 1982); and The National Science Board Commission on Precollege Education in Mathematics, Science, and Technology, *Educating Americans for the 21st Century*, 2 vols. (Washington, DC: National Science Foundation, 1983).

3   Gail Kelly, "The Reports on Excellence: Setting the Boundaries of Debate about Education," in Philip Altback, Gail Kelly, and Lois Weiss (Eds.), *Excellence in Education: Perspectives on Policy and Practice* (Buffalo, NY: Prometheus Press, 1985), 29–40.

4   John Goodlad, *A Place Called School*, 75–76.

5   Theodore Sizer, *Horace's Compromise*, 138–140.

6   The reform effort may fail for other reasons as well, of course. To begin with, reforms on paper are often not implemented. As Kelly points out, the proposed "excellence" reforms are themselves contradictory as well.

7   Paul Willis, *Learning to Labour: How Working Class Kids Get Working Class Jobs* (Westmead, England: Saxon House Press, 1977); Linda Valli, *Becoming Clerical Workers* (Boston: Routledge and Kegan Paul, 1986); Lois Weis, *Between Two Worlds: Black Students in an Urban Community College* (Boston: Routledge and Kegan Paul, 1985); Robert Everhart, *Reading, Writing and Resistance: Adolescence and Labor in a Junior High School* (Boston: Routledge and Kegan Paul, 1983); Angela McRobbie, "Working Class Girls and the Culture of Femininity," in *Women Take Issue*, ed. Women's Studies Group (London: Hutchinson, 1978): 96–108; and John Ogbu, *The Next Generation: An Ethnography of Education in an Urban Neighborhood* (New York: Academic Press, 1974).

8   Paul Willis, *Learning to Labour*, 26.

9   My point here is that the structure of the school promotes the consumption of a specific body of knowledge and set of norms. "Success" is measured by the extent to which students master this knowledge and act in terms of the norms. While "failure" may be functional in terms of the broader social structure, it cannot be argued that school authorities want to promote failure. Tracking may, of course, promote the "success" of one group over another.

10   See Harry Braverman, *Labor and Monopoly Capital* (New York: Monthly Review Press, 1974); and Michael Buroway, "Toward a Marxist Theory of the Labor Process: Braverman and Beyond," *Politics and Society* 8 (no. 3–4, 1978): 247–312.

11   See Paul Willis, *Learning to Labour*, 120–121, for a discussion of this important point.

12   Robert Everhart, *Reading, Writing and Resistance*, 121.

13   The latter point must be seen as a debate with the structuralists such as Althusser and Poulantzas. For a discussion of the culturalist/structuralist controversy, see Michael Apple, ed., *Cultural and Economic Reproduction in Education: Essays on Class, Ideology and the State* (London: Routledge and Kegan Paul, 1982), ch. 1; and Richard Johnson, "Histories of Culture, Theories of Ideology," in *Ideology and Cultural Production*, ed. Michele Barrett et al. (New York: St. Martin's Press, 1979): 49–77. For a structuralist perspective see Nicos Poulantzas, *Classes in Contemporary Capitalism* (London: New Left Books, 1975); Louis Althusser, "Ideology and Ideological

State Apparatuses, in *Lenin and Philosophy, and Other Essays* (London: New Left Books, 1971); and Samuel Bowles and Herbert Gintis, *Schooling in Capitalist America* (New York: Basic Books, 1976).

14 Here I am simplifying a rather complex argument. For elaboration see Paul Willis, *Learning to Labour*, especially chs 5 and 6.

15 Paul Willis, *Learning to Labour*, 119.

16 Robert Everhart, *Reading, Writing and Resistance*, 86.

17 Robert Everhart, *Reading, Writing and Resistance*, 86.

18 Robert Everhart, *Reading, Writing and Resistance*, 125.

19 Robert Everhart, *Reading, Writing and Resistance*, 129.

20 Such valuations on the cultural level are linked to the wider system of commercial youth culture that supplies a lexicography of style, with already connoted meanings that are adapted by various groups to express their own located meanings. These located cultural forms, in turn, affect the shape and form of commercial youth culture. This theme is pursued more extensively by Mike Brake, *The Sociology of Youth Culture and Youth Sub-Cultures* (London: Routledge and Kegan Paul, 1980).

21 Robert Dreeben, *On What is Learned in School* (Reading, MA: Addison Wesley, 1968).

22 Ernest Boyer, *High School*, 5.

23 John Ogbu, *The Next Generation*, 12.

24 John Ogbu, *The Next Generation*, 197.

25 John Ogbu, "Equalization of Educational Opportunity and Racial/Ethnic Inequality," in *Comparative Education*, ed. Philip Altbach, Gail Kelly, and Robert Arnove (New York: Macmillan, 1982): 269–289.

26 This is Omi and Winant's point. See Michael Omi and Howard Winant, "By the Rivers of Babylon: Race in the United States," *Socialist Review* 71 (September/October 1983): 56.

27 Ogbu and I draw different conclusions here. Ogbu stresses the way in which castelike minorities consciously understand their subordination and therefore "blame the system" for their failure. I argue that, at least on the community college level, black students also blame themselves for failure. My point is that a tendency to blame the system exists side by side with the tendency to blame oneself.

28 Michael Olneck, "The Effects of Educaton", in *Who Gets Ahead?* Christopher Jencks et al. [eds] (New York: Basic Books, 1979): 150–170. For a careful analysis of the historical position of blacks in the American economy, see Michael Reich, *Racial Inequality* (Princeton, NJ: Princeton University Press, 1981).

29 See Gail Kelly and Ann Nihlen, "Schooling and the Reproduction of Patriarchy: Unequal Workloads, Unequal Rewards," in *Cultural and Economic Reproduction in Education*, ed, Michael Apple (London: Routledge and Kegan Paul, 1982): 162–180.

30 This is true for class and race meanings as well.

31 Angela McRobbie, "Working Class Girls and the Culture of Femininity," 104.

32 Linda Valli, *Becoming Clerical Workers*, 102.

33 Linda Valli, *Becoming Clerical Workers*, 252.

34 Jane Gaskell points to the way in which sexual harassment also influences "job choice" for women. While there is certainly harassment in an office setting, it is less intense than that which is experienced in a traditionally male working-class area. See Jane Gaskell, "Course Differentiation in the High

School: The Perspective of Working Class Females" (Paper presented in Symposium on Race, Class and Gender Analysis in Education—Implications for Curriculum Theory, Meetings of the American Educational Research Association, Montreal, April 1983).

35 Linda Valli, *Becoming Clerical Workers*, 263.

36 I must point out here that student cultures can serve to inform school practice in positive ways. Resistance in schools based on class, race, and gender cultures can, if understood, be taken into account in some kind of productive manner. One example might be the way in which the assertion of minority culture has impacted upon literature choice.

37 Linda McNeil, "Economic Dimensions of Social Studies Curricula: Curriculum as Institutionalized Knowledge," unpublished Ph.D. diss., University of Wisconsin—Madison, 1977.

38 Sizer's *Horace's Compromise*, for example, recommends the elimination of tracking.

39 Philip Cusick, *Inside High School: The Students' World* (New York: Holt, Rinehart and Winston, 1973).

Chapter 12

Racial Identity Attitudes, School Achievement, and Academic Self-Efficacy among African American High School Students

Karen McCurtis Witherspoon, Suzette L. Speight, and Anita Jones Thomas

African American students "generally earn lower grades, drop out more often, and attain less education than do Whites" (Mickelson, 1990, p. 44). Although there is considerable agreement that ethnic and racial differences in school performance exist, there is little consensus about the causes of these differences (Steinberg, Dornbusch, & Brown, 1991). Both biological and environmental causes are among the explanations for the consistent and disturbing finding that the academic performance of many African American students falls behind other groups.

Steinberg et al. (1991) examined the roles of parenting, familial values, and beliefs about rewards of success with approximately 15,000 high school students. A significant finding related to the African American youngsters was that the absence of peer support seemed to undermine the positive influences of authoritative parenting on students' school performance. Steinberg et al. reported that African American students faced a unique situation because, although their parents were supportive of academic success, it was much more difficult to join a peer group that encouraged the same goal of academic excellence.

The recognition that the peer group is greatly influencing African American students is not a surprising finding in and of itself. After all, developmental theory consistently has talked about the importance of friends and peer acceptance during adolescent years. For African American adolescents, racial identity may be intricately linked with the struggle for peer acceptance. Students from various ethnic backgrounds may experience some negative label for high academic achievement (e.g., brain, nerd, bookworm). Unique to the struggle for peer acceptance by African American adolescents is the fear that peers will accuse them of not "being Black." African American students who get good grades are often accused of trying to "act White" because performing well in school has been deemed as a White behavior by some. Many talented Black students find that one of the most surprising source of obstacles to academic achievement is their peer group (Gregory, 1992).

Fordham (1988) conducted a qualitative investigation exploring the process by which African American students are able to achieve academic success. Fordham suggested that for African American students to succeed in school, they consciously or unconsciously dissociate themselves from the African American community—its values, beliefs, and customs —and embrace the culture of the school. Fordham and Ogbu (1986) described this phenomenon as "the burden of acting White." They proposed that this burden arose partly because White Americans traditionally refused to acknowledge the intellectual capabilities of African Americans, and partly because African Americans began to doubt their own ability, thereby defining success as the White person's prerogative. According to Fordham and Ogbu, students who minimize their connection to their indigenous culture and assimilate into the school culture improve their chances of succeeding in school. Fordham called this deliberate coping strategy cultivating a raceless persona.

The conclusions reached by Fordham (1988) and Fordham and Ogbu (1986) suggest that an adolescent cannot identify with the African American community and be a successful student. The literature on racial identity and achievement in high-achieving African American students has been largely built on the notion that such students are forced to choose between a pro-African American, anti-achievement identity and a pro-White, pro-achievement identity (Rowley & Moore, 2002). Fordham's notion of racelessness as a coping strategy, while perhaps true for some students, may be only one side of the story. In contrast, Ward (1990) proposed another alternative for high-achieving African American high school students. In interviews of approximately twenty students, Ward found that racial identity, personal commitment, and academic achievement were successfully converged during the high school years. The students that Ward interviewed reported feeling good about their race and personally strengthened by their racial status. Ward concluded that the African American adolescent must reject White society's negative evaluation and construct an identity that includes one's Blackness as positively valued and desired.

These two studies, Fordham (1988) and Ward (1990), have yielded conflicting results regarding the relationship of racial group identity and high school achievement. Although both of these studies addressed the impact of the students' race, neither of these studies utilized a popular prevailing theory of Black identity development (e.g., Cross, 1971), nor did these investigations operationalize racial identity attitudes with the Racial Identity Attitude Scale (Parham & Helms, 1981). Fordham and Ward provided qualitative data from a small number of research participants and the transferability of these results to other adolescents has yet to be determined. Variables such as self-esteem and self-concept were not measured by these authors. Nevertheless, many researchers have postulated that a relationship existed among school achievement, self-esteem, and racial identity (e.g., Ford & Harris, 1997; Fordham, 1988; Miller, 1999; Ward, 1990).

Few studies have examined the relationship between racial identity (e.g., the attitudes one holds about his or her Blackness) and high school achievement. Cross (1971, 1978) postulated a four-stage model of racial identity development. The first stage, *preencounter*, is characterized by one's racial attitudes being primarily pro-White or anti-Black. The individual devalues his or her ascribed race and racial group in favor of Euro-American culture. The second stage, *encounter*, begins when the individual has an experience that challenges his or her prior view of Blackness. The third stage, *immersion-emersion*, represents a turning point in the conversion from an old to a new frame of reference. This stage involves learning and experiencing the meaning and value of one's race and culture. This stage is also characterized by the tendency to be pro-Black and anti-White. The fourth stage, *internalization*, is the stage in which the individual achieves pride and security in his or her race and identity. This stage is also illustrated by psychological openness, ideological flexibility, and a general decline of anti-White feelings, though Black reference groups remain primary. More recent developments in the model are outlined by Cross (1991, 1995) and Cross, Parham, and Helms (1991).

In a review of ethnic identity research with adolescents, Phinney (1990) concluded that empirical investigations have yielded conflicting results regarding the relationships of self-concept measures and identity. To capture the complexity and malleability of ethnic identity, it seems critical to recognize how relational and cultural contexts contribute to one's sense of self (Yeh & Hwang, 2000). Spencer and Markstrom-Adams (1990) have suggested that to better understand the complex process of identity formation, investigators should examine both racial or ethnic identity and self-esteem. While research has examined the relationship between self-concept and achievement and between self-esteem and achievement, Grantham and Ford (2003) argued that people of color have been shortchanged in theories of self-concept and self-esteem because these theories have failed to consider racial identity in the context of self-concept, self-esteem, and overall self-perceptions. For this study, self-esteem and academic self-concept (or one's sense of personal efficacy about academic activities) will be measured.

The purpose of the present investigation was to explore the psychosocial-cultural variables related to African American students' school performance. More specifically, a main objective was to examine the extent to which racial identity, self-esteem and academic concept could predict academic success for African American high school students. An additional objective of this investigation was to look at the interplay of family and peer support on school performance. Given the history of inferior academic achievement of African American students and the important role of education for advancement in today's society, rigorous research is warranted to examine the relationship between academic success and racial identity. Based on the literature related to African American school performance, the following research questions were examined: (a) What is the relationship between the various racial identity attitudes, self-esteem, academic self-concept, and grade point average (GPA)? (b) What are the students' perceptions of family support and peer support? and (c) What is the best predictor model of GPA?

METHODS

The participants were 86 African American high school students in Upward Bound programs at two medium-sized universities in the Midwest. Project Upward Bound is a national pre-collegiate program funded by the United States Department of Education that has a curriculum designed to encourage the development of skills, motivation, and sophistication needed for success in education (K. Ingram, personal communication, January 25, 1993). Students chosen for Upward Bound must submit a high school transcript showing classes and grades with a 2.0 GPA or higher and be a member of a low income family and/or will be a first generation college student upon graduation from high school.

Although all Upward Bound students from the two programs were invited to participate in the study, only respondents who identified themselves as Black or African American were used in this study. Thirty-nine of the participants were from one Upward Bound program (59%) and 47 of the participants were from the other Upward Bound Program (41%). Thirty-five percent of the participants were male (n = 30) and 65% (n = 56) were female. Students were divided among class levels as follows: 25 were freshman (29.4 percent), 17 were sophomores (20 percent), 29 were juniors (34.1 percent), and 14 were seniors (16.5 percent). The students' ages ranged from 12 years to 18 years, with an average age of 15.4 years (S.D. = 1.22). Parental consent was obtained for all of the research participants. No financial or credit incentives were given for participation. Both Upward Bound project administrators supplied final cumulative GPAs of participants, which were used as a measure of school performance.

Instruments

Student Questionnaire

A brief questionnaire was presented to respondents asking their age, gender, ethnicity, race, and class rank. In addition, respondents answered five open-ended questions that were used to specifically assess the perceived conflict between being popular with the Black peer group or being smart. These questions were adapted from an inventory utilized by Kunjufu (1988). Only the two questions pertaining to peer and family support were analyzed in this study: "Does your family encourage your academic activities?" and "Do most of your friends encourage your academic activities?"

Personal Orientation Inventory/Self-Regard Subscale

The Personal Orientation Inventory (POI: Shostrom, 1963) is a measure to assess self-actualization. The Self-Regard subscale is a 16-item scale that measures the degree of positive feelings an individual has due to sense of worth and strength, or self-esteem. The inventory consists of pairs of numbered statements from which participants choose the item that most consistently applies to them. Each question is assigned a point value (0 or 1), with possible total scores ranging from 0 to 16. The higher the score, the stronger the esteem. The test-retest reliability for the Self-Regard subscale has been found to be .71 (Parham & Helms, 1985). Parham and Helms (1985) found that positive scores on the Self-Regard subscale were negatively correlated with *preencounter* and *immersion-emersion* attitudes, and that *encounter* attitudes (as measured by the *Racial Identity Attitude Scale* [RIAS]) were positively correlated with high scores of the Self-Regard subscale.

Academic Self-Concept Scale

The Academic Self-Concept Scale (ASCS) was developed by Reynolds, Ramirez, Magrina, and Allen (1980) to assess how positively one feels about his/her academic ability. Where the word *college* appeared in the scale, it was substituted for the word *school* to make the inventory relevant to this high school sample. The ASCS consists of 40 statements with a four-point Likert scale ranging from 1 = *strongly disagree* to 4 = *strongly agree*, with no neutral point. Scores can range from 40 to 160; the higher the score, the stronger the level of academic self-concept. Reynolds et al. reported an internal consistency of .91. The ASCS has been found to correlate with GPA ($r = .40–.52$), SAT scores ($r = .12–.22$), and the Rosenberg Self-Esteem Scale ($r = .45$; Reynolds et al., 1980).

Racial Identity Attitude Scale (Short Form B)

The RIAS (Parham & Helms, 1981) is a 30-item scale that measures attitudes associated with the Cross (1971) model of Black identity development, Psychological Nigrescence. This scale was developed from Hall, Cross, and Freedle's (1972) Q-sort procedure, which asked subjects to sort cards that reflected attitudes at the various stages of racial identity.

Each RIAS item consists of statements to which each participant responds how much each statement describes him or her using a five-point Likert scale (1 = *strongly disagree* to 5 = *strongly agree*). There are four subscales, corresponding to the four stages of Black identity development (*preencounter, encounter, immersion-emersion,* and *internalization*). A mean scale score is computed for each stage by summing the responses to the item keyed in a particular subscale and dividing by the number of items in each subscale.

Internal consistency reliabilities for the subscales were found to be: *preencounter* = .67; *encounter* = .72; *immersion-emersion* = .66; *internalization* = .71 (Parham & Helms, 1981). Ponterotto and Wise (1987), using oblique factor analytic methods and examining alternative factor solutions, found strong support for three of the four constructs described in the Cross (1971) model. They found little statistical support for the *encounter* stage as measured by the RIAS. Furthermore, some of the subscale intercorrelations were high enough to question the independence of the scale constructs. Despite these potential difficulties, there has been consistent evidence for the construct validity of the scale.

Procedure

Upward Bound students from the first university were introduced to the research study at parents' orientation day. Parents were able to turn in consent forms to the investigator that day. Subsequently, parents who were not at the orientation were mailed consent forms with return envelopes. Students were administered surveys as a group at one of their weekly meetings. Students were given up to 45 minutes to answer items as thoroughly as possible. Follow-up phone calls were made to parents of students who needed to complete parent or guardian consent forms. The Upward Bound students from the second university were given individual packets by program administrators that contained surveys and parent or guardian consent forms. The only directions given were to complete surveys as thoroughly as possible and return the completed package along with the consent forms to the Upward Bound office.

RESULTS

Descriptive Data

A series of ANOVAS (analyses of variance) were conducted to assess for possible Upward Bound program location, gender, and class rank differences on all predictor and criterion variables. These preliminary analyses were conducted as a justification for collapsing the different sample subgroups. Adjusting our stated probability level of .05 with the Bonferroni test, no significant mean differences were found for location or class rank. There were significant differences found by gender. Gender was found to be significantly related to GPA and *immersion* scores. Planned Comparisons using Tukey's Honest Significant Difference test (HSD) indicated that women possessed higher mean GPAs than men (2.72 vs. 2.12; $F = 5.99, p < .01$). Men had higher mean *immersion* scores than women (3.25 vs. 2.86; $F = 9.82, p < .05$). Table 12.1 summarizes the means for each of the variables of interest.

Table 12.1 Means, standard deviations, and ranges for all variables

Variables	Mean	SD
GPA	2.51	.77
Pre	2.02	.52
Enc	3.32	.78
Imm	2.99	.69
Int	4.02	.44
ASCS	111.83	14.92
POI	11.98	2.16

Notes: ASCS = Academic Self-Concept Scale scores. POI = Personal Orientation Inventory, Self-Regard subscale.

Reliability coefficients were calculated for the RIAS subscales, and the ASCS inventory. The internal consistency measures for *preencounter, encounter, immersion-emersion,* and *internalization* were .53, .42, .64, and .44, respectively. The Cronbach alpha calculated for ASCS was .90.

A correlation matrix for all of the research variables is presented in Table 12.2. Among the RIAS subscales, *preencounter* attitudes had a significant negative correlation with *internalization* attitudes. *Encounter* attitudes had a high significant correlation with both *immersion* and *internalization* attitudes. *Immersion* attitudes were found to have a significant and positive relationship with *internalization* attitudes. ASCS scores were positively correlated with GPA and POI scores. POI scores were not significantly correlated with any of the RIAS subscales.

Responses to the questions, "Does your family encourage your

Table 12.2 Correlation coefficients for all variables

	GPA	Preencounter	Encounter	Immersion	Internalization	ASCS	POI
GPA	—	-.1193	-.2751*	-.3147**	-.0357	.3702**	.0189
Preencounter		—	-.0067	-.1798	-.2684*	-.1916	-.0401
Encounter			—	.6662**	.5153**	-.1192	.0514
Immersion				—	.4801**	-.1693	-.0682
Internalization					—	.1514	.1865
ASCS						—	.3668**
POI							—

Notes: ASCS = Academic Self-Concept Scale scores. POI = Personal Orientation Inventory, Self-Regard subscale.
* p < .05; **p < .01 (two-tailed).

academic activities?" and "Do most of your friends encourage your academic activities?" on the student information survey were analyzed for content and placed into the following categories by the authors: 89.8 percent of the participants stated that their family encourages their academic activities, 4.5 percent said that their parents do not encourage their academic activities, and 2.3 percent said that sometimes their parents encourage their academic activities, leaving 3.4 percent who did not respond to the question. For the question regarding peer support, 45.5 percent said their friends encourage their academic activities, 30.7 percent said their friends do not encourage their academic activities, 11.4 percent said sometimes their friends encourage their academic activities, 9.1 percent said that some of their friends encourage their academic activities, and 3.4 percent did not respond to the question.

Because the purpose of the study was to test a model that would predict GPA, a simultaneous multiple regression was calculated with POI scores, ASCS scores, and the RIAS subscales. A forced-entry method was chosen over a stepwise method to examine the combined influence of the variables of interest (see Table 12.3).

Table 12.3 Summary of simultaneous regression for grade point average

Variable	R^2	B	T	p<
Preencounter	.00	−.071	−.635	.523
Immersion	.14	−.378	−2.86	.006**
Internalization	.02	.133	.975	.333
ASCS	.13	.362	3.03	.004**
POI	.03	.183	−1.51	.137

Notes: ASCS = Academic Self-Concept Scale scores. POI = Personal Orientation Inventory, Self-Regard subscale.
** $p < .01$.

The best predictor model for GPA was *immersion* attitudes and academic self-concept as measured by ASCS. Together, *immersion-emersion* and ASCS accounted for 27 percent of the variance in GPA scores, $F(7,68) = 3.42$, $R^2 = .27$, $p < .01$. *Immersion* attitudes had an inverse relationship with GPA. Thus, as *immersion* attitudes increased, the student's GPA decreased. ASCS and GPA had a positive relationship. Thus, the higher the ASCS, the higher the GPA.

DISCUSSION

The purpose of this study was to examine the extent to which racial identity, self-esteem, and academic concept could predict school performance for an African American high school student population. The results as they relate to the hypothesis, as well as relevant literature, will be presented in this section. Limitations of the study and implications for future research will also be discussed.

Racial Identity Attitudes and GPA, ASCS, and POI

None of the various racial identity attitudes were significantly correlated with ASCS scores or POI scores. This was somewhat surprising. Prior research had reported that *preencounter* attitudes were related to feelings of inferiority, inadequacy, and lack of self-acceptance (Butler, 1975; Cross, 1971; Parham & Helms, 1985). It is important to recognize that the findings of the present investigation were based on students in a different developmental stage than the previously cited research. POI scores were positively related to ASCS scores. As self-esteem increased, so did academic self-concept. Unfortunately, it is not possible to determine causation from this correlation. Although nonsignificant, the correlations between ASCS scores and *preencounter*, *encounter*, and *immersion* attitudes were all in a negative direction, whereas the correlation between ASCS and *internalization* scores were in a positive direction. These trends are intriguing to consider, and support Oyserman, Harrison, and Bybee's (2001) finding that racial identity can promote academic efficacy in African American youth. Only attitudes reflecting internalized racial identity tend to be positively related to higher academic self-concepts. Furthermore, ASCS scores were significantly correlated with GPA. Self-efficacy theory would predict that student's academic self-concept would be an important mediator of academic performance.

Both *encounter* and *immersion* attitudes were inversely related to GPA. The more that students held *encounter* and *immersion* attitudes, the lower their GPA. *Immersion* attitudes and ASCS scores were significant predictors of GPA. Involving oneself in Black culture is a very central part of *immersion* stage. Gregory (1992) and McCalope (1991) explained that some African American students fear their academic-related events will be associated with White behavior. "Coping strategies that seemingly correspond to the *immersion-emersion* phase appear to occur quite often among Black adolescence who find themselves adrift in White educational systems" (Helms, 1990, p. 27).

Young men endorsed *immersion* attitudes significantly more than young women. The response to an angry, young African American male may operate in the form of not inviting him to fully participate in the learning environment, and/or his withdrawal from the school environment, either one of which could result in lower grades. Adding additional confirmation to this hypothesis is the finding that being female was found to be a significant predictor of GPA. Obviously, some of the young men in this investigation were struggling with both issues of racial identity and achievement. These findings were also replicated by Ford and Harris (1997), who found that males had lower GPAs and higher *immersion* attitudes than females. Certainly causation cannot be inferred from these correlations. We cannot determine which comes first—lower grades or *immersion* attitudes—yet it is interesting to speculate.

Some studies have suggested that African Americans have to give up their racial identification with the Black community to succeed (Fordham, 1988), whereas other studies have found that pride in their race strengthened students and aided their academic success (Ford & Harris, 1997; Oyserman et al., 2001; Ward, 1990). According to the present investigation, neither of these results were wrong. The dichotomous conceptualization of racial identity as either pro-African American or pro-White offers an overly simplistic view of how gifted African American students function (Rowley & Moore, 2002). Instead, it appears that a variety of racial identity attitudes actually exist within the high school student population. This study found high school students with positive Black identity attitudes and good grades. This study also found students with pro-Black/anti-White attitudes who had poor grades. Perhaps the different studies tapped into students holding a preponderance of one racial identity attitude or another.

Family Support and Peer Support

Ninety percent of the sample said that their family encouraged their academic activities. Steinberg et al. (1991) found that in general, African American high school students had active, involved, authoritative parents who were very supportive of academics. It was disturbing to discover that 5 percent of the students reported that their parents did not encourage academics and 2 percent reported that their parents occasionally encouraged academic activities. Respondents were not asked to describe specific ways in which they felt their parents were unsupportive. Nonetheless, the lack of encouraging parents, or worse yet, the effect of disparaging remarks from parents, could be detrimental to a student's academic and personal development. This investigation highlights the importance of understanding the familial context within which African American high school students may find themselves.

Forty-six percent of the students reported that their friends encouraged academic activities and 31 percent of the students reported that friends did not encourage academics. Kunjufu (1988), in his survey of over 300 African American high school students, found that the majority of students reported that their friends encouraged their academic activities. Although Kunjufu's results were corroborated in this study, there was a significant portion of the students in the present sample who described an unsupportive peer group. This suggests that an interest in academics could be a potential hindrance for students who desire to connect with other African American peers. The possibility that these students would choose to downplay school-related activities such as class participation, studying for exams, and participating in nontraditional extracurricular activities exists for a significant number of students in this study. Ultimately, these choices may divert educational and career accomplishments and are therefore of great concern.

Limitations of Present Study

The participants in this study were all recruited from two Upward Bound programs; this particular environment may have had an effect on the results found. For example, in explaining the finding that close to half (46 percent) of the group reported that their friends supported their academic endeavor, it may be that this sample of high school students was surrounded by more friends who readily support academics because they participated in Upward Bound programs. Upward Bound brings together students with the aim of providing support services that would enable them to succeed in college. Consequently, generalizability to the wider African American high school student population at large is limited. The use of cumulative GPA as the only outcome variable for school performance is also problematic because it is such a distal measure. Perhaps more proximal variables (i.e., classroom behavior, time spent on homework, amount of preparation for exams) might have yielded a better assessment of school performance.

Because the instruments used in the study were normed on a college-age population, reliability coefficients were calculated for each of the instruments. The reliability coefficient for the POI (.54) was lower in comparison to previous findings (Shostrom, 1963). However, the Cronbach's alpha for the ASCS (.90) was consistent with other investigations. The reliability coefficients for the RIAS subscales were also lower than those reported in other recent studies (e.g., Stevenson, 1995). It is not clear why this was the case. For some reason, this sample of adolescents did not respond in a consistent manner on the RIAS. During the administration of the survey packet with the first group of Upward Bound students, several of the students made audible disparaging comments about some of the words used in the RIAS (e.g., honky, the man). Perhaps different versions of the RIAS were used in these different investigations. Whether the RIAS can be appropriately used to assess the identity of non-college populations remains to be determined (Helms, 1990). Although the RIAS is written at an eighth-grade reading level, the reliability coefficients calculated for the subscales bring into question whether it is a valid measure for high school students. Moreover, the high correlations among the RIAS subscales affect the stability of the regression analysis that was performed. This investigation did, however, have enough statistical power to achieve adequate results. A power analysis found that with 86 subjects and an alpha level of .01, the power was .985, which was more than adequate.

On the other hand, Stevenson (1995), in a study with 287 adolescents age 14 and 15 years, found support for use of the 50-item RIAS scale. Factor analytic procedures yielded moderately reliable factors corresponding to *preencounter*, *immersion*, and *internalization* stages. Plummer (1995) also successfully used the RIAS with 3,000 adolescents to identify, among other things, gender differences in the expression of *preencounter* attitudes. Taken together, this is a confusing state of affairs for the RIAS. It is difficult to ascertain if the problems with the RIAS are of a conceptual or measurement nature.

Suggestions for Future Research

Given the findings about gender differences in achievement, research is warranted that examines the different ways that Black male and female students are coping in high schools. Laveist and McDonald (2002) suggest that African American females show no signs of buckling under "acting White" pressure. Also, more research on racial identity attitudes in high school populations, including an examination of parental socialization messages around race and achievement, is needed. This would necessitate the development of an age-appropriate measure or revision of the RIAS for high school populations.

In conclusion, this investigation has found that there are indeed within-group differences in racial identity attitudes of African American high school students that may be related to the various ways that students perform in school. According to the National Task Force on the Achievement Gap (McCombs, 2000), there is a limited presence of African Americana among high achieving students at all levels of our educational system. It is hoped that with continued research, psychoeducational interventions could be developed aimed at helping all African American students succeed academically.

ACKNOWLEDGMENT

Witherspoon, K. M., Speight, S. L., and Thomas, A. J. (1997) Racial Attitudes, School Achievement and Academic Self-efficacy among African American High School Students. *Journal of Black Psychology*, 21(4) 344–357. Copyright © 1997. Reprinted by permission of Sage Publications.

REFERENCES

Butler, R. O. (1975). Psychotherapy: Implications of a Black-consciousness process model. *Psychotherapy: Theory, Research, and Practice, 12*, 407–411.

Cross, W. E. (1971). Negro-to-Black conversion experience: Toward a psychology of black liberation. *Black World, 20*, 13–27.

Cross, W. E. (1978). The Thomas and Cross models of psychological nigrescence: A review. *Journal of Black Psychology, 5*, 13–21.

Cross, W. E. (1991). *Shades of Black: Diversity in African American identity.* Philadelphia: Temple University Press.

Cross, W. E. (1995). The psychology of Nigrescence: Revising the Cross model. In J. G. Ponterotto, J. M. Casas, L. A. Suzuki, & C. M. Alexander (Eds.), *Handbook of multicultural counseling* (pp. 93–122). Thousand Oaks, CA: Sage.

Cross, W. E., Parham, T., & Helms, J. (1991). The stages of Black identity development: Nigrescence models. In R. L. Jones (Ed.), *Black Psychology*, New York: Harper & Row.

Ford, D. Y., & Harris, J. J. (1997). A study of the racial identity and achievement of Black males and females. *Roeper Review, 20*, 105–110.

Fordham, S. (1988). Racelessness as a factor in black students' success: Pragmatic victory or pyrrhic victor? *Harvard Educational Review, 58*, 29–84.

Fordham, S., & Ogbu, J. (1986). Black students' school success: Coping with the burden of acting white. *The Urban Review, 18*, 1–31.

Grantham, T. G., & Ford, D. Y. (2003). Beyond self-concept and self-esteem: Racial Identity and Gifted African American Students. *High School Journal, 87*, 18–29.

Gregory, S. S. (1992, March 16). The hidden hurdle. *Time Magazine*, 44–46.

Hall, W., Cross, W., & Freedle, R. (1972). Stages in the development of Black awareness: An exploratory investigation. In R. L. Jones (Ed.), *Black Psychology*. New York: Harper & Row.

Helms, J. E. (1990). *Black and White racial identity: Theory, research, and practice.* Westport, CT: Greenwood Press.

Kunjufu, J. (1988). *To be popular or smart: The Black peer group.* Chicago: African American Images.

LaVesit, T. A., & McDonald, K. B. (2002). Race, gender, and educational advantage in the inner city. *Social Science Quarterly, 83*, 832–852.

McCalope, M. (1991, August 15). Fear of "acting White" causes failure among Black students. *Jet, 80*, 24–26.

McCombs, B. L. (2000). Reducing the achievement gap. *Society, 37*, 29–36.

Mickelson, R. (1990). The attitude-achievement paradox among Black adolescents. *Sociology of Education, 63*, 44–61.

Miller, D. B. (1999). Racial socialization and racial identity: Can they promote resiliency for African American adolescents? *Adolescence, 34*, 493–501.

Oyserman, D., Harrison, K., & Bybee, D. (2001). Can racial identity be promotive of academic efficacy? *International Journal of Behavioral Development, 25*, 379–385.

Parham, T. A., & Helms, J. (1981). The influence of Black students racial identity and attitudes on preferences for counselor race. *Journal of Counseling Psychology, 28*, 250–257.

Parham, T. A., & Helms, J. (1985). Attitudes of racial identity and self-esteem: An exploratory investigation. *Journal of College Student Personnel, 26*, 143–146.

Phinney, J. S. (1990). Ethnic identity in adolescents and adults: Review of research. *Psychological Bulletin, 108*, 499–514.

Plummer, D. L. (1995). Patterns of racial identity development of African American adolescent males and females. *Journal of Black Psychology, 21*, 168–180.

Ponterotto, J. G., & Wise, S. L. (1987). Construct validity study of the Racial Identity Attitudes Scale. *Journal of Counseling Psychology, 34*, 218–223.

Reynolds, W. R., Ramirez, M. P., Magrina, A., & Allen, J. E. (1980). Initial development and validation of the Academic Self-Concept Scale. *Educational and Psychological Measurement, 40*, 1012–1016.

Rowley, S. J., & Moore, J. A. (2002). When who I am impacts how I am represented. *Roeper Review, 24*, 63–67.

Shostrom, E. (1963). *Personal Orientation Inventory*. San Diego: Educational and Industrial Testing Service.

Spencer, M. B., & Markstrom-Adams, C. (1990). Identity processes among racial and ethnic minority children in America. *Child Development, 61*, 290–310.

Steinberg, L., Dornbusch, S. M., & Brown, B. (1991). Ethnic differences in adolescent achievement: An ecological perspective. *American Psychologist, 47*, 723–729.

Stevenson, H. C. (1995). Relationship of adolescent perceptions of racial socialization to racial identity. *Journal of Black Psychology, 21*, 49–70.

Ward, J. V. (1990). Racial identity formation and transformation. In C. Gilligan, N. D. Lyons, & T. J. Hanmer (Eds.), *Making corrections: The relational worlds and adolescent girls at Emma Willard School*. Cambridge, MA: Harvard University Press.

Yeh, C. J., & Hwang, M. Y. (2000). Interdependence in ethnic identity and self: Implications for theory and practice. *Journal of Counseling & Development, 78*, 420–429.

Part III

Reassessment and Methodological Issues

Chapter 13

The Burden of "Acting White"

Do Black Adolescents Disparage Academic Achievement?

Philip J. Cook and Jens Ludwig

> The academic learning and performance problems of black children arise not only from a limited opportunity structure and black people's response to it, but also from the way black people attempt to cope with the burden of "acting white."[1]

Recent ethnographic work suggests that some minority students condemn academic success as a rejection of their cultural identity. The research on African-American students has been particularly influential: a study by Signithia Fordham and John Ogbu has played a major role in making this one of the "chestnut" explanations for Black-White differences in educational outcomes.[2] According to these authors, "one major reason that black students do poorly in school is that they experience inordinate ambivalence and affective dissonance in regard to academic effort and success." Due to the history of racial discrimination in the United States, African Americans "began to doubt their own intellectual ability, began to define academic success as white people's prerogative, and began to discourage their peers, perhaps unconsciously, from emulating White people in academic striving, i.e., from 'acting White.' "[3]

The "acting White" hypothesis seems to suggest that if African-Americans were as committed as Whites to achievement, the educational gap between Blacks and Whites would narrow. This may be true, but before one accepts the argument, one needs to ask whether African-American youth really is alienated from school and hostile to academic effort. While ethnographic and anecdotal evidence indicates that some Black students see academic success as selling out, it cannot say how pervasive this perspective is, nor whether it is more common among blacks than whites. To answer this question, one needs data on nationally representative samples of both Blacks and Whites.

In this chapter we use the National Education Longitudinal Study (NELS), which provides recent data from American tenth graders, to answer three questions:

1   Do African-American adolescents report greater alienation from school than non-Hispanic Whites?
2   Does academic success lead to social ostracism among Black adolescents?
3   Do the social costs or benefits of academic success differ by race?

Our analysis suggests that the answer to each of these questions is "apparently not."

We begin by discussing the "acting White" hypothesis in greater detail, tracing its evolution from an ethnographic finding to a popular media story to conventional wisdom, and reviewing earlier surveys that have explored the issue. We then describe the NELS data. We compare the alienation from school of Black and White tenth graders in 1990, and also look at the social costs of academic success for Blacks and for Whites.

THE "ACTING WHITE" HYPOTHESIS

The notion that Blacks view upward mobility as selling out has been around since at least the 1950s.[4] But concern about the effects of this attitude on the educational efforts and aspirations of Blacks appear to have increased in the past decade.[5] In their 1986 study, Fordham and Ogbu argued that the history of discrimination in the United States has led African-American adolescents to value educational achievement less than other groups, and that Blacks have come to associate academic success with "acting White." Subsequently, Ogbu suggested that African Americans had developed a "folk theory of getting ahead that does not necessarily emphasize the strategy of academic pursuit." He contrasted this with the "folk theories" of most white Americans, who allegedly saw education as a key strategy for upward socioeconomic mobility; and concluded that "castelike minorities [such as African Americans] tend to equate . . . learning Standard English and academic aspects of the school curriculum . . . with linear acculturation, which is threatening to their culture/language, identity; and sense of security."[6]

More recently, Ogbu has introduced the term "cultural inversion," which he described as

a process whereby subordinate group members come to define certain forms of behaviors, events, symbols, and meanings as inappropriate for them because these are characteristic of their oppressors. . . . The target areas in which an oppositional cultural frame of reference is applied appear to be those traditionally defined as prerogatives of white Americans, first defined by whites themselves and then acceded to by blacks. . . . Intellectual performance (IQ scores), scholastic performance, and performance in high-status jobs in [the] mainstream economy represent such areas.[7]

Shelby Steele argued similarly in his 1990 book *The Content of Our Character*.

> The middle-class values by which we [middle-class blacks] were raised—the work ethic, the importance of education, the value of property ownership, of respectability, of "getting ahead," of stable family life, of initiative, of self-reliance, et cetera—are, in themselves, raceless and even assimilationist.... But the particular pattern of racial identification that emerged in the sixties and still prevails today urges middle-class blacks (and all blacks) in the opposite direction.

He writes that one of "the most damning things one black can say about another black [is that] so-and-so is not really black, so-and-so is an Oreo."[8]

Claude Steele argued that African-American students "disidentify" with academic achievement. He described "the assimilationist offer that schools make to blacks" as follows:

> You can be valued and rewarded in school (and society) . . . but you must first master the culture and ways of the American mainstream, and since that mainstream (as it is represented) is essentially white, this means you must give up many particulars of being black—styles of speech and appearance, value priorities, preferences—at least in mainstream sense. This is asking a lot.[9]

He cautioned that

> once disidentification occurs in a school, it can spread like the common cold. . . . Pressure to make it a group norm can evolve quickly and become fierce. Defectors are called 'oreos' or 'incognegroes.' One's identity as an authentic black is held hostage, made incompatible with school identification.[10]

Fordham and Ogbu's study focused on one almost entirely Black high school in Washington, DC, but they suggested that the phenomenon also occurs in other parts of the United States. However, Diana Slaughter-Defoe and colleagues argued that this study probably is not representative of high schools nationally. Indeed, Fordham has acknowledged that the findings are "not necessarily generalizable to all black adolescents."[11]

From Media Story to Conventional Wisdom

Since Fordham and Ogbu first suggested that fear of "acting White" is "a very important but as yet widely unrecognized dilemma of black students," this dilemma has received considerable attention in the mainstream press.[12] A 1992 *Time* magazine feature, with the tag line "Talented black students find that one of the most insidious obstacles to achievement comes from a surprising source: their own peers," described the problem as follows:

> Of all the obstacles to success that inner-city black students face, the most surprising—and discouraging—may be those erected by their own peers. . . . Many teenagers have come to equate black identity with alienation and indifference. "I used to go home and cry," says Tachelle Ross, 18, a senior at Oberlin High in Ohio. "They called me white. I don't know why. I'd say. 'I'm just as black as you are.' " . . . Promising black students are ridiculed for speaking Standard English, showing an interest in ballet or theater, having white friends, not joining activities other than sports. . . .
>
> Honor students may be rebuked for even showing up for class on time. The pattern of abuse is a distinctive variation on the nerd bashing that almost all bright, ambitious students—no matter what their color—face at some point in their lives. The anti-achievement ethic championed by some black youngsters declares formal education useless; those who disagree and study hard face isolation, scorn and violence. While educators have recognized the existence of an anti-achievement culture for at least a decade, it has only recently emerged as a dominant theme among the troubles facing urban schools. . . .
>
> Social success depends partly on academic failure; safety and acceptance lie in rejecting the traditional paths to self-improvement.[13]

These themes are echoed in a 1994 story in the *Wall Street Journal* about a summer program for minority teenagers at the Massachusetts Institute of Technology: "At a lunch table, over cold cuts on whole wheat, talk turns to the ultimate insult: 'wanting to be white.' " The story describes an African-American participant from a low-income area of Washington, DC as knowing few whites; in his world, whites have always been the unseen oppressors: " 'The charge of "wanting to be white," where I'm from . . . is like treason.' "[14]

In an op-ed piece published in the same newspaper a few weeks later, Hugh Pearson connects "acting White" rhetoric to the rise of the Black Power movement. Of his childhood in Fort Wayne, Indiana in the late 1960s he recalled: "Schoolwork, my two Black Power-chanting classmates decided, was for white people. Our take on Black Power meant . . . that we were supposed to stop excelling in 'the white man's school.' " His own attitude toward school changed, and by the sixth grade he had achieved "the greatest improvement in test scores of any student in my predominantly white school." But he quoted a Black classmate commenting, "I guess you think you're like the white students now." Even today, Pearson writes, "numerous black students tell of being made to feel uncomfortable if they apply themselves and get good grades. Such a tactic is the legacy of the type of behavior that I experienced in the sixth grade." He suggests that simply changing Black attitudes toward schooling "could mean that within fifteen years the 15-point gap in black and white IQ averages would be closed."[15]

Although conventional wisdom has now incorporated the notion that Black youths who strive to excel in school are subject to extremely powerful peer sanctions, the evidence that peer pressure accounts for current Black-White differences in test performance is hardly compelling. Ethnographers have documented the existence of anti-achievement norms among Black adolescents. But they have not compared the strength of anti-achievement norms to that of pro-achievement norms. Furthermore, while Black teenagers disparage high achievers for "acting White," White teenagers disparage high achievers for being nerds. Without some evidence that anti-achievement norms are stronger among Blacks than Whites, one cannot conclude that they contribute to racial differences in achievement.

Previous Surveys

Laurence Steinberg, Sanford Dornbusch, and Bradford Brown explored these issues in a survey of nine high schools in California and Wisconsin conducted in 1987–88, which included interviews with 15,000 students of different races. Their conclusions seem to support Ogbu and Fordham:

> Although [African-American] parents were supportive of academic success, these [African-American] youngsters, we learned from our interviews, find it much more difficult to join a peer group that encourages the same goal. Our interviews with high-achieving African-American students indicated that peer support for academic success is so limited that many successful African-American students eschew contact with other African-American students and affiliate primarily with students from other ethnic groups.[16]

Jan Collins-Eaglin and Stuart Karabenick drew quite different conclusions from their interviews of approximately 200 African-American students at Michigan schools, almost three-fourths of whom were attending an academic summer institute.[17] Their sample was probably more academically inclined than the average Black student in Michigan. On the one hand, therefore, the interviewees may have been more aware than other Blacks of whether peer pressure affected their academic behavior. On the other hand, they may have been drawn disproportionately from schools with unusually peer-supportive environments. Only a fifth of the sample reported any agreement with the statement that academic success would be viewed by Black schoolmates as "selling out." Only a quarter reported any agreement with the statement that their Black friends viewed success in school as "acting White."

THE NATIONAL EDUCATION LONGITUDINAL STUDY

The National Education Longitudinal Study sponsored by the U.S. Department of Education surveyed a national sample of eighth grade students in 1988 and interviewed them again in 1990 and 1992. The original sample covered 815 public schools and 237 private schools. From each school, 26 students were chosen to participate in the study, deliberately excluding those with mental handicaps, serious physical or emotional problems, or inadequate command of the English language. We use data from the 1990 follow-up, when most students were in tenth grade. Our sample includes 17,544 students: with appropriate weights, it is intended to be representative of all tenth graders who met the criteria for inclusion. Descriptive statistics for the sample are reported in Appendix Table 13A-1.

Most of our data come from a self-administered questionnaire. This raises the possibility that differences between Black and White students in the accuracy of reports could bias our results. Kurt Bauman found that Black tenth graders in the 1980 High School and Beyond survey overestimate their grades by about a quarter of a letter grade, whereas Whites only overstate them by a fifth of a letter grade. But Blacks do not seem more likely than Whites to overstate time spent on homework.[18] Fortunately, the NELS provides two measures of student behavior that do not rely on self-reports: absences and dropping out. Data on absences are gathered from high school transcripts, and dropout data come from other school records.

In contrast with the ethnographic data, the NELS does not describe students' speech or behavioral patterns, attitudes toward racial identity, or social interactions. But it is a nationally representative sample, and it does allow one to compare Blacks with Whites in ways that existing ethnographic studies do not.

ALIENATION FROM SCHOOL

To measure alienation from school among tenth graders, we look at their educational expectations, their dropout rates, the effort they devote to classes, and parental involvement in their schooling. We first compare the observed means for blacks to those for non-Hispanic Whites. Then we estimate the Black-White difference for students whose parental income, mother's education, and family structure are the same.

Educational Expectations

If African-American teenagers see a conflict between preserving their cultural identity and succeeding in school, one would expect them to devalue staying in school. Table 13.1 shows, however, that about 60 percent of both Black and White tenth graders expect to earn a four-year college degree. This does not mean that Blacks and Whites do in fact graduate from college in equal numbers. In the early 1990s, only about 24 percent of Whites and 13 percent of Blacks completed college.[19] Nonetheless, comparing the NELS measures for Blacks and Whites from similar socioeconomic backgrounds, Blacks on average expect to stay in school longer than Whites.

Dropout Rates

In 1990, almost all the tenth-graders surveyed said that they expected to graduate from high school. The 1992 follow-up survey found that 6.9 percent of the Whites and 9.8 percent of the Blacks were no longer enrolled in school. But this difference disappears when one adjusts for

Table 13.1 Educational expectations, NELS tenth graders, 1990[a]

Measure and summary statistic	Non-Hispanic Whites	Blacks
Percent expecting to complete		
High school or less	9.4	11.2
Some college	29.6	30.5
College or more	61.0	58.3
Expected years of school	15.9	16.0
Adjusted mean[a]	15.8*	16.4*
Summary statistic		
Sample size	12,311	1,742

Source: Authors' calculations based on data from National Center for Education Statistics (1994b)

Notes: Asterisk denotes Black-White difference statistically significant at the 0.05 level.
[a] Adjusted for socioeconomic status, using a probit regression analysis evaluated at the non-Hispanic White mean for gender, race, father in the home, mother's education, and family income.

family background. Earlier studies also found that among students from similar socioeconomic backgrounds, Blacks actually stay in school longer than do Whites.[20]

Effort

If the African-American adolescent community does discourage academic achievement, one would expect Blacks to skip class and miss school more often than Whites. The NELS suggests otherwise. Table 13.2 shows that about 35 percent of both racial groups admit to skipping class at least once during the fall term. And about 10 percent of both groups report missing more than 10 days of school during the fall. After adjusting for family characteristics, Whites miss slightly more days than Blacks. School transcripts for the full academic year tell essentially the same story.

Another indicator of effort is the amount of time students spend on schoolwork when they are not in school. Sixty-eight percent of White and 65 percent of Black respondents said they spent at least two to three hours a week outside school doing homework. Even this small difference disappears once one controls for family background. Note that regardless of race, a third of tenth graders spend less than two hours on homework each week.[21]

Table 13.2 Low levels of effort, NELS tenth graders, 1990[a]

| | Percent | |
Measure and summary statistic	Non-Hispanic Whites	Blacks
Skipped a class, fall 1989		
Observed	34.9	35.5
Adjusted	34.8	33.4
Missed more than ten days of school, fall 1989		
Observed	10.1	9.2
Adjusted	9.7*	6.5*
Transcript shows missed more than ten days of school, 1989–90		
Observed	28.5	28.0
Adjusted	28.4	20.8*
Does less than two hours of homework out of school		
Observed	31.9*	34.8*
Adjusted	31.6	31.1
Summary statistic		
Sample size	12,311	1,742

Source: Authors' calculations based on data from sources for Table 13.1.

Notes: [a] Data are self-reported, unless otherwise indicated. Adjusted percentages are controlled for socioeconomic status; see Table 13.1, note a. Asterisk denotes Black-White difference statistically significant at the 0.05 level.

Similarities in the levels of effort of the typical Black and the typical White student may mask differences between the hardest-working students.

Table 13.3 suggests that among these students, Blacks and Whites differ somewhat in the time that they spend on homework. Focusing on students who spend four or more hours per week on homework (roughly, 40 percent of all students) and those who spend 10 or more hours (roughly 13 percent), Whites are somewhat more likely than Blacks to spend large amounts of time on homework, even after controlling for socioeconomic status.[22] To put these results in perspective, if one compares the homework effort of Black students at the 75th and 90th percentiles of the Black distribution with Whites at similar points in the White distribution (after controlling for socioeconomic status), Whites

Table 13.3 High levels of effort, NELS tenth graders, 1990[a]

	Percent		
Measure and summary statistic	Total	Non-Hispanic Whites	Blacks
Spends four or more hours on homework per week			
Unadjusted	39.6	40.5	34.7*
Adjusted	40.1	40.6	37.4*
Spends ten or more hours on homework per week			
Unadjusted	13.3	14	9.6*
Adjusted	12.9	13.4	10.1*
Participated in science or mathematics fair			
Unadjusted	10.3	9.6	14.9*
Adjusted	10.6	9.6	17.5*
Participates in academic honor society			
Unadjusted	7.6	7.4	8.4
Adjusted	7.2	6.9	8.9*
Receives mostly As in mathematics			
Unadjusted	18.5	19.6	13.0*
Adjusted	18.8	19.4	15.4*
Receives mostly As in English			
Unadjusted	19.4	20.1	16.0*
Adjusted	19.3	19.5	18.4
Won an academic honor			
Unadjusted	16	15.6	18.6*
Adjusted	15.9	15.3	19.6*
Summary statistic			
Sample size	17,753	12,311	1,742

Source: Authors' calculations based on data from sources for Table 13.1.

Notes: [a] Unadjusted percentages are calculated from a probit regression that includes a constant term and a dichotomous variable for gender, evaluated at the White mean for percent male. Adjusted percentages are controlled for socioeconomic status; see Table 13.1, note a. Asterisk denotes Black-White difference statistically significant at the 0.05 level.

spend about one to one-and-a-half more hours on homework per week, or about 10 to 15 minutes per day.[23]

Participation in science or math fairs may be another good measure of effort among the hardest workers. In the 1990 NELS survey, Blacks are somewhat more likely than Whites to participate in these events, as shown in Table 13.3. Moreover, the table shows that Blacks and Whites are equally likely to be recognized by their schools for hard work and high performance. Black students are as likely as Whites to receive an academic award, participate in an honor society, or receive mostly As in English, although they are somewhat less likely to receive high marks in mathematics.

Parental Involvement

Table 13.4 suggests that African-American parents are at least as involved in their children's education as White parents with similar socioeconomic characteristics. Black children are more likely than White children to report that their parents have telephoned a teacher or attended school meetings. Once family socioeconomic status is controlled, African-American children are also more likely to say their parents have attended other school events. Finally, Table 13.4 shows that African-American parents are at least as likely as White parents to check their children's homework.

Table 13.4 Parental involvement in students' education, NELS tenth graders, 1990[a]

	Percent	
Measure and summary statistic	*Non-Hispanic Whites*	*Blacks*
Telephoned teacher at least once, fall 1989		
Observed	57.8	64.5*
Adjusted	57.8	65.9*
Attended school meeting at least once, fall 1989		
Observed	56.4	64.7*
Adjusted	56.8	70.8*
Attended at least one school event, fall 1989		
Observed	62.3	63.1
Adjusted	62.6	68.1*
Checks homework at least sometimes		
Observed	53.1	54.4
Adjusted	53.1	57.3*
Summary statistic		
Sample size	12,311	1,742

Source: Authors' calculations based on data from sources for Table 13.1.

Notes: [a] Adjusted percentages are controlled for socioeconomic status; see Table 13.1, note a. Asterisk denotes Black-White difference statistically significant at the 0.05 level.

SOCIAL COSTS OF ACADEMIC SUCCESS

Although Black and White adolescents have remarkably similar expectations and exert similar amounts of effort, they might still differ in how
much they value doing well in school. Academic success could bring more
peer derision or ostracism to Blacks than to Whites.

Many sociological studies have noted that high school students self-
select into different social cliques, such as "jocks," "populars," "brains,"
"loners," "nerds," and "average students." The affiliation of each student
seems to be widely known throughout the school, even across racial
lines.[24] Student support for academic achievement is highest among the
"brains," lowest among the oppositional crowd, and moderate for other
groups.[25]

In this balkanized social system, a student's status is likely to depend on
two factors: how the student ranks within a given group and how that
group ranks in the school. If each group enjoyed equal social standing,
the status of an individual would depend entirely on his or her standing
within-group. But this is probably not the case. James Coleman wrote
about the 1950s that "in every school, most students saw a leading
crowd, and were willing to say what it took to get in." He noted that
while a few students objected to the idea of such a social hierarchy, a
friend of one such student offered a poignant retort: "You don't see
it because you're in it."[26] As the junior author of the present chapter
can attest, there is no reason to think that today's schools are any less
hierarchical than those that Coleman studied.

The NELS asks students a number of questions about their social
standing and how they are treated by their peers. Table 13.5 presents
results on five of these measures: experience of put-downs and physical
threat; whether a student thinks he or she is popular in general, and with

Table 13.5 Low social standing, NELS tenth graders, 1990

Measure	Percent	
	Non-Hispanic Whites	Blacks
Often feels put down by students in class	19.8	22.3
Says someone threatened to hurt him or her at school last fall	24.3	20.9
Answers "not at all" to whether other students think of him or her as popular	15.9	15.6
Says is not very popular with opposite sex[a]	21.0	26.5
Answers "not at all" to whether other students think of him or her as part of leading crowd	33.0	33.4

Source: Authors' calculations based on data from sources for Table 13.1.

Note: [a] Includes those reporting "true," "mostly true," or "more true than false."

students of the opposite sex, in particular; and whether other students think the respondent is part of the "leading crowd."

With these data, Table 13.6 relates social standing to academic success for high-achieving tenth graders. We measure academic success with two indicators: receiving mostly As in mathematics (reported by 20 percent of Whites versus 13 percent of Blacks) and membership in an academic honor society (7 percent of Whites versus 8 percent of Blacks).[27] We measure the social cost of high achievement as the percentage of high achievers who are "unpopular" minus the percentage of other students

Table 13.6 Effects of high achievement on low social standing, by race and gender, NELS tenth graders, 1990*

Measure of high achievement and sample	Measure of low social standing (Percent[a])				
	Feels put down by students	Threatened at least once last fall	Not popular	Not part of leading crowd	Not popular with opposite sex
Mostly A's in mathematics					
Whites (10,284)	−1	−2	3†	2	0
Blacks (1,289)	−1	−3†	−4	−5	4
Predominantly White schools[b]					
Whites (8,715)	−2	−3†	0	0	−2
Blacks (472)	−1	4	6	10	4††
Predominantly Black schools[c]					
Blacks (399)	7	6	−3	0	−15†,††
Honor society					
Whites (11,586)	−2	−8†	−5†	−11†	−4†
Blacks (1,653)	−1	−6	−12†	−21†	−18†*
Predominantly White schools[b]					
Whites (9,732)	−2	−9†	−4†	−9†	−4†
Blacks (788)	−10	−1	−7	5††	−1††
Predominantly Black schools[c]					
Blacks (514)	6	−5	−18†	−32†,††	−21†,††

Source: Authors' calculations based on data from sources for Table 13.1.

Notes: † denotes "penalty" statistically significant at the 0.05 level. †† denotes "penalty" differs between predominantly Black and predominantly White schools (statistically significant at the 0.05 level). * denotes Black-White difference statistically significant at the 0.05 level. Sample size is shown in parentheses.
[a] Percent of high achievers who report a given measure of low social standing minus percent of other students who report the same measure.
[b] At least 60 percent of total student population is non-Hispanic White. In these schools, 55 Black students earn mostly As in mathematics and 34 are members of an honor society.
[c] At least 60 percent of total student population is Black. In these schools, 58 Black students earn mostly As in mathematics and 63 are members of an honor society.

who are "unpopular." When this value is positive, it indicates that high achievers are paying a social price for their academic success.

Ethnographic evidence suggests that the social cost should be positive for high-achieving Blacks. Table 13.6 does not support this hypothesis. Black tenth graders who mostly earn As in mathematics appear to be marginally more popular than those who mostly earn Bs or Cs, although the difference is never statistically significant. Black honor society members are substantially more popular than their classmates, and these differences are statistically significant.

The "acting White" hypothesis could still help to explain why Blacks score lower than Whites on standardized tests, however, if the positive correlation between academic success and social standing were weaker among Blacks than Whites. But Table 13.6 does not offer any support for this view either. The social benefits of academic success are generally greater for Blacks than for Whites. This racial difference is neither statistically significant nor substantively significant for math grades, but it is large and sometimes statistically significant for honor society members.

If Whites support high achievement more than do Blacks, academic success might be less costly in predominantly White schools than in predominantly Black schools. Recall that Fordham and Ogbu base their conclusions on data from a predominantly Black high school. But Table 13.6 does not support this hypothesis either. Although our samples of high-achieving Blacks are fairly small, several of the differences between predominantly Black and predominantly White schools are statistically significant. These suggest that academic success is more socially beneficial in Black than in White schools.

Conclusion

Black high school students are not particularly alienated from school. They are as likely as Whites to expect to enter and complete college, and their actual rate of high school completion is as high as that among Whites from the same socioeconomic background. Also, Black and White students report that they spend about the same amount of time on homework and have similar rates of absenteeism.

The story is somewhat more complicated for the hardest-working students. Although the typical Black student spends as much time on homework as the typical White student, after controlling for socioeconomic status, the hardest-working White students do about 10 to 15 more minutes of homework a day than the hardest-working Black students. This difference may exist because schools have lower expectations of their top Black students than their top White students. Despite the fact that the hardest-working Black students do less homework than their White counterparts, Blacks are actually more likely than Whites to be members of academic honor societies or to win academic awards, and they are equally likely to receive high marks in English.

Moreover, Black and White tenth graders who excel in school are no more likely to be unpopular than other students. This finding suggests that both Black and White students are able to find peer groups that accept high achievement. Indeed, our evidence indicates that membership in an academic honor society is a social advantage. While ethnographers observe that Black adolescents sometimes taunt high-achieving Black students for "acting White," it appears that either these taunts do not inflict especially grievous social damage or high achievement has offsetting social benefits.

Are there other reasonable interpretations for our results? It is possible that surveys like the National Education Longitudinal Study are misleading because Blacks are more likely than Whites to exaggerate their level of effort. Bauman's results based on tenth graders in the 1980 High School and Beyond survey suggest that Blacks overstate their grades somewhat more than do Whites.[28] Blacks may also overstate their commitment to school. It might be that Black students are heavily influenced by an oppositional culture that penalizes doing well in school, but deny this alienation in response to survey questions, representing themselves as more engaged in schoolwork than they really are. Alienation and misrepresentation would then cancel out, to produce our NELS results.

But if this theory were correct, indicators of effort taken from school records should tell a different story than self-reports. As we have shown, that is not the case; school records show little difference between Blacks and Whites on attendance or graduation rates. Differing bias in survey responses between Blacks and Whites is even less likely to account for our findings concerning popularity because these are based on comparisons of Blacks with Blacks and Whites with Whites; any generalized "race effect" should cancel out.

There is another, more complex, challenge to our interpretation. Suppose students choose between two types of clique: the As, who tolerate effort, and the Ds, who impose prohibitive penalties on effort among themselves but ignore nonmembers. If Black students tend to find the Ds more attractive, high-achieving Black students would suffer no social penalty, but antieffort norms would have a more negative effect on Blacks than Whites, just as ethnographers have suggested. But this theory implies that Blacks should devote less time to schoolwork than Whites, which does not appear to be the case—at least, for the average Black and White students. Furthermore, ethnographic accounts do not, in fact, suggest that high-achieving Blacks are completely insulated from oppositional norms in this way. Quite the contrary.

How then, is one to account for the discrepancy between the NELS survey and the reports in the ethnographic literature and the press?

One possible answer is that such accounts are correct but incomplete. Ethnographers, journalists, and some high-achieving blacks have stressed the social costs of achievement. They have not had much to say one way or the other about the possible social *benefits* of high achievement. To put this point slightly differently, ethnographic accounts of social norms in Black schools say very little about the social costs of not doing well. The NELS suggests that the social costs and benefits of academic achievement roughly offset each other.

The notion that Blacks pay a higher social price than Whites for doing well in school may also reflect the absence of careful ethnographic comparisons between Blacks and Whites. White students do not criticize one another for "acting white," but they have many other derogatory terms for classmates who work "too hard." Blacks stigmatize effort in racial terms whereas Whites do so in other ways, and one cannot predict *a priori* which form of stigma will be most effective. To answer that question, one would need to measure effort directly. When we try to do this using NELS, we find little difference between typical Black and White students and only moderate differences between the top Black and White students.

In sum, our results do not support the belief that group differences in peer attitudes account for the Black-White gap in educational achievement. In contrast, disparities in the family backgrounds of Blacks and Whites do account for the modest differences in effort that we find between the average Black and White students. Policymakers, therefore, should not allow concern about the so-called oppositional culture to distract them from more fundamental issues, such as improving schools and providing adequate motivation, support, and guidance for students weighed down by the burdens of poverty.

That the problem may be more fundamental than racial differences in peer group norms is illustrated by the troubling story of Scott Baylark and Telkia Steward, two of the top students in the class of 1986 at DuSable High School in Chicago.[29] Both took numerous honors classes. Both were given every encouragement by the faculty. Far from being ostracized by their peers, both were elected class officers and served as class leaders. Both went on to matriculate at the University of Illinois. There, they both discovered that they were poorly prepared for the academic demands of freshman year. For that reason among others, both soon dropped out.

APPENDIX: THE NELS SAMPLE

Comment by Ronald F. Ferguson

The first published version of this chapter won Philip Cook and Jens Ludwig the award for the most important paper published by the *Journal of Policy Analysis and Management* in 1997. Many people seem to believe that the authors have put to rest the popular hypothesis that fear of "acting White" is an impediment to closing the Black-White achievement gap. I disagree with this interpretation of their findings.

Before explaining my reasons, however, let me state some points of agreement. First, I agree that the 1988 National Education Longitudinal Study data offer no clear support for the proposition that high-achieving Black students are less popular than low-achieving Black students. Second, the ethnographic literature probably does overstate the amount of negative peer pressure in fact experienced by high-performing Black students. Third, I strongly agree that the Black-White test score gap is, as Cook and Ludwig write, much more fundamental than racial differences in peer group norms. Indeed, my own work describes many other factors that contribute to the gap. Finally, I agree with Cook and Ludwig that policymakers "should not allow concern about the so-called oppositional culture to distract them from more fundamental issues, such as improving schools and providing adequate motivation, support, and guidance for students weighed down by the burdens of poverty."

Two conditions must be met for the "acting White" hypothesis to be true. First, Black and White adolescents must be faced with different peer norms for academic achievement. Second, these norms must affect their academic achievement. Like most other researchers who have tested "cultural" theories about racial differences in behavior, Cook and Ludwig have no measures of peer norms or pressures. Instead, they use measures of academic behavior—such as time spent doing homework, school attendance, and school completion—that they say should be influenced by differential norms if such norms vary by race. When they find that these behaviors hardly differ by race, they conclude that peer norms regarding academic achievement do not differ by race either.

In my judgment, however, the NELS survey does not measure the behaviors that are most indicative of adolescent norms. For example, Black students may hesitate to raise their hands in class, to participate in class discussions, or to seem eager to learn because they fear social ostracism by their peers. Some Blacks may moderate their speech because they worry about sounding too much like an "Oreo." Others may try to "act ghetto" in an effort to assert their racial authenticity, but as a consequence may convince teachers that they are disruptive and uncommitted to academic matters. Indeed, a study by James Ainsworth-Darnell and Douglas Downey (1998), using the same NELS data that Cook and Ludwig used, finds that teachers rate Black students as more frequently disruptive and as putting forth less effort. Both effects remained statistically significant after accounting for family income, parental occupation, and parental education. White students may exhibit similar behaviors, but I suspect that the social pressures against "acting White" are stronger and more effective than those against acting nerdy. This is an empirical question, but it requires assessment of a range of behaviors more subtle than those that the NELS measures. These subtler behaviors might not be correlated at all with attendance rates or homework hours, especially when even Whites do very little homework.

Cook and Ludwig also try to assess racial differences in peer norms regarding academic achievement by examining whether high-achieving students report being less popular than low-achieving students. I do not dispute their basic finding that Black and White tenth graders who excel in school are no more likely to be unpopular than other students. I do wonder, however, about the generality and relevance of this conclusion.

First, the prevalence of accusations about "acting White" probably varies by context. Although Fordham and Ogbu developed the "acting White" hypothesis based on data from an all-Black high school, one would expect peer pressure against "acting White" to be stronger for Black students in racially mixed schools. Cook and Ludwig's data suggest that this could be the case. In Table 13.5, for example, Blacks in predominantly White schools who get mostly As in mathematics have been threatened more and are more likely to be "not popular," "nor part of the leading crowd," and "not popular with the opposite sex." None of these differences, taken singly, is statistically significant. But the sample is very small: only 55 Blacks in White schools earn mostly As in mathematics. Nonetheless, this pattern differs from the pattern for Whites in the same schools, and it contradicts Cook and Ludwig's overall conclusion. Conversely, answers for students in honor societies in predominantly White schools (only 34 such students are Black) indicate no penalty for Blacks, and perhaps even an advantage. Why does the pattern for students who get As differ so much from the pattern for students in an honor society? Is it just statistical noise? One needs to examine much larger samples of high-achieving Blacks in racially mixed settings and more appropriate variables before one can draw any conclusions about whether anti-academic peer pressure discourages achievement in such settings.

I also believe that Cook and Ludwig's analysis is too static. Imagine two runners nearing the end of a one-mile race, separated by 40 yards. Like the bottom three-quarters of Black and White students, who spend very little time outside of school on homework, the runners in this race are jogging along at a leisurely pace. One could ask one of two questions. The first is: Why are the runners 40 yards apart? In effect, this is the question that Cook and Ludwig ask, and they come to the conclusion that the acting White hypothesis is not an important part of the answer. I agree. To my mind, however, as one looks to the future the more relevant question is: Why is the distance between the runners not closing more rapidly? Or, why is the second runner not running faster in order to catch up? After all, the front runner is only jogging. The "acting White" hypothesis probably *does* help to explain why Black students are not closing the gap with Whites who make relatively little effort.

At bottom, then, my criticism is that the NELS data are not adequate for testing the "acting White" hypothesis. Cook and Ludwig recognize this possibility when they suggest that their analysis of peer pressure would be invalid if students self-segregated into peer groups with different norms, and if these peer groups did not interact much. They offer the hypothetical example of students who sort themselves "between two types of clique: the As, who tolerate effort, and the Ds, who impose prohibitive penalties on effort among themselves but ignore nonmembers. If Black students tend to find the Ds more attractive, high-achieving Black students would suffer no social penalty but antieffort norms would have a more negative effect on Blacks than Whites, just as ethnographers have suggested." I believe that this approximates reality in many schools. If so, closing the Black-White achievement gap would probably require group-level "cross-overs" by Black students. To learn whether fear of "acting White" is an impediment to crossing over from the Ds to the As, one would need data on peer group membership, on students' perceptions of how their peers might respond to changes in their academic behavior or group affiliations, and on what happens to Black and White students when they try to change peer groups. This goes far beyond what the NELS can provide.

Cook and Ludwig have helped to stimulate a more carefully crafted debate on the "acting White" hypothesis. For this they should be applauded. Still, I think the NELS data miss the subtle ways in which peer norms influence Black students' effort. I also think that the "acting White" hypothesis is most relevant to the question of why the Black-White gap does not close more during high school. In any case, there is still a lot to learn about the importance of the "acting White" hypothesis for explaining the persistence of the Black-White achievement gap.

Comment by Philip J. Cook and Jens Ludwig

We thank Ronald Ferguson for his thoughtful comments on our chapter. We agree with him that our views overlap considerably. In what follows, we focus on three remaining points of disagreement.

The first concerns African-Americans in mixed-race schools. Ferguson suggests that our findings for predominantly White schools contradict our overall conclusion that high-achieving Black students are not more likely to be unpopular than other Black students, and may be inconsistent with our findings for Blacks who earn As in mostly White schools. Yet none of the "achievement penalties" that we estimate for Black students in predominantly White schools using either of our achievement measures is statistically significant, which means that the confidence intervals around these estimates are consistent with achievement being a social help *or* a hindrance. Of the 10 achievement penalties for African-American students in mostly White schools, five are positive (high-achieving Blacks are less popular than other Blacks) and five are negative (high achievers are more popular)—exactly the pattern that we would expect if the true effect were zero.

Since all the statistically significant estimates for the achievement penalties tell the same story—that high-achieving Blacks are no more likely to be unpopular than other Black students—we think the results in our study are quite consistent. Nevertheless, we agree with Ferguson that additional research on African-American students in mixed-race schools would be valuable, given the small sample of such students in NELS.

The second point concerns potential limitations of our effort measures. If peer norms for student achievement differed by race, we should find differences in the levels of Black and White students' engagement with school. Instead, we find that the typical Black and White student have similar attendance rates and spend similar amounts of time on homework. Ferguson argues that more subtle measures of school engagement might turn up more racial differences. We agree that it would be valuable to uncover other types of student effort that differ by race and to investigate how these different kinds of effort influence academic achievement. However, the absence of racial differences in school attendance and homework effort makes us doubt that differences in other types of effort would be large. The study by James Ainsworth-Darnell and Douglas B. Downey "Assessing the Oppositional Culture Explanation for Racial/Ethnic Differences in School Performance," in *American Sociological Review*, provides support for our view. On the one hand, teachers report that African-American students put forth less effort and are more disruptive than whites, and student self-reports suggest that Blacks are in trouble more frequently than Whites. On the other hand, these differences are quite small, equal to .12, .17, and .01 standard deviations, respectively.

Furthermore, if peer norms differed by race, high-achieving students would need to be socially isolated from other students in order to explain why high-achieving Blacks are as popular as other Blacks. Newspaper accounts of African-American valedictorians and honors students who are elected officers in student government provide some support for our view that high-achieving Blacks are not particularly socially isolated.[30] It seems unlikely that these high achievers would have been elected class president or vice president had their popularity been limited to one small clique within the school.

The third point concerns implications for public policy. One way to narrow the achievement gap between Blacks and Whites is to ask Black students to work harder than Whites from similar backgrounds. But, assuming that effective strategies for improving student motivation can be identified, some students who are currently in low-effort peer groups may receive grief from their friends if they try to increase their effort. In this way, the "acting White" phenomenon could act as an impediment to reducing the Black-White test score gap. Ferguson is correct that our chapter provides few clues about this possibility.

The concern that motivates our study, however, is that the widespread belief that Black students do not work as hard in school as Whites might distract attention from the need to equalize the educational opportunities of Black and White students. We hope we have dispelled the notion that

Table 13A-1 The NELS tenth grade sample[a]

| | | Percent | |
| | | --- | --- |
Characteristic and summary statistic	Total Sample	Non-Hispanic Whites	Blacks
Male	50.0	50.3	49.1
Race			
Non-Hispanic White	71.4	n.a.	n.a.
African-American	12.5	n.a.	n.a.
Hispanic	10.5	n.a.	n.a.
Asian	4.0	n.a.	n.a.
Other	1.6	n.a.	n.a.
Family income, 1988			
Less than $10,000	9.7	5.6	28.3
$10,000–$20,000	14.8	12.5	21.5
$20,000–$35,000	29.7	30.2	27.1
$35,000–$50,000	21.5	24.2	12.1
$50,000–$75,000	16.0	18.1	8.8
More than $75,000	8.1	9.5	2.3
Mother's education			
Less than high school	14.6	10.5	17.5
High school	38.3	40.1	36.4
Some postsecondary	23.0	23.6	27.3
College degree	14.5	15.8	10.7
Postgraduate	9.5	10.1	8.2
No father or male guardian in home	15.0	11.8	38.4
Black tenth graders in high school			
0–25 percent	82.2	90.7	27.8
26–50 percent	9.0	6.7	27.7
51–75 percent	4.6	2.1	20.5
76–100 percent	3.3	0.2	24.2
Summary statistic			
Sample size	17,753	12,311	1,742

Source: Authors' calculations based on data from NCES (1994b).

Note: [a] Missing values for variables are as follows: school demographics, 6.6 percent; family income, 18.5 percent; mother's education, 15.8 percent.

the "acting White" hypothesis is likely to explain much of the Black-White test score gap.

NOTES

1 Fordham and Ogbu (1986, p. 201).
2 Fordham and Ogbu (1986); Claude M. Steele, "Race and the Schooling of Black Americans," *Atlantic Monthly*, April 1992, pp. 68–78. Similar attitudes have been documented among Chicano students and various other ethnic groups; see Portes and Zhou (1994).
3 Fordham and Ogbu (1986, p. 177).
4 See, for example, Frazier (1957).
5 Petroni (1970), in an early description of this phenomenon, notes that black school children were afraid of being called an "Uncle Tom" or accused of "acting white" if they exerted themselves too much at schoolwork; cited by Ogbu (1987, p. 168).
6 Ogbu (1987, pp. 154, 156). Ogbu appears to have changed his view somewhat in recent years: "It is true that in spite of the historical experience of blacks in the opportunity structure, black folk theories for getting ahead stress the importance of education. But this verbal endorsement is not to be accepted at face value. It is often not accompanied by appropriate or necessary effort" (1994, p. 289).
7 Ogbu (1994, pp. 274, 275).
8 Steele (1990, pp. 71, 95, 96).
9 Claude M. Steele, "Race and the Schooling of Black Americans," *Atlantic Monthly*, April 1992, p. 77.
10 Claude M. Steele, "Race and the Schooling of Black Americans," *Atlantic Monthly*, April 1992, p. 75. Shelby Steele and Claude Steele offer different explanations for this phenomenon, but nonetheless their predictions for the effort of African-American students relative to Whites are strikingly similar to those of Fordham and Ogbu (1986).
11 Fordham and Ogbu (1986, p. 200); Slaughter-Defoe and others (1990); Fordham (1988, p. 55).
12 Fordham and Ogbu (1986, p. 202).
13 Sophronia Scott Gregory, "The Hidden Hurdle," *Time*, March 16, 1992, pp. 44–46.
14 Ron Suskind, "Poor, Black, and Smart, an Inner City Teen Tries to Survive MIT," *Wall Street Journal*, September 22, 1994, p. A1.
15 Hugh Pearson, "The Black Academic Environment," *Wall Street Journal*, November 23, 1994, p. A14.
16 Steinberg, Dornbusch, and Brown (1992, p. 728).
17 Collins-Eaglin and Karabenick (1993).
18 Bauman (1996).
19 National Center for Education Statistics (1994a).
20 Jaynes and Williams (1989); Cook and Moore (1993); Ludwig (1994); Haveman and Wolfe (1994).
21 By way of comparison, in a survey of 8,000 students enrolled in Wisconsin and San Francisco public high schools, Brown and Steinberg (1991) find that respondents spend about four to five hours on homework per week, figures apparently similar to those from other national surveys. Brown and

Steinberg's survey may include time spent on homework during school hours, while the NELS focuses on homework time after school. Using data on sophomores in the High School and Beyond survey for 1980, Bauman (1996) finds that Black students spend an average of approximately 30 minutes less on homework than Whites. This difference is fully accounted for by sociodemographic factors. Ainsworth-Darnell and Downey (forthcoming) perform an exercise similar to ours using data from the NELS tenth-graders, but focus on the mean (rather than the median) time spent on homework by Black and White students. They find a statistically significant difference between Blacks and Whites, even after controlling for socioeconomic status, but it is quite small: about 15 minutes per week.

22   In the 1990 NELS survey, homework time is reported in discrete categories (for example, two to three hours per week), so we have chosen the categories that contain the 75th and 90th percentiles.

23   These estimates are based on a linear regression of total homework time on our socioeconomic measures and a race variable. We then compare the regression residuals for White students with those for Blacks (after adding together the residual and the coefficient for the race variable for Black students). The differences at the 80th and 95th percentiles are around 1.5 hours and 1 hour, respectively.

24   Steinberg, Dornbusch, and Brown (1992).

25   In the northern California high schools that they survey, Brown and Steinberg (1991) refer to the oppositional crowd as "druggies."

26   Coleman (1961, p. 36).

27   In regard to the first indicator, we find qualitatively similar patterns to "mostly As in mathematics" when we use "mostly As in English" as the criterion (not reported here). For the second indicator, the question is worded, "Which of the following activities have you participated in during this school year?" Possible answers include "National Honor Society or other academic honor society."

28   Bauman (1996).

29   Alex Kotlowicz, "Upward Fragility," *New York Times Magazine*, April 2, 1995, pp. 36–40, 49, 62–63, 85, 87.

30   Examples include Scott Baylark and Telkia Steward of DuSable High School in Chicago and Lauren Powell of Washington-Lee High School in Arlington, Virginia: see, respectively, Alex Kotlowicz, "Upward Fragility," *New York Times Magazine*, April 2, 1995, pp. 36, 40, 49, 62, 63, 85, 87; Eric L. Wee, "Students Go the Extracurricular Mile for Admission into Elite Colleges," *Washington Post*, May 7, 1996, p. A1.

REFERENCES

Ainsworth-Darnell, J. W., & Downey, D. B. (Forthcoming). Assessing the oppositional culture explanation of racial/ethnic differences in school performance." *American Sociological Review*.

Bauman, K. (1996). *Trying to get ahead: School work and grades in the educational advance of African-Americans*. Working paper. Madison, WI: Institute for Research on Poverty.

Brown, B. B., & Steinberg, L. (1991). *Final Report: Project 2. Noninstructional influences on adolescent engagement and achievement*. Paper prepared for the U.S. Department of Education.

Coleman, J. S. (1961). *The adolescent society: The social life of the teenager and its impact on education.* New York: Free Press.

Collins-Eaglin, J., & Karabenick, S. (1993). *Devaluing of academic success by African-American students: On "acting White" and "selling out."* Paper prepared for the annual meeting of the American Educational Research Association.

Cook, P. J., & Moore, M. (1993). Drinking and schooling. *Journal of Health Economics, 12,* 411–429.

Cook, P. J., & Ludwig, J. (1997). Weighing the burden of "acting White": Are there race differences in attitudes toward education?" *Journal of Policy Analysis and Management, 16*(2), 656–678.

Fordham, S., & Ogbu, J. (1986). Black students' school success: Coping with the burden of "acting White." *The Urban Review, 18*(3), 176–206.

Fordham, S. (1988). Racelessness as a factor in Black students' success. *Harvard Educational Review, 58*(1), 54–84.

Frazier, F. (1957). *Black bourgeoisie: The rise of a new middle class in the United States.* New York: Free Press.

Haveman, R., & Wolfe, B. (1994). *Succeeding generations: On the effects of investments in children.* Thousand Oaks, CA: Russell Sage.

Jaynes, G., & Williams, R., Jr. (1989). *A common destiny: Blacks and American society.* Washington: National Academy Press.

Ludwig, J. (1994). *Information and inner city educational attainment.* Ph.D. dissertation, North Carolina: Duke University.

National Center for Educational Statistics (1994a). Digest of Education Statistics, 1994, NCES 94–115. Washington, DC: Department of Education.

National Center for Educational Statistics (1994b). National Educational Longitudinal Study of 1988 Second Follow-Up: Student Component Data File User's Manual, NCES 94–374, 94–376. Washington, DC: Department of Education.

Ogbu, J. (1987). Opportunity structure, cultural boundaries, and literacy. In Judith Langer (Ed.), *Language, literacy, and culture: Issues of society and schooling.* Norwood, NJ: Ablex.

Ogbu, J. (1994). Racial stratification in the United States: Why inequality persists. *Teachers College Record, 96*(2), 264–298.

Petroni, F. A. (1970). "Uncle Tom": White stereotypes in the Black movement. *Human Organization, 29*(4), 260–266.

Portes, A., & Zhou, M. (1994). Should immigrants assimilate? *Public Interest, 116,* 18–33.

Slaughter-Defoe, D., Nakagawa, K., Takanishi, R., & Johnson, D. (1990). Toward cultural/ecological perspectives on schooling and achievement in African- and Asian-American children. *Child Developments, 61*(2), 363–383.

Steele, S. (1990). *The content of our character: A new vision of race in America.* New York: St Martin's Press.

Steinberg, L., Dornbusch, S., & Brown, B. (1992). Ethnic differences in adolescent achievement: An ecological perspective. *American Psychologist, 47*(6), 723–729.

Chapter 14

A Funny Thing Happened on the Way to Confirming Oppositional Culture Theory

Douglas B. Downey

The Black-White gap in educational performance remains a prime concern to social scientists and rightly so. With education playing such a central role in the stratification process, explaining the race gap in school performance would go a long way toward understanding the persistence of racial stratification in general. In this chapter, I relate how my initial work with Jim Ainsworth, done with the expectation of confirming an oppositional culture, ultimately provided evidence against it. Current disputes surrounding oppositional culture theory depend, in part, on whether the kind of evidence we presented—Blacks' reports of pro-school values—should be believed. Below I make the case for trusting that Blacks mean what they say.

Among the many possible explanations for the Black/White performance gap, there is much to like about Ogbu's oppositional culture theory. Its clever distinction between historically enslaved, colonized, or conquered minorities (involuntary) and those who migrated to the host country of their own free will (immigrant) provides a provocative environmental explanation for why some minority groups (e.g., Blacks) have struggled in school, while others (e.g., Asians) have thrived. In contrast to involuntary minorities who perceive limited job opportunities, immigrant minorities compare their condition to that of relatives in their homelands and conclude that their chances for success in the new country and the payoff for effort in school are good. Perhaps the most compelling element of oppositional culture theory, however, is its link between micro-level behaviors and macro-level characteristics of society. Ogbu argued that Blacks have come to devalue education because they perceive blocked opportunities and are, consequently, skeptical that education will do much to change that. In addition, involuntary minorities tend to eschew practices symbolizing the dominant group. Since schools are White-dominated institutions, Ogbu reasoned that part of Blacks' identity is maintained through opposition to schooling (see Ogbu 1991, 1994, 2003 for a more complete discussion).

This attractive set of ideas has garnered substantial attention in the social sciences. Several researchers have explored whether Blacks really resist school goals, and an initial wave of ethnographies was consistent with Ogbu's claim, generally showing that Blacks perceived limited occupational opportunity and saw little point to school (Dollard, 1957; Gilmore, 1985; Ogbu, 1974; Powdermaker, 1968; Solomon, 1992; Weis, 1985). There was, however, a troubling limitation to this work. Most notably, these researchers *described* the school values of Black adolescents rather than *comparing* the values of Blacks and Whites. It thus remained unclear whether Blacks were more resistant to schooling than similarly situated Whites for two reasons: (1) these studies often focused only on disadvantaged Blacks, and (2) comparative research at the time, most notably Coleman's (1961) book, *Adolescent Society*, suggested that U.S. youths of all racial/ethnic groups lacked interest in school.

It was with this goal in mind, to provide explicit comparisons, that Jim Ainsworth and I first started testing oppositional culture ideas with nationally representative survey data. Both of us expected to confirm the theory and to improve its base of empirical support by making explicit comparisons with Whites and by studying a more generalizable sample of students than earlier studies. But our initial analyses—showing that Blacks valued schooling *more* than Whites—were so puzzling that we found ourselves checking and rechecking our coding for errors. The coding was right and the unexpected patterns were real. Not only did the results demonstrate Blacks' appreciation for school, but, on a wide range of indicators, the *comparison* between Blacks and Whites produced the opposite pattern predicted by oppositional culture theory: Blacks reported *more* pro-school values than Whites. We tried restricting the analysis to youths who dropped out of school, low-socioeconomic students, and males, but evidence of oppositional values among Blacks was completely lacking. While the earlier studies had produced rich descriptions of Blacks' anti-school values, our work showed that when Blacks and Whites were compared on standardized indicators, Blacks valued schooling *more* than Whites (Ainsworth-Darnell & Downey, 1998).

We struggled to reconcile these results with oppositional culture theory. Although we found that Blacks exhibited poorer classroom *behavior* than did Whites, given Blacks' consistently pro-school attitudes, it was hard to make the case that the behaviors represented resistance to schooling, as oppositional culture theory posited. We concluded that Blacks do not devalue school, but are instead less likely than White students to have developed the "toolkit" of cultural skills, habits, and styles that are rewarded by teachers (Swidler, 1986). Despite valuing education, Black students less often exhibit the kinds of school-related behaviors that teachers reward because "[s]kills, habits, and styles are often shaped by the frequency at which they are found in their own community" (Wilson, 1996, p. 72).

Consistent with this position, more recent work has shown how Black students' classroom behavior is rated less favorably by White than Black teachers (Downey & Pribesh, 2004). These less favorable ratings for "mismatched" Black students are evident among eighth graders (NELS), but also among children during the first few weeks of kindergarten (ECLS). Of course, this pattern could be evidence of an oppositional culture if it is a product of Black students' greater tendency to misbehave when placed with White versus Black teachers. But kindergartners (Blacks included) are widely regarded as eager students (Alexander, Entwisle, & Horsey, 1997), and oppositional culture theorists have posited that resistance increases with age (Ogbu, 2003). The fact that matching penalties are evident for Black kindergartners as well as adolescents is especially troubling for the theory. In addition, if we consider what kindergartners have to say, Black children show no preference for their Black versus White teachers (Downey & Pribesh, 2004).

Alternatively, some scholars remain unconvinced that Blacks really value schooling, instead expressing concern that Blacks' reports lack credibility. Proponents of oppositional culture have argued that Blacks' pro-school pronouncements reflect "wishful thinking" (Ogbu, 1991) and that we should dismiss this information because there is a "disjuncture" between Blacks' attitudes and their behaviors (Farkas, Lleras, & Maczuga, 2002). As a result, they have discounted Black students' pro-school attitudes as too good to be true. Although Blacks' pro-school reports may *appear* to provide critical evidence against the theory, their argument goes, they do not because these reports lack credibility. Blacks' resistance to schooling, the argument goes, is largely unconscious and difficult to measure.

WHAT BLACKS SAY

Blacks' optimism has surprised social scientists on a number of research fronts. More than three decades ago, Rosenberg and Simmons (1972) puzzled over why Blacks, despite their disadvantaged social position, reported similar levels of self-esteem relative to Whites. And scholars of education have noted that in many samples, Black students report educational aspirations comparable to those of Whites. Moreover, when we control for background differences in socioeconomic status and family structure, Blacks usually have higher educational aspirations than Whites (Solorzano, 1991).

The most recent studies using the National Education Longitudinal Study (NELS) of 1988 provided important and consistent documentation of this pattern. Cook and Ludwig (1997, 1998) reported no evidence that Black students had lower educational expectations than White students.

Moreover, Ainsworth-Darnell and Downey (1998) demonstrated that Blacks' confident educational expectations are complemented by a wide range of pro-schooling views. We found that Black youths offered *more* optimistic responses than their White counterparts to questions about: (a) the kind of occupation they expected to have at age 30, (b) the importance of education to success, (c) whether they feel that teachers treat them well, (d) whether the teachers in their school are good, (e) whether it is ok to break rules, (f) whether it is ok to cheat, (g) whether other students view them as a "good student," (h) whether other students view them as a "troublemaker," and (i) whether they try as hard as they can in class. These pro-school reports do not appear to be restricted to studies employing survey methods. Indeed, ethnographers have reported the same pattern when they talk to Black students (Ogbu, 1994; MacLeod, 1995; Tyson, 2002).

THE CASE FOR DISMISSING BLACKS' REPORTS

Ogbu (1991) argued that job ceilings shape Blacks' perceptions of job opportunities and the value of schooling, and hence their view of whether school will pay off. But he maintained that we cannot learn about how Blacks' perceive and value school by asking them.

> One learns what blacks believe about how they get ahead in America not necessarily by asking them direct questions about getting ahead; direct questions will generally elicit responses similar to those given by white Americans. A more useful approach is to observe what they do in order to get ahead.
>
> (p. 444)

Blacks' reported values and perceptions lack credibility, the argument goes, because they are saying one thing and doing another. If their deeds do not match their words, then why should we believe what they say? Ogbu (1994) explained:

> It is true that in spite of the historical experience of blacks in the opportunity structure, black folk theories for getting ahead stress the importance of education. But this verbal endorsement is not to be accepted at face value. It is often not accompanied by appropriate or necessary effort.... The students verbally assert that making good grades and obtaining school credentials are important. They also say that in order to make good grades, one must pay attention in class, do what teacher says, answer questions in class, and do homework. However, from our observations in the classroom, in the

family, and in the community I must conclude that many do not do these things.

(p. 289)

Other proponents of oppositional culture theory have made a similar claim. Farkas et al. (2002) discounted Blacks' pro-schooling views because they said that there is a "disjuncture between African American student attitudes and their school behavior" (p. 153).

The idea that Blacks say one thing and do another has significant currency among social scientists. How did so many scholars come to believe that Blacks exhibit attitude-behavior inconsistency? Education scholars have long suspected that something is "wrong" with what Blacks say because their attitudes and expectations are surprisingly positive. In his 1966 report, Coleman and his colleagues concluded that "Blacks ... give a picture of students who report high interest in academic achievement, but whose reported interest is not translated through effective action into achievement" (p. 320). And others have noted difficulty in understanding Black students' optimistic educational expectations. Studying a sample of Black and White high school boys from Indiana, Kerckhoff and Campbell (1977) wrote that: "The expectations of the white boys seem clearly to be based on their past school experience as well as their ability and social background, but there is little understandable basis for the expectations of the blacks" (p. 24).

Skepticism of Blacks' pro-school attitudes grew further as a result of Mickelson's (1990) article, "The attitude-achievement paradox among Black students." Mickelson puzzled over how Blacks can report more pro-schooling attitudes than Whites yet achieve at a lower level. Her solution included the argument that attitudes are multidimensional and that researchers typically measure attitudes with abstract indicators (e.g., "Education is the key to success in the future") that reflect the dominant ideology rather than concrete attitudes that are "rooted in life experience" (Mickelson, 1990, p. 51). The attitude-achievement paradox is resolved, according to Mickelson, by noting that Black students espouse positive, *abstract* attitudes, but they reveal their frustrations with school when asked about their more *concrete* experiences. If we focus on students' *concrete* attitudes regarding their everyday experiences, her argument goes, there is no paradox. This elegant and often-cited solution has influenced scholars for more than a decade now and has played a central role in recent discussions regarding the merits of oppositional culture theory.

Of course, this solution also provides justification for impugning Blacks' attitudes, at least some of them, as untrustworthy. Mickelson's explanation suggests that Blacks' positive attitudes do not predict achievement outcomes, and so it is reasonable to discard them. And she suggested that

Blacks exhibit attitude-behavior inconsistency, wondering why "blacks continue to say that education is important and then behave in ways that have little relationship to their stated attitudes" (p. 46). Below, I challenge the position that Blacks exhibit attitude-behavior inconsistency and that their reports lack credibility.

THE CASE FOR BELIEVING BLACKS' REPORTS

(1) The Myth of Attitude-Behavior Inconsistency

Do Blacks say one thing and do another? The racial/ethnic rank ordering of attitudes at the group level (Blacks' attitudes are better than Whites') does not match the racial/ethnic rank ordering of school behaviors and performance at the group level (Whites' behavior/performance is better than Blacks'). This suggests that something is amiss.

Although the group-level pattern should raise our curiosity, it would be a mistake to conclude that it constitutes evidence of individual-level, attitude-behavior inconsistency among Blacks. Consider an analogy. Among individuals born since 1960, women tend to gain more years of education than men, but earn less income. But this group-level pattern (a result of women entering different occupations and many other factors) does not demonstrate a *disjuncture* between education and income for women. Women with more education, in fact, make more money than women with little education. There is certainly no reason to discount indicators of women's educational attainment as invalid as a result of this group-level paradox.

Another analogy shows the same pattern. Suppose that social scientists and medical scientists were both asked whether obtaining grants to support their research is important and that both groups reported similar levels of enthusiasm for obtaining grant funds. But then suppose that when we looked at outcomes, we noted that medical scientists, on average, obtained substantially more funding than social scientists. In each of these scenarios, a group-level rank ordering on an independent variable did not translate into the expected group-level rank order on the dependent variable. But because we live in a multivariate world, it should be no surprise when this happens, even when our measurement is valid and reliable for all subgroups. Social scientists might report the same enthusiasm for grants as medical scientists, but garner substantially less funding because of fewer grant opportunities, a pattern that would not malign the validity of social scientists' reported enthusiasm. The same is true for race, attitudes, and behaviors. The fact that group-level relationships show that Blacks have more positive attitudes, but poorer behaviors than Whites should not be considered evidence of a *disjuncture* between

Blacks' individual-level attitudes and behaviors or an indication that Blacks' attitudes are untrustworthy.

A better way to assess whether there is an inconsistency between what Blacks say and what they do is to see whether Blacks' attitudes predict their behaviors. If Blacks demonstrate attitude-behavior inconsistency, we should observe puzzling correlations between their stated attitudes and behavioral outcomes, and they should stand out as odd relative to other racial/ethnic groups. Or, a weaker form of this position would predict no association between attitudes and behaviors, especially those attitudes for which Blacks' reports are especially positive (Mickelson, 1990).

It turns out, however, that Blacks' attitude-behavior relationship is comparable to that observed among other racial/ethnic groups. Table 14.1 shows correlations for 16 attitude-behavior pairs for non-Hispanic White, Black, Asian American, and Hispanic students from tenth-grade NELS data. The correlations are modest for all groups, but for our purposes the

Table 14.1 Attitude-behavior correlations by race/ethnicity: high school sophomores from the National Education Longitudinal Study, 1990

Attitude measure and race/ethnicity	Behavior Measure			
	Teacher Report		Student Report	
	Effort	Disruptiveness	Time spent on homework	Grades
"I get a feeling of satisfaction from doing what I am supposed to do in class."				
Non-Hispanic Whites	.205***	−.128***	.220***	.290***
Blacks	.149***	−.077**	.154***	.164***
Asian Americans	.203***	−.103	.165**	.265***
Hispanics	.205***	−.142***	.138***	.273***
"I try as hard as I can in class."				
Non-Hispanic Whites	.236***	−.159***	.212***	.219***
Blacks	.194***	−.093***	.161***	.172***
Asian Americans	.113	−.011	.167**	.013
Hispanics	.136***	−.087**	.173***	.190***
"Education is important to getting a job later on."				
Non-Hispanic Whites	.218***	−.147***	.176***	.260***
Blacks	.150***	−.072**	.123***	.126***
Asian Americans	.140*	−.199**	.123*	.158***
Hispanics	.133***	−.095***	.150***	.185***
Occupation student expects to have at age 30				
Non-Hispanic Whites	.175***	−.102***	.159***	.277***
Blacks	.156***	−.127***	.261***	.231***
Asian Americans	.193***	−.024	.142*	.257***
Hispanics	.115***	−.047	.085***	.239***

Notes: $*p < .05; **p < .01; ***p < .001$ (two-tailed).

question is whether Blacks stand out as an anomalous group. They do not. All 16 of the attitude-behavior correlations for Blacks are in the expected direction, just like the other racial/ethnic groups.

As one example, among Blacks, the correlation between "Education is important to getting a job later on" and teachers' evaluations of students' efforts is .150. For Whites, the correlation is .218, for Asians .140, and for Hispanics .133. This pattern is typical, as the associations are often slightly stronger for Whites and roughly the same for Blacks, Asians, and Hispanics. The fact that Blacks' attitude-behavior correlations are comparable to those of Asians and Hispanics demonstrates that Blacks' attitudes exhibit predictive validity on par with these two other groups. If we were to dismiss Blacks' attitudes because their attitude-behavior correlations are slightly smaller than those of Whites, we would need to discard Asians' and Hispanics' attitudes, too. *One pattern is clear: Knowing Blacks' attitudes consistently helps us predict their behaviors.*[1]

(2) The Myth that Blacks' Attitudes are too Good to be True

Another line of reasoning may allow that Blacks exhibit attitude-behavior consistency based on within-race correlations, but posit instead that Blacks' reports should be discounted because, as Farkas et al. (2002) explained, Blacks give "answers that are typically inconsistent with the students' objective circumstances" (p. 153). If this were the case, we could observe attitude-behavior consistency but still be skeptical if Blacks, as a group, responded *too* optimistically to attitude questions.

The problem with this position, however, is that we have no way of evaluating its validity, given that we do not know what students' attitudes are *supposed to be* relative to their outcomes and behaviors. Consider an example that illustrates the kind of awkward assumptions we have to make to endorse this position. Using the NELS, we can look at students' reports of "how hard they try in school," along with the number of hours they spend on homework each week. Before looking at the data, we probably have our own notions of how much homework "hard-working" students should be doing. For my part, I think that a "hard-working" eighth grader should spend at least 10 hours a week on his or her homework outside of school. But none of the racial/ethnic groups in the NELS meets my standard. Of the students who claimed that they "work as hard as they can every day" on schoolwork, Blacks reported doing an average of 3.9 hours of homework per week, compared to 7.5 for Asian Americans and 5.4 for White students. If we were to stick with my 10 hours/week standard, we would dismiss the reports of all of the racial/ethnic groups in the NELS as overly generous.

But now that we have seen the data, we might be tempted to modify

306 Douglas B. Downey

our position. Perhaps "hard-working" students could be ones who average one hour a day (seven hours per week). If this were the case, one would then believe only the reports of Asians—they are the only ones matching their claim of "hard work" with sufficient time spent on homework. We might be frustrated by losing most of our data (White students), however, and thus succumb to a more lenient standard—5.4 hours a week—so that we can include Whites. The problem with this new standard is not so much that it is low, but that it is so arbitrary, as it assumes that the White attitude-behavior relationship must be the "right" one. And of course, if we somehow were persuaded that 5.4 hours of homework per week really was an objective standard for "hard-working" students, it makes sense to *eliminate all students* (Black, White, Asian, etc.) who do not meet this standard. Finally, it is worth noting that Black students may spend less time on homework than White students for other reasons. If their teachers assign less homework, they will do less—a possibility that would account for Blacks doing less homework without questioning the validity of their attitudes.

As another example, consider the relationship between students' educational expectations and their actual attainment. Nearly equal percentages of Black (67 percent) and White (70 percent) NELS eighth graders expected to graduate from college. Given Blacks' lower average socioeconomic status relative to Whites, their nearly comparable expectations of college completion represent one more example of their optimistic school attitudes. Twelve years later, however, when these eighth graders are about 26 years old, Black students have less frequently turned this expectation into a college degree: only 24 percent of Blacks had earned a college degree compared to 38 percent of Whites (Downey, Ainsworth, & Qian, 2003).

Did the eighth-grade Blacks offer educational expectations that were too optimistic given their objective circumstances? The fact that they less often succeeded in graduating than Whites suggests that they did. But again, we find ourselves assuming that the numbers for Whites should be viewed as "right." We could just as easily argue that Whites' expectations also were too optimistic. Nearly half of those who thought they would graduate from college had not done so by age 26. Although Blacks less often succeeded, viewing the gap between expectation and attainment for Whites as acceptable but defining the gap for Blacks as unacceptable is arbitrary. And if we really thought that we should discard the views of students who did not attain their educational expectation, we should remove all students under this condition, rather than restricting our concern to Blacks based on their *group* patterns. Perhaps the most important reason for not dismissing Blacks' educational expectations, however, is that expectations are not invalid just because they are not attained. Fewer Black students expecting to graduate from college may do so than White students, but the expectation still tells us something important.

(3) Perceptions of Individual Versus Group Opportunities

The questions from the NELS asked students about their own individual occupational futures. Comparing these standardized responses shows that Blacks do not perceive more limited occupational opportunities than Whites. But from other data sources, a different picture emerges if we ask Blacks whether opportunities for their *racial/ethnic* group are similar to those for Whites. When the question is explicitly linked to race, Blacks sometimes view their prospects as more limited than Whites' (Hochschild, 1995; Ogbu, 2003). In his study of Shaker Heights, Ogbu (2003) noted little recognition of a job ceiling among elementary school-age children, but an increasing belief that Blacks lacked the same job possibilities as Whites as children reached middle school and high school. Taken as a whole, the data suggest that Blacks view their own individual occupational chances optimistically, yet recognize potential barriers to Blacks as a racial/ethnic group. We know that Blacks' perceptions of their own individual opportunities are important predictors of behaviors (see Table 14.1); we need to know more about whether these views of societal-level racism affect individual behavioral and educational outcomes to the same degree. And because a non-trivial percentage of Whites believes that Blacks enjoy favored treatment via reverse discrimination (Fraser & Kick, 2000), we also should test the possibility that White students believe that Blacks are advantaged in the labor market and the possibility that this perception might shape White students' school efforts.

Conclusion

Although in our research we initially expected to confirm the theory's predictions, Jim Ainsworth and I were surprised to find that Blacks reported more pro-schooling values than Whites. We struggled to understand this evidence in light of oppositional culture predictions and ultimately viewed these patterns as too robust to dismiss. We also noted that Blacks' pro-schooling attitudes exhibited predictive validity on par with Asians' and Hispanics' and only slightly lower than that of Whites. The view popular among social scientists for more than a decade—that Blacks' pro-school reports can be overlooked because they do not predict outcomes—did not hold up when explored with high-quality, nationally representative data. There is no empirical justification for discarding Blacks' attitudes.

I posit that oppositional culture theory overemphasizes the role of racial identity and underemphasizes the extent to which Blacks' material conditions place them in a more difficult situation than that confronting most other groups. The key empirical finding that motivated Ogbu's theory was that the Black/White gap in school performance persists even once socioeconomic status is statistically controlled. But this simple measure of socioeconomic status (typically measured as parents' education, parents' occupations, and income) does not account fully for the different conditions Blacks and Whites face.

Middle-class Blacks are more frequently first-generation middle class and, as a result, tend to have less wealth than their White counterparts. And it is noteworthy that some researchers have found no Black/White difference in years of education attained when wealth is controlled (Conley, 1999) and no differences in parents' willingness to pay for college when a wide range of background variables are controlled (Steelman & Powell, 1993). In short, while the motivation for oppositional culture theory has been to explain the persistence of a race gap beyond controls for socioeconomic status, it is not clear that race gap exists when more extensive measures are used to control for background differences between Blacks and Whites.

In an attempt to create an ideal comparison, Ogbu went to Shaker Heights, Ohio where the Black/White performance gap persists, but "White and Black social classes are not too dissimilar" (2003, p. 36). With so many professionals of both races, he reasoned, any difference in school performance must be accounted for by culture. He went on to demonstrate Black students' ambivalence toward school and to call for Black parents and community leaders to promote greater school engagement among their children.

But the Black/White comparison in Shaker Heights suffers from a critical error. The material conditions of the Black and White students were not similar, not even close. Ogbu acknowledged that: "According to the 1990 census, about 32.6% of the Black households in Shaker Heights and 58% of the White households, had an average annual family income of $50,000 to over $100,000 (Stupay, 1993, p. 8)" (Ogbu, 2003, p. xii), but then, oddly, proceeded with his argument that the two groups were basically similar. More troubling is what we learn if we compare Blacks and Whites in Shaker Heights more closely, as one reviewer of Ogbu's book did (Bobbitt-Zeher, 2004). It turns out that in 2000 the median value of a home in the city of Shaker Heights was $238,000 for White homeowners and $131,300 for Black homeowners (U.S. Census Bureau, 2000). Unfortunately Blacks and Whites do not typically experience the same material conditions and most comparisons that try to isolate the "race" effect fail to capture the many ways Black students are disadvantaged. Current scholarship typically underestimates these differences.

Finally, it is worth noting that most evidence suggests that Black/White gaps in educational performance have declined during the 1980s (Hedges & Nowell, 1998; U.S. Department of Education, 2000), a pattern seldom emphasized by oppositional culture proponents. Advocates of oppositional culture theory would have to say that the gap has narrowed *in spite of* Blacks' resistance to schooling. But because the best evidence suggests that Blacks have more pro-school values than Whites, a more reasonable explanation is that the gap has diminished, at least in part, *because of* Blacks' pro-school values. Proponents of oppositional culture theory impugn Blacks' cultural values as part of the problem; I see them as part of the solution.

NOTE

1   Perhaps the evidence from Table 14.1 masks the attitude-behavior inconsistency among Blacks because the analyses include all Blacks, as opposed to just those holding the most resistant views toward schooling. In supplemental analyses, I considered whether these attitude/behavior correlations are reversed for (a) the lowest-SES Blacks, (b) a subset of Blacks who admitted that they did not try hard in school, or (c) Blacks who dropped out of school between the 8th and 10th grades. There was no evidence that these disenfranchised groups of Blacks were more likely to exhibit attitude-behavior inconsistency than other Blacks.

REFERENCES

Ainsworth-Darnell, J. W., & Downey, D. B. (1998). Assessing the oppositional culture explanation for racial/ethnic differences in school performance. *American Sociological Review, 63*, 536–553.

Alexander, K. L., Entwisle, D. R., & Horsey, C. S. (1997). From first grade forward: Early foundations of high school dropout. *Sociology of Education, 70*, 87–107.

Bobbitt-Zeher, D. F. (2004). Review of *Black American students in an affluent suburb: A study of academic disengagement,* by John U. Ogbu with the assistance of Astrid Davis in *Contemporary Sociology, 33*(4), 414–416.

Coleman, J. S. (1961). *The adolescent society.* New York: Free Press.

Coleman, J. S., Campbell, E. Q., Jobson, C. J., McPartland, J., Mood, A. M., Weinfeld, F. D., & York, R. L. (1966). *Equality of educational opportunity.* Washington, DC: U.S. Government Printing Office.

Cook, P. J., & Ludwig, J. (1997). Weighing the "burden of acting White": Are there race differences in attitudes toward education? *Journal of Policy Analysis and Management, 16*, 256–278.

Cook, P. J., & Ludwig, J. (1998). The burden of "acting White": Do Black adolescents disparage academic achievement? In C. Jencks & M. Phillips (Eds.), *The Black-White test score gap* (pp. 375–400). Washington, DC: Brookings Institution.

Conley, D. (1999). *Being Black, living in the red*. Berkeley and Los Angeles: University of California Press.

Dollard, J. (1957). *Caste and class in a southern town* (3rd edn). Garden City, NY: Doubleday.

Downey, D. B., Ainsworth, J. W., & Qian, Z. (2003). *Revisiting the attitude-achievement paradox*. Paper to presented at the annual meetings of the American Sociological Association, Atlanta.

Downey, D. B., & Pribesh, S. (2004). When race matters: Teachers' evaluations of students' classroom behavior. *Sociology of Education*, 77(4), 267–282.

Farkas, G., Lleras, C., & Maczuga, S. (2002). Does oppositional culture exist in minority and poverty peer groups? *American Sociological Review*, 67, 148–155.

Fraser, J., & Kick, E. (2000). The interpretive repertoires of whites on race-targeted policies: Claims making of reverse discrimination. *Sociological Perspectives*, 43, 13–28.

Gilmore, P. (1985). "Gimme room": School resistance, attitude, and access to literacy. *Journal of Education*, 167, 111–128.

Hedges, L.V., & Nowell, A. (1998). Black-White test score convergence since 1965. In C. Jencks & M. Philips (Eds.), *The Black-White test score gap* (pp. 148–181). Washington, DC: The Brookings Institution Press.

Hochschild, J. L. (1995). *Facing up to the American dream: Race, class, and the soul of the nation*. Princeton, NJ: Princeton University Press.

Kerckhoff, A. C., & Campbell, R. T. (1977). Black-White differences in the educational attainment process. *Sociology of Education*, 50, 15–27.

MacLeod, J. (1995). *Ain't no makin it: Aspirations and attainment in a low-income neighborhood*. Boulder, CO: Westview Press.

Mickelson, R. A. (1990). The attitude-achievement paradox among Black adolescents. *Sociology of Education*, 63, 44–61.

Ogbu, J. U. (1974). *The next generation: An ethnography of education in an urban neighborhood*. New York: Academic Press.

Ogbu, J. U. (1991). Minority responses and school experiences. *The Journal of Psychohistory*, 18, 433–456.

Ogbu, J. U. (1994). Racial stratification and education in the United States: Why inequality persists. *Teachers College Record*, 96, 264–298.

Ogbu, J. U. (2003). *Black students in an affluent suburb: A study of academic disengagement*. Mahwah, NJ: Lawrence Erlbaum Associates.

Powdermaker, H. (1968). *After freedom: A cultural study in the deep south*. New York: Atheneum.

Rosenberg, M., & Simmons, R.G. (1972). Black and White self-esteem: The urban school child. *Arnold M. and Caroline Rose Monograph Series*. Washington, DC: American Sociological Association.

Solomon, P. R. (1992). *Black resistance in high school*. Albany, NY: State University of New York Press.

Solorzano, D. (1991). Mobility aspirations among racial minorities, controlling for SES. *Sociology and Social Research*, 75, 182–188.

Steelman, L. C., & Powell, B. (1993). Doing the right thing: Race and parental locus of responsibility for funding college. *Sociology of Education*, 66, 223–244.

Stupay, D. S. (1993). *The Shaker Heights City School: An overview.* Shaker Heights, Ohio: Shaker Heights School District.

Swidler, A. (1986). Culture in action: Symbols and strategies. *American Sociological Review, 51,* 273–86.

Tyson, K. (2002). Weighing in: Elementary-age students and the debate on attitudes toward school among Black students. *Social Forces, 80,* 1157–1189.

U.S. Department of Education. (2000). National Center for Education Statistics. *The Condition of Education,* NCES 2000-062. Washington, DC: U.S. Government Printing Office.

Weis, L. (1985). *Between two worlds: Black students in an urban community college.* Boston: Routledge and Kegan Paul.

Wilson, W. J. (1996). *When work disappears: The world of the new urban poor.* New York: Knopf.

U.S. Census Bureau. (2000). HCT42A. Median Value (Dollars) (White Alone Householder). Retrieved October 20, 2003, from <http://factfinder.census.gov/servlet/DTTable?_ts=84741328179>

Chapter 15

Quantitative Studies of Oppositional Culture

Arguments and Evidence

George Farkas

One of the most important research traditions in modern social science began in 1974, when John Ogbu first published the results of his observations of low-income, African American school children in Stockton, California. What he found was a peer-group culture that did not support, and in fact opposed, students' efforts to succeed in school. Through a sustained research program over the following 30 years, Ogbu greatly expanded upon his initial observations. The research area Ogbu pioneered has focused on an African American "oppositional culture," in which doing well in school is negatively sanctioned as "acting White." In recent years, this has emerged as one of the most important, and also one of the most controversial, areas of social science. It is important because it may at least partially answer one of the most perplexing social science and public policy questions of both the twentieth and twenty-first centuries. Why do African American children in inner-city schools perform so poorly? And what can we do to improve the school performance of these children, so that they can attain employment that enables them to participate in the mainstream of American life? It is controversial because its findings have been questioned by other researchers, and its supposed "blaming the victim for not trying hard enough" appears, at least to some social scientists, to come uncomfortably close to being both "unhelpful" and politically incorrect.

Much already has been written on these issues. Yet, the resulting literature has left many readers confused, a situation to which I apparently have contributed. After reading a published exchange on these issues to which I was a party (Farkas, Lleras, & Maczuga, 2002; Downey & Ainsworth-Darnell, 2002), a close friend said, "I still can't tell who's right." This chapter attempts to remedy the situation by clarifying and extending the evidence in this area. I also examine directions for future research.

The basic questions under dispute are relatively straightforward. First, does oppositional culture, as Ogbu described, exist? That is, do African American student peer groups discourage school effort because it is "acting White?" Second, if this behavior does exist, and does in fact reduce African American students' school-related effort, does this reduced effort explain a significant portion of the Black-White school performance gap? Yet, despite the apparent simplicity of these questions, the debate over the evidence used to answer them has introduced a number of related issues that have complicated the discussion. One of these concerns is the relative value of ethnographic (qualitative) versus quantitative evidence.

John Ogbu was trained as an anthropologist. Almost all of his and his collaborators' research has been based on first-hand observations collected during fieldwork. However, the primary challenge to his findings has come from two papers published by quantitative researchers—economists Cook and Ludwig (1997, 1998) and sociologists Ainsworth-Darnell and Downey (1998). These pairs of authors undertook similar calculations from the same national database, the National Educational Longitudinal Study (NELS), and reached similar conclusions: African American high school students do not become less popular than do Whites when they try hard at school. Further, African American students do not even try less hard at school than do White students. Both sets of researchers accompanied their claims with the suggestion that the work of Ogbu and his colleagues may be flawed because, being qualitative, it is less able to accurately and comparatively measure the behaviors at issue than are quantitative analyses of a large database containing information on both Black and White students throughout the United States.

In re-analyses of the NELS data, plus new analyses of National Assessment of Educational Progress (NAEP) data, colleagues and I (Farkas, Lleras, & Maczuga, 2002) disputed these findings and found support for Ogbu's claims. In a reply, Downey and Ainsworth-Darnell (2002) performed further analyses of the NAEP data and reasserted their original claims. As a consequence, the oppositional culture debate now has two strands—that utilizing qualitative, and that utilizing quantitative evidence. It is with the quantitative evidence that I shall be primarily concerned here.

Farkas, Lleras, and Maczuga (2002; hereafter FL&M) argued the following points. First, Ainsworth-Darnell and Downey (1998; hereafter AD&D) reached incorrect conclusions when they used African American students' self-reports to conclude that, far from discouraging academic effort, African American student peer groups actually reward good students by making them more popular. AD&D made this error because (a) they took these students' self-reports at face value, despite prior studies finding that African American and low-income students give unreliable (unrealistically optimistic) answers to survey questions about self-esteem and academic aspirations, effort, and performance (Rosenberg & Simmons, 1972; Mickelson, 1990); and (b) they ignored the strategies that African American good students sometimes use to remain popular despite an oppositional culture that puts them down.

Second, FL&M showed that if AD&D's data are reanalyzed after taking these issues into account, their results are reversed. Finally, FL&M suggested that, by using the NAEP data, which include a more appropriately worded question ("my friends make fun of people who try to do well") and surveying younger children (fourth graders, compared with the tenth graders whom AD&D analyzed), who are less likely to try to give "politically acceptable" survey responses, much could be learned about the true range of variation in oppositional peer group cultures. We presented such a multivariate analysis, finding net effects increasing oppositional peer-group culture for the following: males, African Americans, Hispanics, American Indians, students in central city schools and public schools (compared with Catholic schools), students whose parents are high school dropouts, students who receive free lunches, and students attending poverty (Title I) schools. We concluded that this sort of quantitative analysis, with a more direct question and with younger children, could be expanded so as to further examine these issues.

Downey and Ainsworth-Darnell (2002, D&A-D, hereafter) responded as follows. First, they further analyzed our reanalysis of their original data, and claimed that our findings were not robust and were based on very thin evidence. Second, they further analyzed the NAEP data that we had analyzed, adding eighth and twelfth graders to the fourth graders we analyzed. They showed that the fourth-grade results did not replicate with the eighth and twelfth graders, and that even with the fourth graders, higher Black compared to White oppositional culture explained only 11–15 percent of the Black-White test score gap. Finally, they presented attitude-behavior correlations to argue that Black students' survey responses were just as reliable as those of other students. They accompanied these new analyses with a myriad of additional arguments in support of their position.

D&A-D's response was strongly and skillfully presented. There is little wonder that many readers could not decide who was right! This chapter presents the reply the journal did not permit my colleagues and myself to offer as a response to D&A-D's last contribution to the exchange with FL&M. Following this, I review additional literature, including a recent study by Laura Tach and myself that strongly supported the findings of FL&M. Next, I show new research results that further expand our understanding of the determinants of peer-group oppositional cultures. The chapter ends with a summary of findings and suggestions for new research directions.

RESPONSE TO DOWNEY AND AINSWORTH-DARNELL

Examining D&A-D's first point, we find a complex discussion of our original analysis, which was already quite complex. The subtle points came fast and furious. They included main effects versus interaction effects, the choice of a base comparison for a multi-category variable, statistical significance, and sample sizes. Never did they deny our reported findings, yet they managed to cast doubt with multiple challenges.

D&A-D's claim that our first set of analyses was not robust is false. This is clearly seen in the findings of the large number of preliminary analyses we described, but did not show, because the journal would not provide space. To fully respond to all of D&A-D's assertions would require many paragraphs of "ifs, ands, and buts," whose details are complex, and which would likely still be inconclusive. The real problem is that our analysis was so complex, because, as noted in our text, we were trying to provide an appropriate statistical test, and tease out the truth, in a situation where the survey responses were unreliable. Beginning with such a complex finding, it was relatively easy for D&A-D to make the discussion even more complex. That is why, in our second analysis, we strove to find a simpler situation, where the truth could be seen more easily. It thus seems more useful to focus on D&A-D's response to our second analysis, of the NAEP data.

D&A-D's primary response was to repeat our analysis for eighth and twelfth graders, as well as fourth graders. First they showed that, while the finding replicated for fourth graders, it was absent for eighth and twelfth graders. They used this, plus other arguments, to cast doubt on the significance of the results for fourth graders. They also showed that, even for fourth graders, the oppositional culture variable explained only 11–15 percent of the Black-White test score gap. Finally, in a footnote (#3 on p. 159), they sought to create doubt about the validity of the fourth-grade results, by saying that the race effect on "my friends make fun of" would disappear if we were to control the test score.

I will discuss the last of these points first. The specification that the authors suggested in the footnote was inappropriate, as it would have introduced bias by using an outcome of peer-group oppositional culture to predict peer-group culture. In their Table 1 calculation, they put the causal order the *other* way, with oppositional culture *predicting* test scores. Thus, this argument should be completely rejected.[1]

Now for D&A-D's finding that our results for the fourth graders in the NAEP were not replicated for eighth and twelfth graders. It is apparently true that the net effect of being African American on "my peers make fun of people who try hard" for fourth graders was not replicated for eighth and twelfth graders. However, they seemed to believe that this result was evidence against our belief in the existence of peer-group oppositional culture. Yet our principal argument against D&A-D's position was based on the previously documented unreliability of African American adolescents' answers to questions that were politically sensitive because the students were aware of the disjunction between what they "should" do and their actual practice (Mickelson, 1990). Thus, in the introduction to our analysis, we argued that "fourth-graders are also more likely to answer without concern for impression management or for issues of adolescent identity than are A-D&D's tenth-graders" (FL&M 2002, p. 150). In light of this assertion, the failure of this effect to be replicated with the older NAEP students was exactly what we would have expected.

Which brings me to D&A-D's final point—their Table 2 and extensive argument (see their footnote 6 on p. 161) that Black students' behavior is as consistent with their self-reported attitudes as that of any other group of students. Here, D&A-D adopted a curious strategy. They argued against a finding for which they had already produced evidence (A-D&D, 1998, Table 3) by devising a new and invalid way to test it, and then proceeding to implement this invalid methodology (D&A-D 2002, Table 2). What they originally demonstrated (and had been reported by others) is that African American students *said* positive things about their attitudes toward school, but their school-related behaviors were inconsistent with these positive attitudes. This inconsistency was so large that, as a group, *African American students averaged more positive school-related attitudes than White and Asian students, while actually behaving less positively toward school than did these groups.* For example, as A-D&D (1998, Table 3b) showed, African American students were more likely than White and Asian students to say that they tried hard and obtained satisfaction from doing what they were supposed to do in class. They were also less likely than White and Asian students to say that it was OK to break school rules, that it was OK to cheat at schoolwork, or that other students saw them as a troublemaker. That is, they sounded like great students! And yet, as shown by A-D&D (1998, Table 3a), teachers' reports of African American students' school effort and disruptiveness rated them worse on these behaviors than White and Asian students. Further, Black students themselves reported spending fewer hours on homework than were reported by White and Asian students. (Black students may have reported accurately on this because they had no way of knowing what the "right answer" was. Or, in fact, they may have overreported their homework hours, so that the Black-White "homework gap" was in fact even larger than it appeared.) That is, by their teachers' and their own reports of schoolwork, they were anything but great students.

Having replicated this prior research finding in their original paper, D&A-D (2002, Table 2) replied to our critique by changing the way they tested the hypothesis. Instead of focusing on what they and everyone else had focused on—that Black students reported better attitudes but worse performance than other groups—they instead focused on the correlation between attitudes and behaviors, separately for Blacks, Whites, and other groups. It turned out that all these correlations were relatively small, and D&A-D used this to argue that "Blacks' deeds match their actions" as well as do those of Whites. But the fact that these correlations were relatively modest does not prove this. The model that we and others have in mind, and that A-D&D tested in their original paper, was one in which a variety of forces, including oppositional culture, shift Black students' school effort downward. Now suppose that Black students are similar to White students, with similar behavior-attitude correlations, except that they have had their effort shifted downward. If the effort of all Black students shifts downward by the same amount, the correlation between the behavior and attitudes of each student would be unchanged. (It is as though for Blacks, the midpoint of the scale of behavior has been shifted. But correlations are independent of scale.) That is, in this case, we would *not expect* to see any Black-White differences in the correlations calculated by D&A-D in their Table 2. This entire analysis is a red herring and says nothing about the issue under dispute.

In their footnote 6, D&A-D suggested additional arguments to support their case. The most potentially powerful of these is that White teachers were biased, and that their reports of lower African American student effort were false. If true, this would be a very important finding and could certainly explain the discrepancy between African American students' self-reported attitudes and their behaviors as reported by their teachers. (It would not, however, explain the discrepancy between their attitudes and self-reported time spent on homework. More on this below.) In arguing for this position, the authors claimed that their analyses of the new Early Childhood Longitudinal Study (ECLS) data provided evidence of such White-teacher bias against Black students.

These data, for a large national sample of kindergarten children, certainly provided evidence that, as early as kindergarten, teachers judged African American children to have worse school-related behaviors than White children. For example, when asked whether the students persisted at tasks, teachers responded "yes" for 75 percent of White children, but for only 61 percent of Black children. Similar Black-White behavior gaps were found for related variables, such as "seems eager to learn," "pays attention," "easily gets angry," "argues with others," and "fights with others" (West, Denton, & Reaney, 2001, Tables 6, 7). D&A-D (2002, p. 161, fn. 6) claimed that in these data, "when matched with same-race teachers, however, the behavior of black and white students is comparable." However, my own analyses of these same data do not support this. Rather, in a paper with Laura Tach, I found that being a Black student had a significant, negative effect on the teacher's judgment of these behaviors, and there was no statistically significant interaction between the teacher's and student's race (Tach & Farkas, 2006).[2]

In the same footnote, D&A-D also addressed the question as to why Black students' *self-reports* indicated less time spent on homework, and being in trouble in school more often, than was reported by White students. They stated that "even these patterns could be a result of teacher bias. If teachers assign black students less homework, they will do less, and if teachers more often misinterpret black students' behavior as resistant, they will discipline them more often." While it is difficult to completely rule out this explanation, there is little evidence for it, and this effort to blame White teachers is far-fetched. (Indeed, the teachers of many Black students are themselves Black, and there is no evidence that these students performed better than those with White teachers.) However, D&A-D's line of argument raised the following question: Is there evidence of Black and White students' school-related effort from any source beyond the students and teachers involved? The answer is yes— there are reports from the students' parents. Later in this chapter, I will present such evidence. We will see that *even parent reports indicate that Black students are less engaged in school than are White students.*

It also should be noted that D&A-D were particularly upset that researchers such as Mickelson (1990) and myself believe that Black students' school-related survey responses cannot be taken at face value. Thus, they asked, "What more must black students do before we believe that they mean what they say?" (p. 161) Further, in an e-mail exchange on this issue, Downey challenged me to provide other cases in which Black students' survey self-reports have not matched objective data. But such cases do exist. One is that Black adolescents underreport their involvement in delinquency (Hindelang, Hirschi, & Weis, 1981). Another is that Black adolescents overreport their placement in academic curricular tracks (Lucas, 1999; Lucas & Gamoran, 1991, 2002). Indeed, this overreporting has led to many years of research, which has found that, net of performance, Blacks are overrepresented in higher curricular tracks (Gamoran & Mare, 1989). Only after scholars began using actual transcript data was it discovered that, net of performance, there is no significant Black-White difference in track placement (Lucas, 1999).

This leaves D&A-D's finding that, in the NAEP data for fourth graders, net of control variables, "my friends make fun of people who try hard" explained only 11–15 percent of the Black-White test score gap. This may be the most useful piece of evidence presented by D&A-D. It suggested that peer-group oppositional culture plays a significant role in creating the Black-White test score gap, but that this was far from being the whole story. As I shall discuss later, this is likely the case. Indeed, the major cause of the gap appears to be the cognitive and behavioral gaps stemming from differential family behaviors during the preschool period, which African American children bring to kindergarten and first grade. These in turn develop individual and peer-group test-score and behavior gaps, which feed back upon themselves over time, leading to large test-score, school-engagement, and peer-group differences between the groups by the time they reach adolescence. In the following section, I review the evidence that has accumulated on these matters.

EVIDENCE ON EARLY BEHAVIORAL AND COGNITIVE PERFORMANCE OF LOW-INCOME AND AFRICAN AMERICAN CHILDREN

McLoyd (1998) reviewed an extensive literature on the effects of family socioeconomic disadvantage on child behavioral and cognitive outcomes. She found that a number of family risk factors accounted for the lower performance of disadvantaged children. These included single parenthood, teenage parenthood, persistent poverty, large family size, maternal school dropout and low cognitive skills, maternal substance abuse and delinquent involvement, maternal depression, and homelessness or residence in a low-income and dangerous neighborhood. Since African American mothers are more likely to display these characteristics, both without and with controls for social-class background, these risk factors are higher for African American than for White children.

McLoyd (1998) also discussed the parental behaviors that mediate the relationship between these family risk factors and negative child outcomes. Successful parenting involves cognitive and learning stimulation, expectations for achievement, positive affective relations between parents and children, and effective discipline and control strategies involving strict and directive supervision administered with high levels of warmth and affection. McLoyd (1998, pp. 195–197) also cited studies showing that chronic parental stress, adverse life events, and the disruption of marital bonds lead to parental mental health problems that in turn cause parents to provide little cognitive stimulation and relatively harsh and inconsistent behavioral management of their children. Unfortunately, these negative life situations are more likely to be experienced by African American than by White parents and children.

More recent studies have confirmed and expanded on these findings. McLoyd and Smith (2002) showed that African American mothers are significantly more likely than European American or Hispanic mothers to use physical punishment (spanking) on their children, while at the same time providing them with significantly less emotional support. Further, both spanking and emotional support are significant predictors of children's behavior problems. Bradley, Corwyn, McAdoo, and Coll

(2001a, b) reported similar results, and Oyserman, Bybee, Mowbray, and MacFarlane (2002) provided further analysis of the role of maternal depression in the parenting of African American mothers. In related research, Menaghan, Kowalski-Jones, and Mott (1997), McLeod and Nonnemaker (2000), and Carlson and Corcoran (2001) showed that race, poverty, and their correlates, including single parenthood, mother's depression, and spanking, are associated with lower child cognitive performance and increased child behavior problems.

Tach and Farkas (2006) used the Early Childhood Longitudinal Study—Kindergarten Class of 1998–99 (ECLS-K) data to examine the learning-related behavior and cognitive performance of a national sample of children in kindergarten and first grade. We found strong confirmation of previous findings, particularly the fourth-grade findings of FL&M. In this analysis, the behavior variable was the teacher's judgment of the student's "approaches to learning," combining the teacher's reports of the child's attentiveness, task persistence, eagerness to learn, learning independence, flexibility, and organization into a single variable. Fully consistent with the fourth-grade results of FL&M, teachers identified the following student categories as associated with worse learning-related behavior: males, African Americans, Hispanics, American Indians, younger students, and lower SES students. The same categories of students also showed lower test-score performance. These effects were largely, but not completely, explained by the lower behavior and test scores with which these students entered kindergarten. Further, D&A-D's claim of discrimination by White teachers was explicitly refuted: When the teacher's race and an interaction between the teacher's and student's race was added to the regression, neither was statistically significant.

Thus, we now have very strong evidence that low-income, ethnic minority, and other disadvantaged students arrive at kindergarten with lower cognitive skills and worse learning-related behaviors than the more advantaged students. Arguably, this circumstance creates fertile conditions for the creation of a peer-group culture that opposes school engagement. But how rapidly does this culture come into being? FL&M found it to be fully in place by fourth grade. Interestingly, Elijah Anderson (1999) discussed the timing of the creation of this culture in his ethnographic study of an inner-city, African American neighborhood:

> During the early years, most of the children accept the legitimacy of the school, and then eagerly approach the task of learning. As time passes, however, in their relentless campaign for the respect that will be meaningful in their public environment, youth increasingly embrace the street code. By the fourth grade, enough children have opted for the code of the street that it begins to compete effectively with the culture of the school, and the code begins to dominate

their public culture—in school as well as out—becoming a way of life for many and eventually conflating with the culture of the school itself.

(p. 93)

We thus see that a distinct student culture in opposition to school appears to come into existence between first and fourth grade. It would be interesting to study which school characteristics either promote or retard the formation of this oppositional culture. This question was examined in the second of the new empirical analyses that I report below.

NEW DATA ON PARENTS' JUDGMENTS OF THEIR CHILDREN'S SCHOOL ENGAGEMENT

As noted above, parents' reports of their children's school engagement could be a key feature of the attempt to resolve conflicting findings from previous studies. In particular, conflicting findings regarding racial/ethnic differences in middle and high school engagement appear to depend upon who is reporting the behavior, with teachers reporting that African American and Hispanic students are less engaged in school than European Americans, but these effects becoming smaller or disappearing when student self-reports are used. The use of parents' reports avoids possible inaccuracies from either source. Presumably, parents are not biased against their own children. They also should be better able than the children themselves to accurately report on their children's behavior, avoiding the wishful thinking that children may indulge in when reporting their own behavior.

To examine this issue, I utilized data from the baseline (1997) wave of the National Survey of American Families (NSAF). These data provided information on a national sample of children enrolled in grades 1–7. Parents answered several questions on their child's schooling behavior. These included how often the child cares about doing well in school, how often the child only works on schoolwork when forced to, if the child does just enough schoolwork to get by, and if the child always does his or her homework. I combined these items to construct a scale indicating each child's engagement level in school. I investigated the social patterning of such engagement as students aged through elementary and into middle school. In the first analysis reported below, I studied the effects of family background and grade separately across groups defined by gender and race/ethnicity. The result was an unusually detailed view of parental reports of their child's school engagement, and thus of the early determinants of the child's socioeconomic attainment via schooling.

NEW ANALYSES OF THE EFFECTS OF THE SCHOOL RACIAL CONTEXT ON OPPOSITIONAL CULTURE

The second empirical analysis in this chapter extends my previous analysis of NAEP data for fourth graders (FL&M, 2002). This provides a more elaborate study of the contextual patterning of oppositional culture, measured by the question: "my friends make fun of people who try to do well at school" for fourth graders. I also extended these results to analyze the determinants of students' reading achievement. As we shall see, the results are consistent with the prior research described above, as well as the findings from the first empirical analysis in this chapter using parental reports in the NSAF data. Taken together, these analyses provide an unambiguous view of patterned variation in individual and peer-group school engagement among elementary school students.

It should be noted that FL&M first used the NAEP data for measuring oppositional culture, and these data were further analyzed in D&A-D's reply. The analysis reported in the present paper is an extension of that reported by FL&M. This extension included the use of school percent Black and school percent Hispanic to predict peer-group oppositional culture. It also included the use of the full set of predictors, plus the measure of peer-group oppositional culture itself, as determinants of students' reading achievement.

My analyses focused on the detailed effects of gender, poverty, and race/ethnicity (including Hispanics, whom D&A-D excluded), as well as school race and poverty contextual variables and their interaction with the individual-level variables. These detailed findings were ignored by D&A-D, who concentrated on Blacks alone, and the failure to find the Black peer-group effect in the NAEP data for eighth and twelfth graders. By contrast with D&A-D's focus on poorly understood and perhaps misleading results for eighth- and twelfth-grade Black students, I focused on very clear and consistent results for a wide variety of elementary school student subgroups. These included males versus females; Blacks and Hispanics versus Whites; and children of low-income and less well-educated parents versus middle-class and better-educated parents. I thus extended FL&M's findings to achieve a more complete view of the determinants of peer-group oppositional culture and reading achievement.

DATA AND METHODS

I discuss the data and variables for each analysis in turn.

The First Analysis: NSAF Data on Parent Reports of Individual Student Engagement

In the first analysis, I used the 1997 wave of the NSAF.[3] The NSAF focuses on the social, economic, and health characteristics of adults under the age of 65, their children, and their families. The 1997 wave, yielding interviews with over 44,000 households and over 100,000 people, is representative of the United States as a whole. Although sampling occurred within every state in the nation, the survey over-sampled 13 targeted states (Alabama, California, Colorado, Florida, Massachusetts, Michigan, Minnesota, Mississippi, New Jersey, New York, Texas, Washington, and Wisconsin) so as to compare data among states as well.[4] Certain individuals/households could not be included in the sample, such as the homeless and non-English- and non-Spanish-speaking people.

The sample was drawn separately for each of the 13, targeted states and for the rest of the nation. Researchers either conducted random-digit dialing to choose households with telephones, or they took an area probability sample of households without telephones. For both procedures, researchers conducted a short screening interview to verify that the household was eligible for the survey.

Once households were chosen by either random-digit dialing or area probability sampling, the people within each household were subsampled. If households had children and low incomes, they were given the full interview. However, if households had children and high incomes, or had no children at all, they were subsampled before being given the full interview. This sampling procedure led to over-sampling households with incomes below 200 percent of the federal poverty level. Households that included only adults over the age of 65 were excluded from the study.

Interviews were conducted using computer-assisted telephone interviewing technology. Cellular phones were given to households with no telephones so that all interviews could be conducted in the same way. Up to two children could be sampled from each household, one under the age of 6, and one between the ages of 6 and 17. To obtain information about the children, interviewers spoke with the Most Knowledgeable Adult (MKA), who was the adult that had the most knowledge about the child's well-being, education, and health care. Although some families with more than one child had different MKAs for different children, the MKA was usually the same for all children, and was usually the children's mother.[5] The 1997 wave of the survey resulted in 28,331 interviews that obtained information on children.

In addition to interviewing the MKA, one or two additional adults under the age of 65 living in the household were randomly sampled and interviewed. Also, in households without children, one or two adults under the age of 65 were sampled and interviewed.

For all households (with and without children), survey questions covered various issues, including economic security, such as employment and earnings, welfare program participation, and housing and economic hardship; health and health care, such as health care coverage and health care use and access; family environment, such as family stress, and family structure; attitudes concerning welfare, work, and raising children; demographics; and household composition. For families with children, child well-being issues, such as behavior problems, education and cognitive development, social and positive development, and child care use, also were covered.

Because children tend to drop out of school at increasing rates following the seventh grade, this study only included children in grades 1 through 7. This resulted in information on 10,617 children.

Independent Variables

Various independent variables on the children, their MKAs, and their households were used in the analysis. At the household level, a poverty variable revealed whether the household income was below 200 percent of the federal poverty level (poverty = 1) or above 200 percent of the level (poverty = 0). Family structure was represented as two dummy variables, one signifying that a single mother headed the household, and the other signifying some other family arrangement, such as living with extended family or an older sibling. The reference category included children living in two-parent families where the mother and father were married and living together. A region variable, involving three dummies, denoted the part of the country in which the family resided, such as the Northeast (reference category), the Midwest, the South, or the West.

Demographic variables at the individual level included the MKA's age, education, gender, and race. Age is a continuous variable representing the MKA's age at the time of the interview. The education measure included three dummies, in which less than a high school education or a GED was the reference category. The other three variables indicated a high school education, some college or an associate's degree, and a completed college degree or a higher level of education. Gender was a dichotomous variable, with males coded high (female = 0 and male = 1). Race/ethnicity was only measured for the child in this analysis, using two dummy variables of Black non-Hispanics and Hispanics, and using White non-Hispanics as the reference category. Black non-Hispanics were coded 1 if the child was Black non-Hispanic, and 0 otherwise. Hispanics were coded as 1 if the child was Hispanic, and 0 otherwise.

The final independent variable used in this analysis reflected the immigration status of both the parent and child. Three categories constituted this variable: the MKA and child were both foreign-born; the MKA was foreign-born but the student was U.S.-born; and the MKA was U.S.-born but the child was foreign-born.[6] Immigration status was treated as three dummy variables, with the base category comprised of the MKA and children who were both U.S.-born.

Dependent Variable

The dependent variable used in this study was a scaled measure of the child's school engagement, asked of the MKA. The scale consisted of four questions, asking how often the child "cares about doing well in school," "only works on schoolwork when forced to," "does just enough schoolwork to get by," and "always does homework." The responses to the questions included (1) all of the time, (2) most of the time, (3) some of the time, and (4) none of the time. Responses to the questions concerning only doing schoolwork when forced to and doing just enough schoolwork to get by were reverse coded. By totaling all responses, I created a scale score that ranged from 4 to 16, in which higher scores indicated greater school engagement. If respondents only answered three of the four questions, their scores were standardized to the 16-point scale. If respondents answered two or fewer questions, they were coded as missing.

The Second Analysis: NAEP Data on Student Reports of Peer-group Oppositional Culture

The second analysis used the NAEP data for fourth graders in 1998 (for a discussion of these data, see National Center for Education Statistics, 2001). Students were asked whether "my friends make fun of people who try to do well." Answers were coded 1 = strongly agree, 2 = agree, 3 = disagree, 4 = strongly disagree. Note that this question combines "being made fun of" with "trying to do well" in a single query, avoiding A-D&D's (1998) need to make an inferential leap based on an interaction between self-reports of "being a good student" and either "being popular" or "being put down." Fourth graders were also more likely to answer without concern for impression management, or for issues of adolescent identity, than were A-D&D's tenth graders.

I will examine the determinants of peer-group oppositional culture within this national sample of fourth graders. Independent variables included gender, race/ethnicity, poverty, parent's education, whether the school attended was high poverty, the school's race/ethnic composition (percent Hispanic and percent African American), and the school's geographic location. I also will examine the effects of these independent variables and peer-group oppositional culture on the student's reading performance as measured by the NAEP. Being a high-poverty school was measured by the school's participation in the Title I program.[7] Individual family poverty was measured by the student's eligibility for the National School Lunch Program.

RESULTS

The First Analysis: NSAF Parents' Reports of Individual Student Engagement in Grades 1–7

Table 15.1 shows the means of the variables extracted from the NSAF data, separately by gender and race/ethnicity groups. Beginning with the dependent variable, school engagement, we see quite regular, expected effects of both gender and race/ethnicity. For each race/ethnic group, females showed higher school engagement than do males, confirming the finding from the majority of previous studies. For each gender, the highest school engagement occurred for Whites, followed in order by Hispanics and African Americans. Recall that previous findings for middle and high school students, some based on teacher reports, others based on students' self-reports, some based on reported attitudes, others based on reported behaviors, disagreed about the relative school engagement of ethnic/racial groups. The Table 15.1 results show a pattern that persisted throughout the present study. When we look at parental reports of behavior for students in grades 1–7, ethnic minority (Hispanic and African American) students were less engaged in school than Whites (European Americans). The overall highest school engagement was for White females, with an average of 13.8. They were followed by Hispanic and Black females. Next came White males, followed by Hispanic and Black males. The Black males' school engagement score was 12.2, which was 1.6, or about 2/3 of a standard deviation below the level for White females.

The means of the independent variables are unsurprising. Across these students in grades 1–7, the average grade in which they were enrolled was 3.7–3.8. For parental education (where the base category was less than high school), White parents had the highest shares, with a college education and beyond, followed in order by African Americans and Hispanics. Whites also had the lowest rates in poverty and single-mother or "other" family type (the base category was two-parent household). The highest rates here were for African Americans, followed by Hispanics. Particularly striking was the more than 70 percent of African American children being raised in the single-mother or "other" family type.

The most knowledgeable adult (survey respondent) in these households was approximately 37 years of age across each of the six groups. Less than 3 percent of all White adults and/or children were born outside the United States. Similarly, roughly 4 percent of the African American children were born in the United States to foreign-born parents (second-generation

Table 15.1 Means of the variables from the NSAF data set

	White Female	White Male	Black Female	Black Male	Hispanic Female	Hispanic Male
School engagement	**13.79**	**12.63**	**13.20**	**12.17**	**13.36**	**12.50**
	(2.44)	(2.77)	(2.67)	(2.84)	(2.48)	(2.62)
Student's grade	3.79	3.84	3.83	3.86	3.72	3.80
	(2.05)	(2.03)	(2.00)	(2.03)	(2.03)	(2.04)
MKA's* education (less than HS base)						
High school	0.15	0.15	0.15	0.16	0.15	0.18
	(0.36)	(0.36)	(0.36)	(0.36)	(0.35)	(0.38)
Some college	0.32	0.33	0.29	0.28	0.23	0.23
	(0.47)	(0.47)	(0.45)	(0.45)	(0.42)	(0.42)
College degree or higher	0.23	0.21	0.11	0.11	0.0768	0.0874
	(0.42)	(0.41)	(0.31)	(0.31)	(0.27)	(0.28)
Poverty**	0.16	0.15	0.44	0.44	0.41	0.37
	(0.36)	(0.35)	(0.50)	(0.50)	(0.49)	(0.48)
MKA's age	37.25	37.25	36.53	37.03	36.18	35.98
	(6.93)	(6.81)	(9.71)	(9.88)	(7.98)	(7.75)
Household structure (two parent base)						
Single Mom	0.24	0.23	0.60	0.57	0.32	0.33
	(0.43)	(0.42)	(0.49)	(0.50)	(0.46)	(0.47)
Other	0.05	0.07	0.13	0.14	0.08	0.06
	(0.23)	(0.26)	(0.34)	(0.35)	(0.27)	(0.23)
Immigration status						
MKA and student Foreign born	0.01	0.01	0.01	0.02	0.16	0.14
	(0.07)	(0.07)	(0.12)	(0.15)	(0.37)	(0.35)
MKA foreign born and student US born	0.02	0.02	0.04	0.05	0.23	0.23
	(0.13)	(0.13)	(0.19)	(0.21)	(0.42)	(0.42)
MKA US born and student foreign born	0.01	0.00	0.00	0.00	0.01	0.02
	(0.07)	(0.06)	(0.04)	(0.00)	(0.11)	(0.13)
Student is foreign born	0.02	0.02	0.05	0.07	0.39	0.37
	(0.15)	(0.15)	(0.22)	(0.25)	(0.49)	(0.48)
Region (Northeast base)						
Midwest	0.34	0.33	0.23	0.25	0.10	0.09
	(0.47)	(0.47)	(0.42)	(0.43)	(0.30)	(0.29)
South	0.24	0.27	0.48	0.48	0.30	0.31
	(0.43)	(0.44)	(0.50)	(0.50)	(0.46)	(0.46)
West	0.19	0.17	0.0617	0.0562	0.34	0.33
	(0.39)	(0.38)	(0.24)	(0.23)	(0.47)	(0.47)
Total number	3484	3774	810	837	638	721

Notes: * Higher scores indicate higher levels of engagement.
** MKA refers to the "most knowledgeable adult." This is the adult in the household who is most knowledgeable about the student and who therefore responded to the questionnaire.
*** Coded 1 if household income is below 200% of the U.S. poverty line.

immigrants), whereas slightly less than 2 percent were themselves born outside the United States (first-generation immigrants). However, 14 percent of the Hispanic parents and children were both born outside the United States, and 24 percent were U.S.-born with foreign-born parents. The African American households were most heavily concentrated in the Southern United States; Hispanics in the West.

Table 15.2 shows the OLS regressions to predict school engagement, separately for each of the six groups. Overall, these regressions were quite significant, with many effects in the expected directions, but they also yielded some new findings.

One of the more interesting findings was that school engagement declined significantly with grade level for both male and female Whites and African Americans, but for neither of the Hispanic groups. Thus, the relatively high school engagement scores of Whites were even higher when they were in the early elementary grades, whereas the relatively low school engagement scores of Hispanics were equally low in early elementary and middle school. The school engagement "gap" between Whites and Hispanics, therefore, was at its greatest in the early elementary years. Furthermore, the relatively low average school engagement score of African Americans was combined with significantly declining engagement scores with increasing grade level, suggesting particularly low school engagement for these students by the time they reached middle school.

Consistent with a majority, but not all, of the previous studies, higher levels of parental education significantly increased student engagement across all six groups. At the lower end of the parental education scale, this effect was largest for African American males and females, with the parent being a high school graduate rather than a dropout exerting relatively large effects in increasing the child's school engagement. For both genders of Whites and African Americans, if the parent who responded to the survey (the "Most Knowledgeable Adult" [MKA] regarding the child) had at least some college education, it significantly improved the child's school engagement score. As one goes up the parental educational scale, positive and statistically significant school engagement effects emerged for all groups. At the highest level, where the parent had at least a college degree, the student's engagement increased by relatively large amounts. The largest of these effects were for African Americans and Hispanics, the groups for which such high levels of parental education were most unusual.

With parental education controlled, poverty had at most a modest effect on school engagement. Coefficients were negative for all groups, but attained marginal statistical significance only for White and Hispanic females. As for parental age, for European American students alone, this variable significantly increased student engagement.

Household structures other than the baseline two-parent type (single-mother or "other") showed a reasonably strong tendency to decrease

Table 15.2 Regression analysis of school engagement, separately by race/gender groups, NSAF data (standard errors in parentheses).

	White Female		White Male		Black Female		Black Male		Hispanic Female		Hispanic Male	
Student's grade	-0.13 (0.02)	***	-0.25 (0.02)	***	-0.19 (0.05)	***	-0.11 (0.05)	*	0.00 (0.05)		0.01 (0.05)	
MKA's education (less than HS base)												
High school	0.13 (0.13)		0.13 (0.14)		0.47 (0.28)	+	1.01 (0.25)	***	-0.06 (0.29)		0.31 (0.27)	
Some college	0.25 (0.13)	*	0.39 (0.11)	***	0.47 (0.23)	*	0.78 (0.24)	***	0.26 (0.25)		0.34 (0.25)	
College degree or higher	0.56 (0.12)	***	0.72 (0.13)	***	0.98 (0.33)	**	1.25 (0.33)	***	0.94 (0.39)	*	0.95 (0.37)	*
Poverty	-0.20 (0.12)	+	-0.22 (0.13)		-0.27 (0.21)		-0.21 (0.22)		-0.38 (0.22)	+	-0.11 (0.22)	
MKA's age	0.02 (0.01)	**	0.03 (0.01)	***	-0.00 (0.01)		-0.00 (0.01)		0.01 (0.01)		0.01 (0.01)	
Household structure (two parent base)												
Single mom	-0.45 (0.10)	***	-0.67 (0.11)	***	-0.10 (0.23)		-0.44 (0.24)	+	-0.51 (0.23)	*	-0.44 (0.23)	+
Other	-0.62 (0.19)	***	-0.69 (0.18)	***	-0.69 (0.34)	*	-0.76 (0.36)	*	-0.57 (0.40)		-0.84 (0.44)	+
Immigration status												
MKA and student foreign born	-0.99 (0.56)	+	-1.21 (0.61)	*	-1.59 (0.81)		0.78 (0.68)		0.52 (0.29)	+	0.68 (0.30)	*
MKA foreign born and student US born	0.21 (0.32)		-0.13 (0.34)		-0.09 (0.45)		-0.72 (0.48)		0.49 (0.25)	*	0.10 (0.24)	
MKA US born and student foreign born	0.51 (0.56)		-0.97 (0.70)		0.31 (2.63)		0.00 (0.00)		0.78 (0.88)		-0.45 (0.78)	

(Continued overleaf)

Table 15.2 Continued

	White Female	White Male	Black Female	Black Male	Hispanic Female	Hispanic Male
Region (Northeast base)						
Midwest	0.03	-0.03	-0.21	-0.20	0.36	0.09
	(0.11)	(0.12)	(0.28)	(0.30)	(0.36)	(0.37)
South	-0.06	-0.12	-0.42 +	-0.25	0.14	-0.25
	(0.12)	(0.13)	(0.24)	(0.27)	(0.27)	(0.26)
West	0.02	-0.04	-0.05	-0.33	0.15	0.00
	(0.13)	(0.14)	(0.42)	(0.46)	(0.26)	(0.26)
Constant	13.57	12.61	14.33	12.79	13.06	12.19
R-square	0.04	0.06	0.06	0.06	0.05	0.04
Total number	3484	3774	810	837	638	721

school engagement among children. All 12 coefficients had negative signs, and most had relatively large magnitudes and achieved statistical significance. In many cases, these magnitudes were comparable to those for parental education, indicating that these two variables (family structure and parental education) exerted the largest effects on children's school engagement. While not really surprising, recent research has de-emphasized these effects. For example, A-D&D (1998) estimated, but did not report, the effects of family structure on school engagement, while Smerdon (1999) did not even include this variable in her analysis. Johnson, Crosnoe, and Elder (2001) reported the effects of both family structure and parental education, but failed to find a significant effect of the latter variable.

Where immigration status was concerned, the results were more complex. Among Hispanics, and consistent with the majority of previous findings for this group, having both the parent and the student born outside the United States was associated with higher school engagement when compared with parents and children who were both native born. This effect was statistically significant for both males and females and persisted even when, with a foreign-born parent, the child was U.S. born, but in this case it was significant only for females. This gender difference may have been due to the much greater parental control exerted over females than males in Hispanic culture. By contrast, U.S.-born Hispanic males may have been more strongly influenced by the oppositional culture that (as we shall see below) was quite prevalent among their friends.

A completely different pattern was found for European Americans and African Americans. For three out of four of these groups, when the parent and child were both foreign-born, school engagement was significantly lower than for native-born parents and children (the exception was Black males). No clear pattern emerged when the parent was foreign born and the student was U.S. born. Of course, it should be noted that these findings were based on small samples. Their meaning remains obscure.

To better understand the grade-level pattern of gender-specific and ethnic-specific engagement rates, Figure 15.1 graphs the engagement score of each race-gender category at each grade level, using the White female means for the remaining independent variables. This shows predicted school engagement for race/gender groups with the other variables held constant at the White female means, thereby displaying race/gender differences, net of these other variables.

In first grade, the highest school engagement was by White and Black females, and the lowest was by Hispanic and Black males. As students progressed through the grades, the school engagement of the average White and Black female decreased, and that of the average Hispanic female remained the same, so that by seventh grade, the school engagement rank order was White and Hispanic females tied for highest, with Black females below them. As for males, Hispanic school engagement

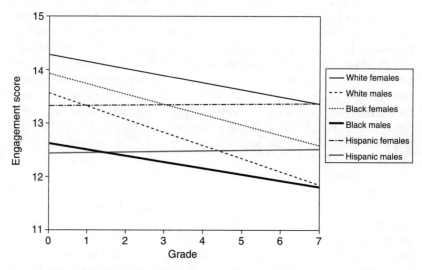

Figure 15.1 Predicted school engagement across grade levels, separately for race/gender groups, with family background set to the White female means*

* These are estimated from the coefficients in Table 15.2, using the White female means from Table 15.1.

stayed relatively constant across grade levels, whereas that for White and Black males declined significantly, so that by grade seven, the Hispanic males had the highest engagement of the three groups, with White and Black males relatively close together below them.

These grade progression patterns of school engagement, separately by gender and race/ethnicity, have not been previously reported. Overall, they show that gender was more important than race/ethnicity in determining school engagement, with females more engaged than males, irrespective of race/ethnicity, at all grade levels.[8]

The Second Analysis: Student Reports of Peer-group Oppositional Culture and Student Reading Test Scores, NAEP Data for Fourth Graders

Table 15.3 shows the means of the variables from the NAEP data. The sample was similar to that analyzed by FL&M (2002), except that I have now included the school's percent Black and percent Hispanic as predictor variables. Since these variables were not available for private and Catholic schools, they were dropped from the sample. Also, consistent with the calculations in the first empirical analysis (above), I dropped Asians and American Indians from the sample.

The peer-group oppositional culture variable ("my friends make fun of

Table 15.3 Means and standard deviations, NAEP data, fourth graders in 1998. (N = 4,952)

Oppositional peer group	
My friends make fun of people who try to do well.	1.98 (1.03)
Achievement	
Reading test score	213.07 (34.75)
Gender	
Male	0.50 (0.50)
Race/ethnicity	
Black	0.19 (0.40)
Hispanic	0.21 (0.41)
Family poverty	
National School Lunch Program	0.47 (0.50)
Parents' level of education	
High school graduate/GED	0.16 (0.36)
Some college	0.20 (0.40)
College degree	0.60 (0.50)
School poverty	
Title I school	0.32 (0.47)
School racial composition	
Percent Black	20.75 (26.86)
Percent Hispanic	16.51 (26.39)
Type of location	
Urban fringe/large town	0.45 (0.50)
Rural/small town	0.16 (0.36)
Region of country	
Southeast	0.32 (0.47)
Central	0.17 (0.37)
West	0.33 (0.47)

people who try to do well at school") was coded 1–4, from "strongly disagree" to "strongly agree." Its mean was 1.98. The mean of the NAEP reading scores was 213. The sample was evenly divided between males and females. It was 19 percent Black and 21 percent Hispanic. Forty-seven percent was in the National School Lunch program, a measure of family poverty. Of the parents, 16 percent was high school graduates, 20 percent had some college, and 60 percent was college graduates. (This distribution appears to be shifted rightward; fourth graders reporting on their parents' education seemed to have erred on the high side. This was unlikely to bias our coefficients for other variables, however.) Thirty-two percent of the children attended Title I schools (as noted, a measure of school-wide poverty). Across these students, the average Percent Black in their school was 20.75; the average Percent Hispanic was 16.51. Forty-five percent of students' schools were located in urban fringe/large towns; 16 percent were rural. Across regions, 32 percent were in the Southeast, 17 percent Central, and 33 percent in the West.

Table 15.4 reports the ordered logic regression analysis of the peer-group oppositional culture variable. (In this case the dependent variable was reverse coded because the ordered logistic statistical program compares the lowest-coded categories to the others.) Column 1 shows, as a baseline for comparison, the same additive model reported by FL&M (2002) in column 1 of their Table 2, but without the private or Catholic school variables (or the Asian or American Indian variables). It should be noted that in their reply to FL&M, D&A-D (2002, footnote 3) reported repeating this calculation with controls for test scores. This, however, was illegitimate and led to biased coefficients, because, as discussed above, it involved selecting on the dependent variable. (Both the original A-D&D paper and all others in this field used school engagement and its determinants, such as peer-group oppositional culture, as *inputs* to the school achievement process.) Accordingly, I did not control achievement in these calculations.[9]

We see that, as reported by FL&M (2002), males, African Americans, Hispanics, students in a low-income (Title I) school, students from a low-income family (National School Lunch Program), and children with parents who were high school dropouts, were significantly more likely to report a peer-group oppositional culture. As before, the largest effects were for Blacks, Hispanics, and children from low-income households, and these three effects were of roughly equal magnitude. Also, as before, since these effects were additive, students who were male, Black or Hispanic, and from a low-income household, with a poorly educated parent and attending a low-income school, had an extraordinarily high likelihood of reporting that their friends made fun of people who tried to do well at school.

Model 2 added interactions between student race and family poverty to the equation. This was to test whether the effects of race may depend upon being from a poor household. The answer is "no": These interactions were not significant. This finding expanded upon FL&M's finding of no significant interactions between race and gender. The additive effects of race did not depend upon either gender or family poverty.

Model 3 added the school's Percent Black and Percent Hispanic to the calculation, testing whether school racial composition affected the existence of oppositional culture. The findings show that the Percent Black variable had a highly significant, positive effect on oppositional culture: the coefficient was seven times its standard error and was significant at better than the .001 level. Percent Hispanic was not significant. Also, with these variables controlled, the effects of the individual-level Black, Hispanic, School Lunch (family poverty) and Title I (school poverty)

Table 15.4 Ordered logistic regression of "My friends make fun of people who try to do well." NAEP, fourth graders in 1998 (standard errors in parentheses)

	Model 1	Model 2	Model 3	Model 4	Model 5
Intercept 1	−2.15(0.16) ***	−2.14(0.16) ***	−2.33 (0.17) ***	−2.34(0.17) ***	−2.35 (0.17) ***
Intercept 2	−1.11(0.16) ***	−1.10(0.16) ***	−1.29 (0.16) ***	−1.30(0.17) ***	−1.30 (0.17) ***
Intercept 3	0.26 (0.16) *	0.27 (0.16) *	0.09 (0.16)	0.08 (0.16)	0.08 (0.17)
Gender					
Male	0.25 (0.05) ***	0.26 (0.05) ***	0.26 (0.05) ***	0.26 (0.05) ***	0.26 (0.05) ***
Race/ethnicity					
Black	0.41 (0.08) ***	0.38 (0.13) ***	0.23 (0.13) *	0.33 (0.16) **	0.31 (0.18)*
Hispanic	0.41 (0.07) ***	0.29 (0.11) **	0.25 (0.11) **	0.14 (0.14)	0.14 (0.14)
Nat. School Lunch Program	0.45 (0.06) ***	0.39 (0.08) ***	0.36 (0.08) ***	0.36 (0.08) ***	0.37 (0.10) ***
Parents' level of education					
High school graduate/GED	−0.29(0.14) **	−0.28(0.14) *	−0.28 (0.14) *	−0.28(0.14) *	−0.28(0.14)*
Some college	−0.39(0.14) ***	−0.38(0.14) ***	−0.38 (0.14) ***	−0.38(0.14) ***	−0.38 (0.14) ***
College degree	−0.35(0.13) ***	−0.34(0.13) ***	−0.35 (0.13) ***	−0.35(0.13) ***	−0.35 (0.13) ***
Title I participation	0.23 (0.06) ***	0.23 (0.06) ***	0.17 (0.06) ***	0.16 (0.06) ***	0.12 (0.09) ***
Type of location					
Urban fringe/large town	−0.14(0.06) **	−0.14(0.06) **	−0.06 (0.06)	−0.06(0.06)	−0.05 (0.06)
Rural/small town	−0.20(0.08) **	−0.20(0.08) **	−0.09 (0.09)	−0.08(0.09)	−0.07 (0.09)
Region of country					
Southeast	−0.05(0.08)	−0.05(0.08)	−0.05 (0.08)	−0.04(0.08)	−0.04 (0.08)
Central	−0.07(0.09)	−0.07(0.09)	0.002 (0.09)	0.01 (0.09)	0.01 (0.09)
West	−0.03(0.08)	−0.03(0.08)	0.06 (0.09)	0.06 (0.09)	0.07 (0.09)
Black * School Lunch Program		0.08 (0.16)	0.01 (0.16)	0.07 (0.17)	0.09 (0.19)
Hispanic * School Lunch Program		0.21 (0.15)	0.18 (0.15)	0.10 (0.16)	0.08 (0.18)
Percent Blacks in school			0.010 (0.001) ***	0.005 (0.002) **	0.006 (0.003)**

Table 15.4 Continued

	Model 1	Model 2	Model 3	Model 4	Model 5
Percent Hispanics in school			0.002 (0.002)	0.004 (0.002) *	0.004 (0.003)
Black * Percent Black				−0.001 (0.003)	−0.001 (0.003)
Black * Percent Hispanic				−0.002 (0.004)	−0.003 (0.004)
Hispanic * Percent Black				0.010 (0.003) ***	0.010 (0.004)***
Hispanic * Percent Hispanic				−0.001 (0.003)	−0.002 (0.003)
School Lunch * Percent Black					−0.001 (0.003)
School Lunch * Percent Hispanic					0.001 (0.003)
Black * Title I participation					0.13 (0.16)
Hispanic * Title I participation					0.05 (0.15)
Likelihood ratio chi-square	323.72***	325.79***	349.02***	362.27***	363.12***
Total number	4952	4952	4952	4952	4952

Notes: *$p < 0.10$; **$p < 0.05$; ***$p < 0.01$.

variables were reduced, although they remained significant. It appears that being in a high Percentage Black school partially explained these other effects. But does this apply to students from all three race/ethnicity groups, or only to African Americans? This was answered by the specification of Model 4, which added interactions between Percent Black, Percent Hispanic, and the Black and Hispanic individual-level variables to the equation.

When these interaction terms were added to the equation, the coefficient on the Percent Black (or Percent Hispanic) variable by itself gave the overall effect of this variable for Whites, Blacks, and Hispanics. This was modified for Blacks and Hispanics by the multiplicative terms involving individual race multiplied by Percent Black (or Percent Hispanic). These overall effects for Percent Black and Percent Hispanic were both positive and significant. For each of the three race/ethnicity groups, being in a higher Percent Black or Hispanic school increased peer-group oppositional culture. This overall effect was then modified by the interaction terms. Only one of these was statistically significant—Hispanics experienced a much larger positive effect of Percent Black on peer-group oppositional culture than did either Whites or Blacks. The increase for Hispanics— .01—raised the effect of Percent Black for them to .015. This was three times the effect of this variable on Whites or Blacks. In accordance with this, the direct effect of the Hispanic individual-level variable in Model 4 fell to approximately one third of its value in Model 1 and was no longer significant. Rather, this variable's effect appeared upon attending a highly Black or Hispanic school. That is, peer-group oppositional culture appeared to arise among Hispanics only when they were in schools with large concentrations of Black or Hispanic students.

As for the other variables in this equation, the male and parental education effects were unchanged, and the positive Black, School Lunch (family poverty), and Title I (school poverty) effects remained relatively large and statistically significant. Because of its striking nature, I repeat the principal finding of Model 4: High schools with a high percentage of Black or Hispanic students appeared to have a school climate that increased oppositional culture among all students, whether White, Black, or Hispanic. The magnitudes of these effects were relatively similar across groups, except that the oppositional culture experienced by Hispanics was particularly strong among those Hispanics in high-percent Black schools. However, these data did not permit the identification of distinct Hispanic subgroups, such as Mexican Americans, Puerto Ricans, and Cubans. Thus, we cannot distinguish between the "high Black school" contextual effect and possible subcultural effects within different segments of the Hispanic community.

Could this effect have been due to interactions between Percent Black and either individual or school-level poverty? Model 5 added interactions between individual poverty (National School Lunch Program participation) and racial composition to the equation. These interactions were insignificant. I also tried interactions with school-level poverty (Title I), but these too were insignificant. In sum, the Model 4 findings were supported. It appears that a higher share of Black or Hispanic students in the school increased peer-group oppositional culture, and this effect was particularly strong for Hispanic students in high-percent Black schools.

Finally, Table 15.5 shows the determinants of reading achievement, using both of the predictor variables used previously, and also the peer-group oppositional culture variable. D&A-D summarized their version of these calculations by reporting that oppositional culture explained only 11 percent of the Black reading deficit. They did not, however, show any of the estimated coefficients. Nor, it appears, did they control the school racial composition, as I did in Table 15.5.

Model 1 shows the basic pattern of inter-group differentials in reading

Table 15.5 Unstandardized OLS of reading test score, NAEP, fourth graders in 1998. Models 1–5 (standard errors in parentheses)

	Model 1	Model 2	Model 3	Model 4	Model 5
Intercept	231.25 (2.53) ***	231.36 (2.54) ***	248.50 (2.54) ***	249.24 (2.64) ***	249.41 (2.68) ***
Gender					
Male	−5.51 (0.84) ***	−5.49 (0.84) ***	−4.24 (0.81) ***	−4.20 (0.81) ***	−4.19 (0.81) ***
Race/ethnicity					
Black	−18.92 (1.24) ***	−20.25 (2.10) ***	−18.24 (2.01) ***	−21.75 (2.78) ***	−21.45 (2.90) ***
Hispanic	−17.43 (1.21) ***	−17.31 (1.83) ***	−15.77 (1.75) ***	−15.64 (2.55) ***	−15.38 (2.64) ***
Nat. School Lunch Program	−16.93 (0.99) ***	−17.29 (1.25) ***	−15.21 (1.19) ***	−15.10 (1.20) ***	−15.71 (2.08) ***
Parents' level of education					
High school graduate/GED	6.33 (2.35) ***	6.27 (2.35) ***	4.83 (2.25) **	4.76 (2.25) **	4.79 (2.25) **
Some college	11.62 (2.30) ***	11.58 (2.30) ***	9.59 (2.20) ***	9.58 (2.20) ***	9.62 (2.20) ***
College degree	7.45 (2.18) ***	7.38 (2.19) ***	5.61 (2.09) ***	5.59 (2.09) ***	5.60 (2.09) ***
Title I participation	−10.31 (0.99) ***	−10.31 (0.99) ***	−9.15 (0.95) ***	−9.18 (0.95) ***	−9.17 (0.95) ***
Type of location					
Urban fringe/large town	1.08 (0.95)	1.09 (0.95)	0.41 (0.91)	0.40 (0.91)	0.40 (0.91)
Rural/small town	0.98 (1.30)	1.01 (1.31)	−0.04 (1.25)	−0.05 (1.25)	−0.05 (1.25)
Region of country					
Southeast	−6.80 (1.25) ***	−6.78 (1.25) ***	−6.96 (1.19) ***	−6.93 (1.19) ***	−6.93 (1.19) ***
Central	−4.69 (1.44) ***	−4.69 (1.44) ***	−5.07 (1.37) ***	−5.09 (1.37) ***	−5.09 (1.37) ***
West	−7.24 (1.27) ***	−7.20 (1.27) ***	−7.31 (1.21) ***	−7.30 (1.21) ***	−7.30 (1.21) ***
Black * School Lunch Program		1.97 (2.58)	2.21 (2.46)	1.68 (2.48)	1.63 (2.48)
Hispanic * School Lunch Program		0.03 (2.34)	0.96 (2.24)	1.02 (2.27)	0.98 (2.27)
My friends make fun of . . .			−8.91 (0.40) ***	−9.33 (0.56) ***	−9.44 (0.64) ***

Black * make fun of . . .				1.81 (1.01) *	1.68 (1.07)
Hispanic * make fun of . . .				−0.02 (0.98)	−0.14 (1.03)
Lunch * make fun of . . .					0.32 (0.89)
Percent Blacks in school					
Percent Hispanics in school					
Black * Percent Black					
Black * Percent Hispanic					
Hispanic * Percent Black					
Hispanic * Percent Hispanic					
School lunch * Percent Black					
School lunch * Percent Hispanic					
Make fun of * Percent Black					
Make fun of * Percent Hispanic					
R-square	0.2747	0.2748	0.3399	0.3403	0.3404
Total number	4952	4952	4952	4952	4952

Notes: *p < 0.10; **p < 0.05; ***p < 0.01.

(*Continued overleaf*)

Table 15.5 Continued, Models 6–9

	Model 6	Model 7	Model 8	Model 9
Intercept	252.75 (2.74) ***	252.42 (2.76) ***	252.33 (2.77) ***	251.78 (2.82) ***
Gender				
Male	-4.30 (0.81) ***	-4.37 (0.81) ***	-4.38 (0.81) ***	-4.37 (0.81) ***
Race/ethnicity				
Black	-18.91 (2.93) ***	-18.24 (3.16) ***	-18.64 (3.29) ***	-19.45 (3.53) ***
Hispanic	-14.62 (2.64) ***	-15.27 (2.80) ***	-15.71 (2.84) ***	-16.87 (3.04) ***
Nat. School Lunch Program	-15.07 (2.08) ***	-14.92 (2.08) ***	-14.41 (2.18) ***	-15.10 (2.27) ***
Parents' level of education				
High school graduate/GED	4.64 (2.24) **	4.77 (2.24) ***	4.72 (2.24) **	4.79 (2.24) **
Some college	9.49 (2.19) ***	9.81 (2.19) ***	9.74 (2.19) ***	9.82 (2.19) ***
College degree	5.46 (2.08) ***	5.78 (2.08) ***	5.73 (2.08) ***	5.81 (2.08) ***
Title I participation	-7.89 (0.98) ***	-7.91 (0.98) ***	-7.89 (0.98) ***	-7.88 (0.98) ***
Type of location				
Urban fringe/large town	-1.06 (0.94)	-1.01 (0.95)	-1.04 (0.95)	-1.04 (0.95)
Rural/small town	-2.15 (1.30) *	-2.25 (1.30) *	-2.25 (1.30) *	-2.23 (1.30) *
Region of country				
Southeast	-7.21 (1.20) ***	-7.85 (1.21) ***	-7.91 (1.22) ***	-7.94 (1.22) ***
Central	-6.46 (1.39) ***	-6.65 (1.39) ***	-6.63 (1.39) ***	-6.63 (1.39) ***
West	-8.01 (1.32) ***	-7.33 (1.35) ***	-7.54 (1.37) ***	-7.52 (1.37) ***
Black * School Lunch Program	2.65 (2.48)	2.83 (2.57)	3.26 (2.88)	2.94 (2.89)
Hispanic * School Lunch Program	2.30 (2.32)	1.60 (2.50)	2.51 (2.70)	2.12 (2.73)
My friends make fun of . . .	-9.35 (0.64) ***	-9.34 (0.64) ***	-9.36 (0.64) ***	-9.09 (0.69) ***

Black * make fun of . . .	1.71 (1.07)	1.69 (1.07)	1.63 (1.08)	2.06 (1.26)
Hispanic * make fun of . . .	−0.03 (1.03)	0.34 (1.04)	0.30 (1.04)	0.90 (1.19)
Lunch * make fun of . . .	0.38 (0.88)	0.39 (0.88)	0.47 (0.89)	0.77 (0.93)
Percent Blacks in school	−0.12 (0.02) ***	−0.05 (0.04)	−0.04 (0.04)	−0.01 (0.05)
Percent Hispanics in school	−0.07 (0.02) ***	−0.16 (0.04) ***	−0.14 (0.05) ***	−0.11 (0.06) *
Black * Percent Black		−0.06 (0.05)	−0.06 (0.05)	−0.06 (0.05)
Black * Percent Hispanic		−0.001 (0.06)	−0.01 (0.06)	−0.01 (0.06)
Hispanic * Percent Black		−0.17 (0.05) ***	−0.17 (0.06) ***	−0.16 (0.06) ***
Hispanic * Percent Hispanic		−0.13 (0.05) ***	−0.13 (0.05) ***	−0.13 (0.05) ***
School lunch * Percent Black			−0.02 (0.05)	−0.01 (0.05)
School lunch * Percent Hispanic			−0.04 (0.05)	−0.03 (0.05)
Make fun of * Percent Black				−0.01 (0.02)
Make fun of * Percent Hispanic				−0.02 (0.02)
R-square	0.3445	0.3483	0.3484	0.3486
Total number	4952	4952	4952	4952

Notes: *$p < 0.10$; **$p < 0.05$; ***$p < 0.01$.

achievement for fourth graders. They are remarkably similar to the school engagement and peer-group oppositional culture patterns reported above, as well as to the findings that Tach and Farkas (2006) and other researchers have reported. Boys scored significantly below girls. Blacks and Hispanics scored significantly lower than Whites. Low-income students (School Lunch Program) scored significantly below higher income students. Students whose parents were high school dropouts scored significantly lower than students whose parents graduated from high school. Students in low-income (Title I) schools scored significantly below students in higher-income schools. There were no urban/rural effects, but there *were* regional effects, with the Northeast scoring highest. As with the determinants of peer-group oppositional culture, the largest of these effects were for Blacks, Hispanics, and low-income students. Each was approximately 0.5 standard deviation.

Model 2 added interactions between race and poverty to the equation. However, neither was significant.

Model 3 added the peer-group oppositional culture variable to the equation. It was strongly and significantly negative. As noted by D&A-D, it explained only about 10 percent of the Black reading deficit and also a similar percent for Hispanics and the other variables. Nevertheless, the magnitude of its effect was not small. Rather, it was similar to that of attending a Title I (low-income) school and was more than twice the size of the significant, negative net effect for males. Further, when oppositional peer culture was added to the equation in Model 3, R-Square increased by a reasonable amount. Overall, this variable clearly had a role to play as a predictor of reading achievement.

Model 4 added interaction terms between peer-group oppositional culture and race to the equation. Coefficients were little changed, but there *was* a (barely) significant, positive interaction between Black and oppositional culture. That is, the negative effect of oppositional culture on reading was slightly smaller for Blacks than for Whites and Hispanics.

Model 5 added an interaction between poverty (free or reduced-price lunch program) and oppositional culture, but it was not significant. Model 6 added the percent of Blacks and Hispanics in the school to the equation. Both were significant and negative, with the Percent Black effect being the larger of the two. This negative effect of Percent Black on student achievement was consistent with previous findings (Roscigno, 1998).

Model 7 added interactions between student race and school racial composition, revealing which groups were most affected by the racial composition of their school. The answer was Hispanics. Compared with both Whites and Blacks, Hispanics in high Black schools showed approximately double the negative effect on reading performance. This was consistent with the similar finding for experiencing an oppositional peer-group culture in Table 15.4. Models 8 and 9 added interactions between racial composition and both poverty (lunch program) and oppositional culture to the equation, but none was significant.

Conclusion

The introduction to this chapter summarized the issues in the published debate regarding the existence of quantitative evidence of oppositional culture between my co-authors and myself (FL&M, 2002) on the one hand, and James Ainsworth-Darnell and Douglas Downey (A-D&D, 1998; D&A-D, 2002) on the other. Following this, the chapter was divided into four parts. In the first part, I replied to D&A-D's arguments, showing that they possessed significantly less merit than the authors supposed. In the second part, I summarized research literature by myself and others, literature that has not previously been considered in this debate. These quantitative, empirical studies all supported the findings of FL&M in favor of the existence of an oppositional culture. They showed that low-income and African American, Hispanic, and American Indian children (and indeed, boys as compared to girls) displayed worse learning-related behavior than did higher-income, and White and Asian children. The third part of this chapter used new data on parental reports of school engagement for first through seventh graders to further examine these issues. Parental reports avoided the possible biases accompanying the use of either student or teacher reports. Once again, our prior findings were supported. As reported by their parents, the following groups had lower school engagement: males, children of less-well-educated parents, African Americans, and Hispanics. The final part of the chapter extended my previous analysis of the NAEP data concerning the determinants of oppositional culture among fourth graders (FL&M, 2002). I found that, net of other variables, a high percentage of African American or Hispanic students in a school increased the oppositional culture experienced by students of all ethnicities. This effect was particularly strong for Hispanic students in highly African American schools. I also found that oppositional culture contributed significantly to the lower reading performance of all children who experienced it, but it only explained a modest proportion of the low-income, Black, and Hispanic reading deficits by comparison with middle-income and White children. (This point was made by D&A-D [2002]. For a similar conclusion, see Ferguson [2001].) Instead, the relatively poor school performance of these students appears to have roots in the weak academic skills with which they emerge from preschool, and the consequent widening gap between these students and middle-class Whites as early elementary school instruction progresses (Alexander, Entwisle, & Horsey, 1997; Ensminger & Slusarcik, 1992; Farkas, 2000; Lee & Burkam, 2002; West et al., 2001).

Thus, the resolution of the debate between FL&M and D&A-D appears to be that John Ogbu was correct. Oppositional culture *is* stronger among ethnic minority and low-income children than among White and middle-class children. However, it only explains a modest proportion of the achievement gap between these groups. Consequently, it may be more a consequence than a cause of poor achievement. More research will be needed to understand how individual and peer-group behavior and cognitive performance evolve and interact as children age through the school grades.

For almost 50 years now, we have struggled with the issues of school segregation and racial and poverty concentrations in our schools. Because of our failure to solve these problems, ethnic minority and low-income children continue to be at a disadvantage where schooling is concerned. The findings in this chapter provide a more detailed view of the nature of this disadvantage. It includes lesser school engagement, increased oppositional culture, and weaker reading performance than that by White and middle-income children. It is present from the earliest years of elementary school. It is more present in schools with higher concentrations of minority and low-income children.

These patterns of disadvantage and inequality show no sign of disappearing. On the basis of these unequal schooling conditions and outcomes, we can already predict unequal occupational and earnings outcomes for children currently enrolled in K-12 education. It is time that these conditions are more aggressively addressed by a society that desires to provide equal opportunity for all.

NOTES

1   This is not the first time that these authors have been too casual with test score controls, appearing to put them in or take them out to produce the results they seek. In the original A-D&D piece, their key analyses in Tables 4 and 5 failed to control the prior test score, even though this was available on the data, logically should have been controlled, and was controlled in my prior work that they cited (Farkas, 1996; Farkas, Grobe, Sheehan, & Shuan, 1990). Further, the body of their Table 5 used the phrase I originally introduced, saying that they were controlling "skills, habits, and styles" even though they left out test scores, the only measure of skills. I had not noticed this error when preparing FL&M, but it alone invalidates A-D&D's findings.

2   Note that Tach and Farkas's (forthcoming) analysis uses the Approaches to Learning measure of student behavior. We find that this teacher judgment of student behavior is unaffected by the teacher's race. Downey and Pribesh (2005) reported the same finding, contrasting it with teacher's judgments of student externalizing behavior, which *are* affected by the teacher's race. But it is the Approaches variables we are concerned with here. Further, Approaches, rather than Externalizing Behavior, is the primary behavioral

determinant of student achievement, controlling prior student achievement in the ECLS-K data.

3   Collection of these data was funded by Westat and the Urban Institute. These data are publicly available online at <http://newfederalism.urban.org/nsaf/index.htm>.

4   For further discussion of the 13 over-sampled states, see report No. 2 of the 1997 Methodology series of the NSAF.

5   For more information concerning the MKAs, see methodology report No. 13 of the NSAF.

6   This final category may reflect either adoptions of foreign-born children or U.S.-born MKAs who have their children while outside the United States.

7   These are schools that, because of their high percentage of children in poverty, receive federal compensatory education funding under Title I of the Elementary and Secondary Education Act. For discussion of Title I targeting of low-income schools, and the failure of this program to achieve its goals, see Farkas and Hall (2000).

8   For related results, using the new Early Childhood Longitudinal Study–Kindergarten data to show the particularly low school engagement and performance with which males enter kindergarten, see Riordan (2002) and Tach and Farkas (forthcoming).

9   In their reply to FL&M, D&A-D chided us for not controlling the minority composition of the schools in the NAEP data. We did not do this at the time because we did not realize that the NAEP had these racial composition measures available. These are the calculations now shown in Table 15.4.

REFERENCES

Ainsworth-Darnell, J. W., & Downey, D. B. (1998). Assessing the oppositional culture explanation for racial/ethnic differences in school performance. *American Sociological Review*, 63, 536–553.

Alexander, K. L., Entwisle, D. R., & Horsey, C. S. (1997). From first grade forward: Early foundations of high school dropout. *Sociology of Education*, 70, 87–107.

Anderson, E. (1999). *Code of the street.* New York: Norton.

Bradley, R., Corwyn, R. F., McAdoo, H. P., & Coll, C. G. (2001a). The home environments of children in the United States. Part I: Variations by age, ethnicity, and poverty status. *Child Development*, 72, 1844–1867.

Bradley, R., Corwyn, R. F., McAdoo, H. P., & Coll, C. G. (2001b). The home environments of children in the United States. Part II: Relations with behavioral development through age thirteen. *Child Development*, 72, 1868–1886.

Carlson, M., & Corcoran, M. (2001). Family structure and children's behavioral and cognitive outcomes. *Journal of Marriage and the Family*, 63, 779–792.

Cook, P. J., & Ludwig, J. (1997). Weighing the "burden of acting White": Are there race differences in attitudes toward education? *Journal of Policy Analysis and Management*, 16, 656–678.

Cook, P. J., & Ludwig, J. (1998). The burden of "acting White": Do Black adolescents disparage academic achievement?" In C. Jencks & M. Phillips (Eds.), *The Black-White test score gap* (pp. 375–400). Washington, DC: Brookings Institution.

Downey, D., & Pribesh, S. (2004). When race matters: Teachers' evaluations of students' classroom behavior. *Sociology of Education* 77: 267–282.

Downey, D., & Ainsworth-Darnell, J. (2002). The search for oppositional culture among black students. *American Sociological Review*, 67(1), 156–164.

Ensminger, M., & Slusarcik, A. (1992). Paths to high school graduation or dropout: A longitudinal study of a first-grade cohort. *Sociology of Education*, 65(April), 95–113.

Farkas, G. (1996). *Human capital or cultural capital? Ethnicity and poverty groups in an urban school district.* Hawthorne, NY: Aldine de Gruyter.

Farkas, G. (2000). Teaching low-income children to read at grade level. *Contemporary Sociology*, 29(1), 53–62.

Farkas, G., Grobe, R. P., Sheehan, D., & Shuan, Y. (1990). Cultural resources and school success: Gender, ethnicity, and poverty groups within an urban school district. *American Sociological Review*, 55, 127–142.

Farkas, G., & Hall, L. S. (2000). Can Title I attain its goal? *Brookings Papers on Education Policy*, 2000, 59–103.

Farkas, G., Lleras, C., & Maczuga, S. (2002). Does oppositional culture exist in minority and poverty peer groups? *American Sociological Review*, 67, 148–155.

Ferguson, R. F. (2001). A diagnostic analysis of Black-White GPA disparities in Shaker Heights, Ohio. *Brookings Papers on Education Policy 2001.* Washington, DC: The Brookings Institution.

Gamoran, A., & Mare, R. D. (1989). Secondary school tracking and educational inequality: compensation, reinforcement, or neutrality? *American Journal of Sociology* 94, 1146–1183.

Hindelang, M., Hirschi, T., & Weis, J. (1981). *Measuring delinquency.* Beverly Hills, CA: Sage.

Johnson, M. K., Crosnoe, R., & Elder, G. H., Jr. (2001). Students' attachment and academic engagement: The role of race and ethnicity. *Sociology of Education*, 74, 318–340.

Lee, V., & Burkam, D. (2002). Inequality at the starting gate: Social background and achievement at kindergarten entry. Paper read at the Annual Meetings of the American Educational Research Association, New Orleans, April 4.

Lucas, S. (1999). *Tracking inequality: Stratification and mobility in American high schools.* New York: Teachers College Press.

Lucas, S., & Gamoran, A. (1991). Race and track assignment: A reconsideration with course-based indicators of track location. Paper presented at the Annual Meetings of the American Sociological Association, Cincinnati, OH.

Lucas, S., & Gamoran, A. (2002). Tracking and the achievement gap. In J. Chubb & T. Loveless (Eds.), *Bridging the achievement gap* (pp. 171–198). Washington, DC: Brookings Institution.

McLeod, J., & Nonnemaker, J. (2000). Poverty and child emotional and behavioral problems: Racial/ethnic differences in processes and effects. *Journal of Health and Social Behavior*, 41, 136–161.

McLoyd, V. (1998). Socioeconomic disadvantage and child development. *American Psychologist*, 53, 185–204.

McLoyd, V., & Smith, J. (2002). Physical discipline and behavior problems in

African American, European American, and Hispanic children: Emotional support as a moderator. *Journal of Marriage and Family*, *64*, 40–53.

Menaghan, E. G., Kowaleski-Jones, L., & Mott, F. L. (1997). The intergenerational costs of parental social stressors: Academic and social difficulties in early adolescence for children of young mothers. *Journal of Health and Social Behavior* 38: 72–86.

Mickelson, R. (1990). The attitude-achievement paradox among Black adolescents. *Sociology of Education*, *63*, 44–61.

National Center for Education Statistics. (2001). National reading summary tables. Retrieved July 25, 2001 at <www.nces.ed.gov/nationsreportcard/tables/REA2000>.

Ogbu, J. U. (1974). *The next generation: An ethnography of education in an urban neighborhood*. New York: Academic Press.

Oyserman, D., Bybee, D., Mowbray, C. T., & MacFarlane, P. (2002). Positive parenting among African American mothers with a serious mental illness. *Journal of Marriage and the Family*, *64*, 65–77.

Riordan, C. (2002). *Male/female early achievement and development: Gender gaps among first time kindergarten children in the public schools*. Paper read at the Annual Meetings of the American Educational Research Association, April 4.

Roscigno, V. (1998). Race and the reproduction of educational disadvantage. *Social Forces*, *76*, 1033–1060.

Rosenberg, M., & Simmons, R. (1972). *Black and White self-esteem: The urban school child*. Arnold and Caroline Rose Monograph Series, Washington, DC: American Sociological Association.

Smerdon, B. A. (1999). Engagement and achievement: Differences between African American and White high school students. *Research in Sociology of Education and Socialization*, *12*, 103–134.

Tach, L., & Farkas, G. (forthcoming). Learning-related behaviors, cognitive skills, and ability grouping when schooling begins. *Social Science Research*.

West, J., Denton, K., & Reaney, L. (2001). *The kindergarten year: Findings from the Early Childhood Longitudinal Study, kindergarten class of 1998–99*. National Center for Education Statistics, U.S. Department of Education. Retrieved July 2001 from <http://nces.ed.gov/pubsearch/pubsinfo.asp?pubid=>.

Chapter 16

The Structure of Opportunity and Adolescents' Academic Achievement Attitudes and Behaviors

Roslyn Arlin Mickelson

African American students still do not perform as well in school as they are able despite over 50 years of efforts to address their academic weaknesses. They are not alone; Latinos and American Indian students underperform as well.[1] Consequently, there is a race gap in grades, test scores, and graduation rates. Through the many efforts of students, parents, educators, and policy makers, the gap narrowed during the 1980s; nevertheless, it persists to this day (Campbell, Hombo, & Mazzeo, 2000; *Education Week*, 2000). The race gap's persistence has stimulated much commentary in the popular media and scholarly research. One promising avenue of inquiry focuses on the intersection between the structures of opportunity in the larger society and educational outcomes. For some time now, social scientists have shown that the opportunity structure is reflected in adolescents' peer culture, attitudes, dispositions, and school behaviors. The results of this line of research suggest that the economic, social, political, and personal opportunities (or lack thereof) that African American adolescents expect to find once they leave school influence their peer culture, their engagement in schooling and, ultimately, their performance. A significant element of John U. Ogbu's cultural-ecological model (CEM) follows this line of theorizing.

In this chapter, I present findings that extend and refine two related lines of inquiry about African American students' underperformance and the opportunity structure. The first line of inquiry is among the most provocative, controversial, and widely debated accounts for the gap—Ogbu's cultural-ecological model of minority achievement. His CEM takes into account historical, economic, social, cultural, and linguistic conditions of minorities in plural societies (Ogbu, 2003). Ogbu theorized that two sets of factors affect minority youth's school engagement and achievement. The first he called "the system," which he identified as the historical and contemporary treatment of minorities by social institutions, especially the schools. The second he termed "community forces," which refers to the ways minority youth perceive, interpret, and respond to education as a result of their history in American society. From these twin forces, every ethnic group develops a cultural frame of reference that shapes its behavior. The cultural frame of reference of many African American, Latino, and American Indian youth manifests as an oppositional cultural framework (OCF), wherein the school's standard curriculum and language are regarded as an imposition of the dominant culture on minority people. In response to the OCF norms, peer pressure leads many minority youth, in varying degrees, to eschew academic engagement. From the perspective of OCF, for African American students to accept White standards of behavior, speech, and academic performance is to accept White judgments that African American language and cultural identity are flawed and inferior to dominant White norms (Ogbu, 2003, p. 189).

The second, and related avenue of investigation updates and extends my previous work wherein I sought to account for adolescents' school performance by examining their attitudes toward education and the future (Mickelson, 1990). I demonstrated that adolescents have idealized attitudes about education and opportunity—what I label abstract attitudes —as well as concrete attitudes—the label I attached to their realistic assessments of future opportunities. Adolescents' concrete attitudes predict their achievement (Mickelson, 1989, 1990, 2001). In this chapter, I replicate my earlier findings with new data that I collected in 1997. I also present new findings that directly test Ogbu's model of OCF with that survey data. These results expand my previous theoretical contribution to the field, the role of abstract and concrete attitudes in explaining school performance.

The chapter has three major sections. The first part summarizes Ogbu's scholarship about OCF, the opportunity structure, and African American student achievement. It then summarizes my earlier work and locates it in relation to Ogbu's earlier studies. The second part of the chapter presents findings from my empirical investigation of adolescents' abstract, concrete, and oppositional attitudes toward achievement, and the extent to which these attitudes predict achievement. Third, I discuss the meaning and significance of the findings for understanding the persistent underperformance of minority youth in the United States and the contributions of Ogbu's cultural-ecological model of minority achievement.

APPROACHES TO MINORITY ACADEMIC UNDERPERFORMANCE

Ogbu: The Job Ceiling

Ogbu's cultural-ecological theory of academic performance, out of which he developed his model of oppositional cultural frameworks (OCF), was the second phase of his theorizing about minority educational performance. In the first phase, he investigated the effects of involuntary minority parents' truncated employment opportunities, which he called the "job ceiling," on minority youth's academic performance.

The job ceiling is based on Ogbu's ethnographic fieldwork in Stockton, California (1974) and a comparative study of minority status and schooling in six nations: Britain, India, Israel, New Zealand, Japan, and the United States (1978). He proposed that in plural societies where caste-like minorities face a rigid stratification system, unequal educational opportunities, and a job ceiling beyond which employment is unlikely irrespective of educational credentials, children perform less well in school than members of the same ethnic group in societal settings that lack these employment barriers. He concluded that minority students' lower academic performance is an adaptation to these anticipated barriers in the structure of opportunities they will face as adults.

Fordham and Ogbu: The Burden of Acting White

In 1986, Signithia Fordham and John Ogbu published an influential article in *The Urban Review* that has taken on an intellectual and political life of its own. They argued that African Americans who study, participate in class, do homework, and speak Standard English face ostracism by their peers, who accuse them of "acting White." This is because, among their networks of fictive kin, these behaviors leading to academic success are associated with White cultural norms. Thus, one factor accounting for African American students' weaker school performance is that, as members of a fictive kinship group that eschews using Standard English, studying, getting good grades, and so on, African American adolescents avoid these behaviors in order to express ethnic group solidarity; in doing so, they also avoid academic success.

In her subsequent work, Fordham (1988, 1996) further explored the ways that academically able African Americans cope with the tensions among identity, negative peer pressure, and academic achievement. She noted the ambivalence that these high achievers feel in an academic environment where school success can threaten membership in the fictive kin network. She argued, for example, that one way those who do well academically cope with the threat of being labeled as "acting White" is to sacrifice their racial identity and become race-less. Fordham's ethnographic work is frequently ignored and, like Ogbu, the corpus of her scholarship often is reduced to their 1986 *Urban Review* article.

"Acting White" has filtered into popular and political discourses about African American education. The phrase has become emblematic of an entire sub-field of research on African American students' achievement. Unfortunately, the expression is used inappropriately as a catchphrase for all of Ogbu's and Fordham's post-1986 works. Critics often fail to make important distinctions between Ogbu's early work, Fordham and Ogbu's 1986 "acting White" argument, and the scholarship completed by both Ogbu and Fordham over the subsequent 15 years.

Ogbu: The Cultural-Ecological Model of Educational Performance

Beginning in the 1990s, Ogbu introduced his cultural-ecological model (CEM) to account for the differences in academic performance among minority groups (Ogbu, 1991; Ogbu & Simons, 1998). CEM extended his earlier work on the effects of truncated opportunities and historical racism on minority achievement. Ogbu argued that such structural barriers (what he called "the system") as segregation, under-funded schools, tracking, and overt racism in schoolyards and classrooms contribute to the race gap. But such barriers are not the sole determinant. He maintained that "community forces" also contribute to the sociocultural adaptations that underlie variable school performances. For example, in his investigation of middle-class African Americans in Shaker Heights, Ogbu (2003) found that many middle-class, African American students were influenced by an oppositional cultural framework, and consequently were disengaged from schooling, despite their parents' high levels of education, professional occupations, and high expectations for their children.

Mickelson: Abstract and Concrete Educational Attitudes

As an urban high school social studies teacher in the 1970s, I had observed that African American students' actual school behavior was often at odds with their expressed positive attitudes toward education. My efforts to understand this paradox of positive educational attitudes mixed with poor academic performance led to the notion of dual educational attitudes (Mickelson, 1989, 1990). I conceptualize people's beliefs about education as multidimensional. The first dimension, abstract attitudes, is based on the dominant American ideology, which holds that education is the solution to most individual and social problems; it unlocks the door to social mobility and is the remedy for poverty and unemployment. Furthermore, according to this view, one's educational credentials are evaluated by the larger society according to merit. Abstract attitudes are ideologically based and essentially reflect the widespread belief that opportunity through education exists for everyone. Abstract attitudes toward education do not vary widely by race, class, or gender.

Race, ethnicity, and class forces that shape individual and group experiences in the opportunity structure influence the second belief system:

concrete attitudes. In 1983 I developed concrete attitudes toward education to test Ogbu's (1978) concept of the job ceiling, wherein people who face barriers to job success, irrespective of their educational credentials, have children who question the value of education for their own status attainment. Concrete attitudes differ from abstract ones in that they reflect neither adherence to ideological shibboleths nor hopes for the future. Instead, they reflect essential, material realities, in which education may or may not lead to status maintenance or upward mobility. Concrete attitudes are derived from a person's family and community experiences in the opportunity structure.

Concrete attitudes can be similar to or quite different from a person's abstract attitudes in the degree to which he or she embraces education. If someone comes from a privileged background where parents' educational credentials have been rewarded by the opportunity structure, his or her concrete and abstract attitudes will display similar confidence in the education-opportunity connection. But if someone's family members have experiences where employment, wages, or promotions are not commensurate with their educational credentials—that is, they face a job ceiling—a person's concrete attitudes will reflect a certain cynicism about schooling and opportunity, while his or her abstract attitudes will remain quite positive. Concrete attitudes are crucial for understanding how the opportunity structure, family background, and racial stratification in the larger society interact to influence school outcomes.

In summary, while the "acting White" hypothesis is related to, and not reducible to the OCF model, the two arguments are often fused in public and scholarly discourse on minority achievement. Because concrete attitudes indicate that *some* students' perceptions of truncated opportunities due to racism depress their achievement—an argument related to Ogbu's OCF—some researchers have included my notion of dual educational attitudes in their critique of the OCF (cf., Ainsworth-Darnell & Downey, 1998). Thus, there is a need to clarify the ways that perceptions of the opportunity structure—past, present, and future—affect minority student achievement. To that end, in this chapter, I report the results of my new investigation of the influence of students' abstract, concrete, and oppositional attitudes on student achievement. The inclusion of oppositional attitudes in my analysis of the attitude-achievement connection tests Ogbu's OCF empirically and clarifies how OCF relates to my earlier work on abstract and concrete attitudes.

Background and Context of the Study

I investigate the issues raised in this chapter with data I have collected over the last 15 years in Charlotte, North Carolina. Charlotte is an excellent site for this research because the community's recent history abounds with conflicts over race and education. The community is a rapidly grow-ing sunbelt city known for its landmark *Swann v. Charlotte-Mecklenburg Schools* (1971) decision, in which the Supreme Court first upheld the constitutionality of within-district mandatory busing as a remedy for segregated schooling. Elsewhere (Mickelson 2001), I demonstrated that the Charlotte-Mecklenburg School (CMS) district's reputation as a suc-cessfully desegregated public system, perhaps, overstated the district's accomplishments. Although the system almost achieved racial balance among its schools during the 1980s, systematic, racially correlated, within-school segregation by tracking and ability grouping meant that African Americans and Whites often learned in very separate environ-ments, even in supposedly desegregated schools. Beginning in the early 1990s, the CMS district slowly began to re-segregate at the school level as well.

At the time the survey data were collected in 1997, the CMS district, with about 100,000 students in roughly 130 schools, was the 25th largest in the nation. The student population was 42 percent African American, 50.3 percent White, and 7.7 percent Hispanic, Asian, and American Indian (CMS, Monthly Reports 1996–1997). In the late 1960s, the time of the original *Swann* order, only a handful of CMS students were neither White nor African American. This particular demographic mix is import-ant because it meant that the CMS district, unlike many larger urban school systems elsewhere across the country, could actually create racially balanced schools.

From roughly 1974 to 1992, the CMS district employed a mandatory busing plan to achieve racial balance among schools. In 1992, it switched from mandatory busing as its primary tool for achieving racial balance to a system of voluntary desegregation through magnet schools. After a bitter, decade-long, community-wide debate over mandatory busing, the school system was sued by Whites seeking to lift the 1971 court order, as well as by African Americans who sought to have it enforced. In 1999, a federal judge ruled in favor of the White plaintiffs and declared CMS unitary. As expected, the African American plaintiffs appealed the deci-sion. After the U.S. Supreme Court declined to hear the African American plaintiffs' appeal of that decision, in the fall of 2002, CMS returned to a neighborhood school-based assignment plan that is re-segregating the district (Mickelson, 2005).

The history of race and education in Charlotte is part of every CMS student's lived reality. As a result of the mandatory busing, most CMS students who participated in this research attended a desegregated school during some portion of their academic careers in Charlotte; in fact, most students spent a majority of their education in racially balanced schools. Nevertheless, about 40 percent of African American and approximately 15 percent of White students spent portions of their elementary educations in racially isolated African American schools (schools whose Black population was more than 15 percent higher than the school system's average). Moreover, most secondary students learned in racially stratified academic classes where the highest-level classes were disproportionately White and the lowest were disproportionately Black. The clear re-segregation of secondary schools by track, and the persistent struggles over desegregation in the CMS district, shaped students' development of trust in their schools and educators and their racial identities.[2] The research reported in this chapter investigates the extent to which these dynamics were captured in students' various educational attitudes, and in turn, it addresses whether the attitudes shaped their achievement.

RESEARCH QUESTIONS AND HYPOTHESES

In the research reported here, I revisited the attitude-achievement connection that I demonstrated in 1990. I add oppositional attitudes to the attitude-achievement model I previously investigated. I conceptualize oppositional attitudes as beliefs that reflect peer group pressure to avoid behaviors leading to academic success—essentially what Ogbu argued is a reflection of an OCF. The survey data I collected in 1997 enabled me to examine (a) if oppositional attitudes are consistent with my prior work that examined the attitude-behavior linkages reflected in students' concrete and abstract attitudes, (b) if an OCF exists, how the oppositional cultural values and attitudes are distributed among those who hold them, (c) if an OCF exists, whether it affects achievement as hypothesized, and (d) what abstract, concrete, and oppositional attitudes tell us about the ways that the structure of opportunity and adolescents' social identities influence their academic achievement. I investigate the following hypotheses:

H_1:   Students possess abstract, concrete, and oppositional attitudes.
H_2:   Oppositional attitudes vary by gender, race, social class, prior achievement, and track.
$H_{2.1}$: Males have stronger oppositional attitudes than females.
$H_{2.2}$: African Americans have stronger oppositional attitudes than Whites.
$H_{2.3}$: Lower-class students have stronger oppositional attitudes than middle-class students.
$H_{2.4}$: Those with lower prior achievement have stronger oppositional attitudes than those with higher achievement.
$H_{2.5}$: Lower-track students have stronger oppositional attitudes than higher-track students.
H_3:   Oppositional, concrete, and abstract attitudes will contribute to the

prediction of student achievement consistent with theory derived from Ogbu's model of OCF and Mickelson's attitude-behavior model.

$H_{3.1}$: Net of individual, family, and school factors, oppositional attitudes have a negative effect on achievement.

$H_{3.2}$: Net of individual, family, and school factors, concrete attitudes have a positive effect on achievement.

$H_{3.3}$: Net of individual, family, and school factors, abstract attitudes have no effect on achievement.

METHODS AND DATA

Data

To test the hypotheses, I drew from my 15-year-long, multi-method study of school reform in Charlotte, NC. I used primarily survey data to test the hypotheses. I then used qualitative data from in-depth structured interviews with adolescents, their parents, and educators to illustrate a few key findings from the survey data.

I collected survey data from CMS eighth and twelfth graders in 1997. The survey ascertained students' attitudes toward education and the future, their educational and occupational aspirations, family involvement, their activities outside the school and the home, their demographic characteristics (age, race, gender), their family's cultural capital, and their self-reported effort. Multiple measures of achievement and the history of prior schools attended by each student were matched by ID numbers to students' survey responses.

Sample

The large representative samples were composed of students enrolled in eighth- and twelfth-grade classrooms randomly selected from master lists of English classes offered each period of the school day in every middle and high school in the school district. At each school at least one class from each of the various English track levels was included in the 50 percent random sample of classes. All students in each selected class were surveyed. To encourage high levels of participation among students in the selected classes, the respondents' names were entered into a lottery for cash prizes. On average, 95 percent of students enrolled in the selected English classes participated in the survey.

Data were obtained for 1,833 high school students: 611 (33.3 percent) were African American, 1,119 (61.1 percent) were White, and 103 (5.6 percent) were Asian, Hispanic, or Native American. Middle-school data were obtained for 2,311 students, 1,010 of whom were African American (43.7 percent), 1,121 of whom were White (48.5 percent), and 180 of whom were Asian, Hispanic, or Native American (7.8 percent). Because there were relatively few Hispanic, Asian, and Native American respondents, I analyzed the data from only African American and White students. The sample of respondents also excluded CMS students who were enrolled in exceptional children's classes, special programs, or special schools. Because of the disproportionate number of African American school drop-outs and students in special education classes, the proportion of African American students in the high school sample (33.3 percent) was lower than the district's overall percent of African American students in 1997 (42 percent). The middle-school sample was somewhat higher than the district's overall average, reflecting the changing demographics of CMSs over time (for example, in 2005 slightly more than 50 percent of CMS students were African Americans).

Variables

Weighted Grade Point Average

Grade 12 students' weighted cumulative grade point averages (GPAs) were used to indicate high school achievement. Weighted GPAs take into account the fact that students in academically gifted (AG) or advanced placement (AP) courses who earn a grade of A receive either five or six grade points; in contrast, grades of A in other courses yield four grade points. In the absence of a cumulative grade point average, grade eight students' fourth-quarter, weighted GPAs indicated their achievement.

Track Placement

High school track placement was coded (1) regular, (2) advanced, (3) academically gifted (AG), and (4) advanced placement (AP) or International Baccalaureate (IB). Middle-school track placement was (1) regular, (2) academically gifted, and (3) Preinternational Baccalaureate (PreIB).

Race

The analyses were confined to African Americans (1) and Whites (0). Whites were the excluded category in the regression analysis.

Gender

Each student's gender was either female (1) or male (0). Males were the excluded category in the regression analyses.

Cultural Capital

Students' cultural capital measured their family background in these analyses. Exposure to high-status culture enhances student achievement because the formal curriculum reflects elite cultural forms, tastes, and distinctions. Although cultural capital is a complex and nuanced social construct that includes much more than private art, music, and dance lessons, I used this measure to reflect families' conscious attempts to expose their children to high culture, an important aspect of cultural capital and the formal curriculum (Bourdieu, 1977; Bourdieu & Passeron, 1977; DiMaggio, 1982; Dumais, 2002; Farkas, 1996; Lamont & Lareau, 1988). The surveys asked whether students had received private art, music, or dance lessons during the previous three years. This construct captures students' access to high-status cultural resources that are distinct from socioeconomic status (yes = 1; no = 0).

Effort

This variable reflects students' self-reports regarding the amount of effort they usually put into their schoolwork. Choices range from (1) "just enough to get by" to (5) "as much effort as possible all the time."

College-Bound Peer Group

For the high school sample only, the measure of peer-group academic orientation is the proportion of each respondent's close friends who were planning to attend a four-year college after high school. Students were asked how many of their close friends were planning after high school to attend a four-year college, attend a two-year college, work full-time, join the military, or be a homemaker. The percent of the respondents' total number of friends planning to attend a four-year college became the indicator of peer-group academic orientation.

Prior Achievement

Twelfth-grade students' sixth-grade CAT Total Language Battery scores were used in the regression analyses as a measure of their prior achievement. To control for an elementary school's effects on CAT scores, students' scores were centered on each student's elementary school's mean on the CAT Total Language Battery. The actual variable used in the analyses, then, was the respondent's score transformed into a deviation from his or her elementary school's mean CAT score. I used the deviated score in order to separate first-order (student-level) from second-order (in this case, elementary school-level) effects on achievement (see Kreft and de Leeuw, 1998 for a discussion of deviation from the mean techniques). Similarly, I used eighth-grade students' second-grade deviated score on the CAT Total Language Battery as a measure of their prior achievement.

Abstract Attitudes

Abstract attitudes are based on the core beliefs of the American Dream: that opportunity through education exists for everyone, that education is the solution to most individual and social problems, and that one's educational credentials are evaluated by the larger society according to merit. The higher the score, the more positive are the student's abstract attitudes toward education and the future.[3] I factor-analyzed the 29 belief statements on which students were surveyed to create the scales. Appendix I presents the belief statements used in the oppositional, concrete, and abstract attitude scales. (For a fuller explication of methodology used to generate the scales, see Mickelson, 2001.)

Concrete Attitudes

Concrete attitudes are grounded in peoples' material realities, particularly the ways that the forces of race, ethnicity, and class shape their experiences in the opportunity structure. Concrete attitudes are influenced by family and community experiences with education and opportunity. As such, they are useful for understanding adolescents' perceptions of their own location in the opportunity structure, and they suggest how these perceptions influence respondents' educational outcomes. The higher the score, the more positive are students' concrete attitudes toward education and the future.

Oppositional Attitudes

I operationalized the OCF construct with an attitude scale that measures the degree to which students and their peers believe that learning the official curriculum, doing homework and getting good grades compromise their social identities. The belief statements that formed this attitude scale were developed specifically to tap Ogbu's OCF construct rooted in his cultural-ecological model of schooling. The oppositional attitude scale differs from concrete attitudes in that it deals specifically with the perceived connection between social identity and school achievement, whereas concrete attitudes address the perceived relationship between barriers in the opportunity structure and school achievement. The higher the respondents' oppositional attitude scores, the stronger their belief that educational achievement compromises their social identity.

If one examines the wording of the belief statements that contribute to the attitude scales, the face validity differences among the three scales become clear. These differences can be summarized as follows: abstract attitudes tap generic beliefs about the relationship between education and opportunity in American society; concrete attitudes reflect beliefs about the student's family and community's lived experiences with the job ceiling and the school-to-work connection; and oppositional attitudes suggest a student's beliefs about whether he or she is subject to peer pressure not to publicly exhibit effort in school, and whether his or her social identity and/or ethnic authenticity are compromised by engaging in certain activities that are associated with academic achievement. Agreement with these propositions is consistent with Ogbu's OCF model.

Proportion of Elementary Education in a Segregated, African American School

This variable measures students' exposure to school-level segregation during the elementary-school years. Using information on students' educational histories in CMS, each school a student attended was coded for its racial composition in the year when the student attended it. I developed an indicator of exposure to school-level segregation by counting the total years (K-6) a student spent in a racially isolated African American elementary school in the CMS district, and then calculating that sum as a proportion of the total years that the student spent in CMS-district elementary schools. In creating this construct, I followed the convention used by the school district: a school was considered to be racially isolated African American if its minority enrollment exceeded by more than 15 percent the system-wide African American elementary-school enrollment in a given year. The variable ranges from 0 to 100 percent of elementary school experience.

Analyses

The analyses of the data proceeded in several steps. I began with the high school data and then repeated the analyses with the middle school sample. I conducted a series of analyses of variance to examine the relationship between certain characteristics of students and their oppositional attitudes. Specifically, I explored the distributions of oppositional attitudes by gender, race, social class, track, and prior achievement.

Once the ANOVAs demonstrated that oppositional attitudes varied in ways that the hypotheses suggested (with important exceptions I will discuss), I explored whether they contributed to differences in student achievement. Because students are nested within schools, the relationship between students' outcomes and the characteristics of the schools they attended needs to be taken into account in any multivariate analysis. I

used multilevel modeling to estimate individual outcomes as a function
of school-level factors and characteristics of students within the schools
(Kreft & de Leeuw, 1998). I used students' abstract, concrete, and
oppositional attitudes; self-reported effort, track level, cultural capital,
exposure to segregated elementary education, gender, and race as individual-level (first-order) predictors of achievement. I performed multilevel
regression analyses with random intercepts using STATA (Rabe-Hesketh
& Everitt, 1999).

FINDINGS

I begin the presentation of the findings with a discussion of the relationship between achievement and the three attitude scales. I examined in
greater detail the relationships of race, gender, social class, prior achievement, and track placement to oppositional attitudes. Table 16.1 presents
the results of the analyses of variance of oppositional attitudes by race,
class, gender, track, and prior achievement for high school students. The
stronger a student's oppositional attitudes, the more the student believed
that doing well in school and studying compromise the authenticity of his
or her cultural identity. Oppositional attitudes significantly differed by
class, gender, track, and prior achievement. Importantly, contrary to my
hypothesis, there were no significant race differences in oppositional attitudes among twelfth graders. Students whose parents had a BA or more
had significantly lower oppositional attitudes compared to those with less
than a college degree; males had higher oppositional attitudes than
females; the higher the tracks, the lower the attitudes; and students who
as sixth graders had lower prior achievement on the CAT had stronger
oppositional attitudes as seniors.

Table 16.2 presents the relationships of oppositional attitudes to class
and race, to class and gender, and to track and race. My examination of
attitudes by race within levels of parental education revealed that for both
African Americans and Whites, oppositional attitudes were strongest
among those whose parents had the least education. However, among the
working class, Whites tended to have stronger oppositional attitudes than
African Americans, and among the middle class, African Americans had
stronger oppositional attitudes than Whites. The analysis of attitudes by
gender within the levels of parental education revealed a consistent pattern across both race groups. At all levels, males had stronger oppositional attitudes than females. In fact, the gender differences are so stark
that the weakest oppositional attitudes of men—those held by men with
the most-educated parents—were higher than the strongest oppositional
attitudes held by women. Attitudes within the track levels also differed by
race. Although both African Americans and Whites in lower tracks had

Table 16.1 Mean oppositional attitudes by race, gender, class, track, and prior achievement, CMS high school seniors, 1996–1997

Attitude	Mean	F
Race		
Blacks	1.959	
Whites	1.927	$F_{1,1744} = 1.226^{n.s.}$
Class (parent's education)		
<High school	1.991	
High school	2.037	
< BA	1.970	
BA	1.904	
>BA	1.885	$F_{4,1726} = 3.428^{**}$
Gender		
Male	2.065	
Female	1.823	$F_{1,1744} = 77.354^{***}$
Track		
Regular	2.044	
Advanced	1.897	
Academically gifted	1.805	
AP/IB	1.772	$F_{3,1726} = 28.544^{***}$
Prior achievement (by deciles)		
First	2.062	
Second	1.969	
Third	2.019	
Fourth	2.035	
Fifth	1.991	
Sixth	2.004	
Seventh	1.925	
Eighth	1.882	
Ninth	1.860	
Tenth	1.742	$F_{9,1359} = 3.931^{*}$

Notes: $^{*}p < .05$; $^{**}p < .01$; $^{***}p < .001$.

stronger oppositional attitudes, Whites in Regular and Advanced levels held stronger oppositional attitudes than African Americans in these tracks. Contrary to predictions based on Ogbu's theory and previous empirical work, there were no differences in attitudes by race in Academically Gifted and Advanced Placement levels.

Next, I examined the relationship among oppositional attitudes, prior achievement, and social class by comparing the mean attitudes by class within each decile. An examination of Table 16.3 reveals two distinct patterns. First, regardless of parental education, oppositional attitudes were strongest among those with the poorest sixth-grade CAT scores and weakest among those with the best scores. This pattern is consistent with

Table 16.2 Mean oppositional attitudes by class by race, class by gender, and race by track, CMS high school seniors, 1996–1997

Attitude	Means	F
Class by race	Blacks	Whites
<High school	2.148	1.812
High school	2.005	2.071
< BA	1.920	2.000
BA	1.930	1.893
>BA	1.885	1.843
		$F_{4,1726} = 2.802**$
Class by gender	Females	Males
<High school	1.833	2.166
High school	1.956	2.149
< BA	1.896	2.050
BA	1.742	2.093
>BA	1.760	1.994
		$F_{9,1705} = 11.432***$
Track by race	Blacks	Whites
Regular	2.044	2.154
Advanced	1.897	1.913
Academically gifted	1.805	1.801
AP/IB	1.772	1.770
		$F_{3,1726} = 28.544***$

Notes: $** p < .01; *** p < .001$.

Table 16.3 Mean oppositional attitudes by prior achievement by class, CMS high school seniors, 1996–1997

Prior achievement (in deciles)	<HS	HS	<BA	BA	>BA
First	1.500	2.178	2.014	1.932	2.300
Second	1.611	2.034	1.907	2.015	2.062
Third	1.555	2.137	2.072	2.000	1.833
Fourth	1.833	1.956	2.103	2.032	2.022
Fifth	1.833	2.110	1.919	1.977	2.065
Sixth	2.833	1.931	2.102	1.954	1.942
Seventh		2.121	1.971	1.925	1.764
Eighth		2.152	1.884	1.847	1.871
Ninth		1.727	1.816	1.852	1.933
Tenth		1.829	1.818	1.636	1.793

Notes: $F_{9,1359} = 3.904***; *** p < .001$.

the construct's underlying logic. The exception is students whose parents had less than a high school education. For them, the pattern was reversed: the strongest oppositional attitudes appeared among those who scored highest on the CAT. The second pattern is extremely intriguing. Among students whose CAT scores were between the first and fifth deciles, oppositional attitudes grew from weak to strong as parental education increased (almost as if consciousness or awareness was heightened among those with less ability). As parental education and student prior achievement increased, oppositional attitudes declined. More privileged students did not appear to consider school achievement as a threat to their identity. However, among students whose CAT scores were between the sixth and tenth deciles, oppositional attitudes decreased as parental education increased. The exception to this was the ninth decile, where the pattern followed the first trend. Overall, among weaker students, attitudes became more oppositional as their backgrounds became more privileged. Among stronger students, attitudes tended to become less oppositional as their backgrounds became more privileged.

I repeated the analyses of variance with the middle school data (see Table 16.4). Middle school students' oppositional attitudes followed the same patterns as those of high school students, with one striking and important difference. As expected, among middle school students there were statistically significant race differences in oppositional attitudes: African Americans had stronger oppositional attitudes than Whites. Overall, middle school students' oppositional attitudes were stronger than those of high school students, but the patterns were the same. Males in lower tracks and those from less-educated families had stronger oppositional attitudes. These findings suggest that among middle school students, oppositional attitudes adhered more closely to what one might predict from Ogbu's OCF.

Table 16.4 Mean oppositional attitudes by race, gender, class, and track for CMS eighth graders, 1996–1997

Attitude	Mean	F
Race		
Blacks	2.22	
Whites	2.15	$F_{1,12728} = 8.73^{**}$
Class		
<High school	2.27	
High school	2.23	
< BA	2.25	
BA	2.08	
>BA	2.12	$F_{4,2724} = 3.96^{**}$
Gender		
Male	2.29	
Female	2.07	$F_{1,2728} = 85.50^{***}$
Track		
Regular	2.25	
Advanced	2.05	
Academically gifted	1.93	$F_{2,2727} = 36.10^{***}$

Notes: $^{**}p < .01$; $^{***}p < .001$.

The results of the multilevel regression analysis appear as unstandard-ized regression coefficients in Table 16.5. The findings for both high school and middle school students support the first hypothesized rela-tionships between achievement and the three attitudes. Oppositional atti-tudes had a significant, negative effect on students' grades. Their concrete attitudes had a positive effect, while their abstract attitudes had no effect on grades.

Oppositional attitudes had a significant, direct, negative effect on achievement for twelfth and eighth graders. As predicted by the OCF, the stronger students' oppositional attitudes are, the lower are their GPAs. Students who believed that doing well in school violates peer norms and that public displays of achievement compromise their cultural identity did more poorly in school. These results are true even when controlling for other individual-, family-, and school-level factors associated with educational outcomes.

The regression analysis also examined the effects of the ascriptive char-acteristics of gender, race, and family background on students' grades. Gender had no significant effect on GPA among high-school students, but being female was associated with higher grades among eighth graders. Being African American had a negative effect on achievement for grade-8 students as well as for grade-12 students, and possession of cultural

Table 16.5 Coefficients of a multilevel regression model of achievement (GPA), CMS 12th and 8th grade students, 1996–1997

Variables	Weighted 4th Quarter GPA (Grade 8)		Weighted Cumulative GPA (Grade 12)	
	β	S.E.	β	S.E
Race (African American)	−.320***	.040	−.346***	.037
Cultural capital (yes)	.117***	.035	.091**	.033
Gender (female)	.166***	.034	.016	.032
Abstract attitudes	.020	.017	.050	.037
Concrete attitudes	.120***	.016	.060*	.029
Oppositional attitudes	−.077***	.017	−.060*	.028
Effort	.301***	.019	.211***	.017
Prior achievement	.005***	.000	.010***	.000
Segregated elementary education	−.174**	.069	−.002***	.000
College track	.278	.042	.301***	.018
College-bound peers	—	—	1.436***	.180
ρ (Rho)	.065		.045	
Constant	1.472		.978	.
N of observations	1727		1253	
N of groups	11		24	

Notes: *$p < .05$; **$p < .01$; ***$p < .001$; — variable not in model.

capital had a positive effect for all respondents. Four other individual characteristics affected achievement. Both middle school and high school students who attended racially isolated African American elementary schools did more poorly than those who attended desegregated ones. For all respondents, the higher their track placement, and the more effort they reported making, the higher were their grades. Among twelfth graders, the greater the proportion of peers going to college, the higher their achievement.

DISCUSSION AND CONCLUSION

This chapter began with reference to the persistent gap between African American students' potential and their actual achievement. To investigate this dilemma, I turned to John U. Ogbu's cultural-ecological model of achievement—specifically, his model of oppositional cultural frameworks and my own prior work that examined the ways that students' perceptions of the structure of opportunity that awaits them are reflected in their attitudes, and how their complex sets of attitudes, in turn, predict their school outcomes. I used data from 1997 surveys of Charlotte-Mecklenburg Schools' grade 8 and grade 12 students to test various hypotheses about the roles of oppositional, concrete, and abstract attitudes on students' academic behaviors.

Findings from the factor analyses I conducted with 29 belief statements offer support for the first hypothesis that students simultaneously hold abstract, concrete, and oppositional attitudes. My separate factor analyses of middle and high school data sets yielded virtually identical results, thereby demonstrating the reliability of the attitude constructs. The second hypothesis, which proposed that oppositional attitudes vary by race, gender, social class, prior achievement, and track level, was supported, with one exception.

While oppositional attitudes differ by race among middle school students in the predicted direction, the absence of a race difference among high school students is striking. At first glance, the absence of race differences in oppositional attitudes among high school seniors appears to undermine Ogbu's argument that an oppositional cultural identity, in part, accounts for the race gap in achievement. The ANOVAs show that White and African American high school seniors have statistically indistinguishable levels of oppositional attitudes net of their gender, track, class, and ability. However, the finding that among middle-school students, African Americans have significantly stronger oppositional attitudes than Whites suggests that there are indeed race differences in cultural frameworks, and that either these differences disappear by the twelfth grade or the students who held them disappear from school.

Given the high Black student drop-out rate between the eighth and twelfth grades (in some cases, less than 50 percent of ninth graders graduated from high school), it is not unreasonable to propose that the absence of a significant race difference in oppositional attitudes arises from the self-selection out of school by those with the strongest (that is, the most anti-achievement) attitudes. This finding, combined with Tyson's (2002) work showing clear, positive achievement orientations among elementary students, suggests that future researchers need to examine the intersection of child development, opportunities to learn, and other school effects relevant to the formation of social identity and attitudes among adolescents.

The multilevel regression analysis revealed that, consistent with social theory and ethnographic research, adolescents' abstract, concrete, and oppositional attitudes effect achievement in predictably different ways. Abstract attitudes have no effect on achievement, while net of family background, individual characteristics, and school factors, concrete attitudes have a positive effect on grades. Students' oppositional attitudes have a negative effect on achievement as predicted. Thus, the oppositional attitude findings presented here challenge the claims of researchers who argue against the existence of an oppositional framework.

The substantively and statistically significant gender, class, ability, and track differences in oppositional attitudes add texture and nuance to the findings that oppositional attitudes affect educational outcomes. The findings suggest that an OCF, operationalized as oppositional attitudes in this study, may be most useful for understanding why low-performing African American students achieve in this manner. Oppositional attitudes are less useful for explaining the race gap at the upper end of the academic continuum. For example, my findings indicate that as ability, social class, and track placement increase, oppositional attitudes decrease. Perhaps we need to look elsewhere to understand why middle-class, academically able, college-bound African Americans under-perform.[4]

But where to look? I conducted an interview with Megan Carter, a high school senior in CMS Advanced Placement classes, where she is often the only African American student. She tutors struggling students in lower grades. She confirmed that in her school, "People associate White with smart, and Black with not smart."[5]

RM: That stereotype, White with smart and Black with not smart, is that something that Blacks and Whites alike believe in at some level?

MC: Yeah, I think, I think so, because I find myself having my own stereotypes. Like if I, I mean, 'cause I know my friends, I know they're smart, Black, White or whatever, but um, I guess if, like I'm an assistant for this class, and it's a majority Black students, and most of them have F's in the class, and like, the few White students, not all of them, a couple of them have bad, lower grades, but none of them, of course, are as bad as the Black students. So I guess that's. . . .

RM: What do you mean "of course?"

MC: I don't know, I don't know why . . . [laughs nervously]. I heard myself do [say] it.

Oh! I don't know why I said, "of course." Um. See I have my OWN stereotypes [emphasis in the original].

To what extent is Megan's off-hand remark that the few White students with bad grades whom she tutors, "of course, do not have grades as poor as the African Americans in that class" a part of her *habitus*, her cultural framework? If this perspective is part of her world view—and she is a high-achieving, motivated student—it is likely that those who do not achieve academically are affected even more strongly by this association.

It is hard to imagine that African American and White students' views about race and achievement are unaffected by this stereotype, or by CMS's repetitive, public struggles over pupil assignment throughout their educations, or the obvious racial stratification of the track system, the gifted program, and the special education classes in their schools. It is entirely reasonable to interpret Megan's off-hand remark as reflecting an unconscious belief that Whites are smart, African Americans are not, and African Americans that are smart are "acting White." Her remark suggests that although she achieves in school, at some level she is aware of the societal stereotype that to be Black means you do not (cannot?) do well in school. If Ogbu is correct, such awareness may fuel a conscious or unconscious disengagement with schooling in order to maintain a student's sense of group identity.

Megan most likely has rather low levels of oppositional attitudes. Yet, her belief that African Americans perform worse than even the least distinguished White students likely influences the courses she takes, the effort she exerts, her decisions to study on a daily basis, and the extent to which her identity as an African American woman is bound up with "being smart." Perhaps among high achievers, like Megan, the OCF operates at a subconscious level, generating only modest ambivalence that ever-so-slightly eats away at effort, self-confidence, and maximum achievement. Perhaps high achievers, like Megan, who do not have oppositional cultural identities, and students who are stimulated by taunts of "acting White" work incredibly hard in order to redefine academic achievement as "acting Black" (Mickelson & Velasco, 2006).

The findings I report here refine and extend my previous work on the attitude-achievement paradox by showing that all students simultaneously hold both abstract, idealized attitudes regarding education and the future and concrete attitudes based on the material realities of their lives, particularly their families' experiences with education and opportunity. By incorporating oppositional attitudes toward education into the models I tested, I am able to extend my own work to include students' social identity and its effects on achievement. And adding the oppositional attitude to my models permits me, at the same time, to investigate Ogbu's cultural-ecological model of schooling.

The results reported here also indicate that all students, irrespective of their race, gender, or social class, simultaneously hold abstract, concrete, and oppositional attitudes toward education. These results confirm earlier work showing that the opportunity structure students are likely to encounter once they are out of school has a powerful impact on their academic performance. I also found that oppositional attitudes, composed of beliefs about the value of education held by the students' peer group, predict achievement. The stronger a student's oppositional attitudes, the lower his or her academic achievement.

The results offer support for the existence of OCFs. The stronger a student's oppositional attitudes, the more likely he or she is to believe that school success compromises his or her social identity. The single challenge to Ogbu's cultural-ecological model and the notion of oppositional frameworks is the absence of race differences in oppositional attitudes among high school students. But the absence of statistically significant differences may have resulted from measurement error in the ways that I captured OCF with my survey, or the systematic sample attrition that occurred as poorer Black students (poor in terms of both meanings of the word) dropped out of school between grades 9 and 12.

Overall, the abstract, concrete, and oppositional attitudes findings reported in this chapter suggest that the structure of opportunity influences adolescents' social identities and their academic achievement. Race, class, and gender discrepancies in opportunities to learn inside schools and to earn a living outside of schools are reflected through concrete attitudes. These attitudes contribute to the gap in African American students' achievement—either measured against their potential or against comparably able Whites, Asians, and Latinos from similar social-class backgrounds. So long as racism confers privileges and handicaps inside and outside schools, and as long as there is neither a predictable nor rational relationship between effort and reward in the social, educational, and economic spheres, African American students will face the dilemma that Theresa Perry (2003) poignantly described—should I commit myself to achieve and work hard in school, even if I cannot predict if and under what circumstance I will be recognized and rewarded for my efforts?

The findings reported in this chapter also support Ogbu's contention that the system (the schools and the economy), as well as community forces (cultural frame of reference), produces each person's cultural framework for negotiating his or her way in the world. According to Ogbu, for many African American youth, this means that an oppositional cultural framework is their guide for being authentic. Oppositional attitudes toward achievement, and the OCF they reflect, do not account for the entire range of academic behaviors among African American youth—witness Morgan—but Ogbu's model offers an important tool for further research on this dilemma.

APPENDIX

Text of Belief Statements Contributing to Abstract Attitudes

1   Education is the key to success in the future.
2   If everyone in America gets a good education, no one has to be poor.
3   Doing well in school does not lead to job success later on.
4   The way for poor people to get ahead is for them to get a good education.
5   Young people have a chance of making it if they do well in school.
6   Effort in school leads to job success.
7   Regardless of where you come from, or who you are, if you work hard and get a good education, you have a chance to make it in America.
8   School success is not a clear path to a better life.

Text of Belief Statements Contributing to Concrete Attitudes

1   I know people who flip burgers for a living even though they finished school.
2   Even if I don't work hard in school I can make future plans come true.
3   I know people who make good money and haven't finished high school.
4   What I don't learn in school I can always pick up later.
5   Students with bad grades often get good jobs after high school.
6   Even without a good education it is likely that I will end up with the kind of job I want.

Text of Belief Statements Contributing to Oppositional Attitudes

1   Most of my friends at home think school is a complete waste of time.
2   Because my friends don't think it's cool, I don't try as hard as I can in school.

3   My friends at home believe that too much education makes a person give up his or her real identity.
4   Most of my friends at school think that education is very important for their future.
5   At this school, it is not cool to be smart.

NOTES

An earlier version of this chapter was presented at the meetings of the American Sociological Association, Chicago, IL, August 16–20, 2002. The author's research is supported by grants from the Ford Foundation (985–1336 and 1000–1430) and the National Science Foundation (RED-9550763). The author is grateful to Deborah G. Berenbach, James Ainsworth, Jan de Leeuw, Douglas Downey, Melissa Herman, and Earl Smith for their comments on earlier drafts.

1   Rather than compare African Americans to Whites, Asa Hilliard (Perry, Steele, & Hilliard, 2003) suggested that we compare African Americans to their potential. Comparing performance to possibility is a more useful formulation of the much-discussed race gap because it does not set up Whites as the source of standards that African Americans need to meet.
2   The struggle over desegregation came to a head in the summer of 1997 when a White family (*Capacchione et al. v. Charlotte-Mecklenburg Board of Education* [1999]) sued the Charlotte-Mecklenburg Schools seeking a declaration of unitary status, an end to mandatory desegregation, and an end to any current and future race-conscious policies. Shortly thereafter, the original *Swann* plaintiffs, perceiving the lawsuit as a threat to the *Swann* ruling, intervened by reactivating their original case against the CMS district. Two young African American families with children currently enrolled in CMS, the Belk and the Collins families, joined the *Swann* plaintiffs. Consequently the case is also known as *Belk v. Charlotte-Mecklenburg Board of Education* (1999). Because the two lawsuits mirrored each other—with the Whites requesting a declaration of unitary status and the African Americans requesting a thorough implementation of the original *Swann* order to desegregate—the judge consolidated the two cases (*Swann sub nom Belk v. Charlotte-Mecklenburg Board of Education* and *Capacchione v. Charlotte-Mecklenburg Board of Education*) into one. In 1999, I served as an expert witness for the defendant in both cases, the Charlotte-Mecklenburg Schools.
    Soon after filing the lawsuit, the Capacchione family moved from Charlotte, NC to Torrance, CA. To sustain the lawsuit's viability, several other White families joined the suit as plaintiff interveners. Although the judge, Robert Potter, had been a citizen activist "unequivocally opposed" to mandatory busing for desegregation before President Reagan appointed him to the federal bench (Morill 1999), he did not recuse himself from the case.
    In September 1999, the district court declared the CMS district to be unitary (*Capacchione v. Charlotte-Mecklenburg Board of Education*, 1999). The trial judge enjoined the school system from using race in any future operations of the school system, and awarded the White plaintiffs attorneys' fees and nominal monetary compensation for damages to their constitutional rights suffered under the school system's use of a race-conscious magnet lottery.

In November 2000, a three-judge panel of the Fourth Circuit Court of Appeals overturned the lower court's unitary decision (*Belk*, 2000). Almost a year later, the full Fourth Circuit Court of Appeals, sitting *en banc*, reversed the three-judge panel and affirmed the lower court's 1999 unitary decision (*Belk*, 2001). The court's majority, however, voted that the race-conscious magnet plan was not unconstitutional, and absent a constitutional violation, the White plaintiffs were not entitled to damages or attorneys' fees.

Both the African American and White plaintiffs appealed the decision to the Supreme Court. In 2002, the Supreme Court denied *certiorari* to both plaintiffs, thereby leaving the unitary decision in place. For details of the case and the legal decisions, see Mickelson (2003a).

3   I simultaneously developed the three attitude scales for abstract, concrete, and oppositional attitudes by factor analyzing 29 belief statements that appeared on the survey. Variables with factor loadings of .6 and greater are included on the attitude scale. The middle school and high school surveys contained almost identical items. Although the attitude scales were developed separately for the middle and high school samples, virtually the same items loaded on the three factors in both the middle and high school samples. The middle school factor analysis then served as a confirmatory factor analysis of the high school data. Respondents' abstract, concrete, and oppositional attitude scores were the mean of the linear sum of their responses to a series of Likert-scaled belief statements scored from (5) strongly agree to (1) strongly disagree.

4   Elsewhere, I have argued that racially correlated opportunities to learn are a major source of the race gap (Mickelson, 2003b).

5   The racial composition of Megan's school is a likely contributing factor to the norms that equate "White with smart, and Black with not smart." The student body at Megan's school is overwhelmingly White. In contrast, Advanced Placement students at desegregated Freedom High, where 50 percent of AP students were Black, reported that being smart was "normal for Black students."

REFERENCES

Ainsworth-Darnell, J. W., & Downey, D. B. (1998). Assessing racial/ethnic differences in school performance. *American Sociological Review*, 63, 536–553.

Belk v. Charlotte-Mecklenburg Board of Education, 99–239 (1999).

Belk. v. Charlotte-Mecklenburg Board of Education, 269 F. 3d 305 (4th Cir. 2001).

Belk. v. Charlotte-Mecklenburg Board of Education, 233 F. 3d 232 (4th Cir. 2000) (vacated).

Bourdieu, P. (1977). *Outline of a theory of practice* (R. Nice, Trans.). Cambridge: Cambridge University Press.

Bourdieu, P., & Passeron, J. (1977). *Reproduction in education, society, and culture*. Beverly Hills, CA: Sage.

Campbell, J. R., Hombo, C. M. & Mazzeo, J. (2000). *NAEP trends in academic progress: Three decades of student performance* (NCES 2000–469). Washington, DC: U.S. Dept. of Education.

Capacchione et al. v. Charlotte-Mecklenburg Schools. Civil Action No.3: 97 CV 482 (1999).

DiMaggio, P. (1982). Cultural capital and school success: The impact of status culture participation on grades of U.S. high school students. *American Sociological Review, 47,* 189–201.

Dumais, S. A. (2002). Cultural capital, gender, and school success: The role of habitus. *Sociology of Education, 75,* 44–68.

Education Week (2000, September 6). NAEP results indicate narrowing of race gap, p. 7.

Farkas, G. (1996). *Human capital or cultural capital: Ethnicity and poverty groups in an urban school district.* Hawthorne, NY: Aldine.

Fordham, S. (1988). Racelessness as a factor in Black students' success. *Harvard Educational Review, 58,* 54–84.

Fordham, S. (1996). *Blacked out: Dilemmas of race, identity, and success at Capital High.* Chicago: University of Chicago Press.

Fordham, S., & Ogbu, J. U. (1986). Black students' school success: Coping with the burden of "acting White." *The Urban Review, 18*(3), 176–206.

Kreft, I., & de Leeuw, J. (1998). *Introducing multilevel modeling.* London: Sage.

Lamont, M., & Lareau, A. (1988). Cultural capital: Allusion, gaps, and glissandos in recent theoretical developments. *Sociological Theory, 6,* 153–168.

Mickelson, R. A. (1989). Why does Jane read and write so well?: The anomaly of women's achievement. *Sociology of Education, 62,* 43–67.

Mickelson, R. A. (1990). The attitude-achievement paradox among Black adolescents. *Sociology of Education, 63,* 44–61.

Mickelson, R. A. (2001). Subverting Swann: First- and second-generation segregation in the Charlotte-Mecklenburg Schools. *American Educational Research Journal, 38,* 215–252.

Mickelson, R. A. (2003a). The academic consequences of desegregation and segregation: Evidence from the Charlotte-Mecklenburg Schools. *North Carolina Law Review, 81*(4), 120–165.

Mickelson, R. A. (2003b). When are racial disparities in education the result of racial discrimination? A social science perspective. *Teachers College Record, 105*(6), 1085–1119.

Mickelson, R. A. (2005). The incomplete desegregation of the Charlotte-Mecklenburg Schools and its consequences, 1971–2004. In J. C. Boger, C. Edley, & G. Orfield (Eds.), *The resegregation of the South?* Chapel Hill, NC: University of North Carolina Press.

Mickelson, R. A., & Velasco, A. E. (2006). "Give me the spotlight!" Diverse responses to "acting White" among academically able Black adolescents." In E. Horvat & C. O'Connor (Eds.), *Beyond acting White: reassessments and new directions in research on Black students and school success.* New York: Routledge.

Morrill, J. (1999, April 18). Trial brings school case full circle. *Charlotte Observer,* p. 16A.

Ogbu, J. U. (1974). *The next generation.* New York: Academic Press.

Ogbu, J. U. (1978). *Minority education and caste.* New York: Academic Press.

Ogbu, J. U. (1991). Immigrant and involuntary minorities in comparative perspective. In M. A. Gibson & J. U. Ogbu (Eds.), *Minority status and schooling: A comparative study of immigrant and involuntary minorities* (pp. 3–36). New York: Garland Press.

Ogbu, J. U. (2003). *Black American students in an affluent suburb: A study of academic disengagement*. Mahwah, NJ: Lawrence Erlbaum & Associates.

Ogbu, J. U., & Simons, H. D. (1998). Voluntary and involuntary minorities: A cultural-ecological theory of school performance with some implications for education. *Anthropology & Education Quarterly, 29*(2), 155–188.

Perry, T. C. (2003). Up from the parched earth: Toward a theory of African American Achievement. In T. C. Perry, C. Steele, & A. Hilliard, III (Eds) *Young, gifted, and Black* (pp. 1–10). New York: Norton.

Perry, T. C., Steele, C., & Hilliard, A. III (Eds) (2003). *Young, gifted, and Black* (pp. 1–10). New York: Norton.

Rabe-Hesketh, S., & Everitt, B. (1999). *A handbook of statistical analysis using Stata*. Boca Raton, FL: Chapman & Hall/CRC.

Swann v. Charlotte-Mecklenburg Schools, 402 U.S. 1, 15 (1971).

Tyson, K. (2002). Weighing in: Elementary-age students and the debate on attitudes toward school among Black students. *Social Problems, 80*, 1157–1189.

Chapter 17

Oppositional Identity and Academic Achievement among African American Males

Miles Anthony Irving and Cynthia Hudley

School failure, high drop-out rates, low college enrollment, over-representation in special education classes, and low standardized test scores reflect a pervasive problem of educational underachievement among African Americans (Sanders, 2000). Over the last 20 years, both educators and researchers have attempted to understand the factors that account for this problem. Much of the research in this area has been framed with a sociological, cultural, or motivational perspective (Caldas & Bankston, 1997; Ferguson, 1998; Gutman & Midgley, 2000; Kozol, 1992). Perhaps one of the most widely cited explanations for African Americans' educational underachievement has been John Ogbu's (1985) cultural-ecological model. The cultural-ecological model posits that cultural and social adaptations to years of discriminatory treatment have resulted in survival strategies among African Americans that contradict their stated educational values. In addition, some African Americans reject the tools and competencies necessary to survive and flourish within the dominant American culture (Ogbu, 1974, 1982).

Recognizing groups' disparate experiences of incorporation into the dominant culture, Ogbu developed a typology that distinguished between minority groups whose incorporation was voluntary and involuntary minority groups, whose incorporation was forced upon them (Ogbu, 1978, 1987). Minorities who chose to immigrate into the United States to improve their social, political, or economic lives are termed voluntary minorities. In contrast, involuntary or caste-like minorities are groups who were involuntarily and permanently incorporated into U.S. society by a process of slavery, conquest, or exploitation (Berreman, 1960; Ogbu, 1978). African Americans fit the description of caste-like minorities because they were brought to America as slaves and after emancipation were relegated to a menial status through legal and illegal means (Ogbu, 1982, 1985). As an involuntary minority group, African Americans have had chronic experiences with racism and discrimination. Therefore, the typology at the heart of the cultural-ecological model has been valuable for examining the unique historical factors that may place African

American students at increased risk for academic underachievement and school drop-out.

Since involuntary minorities were forced to incorporate into the dominant culture, which resulted in severe oppression and victimization, they have a negative perception of their membership in the U.S. society, experiencing it as a loss of former political, spiritual, and cultural freedom (Ogbu, 1978). Further, involuntary minorities typically do not have a homeland with which to compare their current situation. Instead, they compare their current social and economic status with that of the dominant group. They experience economic oppression, discrimination, and racism as part and parcel of their ascribed status as a racial minority, as something they can neither control nor change (Ogbu, 1982, 1985). Social, educational, and economic barriers are seen as permanent conditions of their undeserved oppression as a caste-like minority.

OPPOSITIONAL IDENTITY

The cultural-ecological model has identified particular adaptations that involuntary minorities develop to protect and maintain their group identity and sense of self-worth in the face of oppression and denigration by the dominant culture (Ogbu, 1985, 1991). One such protective adaptation that some African Americans have manifested is an oppositional identity (Ogbu, 1997), which occurs when an individual's cultural values and practices are in direct contrast to those of the dominant culture. Specifically, an oppositional identity is the composite of one's cultural frame of reference for appropriate beliefs and behavior, as well as a sense of cultural mistrust toward the dominant group (Emerson, 1999; Ogbu, 1993, 1994). This cognitive orientation leads involuntary minorities to consciously and unconsciously perceive cultural practices and behaviors that they associate with the dominant culture to be inappropriate for themselves. An individual with an oppositional identity will not feel comfortable dressing, acting, speaking, or engaging in activities in ways that are consistent with the dominant culture (Arroyo & Ziggler, 1995; Cross, 1995).

While some research has supported the cultural-ecological model, and the model appears to be salient for some African Americans (Ford, 1992; Gibson, 1997), Ogbu's theory also has received a considerable amount of criticism (Ainsworth-Darnell & Downey, 1998; Cook & Ludwig, 1998; Goto, 1997; Trueba, 1988). Many of the critiques have cited the model's inability to account for the intra-group variability found within the African American population. For example, critics have claimed that John Ogbu's theory does not explain why some African Americans who place significant importance on their ethnic identity when defining themselves also are high achievers in education.

ALTERNATIVES TO OPPOSITIONAL IDENTITY

African Americans are a diverse group with varying experiences and economic statuses. If an individual African American enjoys economic affluence and has many friends who are members of the dominant culture, it is not clear that their life experiences will support the development of a strong oppositional identity. For example, attaining a relatively high socioeconomic status (SES) can reduce the perception that racial barriers are obstacles that cannot be overcome (Fordham, 1996). Working-class parents who have used education to improve their economic condition also might value educational achievement strongly, based on their personal experiences with success (Gutman & Midgley, 2000). In sum, personal experiences may influence the degree to which an individual African American's identity assumes the characteristics described for involuntary minorities. Thus, many African Americans may not possess what Ogbu described as an oppositional identity.

Many African Americans display high achievement in academic settings and have an achievement ideology that is conducive to school success (Fordham, 1996). Research has shown, for example, that students who participated in the Advancement Via Individual Determination (AVID) program did not exhibit an oppositional pattern towards the dominant culture (Mehan, Hubbard, Villanueva, & Lintz, 1996). In fact, these students felt comfortable developing linguistic styles, social behavior, and academic skills that those in the dominant culture value. Further, students developed these skills without erasing the cultural identity they enjoyed in their home and community environments. In essence, these students developed a dual identity and could "accommodate without assimilating" successfully (Mehan et al., 1996).

CAPTURING THE VARIABILITY IN IDENTITY AMONG AFRICAN AMERICANS

The core of our research program has been the systematic development of a reliable means to assess variability in cultural identification among African American children and youths. The particular study that we will describe here sought to empirically define a psychometric construct of African Americans' oppositional identity by investigating whether cultural mistrust, cultural attitudes, ethnic identity, outcome expectations, and outcome value converged as a coherent marker of an individual's oppositional identity. In addition, this study examined that construct in relationship to cultural identification and educational achievement.

Most of the research investigating John Ogbu's theory has consisted of qualitative investigations (Fordham, 1996; Gibson, 1987; Ogbu, 2003;

Solomon, 1992), and it is not clear that these studies captured important variability in oppositional identity. We thus concluded that a quantitative instrument of oppositional identity would be a useful tool to assess intragroup variability in oppositional identity among African Americans. Understanding oppositional identity as an individual difference variable may further our understanding of factors that uniquely affect African Americans' academic achievement motivation. Variations in oppositional identity are quite likely a function of students' personal and social experiences; thus, a quantitative measure will make it possible to assess and compare relatively large numbers of individual students, who represent a sufficiently broad array of personal histories.

ASSESSING OPPOSITIONAL IDENTITY

In this initial investigation, we began by defining oppositional identity as a composite of attitudinal variables that included cultural mistrust, a resistant cultural frame of reference for beliefs and behavior, academic outcome expectations, and academic outcome value (Emerson, 1999; Ogbu, 1993, 1994). A resistant cultural frame of reference was operationalized as a construct comprising two variables: resistant cultural attitudes and ethnic identity affirmation. We contend that ethnic identity affirmation in and of itself is no indication of an oppositional identity. Rather, ethnic identity affirmation is included in this initial study to clarify the extent to which an individual's oppositional identity might be grounded in an affirming sense of ethnic identity.

Within John Ogbu's framework, an individual who scored high on measures of cultural mistrust and/or resistant cultural attitudes and low on ethnic identity affirmation would not be considered to have an oppositional identity. Ogbu argued that in coping with caste-like status, African Americans developed an oppositional identity that affirms and establishes the meaning of a Black self in opposition to what it means to be White. Oppositional identity is thus grounded in an embracing of membership in a racial or ethnic group that is oppressed due to visible markers of identity (e.g., skin color). Importantly, this conceptualization of oppositional identity is theoretically distinct from attitudes that might derive solely from being poor, culturally different, and/or uneducated.

In addition, given the widely accepted and established finding that SES and academic achievement are positively related, we also investigated the relationship between SES and our model of oppositional identity (Caldas & Bankston, 1997). Some researchers have suggested that oppositional identity is more a function of low-income status rather than racial-group membership *per se*, as described in Ogbu's theory (Ainsworth,

2002). Therefore, we felt it was important to assess the validity of our model relative to SES.

In sum, we developed an initial model grounded in the cultural-ecological model comprising ethnic identity affirmation, cultural mistrust, resistant cultural attitudes, and outcome expectations. However, to test the theoretical accuracy of the cultural-ecological model, we examined multiple models. We began with the hypothesis that cultural mistrust, resistant cultural attitudes, and ethnic identity would be positively intercorrelated. Based on the first author's prior research, we also expected academic outcome expectations and outcome value to be inversely related to cultural mistrust, resistant cultural attitudes, and ethnic identity affirmation (Irving, 2000). Finally, consistent with prior research, we expected our model of oppositional identity to have an inverse relationship to socio-economic status and academic achievement.

RESEARCH METHODOLOGY

In order to capture the complex cognitive processes related to cultural identification, we surveyed adolescents 16 years and older to ensure that cognitive processes and identity formation had been adequately developed (Erikson, 1980). High school students are able to think about the complex interactions of social, personal, and cultural issues in their lives. In addition, as high school students approach graduation, they more actively assess possible future outcomes related to education (Cinnerella, 1998). Thus, high school is an excellent point in development to assess oppositional identity.

Prior research has indicated that the variables included in our model may function differently in the lives and identities of females and males (Fordham, 1996; Graham, Taylor, & Hudley, 1998; Osborne, 1997). Consequently, it is quite plausible that gender may moderate a number of our hypothesized relationships substantially. Given that research in this area has been relatively limited, in our initial study we opted to control for gender by focusing only on males.

Data were collected at a multiethnic high school consisting of 27 percent African Americans, 12 percent Hispanics, 15 percent European Americans, 44 percent Asian Americans, and 2 percent Pacific Islanders (School Accountability Report, 2000). The neighborhood surrounding the high school is a lower-middle- to working-class community with 24 percent European Americans, 34 percent Hispanics, 16.5 percent African Americans, and 23 percent Asians and Pacific Islanders (U.S. Census, 1990). The majority of the people (76 percent) who reside in the community have service sector, production, machine operation, and sales occupations (U.S. Census, 1990). The high school has two high-achievement magnet programs that attract many European Americans from an affluent neighborhood outside the immediate school community.

Participants were 115 male African American high school students enrolled in the 11th and 12th grades. Students represented a balance of high-, medium-, and low-track classes to avoid any potential achievement-level selection bias.

Instruments

An instrument comprising 72 items was compiled to measure oppositional identity. Items were selected from four existing instruments that tap cultural mistrust, academic outcome expectations, outcome values, cultural attitudes, and ethnic identity affirmation. All items are rated on a four-point, Likert-like scale, ranging from *strongly disagree* to *strongly agree*.

Cultural Mistrust

The Revised Cultural Mistrust Inventory (CMI) (Irving, 2000) is a measure of African Americans' mistrust of the dominant culture (Terrell & Terrell, 1981). The Cultural Mistrust Inventory was designed to measure the degree to which African Americans trust the intentions and actions of Whites and the institutions they control. This instrument was used initially with 18- and 19-year-old African American males and females attending college (Terrell & Terrell, 1981) and subsequently with African American junior high school students (Terrell & Terrell, 1993).

Originally, the Cultural Mistrust Inventory was a 48-item measure with four subscales: politics and law, business and workplace, education and training, and interpersonal relationships. When designing the Cultural Mistrust Inventory, Terrell and Terrell used the Jackson social desirability scale to eliminate items from the measure that might be influenced by social desirability (Jackson, 1970). Thus, all items with a significant correlation with the social desirability scale, at the $p = .05$ level, were removed from the inventory. A test-retest reliability estimate of .86 was obtained (Terrell & Terrell, 1981).

In previous research (Irving, 2000), responses within each of the four subscales (business and work, education and training, politics and law, and interpersonal relationships) had high inter-correlations. The inter-correlations between the subscales were all significant at $p < .05$, ranging from $r = .75$ to $r = .88$ (Irving, 2000). These findings among the subscales prompted the first author to run factor analyses to examine the subscales and thus discern which model best described the data. A one-factor model explained 43 percent of the variance. The two-, three-, and four-factor models explained an additional 6 percent, 4 percent, and 3 percent of the variance, respectively (Irving, 2000). Due to high inter-correlations among the subscales and the results of the factor analysis, we decided to analyze the Cultural Mistrust Inventory as one composite score.

Further, given that 48 items is an exhaustive number for measuring a one-factor construct, the number of items on the scale was reduced by eliminating items with low factor loadings, and the 10 questions that best reflected John Ogbu's description of mistrust towards the dominant culture were maintained. The revised Cultural Mistrust Inventory is a 10-item measure with a reliability coefficient of $a = .91$. Low scores indicate that an individual has a low level of mistrust. High scores on an item indicate that an individual has a high level of mistrust towards White people.

Outcome Expectations and Outcome Value

Outcome expectations were assessed using the African American Academic Outcome Expectations Scale (Irving, 2000). This 20-item measure investigates the benefits that respondents expect to gain from academic achievement, as well as how much they value these outcomes. The inventory is divided into two sections. The first section consists of 10 questions measuring the outcomes that students expect to result from high school graduation. The second section measures how much individuals value the outcomes listed in section one. High scores indicate that an individual has a high outcome expectation or values a given item highly. Low scores indicate that an individual has a low outcome expectation or a low valuation of a given item. The Cronbach alpha coefficients for outcome expectations and value were .89 and .91, respectively (Irving, 2000).

Ethnic Identity Affirmation

Ethnic identity affirmation was assessed using Jean Phinney's seven-item affirmation and belonging subscale of the Multigroup Ethnic Identity Measure (MEIM) (Roberts, Phinney, Masse, Chen, Roberts, & Romero, 1999). The affirmation and belonging subscale measures a person's ethnic identity status by assessing his or her degree of agreement on questions concerning their ethnic group membership (e.g., "I have a clear sense of our ethnic group and what it means to me" and "I have a strong sense of belonging to our own ethnic group") (Roberts et al., 1999). Low scores indicate that individuals have a low sense of affirmation and belonging to their ethnic group, while high scores indicate an achieved sense of affirmation and belonging to their ethnic group. Previous studies have indicated reasonable reliability coefficients for the achievement subscale (Cronbach, 1951) for fourth- and fifth-grade African American children: $a = .71$ (Reese, Vera, & Paikoff, 1998); for African American high school students, $a = .75$ (Phinney, 1992); and for a sample of college students, $a = .86$ (Phinney, 1992).

Resistant Cultural Attitudes

The students' frame of reference for appropriate beliefs and behavior was assessed using the cultural subscale of the Self-Perception of School, Peers, and Achievement Survey (SPSAS) (Ford, 1992). This 35-item subscale was designed to measure students' cultural attitudes, beliefs, and values regarding achievement motivation (e.g., "School is more exciting when I learn about Black people") (Ford, 1992). In addition, the cultural subscale measures students' perceptions of parental and community beliefs and attitudes about school (e.g., "My parents believe that going to school is important"). The questions focus on beliefs and values characteristically espoused in the dominant White culture, as well as beliefs and values that oppose them. Items that are reflective of White cultural norms and values are reversed to reflect resistant cultural attitudes. The items are scored and coded such that high scores represent resistant cultural attitudes that are in opposition or resistant to the values and norms of the dominant White culture. The Cronbach alpha is .92 for the cultural attitudes subscale (Addo, 1997).

Socioeconomic Status

SES was measured using a two-item scale attached to the parental informed consent form. These items are categorical variables scored on a 12-point Likert scale. The first categorical variable assessed the education of the parent in the household who had attained the highest level of education. The second categorical variable assessed the combined parental income. The two categorical responses were summed and divided by two to obtain a single mean score of SES.

Academic Achievement

Students' academic achievement was measured using their cumulative academic grade point average (GPA). The academic GPA does not take into consideration non-academic electives like physical education, nor does it take into account the extra grade point available in advanced placement (AP) courses. The academic GPA is an appropriate measure of the students' grade point average and academic achievement because it includes the academic classes that all of the students are required to take to graduate from high school.

RESULTS

The Cronbach alpha reliability coefficients for cultural mistrust, cultural attitudes, and ethnic identity affirmation were $a = .91$, $a = .85$, and $a = .74$, respectively. The Cronbach alpha reliability coefficients for outcome expectations and outcome value were $a = .84$ and $a = .68$, respectively. Descriptive data on all measures are displayed in Table 17.1. The ethnic identity affirmation scale was negatively skewed.

Correlations

Our hypothesis concerning the positive relationships among the variables of cultural mistrust, resistant cultural attitudes, and ethnic identity affirmation was partially supported (see Table 17.2). Cultural mistrust was related to resistant cultural attitudes, $r = .61$, $p < .01$. Our hypotheses concerning cultural mistrust and outcome expectations, outcome value, SES, and GPA were partially supported (see Table 17.2). Cultural mistrust had a significant, inverse relationship with outcome expectations, $r = -.46$, $p < .01$, SES, $r = -.36$, $p < .01$, and GPA, $r = -.43$, $p < .01$. Cultural mistrust was related to neither ethnic identity affirmation nor outcome value. Resistant cultural attitudes were not significantly related to ethnic identity affirmation.

Our hypothesis concerning outcome expectations, outcome value, SES, and GPA was partially supported (see Table 17.2). Resistant cultural attitudes were related to outcome expectations, $r = -.46$, $p < .01$, outcome value, $r = -.31$, $p = < .01$, SES, $r = -.28$, $p = < .01$, and GPA, $r = -.37$, $p = < .01$. Ethnic identity affirmation was only significantly related to outcome value, $r = .18$, $p = < .05$.

Table 17.1 Mean and standard deviation for cultural mistrust, resistant cultural attitudes and ethnic identity affirmation outcome expectations, outcome value, SES, and grade point averages.

N=115	M	SD
1. Cultural mistrust	2.7	.62
2. Resistant cultural attitudes	1.8	.30
3. Ethnic identity affirmation	3.8	.29
4. Outcome expectations	3.1	.47
5. Outcome value	3.5	.34
6. Socioeconomic status	6.6	2.40
7. Grade point average	2	.65

Table 17.2 Intercorrelation of variables

	N = 115						
Variable	1	2	3	4	5	6	7
1. Cultural mistrust		.61**	.02	−.46**	−.14	−.36**	−.42**
2. Resistant cultural attitudes		—	−.12	−.44**	−.31**	−.28**	−.37**
3. Ethnic identity affirmation			—	−.04	.18*	.07	.12
4. Outcome expectations				—	.41**	.17	.21*
5. Outcome value					—	.18*	.20*
6. SES						—	.28**
7. GPA							

Notes: **$p < .01$; *$p < .05$.

Structural Equation Modeling

We next took a structural equation modeling (SEM) approach to test the adequacy of the hypothesized models (Bentler & Weeks, 1980; Jöreskog & Sörbom, 1993), using the EQS (computer software used in equation modeling) program. The significance of the chi-square value, the chi-square value and degrees of freedom ratio, the Bentler-Bonnett normed fit index (NFI), the comparative fit index (CFI), the lisrel (computer program) adjusted goodness of fit index (AGFI), the standardized root mean squared residual (SRMR), and the root mean square error of approximation (RMSEA) were utilized to assess the model fit. It is preferable that the chi-square not be significant and that the ratio between the chi-square value and the degrees of freedom be small. NFI, CFI, and AGFI values above .90 and SRMR and RMSEA values below .08 typically are considered to indicate an acceptable fit to the model (Kline, 1998; Loehlin, 1998).[1]

Three models were created to test our hypothesis that oppositional identity is a reliable factor and that oppositional identity has a relationship with GPAs and SES. Model 1 used cultural mistrust (CM), resistant cultural attitudes (RCA), and ethnic identity affirmation (EIA) as the

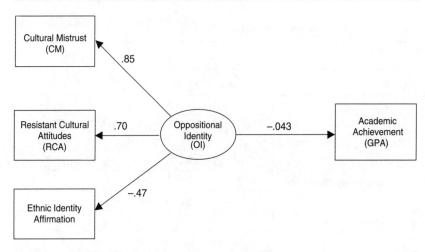

Figure 17.1 Model 1: CM, RCA and ethnic identity affirmation, as oppositional identity and relationship to GPA. X^2(2, N = 115) = 4.69, p = .09, NFI = .93, CFI = .96, AGFI = .90, SRMR = .046, and RMSEA = .11. All of the free loading parameters were significant at $p < .05$ with the exception of academic achievement. CFI = Comparative Fit Index; AGFI = Adjusted Goodness of Fit; SRMR = Standardized Root Mean Squared Residual; RMSEA = Root Mean Square Error of Approximation. Note: The factor loadings presented in the figure represent the standardized coefficients.

measured variables to comprise oppositional identity, the latent variable (see Figure 17.1). In addition, model 1 used GPA as a measured variable to investigate its relationship with oppositional identity. The rationale for this model design was based on John Ogbu's cultural-ecological model, in which he posited that African Americans develop an oppositional identity consisting of a mistrust of the dominant culture and resistant cultural attitudes that are grounded in strong feelings of ethnic identity affirmation (Ogbu, 1987). The fourth measured variable of this model was academic achievement (GPA). Ogbu (1991) argued that oppositional identity contributes to lower academic achievement among African Americans. Therefore, the model was designed to test the hypothesis that cultural mistrust, resistant cultural values, and ethnic identity affirmation will converge to form a single factor. Further, this model assessed whether oppositional identity was related to academic achievement. In model 1, the fit was unacceptable, X^2(2, N = 115) = 4.69, p = .09, NFI = .93, CFI = .96, AGFI = .90, SRMR = .04, and RMSEA = .11. The chi-square and RMSEA were particularly marginal. In addition, the free parameter loading of academic achievement was not significant (see Figure 17.1).

The poor fit of model 1 prompted us to investigate a second model of oppositional identity. In model 2, ethnic identity affirmation was dropped from the model and academic outcome expectations was added. Recall, that previous research has suggested that ethnic identity affirmation is an important component of oppositional identity. However, the negative skewness and the correlation results suggest that our entire sample tended to score high on the measure of ethnic identity affirmation. There is both statistical and theoretical support for this proposed second model. The correlation matrix of this present study found a moderate, inverse relationship with academic outcome expectations, cultural mistrust and resistant cultural attitudes, supporting Ogbu's delineation of these variables. Irving (2000) also found that academic outcome expectations were inversely related to cultural mistrust, and that cultural mistrust was a significant predicator of academic outcome expectations. The moderate correlations found in this study coupled with Irving's previous findings give further statistical support to the development of an oppositional identity model with academic outcome expectations as a measured variable.

Ogbu's cultural ecological model posits low academic outcome expectations as being a component of oppositional identity. While individuals with an oppositional identity may value certain life outcomes, like making a high salary, they maintain low expectations of being able to attain these desired outcomes through educational institutions controlled by the dominant culture (Ogbu, 1991). Ogbu contended that years of discrimination and racism led to the development of an oppositional identity in which African Americans not only mistrust the dominant culture, but also have low expectations that institutions of the dominant culture will enhance their status. Further, Ogbu (1991) argued that African Americans' academic achievement was undermined by their low outcome expectations related to education.

Therefore, in model 2, cultural mistrust, resistant cultural attitudes, academic outcome expectations, and academic achievements were the measured variables and oppositional identity was the latent variable (see Figure 17.2). This model, like model 1, tested the hypothesis that cultural mistrust, resistant cultural attitudes, and academic outcome expectations form a reliable factor of oppositional identity. This model also investigated whether oppositional identity has a significant relationship with academic GPA. In model 2, the fit was adequate, $X^2(2, N = 115) = 1.51, p = .47$, NFI = .98, CFI = 1, AGFI = .96, SRMR = .007, and RMSEA = .00. All of the free-loading parameters were significant at $p < .05$ (see Figure 17.2).

Model 3 was designed to investigate the relationship between SES and oppositional identity. Previous research has suggested that SES influences the development of oppositional identity (Ainsworth-Darnell & Downey, 1998). As previously discussed, varying levels of SES are likely to reflect the different lived experiences of African Americans. For example, African American students who reside in low-income households and come from families with limited levels of educational attainment may be

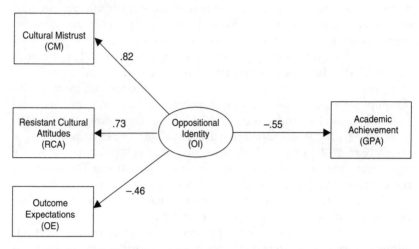

Figure 17.2 Model 2: CM, RCA and OE as oppositional identity and relationship to GPA. Full process model, $X^2(2, N = 115) = 1.51, p = .47$, NFI = .98, CFI = 1, AGFI = .96, SRMR = .007, and RMSEA = .00. All of the free-loading parameters were significant at $p < .05$; NFI = Normed Fit Index; CFI = Comparative Fit Index; AGFI = Adjusted Goodness of Fit; SRMR = Standardized Root Mean Squared Residual; RMSEA = Root Mean Square Error of Approximation. Note: The factor loadings presented in the figure represent the standardized coefficients.

more likely to perceive the myriad of negative outcomes associated with being a person of color in the United States.

Model 3 examines how one's SES impacts the development of oppositional identity. This final model testing the effect of SES retains the construct of oppositional identity as defined by model 2. In model 3 the fit was adequate, $X^2(5, N = 115) = 1.51$, $p = .47$, NFI = .97, CFI = 1, AGFI = .96, SRMR = .03, and RMSEA = .00. All of the free-loading parameters were significant at $p < .05$ (see Figure 17.3).

DISCUSSION

Using a cultural-ecological perspective, this study measured oppositional identity among African American males. The oppositional identity instruments developed for this study demonstrated adequate construct validity and reliability. The study's first two hypotheses predicted that the variables included in our model would be related in specific ways as described by John Ogbu's cultural-ecological model. Additional hypotheses predicted that our operational definition of oppositional identity would be negatively related to academic achievement. Prior research has looked extensively at ethnic minorities' beliefs about themselves and education

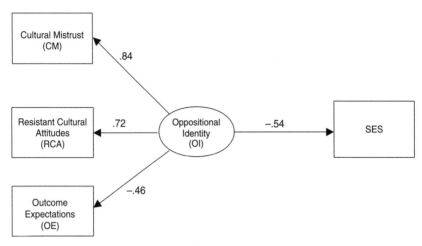

Figure 17.3 Model 3: CM, RCA, OE as oppositional identity and relationship to SES. Full process model, $X^2(5, N = 115) = 1.51, p = .47, NFI = .97, CFI = 1, AGFI = .96$, SRMR = .03, and RMSEA = .00. All of the free-loading parameters were significant at $p < .05$; NFI = Normed Fit Index; CFI = Comparative Fit Index; AGFI = Adjusted Goodness of Fit; SRMR = Standardized Root Mean Squared Residual; RMSEA = Root Mean Square Error of Approximation. Note: The factor loadings presented in the figure represent the standardized coefficients.

(Arroyo & Zigler, 1995; Witherspoon, Speight, & Thomas, 1997). Other previous studies have used qualitative indicators to understand involuntary minorities' oppositional and resistant cultural identification (Fordham, 1996; Fordham & Ogbu, 1986). Only recently have researchers conducted quantitative studies to investigate oppositional identity (Addo, 1997; Ainsworth-Darnell & Downey, 1998; Cook & Ludwig, 1998; Emerson, 1999). The present study was the first attempt to create and empirically test a full quantitative model of oppositional identity and investigate its relationship to academic achievement. In model 1, even though the variables of cultural mistrust, resistant cultural attitudes, and ethnic identity affirmation did form a factor, counter to the hypothesized relationship ethnic identity affirmation had a negative parameter loading with oppositional identity. In addition, oppositional identity did not have a significant relationship with academic achievement. Based upon these findings, model 1 did not support our hypothesis. The skewed distribution and restricted range of responses of the ethnic identity affirmation scale may have contributed to model 1's inconsistencies and insignificant findings.

In model 2, when ethnic identity affirmation was dropped and academic outcome expectations was added, both the overall model and parameter loadings improved considerably. The variables of cultural mistrust, resistant cultural attitudes, and academic outcome expectations converged in the expected directions and formed a factor called oppositional identity. In addition, oppositional identity had a significant relationship with academic achievement. Based upon these findings, it appears that cultural mistrust, resistant cultural attitudes, and academic outcome expectations are reasonable markers of oppositional identity. In addition, the results of model 2 support the hypothesis that oppositional identity is negatively related to academic achievement. In model 3, when SES was added to the model, the model and parameter loadings were an overall very good fit. In support of our hypothesis, SES did have an inverse relationship with oppositional identity. These findings indicate that SES may influence an oppositional identity's development.

This study explored the variability of individual African Americans' cultural identification by examining the concept of oppositional identity. While Ogbu's theory of oppositional identity has received considerable criticism for its rigid typology, this present study was successful in creating a quantitative model capable of capturing the variability of African Americans' cultural identification (Gonzalez, 1999; Trueba, 1988). The quantitative model developed and tested in this study is significant in that it can explain the variability in achievement among African Americans.

John Ogbu's cultural-ecological model has been one of the most-cited explanations for African American's academic achievement over the last 18 years. In addition, his model has sparked a wealth of intellectual dialogue, both supporting and challenging the premises of his theoretical model. Supporting Ogbu's framework, it is clear from our study that oppositional identity exists and has a negative influence on academic achievement. However, our data also call into question the rigid typology of Ogbu's model. Oppositional identity and academic achievement varied among our sample. As the predicament of African American males' underachievement continues to persist, the findings of this study suggest that oppositional identity may be important in understanding school failure. School success for most students depends on consistent effort and persistence. The development of the attitudinal and behavioral characteristics associated with oppositional identity is likely to undermine students' school engagement.

In this study, cultural mistrust, resistant cultural attitudes, and low academic outcome expectations emerged as the salient features of oppositional identity. These findings are supported by previous studies of African Americans' cultural identification. Solomon (1992) found that the students in his sample had an oppositional identity towards the dominant culture consisting of a mistrust of the school system, resistant cultural attitudes, and limited educational outcome expectations. The present study expands Solomon's findings in that it investigated the relationship between oppositional identity and a direct measure of academic achievement (cumulative academic GPAs).

Oppositional Identity and Academic Achievement

Oppositional identity had an inverse relationship with academic achievement. Students who were high in oppositional identity tended to have low GPAs. In their studies of African American students' oppositional or resistant cultural identification, Addo (1997) and Emerson (1999) found that students tended to have positive attitudes towards education. This present study investigated students' actual academic achievement as a function of their cultural identification and found that students' grades did vary depending on their level of oppositional identity.

These data suggest that as African American males' mistrust increased, their academic outcome expectations decreased. In addition, this study found that as students' mistrust increased, their resistant cultural attitudes increased. The cumulative effect of these variables had a negative influence on academic achievement. Given the questions on the Cultural Mistrust Inventory, students who had high responses on this measure may have some reservations concerning the willingness of a White-controlled system to reward African Americans. Further, African American males with high scores on the Cultural Mistrust Inventory may have a greater awareness of institutional racism. Students with an oppositional identity may be sensitive to the cultural stereotypes described by Claude Steele (1997), and thus African American males may disidentify themselves from the goal of achieving academic success.

Socioeconomic Status

In our study, SES maintained an inverse relationship with cultural mistrust and resistant cultural attitudes, and a positive relationship with outcome value and grade point averages. However, SES was not significantly related to academic outcome expectations and ethnic identity affirmation.

Some researchers have suggested that oppositional identity is a function of poverty rather than a resistant cultural identification in response to racism (Ainsworth-Darnell & Downey, 1998). Although we found a relatively strong relationship of SES to oppositional identity, it is clear that cultural mistrust maintained the most powerful relationship with academic achievement in the SEM models. Given the strength of cultural mistrust in the models, it appears that oppositional identity exists beyond the influence of an individual's social circumstances. Some students from high-SES households still maintain the characteristics of oppositional identity. Ogbu's (2003) research in an affluent African American suburb found that students engaged in a variety of oppositional behaviors that impacted school achievement. The work of Osborne (1997) and Steele (1992) also contended that African American disidentification with the school system extends beyond the boundaries of class or social status. Steele's (1992) research acknowledged the impact of SES on an individual's orientation towards school success; however, his research also found that the threat of African Americans' disidentification extends beyond factors related to economic class and social status. In addition, Osborne (1997) found that even when controlling for SES, African American males remained more prone to academic disidentification. While disidentification from education is not the same as oppositional identity, both reflect a resistant cultural identification that is grounded in racial group membership.

LIMITATIONS, IMPLICATIONS, AND FUTURE STUDIES

This study has several limitations, and more research is needed to confirm the generalizability of its findings. This study was conducted at one urban high school campus in southern California. The socio-cultural environments in which African Americans live differ from region to region. Many southern Californian schools and neighborhoods maintain a diverse population of Black, White, Arab, Latino, Asian, East Indian, Southeast Asian, and South Pacific Islander residents. These differing socio-cultural conditions could contribute to unique manifestations of African Americans' cultural identification that may or may not support the present study findings.

The findings of this study have implications for policy makers, educators, and parents of African American males living in urban environments. An instrument with the ability to detect when students are developing an oppositional identity may enable school personnel to identify students who are ideal for educational interventions. Early detection of students' oppositional identity would help educators recognize those who are at risk of school failure. School policy that implements interventions similar to the AVID program may help more African Americans develop a cultural identification that is conducive to an evolution of social awareness, as well as students' academic achievement. African Americans in this study did value outcomes associated with education, yet those with an oppositional identity did not anticipate being able to achieve those outcomes through educational means. It may be that many students fall victim to institutional barriers and oppositional coping responses that create obstacles to academic success. Programs designed to help students proactively become change agents in the current system while simultaneously creating successful educational experiences may help students with an oppositional identity develop a more progressive cultural identification. This study was successful in creating what appears to be a reliable and valid measure of oppositional identity. In addition, this study found that oppositional identity has a negative relationship with academic achievement. A reliable instrument capable of measuring oppositional identity is a major contribution to the fields of educational anthropology, sociology, and educational psychology, where researchers have struggled to understand the relationship between oppositional identity and school achievement. However, given the numerous limitations previously mentioned in this chapter, more research is needed to expand our knowledge of these issues.

NOTE

1   More extensive explanation for this model-fit criteria is beyond the scope of this chapter; for full discussions of this topic, see Mueller (1996) and Jöreskog and Sörbom (1993).

REFERENCES

Addo, L. A. (1997). *Oppositional behavior in Black male early adolescents* (Doctoral dissertation, Boston University). UMI No. 9713656.

Ainsworth-Darnell, J., & Downey, D. B. (1998). Assessing the oppositional identity culture explanation for racial/ethnic differences in school performance. *American Sociological Review, 63*, 536–553.

Ainsworth, J. W. (2002). Why does it take a village? The mediation of neighborhood effects on educational achievement. *Social Forces, 81*(1), 117–152.

Arroyo, C. G., & Zigler, E. (1995). Racial identity, academic achievement and the psychological well being of economically disadvantaged adolescents. *Journal of Personality & Social Psychology, 69*, 903–914.

Bentler, P. M., & Weeks, D. G. (1980). Linear structural equations with latent variables. *Psychometrika, 45*(3), 289–308.

Berreman, G. (1960). Caste in India and the United States. *American Journal of Sociology, 66*(2), 120–127.

Caldas, S. J., & Bankston, C. (1997). Effect of school population socioeconomic status on individual academic achievement. *Journal of Educational Research, 5*, 267–277.

Cinnirella, M. (1998). Exploring temporal aspects of social identity: the concept of possible social identities. *European Journal of Social Psychology, 28*(2), 227–248.

Cook, P. J., & Ludwig, J. (1998). The burden of "acting White": Do Black adolescents disparage academic achievement? In C. Jencks & M. Phillips (Eds.),

The Black-White test score gap (pp. 375–400). Washington, DC: Brookings Institution.

Cronbach, L. J. (1951). Coefficient alpha and the internal structure of tests. *Psychometrika, 16,* 297–334.

Cross, W. (1995). Oppositional identity and African American youth: Issues and prospects. In W. D. Hawley & A. W. Jackson (Eds.), *Toward a common destiny: Improving race and ethnic relations in America* (pp. 185–204). San Francisco: Jossey-Bass.

Emerson, B. K. (1999). The extreme peer group: Its negative influence on the academic and social outcomes of African American adolescents. *Dissertation Abstracts International* (UMI No. 9941584).

Erikson, E. (1980). *Identity: Youth and crisis.* New York: Norton.

Ferguson, R. F. (1998). Can schools narrow the Black-White test score gap? In C. Jencks & M. Phillips (Eds.), *The Black-White test score gap* (pp. 318–374). Washington, DC: Brookings Institution.

Ford, D. Y. (1992). Self-perceptions of underachievement and support for the achievement ideology among early adolescent African Americans. *Journal of Early Adolescence, 12,* 228–252.

Fordham, S. (1996). *Blacked out: Dilemmas of race, identity, and success at Capital High.* Chicago: University of Chicago Press.

Fordham, S. & Ogbu, J. U. (1986). Black students' school success: Coping with the "burden of acting White." *The Urban Review, 18*(3), 176–206.

Gibson, M. (1987). The school performance of immigrant minorities: A comparative view. *Anthropology & Education Quarterly, 18,* 262–275.

Gonzalez, N. F. (1999). Puerto Rican high achievers: An example of ethnic and academic identity compatibility. *Anthropology & Education Quarterly, 30,* 343–362.

Goto, S. T. (1997). Nerds, normal people, and homeboys: Accommodation and resistance among Chinese American students. *Anthropology and Education Quarterly, 28*(1), 70–84.

Graham, S., Taylor, A., and Hudley, C. (1998). Exploring achievement among ethnic minority early adolescents. *Journal of Educational Psychology, 90,* 606–620.

Gutman, L. M., & Midgley, C. (2000). The role of protective factors in supporting the academic achievement of poor African American students during the middle school transition. *Journal of Youth & Adolescence, 2,* 223–248.

Irving, M. A. (2000). Oppositional identity, academic outcome expectations, and outcome values among African American males. Unpublished Master's thesis, University of California, Santa Barbara.

Irving, M.A. (2002) Oppositional identity and academic achievement among African American males. *Dissertation Abstracts International, 63*(06), 2129 (UMI No. AAT 3055998).

Jackson, D. N. A. (1970). A sequential system for personality scale development. *Current Topics in Clinical and Community Psychology, 2,* 61–96.

Jöreskog, K. G., & Sörbom, D. (1993). *LISREL 8: Structural equation modeling with SIMPLIS command language.* Chicago: Scientific Software.

Kline, R. B. (1998). *Principles and practice of structural equation modeling.* New York: Guilford.

Kozol, J. (1992). *Savage inequalities: Children in American schools*. New York: Harper Collins.

Loehlin, J. C. (1998). *Latent variable models: An introduction to factor, path, and structural analysis*. Mahwah, NJ: Lawrence Erlbaum.

Mehan, H., Villanueva, I., Hubbard, L., & Lintz, A. (1996). *Constructing school success: The consequences of untracking low-achieving students*. Cambridge: Cambridge University Press.

Mueller, R. O. (1996). *Basic principles of structural equation modeling: An introduction to LISREL and EQ*. New York: Springer.

Ogbu, J. (1974). *The next generation: An ethnography of education in an urban neighborhood*. New York: Academic Press.

Ogbu, J. (1978). *Minority education and caste: The American system in cross-cultural perspective*. New York: Academic Press.

Ogbu, J. (1982). Cultural discontinuities and schooling. *Anthropology & Education Quarterly, 13*, 290–307.

Ogbu, J. (1985). A cultural ecology of competence among inner-city blacks. In M. B. Spencer & G. K. Brookins (Eds.), *Beginnings: The social and affective development of Black children* (pp. 45–66). Hillsdale, NJ: Lawrence Erlbaum Associates, Inc.

Ogbu, J. (1987). Variability in minority school performance: A problem in search of an explanation. *Anthropology & Education Quarterly, 18*, 312–334.

Ogbu, J. (1991). Minority coping responses and school experience. *Journal of Psychohistory, 18*, 433–456.

Ogbu, J. (1993). Differences in cultural frame of reference. *International Journal of Behavioral Development, 16*, 483–506.

Ogbu, J. (1994). Understanding cultural diversity and learning. *Journal for the Education of the Gifted, 17*, 354–383.

Ogbu, J. (1997). Understanding the school performance of urban Blacks: Some essential background knowledge, children and youth. In H. Walberg (Ed.), *Interdisciplinary perspectives. Issues in children's and families' lives* (pp. 190–222). Thousand Oaks, CA: Sage Publications, Inc.

Ogbu, J. (2003). *Black American students in an affluent suburb: A study of academic disengagement*. Mahwah, NJ: Erlbaum.

Osborne, J. (1997). Race and academic disidentification. *Journal of Educational Psychology, 89*, 728–735.

Phinney, J. S. (1992). The multigroup ethnic identity measure: A new scale for use with diverse groups. *Journal of Adolescent Research, 2*, 156–176.

Reese, L. E., Vera, E. M., & Paikoff, R. L. (1998). Ethnic identity assessment among inner-city African American children: Evaluating the applicability of the Multigroup Ethnic Identity Measure. *Journal of Black Psychology, 63*, 289–303.

Roberts, R., Phinney, J., Masse, L., Chen, R., Roberts, C., & Romero, A. (1999). The structure of ethnic identity of young adolescents from diverse ethnocultural groups. *Journal of Early Adolescence, 19*, 301–322.

Sanders, M. G. (Ed.) (2000). *Schooling students placed at risk: Research, policy, and practice in the education of poor and minority adolescents*. Mahwah, NJ: Lawrence Erlbaum Associates, Inc.

School Accountability Report (2000). *Polytechnic High School*. Long Beach, CA: Long Beach Unified School District.

Solomon, P. (1992). *Black resistance in high school*. Albany: State University of New York Press.

Steele, C. M. (1997). A threat in the air: How stereotypes shape intellectual identity and performance. *American Psychologist, 52*(6), 613–629.

Terrell, F., & Terrell, S. L. (1981). An inventory to measure cultural mistrust among blacks. *Western Journal of Black Studies, 3*, 180–185.

Terrell, F., & Terrell, S. L. (1993). Level of cultural mistrust as function of educational and occupational expectations among Black students. *Adolescence, 28*, 572–578.

Trueba, H. T. (1988). Culturally based explanations of minority students' academic achievement. *Anthropology & Education Quarterly, 19*, 270–287.

U.S. Census Bureau. (1990). *U.S. Gazetteer* [On-line]. Available.

Witherspoon, K. M., Speight, S. L., & Thomas, A. J. (1997). Racial identity attitudes, school achievement, and academic self-efficacy among African American high school students. *Journal of Black Psychology, 23*(4), 344–357.

Part IV

Cross-Cultural Studies of Identity

Situational Ethnicity and Patterns of School Performance among Immigrant and Nonimmigrant Mexican-Descent Students

Maria Eugenia Matute-Bianchi

Persistent school failure among large numbers of Mexican-descent students and other Hispanic groups in the United States is a pervasive, well-documented and enduring problem (The Achievement Council, 1984; Arias, 1986; Brown et al., 1980; California Postsecondary Education Commission [CPEC], 1982; Carter, 1970; Carter & Segura, 1979; Coleman et al., 1966; Ogbu, 1974, 1978; Ogbu & Matute-Bianchi, 1986; U.S. Commission on Civil Rights, 1971). The majority of Hispanic students has suffered and continues to suffer the negative consequences of unsuccessful schooling experiences. As a group, these children participate less and do less well academically than any other group in the Southwest except for Native Americans, with indications of a widening achievement gap between these students and other groups in school (The Achievement Council, 1984).

The history of Mexican-descent students in California schools has been one of segregation and inequality, thus frustrating the achievement of economic and social advancement (Cameron, 1976; Wollenberg, 1976). Many Mexican-descent children continue to attend segregated schools throughout the state, indicating that little progress has been made in integrating these students with more advantaged Anglo students in the public schools (Orfield, 1986). The descriptions of their schooling experiences, both from historical and contemporary perspectives, show clearly that many Mexican-descent students continue to perform less well in school than majority group students despite various intervention efforts to improve their academic achievement. Hence, the cycle of unsuccessful schooling continues for this group—a group which is now the fastest-growing school-age population in California and which is projected to become the state's largest ethnic group, representing almost 35 percent of the population by the year 2010 (Assembly Office of Research, 1986).

Despite the enduring cycle of disproportionate school failure among the Mexican-descent population, there is now evidence to suggest that not all of these students are unsuccessful in school (Matute-Bianchi, 1986; Ogbu, 1974; Romo, 1984; Valverde, 1987). My fieldwork in a California community, which has focused on variations in school performance patterns among Mexican-descent high school students, points to a relationship between academic performance and students' perceptions of ethnic identities (Matute-Bianchi, 1986). I found that more recent Mexican immigrants, as well as the descendants of Mexican immigrants who maintain a separate identity as Mexicanos within the context of their experiences in the United States, tend to perform relatively well in school and in many cases outperform nonimmigrant Chicano students. The emerging documentation of intragroup variability requires that we define the group more precisely, describe more accurately the range of cultural orientations and intragroup variations, and examine critically the traditional single-cause explanations of the underachievement of Mexican-descent students in U.S. schools. The analysis I present here is an attempt to contribute to these efforts.

As researchers have begun to examine the large Mexican-descent population in the United States, taking into account the context of historical and economic developments in both Mexico and the United States, the context of continuing immigration and the impact of subordination, discrimination and limited opportunity structures in the evolution of adaptive strategies that different groups of Mexican-descent persons have made to life in the United States, they have found and have begun to describe differences in a very heterogeneous population (Baca & Bryan, 1980; Bowman, 1981; Browning & de la Garza, 1986; Dinerman, 1982; Keefe & Padilla, 1987; Mines, 1981; Portes & Bach, 1985; Rios-Bustamante, 1981). The function of ethnic identity, for example, among different groups of Mexican-descent people in the United States suggests that there are different meanings for ethnic categories in different social settings for different individuals. As a result, we can observe variations in forms of ethnic identification and consciousness among various groups of Mexican-descent people in the United States: *Mexicanos*, *Mexican Americans*, *Pochos*, *Chicanos*, *Cholos*, *Low Riders*, *Homeboys*, etc. The emphasis on one ethnic category versus another, therefore, is best understood as an adaptive strategy; the specific ethnic label serves as a cognitive resource developed in an interactive response that is strategically exploited and manipulated within specific contexts as the various groups compete for scarce resources (material and/or social) within a system of structured inequality. These ethnic categories, which may change over time and be used for different purposes, are emblematic and have meaning both for members of the group and for analysts of situational contexts in which ethnicity emerges as a salient category. My particular interest in the study presented here is the different forms and functions of ethnic labels and identificational consciousness between immigrant Mexicanos and nonimmigrant Mexican-descent student groups in the United States and their relationship to variations in observed patterns of school performance.

The distinctions between immigrant and nonimmigrant Mexican people in the United States are complex and multifaceted. Yet it has been only relatively recently that researchers have begun to recognize these two groups as distinct communities in the United States or to describe the continuum of adaptive strategies and accommodations various subgroups within these communities have developed in response to the situations they find themselves in here. The earlier literature on Mexican-descent people, whether from assimilationist or ethnic-resistance perspectives, assumed an intragroup homogeneity and a cultural continuum of social, religious, linguistic, and political values. Nonimmigrant Chicanos and other Mexican Americans were viewed as heirs or somewhat distant relatives of a Mexican heritage; immigrant Mexicanos were seen as bearers of the Mexican culture, a source of cultural replenishment for the Mexican-descent population in the United States (Bowman, 1981; Browning & de la Garza, 1986; Rodriguez & Nunez, 1986). The continuum was described in cultural terms with Mexican and American end-points.

Distinctions within the group were described broadly in terms of relative placement along a linear acculturation/non-acculturation dimension, frequently obscuring more important historical and structural antecedents that shaped attitudinal and behavioral distinctions between the two groups, as well as leaving unexamined the different social, economic, and cultural conditions of their experiences in the United States and differences in the manipulation of various ethnic labels as adaptive strategies of accommodations.

John Ogbu and I have proposed a theoretical framework for understanding the differences between immigrant Mexicanos and nonimmigrant Mexican Americans and Chicanos in terms of: (a) differences in minority status, (b) differences in the process of incorporation into the United States, and (c) differences in perceptions of and responses to the experiences of discrimination, limited opportunities and subordination in a system of structured inequality (Ogbu, 1978; Ogbu & Matute-Bianchi, 1986).

While more conventional theories of school performance explain differences between immigrant and nonimmigrant Mexican-descent students in terms of levels of acculturation and assimilation of American culture versus retention of Mexican cultural content, we have proposed an alternative interpretation (Ogbu, 1978, 1982, 1983; Ogbu & Matute-Bianchi, 1986). In our view, what distinguishes the two groups, in general, is their perception of their economic position in the United States as a subordinate, stigmatized minority and their responses to the legitimating, racist ideologies directed against them. Both immigrant Mexicanos and nonimmigrant persons of Mexican descent (Mexican Americans and

Chicanos) are victims of instrumental and expressive exploitation, but they manifest different perceptions, interpretations and responses to such exploitation. The immigrant and nonimmigrant groups also utilize different strategies to respond to the barriers to assimilation and mobility. With respect to education, the response of many nonimmigrants has been to deemphasize striving for academic achievement as an essential component of their efforts to succeed. Many immigrant Mexicanos, on the other hand, see academic success and school credentials as very important elements in their strategies to improve their employment status and access to material benefits (see Ogbu & Matute-Bianchi, 1986, pp. 79–98).

Many earlier studies of Mexican-descent students in U.S. schools noted the persistence of "traditional" Mexican cultural traits and identified such traits as impeding the educational progress of these students. Intervention strategies designed to improve the educational performance of Mexican American children (e.g., Americanization and English-language training) assumed that greater knowledge of English and American cultural values would lead to more positive experiences in school. In fact, even the more recent federal Bilingual Education Act in 1968 was premised on the single-cause explanation of limited proficiency in speaking English as the primary cause of school failure among Mexican-descent students, thus obscuring the reality that many of these children are U.S.-born English speakers. These studies and the educational policies they generated assumed that virtually all persons of Mexican descent in the United States were relatively recent immigrants who lacked sufficient knowledge of the English language and the American culture. The academic progress of Mexican-descent students was perceived to be linked to higher levels of acculturation to the American mainstream and to fluency in English. The reality, of course, is that many people of Mexican descent have been in the United States for several generations, are fluent English speakers and are thoroughly familiar with the values and lifestyle of the American mainstream, yet continue to experience disproportionate school failure. The earlier literature also emphasized the school failure of Mexican-descent students and did not address the fact that some, albeit proportionately fewer, Mexican-descent students have succeeded in school.

The Mexican-descent population is, indeed, a heterogeneous one, and there are distinct subgroups within the population, manifesting different experiences and different adaptations to and strategies for life in the United States. For example, Chicanos have developed a distinct ethnic consciousness that is neither Mexican nor American. It is an identity system in opposition to the American mainstream and has served as a strategic tool of resistance to the systemic exploitation, both instrumental and expressive, that people of Mexican descent have experienced in the United States. Others, as Browning and de la Garza (1986) noted, have had different experiences during different periods in U.S. history, with some members achieving greater success and mobility than others and with some becoming more integrated into U.S. society than others. As a result, there are class differences, differences in cultural orientation and differences in ethnic identification and consciousness, as well as differences between immigrants and nonimmigrants in this large and growing population.

VARIABILITY IN PATTERNS OF SCHOOL ACHIEVEMENT AMONG MEXICAN-DESCENT STUDENTS: A COMMUNITY STUDY

The analysis which follows draws upon my fieldwork in a largely agricultural community in the California central coast area, carried out between 1983 and 1985. It focuses on the differences between successful immigrant Mexicano students and unsuccessful nonimmigrant Chicano students at a high school that will be referred to here as Field High School. The study describes very diverse, distinctive social groups of Mexican-descent students within a single school, and it indicates differences in these students' expectations regarding the value of formal education in their adult lives, their self-definitions, and their perceptions of success and failure, as well as differences in the way the students are perceived by the school community. I interviewed a subsample of 35 Mexican-descent students over a two-year period to assess their aspirations for the future, their perceptions of their adult future, their knowledge of adult occupations, their understanding of strategies to achieve adult success, their definitions of adult success and failure and their perceptions of the value of schooling in achieving their expressed goals. I identified a range of ethnic identities and behaviors. Five major categories emerged within which most of these students could be placed: (a) recent Mexican immigrants, (b) Mexican-oriented, (c) Mexican American, (d) Chicano and (e) Cholo.

In the analysis here, I highlight the pattern of school success I observed among immigrant Mexican-oriented students and the pattern of school failure among nonimmigrant Chicanos. I discuss these patterns within the context of differences in students' perceptions of their adult futures and differences in staff perceptions of these two groups of Mexican-descent students in the school. My analysis also indicates that the students in the Mexican American category do not fit neatly into either the immigrant or nonimmigrant ethnic identificational system. The findings raised important new research questions and policy considerations.

THE COMMUNITY'S HISTORICAL AND STRUCTURAL LEGACY

The historical and structural forces contextualizing this study have left the community with a legacy of paternalistic patterns of interaction between an Anglo majority and the Mexican minority, dating back to the 1848 annexation of California by the United States. Between 1848 and 1955 the region was transformed from a pastoral *Californio/Mexicano* cattle-raising economy to a predominantly Anglo-American farming community specializing in the production of apples, strawberries, berries and lettuce. The development of large-scale agriculture in the area has always depended on cheap immigrant labor, beginning with Chinese laborers in the 1860s, followed by Japanese workers at the turn of the century and later by Filipino workers in the 1920s. Although Mexicans have always been used as a source of exploitable agricultural labor in the area, they did not begin to settle permanently there until after World War II and the development of the Bracero Program. In this postwar period, technological changes in agricultural production created a demand for more Mexican labor to satisfy the region's expansion into one of the richest agricultural regions in California.

Although they made up a relatively small, ignored minority in the region prior to 1946, Mexican people have always been a presence in the community, albeit as a stigmatized subordinate group. With the transformation from the pastoral *Californio/Mexicano* society to a predominantly Anglo-American agricultural economy dependent on a racial division of labor, the social hierarchy was transformed into one in which Mexicans and subsequent nonwhite immigrant laborers were relegated to subordinate positions within all the major institutions in the community. The transformation provided a paternalistic context of inter-ethnic social relations, with Anglo Americans dominating successive influxes of nonwhite immigrant labor.

During this early period there were few significant differences between Mexican-origin residents and the occasional migrant Mexican in search of seasonal work. In 1900, the Mexican-descent population comprised only 118 persons, or 3.3 percent of a total community population of 3,528; by 1940, the Mexican-descent population had increased to 757 persons or 8.4 percent out of a total community of 8,937 (Donato, 1987, p. 40). A review of city directories from this period indicates very few businesses owned by Mexican-descent people, a lack that can be viewed as a result of both their sparse numbers and a discriminatory opportunity structure. In 1930, there were no Spanish-surnamed graduates of the community's one high school, Field High School; by 1940, out of a total of 202 graduates, only 3 were Spanish-surnamed (Donato, 1987, p. 54). By all indications, the Mexican-origin population in this region between

1900 and World War II was an invisible minority, excluded from virtually all aspects of the Anglo-American society.

It was not until well after World War II and the beginning of the Bracero Program that the Mexican-descent population began to grow rapidly in the area. By the 1960s the increasing population of Mexican-descent people began to develop some internal differentiation among those who were long-term residents and those who were relative new-comers (Takash, personal communication, 1988). By the late 1960s, there was a phenomenal increase in the Mexican-descent population, and the community's stable pattern of paternalistic interethnic relations began to change. Not only was the Mexican presence greater, but the community found it was not immune to the larger social and political influences of the Civil Rights Movement, with its mobilization of ethnic consciousness and the ensuing controversies over desegregation, bilingual education, equal educational opportunity and affirmative action. This once quiet, conservative Anglo-American farming community entered the decade of the 1970s as a community of turmoil and interethnic tension.

The schools, in particular, were the focus of continuing conflict in the 1970s and 1980s, serving as a focal point of heated school/community controversies, as well as reflecting an emerging agenda for change among an increasingly more vocal Mexican American leadership. During this period, the conflicts have been heightened by periodic labor unrest in the agricultural fields, a bitter, protracted cannery strike and litigation against the city aimed at political enfranchisement of the Mexican-descent population in the community. The intensity of the conflicts has, of course, been stimulated by the dramatic increase in the Mexican-descent population in the schools as well as in the community as a whole. By 1980, the Mexican-descent student population represented the major-ity in 13 of the district's 24 schools and composed 51 percent of the community's population of 30,000. As the school district's proportion of Spanish-surnamed grew, their social and academic adjustment and devel-opment became a focus of great tension and debate. Issues of concern centered primarily on efforts to desegregate racially impacted schools and the development of bilingual education. The politics of this highly charged arena tended to obscure the differences between the immigrant and nonimmigrant Mexican-descent people in the community. The lead-ership which emerged on behalf of this population came from English-speaking Mexican-American and Chicano professionals, business people and activists (Donato, 1987).

Since the 1970s the turmoil of ethnic conflict in this community has been accompanied by a tremendous increase in the number of immigrant Mexicanos, of both legal and illegal status, seeking work in the fields or canneries. The Mexicanos tend to function in separate occupational contexts from nonimmigrant Chicanos and Mexican Americans who, if employed, are more likely to be found in blue-collar or semiskilled occupations. There is some indication that Mexicanos participate in separate social and organizational contexts, e.g., attending different masses at the same church and different dances in the community and congregating in different parks and plazas. Additionally, there is now a small but very visible Mexican-descent middle class in the community, represented by a few merchants, professionals, salaried white-collar workers and school district employees (administrators and teachers). Such internal differentiation within the community's Mexican-descent population reflects differences between immigrants and nonimmigrants in terms of both social and structural contexts in which they operate, as well as social class differences within the nonimmigrant group. Although there is now a small business and professional class within this population, the overwhelming majority are employed in low status, marginal jobs in agriculture and are stratified at the bottom of the employment structure, as indicated by the community's publicly employed labor force (see Table 18.1).

These differences represent a complexity in the social context which defies easy description. On the one hand, there are observable differences among the various groups in terms of behavior (dress, language, self-presentation, etc.) and attitudes; on the other hand, there is a sense of collective peoplehood as members of a generic Mexican "family." This presumed bond of kinship is often invoked during times of intense controversy over such issues as local elections, immigration, bilingual education and litigation strategies against the city or school district. Hence, my impression is that the bonding agent in this community among the Mexican-descent people is their sense of sharing a common stigma as a low-status subordinate minority group. There are times when the bonding is more palpable and other times, more diffuse.

Table 18.1 Field community workforce composition and distribution, full-time employees, 1984

Job category	Total employees (n = 232)	White %	Hispanic %	Asian American %	American Indian %
Officials and administrators	11	100	0	0	0
Professionals	29	100	0	0	0
Technicians	21	76	10	14	0
Protective services	41	73	17	10	0
Para-professionals	9	77	11	11	0
Office and clerical	41	78	15	7	0
Skilled craft	43	65	28	5	2
Service / maintenance	37	43	49	8	0

Source: Equal Employment Opportunity Commission, State and Local Government Information (EEO-4), Community of Field.

CATEGORIES OF MEXICAN-DESCENT STUDENTS

There is a generic category of "Mexican" within Field High School and it is this category which is accorded lower status than Filipino Americans and Japanese Americans, the other obvious minority student groups in the school. Mexican-descent students are particularly sensitive to the negative perceptions of, and stereotypes attributed to, people of Mexican descent. While students recognize that not everyone holds pejorative views of Mexican people and culture, it is generally accepted that people of Mexican descent face discrimination, prejudice and other difficulties in much greater proportion than other groups in the school and community.

Despite membership in the low-status "Mexican" ranking in the school, not all students of Mexican descent are perceived to be the same. The ethnographic data indicate that many persons within the school community differentiate among the Mexican-descent clientele in the school and in the community, reflecting the great variability and cultural heterogeneity within the group. The five-category typology that I use below to describe the modal characteristics within the heterogenous "Mexican" student enrollment at Field High emerged from interviews with teachers, counselors, administrators, teacher aides, and Mexican-descent students, as well as observations of classes and school functions.

Recent Mexican Immigrant

"Recent" immigrant, according to my usage, means one who has arrived within the last three to five years. Students in this category are also identified as "*recien llegados*," "Mexican nationals," "citizens of Mexico," "Mexicanos" and "*mojados*." These students identify themselves as Mexicanos and refer to Mexico as home. They are Spanish-speaking, Mexican-born and are frequently identified as Limited English Proficient (LEP) by the school, according to diagnostic English placement tests. These students are identified by other Mexican-descent students and by some teachers and school staff as dressing differently from the rest of the student body and their clothing style is considered unstylish by other students. Recent immigrants frequently cite economic opportunity as the reason for their having come to the United States. Some have come here legally, others illegally. Some have established a relatively permanent base in the community and do not migrate seasonally back to Mexico.

Students within this group make distinctions among themselves, using the class-based reference framework of Mexico (e.g., rural versus urban, upper-class versus working-class, *mestizo* versus *indio*). Students in this immigrant Mexican category vary in their level of proficiency in Spanish. Some are functioning below grade level in Spanish, perhaps at the

406 Maria Eugenia Matute-Bianchi

fourth- or fifth-grade level. These students are usually placed in a special curriculum that includes beginning English as a Second Language (ESL). Students functioning approximately at grade level in Spanish are typically enrolled in one or two ESL classes, bilingual math, bilingual science, and in beginning English reading. Among these recent immigrants, those who are relatively proficient in Spanish (both oral and written) tend to be more academically successful than those who are functioning well below grade level in Spanish. Hence, proficiency in their primary language appears to be related to their subsequent academic experience in the school. Many of these more proficient students have successfully completed *primaria* (grammar school) and in some cases, have entered the precollegiate curriculum of the *secundaria* or the *preparatoria* in Mexico.

Mexican-Oriented

Students in the second category are also self-identified as "Mexicanos," but they are distinct from the first group in several obvious ways. Most of the students in this group, which I have labeled "Mexican-oriented," tend to be bilingual. Because they have received most of their schooling in the United States, they are more likely than recent immigrants to be adept in carrying on academic work in English-only classes. They use English and Spanish interchangeably with their peers, but speak English exclusively with most of the school personnel. Typically, these students are identified as Fluent English Proficient (FEP) and speak Spanish in the home and in other community contexts. Many of the fluent English speakers in this group are found in the general or remedial classes, but not in the ESL or beginning reading courses. Many of the Spanish-surname students in the college prep track in the school are from this Mexican-oriented category. The most active and visible Mexican-descent students in the school are in this category, especially those active in the leadership of *Sociedad Bilngue*, considered to be the most active club of Mexican-descent students in the school. Their parents are Mexican-born immigrants, typically from the Mexican states of Jalisco, Michoacan, Guanajuato, and San Luis Potosi.

Students in this group maintain a strong identity as Mexicanos although many have lived most of their lives in this country. They see themselves as being different from the recent Mexican immigrant, Mexican-American, Chicano and Cholo groups in the school. They usually cite pride in their Mexican heritage as a primary difference between themselves and the more "*agabachados*" (Americanized) students of Mexican descent in the school. They do not identify themselves as Mexican Americans or as Chicanos or Cholos. They view the ethnic labels Chicano and Cholo as derogatory and would not use them as self-descriptors; these labels are viewed as symbols of gang membership and a host of offensive qualities.

Frequently, these students are Mexican born and have lived in the United States for at least five years, and usually longer. They have attended junior high and elementary school here, although some may have attended the first year or two of *primaria* in Mexico. Their manner of self-presentation, especially style of clothing and language usage, is considered more "American," but is not what is considered "quaddie" or "preppie" at the school.

Mexican American

Students in the "Mexican American" group are almost always U.S.-born English speakers. Students in this category can be further subdivided into various groupings: (a) some are Mexican in last name only, are very acculturated and do not manifest any of the overt ethnic symbols associated with other Mexican-descent students; (b) others, while acknowledging their Mexican parentage, see themselves as having moved away from a more traditional Mexican culture and as now being members of a contemporary, more advantaged American present; and (c) still others in the group can be labeled "cultural codeswitchers" or "cultural switch-hitters" for they function as Mexicanos at home and Anglos at school. As a category, the Mexican Americans are much more American-oriented than either of the two previously described student categories. They are likely to be described by the school personnel as "totally acculturated." They often do not speak Spanish well or, even if they do, prefer to speak in English at school. There is a range of oral Spanish-language proficiency within this group, depending on the extent to which the student must use Spanish in the home and community context.

Students in this category see differences between themselves and the recent Mexican immigrant and the Mexican-oriented students, as well as between themselves and the Chicano and Cholo groups. They view the label Chicano as an offensive one and consider it to be synonymous with other low-status labels, such as Cholo and Low Rider. Some of the active, most esteemed Mexican-descent students in the school can be identified as members of this category. They tend to participate more in the mainstream school clubs and activities than either of the Mexican-immigrant student groups do. They are members of clubs and activity efforts in which Whites and Japanese American students participate. For the most part, they do not participate in the organizations and activities that are considered more Mexican, such as the *Sociedad Bilingue* or more Chicano, such as Mexican Americans Taking Action (MATA). With the exception of the "switch-hitters" in this category, the Mexican Americans appear more ambivalent, more uncommitted to ethnic labels than students in the other categories. They tend not to call attention to themselves in ethnically explicit ways observed among other groups of students. Additionally, they are not explicitly immigrant or nonimmigrant (as these terms are defined in this book), manifesting neither modal orientation.

Chicano

The term "Chicano" has been selected to differentiate another subgroup of Mexican-descent students from the above three categories. However, it must be understood that the term Chicano in this school community is not salient, nor does it carry the political connotations of the term as it is used in university settings or academic discourse. The term as it is used in this analysis serves to differentiate among the distinct groupings of Mexican-descent students in the school population. These students are typically English-speaking and usually at least the second generation of their family in the United States. The Chicano category comprises students who are among the most alienated Mexican-descent students in the school. They tend not to participate in school activities, exhibit poor attendance and performance in class and are usually described by teachers and staff as being unsuccessful or uninterested in school. Not all students who could be considered members of this subgroup are unsuccessful students, but many of the Mexican-descent students who are considered to be unsuccessful by school-defined criteria emerge from this subgroup.

When asked, these students will first identify themselves as Mexican or Mexicano, but they do not find the term Chicano offensive or derogatory. Often they will call themselves "homeboys" or "homegirls." Academically successful Mexican-descent students—those who attend classes regularly, participate in mainstream activities and who generally conform to school expectations for academic achievement—they call "schoolboys" and "schoolgirls," especially those from the Mexican American category. These terms are used derisively. Another term used by Chicano students to ridicule the "schoolboys" and "schoolgirls" is "Wannabe," which is understood as meaning "wants to be white" or "wants to be Anglo." "Wannabe" was frequently used to describe Mexican-descent girls who dated Anglo boys or who associated almost exclusively with an Anglo peer group.

Many teachers describe these students as being more concerned with loyalty to the Chicano group and displaying an attitude and behavioral orientation that indicates apathy or outright defiance of the school culture. If Chicano students are active in any club or organization, it is the MATA club, but club membership is small and the level of activity minimal. Students in this group may try to do well in school and often declare a desire to do well in school, but they behave in ways that are counterproductive to academic achievement: their characteristics include frequent absences, disruptive behavior, failure to bring books to class and to do homework, and failure to pass enough classes each year to maintain their academic standing.

Cholo

The "Cholo" subgroup is by far the smallest of the five categories of Mexican-descent students at Field High School (almost to the point of disappearing from the school community at the time I conducted field-work), but it is the most distinguishable because of certain obvious stylistic cultural symbols that are readily identifiable to the entire school community. Particular kinds of pants, shirts, shoes, make-up styles and ways of walking are identified as distinctly Cholo. Visually, this particular style of dress stands out in the school community and identifies the wearer as Cholo/Chola.

Students who affect the stylistic symbols of this category are frequently identified by others as "gang-oriented," "gang-bangers" or "gang-sympathizers." Not all students who manifest the sartorial symbols of the Cholo are members of gangs, but because they affect the Cholo style they are usually considered to be sympathetic to Cholos. The manner of the Cholo style is a distinct symbol of an identity which is definitely not "Mexican" or "American." Cholos are also often called "Low Riders," which is another term used to describe Mexican-descent youth who drive distinctively styled cars. Low Riders are not necessarily gang members or gang-affiliated, but are generally perceived as such by others. Chicanos and Cholos are held in low esteem by the other Mexican-descent students in the school, as well as by mainstream students, who often express fear or contempt of what they recognize as Cholo.

Differences among these categories of Mexican-descent students are sometimes quite explicit, as is the case between recently arrived Mexican immigrants and Mexican Americans, or blurred, as between Chicanos and Cholos. Additionally, within each group there are further refinements which can be discerned. However, in general, these five major groupings are the most obvious within which the majority of Mexican-descent students in this school can be placed.

SCHOOL FAILURE AMONG MEXICAN-DESCENT STUDENTS

There has been a virtual shift over a 13-year period in the relative proportions of White and Spanish-surname students enrolled at Field High School. In 1971, the Spanish-surname enrollment was 34 percent of the total school. By 1984, it composed 57 percent of the total. The

White enrollment in 1971 was 60 percent and by 1984 it was reduced to 33 percent.

During this period of rapid increase in the Spanish-surname population, the proportion of students entering the ninth grade from one of the district's local junior high schools who were reading substantially below grade level increased. School documents reporting the reading levels of all entering ninth grade students from 1976 to 1982 indicate that 34 percent were reading at the sixth-grade level or below. In 1982, the percentage of students reading at the sixth-grade level or below had jumped to 50 percent of those entering as freshmen. While these data are not identified by ethnicity or language dominance, but rather as aggregate data for all students entering from the local feeder junior high schools in the district, it is important to remember that the school district and high school were both experiencing large increases in Mexican-descent students.

Perhaps a clearer indication of the patterns of school failure is reflected in the attrition rate in the class of 1985. When the class entered Field High School in 1981, 386 students, or 60 percent of the class ($n = 643$), were Spanish-surname students. Four years later, 232 of the original 386 Spanish-surname students entering as freshmen were identified as dropouts, reflecting a 60 percent attrition rate.

An analysis of the dropouts by place of birth indicates that the majority (61 percent) were born in the United States and, within this group, that 78 percent were born in the local county or an adjacent one (see Table 18.2). Most of the dropouts, moreover, had entered Field High School from one of the local junior high schools (see Table 18.3).

Another indication of school failure is found in the list of ninth grade demotions. Regularly enrolled ninth grade students in the school are expected to earn at least 40 credits by the beginning of their sophomore year to qualify for sophomore standing. If they fail to earn enough credits at the end of their ninth grade year, they are demoted in standing. Such students will consider themselves sophomores, but in order to earn the credits to graduate with their class, they will need to pass enough classes in the next three years, as well as make up the credits they failed to earn as

Table 18.2 Field High School, class of 1985: non-continuing Spanish-surname students by place of birth.

Born in Santa Cruz County	91
Born in adjacent county	20
Born in California	20
Born out of state	11
Born in Mexico	90

Table 18.3 Non-continuing Spanish-surname students, Field High School, in the class of 1985 (*n* = 232)

Category	Number of Drops
Entered from local junior high	184
Entered from school outside district	20
Entered from local parochial school	6
Entered from Mexico	20
Other	2

ninth graders. Students can do this by attending summer school and, if need be, by going to adult school when they turn 17.

The school does not keep official records on those students who are demoted at the end of their ninth-grade year, but unofficial tallies of ninth-grade students demoted at the end of their freshman year in June 1985 indicate that there were a total of 105 such students. As of September 1985, there were 80 Spanish-surname demotees (76 percent of all demotees), while Spanish-surname students made up less than 60 percent of the class. Such students can be considered "at risk" for non-continuation. They will have already begun to manifest other behaviors associated with poor school performance, such as frequent absenteeism and poor performance in class. Once this pattern has been established, many students find it difficult to develop and maintain more successful responses to the demands of schooling. Many of these ninth-grade demotees are located in the Chicano category.

SCHOOL SUCCESS AMONG MEXICAN-DESCENT STUDENTS

Many students of Mexican descent at Field School are successful in meeting the demands of the school program. In fact, there is considerable evidence indicating that some Mexican-descent students are very successful in school. Mexican-descent students are enrolled in college preparatory courses, are active in school activities, earn above-average grades, maintain regular attendance and go on to college—all school-defined measures of success.

An examination of the 1983–84 class lists for college-preparatory English, mathematics and science reveals that Spanish-surname students are represented in this higher-track curriculum. Most of these students could be identified as either Mexican-oriented or Mexican American; virtually no Chicanos or Cholos were found in college-preparatory courses.

One of the best indications of success among Mexican-descent students, especially among the Mexican-oriented, is reflected in the class rankings compiled at the end of the senior year. An examination of these rankings for the years 1983, 1984, and 1985 reveals that Spanish-surname students are represented in the top 10 percent of their graduating classes. In 1983, the top 10 percent of the graduating class was made up of 38 students of whom 26 percent ($n = 10$) were Spanish-surname students. Of these 10 students, 7 were girls and 3 were boys. Although 26 percent underrepresents the proportion of Spanish-surname students in the class (which was more than 50 percent), it does indicate that a not-insignificant proportion of these students were academically successful in their four years at the school.

The class of 1984 had 375 students in the graduating class, of whom 53 percent ($n = 197$) were Spanish-surname students. This class had 37 students in the top 10 percent, of whom 35 percent ($n = 13$) were Spanish-surname students. Moreover, there were 83 students in the entire class with a grade point of 3.0 (an average of "B") or above. Of these latter students, 42 percent ($n = 32$) were Spanish-surname students. Once again, somewhat more than two-thirds of the high-achieving Spanish-surname students were female: 22 girls and 10 boys.

In the class of 1985, there were 377 students who received diplomas, of whom 57 percent ($n = 214$) were Spanish-surname students. The top 10 percent of the graduating class was composed of 37 students, of whom 43 percent ($n = 16$) were Spanish-surname students. Of these 16 Spanish-surname students, 81 percent ($n = 13$) were girls and 19 percent ($n = 3$) were boys.

An examination of the Spanish-surname students in the top 10 percent of the classes of 1984 and 1985 indicates that these students had been regularly enrolled in college-prep courses during their four years in the school, had good attendance, were active in school activities and had plans to attend college upon graduation. In fact, many of these students received substantial scholarships to attend leading four-year institutions of higher education. They were considered by their teachers and counselors to be hard working, conscientious, motivated students. Virtually all of these students identified themselves as Mexicanos and could be described as students in the Mexican-oriented category. A few others could be categorized as Mexican Americans.

The above data clearly indicate that the Mexican-oriented girls consistently were more conspicuous in the rankings of the top 10 percent in at least three of the most recent graduating classes. These same girls were the ones who provided most of the leadership in the *Sociedad Bilingue* and were among the most visible, active, and esteemed Mexican-descent students in the school. This apparent pattern raises important gender implications which warrant more careful scrutiny in any future studies of this kind.

What is clear from the data presented thus far is that academic persistence and success are much more likely to be found among the immigrant Mexican-oriented students and that poor performance is more likely to be found among the nonimmigrant Chicano/Cholo groups. This is not to suggest that the patterns of success and failure are restricted to these groups. However, the data do indicate that variations in patterns of school success and failure reflect a continuum in the variations in ethnic identities observed among the Mexican-descent students in the school and that these variations are broadly reflective of the differences between immigrant versus nonimmigrant accommodations to the demands of schooling. The one group that does not fit easily into either of these two modal patterns of success or failure is the group I have described as Mexican Americans. This group will be discussed later in the context of the research and policy issues they raise.

STAFF PERCEPTIONS OF MEXICAN-DESCENT STUDENTS

The problem of poor performance among many Mexican-descent students is one that is generally recognized by teachers, counselors, administrators, and staff. Perceptions of what accounts for the poor performance, which vary greatly among the school personnel, include: migrancy and frequent travels back and forth to Mexico during the school year, lack of parental support and interest in school, lack of successful role models, poor school habits. and a peer culture which rejects school achievement.

Many adults in the school community also recognize the heterogeneity within the large Mexican-descent student clientele and acknowledge that some of the schools' most visibly successful students are of Mexican descent. Teachers may identify a Spanish-surname student as the recipient of a scholarship to a prestigious Ivy League college or cite the recent accomplishments of a Spanish-surname student elected to a student body office as examples of Mexican-descent students who have been successful in school.

Many teachers describe the differences they have observed among the Mexican-descent students in general terms, distinguishing between those students who are "more acculturated to American culture" and those who are less so. Others describe the differences in terms of those who have been in the United States longer and who speak more English. Only a few of the school personnel link up the strong, positive Mexicano identity with the academically successful Mexican-descent students, but most identify the unsuccessful Mexican-descent students in terms of their perceived Chicano or "anti-school" orientations.

In general, the stereotypic view of the "more Mexican" students is that they are more polite and respectful, more serious about school, more eager to please, more motivated and much less sophisticated in ways to undermine school rules and practices than are "more Americanized" Mexican-descent students, especially Chicano/Cholo students. When asked to describe the differences between students more oriented to Mexico and Mexican culture and Chicano students, for example, many adults described Chicano students as "less interested in school," "more irresponsible," "more smart-mouth," "more street tough," and "less motivated" than students they perceive to be "more Mexican." As one teacher with more than 20 years in the school said:

> The "more Mexican" students in the school, the ones who are active in the *Sociedad Bilingue*, for example, are high-achievement-oriented. They take leadership roles in the school, they get good grades, they follow the school rules, they are law abiding. We now have so many students like this that it is no longer a surprise among the staff that Mexican students can succeed in school. The typical Chicano students, on the other hand, are associated in the school with a "school isn't important" attitude. Doing well in school among this group is not encouraged. In fact, it is derogatory to [be viewed as doing] well in school. To do well would mean running the risk of being called a "schoolboy." Among Chicanos, loyalty to the group is high. And this is a problem that sometimes leads to gang involvement.

Sociedad Bilingue is generally recognized among the staff as being the preeminent "Mexican" organization on the campus, serving as the most visible organizational symbol of Mexican students' involvement in the school. The club is active throughout the year, raising funds for scholarships which the group awards at the end of the year to students going on to college, organizing dances, sponsoring cultural events such as *Semana de la Raza* during the *Cinco de Mayo* week in May and planning field trips to university campuses to encourage student interest in college. The school staff is divided on the importance of this club on the campus. Some view the club as promoting "too much" Mexican culture and being "too activist-oriented." They think it should, instead, be promoting "acculturation into the campus mainstream." Those who hold this view tend to express the belief that rapid acquisition of English and acculturation into the "American mainstream" are the most important vehicles for school success. They see *Sociedad Bilingue* as "maintaining cultural separatism" between Mexican students and the mainstream students in the school. Another criticism is that the club is "too disruptive of the academic program in the school" by encouraging students to be "too active in the club's activities and not [active] enough in their school work." A few see the club as providing a valuable resource and sense of belonging for the

Mexican students in the school and express the wish that other clubs would function as actively for other groups in the school.

Sociedad Bilingue was founded in the late 1970s by a group of recent Mexican immigrant and Mexican-oriented students in the school who wanted an organization to bridge the apparent social distance between themselves and the Anglos in the school. Hence, the name *Sociedad Bilngue* was coined. Initial efforts were aimed at having both "Anglos" and "Mexicans" in the club. However, the club's membership has been virtually exclusively "Mexican" and the club's activities attract the Mexican-descent students, particularly the Mexican-oriented students in the school. The organization is viewed by the general student body as the club for the Mexican students.

A teacher with more than eight years at Field School indicated that there are now so many Mexican-descent students in the school that the staff has been "forced" to make distinctions among this growing student population. The general image of Mexican-descent students, according to this teacher, has changed from a distinctly negative one to one that is now more positive or at least more "ambivalent":

> When I first got here the image was one that was very electrically charged. Now it is more one of we have our good Mexicans and we've got our bad ones. It was a time of militancy when I got here [early 1970s] and now in the Reagan era ethnic groups are less militant. Also, the passing of fashion of the Cholo and Pachuco image here in the school makes the Mexican presence in general much less threatening. Also, we have had some very successful Mexican students here. This has forced people here to look more closely at this population.

Many of the more "Mexican" students are perceived by the staff to have difficulty in school. However, these troubles are perceived differently from the difficulties attributed to Chicano/Cholo students who are unsuccessful in school. The unsuccessful "more Mexican" students are perceived to have difficulty in school because they do not have satisfactory English-language skills and/or because they lack competence in academic skills in Spanish and English and because they are perceived to come from a rural peasant Mexican background which has not prepared them to meet the demands of schooling in the United States. Despite such difficulties in school, these students are frequently described by the staff as "shy but unfailingly courteous," "cheerful," "grateful for what you can do for them" and "well-behaved."

Chicano and Cholo students who are unsuccessful, on the other hand, are perceived to be unsuccessful because they lack the "motivation, interest, and respect for schooling." They are perceived to fail in school because they reject what the school has to offer. They are also viewed as more "apathetic," "sullen," "withdrawn," "mistrusting," and "discourteous" in general than are the "more Mexican" students. They are likely to be described as coming from families unsupportive or uninterested in the academic success of their children. Successful Mexican-descent students, in contrast, are described as hard-working, goal-oriented, respectful, active, conscientious students who come from supportive, intact families. These students are typically not described with reference to their identity as "Mexicanos." Some adults appear to be keenly sensitive to differences that Mexican-descent people in the school see in themselves—differences that are often too subtle to be noticed or are overlooked by many in the school. Other adults appear to be less aware of these differences or describe them in terms of a continuum of "less," "more," and "totally acculturated."

There are differences, then, in the perceptions school personnel have of students who are easily identified as immigrants (the recent Mexican immigrant and the Mexican-oriented) and those who can be identified as nonimmigrants (the Chicanos and Cholos). The differences are marked. It could be that the very behaviors which are rewarded among the more "Mexican" students are those which do not violate the cultural expectations of the mainstream of appropriate "Mexican" behavior. That is, the cultural expectation in the school is that the "more Mexican" students are obedient, respectful, timid and appreciative. Mexican-descent students manifesting these behaviors are positively acknowledged. Other behaviors, such as being outspoken, assertive, critical, and aggressive—behaviors that are often esteemed in Anglo students—are not associated with these Mexican students. The same behaviors, however, could be applied to the more Chicano-oriented students but with a different interpretation. That is, common staff perceptions are that Chicanos are "smart-mouth" (outspoken), "discourteous" (critical), and "resistant" (assertive), etc. It could very well be that these descriptors of student behavior are related to staff perceptions of what is appropriate behavior for "successful" and "unsuccessful" low-status Mexican-descent students in the school. Mexican-descent students succeed in school because they conform to what is considered the culturally appropriate behavior of the "successful" Mexican student: obedient, appreciative and docile. Chicanos fail in school because they, too, conform to what is considered the culturally appropriate behavior for them: defiant, disobedient, rude and lazy. Interestingly, the failure of the Mexican immigrant or "more Mexican" student is perceived to be the result of factors essentially beyond the student's control (migrancy, rural background, poverty, etc.), while the failure of Chicano students is perceived to be the result of characteristics in the individual students themselves.

Another interesting aspect of some of the staff's perceptions of differences in Mexican-descent students is their emphasis on "less acculturated" versus "more acculturated." The staff makes no discernible linkages between the various forms of Mexican identity systems present in the school and the various patterns of school performance and participation found in the Mexican-descent students. These kinds of staff perceptions were much more common among those who were less knowledgeable and sensitive to the subtleties and nuances of the ethnic peer cultures in the school. Such perceptions could be associated with conventional interpretations linking academic success and social mobility to assimilation and the "melting pot" ideology. The contradiction to these conventional explanations presented by the obvious success of the bilingual students with a strong identity as Mexicanos was not readily apparent to teachers and staff members.

DIFFERENCES IN PERCEPTIONS OF THE FUTURE AMONG SUCCESSFUL AND UNSUCCESSFUL STUDENTS

Successful Mexican-Oriented Students

The more successful Mexican-descent students tend to emerge from the Mexican-oriented category; they are achievement-oriented and goal-oriented, even if they lack a specific career goal. They want to be successful. Moreover, they see a definite connection between their experiences in high school and their success as adults. Virtually all of these students express an interest in going on to college, although some indicate that family circumstances (e.g., return to Mexico, financial difficulties) may make this difficult or impossible. Many of these students look to adults in the school—Anglo as well as Mexican descent—as role models of success. They recognize a practical value in meeting the demands of high school and manifest a marked sense of purpose in doing well in school. They know generally which are the "right" courses to take in order to go on to college; they know that it is important for them to be active in school activities in order to go on to college, and they have a generalized understanding that what they do today will serve them well later on in life.

Many of these students were born in Mexico and received their earliest schooling there. Others were born in the United States but traveled frequently back and forth to Mexico, typically having an extended family network on both sides of the border. They had received virtually all of their schooling in the California Central Coast region incorporating the Pajaro Valley. All were the sons and daughters of agricultural workers, cannery workers or laborers in some kind of low-skilled occupation.

For the successful Mexican-descent students, adult success is often defined in terms of "having a nice car, a nice house, a nice job," and enough "money that you don't have to worry about it anymore." A few of the students expressed a definite occupational choice, such as interior designer, engineer, or lawyer. But for the most part, the students were no more specific than expressing an interest in working in "a big company," "in a large corporation," "with something in computers," or "for a bank." One student, a senior going on to a University of California campus, said: "I guess I want to hold a job that pays at least $10 an hour, a job where I can make at least more than my brother [a computer assembly line worker]."

Another, also a twelfth grader, said: "I would like to have a very good job where I could get good money and meet new people, like working in a bank or as an accountant." Another senior said: "I don't know exactly what. Probably working for a big company, like the telephone company."

When asked about their purpose in going to school, the successful Mexican-descent students expressed a strong belief in the linkage between doing well in school and being a successful adult, in "being someone" and "earning good money." As one eleventh grader expressed it: "*Es una preparación que te esta llevando a pasos mas grandes* [It is a preparation which is taking you to greater things]."

These students definitely feel motivated to do well in school so that they can have what they perceive to be greater opportunities for higher-paying, more satisfying jobs than their parents. Another eleventh grader commented:

> My mother keeps telling me, "*Ai mi hija, tienes que sacar buenas califica-ciones en la high school para que no te estes chingando igual que yo* [You have to earn good grades in high school so you won't have to struggle the way I had to]." And you know, she has a point. I don't want to be doing that. I've been in the cannery before. Like taking things to my uncle who works there with my mother. Just being there I can tell I wouldn't want to work there. I don't like it. I've got to do well in school so that I don't have to face this in my future.

Despite the fact that these students are remarkably achievement-oriented in school, they do not know people with the jobs they would like to have as adults and they do not have extensive knowledge of these kinds of jobs. They may know "a friend" or "my cousin's friend" who works in a bank or they may have visited a computer firm, but in general, they lack intimate knowledge or experience with adults who have the types of higher-status jobs and occupations they aspire to. Nonetheless, these students express a definite belief in the linkage between doing well in school and succeeding in what they perceive to be more rewarding, higher-status adult occupations. And "doing well in school," according to these students, means attending classes regularly, doing the homework, asking teachers for help when they do not understand, trying as "hard as you can" and getting along well with their teachers.

Most, but not all, of these successful Mexican-descent students indicated that one reason for their success in school was their parents' interest and support. Family encouragement stemmed from a strong parental desire that their children achieve more than they had been able to here or in Mexico. Some of the girls, however, indicated that their parents had not been particularly supportive and that their encouragement to do well in school had come from teachers and counselors. These same girls indicated that their parents feared their going on to a university or college setting where they would live away from home. They also thought that their parents would probably move back to Mexico rather than have them begin postsecondary schooling in the United States, a fact which disturbed some of these girls. As one said, "I think the real reason why my parents don't want me going away to college is that they are afraid I might get pregnant or something. That plus they want me to work in the restaurant like my older sister. And that is something I don't want to do."

Many of these girls feel torn between wanting to conform to their parents' expectations, on the one hand, and their desire to chart a different course for themselves, on the other. This dilemma is a source of confusion and difficulty. They have long been accorded recognition and praise for their scholastic achievement and yet, as they approach an important step in their academic careers, they are expected to suspend or terminate postsecondary education in order to pursue the perceived gender-appropriate roles as obedient daughter, prospective wife and mother. These gender role conflicts among the successful Mexican-descent girls raise important research questions, especially as they relate to the postsecondary academic persistence of such students.

Unsuccessful Mexican-Descent Students

Unsuccessful Mexican-descent students are among the more visible on campus. Their manners of dress, walk, and speech frequently identify them as Chicanos or Cholos. Moreover, they congregate in specific places on campus that are considered their "turf." Just as the mainstream "quaddie" students "hang out" in the area between the main administration building and the swimming pool, the Chicano and Cholo students are most often found congregating further away from the center of the campus. The students perceived to be more gang-oriented tend to be even more exclusive in their choice of where to "hang out" because certain areas are considered the exclusive province of one of the two major gangs in the community.

Another marker of the visibility of the Chicano and Cholo students is the fact that they are frequently visible roaming the campus after the class bell has rung. They walk across the street to a fast-food stand, meet friends in the faculty parking lot or just "hang out" in the corridors of remote hallways. They are also quite visible in the "study center," which is located in the cafeteria during each class period. This "study center" is reserved for students who are late to class and are thus prevented from entering, or who have been permanently ejected from a class and have no other class in which to reenroll. As the semester progresses, there are more and more students assigned permanently to the "study center." It is monitored each period by an "attendance specialist" who makes sure the students do not leave the room. Although students are asked to bring books and materials, they rest their heads on the table, as if asleep.

Chicano- and Cholo-oriented students are much more likely to be enrolled than other students in the high school's "school within a school" (SWAS) program. This is an alternative program established for students considered to have attendance problems and/or an inability to function effectively in the regular school program. Classes in the program are shorter and the curriculum is less structured or rigorous than in the regular program, although students are required to participate in reading, writing and discussion exercises in class. Other courses are less traditional and, in some cases, perceived to be "much easier" than the regular curriculum. For example, during one grading period in a class containing all boys, the main activity consisted of assembling model cars, many of them in the Low Rider style. The program is considered to be one for students who are unsuccessful and in danger of dropping out of school. Students enrolled in the program are keenly aware of this school-wide perception and of their precarious, unesteemed position in the school community. Hence, the content and structure of the program appear to reinforce the students' marginality and alienation in the school community.

Interviews with unsuccessful Chicano students indicate that some express high-status career aspirations and that others have no definite plans once they leave high school. Initially, these students espouse the conventional notions about going to school to get "good jobs," but in successive interviews, it becomes clearer that most of them anticipate having continuing difficulties in school, as they express uncertainty about their future and doubt about their chances of graduating from school. One of the students, for example, expresses a commonly shared sentiment: "I would like to graduate, but I don't know if I will."

Unsuccessful Chicano students in the study present a decidedly different set of perceptions, experiences, and accommodations than successful immigrant Mexicano students. The form and substance of much of their schooling appear to reinforce their marginality and alienation, thus heightening their sense of being "different" from the dominant group and from Mexicanos. They tend to be concentrated in either the general or low-track classes and are not particularly active in student activities. They are much less goal-oriented or goal-specific than the Mexicano students.

The parents of these students I talked with were employed in marginal occupations, such as seasonal cannery work, laborers, gardeners, or were unemployed. The unsuccessful Chicano students frequently talked about wanting to work in an office or in some occupation which is less physically demanding or "more interesting" than the work their parents, siblings or relatives are engaged in, yet they frequently did not know how one goes about getting a job as a medical secretary, a bank teller or a disk jockey. Or, they were misinformed about securing a job with such companies. For example, unsuccessful Chicano students expressed interest in leaving school early to get a job in a local computer firm. When I asked them, "Do you think it is possible to get a job with such a firm if a person has not graduated from high school or can't read above the sixth-grade level?," some students indicated that they believed a computer firm would teach the person the skills they would need for the job "if the company decided to hire you."

With respect to perceptions about jobs and career paths open to them, these Chicano students are not that much different from the successful Mexican-immigrant students in that they have limited exposure to these occupations and to the cultural knowledge about how to successfully pursue these careers. Their individual family members, as well as their community role models, are typically engaged in low-status occupations.

This society places little, if any, social value on the labor of field hands or cannery workers. Consequently, a parent who raises seven or eight children from his or her labor in these occupations is not viewed as a model of adult success as defined by society. Furthermore, these parents, and others like them who serve as role models, are not in a position materially or structurally to expose the students to worlds and alternatives which they themselves do not know. The structural connection here is an obvious one: the job ceiling experienced by students' parents and other adult community role models also serves to create a ceiling on experiences from which to expose, instruct or inspire these students about a more-advantaged adult opportunity structure and the alternatives within it.

Where the successful Mexican-immigrant students differ is that they and their parents continue to believe in the future value of educational credentials in securing more advantaged futures regardless of present circumstances. The parents of unsuccessful Chicano students, on the other hand, were typically unsuccessful in school themselves or were forced to quit school very early and very possibly do not see school as important in their lives or in the kinds of jobs they or their children are likely to get. Very often these students indicated that "it would be okay" with their parents if they dropped out of school before graduation.

Many of the unsuccessful students also noted that they did not know what kind of job their parents or family would like them to pursue nor had they discussed this with them. Again, this appears to be a difference between the unsuccessful Chicano students and the successful immigrant Mexicano students. The latter were usually able to give ready examples of discussions they had with their parents about their futures and the kinds of jobs and careers they aspired to. Differences in parental aspirations for their children, as well as family ideology about preparing for the future and one's place in it, appear to be significant in the messages that are communicated to unsuccessful Chicano students and successful immigrant Mexicano students. Although extensive interviews with parents were not a part of this initial study and the data I refer to here are impressionistic, I recognize its critical importance. I underscore here the need to collect much more extensive data in this domain.

All students in the sub-sample were asked to describe successful and unsuccessful adults and to elaborate on the reasons for becoming successful or unsuccessful. Many of the Chicano students could not describe a successful Mexican-descent adult whom they knew well. They were more likely to describe an Anglo teacher or youth counselor. Of, if they could describe a Mexican-descent adult whom they considered to be successful, the adult was engaged in activities which would not be valued or would be considered unsuccessful by others. For example, one Chicano tenth grader carefully described his uncle as a "successful adult." The uncle was a leader in Northside (a local gang) and he was "smart with money." He became successful because of "being on the streets" and "knowing what's happening." Another tenth grade student described his grandmother as a successful adult: "She used to own several restaurants and bars in town but she isn't here no more because they kept closing her places down because of the gangs and stuff."

When asked to explain how people become unsuccessful adults, Chicano students articulate a range of responses, indicating the extent to which they may have internalized conventional notions which link success and failure to individual efforts. Typical responses were: "They are lazy and dropped out of school"; "they got too much into partying and doing drugs"; and "they are just lazy and before they realize it, they have messed up too much to start going right." Responses also suggested the extent to which students perceive structural discrimination and limitations: "They work in the fields and they never went to school"; "they got a rotten education"; "Mexicans don't have a chance to go on to college and make something of themselves"; "people like us face a lot of prejudice because there are a lot of people who don't like Mexicans"; and "there aren't enough good jobs to go around." Whether indicative of a conventional ideological interpretation or a perception of structural determination of adult failure, it was much easier for these students to elaborate on and give details of strategies for failure than on strategies for success.

Among this group of students there is a pervading sense that they really do not know what the future holds for them. Unlike the more successful students in the sub-sample, they have a difficult time articulating what they expect to be doing in 10 years. "Gee, I don't know. I hope I have a job, but I don't know," "I haven't really thought that far ahead but I hope I finish school," and, "It's hard to think that far ahead" were characteristic responses. The unsuccessful Chicano students are much more likely to discuss at length their concerns and hopes for today, tomorrow, or possibly the weekend. This focus on the present or immediate future is no doubt reflective of the daily struggles and constrained material realities these students and their families face. The uncertainties and stress of these conditions extract a certain psychological and emotional energy and must be understood as important contextual influences in the schooling experiences of these students and in the processes of negotiation through which their identities are established and affirmed.

ETHNICITY AS A STRATEGICALLY EXPLOITED RESPONSE TO THE DEMANDS OF SCHOOLING AND TO STRUCTURED INEQUALITY

The foregoing discussion presents us with an opportunity to reexamine our understanding of ethnicity and ethnic identity systems, especially as they relate to the variations in patterns of school performance of Mexican-descent students. The data I have presented here indicate that school success and failure among these students do not correlate with a "less acculturated/more acculturated" continuum of ethnic identity and, in fact, speak to a much more complex, interactive set of phenomena.

There are several different ways of defining ethnic groups. One approach is to define an ethnic group objectively in terms of observable traits, behavioral orientations, or combinations of such traits and feelings. Another approach involves defining ethnic groups in terms of subjective criteria. Individuals either identify themselves as being different from others or as belonging to a different group, are identified as different by others, or both identify themselves and are identified by others as different.

These approaches to ethnicity and ethnic identity are limited in their usefulness in understanding the interactive nature of ethnicity or the situational context in which ethnic identity is employed—or not employed—as a specific strategy. Nor are these approaches particularly successful in making cross-cultural comparisons or in suggesting generalizations about ethnic identity.

A more useful approach to ethnicity is proposed by the Social Science Research Council (1973). The Council presents criteria that are useful in understanding what it means to be Chicano, Cholo, Mexicano and Mexican American at Field High School. The Council's criteria suggest that ethnic categories have different meanings in different social settings and for different individuals. So, for example, it means different things to be a Chicano or Mexicano at Field High School. It means one thing to be a Mexicano/a at home and something else to be Mexican American at school or in some other situational context. For some it might mean being a Pocho/a (person of Mexican-descent who speaks Spanish with an American "gringo" accent) at home among family members and something entirely different to be a Mexican American or Cholo/a outside the home. Similarly, it means one thing to be a Chicano (activist or politically sensitive) rather than a Mexican American ("*tapado*," "*vendido*" or "sell out") in a university or college setting.

Another of the Council's criteria deals with the emblematic character of ethnicity and addresses the symbolic nature of ethnic categories. The symbolic content of the identity has meaning for both members of the group and for analysts of ethnic phenomena. Hence, the ethnic labels Chicano, Mexicano, Cholo, Mexican American, Pachuco, etc. are by themselves powerful symbols around which the negotiation of identity takes place. Labels with negative implications, such as the term Chicano as it is used by many Mexicanos at Field High School, can be used to impose a sense of social distance from those perceived to be deviant or a sense of inferiority on other Mexican-descent people, or it may be used to define a dominant-subordinate relationship.

Groups concerned with changing the status or image of the group may change the label by which they are known or imbue an existing label with new meaning. For example, prior to the 1960s, Mexicans in the United States identified themselves primarily as Mexicans, Mexicanos, or Mexican Americans, but with the evolution of the civil rights movement the more politically active, social activist members of the group preferred to identify themselves as Chicanos. Frequently, students who identified themselves as Mexicanos at Field High School found themselves in some university contexts preferring to be identified as Chicanos. This was in recognition of the Chicano label as a symbol of solidarity with the sociopolitical struggle of Mexican Americans against discrimination and domination.

A useful way to understand ethnicity is an interactionist approach—one that emphasizes interaction and contact with others who are different. Such an approach focuses on how contact with, as opposed to isolation from, others heightens the ethnic group's sense of identity. Such an approach is advanced by Spicer (1971), who maintains that opposition is an essential factor in the maintenance of a persistent ethnic identity system. Spicer persuades us that the development of a persistent ethnic identity in opposition to the dominant group has both historical and structural antecedents. Moreover, it is not a mere epiphenomenon or byproduct of the interethnic contact. Rather, Spicer views an oppositional process as the essential ingredient of an enduring, collectively developed identity.

Spicer's model of the persistent identity system and the oppositional process is particularly useful in understanding what it means to be a Chicano or Cholo at Field High School. Spicer's model suggests that involuntary minorities, as opposed to autonomous minorities (described in Ogbu & Matute-Bianchi, 1986, p. 87), form a sense of peoplehood or collective social identity in opposition collective social identity of the dominant group. In response to the enduring system of structured inequality and domination that characterizes their life in the United States, some Mexican-descent people have developed a bonding, collective oppositional identity which is best understood as an adaptive strategy that enables them to endure their status as a stigmatized minority within a system institutionalized inequality.

I am not suggesting here that Chicanos and Cholos at Field High School are consciously aware of their history and the history of other Mexican-descent people as involuntarily enclaved subordinate minorities in the United States. They do not know their history nor have they been provided with the tools to learn that history. But they do have an explicit awareness of their lives in this community as a stigmatized, low-status group with decidedly fewer opportunities than the dominant group. They are keenly aware of the low status they have in the community, a status which is reflected back to them by the school personnel and by other students. To a large extent their world is restricted to this particular community; it is what they live each day. Their reality is one which teaches them that Mexicans mostly work in the fields or in the canneries or are unemployed, a reality which tells them that most people like themselves do not do very well in school, and a reality which imposes strict limits on their future. It matters little whether their grandparents were immigrants or long-term residents of the United States. What matters is that they understand their structural and social position in this community and they have some sense that "this is how it has always been for our race." This collective understanding is an essential part of their identity, which in turn is part of an oppositional process in which the identification with others who share their origins, traditions and experiences has been critical in developing feelings of efficacy and value in their own eyes.

The maintenance of a Mexicano identity at Field High represents a far different ethnic strategy. The immigrant Mexicanos and those who maintain a separate identity as the descendants of Mexicano immigrants are either optimistic about their chances of succeeding here in the United

States or at least share a perception that there are more economic opportunities for them here than in Mexico. Although they are aware of discrimination and prejudice against Mexican people here, they perceive it differently than Chicanos. Either they see these barriers as hurdles to be overcome or as reasons for returning to Mexico. They see the obstacles as part of their reality here but they are optimistic about their chances of overcoming them and becoming successful adults in occupations that earn more money and have higher status than those of their parents. For them, hard work and belief in the future value of educational credentials are an explicit part of their response to the demands of schooling. Others see these barriers as the way life is here and if they are not successful in "making a go of it here," they can "always go back home to Mexico." For many of the recent immigrants, their material conditions in the United States are demonstrably better than what they knew in Mexico, and from their frame of reference life is in some ways much better than it was in Mexico even if there is discrimination and prejudice against Mexicanos. Chicanos, on the other hand, see no dramatic improvement in their standard of living for they have no basis for comparing one situation to another. Their only frame of reference is what they know in this coastal community. That reality has not improved.

For successful immigrant Mexicano students there is an expression of self-confidence about their futures or at least an extreme desire to try hard to be successful in that future. Hence, those students with a strong Mexicano identity reflect a different accommodation to the sociocultural context, an accommodation that is based on very different interpretations of their opportunities and very different frames of reference. This identity is frequently linked to relative optimism about the future and about their ability to direct that future.

The oppositional identity system of the nonimmigrant Chicanos is linked to futures that are seen as limited and unknowable, to life chances that are perceived as limited and to goals that are seen as unattainable. The identity is developed through collectively experienced and interpreted processes of exclusion and subordination which are an enduring part of their daily realities, including their lives in school.

SUMMARY AND RECOMMENDATIONS

The foregoing presentation indicates seven major findings:

1   The Mexican-descent student clientele is indeed a heterogeneous one, broadly reflective of a range of strategies and accommodations to the schooling process. This heterogeneity can be delineated by a five-category typology of Mexican-descent students: recent Mexican

immigrant, Mexican-oriented, Mexican American, Chicano and Cholo.

2   School success is much more likely to be found among the Mexican-oriented students who maintain strong, positive identities as Mexicanos as well as immigrant perspectives about the value of educational credentials in achieving adult success.

3   Patterns of school failure are more likely to be found in the non-immigrant Chicano/Cholo students who have a sense of themselves as a stigmatized group with comparatively limited adult opportunities and with futures that do not require educational credentials.

4   The obvious scholastic success of bilingual students with a strong identity as Mexicanos contradicts the conventional wisdom—and educational policies based on this presumed wisdom—that academic success belongs to those who acculturate and are monolingual English speakers.

5   School success among Mexican-oriented girls is more pronounced than it is for any other category of Mexican-descent students, with the possible exception of Mexican American girls. This raises important questions for subsequent research and bears more careful study.

6   The choice of ethnic labels and symbols, as well as variations in ethnic consciousness among Mexican-descent students, reflects an interactive process between the perceptions Mexican-descent students have of themselves and the perceptions school personnel, other students in the school, and the larger community have of them.

7   There is a relationship between student perceptions of the job ceiling and adult opportunities that their families have experienced, their explanations of the opportunities and the strategies developed in response to them that accords with variations in patterns of school success and failure. In other words, these patterns are broadly reflective of differences in student perceptions of the adult opportunity structure, their chances of becoming a successful adult and the importance of school achievement in achieving adult success.

The one group in my study that defies easy description is the Mexican American. It does not fit easily into the immigrant versus nonimmigrant continuum. As indicated earlier, there are at least three subgroups in the Mexican American category: students who are "totally acculturated" so that all that remains of their Mexican roots is their last name; students who are "cultural switch-hitters" who alternate easily between being Mexicano at home and "American" at school; and students who see themselves as neither "purely American" nor "purely Mexican" but as some combination of the two. With the exception of the "switch-hitters," the students in this category are more ambivalent and uncommitted in their ethnic orientation. They do not manifest the behavioral symbols or styles of the Chicano/Cholo identities nor do they affect any of the overt symbols associated with the Mexicano identities. Some of these students are active and successful in school, but many appear to drift, to be disengaged and withdrawn from much of what the school offers. They can be found in all curriculum tracks in the school, but probably are more likely to be found in the general or low tracks. They are more likely to be seen and not heard. They do not really fit into any of the modal categories I have defined along the immigrant versus nonimmigrant continuum, nor do they fit any of the generalizations I have made about students in other categories.

That the Mexican Americans at Field High School do not neatly fit into these generalizations or into the immigrant versus nonimmigrant categories does not necessarily invalidate the theoretical foundation upon which I framed my study. Rather, I think the difficulty in categorization that the Mexican American group presents reflects the complexity and diversity of sociocultural adaptations that Mexican-descent students and their families have made and are making to an ever-changing context. We started to identify the heterogeneity of this large Mexican-descent population and to describe some of its internal differentiation. One of the next research questions should be to what extent this five-category classification of Mexican-descent students is found in other similar agricultural communities and to what extent it is reflective of Mexican-descent students in urban communities, especially those with non-White minorities (Blacks, Koreans, Vietnamese, Filipinos) and other Latino groups (Central and South Americans). What other categories might we find? What refinements might be made? What other kinds of accommodations and adaptive strategies are being worked out?

The elusiveness that I have described among the more ambivalent and uncommitted Mexican American students raises another issue. Educational intervention programs and policies aimed at improving academic achievement among Mexican-descent students assume a cultural homogeneity that does not exist and typically focus on single-cause assessments and solutions to perceived problems. The students' failure to achieve in school has been explained by some in terms of their inability to speak English, their culturally impoverished homes and/or the mismatch between the language and culture of the home and school. Based on these perceived causes of school failure, simplistic educational solutions are proposed to fit stereotypic categories of students: ESL for the non-English speaker, multicultural education for the "culturally deprived," and special programs for the "at risk," the migrants and the learning-handicapped. The response has been to create categorical programs for categorical students, with the expectation, if not fervent hope, that we can change the students to fit the "regular" school program. The situation of the Mexican American students at Field High School indicates the high cost to those students who do not fit any of the single-cause assessments of school failure, who do not warrant special attention as either "at risk" or as "gifted and talented" and who are neither "gang bangers" nor *mojados* at either extreme. The students are ignored. They drift politely and quietly, remaining bored and unchallenged, and they spend the majority of their time in school just getting by.

I have developed the typology of the students I observed at this school for the purposes of making generalizations about a student population that has long been perceived as a homogeneous one. The typology presents a useful starting point in understanding the intragroup variability and diversity of adaptations that can be found within the group. The case I have presented of the ambivalent, uncommitted Mexican Americans, however, raises an important caution in the interpretation of this typology. It would be a gross misinterpretation of my study to develop specific interventions and programs to "fit" the modal characteristics of the students I have identified by the typology. A more appropriate response to these findings would be to stop creating special programs to fit stereotypic perceptions of students and their perceived problems and to begin changing the school climate, structure and practices to ones that are more broadly sensitive, responsive and challenging to this diverse student clientele.

This study documents variations in patterns of school performance among Mexican-descent students. It suggests a new way for educators to look at ethnic identity as an interactive process which includes all the participants in a social context, including the school. In particular, it calls upon educators to examine closely the relationship between a strong, positive Mexicano identity and academic achievement and to see such an identity system not as a liability but as a source of strength in helping students to succeed in school. The academic success of the Mexican-oriented students suggests that assimilation and acculturation are not necessarily the *sine qua non* of scholastic achievement. The success of these students, especially the support for academic achievement that is provided by their involvement in *Sociedad Bilingue*, suggests not only the role of ethnic pride in promoting school achievement but also the importance of the peer culture in legitimating academic success. *Sociedad Bilingue* functioned as an important source of ethnic pride and leadership development in the lives of many Mexicano students and as a decidedly positive influence in a school where the various peer cultures were often "anti-school" in orientation.

The study also indicates that the job ceiling constraining a student's future creates a ceiling on exposure to and experiences with alternative futures and opportunities. How can students aspire to something that they and their families do not know exists? In this regard, the school has an important role to play in providing these students with the exposure to careers and jobs in a world beyond what the students know as their daily reality, providing access to information and successful role models in esteemed occupations. Schools must become active partners with the larger community, with private industry and the business community and with service organizations in providing these students with mentors, internships, apprenticeships and other enhancements. The schools by themselves cannot be expected to provide the necessary exposure and access to information. The effort must involve the community beyond the school.

I have suggested here the crucial importance of ethnic identity and minority status for patterns of school performance within distinct groups of Mexican-descent high school students. Of issue in subsequent research is the process of recruitment into a particular identity system. My impression of these students is that the particular identity a student claims is made long before he/she reaches Field High School, and that the process of recruitment begins much earlier. Just as the high dropout rate among Mexican-descent students must be understood as a process which begins early in the elementary school grades, my hunch is that the recruitment into the Chicano/Cholo identity systems begins about this time, and that the particular identity is confirmed by the time the student reaches junior high, about the time when the peer groups begin to assume much greater influence in the lives of students. By the same token, I think students who enter the schools with a strong, positive identity as Mexicanos probably have different sets of experiences at home and in school that allow them to maintain this self-confident identity system. A fruitful venture for subsequent research would be to follow Mexican-descent students longitudinally through a particular school system, documenting the internal differentiation in ethnic identification as it begins to develop, identifying emerging patterns of school performance, documenting variations in schooling experiences and other school input factors, and relating these developments to family histories, ideologies and other sociocultural variables.

The variations in ethnic identities among the Mexican-descent students are inextricably linked to the development of their identities as students long before they reached Field High School. In a larger sense, their identity systems are anchored to broader historical and structural antecedents in a community that has undergone rapid, dramatic changes. The community's established interethnic structures of domination and subordination are changing, thus providing a complex, multifaceted, interactive context in which students learn the significance of what it means to be "Mexican" and thus "different" from others. This context exerts a powerful influence not only on what students learn but on what they do with that knowledge, on the opportunities they have to acquire and apply socially valued knowledge, on how they see themselves today and tomorrow, and on the value they place on schooling in getting them from today into the future.

ACKNOWLEDGMENT

Copyright (1991) *Situational ethnicity and patterns of schooling perform-ance among immigrant and nonimmigrant Mexican-descent students* by Maria Eugenia Matute-Bianchi. Reproduced by permission of Routledge/ Taylor and Francis Books Inc.

REFERENCES

Achievement Council, The (1984). *Excellence for whom? A report from the Planning Committee*. Oakland, CA: Author.
Arias, B. (1986). The context of education for Hispanic students: An overview. American Journal of Education, 95(1), 26–57.
Assembly Office of Research (1986). *California 2000: A people in Transition. Major issues affecting human resources*. A report prepared by the Assembly Office of Research. Sacramento, California.
Baca, R., & Bryan, D. (1980). *Citizenship aspirations and residency preference: The Mexican undocumented worker in the binational community*. Compton, CA: SEPA-OPTION, Inc.
Bowman, C. (1981). Between cultures: Toward an understanding of the cultural production of Chicanos. In M. Tienda in collaboration with C. Bowman & C. M. Snipp (Eds.), *Socioeconomic attainment and ethnicity: Toward an understanding of the labor market experience of Chicanos*. Springfield, VA: National Technical Information Service.
Brown, G., et al. (1980). *The condition of education for Hispanic Americans*. National Center for Education Statistics. Washington, DC: U.S. Government Printing Office.
Browning, H., & de la Garza, R. O. (1986). *Mexican immigrants and Mexican Americans: An evolving relation*. Austin: CMAS Publications, University of Texas at Austin.
California Postsecondary Education Commission (1982). Equal education opportunity in California education. Part IV. Sacramento, CA: Author.
Cameron, J. W. (1976). *The history of Mexican public education in Los Angeles, 1910–1930*. Unpublished Ph.D. dissertation, University of Southern California.
Carter, T. P. (1970). *Mexican Americans in school: A decade of change*. New York: College Entrance Examination Board.
Carter, T. P., & Segura, R. D. (1979). *Mexican Americans in school: A decade of change*. New York: College Entrance Examination Board.
Coleman, J., et al. (1966). *Equality of educational opportunity*. Washington, DC: U.S. Government Printing Office.
Dinerrman, I. R. (1982). *Migrants and stay-at-homes: A comparative study of rural migration from Michoacan, Mexico*. San Diego: Center for U.S. Mexican Studies, University of California, Monograph Series #5.

Donato, R. (1987). *Pajaro Valley Unified Schools: Bilingual education and desegregation.* Unpublished Ph.D. dissertation, Stanford University.

Keefe, S., & Padilla, A. (1987). *Chicano ethnicity.* Albuquerque: University of New Mexico Press.

Matute-Bianchi, M. E. (1986). Ethnic identities and patterns of school success and failure among Mexican-descent and Japanese American students in a California high school: An ethnographic analysis. *American Journal of Education, 95*(1), 233–255.

Mines, R. (1981). *Developing a community tradition of migration: A field study in rural Zacatecas, Mexico and California settlement areas.* San Diego: Center for U.S. Mexican Studies, University of California, Monograph #3.

Ogbu, J. U. (1974). *The next generation: An ethnography of education in an urban neighborhood.* New York: Academic Press.

Ogbu, J. U. (1978). *Minority education and caste: The American system in cross-cultural perspective.* Orlando, FL: Academic Press.

Ogbu, J. U. (1982). Cultural discontinuities and schooling. *Anthropology and Education Quarterly, 13*(4), 290–307.

Ogbu, J. U. (1983). Minority status and schooling in plural societies. *Comparative Education Review, 27*(2), 168–190.

Ogbu, J. U., & Matute-Bianchi, M. E. (1986). Understanding sociocultural factors: Knowledge, identity and school adjustment. In *Beyond language: Social and cultural factors in schooling language minority students* (pp. 73–142). Sacramento, CA: State Department of Education, Bilingual Education Office.

Orfield, G. (1986). Hispanic education: Challenges, research and policies. *American Journal of Education, 95*(1), 1–25.

Portes, A., & Bach, R.L. (1985). *Latin journey.* Berkeley: University of California Press.

Rios-Bustamante, A. J. (1981). *Mexican immigrant workers in the United States.* Los Angeles: Los Angeles Chicano Research Center, University of California, Los Angeles.

Rodriguez, N., & Nunez, R. T. (1986). An exploration of factors that contribute to differentiation between Chicanos and Indocumentados. In H. Browning & R. O. de la Garza (Eds.), *Mexican immigrants and Mexican Americans: An evolving relation* (pp. 138–155). Austin: CMAS Publications, University of Texas at Austin.

Romo, H. (1984). The Mexican origin populations' differing perceptions of their children's schooling. *Social Science Quarterly, 65*(2), 635–650.

Social Science Research Council (1973). Comparative research on ethnicity: A conference report. *Items, 28*, 61–64.

Spicer, E. (1971). Persistent identity system. *Science, 4011*, 795–800.

U.S. Commission on Civil Rights. (1971). *Mexican American education study. Reports 1–4.* Washington, DC: U.S. Government Printing Office.

Valverde, S. (1987). A comparative study of Hispanic high school dropouts and graduates—Why do some leave school early and some finish? *Education and Urban Society, 19*(3), 320–329.

Wollenberg, C. (1976). *With all deliberate speed: Segregation and exclusion in California schools, 1955–1975.* Berkeley: University of California Press.

Chapter 19

Navajo Youth and Anglo Racism

Cultural Integrity and Resistance

Donna Deyhle

Graduation day was near at Navajo High School.[1] Young Navajo men wearing blue jeans, T-shirts, and Nikes stood in the hall talking to the vocational education teacher. "You learned lots of skills in my class. Try the job services office in town. They can help you find jobs," he told them. One student disagreed. "I haven't really seen any Navajo people working, like in convenience stores or grocery stores. So, the job outlook is pretty slim. Unless you figure out something else to do. Like shoveling snow or something. But the outlook isn't really great. For Indians, you know."

Several of the students nodded in agreement. The teacher continued, "There are lots of jobs out there. You just have to look for them." As I passed them, I remembered a Navajo parent's comment: "It's the way it has always been. The Anglos keep the jobs for themselves, they don't hire real Navajo. That's the way it is."[2]

I continued down the hall to the library to interview one of the graduating seniors. She was in the top 10 percent of her class and had turned down two college scholarships to stay home with her family on the reservation. "I've always wanted to do things but it's like I couldn't because of school. That's what has held me back. I feel that." Going to college away from the reservation would cause her to miss opportunities to participate in, for example, traditional Navajo ceremonies. She explained her decision: "If I go to college, I will get a job in the city and then I won't come back very often. When am I going to have time to spend with my grandmother learning about my culture? I feel that kind of resentment towards school. I feel cheated out of my own culture."

This chapter is about the lives, in and out of school, of young Navajo men and women in a border reservation community.[3] Here, school success and failure are understood as one part of the larger process of racial conflict, which I have seen fought out in the workplace and in schools in this polarized community. This chapter will illustrate how Anglos maneuver to acquire the best jobs (some of which are teaching jobs) and how they systematically prepare Navajos for the lowest level jobs. These Navajo people are subject to racial discrimination in the workplace and at school. Young Navajos may respond to the vocational, assimilationist curriculum in their schools by withdrawing or resisting "education." For Navajo students, one of the most life-affirming strategies is to embrace reservation life and traditional Navajo culture. Indeed, the students in my study who were able to maintain Navajo/reservation connections gained a solid place in Navajo society and were also more successful in the Anglo world of school and workplace.

As an anthropologist interested in issues related to American Indian education, I discovered an absence of ethnographic research on American Indian adolescents' lives in and out of school since Murray Wax, Rosalie Wax, and Robert Dumont published *Formal Education in an American Indian Community* in 1964.[4] No such studies existed on the Navajo. In the early 1980s, a doctoral student, who at the time was an elementary school principal in the local school district, invited me to conduct a similar study in his community. District administrators and Navajo parents were concerned with the high dropout rate of Navajo youth, and requested a study that would examine the reasons for the school success and failure of these students. In the fall of 1984, I moved to the community as an ethnographer to start this study. Over the next two and a half decades, I listened to Navajo youth talk about their lives and watched them grow up and have families of their own. I attended their high schools, joining them in over three hundred classes, watching their struggles, successes, and failures. With field notes of observations and casual conversations, audiotapes of meetings and interviews, and ethnohistorical archival data, I documented their lives since 1984.

Border High School (BHS) is located in a small town of 3,500 people about 20 miles from the Navajo reservation. Almost half of the student population is Navajo. Navajo High School (NHS) is located on the Navajo reservation, and almost 99 percent of the student population is Navajo. Both high schools, as part of one large public school district in one county, are administered from a central district office. They use both state and local standardized curricula.

For this study, I developed a main database that tracked by name all Navajo students who attended BHS and NHS during the school years from 1980–1981 to 1988–1989. This master list contained attendance data, grade point averages, standardized test scores, dropout and graduation rates, community locations, current employment situations, post-high school training, and General Education Diploma (GED) or regular high school graduation diploma received for 1,489 youth. Formal interviews took place with 168 youth who had left school and another 100 who were either still in school or had successfully graduated. Teachers, administrators, political leaders, parents, and community members also answered my endless questions within the context of formal and casual conversations over the past 10 years. During this time, I became involved in extracurricular school activities, including athletic games, plays, dances, and carnivals, and "hanging out" on Main Street and at local fast food restaurants. I attended school and community meetings with Navajo parents. After several years, I was invited to participate in discussions with Navajo parents and to help develop strategies to intervene in school district decisions, such as disciplinary codes, attendance regulations, busing schedules, equal band equipment, and bilingual education. I watched and participated as parents fought for local political control over their children's education and struggled through racist treatment by the Anglo community. These parents were clearly aware of racist practices that occurred, and which I observed, on a daily basis.

I lived for two summers with a Navajo family on the reservation, herding sheep and cooking with children and adolescents. Over the years, as I continually returned to their community, they decided it was worth their time and energy to "educate" me about their cultural norms and values. The oldest daughter, Jan, was a student I had come to know from my initial observations at BHS. She explained her family's decision: "That first year, my Dad said you wouldn't come back. Most people come and study Navajos and leave. He was surprised you came back the next year. And every year you came back. So he said we could trust you." This family introduced me to others, who in turn introduced me to still other families. My hosts graciously explained their perceptions of life, school, and education. I was invited to attend traditional ceremonies as "part of the family." From the ceremony I describe in this chapter, I have chosen to reveal only dialogue that is relevant to education in order to avoid disclosing any confidential religious beliefs. I have shared drafts of this chapter over the years with Navajos in the community who have confirmed my observations and who have helped me represent their experiences and concerns more accurately. They have agreed that this chapter should be published, in order to share with others both the concerns Navajos have for their children's education and the importance of having their children remain faithful to their Navajo traditions.

Anglos living in the community on the border of the reservation also patiently answered my endless questions in over 100 informal interviews. Approximately 85 percent of the Anglos in 1984 were members of the Church of Latter Day Saints (LDS), commonly called Mormons. I attended religious meetings at the Indian Ward (a local unit of the LDS Church), seminary classes (religious training) at the two high schools, and interviewed several religion teachers who were bishops in the LDS Church. My research with Navajo youth was a frequent topic of conversations at picnics, dinners, and socials, where Anglos carefully explained their personal understanding, as well as the LDS Church's views, of American Indians. The Anglo voices in this community do not represent a definitive Mormon perspective, but they do illustrate a cultural view that is influenced, in part, by religious beliefs. In the context of this community, Mormon and non-Mormon Anglo voices are consistent in opposition to their Navajo neighbors.[5] As an outsider to both the Navajo and Anglo communities, I was supported, tolerated, and educated by many local people in my efforts to understand the contemporary lives of Navajo people.[6]

THEORETICAL FRAMEWORK

Educational anthropologists and sociologists who attempt to explain minority youths' responses to school primarily present either a cultural difference theory or a sociostructural theory.[7] Cultural difference theorists such as Cummins argue that cultural conflicts and other problems develop in minority classrooms because of the differences between students' home and school cultures.[8] Sociostructural theorists such as Ogbu argue that the explanations for minority school failure lie outside the school itself, specifically in the racial stratification of U.S. society and the economy.[9] Both of these positions provide a useful perspective and have contributed to our understanding of cultural conflict. In particular, I find Ogbu's[10] structural analysis of castelike or involuntary minorities and the job ceiling they face and Cummins's analysis of cultural differences and cultural integrity useful in understanding the situation faced by these Navajo youth.[11]

My research represents a more traditional anthropological approach. I am not attempting to create a general theory of castelike minorities, but rather to represent the specific Navajo experience. In so doing, I take a different position than Ogbu. This ethnographic study speaks to some general claims made by Ogbu, but it does not replace his theory. Specifically, I speak about "racial warfare" to capture two points on which my interpretation and Ogbu's theory diverge: first, Navajos and Anglos conflict economically, politically, and culturally in both the schools and workplace. While Ogbu views the schools as a relatively neutral terrain, I portray the ways in which teachers and students play out this racial conflict. Second, Navajos have substantive ethical disagreements with the Anglo values manifested in the schools and the greater economy. The concept of racial warfare is intended to represent the integrity of Navajo culture and to avoid reducing this culture to a reinterpretation of traditional values in reaction to denial of opportunity in the Anglo-dominated schools and businesses, as I believe Ogbu does.

Young Navajo men and women face a racially polarized landscape, in which historically defined racial conflicts between Navajos and Anglos continue to engulf their lives. As a result, political and economic power remains in the hands of local Anglos who maintain a limited "place" for Navajos. This discrimination is basic to Navajos' attitudes toward schools. As Ogbu has pointed out, any comprehensive understanding of minority students' responses to school must include the power and status relations between minority and majority groups, as well as the variability among different minority groups.

According to Ogbu, the main factor differentiating the more successful from the less successful minorities appears to be the nature of the history of subordination and exploitation of the minorities, and the nature of the minorities' own instrumental and expressive responses to their treatment. In Ogbu's analysis, immigrant groups who came to this country more or less voluntarily arrived with an intact culture developed *before* contact with the dominant group. They viewed schooling as a means for increased opportunity and economic mobility, not as a threat to their cultural identity. In contrast, castelike minorities, which include African Americans, Mexican Americans, and American Indians, have been historically positioned as involuntary subordinates through slavery, conquest, or colonization. Ogbu argued that castelike minorities face schooling with a set of secondary cultural characteristics—a reinterpretation of traditional culture that is developed *after* contact with the dominant White group—to help them cope with the social, economic, political, and psychological history of rejection by the dominant group and its institutions. Schools, as sites of conflict with the dominant group, are seen as a threat to their cultural identity. These castelike minorities have developed oppositional cultural responses to schooling as they reject a system that has rejected them. Ogbu saw this resistance, which takes the form of truancy, lack of serious effort in and negative attitudes towards school, refusal to do classwork or assignments, and delinquency, as an adaptation to their lower social and occupational positions, which do not require high educational qualifications. This, in turn, has been counterproductive to school success. Specifically, pressure from the minority community not to "act White," coupled with feelings that they will not get jobs anyway, further decreases students' school efforts because they struggle with the fear of being estranged from their community if they are successful. The dominant group maintains this "adaptation" by providing inferior education and by channeling the students to inferior jobs after they finish high school.

Although Ogbu's general framework, which combines structural barriers and culturally based reactions, generally "fits" the Navajo situation, there are also striking differences between Navajos and other "castelike" minorities. Navajos have not played the same role in the national economy as other castelike minorities. African Americans, for example, have historically played a central role in the White-dominated economy. Navajos, in contrast, have never been an essential part of the White-dominated economy, except in regard to land procurement. Navajos accurately perceive that they are shut out of the job market, and that their school success is not linked to their economic prosperity.

Whereas Ogbu viewed the cultures of castelike minorities as a reaction to the dominant White group, I believe that Navajo practices and culture represent a distinct and independent tradition. Navajos do occupy a castelike, subordinate position in the larger social context. However, only a small part of Navajo cultural characteristics can appropriately be called "secondary" or "oppositional." Navajos face and resist the domination of their Anglo neighbors from an intact cultural base that was not developed in reaction to Anglo subordination. An oppositional description of Navajo culture ignores the integrity of Navajo culture and neglects the substantive value disagreements between Navajos and Anglos.

Navajo success is closely tied to family and reservation economic and cultural networks. It is these traditional values that parents seek to pass on to their children. For example, traditional Anglo notions of "success"—school credentials, individual careers, and individual economic prosperity—do not reflect those of the Navajo. The successful Navajo is judged on intact, extended familial relations, where individual jobs and educational success are used to enhance the family and the community and aggressive individualism is suppressed for the cooperation of the group. These Navajo values—the communal nature of success and the primacy of the family—exist in well-developed institutional structures on the reservation independent of Anglo culture, and during social and economic crises, help secure the Navajos' identity as a people.

These cultural characteristics in themselves do not necessarily result in school failure, although they contribute to the tension and misunderstanding between Navajos and Anglos. Youth who have little identity as Navajos and who are not accepted by Anglos because they are not White face the greatest risk of school failure and unemployment. To understand this position more fully, it is necessary to turn to Cummins, who argued that the strength of one's cultural identity is a vital factor in the expressive responses to the schooling experience. Cummins stated that "widespread school failure does not occur in minority groups that are positively oriented towards both their own and the dominant culture, that they do not perceive themselves as inferior to the dominant group, and that they are not alienated from their own cultural values."[12] This position suggests that Navajo youth who are better integrated into their home culture will be more successful students, regardless of the structural barriers they face. In other words, the more Navajo students resist assimilation while simultaneously maintaining their culture, the more successful they are in school.

In this chapter, I draw upon three events—a racial fight, a meeting of the Native American Church, and a high school career day—to portray the race struggle between Navajos and Anglos and the way that struggle manifests itself in schools. My position captures, but also moves beyond, central insights from both cultural difference theory and structural theory. Like cultural difference theorists, I believe that differences in culture play a role in the divisions between Anglo teachers and Navajo students. Anglos do not understand Navajo values, and thus manufacture deficit explanations to account for behavior they assume is unguided by specific beliefs. When Navajo students act on their beliefs, they act in contrast to existing institutional values.

Furthermore, like Ogbu, I believe that these cultural differences become barriers because of the power relations involved. However, Ogbu implied that castelike minority students withdraw from academic effort not only because of the power relations in schools, but also because of the job ceiling and their own communities' social realities or folk theories that undermine the importance of school success. As a result, he took the accommodationist position that castelike minorities would do better to adopt the strategies of immigrant groups, accept the school's regime, and succeed by its standards. Ogbu did not see culture as a terrain of conflict, nor does he perceive the significance of race as contributing to racial warfare, as I do; rather he believed it is possible for the culture of the student to be left "safely" at home so that his or her cultural identity can be disconnected from what occurs in school.

This is not possible for Navajo youth. My data support Navajo students' perception that Anglos discriminate against them and that they have no reason to believe that their cooperation with the educational regime would bring advantages in either schools or in the workplace. The issue for Navajo students is not that doing well in school is to "act White," but that playing by the rules of the classroom represents a "stacked deck." Educational compliance, or succeeding in the *kind* of schooling available to them, does not result in economic and social equality in the Anglo-dominated community. I argue, in this chapter, that the Navajos' experiences of racial and cultural warfare must be placed at the center of an explanatory model of their education and work experiences.

THE FIGHT: RACIAL CONFLICT

Racial polarization is a fact of life in San Juan County, a border community next to the Navajo Nation. In 1989, a fight broke out between a Navajo and an Anglo student at BHS. Claiming his younger cousin had been verbally and physically assaulted, a Navajo junior struck an Anglo student across the face in the school hallway during lunch. Navajo and Anglo students quickly gathered at the scene as the principal and the football coach pulled the boys apart. Police were called to the school; the Anglo student was released to his parents, while the Navajo student was taken to jail. The Navajo community demanded a meeting with school officials to discuss the incident, which more than 75 Navajo parents attended. The superintendent, the two high school principals, and several teachers also attended, along with the school district lawyer, the DNA lawyer,[13] the local sheriff, and myself. The tension felt in the meeting was a reflection of the larger battles lived out between Navajos and Anglos in the community each day.

The president of the parent association, who served as the meeting translator, spoke first in Navajo and then in English. The Navajo youth who was involved in the incident was his son-in-law.

> It kinda hurts to hear this information. The parents hurt over this. The parents have come to me with the problem. It hurts the parents and the students. We have to get over this problem. When kids come home and say they have been thrown around, they can't concentrate on their work. It hurts. Word gets around that the Indians are having an uprising. No. It is not true. We want our kids to go to school and do well. They are far behind. We want them to do well in academics. I hope we can talk about this. It gets worse every time we talk. I hear the police came into school and took him away. This is not fair, to knock around youth. If this is happening in school, I want to know about it.

As he sat down, the principal from the high school where the fight occurred stood up. He glanced at notes on a yellow pad, cleared his throat, and spoke:

> Let me express very strongly that there are a lot of things that cannot occur in a school for students to succeed. One thing is that they must feel safe. One of our goals is that it be a safe place. A week ago, following a school dance, a group of Anglos and Navajos got into a fight. They have a history of not getting along. The following week there was a fight in school, only one blow. I didn't talk to the Anglo boy because the police did.

The Navajo student accused of starting the fight interrupted the principal. "You have a problem. The Anglo started it. He was picking on a little kid and I told him to stop. Then he fought me."

The vice principal shook his head in disagreement. Several Navajo students shouted that Anglo students were always picking on and making fun of Navajos.

The principal, still standing, responded, "This is the first time I have heard this. I didn't know the Indian students were being picked on."

Sharon, a Navajo senior who witnessed the fight, stood and faced the principal. "We are never asked. I was not asked. I never get anything from Anglos." Her mother asked, "Why is it so hard for the kids to go to you with their problems?" Sharon persisted in questioning the principal. "I don't like the way Whites treat Indians. Why do you believe what the Anglo students say only? It's one side in this case. Can you guarantee that they won't continue?" The Navajo crowd clapped.

The principal responded, "We can talk about it. No, I guarantee. That's what you have to do as an individual. You have to take it." Murmurs of discontent echoed throughout the room. The principal continued, "Rumors of a fight were all around the school on Thursday, so I called in the police. There was no fight that day. Because of the tension we invited the police to investigate. On Friday morning there was a fight. Both the students were taken in and charged."

The DNA lawyer stood and asked the principal, "Is it true that the Anglo student was not charged and the Navajo student was?" The principal uttered softly, "Yes." Again the crowd muttered their disapproval.

"That cop tried to get me to fight him," shouted the Navajo youth involved in the fight. "He said, 'Come and fight me.' They told me not to step a foot in the school. Not to ever come back."

After a pause for a translation into Navajo, the principal urged parents to come to him with their problems. "If you feel your kids have been made fun of, you should come up to the school. You must come up to the school. We will do everything we can to help. If I can't help, you can go to the superintendent and say, 'That crazy principal can't help us.' That is the avenue we have in the district. We will do everything to help." At this point the superintendent stood and moved to the front of the room to stand by the principal:

> I want to say two things. We expect a lot of our principals, but not to be policemen. We don't expect them to do that. We have a good relationship with the police, so we turn problems over to the police. And then the school gives up jurisdiction. The world is a great place. I hope that the students we turn out have great opportunities. Our schools are good schools, but not perfect.

An elderly Navajo woman brought the discussion back to the issue of discrimination. "Why is it so hard for us to understand that we have this problem? It has been this way for years. I think the problem is that we have the police treating people differently. So you see, the policeman is the problem." A mother added, "I used to go to that high school. I bear the tragedy with the students now. The higher I went, the greater pressure I got. So I left and went to another high school to graduate." An elderly medicine man spoke last:

> We are just telling stories about each other now. Who was in the incident should be up front talking. When my kids were in school it was the same. And we are still trying to solve this problem. These kids who were talking tonight were in elementary school when my kids had this problem in high school. And I think the kids who are in elementary school now will also have this problem. We need to talk about it. Each time we talk about it the problem continues.

The meeting ended shortly before midnight. The school officials quickly left the building. Many of the Navajo parents and children continued to talk in small groups. Although charges against the youth had been dropped, he was not allowed to return to school. "They told me I was 18 so I could not go to high school any more. I was told to go to adult education to finish."

As I sat with his family, his mother-in-law bitterly complained she should have said the following to the vice principal, with whom she had gone to school twenty years before: "You know what it is like for the high school kids. You used to do the same things the kids are doing now against the Indians. You remember when you put pins in my seat. All the things that you used to do to Indians, it is still going on here and now. You did it, and now your kids are doing it."

I left with Sharon, the senior who spoke during the meeting, and her mother. We went to my house and continued talking about the incident. Sharon spoke of her own experiences in the racially mixed school. "They always give us trouble. Like there is this one group of guys. I told one, 'Shut up you pale face, or you red neck!' When they are rude to me I call them everything I know. They think Indians stink. I tell them, if you don't like Indians, why did you move here!"

Important public officials, like those who attended the meeting, are Anglos, and their ability to ignore Navajo concerns speaks to the security of their power base. All public institutions in the county are controlled by Anglos and by members of the Mormon Church.[14] The school superintendent, all four high school principals, four out of five elementary school principals, and the administration of the local community college are all LDS members. Over half of the county's population is Navajo, but Navajos account for only 15 percent of the teaching staff, and more than half of those have converted to Mormonism. The few Navajos in power have been sponsored for upward mobility since they joined the LDS church.[15] Locally, these converted Navajos are described by Anglos as "responsible," "good," and the "right kind" of Navajo. Anglo-controlled political and economic networks open slightly for these few individuals. Even for Navajos who hold middle-class jobs, racial stratification limits their place in the community. Navajos and Anglos do not socialize, and they pass each other without acknowledgment in stores, banks, and restaurants. As the meeting revealed, even when Navajos speak they are seldom heard, contributing to a strong sense of disempowerment.

Over the last 100 years, the Anglo population has expanded and prospered.[16] The Navajo population has also expanded, now comprising 54 percent of the county's population, but they have not prospered. Their life conditions speak loudly of discrimination. A colonized form of government exists in the county where the Anglo population benefits disproportionately from Navajo resources: 60 percent of the county's economic resources comes from the reservation, but only 40 percent is returned in goods and services. Almost 50 percent of the Navajo in the county live without running water or utilities. Their per capita income is $3,572 compared to $11,029 for Anglos. Almost 60 percent of Navajo families have incomes below the poverty level, compared to less than 10 percent of Anglo families. Nearly 90 percent of those in the county on public assistance are American Indian—Navajos or Utes. The unemployment rate of Indians is over 40 percent, four times the unemployment rate for Anglos. Navajo youth and their families are well aware of this economic marginalization. Shoveling snow, envisioned as a job possibility by a young Navajo student at the beginning of this chapter, speaks powerfully of the job ceiling in this arid, high desert community.

RACIAL CONFLICT IN THE SCHOOLS

Racism and cultural beliefs, particularly the issues of assimilation and resistance, are at the heart of the interactions between Navajos and Anglos. The Anglo perspective is informed by a century-old model of assimilation that views Navajo culture and language as a problem to be eradicated. During this period, the Navajo have resisted assimilation and successfully struggled to maintain a Navajo way of life. Faced with continued colonization and discrimination, few Navajos remain silent.

The antagonisms apparent at the meeting also produce tensions in schools. Discrimination takes different forms between teachers and students in classes and in the hallways. Some racism is overt: Anglo students and teachers speak openly about disliking Navajos. Other interactions are more subtle, disguising racism in ostensibly well-intentioned actions, such as teachers lowering their academic expectations to "accommodate" the culture of their Navajo students. Some paternalistic racism exists, such as when teachers assume Navajos are "childlike" and that educators know what is best for "their Navajos." Still other racism is based on superficial stereotypes of Navajo culture, which assume that because Navajo families do not share middle-class Anglo values they hinder their children's success in schools. This section depicts the cultural and racial warfare that comes as a result of dismissing Navajos as being culturally inferior.

Daily encounters with Anglo peers and teachers demonstrate the power of the racial and cultural struggle occurring in schools. Shortly after the meeting, Sharon spoke of her embarrassment and the anger she had towards the science teacher:

> He is prejudiced. He talks about Navajos and welfare. "You all listen, you aren't going to be on welfare like all the other Navajos." He shouldn't talk like that! And then the White students say things like that to us. Like all Navajo are on welfare. I'm not like that. We work for what we have. He shouldn't say things like that. It makes us feel bad.

Some youth use subtle counterattacks when put down by their non-Indian peers. One day in class, two Anglo students teased a young Navajo studying to be a medicine man about his hair bun, lice, and the length of his hair: "Hey, how long did it take you to grow that?" The Navajo boy replied with a soft smile, "Ten minutes." Other confrontations are not so subtle. One young woman, whose last name was Cantsee, explained why she was no longer in math class: "When I came into class late, that teacher said, 'Oh, here is another Indian who can't see how to get to class.' I told him to go to hell and left class."

Teachers' lack of experience in the Navajo community and stereotyping of Navajos results in both the distortion and the dismissal of Navajo culture. During an English class I attended, a teacher was discussing the romantic and realist periods in literature:

> Have you ever dreamed about something that you can't get? That is romanticism, when you dreamed that everything would work out. But then there is the realism period. Some people during this time in your literature text, they lived together six to a room with fleas and lice and everything. They had dreams but they weren't coming true. I hope all of you have bigger dreams than that.

A Navajo student whispered to a friend, "It sounds like he is describing a *hogan* [the traditional Navajo one-room round home]!" In a reading class I observed, the teacher said, "We are studying tall tales. This is something that cannot be true. Like Pecos Bill. They said he lived with the coyotes. You see, it can't be true." Two Navajo students looked at each other and in unison said, "But us Navajo, we live on the reservation with the coyotes." The teacher replied, "Well, I don't know anything about that. Let's talk about parables now."

Although some teachers' actions may be seen as "innocent" or "ignorant," others clearly reveal a hostile edge. Some teachers do know that coyotes are a fact of life on the reservation and still dismiss and mock students' lives. For example, during Sharon's senior year, her career education teacher lectured the class on the importance of filling out job applications. "You must put your address. When you were born, you are born into a community. You are not isolated. You are part of a community at birth. So you have an address." To which a student replied, "But I was born waaaaaaay out on the reservation! Not in a community." "I don't care if you were born out there with the coyotes. You have an address," argued the teacher. Students hooted, groaned, and laughed as several shouted, "Yessss, lady!" to which the teacher shouted back, "You sound like you are all on peyote. Let's go to the occupations quiz in your books."

Just as all Navajo youth are not dropouts, all Anglo teachers are not racist. Some teachers care deeply about their Navajo students. However, continued resistance to their educational efforts frustrates even the best teachers. I shared the frustration of Sharon's English teacher, who urged her Navajo students to perform in class: "You guys all speak two languages. Research shows that bilinguals are twice as smart. Language is not your problem. It's your attitude. You have given up because Whites intimidate you. Don't you want to be a top student?" "No!" the class responded loudly, "We don't care." This teacher, who had expressed a great deal of concern and empathy for her Navajo students three years earlier, recently told me, "You are not going to like what I say about Indians now. I am a racist! I'm not kidding. Working with these Indian kids makes you a racist. They just sit here and do nothing." Throughout the district, at both elementary and high school levels, administrators and teachers believe Navajo students have difficulties in school because of their language and culture.

Equally damaging to Navajo students' school experiences are teachers who refuse to acknowledge the racial discrimination in the community. By reducing racial conflict to "others' problems" or a thing of the past, the local power struggle is kept out of the classroom. During the last week of studying *To Kill a Mockingbird* in a twelfth-grade English class, the teacher focused on racial conflict between Whites and Blacks, and summarized the discussion of the book by saying:

> It used to be that Whites treated Blacks badly. Remember, this is racial discrimination, when one group treats another badly just because of the color of their skin, and it is against the law. It was a sad part of history and I'm glad it doesn't happen any more.

A Navajo student turned to me and said, "But it happens to us! Why didn't he say that? What about what happens to us?"

Navajo students' attempts to make racial discrimination visible within the school have been silenced by the Anglo students and school administrators. Shortly after the fight and community meeting, Sharon's journalism class called a "press conference" to discuss Navajo education and racial prejudice for an article in the school paper. The journalism teacher, who was also the faculty advisor for the school paper, suggested the conflict between Navajo and Anglo students was an important topic to be covered by the newspaper. The students, 14 Anglos and 2 Navajos, voted to invite Navajo parents, the high school principal, the Indian advisor, and myself to be interviewed. We had all attended the community meeting following the fight. At the press conference, an Anglo student who was new to the district spoke first:

> When I came I didn't know about Indians. The kids here tried to scare me, told me about Indian witches and evil spirits. It made me afraid of Indians, that they were weird or gross and they were out to scalp Whites!

The principal suggested that when students hear discriminatory comments they should correct them. Another Anglo student replied, "What do we do when teachers say bad things about Indians? Like the AP [advanced placement] history teacher. We don't have any Indians in there, and he says really awful things about Indians." The principal shook his head, "I'm sure most teachers don't do that. If they do you kids can tell us." He continued, "All students, Anglo and Navajo, are just the same. I don't see the difference. Kids are just kids. The fight between the Anglo and Navajo boy was an isolated incident. We have taken care of the problem." A Navajo parent, who had been silent, then stood and said:

> I hear that there was this Anglo kid who was caught stealing a little radio. But then the teacher found out the boy was from an important family here, so the teacher did nothing to the boy. So, you see, we still have this problem.

The bell rang. The press conference was concluded. The students, concerned that discussions of racial prejudice would both demoralize Navajo students and embarrass Anglo students, decided not to print the story.

Racial attitudes are also evident in teachers' and administrators' expectations of Navajo students. These attitudes include assumptions about the "academic place" for Navajos. The sixth-graders from an elementary school feeding into Border High School all scored above the national norm in mathematics on the Stanford Achievement Test. Yet upon entering high school, Navajo children were systematically placed in the lowest level mathematics class. When asked about the placement the principal explained, "I didn't look at the scores, and elementary grades are always inflated. Our Navajo students always do better in the basic classes." These attitudes about race and culture place a ceiling on learners; in a school-administered survey, 85 percent of the teachers in one school indicated that Navajo students had learned "almost all they can learn." Standardized test scores showed an average seventh percentile for the school, the lowest in the state, which the principal explained, saying, "Our district-level scores are low and dropout rate high because we have Navajo students."

Racism surfaces not only in ill-intentioned treatment of Navajo students, but also when well-intentioned educators make demeaning assumptions about them, representing a cultural mismatch. Anglos frequently distort Navajo values and view them as inadequate compared to their own cultural values. For example, Navajos are viewed as present-oriented and practical-minded. "I've never met a Navajo that planned far in the future, to like go to college. It's more [about] what to do tomorrow and the day after," said an Anglo school counselor. Another explained, "The Navajo are very practical minded. They think, 'What value is it to me in everyday life?' A lot of abstract ideas in education just don't mean anything." Anglo stereotypes of Navajos also include the perception that they work well with their hands. A career education teacher said, "Well, I mean, they are good in spatial things. Working hands-on. They don't learn theoretically. You can talk until you are blue in the face. It's much better if there is practical hands-on application." Anglos intertwine such "descriptions" of Navajo culture with the belief that the Navajo family does not teach children school-appropriate values. A counselor explained:

> We [Anglos] were brought up every day with the question, "What are you going to be when you grow up?" And that is something that the Navajo parents never ask. And then I bring them in the counseling office and I ask, "What are you going to be when you finish high school?" That is the first time they have even heard the question. It's just not done at home. And it's my values. The importance of an education and a job. They don't think to the future.

Embedded in this cultural distortion of Navajo values is the assumption that the closeness of Navajo family ties (i.e., "cultural pressure") is problematic for "progress" and that it "causes" school failure. One of the teachers explained it graphically with a story about lobsters:

> You know what they say about lobsters? You can put them in water this high [indicating a depth of a few inches] and they won't get out. As soon as one tries to climb out the others pull him back in. [Laughter] That's what it is like with the Indians. As soon as one of their kind tries to better himself, the others pull him back in.

The owner of a local pottery factory, who employs work-study students from the high school, also saw the problem not as a lack of individual skills, but of the demands of family responsibilities:

> Many of them have been through all sorts of training programs. Take Tom. He is a graduate from technical school. A welder. But he came back here and is working here painting pottery. . . . They come back here to live with their families. There is a good and a bad side to that. Over there on the reservation they are getting strangled. It really strangles them over there with families. They can't make it on their own and their families strangle them with responsibilities.

It is within this racially divided community that Navajo youth must navigate the school system. Over 10 years, from 1984, in a district with 48 percent Navajos, one out of every three Navajo students left school before graduation; almost 80 percent of the district's dropouts are Navajos.[17] During a district-wide meeting, administrators identified the following as the causes of these youths' school failure: lack of self-esteem; inadequate homes; inadequate preparation for school; lack of parenting skills; poor communication between home and school; poor student attendance; limited vocabulary and language development; limited cultural enrichment opportunities; too academic a curriculum; poor attitude and motivation; and fetal alcohol syndrome. All of these place the blame on deficits of the students and their families. In contrast, only three causes listed found fault with the schools: questionable teacher support, lack of counseling, and non-relevant curriculum.

Navajo students paint a different picture. Acknowledging racism (i.e., citing it as one of the central reasons they leave school), over half of the 168 students I interviewed who had left school said simply, "I was not wanted in school." Over 40 percent of those who left school saw the curriculum as having little relevance for their lives. Although they acknowledge home difficulties, over half of the Navajo youth who left school complained of problems with administrators and uncaring teachers who would not help them with their work.

ASSIMILATION: "NAVAJONESS" AS THE PROBLEM

Navajos became wards of the federal government in 1868. In accordance with treaty provisions signed at that time, the federal government was to provide schooling for all Navajos. Ever since, schooling has been used by policymakers and educators at the district and federal levels as a vehicle for cultural assimilation. Because public officials considered Navajo culture and language problematic and superfluous, education became a way to eliminate the "Indian problem."

In 1976, the district lost a suit filed by Navajo parents. As a result of the court's decision, the district was required to build two high schools on the reservation and to develop a bilingual and bicultural program for all grades. Construction of the high schools took eight years. The bilingual and bicultural program sat unused, gathering dust in the district's materials center for fifteen years. In 1991, after an investigation by the Office for Civil Rights in the Department of Education, the district was again found out of compliance with federal requirements concerning English as a Second Language (ESL).[18]

The district then created a new bilingual plan, which the newly appointed director of bilingual education presented at a parent meeting at the beginning of the 1993 school year. The district's latest plan calls for the total immersion of Navajo students in the English language to eradicate the Navajo language "problem." It requires that all Navajo students be tested for English-language proficiency, after which, the proposal states, "All Limited English Proficient (LEP) (ESL) [the two terms are used interchangeably] students are placed in the regular classroom with fluent English proficient students to ensure optimal modeling of language." This plan will operate even in schools with a 99 percent Navajo population. No special ESL classes will be provided for students who are Navajo-language dominant.

Navajo parents expressed disbelief that the new program would be implemented, and questioned whether Navajo would actually be used for instruction in their children's classrooms. The parents had reason to be concerned. The district had agreed to such a program 17 years earlier and it still did not exist. The bilingual project director responded, "Trust us. We are now sincere."

The Office for Civil Rights rejected the plan, issuing a citation of non-compliance to the district and turning the investigation over to the Education Litigation Division of the Justice Department. During the summer of 1994, U.S. Attorney General Janet Reno authorized the Justice Department to intervene in this case as "party-plaintiff." Based on the preliminary investigation, the Justice Department believed the school district had discriminated against American Indian students, violating federal law and the Fourteenth Amendment, by failing to adopt and implement and alternative language program for Limited English Proficient students. The district is accused of denying American Indian students the same educational opportunities and services, such as equal access to certain academic programs, provided to Anglo students, and of denying qualified American Indians employment opportunities equal to those provided to Anglos.

Throughout the district (at both Navajo and Border High Schools), administrators and teachers believe Navajo students have difficulties in school because of their language and culture. This explains, in part, why the district refuses to implement a bilingual program that uses Navajo as a language of instruction. "These kids we get are learning disabled with their reading. Because they speak Navajo, you know." The ESL teacher explained, "The Indian students need to learn English and basic skills to survive in the Anglo world. That bilingual and bicultural stuff is not important for them. The jobs are off the reservation, so they need to learn how to work in the Anglo world." Another teacher, in a letter to the editor of the local newspaper, argued, "Bilingual education will become the greatest obstacle a Navajo student has to overcome and an impediment to the education of all other students."

English language difficulties are acknowledged by Navajo parents; over a two-year period, the topic was brought up at 18 parent meetings. "Our kids speak Navajo, they need more of those ESL classes to help them learn." But at the same time, they speak of the importance of Navajo culture. "Our kids learn White history. When are you going to have Navajo language and culture, too?" At each meeting, school administrators and teachers assured the parents that language and culture were part of the school's curriculum. During the first 10 years of my fieldwork, only four semester-long classes were offered in Navajo language, history, or culture. All ESL classes have been eliminated in the high schools and replaced with general reading classes, even though few teachers in the district are certified in reading education.

This model of assimilation, which views native culture and language as a barrier to be overcome, has always framed educational policy in schools for American Indians.[19] Various programs have attempted to eliminate native cultures, measuring success in part by how many students do not return to their homes and families on the reservation. In the late 1890s, the superintendent of the Carlisle Indian School, the first boarding school for American Indian students, informed a congressional committee that between 25 percent and 30 percent of their students found a job and earned a livelihood away from their home; the remainder returned to the reservation. Even a year or two at school, he said, gave the youth a new life, and only a small percentage go "back to the blanket" and "do nothing."[20]

While the structure has changed somewhat, this educational practice has changed very little in the past 100 years. In 1990, Sharon's counselor explained, "Most of the kids want to stay right here. On the reservation. It's kinda like, we say, they have 'gone back to the blanket.' They will sit in their *hogan* and do nothing." Counselors cannot comprehend that a youth does not want to leave the reservation. Their typical comments include: "He said he wanted to be a medicine man![21] He can't really mean it. His card [counselor's student aspiration list] says the military," and "It's real progress when they want to get off the reservation. There is nothing for them to do out there." Today, as throughout history,

American Indians who resist assimilation by maintaining their culture and remaining on the reservation are described as failures. Such was the case with Sharon. Upon her return to the reservation after college in 1992, I was told by her counselor, "It's too bad. She didn't make it away from here. And I had so much hope for her succeeding." The college graduate is viewed positively, but those who "come home" are labeled "failures" by the Anglo community.

Racial beliefs about Navajos, embedded in a model of assimilation, guide Anglos' "understandings" of how to teach or interact with Navajos. For Anglos, these assimilationist beliefs are generally used to frame either the need to "change" Navajos to fit into the outside world or to adjust educational and economic opportunities downward to be "appropriate" for Navajo culture. Either way, Navajo culture is seen as undesirable. Teachers and administrators believe students fail because of their impoverished homes, culture, and language. Counselors assume Navajo students are not bound for college, and that they therefore should receive practical, vocation-oriented instruction; additionally, they should be encouraged to leave their families for jobs off the reservation. The educational assimilation policies described in this section are part of the larger race war in the community. Within this context, the school curriculum is not "neutral." Navajo youth who resist school are in fact resisting the district's educational goal of taking the "Navajoness" out of their Navajo students.

As Cummins pointed out, virtually all the evidence indicates that, at the very least, incorporating minority students' culture and language into the school curriculum does not impede academic progress. He argued that Anglos' resistance to recognize and incorporate the minority group's language and culture into school programs represents a resistance to confer status and power (with jobs, for example) on the minority group.[22]

From this angle, Navajo culture is considered *the* reason for academic failure. To accept Navajo culture and language would be to confer equal status, which is unacceptable to the Anglo community. Navajo culture and students' lives are effectively silenced by the surrounding Anglo community. Navajo language and traditions are absent from the school curriculum. Teachers' ignorance of Navajo students' lives results in the dismissal of the credibility of Navajo life. Racial conflict is silenced, either on the premise that it does not exist or that to acknowledge racism is the "cause of problems." This "silencing" is a clear denial of the value of the Navajo people's way of life.

NAVAJONESS AND SCHOOL SUCCESS

The Anglo community views assimilation as a necessary path to school success. In this view, the less "Indian" one is, the more academically "successful" one will become. Anglos perceive living in town, off the reservation, to be a socially progressive, economically advantageous move for Navajos. In fact, the opposite is true. The more academically successful Navajo students are more likely to be those who are firmly rooted in their Navajo community. This is consistent with Cummins's position that school failure is *less* likely for the minority youth who are not alienated from their own cultural values and who do not perceive themselves as inferior to the dominant group. Failure rates are *more* likely for youth who feel disenfranchised from their culture and at the same time experience racial conflict. Rather than viewing the Navajo culture as a barrier, as does an assimilation model, "culturally intact" youth are, in fact, more successful students.

Located on the Navajo reservation, Navajo High School (NHS) is more "successful" than Border High School in retaining and graduating Navajo students. The dropout rate from this school, 28 percent, is slightly less than the national average.[23] These students come from some of the most traditional parts of the reservation. Navajo is the dominant language in most of the homes, and 90 percent of them qualify for subsidized school meals. NHS has four certified Navajo teachers, a group of Anglo teachers with an average of five years' experience, and a school curriculum that is identical to other schools in the district. The differences in Navajo students' performance between BHS and NHS indicate the importance not only of the student's cultural identity, but also of the sympathetic connection between the community and its school. Where there are fewer Anglo students and more Navajo teachers, racial conflict is minimal and youth move through their school careers in a more secure and supportive community context. Nevertheless, even NHS students experience "well-intentioned" racism from some teachers and a vocationalized curriculum.

This pattern—reservation youth succeeding academically more than Navajo town youth—is also repeated *within* the Navajo student population at Border High School (BHS). Almost half the Navajos who attend BHS are bused to school from the reservation. Among Navajos living in town, only 55 percent graduate from BHS, whereas almost 70 percent of the Navajo students living on the reservation graduate from Border High School.[24] In other words, Navajo students who live in town and attend BHS are less successful than those who live on the reservation and attend NHS. Also, within the BHS Navajo population, the Navajos who are bused from the reservation do better than those who live in town. The most successful students, like Sharon, are from one of the most traditional areas of the reservation. In contrast, those who are not academically successful are both estranged from the reservation community and bitterly resent the racially polarized school context they face daily.

Many of the Navajo BHS students who live in town take a confrontational stance towards school: many of their teachers express fear and discomfort with them in their classrooms. Over three-fourths of the school's disciplinary actions involve these Navajo youth. These students' resistance is clear: the schools don't want them and they don't want the schools. The racial conflict in this school is highly charged, with each side blaming the other for the problem.

Faced with a school and community that refuse to acknowledge their "Navajoness" positively, and coming from homes that transmit little of "traditional" Navajo life, these youth clearly are living on a sociocultural border, with little hope of succeeding in either cultural context. Only 15 percent are employed and fewer than 10 percent of those who leave school attempt educational training later on.

Navajo youth respond in a variety of ways to the racial treatment they experience. Many leave school, while others simply fade into the background of their classrooms. Most report suffering racial discrimination. Sharon's experiences mirror those of many high school graduates. Although Sharon felt unwanted in school, she persisted, and graduated in 1991. Of her six elementary school girlfriends, Sharon was the only one to finish school. Her persistence was framed by her experience growing up on the reservation. Sharon's ability to speak at the meeting and her school success reflect her own sense of confidence—a confidence supported by traditional influences. Her early years were spent with her grandparents in a *hogan* on the reservation. As she explains:

> After I was born my mom was working. My grandma and grandpa, they were the ones that raised me until I started going to school. He was a traditional, a medicine man, so he was strict with us. And he made us go to school all the time. I am thankful to him. His influence is all around me now. . . . I'm modern. I guess I'm kind of old-fashioned, too. I keep all those traditions. I really respect them. I really respect those old people. Like they tell me not to do something. I listen to them. I go to all kinds of ceremonies. I'm proud to be a Navajo.

Sharon places her traditional beliefs alongside those of the dominant culture and honors both. Her grandfather's advice supports her decision. "He told me that it was okay for me to go to both. He said, 'take what was good from both and just make it your life.' So that's what I did. If some old medicine man or somebody told me I needed some kind of ceremony, I'd do it. I'd do it both ways. I'd go for the blessing too."

Sharon was an academically successful high school and college student. She completed her freshman year at the state university with a 2.8 grade point average, and then decided to return home. This choice securely embedded Sharon within her family and the Navajo community. She reflects on her decision:

> I used to think those people that go to college never come back. They always promise to come back to the reservation, but they never do. And now I understand why, because all the jobs are up there [in the city] and I mean, if I major in physical therapy, there is nothing I can do with that down here at home. I thought I could do it without Indians. I thought I could do it by myself, but it does make a difference. It makes me feel more at home. It is good to see some Indian people once in awhile. It really motivates me.

Sharon now lives with her mother on the reservation. She took community college classes for one year to certify as a Licensed Practical Nurse, but left after deciding the classes were boring. "You see, they make the classes easy because most of the students are Navajo. It was too easy and I got tired of it." She occasionally works as a medic on the county's ambulance. With a characteristically broad smile, she said:

> Maybe I'll go back [to the university] someday. I sometimes feel sucked in here. Like I'm stuck here. It's so hard to get out. But it feels good to be at my home with Navajo people, even though those Whites sometimes give us trouble. [Reflecting back on the racial fight and community meeting, she said little had changed.] . . . My brother, he is still at that school. And he is fighting back. You just have to keep doing it. Otherwise they just treat you like a dumb Indian. I will always fight. And someday my children will also go to school and fight to get jobs and be Indian.

Despite their treatment by a racist Anglo community that continues to dismiss the values and viability of Navajo life, the Navajo remain a culturally distinct and unified group of people. The continuity of Navajo culture provides a supportive framework or network of family and community for young Navajos, which increases their chances of academic success. This insistence on cultural integrity is visible in life on and near the reservation—where 70 percent of the Navajo youth will choose to live their lives.

THE NATIVE AMERICAN CHURCH: CULTURAL INTEGRITY

The Native American Church (NAC) and traditional Navajo ceremonies have a central place in the lives of almost all of these Navajo youth. Embedded in Navajo ceremonies are beliefs about the communal nature of success and the primacy of the family. Jobs and educational success are means to enhance the group, not just the individual. Jobs are seen as a means of earning necessary money, not as "good" in and of themselves. This contrasts sharply with Anglo values of hard work for individual mobility, agency, and economic success. To understand the Navajo perspective, it is necessary to experience Navajo life on the reservation, to see the goals and vitality of the Navajo community.

One ceremony I was invited to attend reveals a glimpse into this life. I had been invited by Joe, the father of the family with whom I had lived on the reservation:

> We are going to have a Peyote meeting for the girls.[25] For Jan's birthday, too. To help pray for them to finish school. Jan is trying to graduate this year. If you could come it would help to have an educated person like yourself, a professor.

I was asked to "go in," joining the family and friends for the all-night ceremony in a *tipi* [a traditional Plains Indian structure used for most Native American Church meetings]. Of the 28 participants, I was the only *bilangaana* [Navajo for White person]. We sat around a central fire and a half-moon shaped altar that represented the path of life—from birth to death. The fire and altar were attended to by the Fire Chief. Songs and prayers started with the passing of prayer sticks and a drum, and continued over the next four hours until holy water was brought into the *tipi* at midnight. I spoke and offered prayers during the meeting when I was invited to do so by the Fire Chief, who spoke to Jan and her sister first in Navajo, and then for my benefit in English:

> You are young still. You do not know what will happen to you in ten years. It is important that you take this path, and finish school. Your parents love you very much. You must get your education. I pray for you, it is so important.

He spoke passionately for 20 minutes. Tears were rolling down his face as he pleaded with his kin to succeed in school. As the singing resumed, more participants spoke of their own problems and offered prayers for the hosts' daughters. An uncle spoke:

> I want you to have the good in life. It is hard. It is like a job. You are in school and you must work hard, like a job. We want you to get a good education, and then someday you might have a job like a secretary or something like that, in an office. I can see that. Your parents try hard, but it is up to you to get an education. We know it is hard, but it is important.

The meeting ended at dawn, with a second pail of holy water and ceremonial food. Afterwards, the men remained in the *tipi*, stretched out comfortably as they smoked and told stories. They allowed me to remain and took the opportunity to educate me. The Fire Chief spoke seriously about the general concerns Navajo parents had for their children:

> The things our grandparents knew, we do not know now, and our children will never know. There is a new life, forward, to live in this here dominant culture. This is what I think. Our children need to go out and get the best they can. Go to school and college and get everything they want, and then come back here, to their homes, here between the four sacred mountains. In the past Navajo parents told their children to go out and get an education. Go to college. And they did and they stayed in Albuquerque, in the towns, and then the parents were sad because they said they never saw their children again. But Navajo parents now have to tell their children to go out and get their education. To college. And graduate school. And then to come back home, where they belong. Here on this land. This is where they belong. They need to bring their education back here to the reservation, their home. Then we can be a whole people. This is what I think.

The Native American Church meeting captures the solidarity of the Navajo community and the cultural vitality of its people. Although often invisible to their Anglo neighbors, who view Navajo youths' lives as a "cultural vacuum," ceremonies and family gatherings cloak and support these Navajo youth.[26] The Enemy Way, a five-day ceremony for the purpose of curing illness caused by a ghost, an alien, or an enemy, occurs frequently during the summer months. Additional ceremonial dances occur in the area at least monthly, and a strong Native American Church is active weekly on the reservation. All but one of the young women in the study had their *Kinaalda*, a Navajo puberty ceremony that marks the beginning of Navajo womanhood.[27] Ceremonies are frequently used to bless and support youths' life paths, including their progress in schools and at jobs. In all ceremonies and events, the group serves to support and bond the individual to the Navajo community. Individual economic success becomes a part of the Navajo community's larger economic network.

As was expressed in the NAC meeting, Navajo parents want their children to succeed in both the Anglo and Navajo worlds. However, it is clear that the family and community are of paramount importance, and that educational success brings community and family responsibility. There is a dual side to this message. Navajos are not trying to "get away" from Anglo culture, just from assimilation. Thus, they do want certain material goods and school success, but not at the expense of their cultural identity.

As Jan said shortly after her NAC ceremony, "They [parents] tell us to do good in school, but that we will always be Navajo."

CULTURAL INTEGRITY AND RESISTANCE

Traditional Navajo cultural values still frame, shape, and guide appropriate behavior in the Navajo community. Navajo youths' choice to remain a part of the community assures them economic support through local kinship networks unavailable off the reservation. This choice also puts these youth in opposition to the goals set for them by school officials. Specifically, the choice to remain on the reservation, and the insistence on maintaining culturally different values are central to the power struggle in the larger community, because these choices are defined as impoverished by Anglos. However, if one understands the viability of the Navajo community, resistance to assimilation is seen as a rational and appropriate choice.

The Navajos are a conquered and colonized people who have successfully resisted assimilation. They have survived over 400 years of Anglo subjugation and exploitation with a culture that, although changed, has remained distinct in its values, beliefs, and practices. These Navajos have remained on their ancestral land; Anglos are immigrants. The Navajo Nation, the largest American Indian reservation in the United States, comprises 26,897 square miles, an area approximately the size of West Virginia. Treaty rights recognize sovereignty status, a separate "nation within a nation," for the 210,000-strong Navajo nation. John David reports that the total personal income in 1991, including wages and salaries, transfer payments, livestock, and crops, was $900,032,754, with a per capita income of $4,106.[28] Accurate portraits of reservation poverty, however, leave non-reservation residents unprepared to understand that there are viable economic and social institutions on the reservation. The Navajo Nation's budget supports an infrastructure of education, law enforcement, and health and human social services with revenues from oil, gas, mining, timber, taxes, and federal and state funds.

Unique to this governmental structure is the infusion of Navajo culture. Traditional home sites that are determined by sheep and cattle grazing rights are maintained by a Land Permit Office; a tribal court system relies on a Navajo legal code, as well as a federal legal code; the Navajo Medicine Men's Association is housed in the complex of the tribal headquarters, with an office at the local hospital; all significant tribal meetings are prefaced with a traditional prayer from a Medicine Man; and the Navajo Nation publishes its own newspaper to provide a Navajo perspective on local and national matters. In 1986, 286 retail businesses, 94 of them Navajo owned, operated on the reservation. The Navajo

Communication Company provides cable television and telephones to homes with electricity, and the Native American Public Broadcasting Consortium provides local news to radio listeners. The Navajo Community College, a multi-campus institution with seven branches, serves over two thousand students.[29] In 1992, a total of 3,000 students were awarded tribal scholarships totaling $3,320,377. This insistence on tribal autonomy and resistance to "blending in" has assured their youth their continuity as Navajos. Specifically, Navajo choices cannot be compared, as in Ogbu's theories, to other minorities, because Navajos stand to lose only by integration into the larger society. The U.S. Commission on Civil Rights explains this unique position:

> Politically, other minorities started with nothing and attempted to obtain a voice in the existing economic and political structure. Indians started with everything and have gradually lost much of what they had to an advancing alien civilization. . . . Indian tribes have always been separate political entities interested in maintaining their own institutions and beliefs. . . . So while other minorities have sought integration into the larger society, much of Indian society is motivated to retain its political and cultural separateness.[30]

It is important to realize that Navajo individuals do not monolithically represent "the" Navajo culture. There are hundreds of different ways of "being" Navajo. However, within this cultural constellation, specific values are maintained. These Navajo beliefs and values surround the young as they learn how and what it means to be Navajo. Although the autonomy of the individual regarding possessions and actions is strongly maintained, consensus and cooperation for the good of the group is emphasized over aggressive individualism.[31]

The insistence on recognizing Navajo cultural allegiance begins at an early age and continues throughout life. Children learn to support and be supported by families. "Like there are all these things we do differently," explained Jan, "but I don't know them all. You learn them when you do something wrong. Then they show you what to do right." These lessons are learned and challenged against the backdrop of an Anglo world. Sometimes these worlds successfully co-exist. Matt, Jan's youngest brother, explained how a Navajo ceremony made things "right." Lightning, which is a powerfully negative force in Navajo beliefs, hit the transformer at the trading post. He continued, "We were afraid we could never drink a coke or get candy from there again! But then they had a medicine man do something and it was okay to eat there again."

Other situations provide challenges to the adherence of Navajo values. Navajos feel it is arrogant to try to control nature by planning every detail in the future. After a counseling session during her senior year, Jan explained, "It's dangerous. You can't change things that happen. That's the way it is. But my counselor said I could change everything by planning on a career. I don't think that would work." Navajos have a more humble view of "individual choice," which acknowledges both the dependence of the individual on the group and the importance of the extended family. When receiving sharply negative comments from an Anglo friend about the crowded living conditions at her home, Jan "turned the lens" and expressed disapproval of the Anglo nuclear family: "The way Whites live seems to be lonely. To live alone is kind of like poverty."

The Navajo depend upon extended family networks of economic and social support, critical factors in their lifestyle. On the reservation, the extended family relies on multiple (often minimum wage) incomes to provide support for the group. Joe's 1990 tax forms claimed 12 dependants supported on a $26,000 salary from a uranium plant. Their new pink, double-wide, three-bedroom trailer houses four daughters, two sons, five grandchildren, and the husbands of two of their daughters. Over the past several years, family members supplemented Joe's income with work in the uranium plant and on road construction crews, and as clerks, waitresses, cooks, motel maids, pottery painters, and temporary tribal employees. Sons and daughters move off the reservation in search of employment, and return when temporary employment ends. The family makes "kneel-down bread" with corn from the garden and sells it at fairs and in town.[32] All who can, work at jobs or at home. Pooled resources buy food, clothing, and necessities, and pay for car and insurance bills.

Along with the economic stability the extended family supplies, there is pressure to place the family ahead of individual prosperity and careers. As an elderly Navajo man said, "You can't get rich if you look after your relatives right. You can't get rich without cheating some people."[33] And as Jan said, "In the traditional way and now, the family is the most important thing you can do. Life is too short to worry about jobs. The family is needed for all those ceremonies." Jobs are seen as a way of earning necessary money, not as the way of life in and of itself.

Navajo families struggle with racial and economic discrimination imposed by their Anglo neighbors at the same time as they speak with pride of their "freedom" on the reservation. As Jan's father explained, "We don't have electricity, and don't have electric bills. We haul water, and we don't have water bills. And out here we don't have to pay for a [trailer] space." Nightly television watching, lights, and the vacuum cleaner only require an adapter and a car battery. Jan's aunt added,

> A medicine man warned us about what happens when you leave. He said, "They educate us to be pawns. We are educated to do a thing, and then we become pawns. Must work for money to pay for the water

bills, the electricity. We become pawns." So you see, we have our water, even though we haul it from sixteen miles away, we have our warm house, and our meat, and food from the land. In town we have to pay for these things, and then we become dependent.

A move to the city does not necessarily mean an increase in standard of living or "success." For example, in 1992, Jan and her husband moved to a large city to stay with his relatives and seek employment. After three months with only sporadic employment, they returned to her family. "It was lonely in the city," Jan said. "My mother needed us, her daughters, so we moved back. The family is real important. That is the main thing. You depend on the family to teach each other, and to be brought up right. If it is not the whole family being involved in it, then it is like lack of communication." Jan reminded me of a Navajo insult: "She acts as if she doesn't have any relatives." The individual without family is an isolated and unsatisfied person. This echoes the Fire Chief's plea at the Native American Church meeting: ". . . and then come back home. Then we can be a whole people." Jan has successfully followed this life path. She has settled into rearing her own children in the home of her mother on the Navajo reservation.

Submerged in an Anglo-controlled social landscape that restricts employment opportunities for Navajos, over half of the youth who remain on the reservation try, like Jan, to continue their schooling to enhance their chances for employment. After graduating from high school, almost all of them attend the local community college, their last chance to learn job skills to qualify for local employment. This path, starting with the traditional "Career Day" experienced by most U.S. high school seniors, appears egalitarian in that a multitude of opportunities and choices are "open" to youth after high school. For these Navajo youth, however, the Anglo belief of "equal educational opportunity for all" leading to "equal employment opportunities" is racially restricted. Anglos construct educational "choices" or paths for Navajo youth that lead through a vocationalized curriculum in both high school and college. This path dead ends, however, in the secondary labor market.

Post-high school options offered Navajo youth include a combination of local job ceilings, impersonal universities, and the local community college. Navajo students face a world segmented by unattractive choices with which schools and career counselors never come to grips. Although Navajo youth enter high school with aspirations about their future opportunities, their future aspirations are thwarted by the racism they experience in school. After high school, Navajo youth face a choice between a university-city route that works against their cultural beliefs, and a local job and school market that is totally subject to the racial struggle in the community.

HIGH SCHOOL CAREER DAY: RACIALLY DEFINED CHOICES

On one of my days of observation, I pulled into the small paved parking lot in front of Navajo High School five minutes before school began. The green athletic field stood in sharp contrast to the red dirt and sandstone bluffs. Sheep grazed on the lush lawn, rubbing against the chain-link fence that separated the school from the surrounding Navajo reservation. As I entered the windowless one-story, red brick school for another day of field-work, I was joined by Vangie, a Navajo friend. "It's career day, so you can come with me, Professor, while I learn about schools!" she exclaimed. The juniors and seniors were excused from classes to attend presentations from seven regional colleges and universities, two vocational or technical schools, and the Job Corps. The Navajo Nation's Education Office had a representative to explain tribal scholarships. Students were to attend four information sessions located throughout the school.

Vangie and I attended two regional college presentations. "Some classes are outside and are so much fun. Then there is the choir. You should take that your first year, it is really fun. And you meet all sorts of nice people," a recruiter said. A professionally developed video accompanied the presentation. The second recruiter also showed a polished, upbeat video with smiling faces, a brief glimpse of a professor lecturing in a large amphitheater, shots of athletic events, tennis courts, and leisurely images of students reading books on rolling campus greens. The recruiter said:

> If you want to be a policeman don't come here. But if you want to go into the computer field, or nursing, or in-flight training, come here. It is beautiful and the campus is lots of fun. You can do all sorts of things while you are in school.

Students talked excitedly about which college would be more fun.

The representative from a local vocational training school slowly went through a slide presentation as he explained the school's program:

> And that girl there, she is working at a real good job in a TV station. And that one, she is underemployed. She could get a real good job if she would ever leave here! See, in all these pictures we have the old and the totally up-to-date equipment. You never know when you will be working in a small place that has old equipment. So we teach with the old and the new.

Looking at a student audience of only seven Navajo females, he backed up to a previous slide:

> See that computer on that slide. If you are going to work in a big office, you have to learn about computers. And then we have a heavy equipment program. We could use more girls. Because of the Equal Opportunity Program, we could place 40 girls a year if they completed the program.

The students were quiet and attentive.

We stopped in the library to look at the literature brought by the local community college. District school staff were discussing with the Dean of the college their success in sending many of the Navajo youth away to school after graduation. One of the counselors said, "Over 60 percent of the graduating class got accepted to college. Some went to the Job Corps. One year later they are all back. Every one of them!" The Dean of the local community college explained:

> We don't recruit our students. They come to us. Many of the Indian students go to large universities and they fail. Then they come to us. After they have been with us, they all—100 percent who go to larger colleges —will succeed. If we recruited them to start with us, they might think they have been missing something. They can get what they need here.

The booth was full of pictures of Navajo students sitting at computers, building houses, working in hospitals, and sitting in lectures. The recruiter was the only Navajo on the professional staff at the college. Raised by a Mormon family, he had recently returned to work at the college.[34] He spoke softly to several Navajo students. "You can get a good education here. And your Pell Grant[35] will pay for everything. It's close to home so your parents can watch you girls!" They laughed and moved on to examine the pamphlets in the Job Corps booth.

The last presentation was by the state's largest university, my employer. Two student recruiters stood in front of a small group and emphasized the importance of filling out the applications correctly and getting financial aid forms into the university on time. "It is very important that you do things on time and correctly. It is a huge university. But we also have support for minority students and we want you to seriously consider coming to the university." The presentation continued with a list of the academic fields offered by the university and the statement, "The classes may be hard, but they are real interesting. And you can get a good education at our university." The presentation was dry, the "fun" of college life was presented as "getting an education," and the recruiters did not smile.

After these presentations, students moved into the auditorium for two films by the College Board on financial aid. Students filled the room, talking about the sessions they had attended, graduation plans, their personal relationships, and after-school activities. The first film pictured an African American man, one of several individuals interviewed who had "made it." He urged others to attend college. "Anyone can go to college. It is worth it. A small sacrifice now to have the money to go to college. But it is worth it. I am glad I went." The second film, a cartoon on how to correctly fill out financial aid forms, covered topics from estimating summer earnings to who in the household was a legal "provider." Students were bored and restless with the films and cheered when the lights came on, and then left for lunch. A counselor spoke to me as we were leaving the auditorium:

> We are the ones that fill out the forms. The students don't do it. About half will go on to some kind of school and almost all of them will be on financial aid grants. And the other half will sit out on the reservation and do nothing.

We left school early. As I was driving Vangie, her brother Sam, and several of their friends home, the conversation turned to what they were going to do after graduation. "I'm thinking about going to Dartmouth. They have a special Indian program. But I don't know if I want to be so far away from home. I might go into the Army. They will pay for my college." Another said, "I'll probably end up with a baby and be stuck here." She laughed, "I really want a baby of my own. I would be really happy, then, at home with a baby. That's what us Navajo do." Vangie jumped into the conversation. "There are a lot of girls that get pregnant. I'm just not going to do it. It will ruin your life if you have a baby. I want to go to college and get away from here so I can get a good job!" One said, "My parents tell me to do what I feel I want to do. I want to go to college. I hear college is a lot of fun. I want to have a business or something and come back to the reservation and live and help my people. I go crazy about thinking and taking care of my parents in the future." Another, who had been silent, softly spoke, "I want to be a race car driver. But my mom thinks it's too dangerous. So I guess I can be a secretary or nurse. She wants me to have a good job like secretary or something and live at home." Vangie and Sam's home was the last stop. As they climbed out of my car, Sam teased his sister, "I'm not going to have a baby either! At least till I get married and have a job."

EDUCATIONAL AND ECONOMIC MARGINALIZATION

The images shown during Career Day of youth lounging on green fields, smiling faces in a choir, a class, using computers, and laboratories, filled the picture window of opportunities facing youth beyond high school.

Few Navajo youth will realize the life depicted in these tableaux. Their dreams of a wide range of occupational choices and jobs in distant big cities dim with the reality of their limited academic skills, which relegate them to semi-skilled jobs. High school career days present hollow images for Sam and most of his peers, who do not face "unlimited" opportunities dependent only on individual achievement, but rather a set of political, economic, and social constraints that intertwine in schools and communities to limit their possibilities. Economic disparity is maintained by the continued role of vocational education in local schools and colleges as one aspect of an ongoing racist strategy to limit the opportunities of Navajo and secure opportunities for Anglos. Navajo youth are trained to remain below the job ceiling.

Sam's experiences, which follow in this section, mirror that of many Navajo youth. Sam and Vangie have 10 brothers and sisters. They live on the reservation 10 miles from the bus stop in a complex that includes 18 relatives, a new government home, and older stone home, traditional *hogans*, and a satellite dish. They haul their water from a well six miles away, but have electricity from a nearby oil rig. Shortly before graduation in 1989, while flying kites near their home, Sam talked about what he wanted to do with his life: "I want to go into business or finance. Or maybe electronic engineering. Or maybe the military. I would like to go to Berkeley, in California, but I will need a tribal scholarship. I am working on getting my grades up." He had a 2.1 grade point average. Navajo tribal scholarships require a 3.5, a goal he did not reach. The rhythmic whishing of the oil pump was the only sound on the mesa. Sam proudly pointed out the canyon where their livestock grazed and to the far mountains where his father was born. "I have relatives up there that I don't even know. I would like to come back here to live on the reservation. It would be all right. But it is better to get off the reservation to get jobs." His brother was an example. "My brother, he travels all over the world with his job. He works with computers." But there remains the pull of home. "There are not many jobs here. But I like it here. It is home for us Navajo."

Students' experiences in and out of school modify their expectations about future job possibilities. For the Anglo students, future possibilities increase as students approach graduation. Navajo youths' aspirations, on the other hand, are greater than the future envisioned for them by the schools. After four years in high school, their aspirations often match the vocational orientation constructed by their schools. Even though Sam intended to go to college, with the help of a counselor, he filled his senior year schedule with basic and vocational level classes. The counselor explained:

We are not supposed to track kids, it is against the law. But by the time these kids are in high school they know what they are going to do. So we have most of our Indian students in vocational classes. After all, most won't go to college anyway.

The assumption that Navajo youth knew they wanted a future in vocational jobs early in high school was not supported by my data. During the 1987–1988 school year, 132 Anglo and Navajo students in grades nine through twelve completed the JOBO, a career inventory test that translated student "interest" into job fields. Although 20 percent of the Navajo ninth-graders indicated interest in professional careers requiring college, twice as many Anglo ninth-graders saw their future jobs as being in professional fields. The reverse was true regarding vocational, semi-skilled jobs. Almost half, 47 percent, of the Navajo ninth-graders were interested in such jobs, whereas only 30 percent of the Anglo students saw vocational jobs as part of their desired future. This pattern changed by the twelfth grade. The Anglo students desiring vocational jobs dropped by half, from 30 percent to 15 percent, and over 60 percent now desired professional careers. Just the opposite occurred with the Navajo seniors: 62 percent of these students had readjusted their goals downward, towards vocational jobs, and only 15 percent remained determined to achieve professional careers. These figures must be viewed against the backdrop of the dropout rate: by their senior year, close to 40 percent of Navajo youth had already left school—leaving behind the most academically successful Navajo youth.

Navajo culture and local employment opportunities are used by the Anglo educators as a rationale to limit Navajo students' educational opportunities, while, in reality, a vocational curriculum assures the continuity of the local job ceiling for Navajos. The principal at Sam's high school explained the school's vocational orientation:

I'm interested in equal educational opportunity. I have been here for ten years. We used to be 75 percent academic and 25 percent vocational. Now we have 75 percent vocational and 25 percent academic. We need to recognize the needs of the people in this local area. I'm not saying we should ignore the academic classes. But the vocational training is where the jobs are for the local Navajo people.

His vice principal added:

Academics are very important in this world, but we've got to realize that half the kids or more out of this high school are not going into academic jobs. They are going to go into vocational. In fact, the majority of jobs in the future are still going to be vocational. They're not going to be in the white-collar type job. But how do you tell them that?

In 1990, the district received a $3.5 million grant to construct a vocational career center. In an open letter to the community, an administrator explained the new thrust of the school district into technology and job preparation. Citing a state statistic that 40 percent of youth finish college or university training when only 20 percent of the available jobs require a four-year degree, he told of the shock facing graduates who have to be retrained in vocational and technical areas. "Since only 20 percent of the jobs in Utah will require a college degree, the secondary schools must take a more active role in preparing students for employment." He explained the necessity for the curriculum to be responsive to employers' needs:

> This concept does not mean a lowering of academic standards; to the contrary, most technical jobs now require a strong background in math, physics, and language. Nor does this concept infer that all students should know a specific vocational skill prior to leaving high school. The jobs in our society are changing so rapidly that students will be much better served if they develop certain basic skills and attitudes toward work. Most employers now prefer to train their own employees in specific skill areas. What they want from high schools are students with basic understandings of technology, good basic academic skills, and the flexibility to be retrained as often as the job market requires.

This emphasis in high schools sets the stage for focusing the educational careers of Navajo youth onto vocational paths. The district's "state of the art" vocational school is Navajo High School; the predominantly Anglo high school in the northern part of the district remains college preparatory. This assures college-educated Anglo youth a brighter job future in the community.[36] The administrator's state statistic that 40 percent of youth finish college or university reflects the 97 percent Anglo population of the state, not the local Navajo population served by the district. Almost half of the Navajo youth from the local school district attempt some kind of post-high school education. Out of 1,000 youth, one-third eventually attend the local community college, 6 percent attend universities, and 7 percent attend vocational institutions. Regardless of these efforts, less than one-half of 1 percent complete a four-year degree, only 2 percent complete two-year degrees, and 5 percent receive a vocational certificate. None of the youth who attend the community college go on to finish a four-year degree. Over 90 percent of the Navajo youth do not receive a degree higher than their high school diploma. Sam and his friends are in this group.

Sam graduated in 1989 from Navajo High School. During his senior year, he fluctuated among wanting to study business or finance, joining the military, or wanting to go to technical school to learn electronics. He decided to go to the city to hunt for a job. Off the reservation, Navajo family networks are utilized for economic support—both for the family left behind and the person moving to the city. Youth who leave for the city do so only if there is a relative who can assist with housing and the location of a job. The housing tends to be low-income and jobs are usually minimum-wage labor in fast food restaurants, motels, and factories. During the two years following high school, Sam worked at an airplane parts factory in Salt Lake City and did construction work in Phoenix. He lived with relatives in both cities. Back on the reservation to visit his family, he stopped by my house:

> It has been two years since I graduated and I haven't gotten it together to go to college. And now my younger brother is already up at the university ahead of me! I would like to come back here to live on the reservation. It would be all right. But they say that it is better to get off the reservation to get jobs. That's what I did. There are not many jobs here. But I like it here. It is my home. And the air is clear.

Sam stayed on the reservation. He enrolled in the community college in a program that promised good local employment. "It's for electronics. Job Services and the college are running it. I will be able to get a good job with the certificate."

The two-year community college Sam attended is where most Navajos finish their time in higher education. The creation of this community college in the early 1980s has been an economic boom for the local Anglo community, whose members occupy all of the teaching positions and 99 percent of the administrative and support staff. The college is supported, due to its two-thirds Navajo student population, by federal tuition grants targeted for "disadvantaged" youth and from the Navajos' own oil royalties money.[37]

One Navajo high school counselor explained, "The college comes with scholarship money and says they [youth] can come to the college free. Many don't know about other places. And they need the money to go. And the college needs them to survive." Last year the community college established a scholarship fund for all county residents, using $500,000 from Navajo royalty money to establish matching funds from the state.[38] Prior to this, Navajo students could use their scholarships to attend the college of their choice. Now, under the guidelines of the new scholarship fund, all scholarships are limited to attendance at the local college. By putting these stipulations on the funding, the community college has insured middle-class jobs for the Anglos and vocational training for jobs that do not exist for Navajos.

As in high school, Navajo youth at the community college are encouraged to seek terminal degrees in vocational areas. As the academic dean explained, "We have looked into the economic development of the next decade and it is in the service industry. Our students want to stay in this community and these are where the jobs will be." I argued for encouraging more students to go for four-year professional degrees, reminding him that the better jobs in the county required a college degree. He argued, "Most of the jobs here are in the service industry. We are happy if we can keep a Navajo student for a one-year program. That is success." The mission statement of the college supported his emphasis. Only its concluding goal mentioned preparing students to go on to four-year institutions.[39]

The college has a large vocational program. During the 1992 winter quarter, out of almost 100 courses offered, two-thirds were in vocational or technical areas. Certificates of Completion, requiring one year of study, are offered in accounting, auto mechanics, general clerical, secretarial occupations, office systems, practical nursing (LPN), stenography, and welding. In addition to these specialties available to all its students, the college offers special vocational programs for Navajo students that are cosponsored by the Navajo tribe. Designed to fill immediate job needs, these latter certificates are offered in marina hospitality training, needle trades (sewing), building trades, sales personnel training for supermarket employment, security officers, building maintenance training, pottery trades, modern office occupation, restaurant management, and truck driving. These latter "Navajo only" certificates are designed to prepare students for local employment. An instructor explained,

> These programs are designed to prepare the student for good jobs that are out there. They are extensive, lasting for three quarters. One quarter they are prepared with communication skills. And then how to get along with their bosses. It is the general social skills, work skills, and the particular skills for the job.[40]

These programs are not without criticism. Another instructor explained:

> We trained 40 or 50 people at a time to run cash registers. That's good. But how many stores around here are going to hire all those people? They're training for limited jobs. Why send everyone to carpenter's school? In this small area we have tons of carpenters. Why teach them all welding? You can do it at home, but how many welders are there in your area? Probably every other person is a welder.

During the last decade at this community college, 95 percent of the vocational certificates were earned by Navajo youth and adults. Even this training, however, did not necessarily result in a job. The Dean of the college explained:

Our marina hospitality program was a good one. And it was going to get a lot of Navajo jobs. The tribe had built a new marina and the tourist dollars were going to be good. But then they had the flood. It wiped out the marina. It hasn't been built again. So all those people, almost 100, were trained for jobs that never happened.

And then there was the needle trades program.

We trained 24 women, but there weren't many jobs. The one sewing factory closed down. The other only hired a few.

The employment results from the truck driver program were minimal.

We trained over thirty for that program. The uranium tailings over on the reservation were supposed to be hauled away, so we trained truck drivers. It's still in the courts and so no one was hired. We could have gotten them good jobs in other states, like Oklahoma, but they didn't want to leave the reservation.

And the largest program, sales personnel, a joint effort of business, the tribe, and the college, placed students in local supermarkets for "on-the-job training" with the understanding they would receive employment after completing the program. The supermarkets supervised the student trainees for three months while they learned job-required skills, such as boxing, shelf stocking, and check-out packing:

We had a real good success with this one. A lot of our students were working in the supermarkets in towns. But then there were problems with the supermarkets not hiring them after the training. Cutbacks, you know. But some people thought they were just using the Navajo students for cheap labor. And then they didn't hire them.

Some vocational training programs lead to jobs. Most do not.

After completing the one-year certificate in electronics, Sam found a job—at a factory in the city. Again, he left the reservation. After 18 months, he was laid off. In 1993, he returned to his home, this time with a wife and child. Sam said,

I'll find something around here, or we will try the city again. Right now I have things to do at home. My parents need help, after my sister died in the car accident, so I need to be here. I have things to do, you know. My younger sister is going to have her *Kinaalda* and the wood has to be gathered. I can get a job around here.

After six months without a job, he enrolled at the community college again. He is studying building trades in a community that saw a 9 percent reduction in the construction industry in 1992.

The only successful job networks Navajo youth have are through their parents or relatives, which are for low-level jobs. Mothers grew up working in the local restaurants and school cafeterias, or as maids in the three local motels. Fathers worked at temporary construction jobs, and in the local oil and uranium fields. Sons and daughters have access into the same lines of employment, especially when the training paths available to them in high school and at the community college limit them to these kinds of jobs.[41] If they remain in their home community (as most do), even Navajo youth with a high school diploma face a future of semi-skilled jobs, training programs, and seasonal work, mirroring the lives of their parents.

High school graduates are twice as likely to have jobs as those who do not finish school.[42] On the surface, this seems like an incentive for youth to finish high school. However, there is little difference in the *kinds* of jobs held by graduates and non-graduates. With rare exceptions, both groups of employed youth work at the same kinds of service industry jobs characterized by low pay with few or no benefits, seasonal employment, and a highly transitional work force: cooks, motel maids, school aides, bus drivers, tour guides, making or painting pottery, clerical workers, electrical assistants, janitors, waitresses, seamstresses, the military, uranium and oil workers, and construction. Working at the same job alongside peers who dropped out of school, many Navajo youths question the relevance of the high school and college diplomas. At the very least, Navajo youth see a successful academic effort paying off less for them than for their Anglo peers. On the one hand, leaving school is not the route most youth choose, as it affects their chances for employment, and completing school is a goal encouraged by their families and the community. On the other hand, they are acutely aware that completing school does not guarantee employment at other than menial jobs. The Navajo youths mentioned at the beginning of this chapter who disagreed with their vocational education teacher about the limited job opportunities facing them after high school clearly understood this dilemma.

Regardless of school success or failure, after high school, all of these youth face the same structural barriers in the community because they are Navajo. Here, Ogbu's model partly explains this situation. He argued that the existence of a "job ceiling," intertwined with a "rejection" of the Anglo world, mediates against school success for some castelike minorities. Ogbu stated:

Members of a castelike minority group generally have limited access to the social goods of society by virtue of their group membership and not because they lack training and ability or education. In particular, they face a job ceiling—that is highly consistent pressures and obstacles that selectively assign blacks and similar minority groups to jobs at the lowest level of status, power, dignity, and income while allowing members of the dominant white group to compete more easily for more desirable jobs above that ceiling.[43]

Ogbu implied that the job ceiling affects student attitudes towards school and that vocational tracking is the school's adaptation to the job market. A picture of the economic landscape of the community illustrates the racial stratification that frames the employment possibilities of Navajo youth like Sharon, Jan, and Sam. Although American Indians comprise over half of the local population, they are marginalized to either low-paying jobs or no jobs.[44] The unemployment rate for Indians, 41 percent, is over four times the unemployment rate for Anglos. A breakdown of the jobs in the county by occupation illustrates the different opportunity structures faced by Anglo and American Indian workers. Over 90 percent of official and management jobs are held by Anglos. Only 8 percent of these top-level jobs are held by American Indians. In other professional positions, Anglos hold over two-thirds of the jobs. Twenty-five percent of all jobs in the county are classified in these two management and professional categories, but few American Indians make it into these powerful positions. In other areas, Anglos occupy almost 90 percent of the jobs as technicians, 91 percent of the sales workers, 80 percent of office and clerical workers, 63 percent of skilled craft workers. American Indians are employed in the service-maintenance and the construction trades, and as laborers and para-professionals. All of the assemblers and hand-working jobs, 75 percent of non-precision machine operators, 50 percent of construction, 61 percent of cleaning and building services, 50 percent of laborers, and 47 percent of food preparation and service jobs are held by American Indians. This job ceiling is faced by all Navajo youth—dropouts, graduates, and community college students.

The Navajo in this community experience a racially defined job ceiling, but student attitudes toward the job ceiling do not result in the rejection of schooling or of the Anglo world. Rather, Navajo reject assimilation as a path they must follow in order to be defined as "successful." Navajo students on the reservation, where there are fewer jobs than in town, are more successful in school, even though they are acutely aware of their limited economic opportunities in the community. Historical experiences and the job ceiling, by themselves, do not explain how Navajo youth respond to school: rather, their response to school is mediated by culture, especially the cultural integrity of the group.

Regardless of students' "cultural stance" (degree of acculturation or assimilation), a key factor in the relationship between schools and students seems to be what schools *do* to students—successful students are still limited by the *quality* of their schooling experience. In viewing schools as sites of conflict, vocational tracking is one part of the racial struggle in this community.

Navajo students are counseled into vocational classes in high school, limiting their access to college preparatory classes. By the time these youth leave high school, their "academic fate" is assured. Almost half of them try schools away from the area, but with minimal academic skills and limited economic resources, they drop out and return home. They then move into the "arms" of the community college to complete the education they will "need" to live, training locally for semi-skilled jobs.[45] Ironically, Navajo youths' failure to succeed educationally "outside" actually enhances the local Anglo economic power base by assuring the continuity of the community college.

Navajo youth are encouraged to leave the area for "good" jobs, which in turn also fits with the Anglos' interest in maintaining good local jobs for their group. Many Navajos work in factories in cities for a while, but, separated from their families, they remain detached, isolated, and poor. Most return home and seek whatever paying job they can find. Unlike middle-class youth, who attach their self-image to the kinds of job they strive for, these Navajo youth view a job as a means of making money, which is necessary for survival. The kind of job they work at does not define their "goodness." That is defined by their family relationships. As Paul Willis argued, the concept of "job choice," from semi-skilled to professional jobs, is a middle-class construct.[46] Some people get "jobs," others have "careers." Structural and economic determinants restrict individual alternatives, but choices are made among the remaining possible choices. Navajo youth seek whatever jobs are available to them in their community. In doing so, they support their families with an income and secure the continuity of Navajo culture.

Regardless of the dismal job ceiling, Navajos are persistent in their schooling efforts to enhance their employability. Navajo men and women who do hold the credentials necessary for better jobs are increasingly competitive for those positions. Almost without exception, these educational credentials are earned at schools outside the county. These few hold positions as teachers, social workers, health care providers, and administrators for tribal and county programs. Without these credentials, however, Navajo people are guaranteed to lack qualifications for positions of leadership and power in the community—a community that has always been their "home" and where most of them will live their lives.

NAVAJO LIVES: CULTURAL INTEGRITY

Navajos are treated differently from Anglos in this community's educational and economic institutions. However, as John Ogbu, Margaret Eisenhart and M. Elizabeth Grauer, and Margaret Gibson have pointed out, there is intra-group variability in responses to schooling within each minority group.[47] The Navajos are no exception. Clearly, Navajo youth are not homogeneous in their responses to schooling. Some, like Sharon, Jan, and Sam, follow paths that Gibson called "accommodation without assimilation" and that Ogbu called an "alternative strategy or the immigrant strategy," even though they are from a "castelike" group. They are successful in the educational system, even though this does not necessarily translate into economic stability. At the same time, they insist on maintaining their place as Navajos within the community. By refusing to accept either assimilation or rejection, these youth force us to look at new ways of viewing success. The school success of these Navajo students, with strong traditions intact, is explained, in part, by a model of "cultural integrity." Supported by a solid cultural foundation, they resist by moving through high school as a short "interruption" in their progression to lives as adult Navajo men and women. For them, high school is something one tolerates and sometimes enjoys; school success does not pose a serious threat to their cultural identity. What is clear from the lives of these Navajo youth, however, is that rather than attempting to erase Native culture and language, schools should do everything in their power to use, affirm, and maintain these if they truly want to achieve equity and promote Navajo students' academic success.

Even though Navajo youth develop a variety of responses to their schooling experiences, what is significant is that the school system issues a homogeneous institutional response to the Navajo youth, regardless of their "good" or "bad" student status. Focusing on student behaviors and their values towards school must be coupled with what schools *do* to these students, such as subjecting them to racial humiliation and vocational tracking. As I have illustrated in this chapter, the school context and curriculum are not neutral. Racism frames the stage and remains a barrier for all Navajo youth, regardless of their academic success or social compliance. Ironically, academic achievement under these conditions is questionable because of the watered-down curriculum and the persistent discrimination in the job market. This suggests that school reform and changes in the job market must be connected in order to talk about educational success in a meaningful way.

In looking at the variability of Navajo youths' responses to education and the homogeneity of Anglo responses, "cultural identity" is used by both to establish cultural boundaries and borders.[48] Cultural boundaries can be thought of as behavioral evidence of different cultural standards and appropriateness. These can be manifested in different speech patterns, child-rearing practices, and learning styles. The presence of these cultural differences, by themselves, is a politically neutral phenomenon. Navajo youth, securely rooted in their culture, move back and forth between their community and the surrounding Anglo community. The cultural framework surrounding Navajo youth, unlike secondary cultural differences, did not initially arise to maintain boundaries and to provide the ability to cope with Anglo subordination. Cultural boundaries, however, are often turned into cultural borders or barriers during inter-group conflict. In this situation, cultural differences become politically charged when rights and obligations are allocated differently. The Anglo community uses Navajo culture as a border, a reason to deny equality by claiming the privilege of one kind of knowledge over another. Navajo families are judged by what they don't have—money, middle-class Anglo values, higher education, and professional jobs—rather than by what they do have—extended families, permanent homes, strong Navajo values and religious beliefs.

Remaining Navajo is a desired goal, not one settled on by default. Life in homes on the reservation, surrounded by family, friends, and similar "others," is a sound choice for youth, with or without school credentials. The choice to remain on the reservation represents failed attempts to find security and happiness in towns and cities amid racial isolation and under- or unemployment. This choice also represents an ethical commitment and valuing of families and Navajo traditions. The Navajo community provides a place of social acceptance and economic survival unavailable in Anglo-dominated communities off the reservation. This choice, however, situates Navajo youth within a local Anglo community structure that dismisses their lives and limits their educational and economic opportunities.

Cultural and racial differences serve both as reasons used by the Anglo community to deny equal educational or economic opportunity to Navajos and as a means Navajos use to resist cultural homogeneity. Jan, Sharon, and Sam chose a "boundary" strategy, resisting assimilation by maintaining pride in their culture and language, which led them successfully through school. They followed the "rules of the game," even though they knew they faced a "stacked deck." This path, fraught with conflict, uncertainty, and pain, was not easy. For some Navajo youth, however, boundaries become borders. A few cross over and leave their families and lives on the reservation. Most, however, choose their families and Navajo traditions over the illusory promises of wealth in the larger society. As Jan said earlier in this chapter, "The [parents] tell us to do good in school, but that we will always be Navajo." This choice assures the continuity of the Navajo people, and answers the plea expressed in the NAC meeting: "They need to bring their education back here to the reservation, their home. Then we can be a whole people."

ACKNOWLEDGMENT

Donna Deyhle, "Navajo youth and Anglo racism: Cultural integrity and resistance", pp. 403–444. Copyright © 1995 by the President and Fellows of Harvard College. All rights reserved.

NOTES

1   In this article, I use pseudonyms for the schools and the individuals who participated in my research.
2   Although somewhat contested as a term that attempts to represent all majority people, I use the term "Anglo" as it is used by the Navajos in this community, as a political category that unifies all White people.
3   "Border" refers to the economic, social, and political marginalization of the Navajo. It also describes the literal "border" of the reservation community, which is divided geographically by a river. Most of the Anglos live in the North and almost all Navajo live in the South.
4   Murray Wax, Rosalie Wax, and Robert Dumont, *Formal Education in an American Indian Community* (Prospect Heights, IL: Waveland Press, 1989). The original study was published in 1964 by another publisher.
5   I shared my research with LDS and non-LDS Anglos. They also helped me correct my understandings of the Mormon Church.
6   For a more detailed analysis of my fieldwork relations, see D. Deyhle, G. A. Hess, and M. LeCompte, "Approaching Ethical Issues for Qualitative Researchers in Education," in *Handbook of Qualitative Research*, ed. M. LeCompte, W. Millroy, and J. Preissle (San Diego: Academic Press, 1992); Donna Deyhle, "The Role of the Applied Educational Anthropologist: Between Schools and the Navajo Nation," in Kathleen Bennett deMarrais, *Inside Stories: Reflections on Our Methods and Ethics in Qualitative Research* (New York: St. Martin's Press, 1998).
7   See Frederick Erickson, "Transformation and School Success: The Politics and Culture of Educational Achievement," *Anthropology & Education Quarterly*, 18 (1987), 335–356; John Ogbu, "Variability in Minority School Performance: A Problem in Search of an Explanation," *Anthropology & Education Quarterly*, 18 (1987), 312–334; and Henry T. Trueba, "Culturally Based Explanations of Minority Students' Academic Achievement," *Anthropology & Education Quarterly*, 19 (1988), 270–287, for debates on these positions.
8   Jim Cummins, "Empowering Minority Students: A Framework for Intervention" *Harvard Educational Review*, 56 (1986), 18–36.
9   John Ogbu, *Minority Education and Caste: The American System in Cross-Cultural Perspective* (New York: Academic Press, 1978).
10 Ogbu, *Minority Education and Caste.*
11 Cummins, "Empowering Minority Students," p. 22.
12 Cummins, "Empowering Minority Students," p. 22.
13 DNA is short for *Dinebeiina Nahiilna be Agadithe*, which translates to English as "people who talk fast to help people out." The DNA is a legal service that provides free legal counsel to low-income Navajos.
14 Racial issues in the county are made more complex by the relationship between the dominant religion, The Church of Latter Day Saints (LDS), or Mormons, and non-Mormons. A majority of the Anglos in the county are

Mormons. A majority of the Navajos were either traditionalists or members
of the Native American Church. The LDS church teaches that American
Indians are "Lamanites," descendants of Laman, Lemuel, and others who,
having emigrated to the Americas, rejected the gospel. Righteous groups are
White, while those who had rejected the covenants they had made with God
received a "sore cursing," even "a skin of blackness . . . that their seed might
be distinguished from the seed of the brethren" (*Book of Mormon*, 2, Nephi.
5:21; Alma 3:14). Converting back to the gospel results in the "scales of
darkness" falling from Lamanite's eyes and a return to a "white and delight-
some" being.

15   For an analysis of the relationship between Mormons and American Indians,
see Mark P. Leone, *Roots of Modern Mormonism* (Cambridge: Harvard
University Press, 1979); Dan Vogel, *Indian Origins and the Book of Mormon*
(Signature Books, 1986); and Wallace Stegner, *Mormon Country* (Lincoln:
University of Nebraska Press, 1970).

16   The Anglo population in this county arrived in the 1800s as pioneers from
the Church of Jesus Christ of Latter-day Saints (Mormons). Sent by Brigham
Young, the 236 settlers were to start a colonizing mission among Navajos
and to increase the land base and religious influence of the LDS church
throughout the region. From the beginning, cloaked within the assimilationist philosophy of the LDS church, the Mormons dismissed Indians' claim to
political and cultural sovereignty.

17   I determined the graduation and dropout rates in this community by following "cohorts" of Navajo youth throughout their school careers. A total of
629 students forming six different cohorts from two schools, from the class
of 1984 to the class of 1989, are represented with complete four-year high
school records. Combining the data from both schools revealed that 59 percent graduated through either traditional or nontraditional means, 34 percent left school, and 7 percent remained "unknown." The graduation rate of
59 percent is lowered to 49 percent when reporting only students who
graduated on time in the traditional high school program. Over half,
55 percent, of the youth that dropped out did so during the twelfth grade.

18   This was based on the *Lau v. Nichols* court decision, which mandated that
school districts test and provide special English instruction to non-native
English speakers. See, for example, Courtney B. Cazden and Ellen L. Leggertt,
"Culturally Responsive Education: Recommendations for Achieving Lau
Remedies II," in *Culture and the Bilingual Classroom*, ed. Henry T. Trueba,
Grace Pung Guthrie, and Kathryn Hu-Pei Au (Rowley, MA: Newbury
House, 1981), pp. 69–86, for the educational implications of this court
decision.

19   See, for example, Margaret C. Szasz, *Education and the American Indian:
The Road to Self-Determination since 1928* (Albuquerque: University of
New Mexico Press, 1977); Gloria Emerson, "Navajo Education," in *Hand-
book of North American Indians*, 10, ed. Alfonso Ortiz (Washington, DC:
Smithsonian Institution, 1983), pp. 659–671; and Estelle Fuch and Robert
Havighurst, *To Live on This Earth: American Indian Education* (Albu-
querque: University of New Mexico Press, 1972).

20   Robert A. Trennert Jr., *The Phoenix Indian School: Forced Assimilation in
Arizona, 1891–1935* (Norman: University of Oklahoma Press, 1988).

21   Navajo medicine men and women are regarded as the most powerful people
within Navajo culture. One studies to obtain the knowledge and practices
throughout a lifetime, as all of Navajo beliefs about their origin, and reasons

and ways to live one's life are intertwined with ceremonies to "balance" and guide themselves for a healthy life. The medicine men and women are the mediators between the beliefs of a tradition and personal health. In addition to conducting large-scale religious ceremonies, such as the Enemy Way, Navajo medicine men and women perform traditional weddings and *Kinaaldas*, as well as being called upon by families for curing illnesses that range from headaches and nightmares to cancer and diabetes. Most Navajo use the services of both the traditional medicine men and women and Western-trained medical doctors. See, for example, Clyde Kluckhohn and Dorothea Leighton, *The Navajo* (Cambridge, MA: Harvard University Press, 1974); Gladys Reichard, *Navaho Religion* (Tucson: University of Arizona Press, 1983); and Leland C. Wyman, "Navajo Ceremonial System," in *Handbook of North American Indians*, 10, ed. Alfonso Ortiz (Washington, DC: Smithsonian Institution, 1983), pp. 536–557.

22   Cummins, "Empowering Minority Students," p.25.

23   U.S. Department of Education, *State Education Statistics* (Washington, DC: U.S. Department of Education, January 1984 and January 1986).

24   The situation has worsened. The dropout rate among Navajo students increased throughout the 1980s. Although the combined cohort rate at BHS shows only a dropout average of 41 percent, 75 percent of the 1991 class at Border High School did not graduate. In 1991, the district reported that the dropout rate for Navajo students was five times higher than for Anglo students; 80 percent of the dropouts were Navajos.

25   The Native American Church, commonly referred to as the Peyote religion, is a pan-Indian, semi-Christian, nativistic religious movement in the course of whose ritual believers eat the Peyote cactus, a substance containing more than 10 alkaloids, the best known of which is mescaline. It is pan-Indian in the sense that its ideology emphasizes the unity of Indians and their distinctness from Whites. Its origins are traced to the Plains Indian nativistic religious movements at the turn of the century. It was introduced to the Navajo by the Ute, their neighbors to the north of the reservation. See David Aberle, *The Peyote Religion among the Navajo* (Chicago: University of Chicago Press, 1982). Peyote meetings are jointly conducted by a Fire Chief and a Roadman.

26   This ideology asserts that the Indian home and the mind of the Indian child is meager, empty, or lacking a pattern. See Wax, Wax, and Dumont, *Formal Education*, for an excellent examination of this ideology. This study of a Sioux community and its school was conducted over 40 years ago; many of these researchers' results were mirrored in this Navajo community.

27   With a Navajo girl's first menses, she becomes a young woman and has a "coming of age" ceremony to usher her into adult society. The chief aim of the four-day ceremony is to impart the physical, moral, and intellectual strength she will need to carry out the duties of a Navajo woman, following the example set by Changing Woman in the creation story. Details of the ceremony are reported by Shirley M. Begay, Kinaalda: *A Navajo Puberty Ceremony* (Rough Rock, AZ: Rough Rock Demonstration School, Navajo Curriculum Center, 1983), and Charlotte J. Frisbe, Kinallda: *A Study of the Navaho Girl's Puberty Ceremony* (Middletown, CT: Wesleyan University Press, 1964).

28   David L. John, *Navajo Nation Overall Economic Development Plan 1992–93* (Window Rock, AZ: The Navajo Nation, 1992).

29   Both Anglos and Navajos teach at the College. The President and Board

478 Donna Deyhle

are Navajo—this is a strong, Navajo-controlled organization. Navajo philosophy, language, and culture are part of the curriculum. The school is currently working on developing a Navajo teacher-training program.

30 U.S. Commission on Civil Rights, *Indian Tribes: A Continuing Quest for Survival* (Washington, DC: U.S. Government Printing House, 1981), pp. 32–33.

31 Louise Lamphere, *To Run after Them: Cultural and Social Bases of Cooperation in a Navajo Community* (Tucson: University of Arizona Press, 1977).

32 "Kneel-down" bread is a traditional food of the Navajo. A fist-sized ball of ground corn is wrapped in fresh corn leaves and buried in an underground pit oven. The name comes from the process of having to "kneel down" when putting the bread into the pit.

33 Kluckhohn and Leighton, *The Navajo*, p. 300.

34 In 1954, the LDS Church officially adopted, as part of their missionary activities, the Indian Student Placement Program, in which American Indian children were "adopted" by a Mormon family. American Indian youth lived with foster families during the year, went to public schools, and were educated into the LDS Church. Home visits occurred for a few weeks or months during the summer. By 1980, approximately 20,000 Indian students from various tribes had been placed in LDS foster homes. The program is no longer expanding, placing only 1,968 in 1980, and in the future will be focusing on high-school-age children. This program had touched almost all of the Navajo families in this area. In every family, close or distant clan members have experienced LDS foster homes. For some example of the experiences of the program see: J. Neil Birch, "Helen John: The Beginnings of Indian Placement," *Dialogue: A Journal of Mormon Thought*, 18 (Winter 1985), 119–129; Lacee A. Harris, "To Be Native American—and Mormon," *Dialogue: A Journal of Mormon Thought*, 18 (Winter 1985), 143–152; and M. D. Topper, "Mormon Placement: The Effects of Missionary Foster Families on Navajo Adolescents," *Ethos*, 7, No. 2 (1979), 142–160. There were many reasons for parents to put their children in this program, including a chance for better educational opportunities in the cities, more economic security in White families, and, in some situations of extreme poverty, better food.

35 Pell Grant is a post-secondary school federal grant sponsored by the U.S. Department of Education. The grant is based on financial need.

36 A local county report revealed that two-thirds of the jobs in the county were located in the northern portion of the country, where almost 75 percent of the Anglo population lived. The government ranked as the number one employer, the school district the second, and the county the third. These three provided a total of 750 jobs, or 23 percent of the county's employment. A majority of these jobs required either a college degree or some college education. Specifically, 20 percent of jobs in the state of Utah will require a college degree, 40 percent will require six months to four years post-high school training, and 40 percent will require less than six months of training.

37 In 1933, Congress passed a bill that added this area to the Navajo reservation located in Utah. The bill gave the Navajo people in these areas the right to 37.5 percent of any gas or oil royalties, to be used for tuition of Navajo children, for building or maintaining roads on the lands added to the reservation, and for other benefits for these residents. The state of Utah was the trustee of this trust. In 1956, great quantities of oil were discovered in this area. In lawsuits filed in 1961, 1963, 1977, 1984, and 1987, the Court found

in favor of Navajos who claimed the Utah Division of Indian Affairs had failed to comply with the terms of the 1933 Act by using money for the benefit of non-Navajos. In the most recent lawsuit, in 1992, the Navajos accused the state of breach of trust and breach of fiduciary duties, and are suing to recover millions of dollars lost through this mismanagement. Estimates of how much could be awarded in the case run to more than 50 million dollars.

38   After Navajo complaints of mismanagement, the state attorney general's office audited the trust fund. The audit found a questionable use of funds, including $146,000 to finance the administration building, science building, and dormitories; $35,000 for nursing faculty; and $43,500 for a counselor who administered the scholarship program. The audit questioned using Navajo monies to defray the costs of a state institution.

39   "[T]he curriculum includes associate degree programs, vocation-technical programs, developmental programs, adult and community education programs and courses which are transferable towards four-year degrees."

40   During the 1992 Winter Quarter, this instructor taught 24 one- to six-credit cooperative education classes. Each class covered a different subject area, such as anthropology, auto mechanics, geology, drafting, and secretarial work, with a title that included "Work Experience."

41   Out of 200 employed graduates from my database, 25 percent of the males were in the military, the National Guard, or the Marines, and 75 percent were in trade types of occupations, particularly construction, welding, electrical, and oilfield work. Most of the women were in traditional low-paying, pink-collar jobs, such as LPN, office worker, seamstress, pottery painter, and clerk. One woman had a bachelor's degree and was teaching; one other was a supervisor at K-Mart.

42   All the Navajo youth, from the high school classes of 1982 to 1989 in two different schools, were tracked in my database over the past eight years to determine what happened to them after they had graduated or left school. Two-thirds of these youth were successfully located. The percentages given are based on these youth. Out of 732 youth, both graduates and non-graduates, 32 percent were employed, 39 percent were unemployed, and 29 percent were students. Higher employment, lower unemployment, and more student status were revealed by examining the high school graduates separately. Out of 499 graduates, 39 percent were employed, 26 percent unemployed, and 35 percent were students. The image is bleaker when looking at the youth who left school prior to graduation. Of these 233 youth, only 19 percent were employed, 66 were unemployed, and 15 percent were students. There were slight gender differences. More men were employed, 37 percent, compared to 27 percent of the women. Close to half, 47 percent, of the women were unemployed, compared to 34 percent of the men. An equal number of men and women were students. The label "student" is one that needs to be viewed cautiously. Over 80 percent of these were enrolled in the local community college. Many of these youth attended school on a part-time basis, lived at home, and were otherwise unemployed.

43   John Ogbu, "Societal Forces as a Context of Ghetto Children's School Failure," in *The Language of Children Reared in Poverty*, ed. Lynne Feagans and Dale C. Farren (San Diego: Academic Press, 1982), p. 124.

44   In this rural county, existing jobs are limited. The services industry sector (lodging, personal, business, repair, health, and educational services) was the largest contributor of jobs in the county, accounting for 21 percent in 1986.

The largest occupational group, representing 36 percent of all jobs in 1986 and 37 percent in 1991, was in production, operations, and maintenance—basically in the blue-collar group of occupations. These jobs were concentrated primarily in the goods-producing industries of agriculture, mining, construction, and manufacturing. Second in the number of jobs hierarchy are the professional, paraprofessional, and technical groups, followed by service and clerical occupations. The Utah Department of Employment Security published a projected occupations outlook from 1986 to 1991 specific for this county. The occupations listed as being in demand included: blue-collar workers, supervisors, cashiers, combined food preparation and service workers, continuous mining machinery operators, conveyor operators and tenders, electricians, underground mining machinery mechanics, maintenance repairers (general utility), roof bolters, secretaries, sewing machine operators, and shuttle car operators. This local profile mirrors that of the state in general. The services and trade industry will account for half of all jobs in Utah by 1991 and will claim 58 percent of all new growth over the same period. Brad M. McGarry, "Utah's Affirmative Action Information 1987: A Blueprint for Hiring," Utah Department of Employment Security Labor Market Information Services, May 1988; John T. Matthews and Michael B. Sylvester, "Utah Job Outlook: Statewide and Service Delivery Areas 1990–1995," Utah Department of Employment Security Labor Market Information Services, January 1990.

45 For a discussion of how community colleges function to "cool out" students, limiting rather than leading them to professional degrees, see Steven Brint and Jerome Karabel, *The Diverted Dream* (New York: Oxford University Press, 1989); Burton Clark, "The 'Cooling-Out' Function in Higher Education," *American Journal of Sociology, 45* (1960), 569–576; Kevin J. Doughtery, "The Community College at the Crossroads: The Need for Structural Reform," *Harvard Educational Review, 61* (August 1991), 311–336; and W. Norton Grubb, "The Decline of Community College Transfer Rates," *Journal of Higher Education, 62* (March/April 1991), 194–222.

46 Paul Willis, *Learning to Labour* (Westmead, Eng.: Saxon House, 1977).

47 Ogbu, *Minority Education and Caste*; John Ogbu, "Variability in Minority School Performance: A Problem in Search of an Explanation," *Anthropology & Education Quarterly, 18* (1987) 312–334; John Ogbu, "Understanding Cultural Diversity and Learning," *Educational Researcher, 21* (November 1992), 5–14; Margaret A. Eisenhart and M. Elizabeth Grauer, "Constructing Cultural Differences and Educational Achievement in Schools," in *Minority Education: Anthropological Perspectives*, ed. Evelyn Jacob and Cathie Jordan (Norwood, NJ: Ablex, 1993); and Margaret A. Gibson, *Accommodation Without Assimilation: Sikh Immigrants in an American High School* (Ithaca: Cornell University Press, 1988).

48 Erickson, "Transformation and School Success," p. 346.

Chapter 20

A Quantitative Examination of Oppositional Identity among African American and Latino Middle-School Students

April Taylor

Although poor performance and academic underachievement are experienced across ethnicities, for minority, school-aged children, they are a well-documented and pervasive problem. The achievement gap continues to increase, with only 13 percent of African American and 16 percent of Latino fourth graders demonstrating reading ability proficient for their grade level (National Center for Educational Statistics, NCES, 2006a). Similarly, only 13 percent of African American and 19 percent of Latino fourth graders demonstrate grade-level proficiency in mathematics (NCES, 2006b). This underachievement persists throughout middle and high school, with African American students continuing to experience school failure and dropout at disproportionate rates compared to their White peers (NCES, 2004).

One explanation for this underperformance that has received much attention is that minority students devalue academic achievement. This devaluing has been attributed to a variety of causes, such as a desire to protect one's self-esteem (Crocker & Major, 1989), a response to one's perceptions of barriers to socioeconomic mobility (Ford, 1992; Ogbu, 1997), and a consequence of one's cultural and historical experiences (Ogbu, 1991, 1997). Yet, what do we really know about the potential social-psychological precursors to minority students' devaluation of academic achievement? Most researchers who have studied the devaluing of achievement have used qualitative approaches. The current study represents a quantitative investigation of theoretical constructs hypothesized as shaping minority students' attitudes toward academic effort and achievement.

Like researchers from many other disciplines, anthropologists have attributed ethnic minority students' underachievement to their devaluing of academics. Anthropologists whose work is relevant to achievement have focused on the historical circumstances and cultural forces that have shaped U.S. minorities' experiences. John Ogbu's cultural-ecological model distinguishes between voluntary minorities, those who voluntarily immigrated to the United States to improve their social, political, or economic conditions, and caste-like or involuntary minorities, like African Americans and Chicanos, who have become part of the U.S. fabric not by choice, but as a result of slavery, conquest, or colonization (Fordham & Ogbu, 1986; Ogbu, 1997).

According to Fordham and Ogbu's 1986 thesis, one consequence of African American students' involuntary status is the development of an "oppositional identity," which is characterized by the adoption of values that conflict with those held by mainstream, middle-class, White Americans. Among these rejected values is that of working hard to succeed in school. Involuntary minorities perceive endorsing White American values as threatening to their social and ethnic identities. Particularly during adolescence, African Americans may adopt oppositional identities whereby they show relative indifference, or even disdain, towards achievement behaviors that the larger society values.

A CONCEPTUAL MODEL OF OPPOSITIONAL IDENTITY

The social-ecological literature has identified several attitudes, beliefs, and behaviors that contribute to students' development of an oppositional identity. Based on the literature, I have developed a multidimensional model of oppositional identity (see Figure 20.1). Elements represented in the model are described in the relevant literature as contributing to minority students' attitudes and approaches to academic achievement. Each element's specific relationship to the academic attitudes of involuntary ethnic minority group members is discussed below.

Cultural Inversion

The first element of the model, cultural inversion, describes the tendency for involuntary minority groups to regard certain behaviors as inappropriate for them because they are characteristic of the dominant ethnic population. Instead, minority group members adopt behaviors that are opposite to those of the dominant group. Fordham and Ogbu (1986) identified several behaviors depicting cultural inversion and coined the term "acting White" to describe African American high school students' perceptions of their same-race peers who worked hard to do well in school. To these students, academics are considered the domain of White Americans. To achieve academically would require African Americans to go against their culture and attempt to adopt behaviors of the dominant group. Other unacceptable "White" behaviors that Fordham and Ogbu noted include speaking Standard English, spending time in the library, getting good grades, and being on time. Engaging in cultural inversion

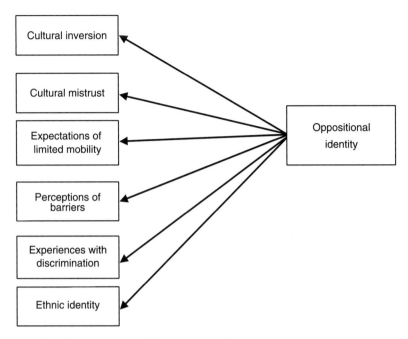

Figure 20.1 Conceptual model of oppositional identity.

and resisting the adoption of some mainstream qualities of the dominant group obviously could be detrimental to academic achievement. Minority students are faced with the dilemma of striving for success in the academic arena, despite their peers' opposition and the threat that academic achievement poses to their ethnic identity.

Cultural Mistrust

Involuntary minority group members' attitudes towards school are more generally described as being shaped by their negative perceptions of institutions as a whole, or cultural mistrust. According to Ogbu, episodes and events throughout history compel involuntary minorities to believe that Whites and the institutions they control cannot be trusted. In the case of schooling, involuntary minorities tend not to trust that they or their children are being given the best education or that the school guidelines reflect minority group members' best interests. This distrust arises out of their experiences of discrimination and marginalization and results in involuntary minorities' rejection of the dominant group's rules and standards.

Consistent with a distrust of White institutions, involuntary minority students' academic motivation is debilitated by their belief in socioeconomic mobility. For them, hard work does not pay off. Instead, they believe that they face a job ceiling that prohibits them from competing for the most desirable positions (Ford, 1992; Ogbu, 1982, 1997). It is a classic notion that ethnic minority group members are socially barred from achieving their fair share in the labor market, with social historians documenting racial job ceilings beginning in the mid 1800s (Olneck & Lazerson, 1974). In response, involuntary minorities believe that educational attainment and effort do not necessarily result in occupational opportunity.

Perceptions of Barriers

Similar to perceptions of a lack of mobility, minority group members' strong perceptions of barriers to opportunity lead to diminished regard for academic achievement (Mickelson, 1990; Taylor, 2001). Mickelson (1990) found that despite high endorsement for education in the face of low achievement, African American students' experiential attitudes regarding education revealed that they were more pessimistic about *their own* occupational gains to be reaped through academic effort than were their White peers. Taylor (2001) found that perceptions of barriers were a significant predictor of low academic-achievement values among middle-school males. These findings further suggested that ethnic minorities' perceptions of barriers might negatively impact their educational and occupational expectations. It is clear that considering school achievement as being unrelated to future gains may subsequently contribute to an attitude that does not facilitate academic motivation.

Experiences with Discrimination and Ethnic Identity

Taken as a whole, cultural inversion, cultural mistrust, and perceptions of immobility and barriers to opportunity are rooted in minority group members' personal experiences with discrimination and the importance and meaning they attach to their ethnicity. As such, experiences with discrimination and the degree to which ethnic minority students identify with their ethnic group might shape the degree to which they adopt an oppositional identity.

GOALS OF THE RESEARCH

Despite the cultural-ecological model's contribution to understanding minority students' underachievement, there has been relatively little empirical work in this area other than the qualitative studies of Ogbu and his critics (see Ainsworth-Darnell & Downey, 1998). Some researchers have viewed the concept of oppositional identity as a largely unproductive way to think about the problems of minority youths (Spencer, Noll, Stoltzfus, & Harpalani, 2001). As such, the potential practical contributions of this theoretically rich concept remain unexamined. The usefulness of the concept of an oppositional identity in understanding academic underachievement depends on its ability to assess the degree to which students adopt such an identity and the relation between such adoption and resultant behaviors.

The goals of this study are two-fold. The first goal is to quantitatively examine the theoretical constructs hypothesized as contributing to minority students' oppositional attitudes regarding academic effort and achievement. The second goal is to construct a measure of oppositional identity that can be used in future investigations. Despite the attention and resources committed to educational equity, minority students' persistent academic lag highlights the need for additional study in this area.

METHOD

Participants

Study participants included 300 middle-school-aged boys and girls from two ethnic groups (African American and American-born Latino). Among the African Americans, there were 45 boys and 65 girls (M age = 12.42). The Latino sample consisted of 88 boys and 102 girls (M age = 12.51). The groups included in the study are theoretically identified as representing involuntary minority groups. Of the total recruited for the study, 48 students were excluded because they reported that they were first-generation Latino or of mixed ethnicity, or because they failed to report their ethnicity.

Students were recruited from a predominantly bi-ethnic middle school located in an economically depressed neighborhood in greater metropolitan Los Angeles. The school received Title 1 compensatory education funds and had a large percentage of students who qualified for the district's free lunch program. Thus by all available indicators, the great majority of participants in this study reasonably could be classified as having a low socioeconomic status (SES). A school in a lower-SES area was purposefully chosen. Because perceptions of barriers and immobility are key constructs in this study, it was important to recruit a sample that might perceive obstacles to opportunities in their lives. That is more likely to be the case in lower- versus middle- or higher-SES communities.

Procedure

One African American female senior researcher and one Latino male graduate student administered the study measures as a pair.[1] Students were instructed to move away from their neighboring classmates and to put up notebooks to separate them. The researchers then passed out the response booklets; one of the researchers read the questions aloud as the other circulated around the classroom, assisting respondents as needed. During the procedure, the researchers stressed the importance of students answering the questions honestly and keeping their responses confidential. The entire procedure lasted about 45 minutes.

Outcome Measures[2]

Cultural Inversion

Students' degree of cultural inversion was assessed by having students rate the degree to which they endorsed: (a) engaging in school-related oppositional *behaviors* (e.g., turning homework in on time, speaking Standard English) and (b) holding oppositional *beliefs* (e.g., "Some kids feel that they should be in class *on time* and before the bell rings BUT other kids think that it's *not cool* to be in class before the bell rings") (see Fordham, 1996; Fordham & Ogbu, 1986). Students indicated the belief that most closely expressed what they thought, as well as the strength of this belief.

Cultural Mistrust

Cultural mistrust was measured using a modified version of the Cultural Mistrust Inventory (CMI) (Terrell & Terrell, 1981). For the purposes of this study, only items related to the education and training subscale of the CMI were used (e.g., "Teachers from ethnic groups other than my own present materials in class on purpose to make my ethnic group look dumb").

Perceptions of Mobility

Perceptions of mobility were measured using a revised version of the African American Career Outcome Expectancy Inventory (Brown, 1994), which investigates the future occupational benefits that respondents expect to gain after graduating from high school and college (e.g., make a lot of money, avoid being treated unfairly).

Perceptions of Barriers

Participants responded to questions regarding their perceptions of educational barriers being present in their lives. Barriers were measured using a cartoon-based pictorial assessment adapted from Cook, Church, Ajanaku, Shadish, Kim, and Cohen (1996). For each barrier, students were asked to indicate the degree to which they believed the barrier would keep them from going to school. Educational barrier items included: "not smart enough," "didn't try hard enough," "no good schools nearby," and "you have a bad teacher."

Students' perceptions of occupational barriers were measured and computed in a similar manner. In this case, students were asked the degree to which seven occupational barriers would keep them from getting the job they wanted. Occupational barrier items included: "don't know what to do," "there are no jobs," and "they don't want to hire people like you."

Perceptions of Discrimination

The educational, institutional, and peer discrimination subscales from the Adolescent Discrimination Distress Index (ADDI; Fisher, Wallace & Fenton, 2000) were used to assess the frequency of students' experiences of discrimination (e.g., put in a lower ability class or group because of your ethnicity, people acted as though they were suspicious of you because of your ethnicity, threatened by other kids because of your ethnicity).

Ethnic Identity

Ethnic group identity was measured using a modified version of the Multidimensional Inventory of Black Identity (MIBI; Sellers, Smith, Shelton, Rowley, & Chavous, 1998). Students' attitudes regarding how they felt and thought about being a member of their ethnic group (e.g., "I really like belonging to my ethnic group"), their perceptions of how others in society perceive their ethnic group (e.g., "Overall, people in my ethnic group are considered good by others"), and the importance of a student's ethnic group to his or her self-concept (e.g., "My future depends on what happens to other people in my ethnic group") were measured.

Student Attitudes Towards School

Students' attitudes towards school were assessed using an adapted version of the school climate subscale of the Effective School Battery (ESB; Gottfredson, 1984). Students' attitudes about how much they like school (e.g., I like school) and the clarity, fairness and respectfulness of school rules and administrators (e.g., the school rules are fair) were assessed.

RESULTS

Factor Analysis

This study used multiple constructs to operationalize oppositional identity. To identify general categories of beliefs or behaviors that might vary differently depending on the gender or ethnicity of respondents or uniquely influence students' adoption of an oppositional behavior, a factor analysis of students' responses to the subscales was conducted.

Principal components extraction with varimax rotation was performed on the 14 scales and/or subscales. Four factors, accounting for 62 percent of the variance, were extracted (factor loadings, communalities, and percents of variance and covariance are shown in Table 20.1).

The first factor accounted for 19 percent of the variance (eigenvalue = 3.61). Each of the three perceptions of discrimination subscales, cultural mistrust, and the ethnic identity public regard subscale loaded on this factor. This factor is labeled Perceptions of Ethnic Victimization and had a Cronbach's alpha of .70.

The second factor accounted for 17 percent of the variance (eigenvalue = 2.04). This factor included agreement with each of the two attitudes towards school subscales and measures of oppositional beliefs and behaviors. This factor was labeled Unconstructive School Attitudes, and Cronbach's alpha equaled .58.

Each of the remaining two factors accounted for 13 percent of the variance. The third factor (eigenvalue = 1.76) included the remaining two of the three ethnic identity subscales—centrality and private regard—as well as perceptions of mobility. This factor is labeled Optimistic Ethnic Identity and had a Cronbach's alpha of .70.

The fourth factor (eigenvalue = 1.20) was labeled Perceptions of Barriers and included measures of perceptions of educational and occupational barriers. Cronbach's alpha equaled .90.

Analyses of Variance

Ethnographic research has suggested that the underachievement of U.S.-born involuntary minority students can be explained by examining particular attitudes and beliefs that these students hold as a result of specific historical and life experiences. In order to examine ethnic and gender differences, students' mean responses on each factor were analyzed in a 2 (gender) × 2 (race), analysis of variance (ANOVA), and significant models were followed by one-way analyses where appropriate to interpret the effects. For each analysis, there were no significant main effects of gender and no interactions.

Table 20.1 Component loadings, communalities, percents of variance and covariance for principal components extraction and varimax rotation on model variables.

Scale	Ethnic victimization	Unconstructive school attitudes	Optimistic ethnic identity	Perceptions of barriers	Communalities
Perceptions of discrimination: institutional subscale	**.80**	.17	.03	-.06	.67
Perceptions of discrimination: peer subscale	**.78**	-.22	-.15	.08	.69
Perceptions of discrimination: educational subscale	**.84**	.13	-.09	.03	.74
Cultural mistrust	**.55**	.25	.03	.23	.42
School attitudes: belonging subscale	-.02	-.66	.29	.08	.52
School attitudes: fairness subscale	-.35	-.65	.11	.25	.62
Oppositional behaviors	.06	**.77**	-.04	.26	.67
Oppositional beliefs	.06	**.82**	-.06	.14	.70
Ethnic identity: centrality subscale	.03	-.08	**.77**	-.04	.63
Ethnic identity: private regard subscale	-.08	-.08	**.80**	-.12	.67
Ethnic identity: public regard subscale	-.46	-.07	-.07	-.22	.29
Perception of mobility	-.01	-.08	**.62**	-.15	.41
Occupational barriers	.16	.02	-.23	**.86**	.82
Educational barriers	.14	.09	-.15	**.86**	.79
Percent of variance	.19	.17	.13	.13	
Percent of covariance	.31	.27	.21	.20	.62

Ethnic Victimization

African Americans reported significantly higher perceptions of ethnic victimization than Latinos, $F (1, 276) = 8.63$, $p < .004$ respectively ($Ms = 2.17$ vs. 1.99).

Unconstructive School Attitudes

For the measure of students' unconstructive school attitudes, there were no significant differences as a function of ethnicity or gender, $F (1, 267) = 2.146$.

Optimistic Ethnic Identity

Students' positive perceptions of their ethnic group and mobility varied significantly by ethnicity, with Blacks reporting higher scores than Latinos ($Ms = 4.03$ vs. 3.84), $F (1, 282) = 11.94$, $p < .001$.

Perceptions of Barriers

Consistent with findings of optimistic ethnic identity, African Americans reported significantly lower perceptions of barriers than Latinos ($Ms = 2.22$ vs. 2.46, respectively), $F (1, 292) = 10.31$, $p < .001$.

DISCUSSION

Much of what we know about oppositional identity is rooted in the qualitative studies and theoretical work of Ogbu and his colleagues. To make this work meaningful to educators and practitioners, we must find ecologically valid ways to operationalize oppositional identity. Towards this aim, the research presented here has attempted to quantitatively examine the theoretical constructs that have been hypothesized as contributing to involuntary minority students' oppositional attitudes regarding academic effort and achievement.

There were two major findings, each related to this study's two goals. The first goal was to construct a measure of oppositional identity that can be used in future investigations. Results of a factor analysis revealed the potential higher-order components of oppositional identity. An additional goal was to quantitatively examine theoretical constructs hypothesized as contributing to minority students' oppositional attitudes regarding academic effort and achievement. Results showed ethnic differences in students' responses, even though all respondents were involuntary minority group members.

Ethnic Differences in Oppositional Identity

The findings showed clear ethnic differences in terms of students' responses to construct measures. African American students reported strong beliefs of discrimination and cultural mistrust, unfair school rules, immobility, and strong ethnic identity. In contrast, Latinos reported that they liked school despite having strong perceptions of barriers. This latter finding is consistent with previous literature (Taylor & Graham, 2007), in which middle-school Latinos reported having stronger perceptions of barriers than Blacks.

These findings suggest that African Americans perceive that they are treated unfairly as a group. Although they perceive institutional barriers, African Americans also have a sense that they will be able to overcome personal barriers. Blacks possess elements of oppositional identity in that they recognize institutional inequity, but do not generalize this inequity to personal obstacles. In contrast, Latinos perceive that the rules are fair and that they are not targets of discrimination. They are, however, less certain about their ability to overcome personal barriers. Despite Latinos' perception of personal obstacles to success, they do not seem to develop a generally negative worldview as do African Americans.

This study's results suggest that oppositional identity is complex and might not be adequately represented by a general set of constructs. Oppositional identity might be composed of different dimensions across ethnic groups and possibly across generations. In order to identify how the relation between oppositional identity and academic outcomes is moderated by component factors, such as those examined in this study, in addition to the minority group identifiers defined by Ogbu (i.e., voluntary or involuntary), more work is needed.

No differences were found between students' self-reports of oppositional beliefs and behaviors. This might reflect that students responded in a socially desirable manner. This is consistent with previous research in which students reported that they valued doing well in school despite poor performance and underlying differences in beliefs (e.g., Ford, 1992; Goodenow & Grady, 1995; Mickelson, 1990; Steinberg, Dornbusch, & Brown, 1992).

Results of the factor analysis lend support to the model of oppositional identity described in this study. Variables loaded logically on factors consistent with those defined by the literature and hypothesized in the present research. In addition, within-scale distinctions were identified, supporting the development of a revised model of oppositional identity, as presented in Figure 20.2. Taken as a whole, the data presented here suggest that efforts to improve minority students' academic outcomes by improving their behaviors might be misdirected in that such efforts neglect to recognize that these behaviors arise from deep-rooted worldviews.

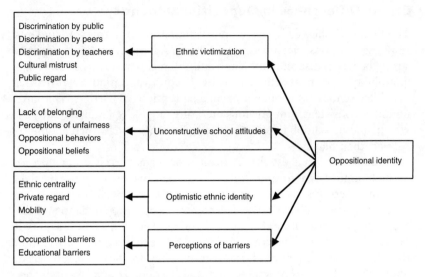

Figure 20.2 Revised conceptual model of oppositional identity.

Limitations and Future Directions

This study found many ethnic differences in involuntary minority students' endorsement of the constructs that were hypothesized as comprising oppositional identity. Participants consisted of African American and Latinos with at least second-generation-American status. This operationalization of involuntary status did not account for the possibility that second-generation status might not be a necessary or sufficient determinant of adopting an involuntary minority mindset. This study did not measure the degree of immigrant (voluntary) vs. involuntary mentality that the students possessed. Both African American and Latino students endorsed constructs indicative of oppositional identity. However, it is necessary to conduct similar investigations with non-ethnic minority and/or non-involuntary minorities to determine whether these findings are indeed unique to involuntary minorities rather than characteristic of adolescents in general. Future investigations could incorporate some of these additional factors to further clarify our understanding of oppositional identity. It is our goal to investigate the relations between oppositional identity and student achievement and value for academic achievement, as well as teachers' perceptions of social and academic behavior.

Conclusion

John Ogbu's cultural-ecological model provides us with a rich framework for understanding the historical, sociological, and social-psychological factors that contribute to individuals' achievement strivings. The focus on the African American experience in particular and socially stratified groups in general offers a means to understand and promote academic achievement among not only historically disenfranchised groups, but students of all ethnic backgrounds.

Researchers' and practitioners' attempts to appreciate and respond to the needs of an increasingly diverse student population have resulted in such concepts as multicultural education, culturally relevant teaching, and antiracist curricula. We would do well to incorporate into these efforts the broad historical perspective that Ogbu's work contributes. However, to most effectively move from theory to practice and ultimately prevention, we must develop a means of measuring oppositional identity and its componential constructs. The research presented here is one of several initial attempts to quantify Ogbu's theoretical concepts. This chapter has described the relations among theoretical factors underlying oppositional identity and identified how these components vary uniquely for two involuntary minority groups in America, thus suggesting that (a) an area ripe for future research involves examining within-typology yet between-group differences, and (b) intervention efforts guided by Ogbu's typologies must acknowledge the multiple causal origins of oppositional beliefs and behaviors.

NOTES

1   The interviewers on this project were bilingual, English-Spanish, and all classroom procedures were conducted bilingually.
2   Unless otherwise noted, all items for each measure were rated on a five-point scale with higher numbers corresponding to stronger endorsement for the item. A full description of the measures used in this study is available in Taylor (2003).

REFERENCES

Ainsworth-Darnell, J. W., & Downey, D. B (1998). Assessing the oppositional culture explanation for racial/ethnic differences in school performance. *American Sociological Review*, 63, 536–553.

Brown, M. (1994). *The African American Career Outcome Expectancy Inventory*, University of California, Santa Barbara. Unpublished manuscript.

Cook, T. D., Church, M. B., Sjanaku, S., Shadish, W. R., Kim, J., & Cohen, R. (1996). The development of occupational aspirations and expectations among inner-city boys. *Child Development*, 67, 3368–3385.

Crocker, J., & Major, B. (1989). Social stigma and self-esteem: The self-protective properties of stigma. *Psychological Review*, 96(4), 608–630.

Fisher, C. B., Wallace, S. A., & Fenton, R. E. (2000). Discrimination distress during adolescence. *Journal of Youth and Adolescence, 29*(6), 679–695.

Ford, D. Y. (1992). Self-perceptions of underachievement and support for the achievement ideology among early adolescent African-Americans. *Journal of Early Adolescence, 12*(3), 228–252.

Fordham, S. (1996). *Blacked out: Dilemmas of race, identity, and success at Capital High.* Chicago: University of Chicago Press.

Fordham, S., & Ogbu, J. U. (1986). Black students' school success: Coping with the burden of acting White. *The Urban Review, 18*(3), 176–206.

Goodenow, C., & Grady, K. (1995). The relationship of school belonging and friends' values to academic motivation among urban adolescent students. *Journal of Experimental Education, 62,* 60–71.

Gottfredson, G. D. (1984). *Effective School Battery*: Psychological Assessment.

Mickelson, R. A. (1990). The attitude-achievement paradox among Black adolescents. *Sociology of Education, 63*(1), 44–61.

National Center for Educational Statistics (2004). *Digest of Education Statistics, 2004.* Chapter 2, Elementary and Secondary Education. Retrieved February 20, 2006, from <http://nces.ed.gov/programs/digest/d04/tables/dt04_107.asp>.

National Center for Educational Statistics (2006a). *The Nation's Report Card: Reading 2005.* Retrieved February 20, 2006, from <http://nces.ed.gov/nationsreportcard/reading/>.

National Center for Educational Statistics (2006b). *The Nation's Report Card: Mathematics 2005.* Retrieved February 20, 2006, from <http://nces.ed.gov/nationsreportcard/mathematics/>.

Ogbu, J. U. (1982). Societal forces as a context of ghetto children's school failure. In L. Feagans & D. Farron (Eds.), *The language of children reared in poverty: Implications for evaluation and intervention,* pp. 117–138.

Ogbu, J. U. (1991). Minority coping responses and school experience. *Journal of Psychohistory, 18*(4), 433–456.

Ogbu, J. U. (1997). Understanding the school performance of urban Blacks: Some essential background knowledge. In H. J. Walberg, O. Reyes, & R. P. Weissburg (Eds.), *Children and youth: Interdisciplinary perspectives. Issues in children's and families' lives,* vol. 7 (pp. 190–222). Thousand Oaks, CA: Sage.

Olneck, M. R., & Lazerson, M. (1974). The school achievement of immigrant children: 1990–1930. *History of Education Quarterly, 14,* 453–482.

Sellers, R., Smith, M. A., Shelton, J. N., Rowley, S. A. J., & Chavous, T. M. (1998). Multidimensional model of racial identity: A reconceptualization of African American racial identity. *Personality and Social Psychology Review, 2*(1), 18–39.

Spencer, M. B., Noll, E., Stoltzfus, J., & Harpalani, V. (2001). Identity and school adjustment: Revisiting the "acting White" assumption. *Educational Psychologist.* Special Issue: The schooling of ethnic minority children and youth, *36*(1), 21–30.

Steinberg, L., Dornbusch, S., & Brown, B. (1992). Ethnic differences in adolescent achievement: An ecological perspective. *American Psychologist, 47,* 723–729.

Taylor, A. (2001). *Writing off ambition: A developmental study of gender, ethnicity, and achievement values.* Graduate School of Education, University of California, Los Angeles. Unpublished dissertation.

Taylor, A. (2003). *Cultural identification, resistance, oppositional identity, perceived discrimination, and school achievement: African American and Latino experiences.* Paper symposium conducted at the meeting of the American Educational Research Association, Chicago.

Taylor, A., & Graham, S. (2007 in press). An examination of the relationship between achievement values and perceptions of barriers among low SES American and Latino students. *Journal of Education Psychology, 99*(1), 52–64.

Terrell, F., & Terrell, S. L. (1981). An inventory to measure cultural mistrust among Blacks. *Western Journal of Black Studies, 5*(3), 180–184.

Chapter 21

Ogbu's Voluntary and Involuntary Minority Hypothesis and the Politics of Caring*

Angela Valenzuela

While John Ogbu did not engage the voluminous scholarship on caring or caring theory (e.g., Danin, 1994; Fisher & Tronto, 1990; Gilligan, 1982; Noblit, 1994; Noddings, 1984, 1992), neither have caring theorists engaged Ogbu's research and theorizing on U.S. ethnic minorities. Such engagement would have been mutually beneficial. For Ogbu, the etiology of oppositionality might have been placed more squarely on schools, where the micro-political dynamics between majority teachers and minority students, through a discourse on caring, reinscribe the larger social relations of power about which he wrote. In addition, the predicate in Ogbu's argument about oppositionality might have been that oppositional youth reject not achievement or education, but rather, *schooling*. By schooling, I refer to a system of unequal power relations in which schools objectify or treat students and their families like objects. They are done *to* rather than *with*. Indeed, Ogbu (1974) accorded importance to this process of objectification when he referred to relations between school officials and minority youth in terms of a "patron-client relationship" that is in turn linked to broader historical, cultural, and structural factors that generate school failure.

For caring theorists, attention to Ogbu might have informed theorizing regarding the underlying dynamics of race, culture, power, and difference that track back to minorities' forced incorporation into the U.S. political economy and that today permeate all relations between dispossessed urban, minority youth and their teachers and school administrators. The failure to incorporate this view blinds analysts from the historic elements of coercion and cultural chauvinism that pervade the English language curriculum and associated instructional practices that objectify and sort students according to a factory model approach for educating regular-track youth. More pointedly, it keeps them from seeing how caring gets politicized, embodying unequal power relations between "Whitestream" schools and the communities they serve (Urrieta, 2004). In such settings, as this case study of Seguín High School[1] in Houston,

Texas demonstrates, teacher caring can equate to an exercise of dominion and control rather than to social justice.

In the present study on teacher-student relations at Seguín, Ogbu's complementary concepts of *voluntary* and *involuntary minorities* succinctly convey this dynamic that finds expression both through a naturalistic discourse on caring and in the attitudes and predispositions that characterize, in particular, acculturated youth, the majority of whom are U.S.-born. Seguín, an over-crowded, underperforming urban school is fraught with vexed relations between its predominantly non-Latina/o teaching staff and its predominantly Latina/o school population.

This chapter is divided into three parts. The first describes the larger study from which the present data are drawn, noting current evidence of persistent underachievement, as well as key findings that lend credence to Ogbu's theorizing on voluntary and involuntary minorities. The second part posits a synthesis between Ogbu's work and caring theory that is conveyed in the concept of *politically aware, authentic caring*. While Ogbu's hypothesis on voluntary and involuntary minorities should not be over-generalized, I maintain that his theorizing nevertheless helps illuminate the bases of conflict and student disaffection at Seguín—most notably between teachers and acculturated, U.S.-born Mexican American youth. Caring theory offers a different, yet compatible, angle of vision. That is, though relations between immigrant youth and teachers are less overtly conflictive than those involving their U.S.-born counterparts, an ethic of authentic caring clearly exists among both groups.

The last section examines teachers' and students' respective perceptions of caring at Seguín. It begins with a description of the "Uncaring Student Prototype" for whom their putative lack of caring constitutes an oppositional stance not to education, but rather to *schooling*. The significance of many of the findings in this account is that by re-establishing schooling and not education or achievement as the predicate for student disaffection, the onus for the students' putative lack of caring is the school's approach to "caring." Due to space limitations, minimal, but important attention is accorded to immigrant youth to illustrate how Ogbu's notion of involuntary minority status is not a static identity, but is itself a product of subtractive schooling, of which teacher caring (or the lack thereof) is a part.

SEGUÍN HIGH SCHOOL REVISITED

Context

Seguín High is a large, comprehensive, inner-city high school located in the Houston Independent School District (HISD). Throughout the 1990s, its 3,000-plus student body was virtually all Mexican and generationally diverse (45 percent immigrant and 55 percent U.S. born).[2] At the time of the study (1992–95), 81 percent of teachers were non-Latino, while only 19 percent were Latino (mostly Mexican American). According to Texas Education Agency (TEA) (2003–04) data (www.tea.state.tx.us/cgi/sas/broker), these staff demographics remain virtually unchanged today. Although this school has improved its underachieving profile, it, like many other schools in the HISD, has been subject to various investigations involving test abuse and fraudulent reporting practices (Axtman, 2005; Kimball, 2004; Spencer, 2005). These reports render questionable any test-score data reported by the district, particularly when coupled with state-level data, which show that the Houston ISD's dropout rate for the district (18.2 percent) is two-and-a-half times higher than the overall state average (7.1 percent) (Texas Education Agency, 2004).[3]

Student retention rates at Seguín are also very high. In 1992, a full quarter of the freshman class repeated the grade for at least a second time, and a significant portion of these students were repeating the ninth grade a third or fourth time. An average of 300 students skipped school daily. Low expectations were virtually built into this school: were students to progress normally from one grade to the next, there would be no space to house them. Seguín's 3,000-plus student body was crammed into a physical facility capable of housing no more than 2,600 students. Because of the school's high retention rate, the freshman class made up more than half of the school population.

Although the building in 2000 of a new high school in Houston's east side helped to significantly lower Seguín's annual enrollment figures to slightly more than 2,000 students for the past several years, state data show that it still only graduated between 313 and 425 students annually (Texas Education Agency, 2001, 2002, 2003, 2004). Except for those participating in the privileged rungs of the curriculum—that is, honors classes, the magnet school program, and the upper levels of the Career and Technology Education (CTE) vocational program—the academic trajectories of the vast majority are highly circumscribed.[4]

An ethnic brand of politics that has focused on problems in the school has made for a contentious relationship between Seguín and its surrounding community. Although local community activists historically have supported numerous causes, including legal challenges against segregation during the early 1970s, a massive student walkout in October 1989, and a number of school reforms like site-based management, little has changed to significantly alter Seguín's underachieving profile. Steeped in a logic of technical rationality, schooling centers on questions of how best to administer the curriculum rather than on why, as presently organized, it tends to block the educational mobility of huge segments of its student body. Lamentably, though more than a decade has passed since I conducted the study at Seguín, evidence of positive change is simply not evident. This justifies my use of the present tense.

The Seguín High School Study

My study makes use of quantitative data, participant observation, and open-ended interviews with individuals and groups of students. Although data for this chapter derive primarily from pertinent surveys,[5] individual interviews, and classroom observations, group interviews significantly informed the larger analysis. They allowed me to tap into peer-group culture and also to investigate the social, cultural, and linguistic divisions that I observed among teenagers at Seguín. Regarding survey data, findings on parental education, schooling orientations, and generational differences in achievement are relevant to the present focus on teacher-student relations.

With respect to parental education, estimates hover around nine years of schooling completed for third-generation students.[6] This means that the major responsibility for education falls on the school by default. School officials, however, tend not to see it this way. As conveyed in a naturalistic discourse on caring that emerged organically from this schooling context, school officials tend to blame the students, their parents, their culture, and their community for *their own* educational failure. Complicating matters—and reinforcing many teachers' and other school officials' opinions that students "don't care" about school—is that a significant proportion of students, mostly U.S.-born, has become adept at breaking school rules. For example, students skip class and attend all three lunch periods, knowing that the numbers are on their side. Violations of school policies are so common that they outstrip the administration's capacity to address them, making Seguín a capricious environment that minimizes many students' sense of control, on the one hand, and their respect toward authority, on the other. Despite the fact that certain types of students consistently succeed and that most students actually do follow school rules, the prevailing view is that students "don't care." Absent is an awareness of the students' countervailing perspective that the reverse is true—that is, teachers and principals are the ones who do not care.

Another finding from the survey data corroborated in the ethnographic account is that immigrant youth experience school significantly more positively than do their U.S.-born peers (see Tables 21.1 and 21.2). That is, they see teachers as more caring and accessible than do their U.S.-born counterparts, and they rate the school climate in more positive terms as well. They are also much less likely to evade school rules and policies. These students' attitudes contrast markedly with those of their second- and third-generation counterparts, whose responses in turn are not

Table 21.1 Analysis of variance of teacher-caring items by generational status (total sample)

Survey items	F-ratio	Gen I	Gen 2	Gen 3+
		$\bar{X}$ (n) sd	$\bar{X}$ (n) sd	$\bar{X}$ (n) sd
My teachers give me the moral support I need to do well in school	11.80***	2.92 (643) .68	2.78 (485) .67	2.72 (362) .70
I rely on my teachers for advice and guidance in making important school-related decisions	7.10***	2.67 (635) .77	2.58 (479) .70	2.49 (355) .76
My teachers are sensitive to my personal needs	4.17*	2.49 (625) .71	2.40 (477) .70	2.37 (352) .72
My teachers are good in helping me solve school-related or academic problems	.03	2.67 (623) .73	2.67 (474) .68	2.68 (351) .69
My teachers are good in helping me solve personal problems	22.30***	2.55 (606) .78	2.32 (458) .73	2.24 (341) .76
I have a friendly and trusting relationship with at least one teacher	3.65*	2.89 (615) .79	2.77 (472) .80	2.78 (348) .80

Notes: Response categories ranged from "Strongly Agree" = 1 to "Strongly Disagree" = 4. A high score thus signifies high teacher caring. In analyses controlling for gender and curriculum track placement, none of the items reached statistical significance.
*$p = \leq .05$; **$p = \leq .01$; ***$p = \leq .001$.

significantly different from one another. Particularly striking is how generational status—and not gender or curriculum track placement—influences orientations toward schooling. Notwithstanding the complexity and fluidity of students' identities, these findings on generational differences lend credence to Ogbu's theorizing on the significance of voluntary and involuntary status for U.S. minorities.

Because of its relevance, I interject at this point how ethnographic evidence additionally reveals that immigrant, more than U.S.-born, youth belong to informal peer groups that exhibit an esprit-de-corps, pro-school ethos. Immigrants' collective achievement strategies, when combined with the academic competence that their prior schooling provides, directly affect their achievement levels (see Fry, 2005, for national-level data that corroborate the positive impact of prior educational experiences abroad for Latina/o youth).

Table 21.2 Analysis of variance of school-climate items by generational status (total sample)

Survey Items	F-Ratio	Gen 1	Gen 2	Gen 3+
		$\bar{X}$ (n) sd	$\bar{X}$ (n) sd	$\bar{X}$ (n) sd
Students get along well with teachers	15.70***	2.75 (694) .66	2.58 (505) .63	2.56 (375) .60
There is real good school spirit	8.10**	2.69 (684) .70	2.54 (506) .68	2.56 (378) .72
Discipline is fair	4.60*	2.74 (675) .70	2.64 (506) .67	2.63 (379) .69
Other students often disrupt class*	.29	2.08 (670) .66	2.10 (505) .63	2.09 (379) .67
The teaching is good	13.60***	2.92 (671) .68	2.75 (502) .66	2.72 (370) .66
Teachers are interested in students	5.10**	2.84 (654) .70	2.72 (489) .69	2.74 (367) .65
When I work hard on schoolwork, my teachers praise my effort	7.90***	2.78 .75 (667)	2.63 (494) .70	2.63 (369) .70
Most of my teachers listen to what I have to say	6.10**	2.87 (652) .70	2.73 (492) .66	2.76 (369) .66

Notes: Response categories ranged from "Strongly Agree" = 1 to "Strongly Disagree" = 4; the daggered item was not reversed. A high score thus signifies a positive school climate. Except for one item, "Discipline is fair," gender differences were not statistically significant. In terms of curriculum track placement, none of the items reached statistical significance.
$*p = \le .05; **p = \le .01; ***p = \le .001$.

Academic competence thus functions as a human-capital variable that, when marshaled in the context of the peer group, *becomes* a social-capital variable (Coleman, 1988, 1990). This process is especially evident among females in Seguín's immigrant student population (see Valenzuela, 1999). In contrast, and borrowing from Putnam (1993, 1995), regular-track, U.S.-born youth are "socially de-capitalized." Through a protracted, institutionally mediated process of de-Mexicanization that results in a de-identification from the Spanish language, Mexico, and things Mexican, they lose an organic connection to those among them who are academically oriented. U.S.-born youth are no less solidaristic; their social ties are simply devoid of academically productive social capital.

Finally, quantitative evidence points to significantly higher academic achievement among immigrants than among U.S.-born youth located in the regular track.[7] Though not controlling for curriculum track placement, other scholars have observed this tendency among Mexican and Central American students (Buriel, 1984; Buriel & Cardoza, 1988; Matute-Bianchi, 1991; Ogbu, 1991; Reed, Hill, Jepsen, & Johnson, 2005; Suárez-Orozco, 1991). This finding has been primarily interpreted from an individual assimilationist perspective rather than from a critical analysis of assimilating institutions. By this, I refer less to students' dispositions and more to the policies, practices, and organization of schooling that culminate in what may be termed *subtractive cultural assimilation* or simply, *subtractive schooling*.

An important caveat is that this observed pattern of higher immigrant achievement vis-à-vis U.S.-born underachievement is *only* evident among youth located within the regular, non-college-bound track. In other words, as one would expect, location in the college-bound track erases these differences. At Seguín, however, the vast majority of youth are located in the regular academic track. Olsen's (1997) ethnographic study in a northern California high school underscores the importance of track placement as a highly consequential variable that structures the schooling experiences and academic trajectories of immigrant and U.S.-born youth alike. At Seguín, only between 10 and 14 percent of the entire student body is ever located in the honors courses, the magnet school program, or the upper-levels of the Career and Technology Education (CTE) vocational program.

Taken together, these quantitative findings on generational differences *among regular-track youth* in parents' education levels, perceptions of caring, social capital, and school climate demonstrate the significance of being an immigrant, as Ogbu's voluntary-involuntary typology suggests. These findings, coupled with those on teacher-student relations provided below, complexify Ogbu's typology, which, if used reductively, risks essentialist constructions of groups whose identities are in a constant state of negotiation and modification.[8] Stated differently, oppositionality toward either achievement or schooling, as the present account suggests, may cut across groups, blurring the distinctions within Ogbu's voluntary-involuntary framework. With these considerations in mind, I turn now to the linkages between Ogbu's typology and caring theory. In particular, I posit a synthesis that is conveyed with the concept of politically aware, authentic caring.

SYNTHESIZING OGBU'S TYPOLOGY AND CARING THEORY

The Voluntary and Involuntary Minority Hypothesis

While, as Gibson (1997) cautioned, it is important not to over-generalize the distinctions between voluntary and involuntary minority youth, it is also incumbent upon researchers to acknowledge their relevance when empirically validated. At the macro level, Ogbu (1991) elaborated the notion of voluntary and involuntary minorities to signify the means through which groups were historically incorporated into the U.S. political economy, on the one hand, and to delineate the resulting schooling orientations that develop among youth, on the other. Immigrants enter the United States voluntarily, whereas others do so involuntarily as a result of slavery, conquest, or colonization.

At the micro level, conditions of institutionalized oppression lead students to collectively develop ethnic minority identities that enable them to buffer the more psychologically damaging elements in schools and society that are associated with the dominant, individualistic model of mobility. Ogbu referred to this in terms of students' oppositionality to dehumanizing forms of exploitation and control.

In the schooling context, Ogbu (1991) maintained that the manner in which a child's group is incorporated has an enormous bearing on the dispositions that he or she holds toward school. Accordingly, there is corroborating evidence in other research that immigrant youth are more able to transcend cultural boundaries than their U.S.-born counterparts, who develop and maintain boundaries that reflect an oppositional standpoint with respect to the dominant group (e.g., Buriel, 1984; Buriel & Cardoza, 1988; Matute-Bianchi, 1991; Ogbu, 1991; Suárez-Orozco, 1991). While this generalization applies to U.S. minorities, it also may apply to some immigrant youth, as the next section on teacher-student relations reveals.

Caring Theory

According to Noddings's (1984, 1992) theorizing on caring relations, teachers expect students to demonstrate caring for schooling with a superficial, or *aesthetic* commitment to ideas or practices that purportedly lead to achievement. This contrasts with *authentic caring*, in which all instruction is premised on respectful, caring relations. The Spanish language term, *educación*, closely resembles Noddings's (1992) concept of authentic caring, which views sustained, reciprocal relationships between teachers and students as the basis for all learning. Moreover, a caring relationship may be said to exist only when this caring is received by the *cared-for*. Without this complete circle of care, a caring relationship does not exist, regardless of how much a teacher believes that she or he cares.

Noddings (1984, 1992) argued that teachers' ultimate goal of apprehending their students' subjective reality is best achieved through an emotional displacement characterized by engrossment in their welfare. That is, an authentically caring teacher is seized by the *other* with energy flowing toward his or her project and needs. The benefit of such profound relatedness for the student is the development of a sense of competence and mastery over worldly tasks. In the absence of such connectedness, students are not only reduced to the level of objects; they also may be diverted from learning the skills necessary for mastering their academic and social environment. Thus, the difference in the ways students and teachers perceive school-based relationships can bear directly on students' potential to achieve.

Synthesis

Within caring theory, a penchant for aesthetic caring, coupled with a systematically incomplete circle of care, provides the conceptual space within which to insert the problematic nature of schooling for many, if not most, immigrant and U.S.-born, Mexican youth alike. A mutual sense of alienation evolves when teachers and students hold different understandings about school. Because teachers and administrators are better positioned than students to impose their perspective on the conduct of schooling, aesthetic caring comes to shape and sustain a subtractive logic. This means that the demand that students embrace their teachers' view of caring is akin to requiring their active participation in a process of cultural and linguistic erasure (Bartolomé, 1994). The curriculum they are asked to value and support is one that dismisses or derogates their language, culture, and community.

Rather than building on students' cultural, linguistic, and community-based knowledge, schools like Seguín typically subtract these resources, to their detriment. Psychic and emotional withdrawal from schooling is symptomatic of students' rejection of subtractive schooling and a curriculum they perceive as uninteresting, irrelevant, and de-humanizing (also see Valenzuela, 2004). Moreover, because their critique of the aesthetic-caring status quo is sometimes lodged in acts of resistance—not to education, but to schooling—school officials typically misinterpret the meanings of these challenges.

Complicating most teachers' demands that students care about school is their displeasure with students' self-representations, on the one hand, and the debilitating institutional barriers they face on a daily basis that impede their abilities to connect effectively with youths' social world, on the other. From these adults' perspective, the way youth dress, talk, and generally deport themselves "proves" that they do not care about school. For their part, students argue that they should be assessed, valued, and engaged as whole people, and not as interchangeable or disposable fragments of the school machinery.

Ogbu's voluntary and involuntary minority typology accurately captures, albeit in a very general sense, how differential responses to discriminatory and exclusionary forces exist across these two major categories of youth. It fails to note, however, an ethic of care that is common to both groups. This ethic is further embodied in the Spanish language term, *educación*, representing a folk model of schooling that is characterized by relations of reciprocity between teachers and students (Noddings, 1984, 1992; Valenzuela, 1999). Conversely, caring theory fails to recognize the political, anti-democratic, and even imperialistic dimensions of caring, where caring can "work" to either empower or disempower youth and their communities.

A synthesis thus requires that we at once view voluntary and involuntary Mexican-origin youth as sharing an ethic of care, on the one hand, and caring as power-laden, on the other. To this end, I propose the concept of *politically aware, authentic caring*. This construct retains notions of emotional displacement, engrossment in students' welfare, and *educación*, but is also affixed to the concept of political awareness (Bartolomé, 1994). This re-framing acknowledges that subtractive schooling has deep roots, as Ogbu (1974; 1978; 1991) so eloquently expounded in his many writings. Politically aware, authentic caring embraces a commitment to social justice in ways that represent the authentic, collective interests of the Mexican American community's historic struggle for equity, fairness, and due process. The final section delves into the qualitative evidence on vexed relations between students and teachers at Seguín, revealing the school's penchant for aesthetic caring, and as a result, the incomplete circle of care. The data allow me to develop the argument that students' putative lack of caring constitutes an oppositional stance not to education, but rather to *schooling*.

STUDENT AND TEACHER PERCEPTIONS, THE STRUCTURE OF TEACHER BIAS, AND STUDENT RESISTANCE

The "Uncaring Student" Prototype

U.S.-born, Seguín ninth-graders are especially preoccupied with looking and acting in ways that make them seem cool. Males tend to be more involved than females in countercultural styles, but many females share these same preoccupations. Boys wear tennis shoes, long t-shirts, and baggy pants with crotches that hang anywhere between mid thigh and the knees. Also popular are *pecheras* (overalls) with the top flap folded over the stomach, dickies, khaki pants, earrings, and, sometimes, tattoos (many of which are self-inflicted) on the hands and arms. Boys, and some girls, also may shave their heads partially or fully. Gold-colored chains, crucifixes, and name pendants often dangle from students' necks. The tastes of these urban teens closely resemble those of Latino Angelino youth (see Patthey-Chavez's [1993] ethnography of a Los Angeles high school).

The mainstream values of the high school and its school-sponsored organizations tend to assure that high achievers and students involved in school activities will be under-represented in the ranks of the "uncaring-student" prototype. Average- and low-achieving ninth-graders concentrated in the school's regular track, in contrast, are likely to fit the type. This alignment between student type and student attire leads teachers and administrators to use (consciously and unconsciously) greater amounts of garb as a signal. Although most Seguín students do not belong to gangs, school personnel readily identify certain clothing as gang apparel. Most Seguín parents, by contrast, staunchly maintain that the way their children dress has much more to do with their adolescent need to "fit in" than their proclivity for trouble or their membership in any particular gang.

Though the school disapproves of urban Hip-Hop styles and views the more exaggerated manifestations as a "problem" that needs to be "fixed," the school itself cultivates this taste in attire through its Channel 1 television programming, which is accessible in virtually every school space where students congregate. Students huddled around Rap exhibitions on TV in the cafeteria or in a homeroom classroom is a familiar sight. Not all youth, of course, prefer Rap and Hip-Hop, but the vast majority of U.S.-born youth appreciate it.

It is not hard to pick out Seguín's "hip" urban youth. They strut about campus in a stiff-legged, but rhythmic, slightly forward-bouncing fashion and act like they do not care much about anything. This posturing helps mark group boundaries and communicates solidarity. Exaggerated posturing is evident in certain situations, such as before a fight, or when students get into trouble with school authorities, either as a face-saving strategy or to communicate righteous indignation.

Whereas the findings on generational differences in perceptions of school in the quantitative account signal strikingly divergent experiences between immigrant and U.S.-born youth, this ethnographic description provides still yet further texture and context within which teacher-student caring (or non-caring) finds expression. Although the irreverent symbols of gangster attire are frequently donned and open hostility to school authority occasionally surfaces, far more students are simply withdrawn and disaffected from school.

Ninth graders are over-represented in the "uncaring student" category. This is attributable to three factors. First, many of these students have not yet shed their middle-school personae. They are still carrying on with their tough, gangster-type attitudes and a clothing style to match. The social pressure to continue in this mode is abetted by the school's high dropout and failure rates, which leave freshmen to make up more than half of the school's total population. Academic failure is so common that a full quarter of the students have to repeat the ninth grade for at least a second time. School officials refer to many of these students as "career ninth-graders."

Second, because many of the ninth graders were members of middle-school "gangs," loosely defined, they are subjected to intense scrutiny by an aggressive, discipline-focused, "zero-tolerance" administration that tends to approach disciplinary problems in a reactive and punitive fashion. "Withdrawing students for inattendance," for example, is a customary way of handling students like these with high absentee rates. In this environment, even the appearance of gang membership often results in students receiving unwelcome attention from school authorities. A self-fulfilling prophecy develops when youth react negatively against school authorities who breathe heavily on them.

Third, upperclassmen tone down their appearance. Tenth- but especially, eleventh- and twelfth-grade students make a point of distinguishing themselves from freshmen by dressing differently. Whereas the upperclassmen may still wear baggy jeans or khakis low around their hips, their pants may be pressed and only somewhat baggy. One student I interviewed reminisced about having been a "punk" himself when he was a freshman. Now that he was a football player and working part-time, he felt he had to "grow up."

While it is certainly possible to find immigrant youth at Seguín who conform to this depiction of the uncaring student, this prototype is largely a U.S.-born, regular-track phenomenon. The reason for this appears not to be fewer barriers or less discrimination, as the opposite actually appears true. Rather, immigrant youth process these barriers differently than U.S.-born youth. That is, they *subjectively* experience schooling as *additive*, expanding their cultural and linguistic repertoires, though *subtractive schooling* begins in earnest with their generation.

Exceptional cases, such as that of Elvia, a first-generation immigrant, exist in increasing numbers. They reveal how both rapid cultural assimilation (i.e., "Americanization") and curricular track placement are key mediating factors that correlate to this status of the so-called uncaring student (for more evidence of this type, see Valenzuela, 1999). Such blurring of the distinction between immigrant and involuntary minority youth further reveals that many of the cultural characteristics associated with the categories of "immigrant" and "U.S.-born" youth are neither *a priori* nor "handed down" from parents to children. That is, adolescents' identities are neither static nor unchanging; rather, they develop and change in ways that reveal the complexity of their social and historical location, including the underlying logic of schooling to standardize and sterilize their ethnic identities. As Elvia's account reveals, the very micro-level negotiations of student identity that normally occur are themselves embedded within a much larger and historic agenda of de-Mexicanization (Valenzuela, 1999).

"Americanized" Immigrant Youth

In a schooling context that privileges a North American or English-speaking identity over a Mexican or Spanish-speaking one, there is strong pressure to assimilate subtractively. Immigrant youth necessarily emulate a marginal subculture when fulfilling their desire to "fit in." The following situations provide some insights that help explain the finding of "accelerated subtractive assimilation" among some immigrant youth. These youth share many of the same problems as U.S.-born youth.

Outside Seguín's attendance office in spring 1994, I spoke at length with an immigrant mother whose daughter had not attended any classes during the previous six-week grading period. Had a family emergency not brought the mother to campus that day, she might never have discovered that her daughter had been "withdrawn for inattendance." Until that day, she thought that her daughter had been attending school daily. The mother had approached an attendance officer to find out which class her daughter was in that period, only to discover that her daughter's name was not listed on any class roster. Because this woman was visibly distressed and the attendance officers were obviously busy with other students and parents, I approached her and offered my assistance.

With her arms wrapped around her waist, Mrs. Treviño doubled over and wept softly as I tried to guide her to the nearby steps in the center of the hall, where she could sit down. *"Ha fallecido mi papá y tenemos que irnos a México, y vengo a la escuela a descubrir esto?"* she cried. ("My father has died and we have to go to Mexico, and I come to school to discover this?") I told her that I was sorry, and I suggested that perhaps her daughter could make up the work in summer school. With an incredulous tone in her voice, Mrs. Treviño vented her anger with the school for failing to notify her of her daughter's lack of attendance:

> Uno deja a sus hijos esperando que las escuelas los esten cuidando, y no nos informan que nuestros hijos no han estado asistiendo. O esperan que nos digan nuestros hijos. ¿Cómo nos van a decir ellos si ellos

mismos son los que estan quebrando las reglas? ¿Y que si le hubiera pasado algo a mi'jita . . .? ¿Entonces que? (One leaves one's children trusting that the schools are taking care of them, and they do not inform us that our children are not attending. Or they expect our children to tell us. How are they going to tell us if they're the ones breaking the rules? And what if something would have happened to my daughter . . .? Then what?)

Mrs. Treviño's daughter rounded the corner carrying textbooks in her arms. She was in the process of withdrawing from school and was returning her books to the registrar's office. I realized that I recognized her from a lunchtime discussion during the previous fall semester. I was struck by the incongruity of this young woman being Mrs. Treviño's daughter. She wore extraordinarily baggy khaki pants—which somehow at the same time clung to her narrow hips—and her head was partially shaved in broad strokes around her ears, exposing olive-brown skin. She sported a tiny, golden nose earring. "Yes, I know you. You're Elvia, right? Do you remember me?" I asked. She acknowledged me with a slight nod. I also realized for the first time that she spoke Spanish. In a soft voice with her head lowered, the daughter said, "*Amá, tengo que entregar estos libros. Ahorita vuelvo por usted.*" ("Mom, I have to turn in these books. I'll come back for you in a minute.") I also noted that she spoke formally to her mother, using the formal pronoun "*usted,*" instead of the more familiar form, "*tú.*" Her mother's voice trembled as she told her daughter that now she would have to contend with her father. Looking humiliated, Elvia glanced at me and walked away. "*Me da verguenza como se mira y como se viste. ¡Verdaderamente me da verguenza! ¿Y cómo la puedo llevar a México vestida así? ¿Y con ese aretito? ¿Imagínate? ¡Ni parece Mexicana!*" Mrs. Treviño lamented. ("The way she looks and dresses embarrasses me. It really embarrasses me! And how can I take her to Mexico like that? And with that little earring? Can you imagine? She doesn't even look Mexican!") She then assured me that her daughter did not learn to be this way in their home. The mother added that she had two older sons and an older daughter, none of whom ever caused her any serious problems. "*Pero ésta, la mas chiquita, es fuerte de carácter!*" ("But this one, the youngest one, has a stubborn character!")

The family situation had been very unstable. Mr. Treviño was a migrant laborer who spent part of the year in Michigan harvesting beets and other vegetables. For the previous two years, he also had spent months at a time in Mexico helping take care of his father, who was dying slowly from cancer. The family's story gushed out of Mrs. Treviño's mouth as she repeatedly wiped tears from her face. I embraced her and told her not to feel obligated to tell me anything. "*Al contrario, no quiero ser una molestia para usted,*" she said. ("To the contrary, it is I who does not wish to trouble you.") *"No es ninguna molestia,"* I assured her. ("It's no trouble whatsoever.")

So she continued, explaining that she worked evenings as a waitress, while her older daughter, who held a daytime job, stayed at home with Elvia during the evenings. Elvia continually challenged her sister's authority and also had her friends over on a regular basis. They spent most of their time talking, although the mother also suspected that Elvia was taking drugs. She noted dryly that Elvia always underestimated her ability to detect the smell of marijuana or to recognize when she and her friends were high.

Mrs. Treviño thought that perhaps she had made a mistake by allowing Elvia to have her current set of friends. But she also admitted that her daughter had shown troubling tendencies since middle school. *"Es cuando empezó a vestirse como un Chicano. Siempre ha sido importante para ella ser aceptada por sus amigas y la influyen mucho,"* she mused. ("It's when she began to dress like a Chicano. It has always been important for her to be accepted by her friends and they influence her a lot.") By the time Elvia entered high school, Mrs. Treviño had decided not to make an issue of her daughter's attire. The haircut and the earring were recent additions. They had appeared this year when Elvia began hanging out with friends who spoke to one another in either English or "Span-glish," a dialect that uses both languages. She lamented that although she spoke to Elvia in Spanish, Elvia responded primarily in English: *"Y si puede hablar al Español pero parece que no le gusta."* ("And she can speak Spanish, but it seems as if she does not like to.") She found it strange that the daughter she had attempted to spare from the kind of hardships the family had endured earlier is the same one that she had now "lost." I asked her to elaborate. How had she "lost" Elvia?

A few moments later, Elvia returned. I asked her if everything was okay. "Yeah, I just checked out of school," she replied, her eyes glistening, as if she might burst into tears at any moment.

"Don't worry, Mom," she said, "I'll make it up. I'll take summer school. I promise."

Her mother shook her head and rolled her eyes in disbelief. When her mother stepped away to use the restroom, I was able to talk to Elvia alone.

> AV: It's pretty bad, huh?
>
> ET: Yeah, I can't stand it. . . . I wish she was mad at me instead.
>
> AV: So what's the problem? Why haven't you been going to classes?
>
> ET: I just don't like school, and I used to like it. I just can't get into my classes this year. They're all so boring, and no one seems to care if I show up. And then they talk down to you when you do show up.
>
> AV: What do you mean?

ET: It's like all of our teachers have given up, and they don't want to teach us no more. In one class, I had a sub [substitute teacher] for all the time I was there, for four weeks! And he can't teach us nothing because he don't know math. The dude tried, but that wasn't good enough, man! God, it just kills me to give that man even just a little bit of my time! If the *school* doesn't care about my learning, why should *I* care? Answer me that. Just answer me that! A friend of mine dropped out of high school, took her GED, and went on to college. I tell my Mom that's what I want to do, but it's like she don't get it.

AV: So what was your brothers' and sister's experience here at Seguín?

ET: They just took all the crap you get here. It's like, "You're Mexican; take crap." Well, man, I got some pride and self-respect. "Sorry to disappoint you, but *this* Mexican don't take crap." Mexicans who do, embarrass the hell out of me. I just want to tell them, "Lay off the humble trip, man. You some damn *Indio* [Indian] or something?"

Elvia's anger with and alienation from schooling are unmistakable. Further complicating matters at school was a lack of authentic caring, as well as a lack of aesthetic caring in one of her classes that stretched Elvia beyond her limits. Her story made me wonder whether, if she and I traded places, I would be able to tolerate such a bad situation for very long. Elvia's case also brings to the foreground a schooling strategy that is increasingly common among youth in HISD schools: they drop out of high school, secure a General Equivalency Diploma, and enroll in community college.

Elvia's dramatic departure from her siblings' educational experiences was partly evident in her unflattering portrayal of Mexican immigrants. She saw them as spineless individuals, lacking in "pride and self-respect." She further attributed this weakness to cultural factors—that is, to their "Indian-ness." Although expressed off-handedly, Elvia's dismissal of immigrants reveals the complexities of a colonized *mestiza* (Spanish and Indian mixed-blood) undergoing a personal de-colonization process. Even as Elvia asserted her Mexican identity in a U.S. context, she negated her indigenous ancestry. "De-Indianization" is a manifestation of the subtractive assimilation processes that operate at a transnational level wherever indigenous communities are viewed with contempt. I never saw Elvia again, but I noted with relief and pleasure that her name was included on the school roster in the attendance office the following year.

Rapid cultural assimilation, marked by a strong orientation either to the peer group or to the culture of the peer group, characterized every immigrant youth I observed who conformed to the "uncaring" student prototype. The contrast in language, clothing, demeanor, and other cultural markers between these young people and their parents is stark. Whatever its source, a need for acceptance by the more Americanized peer group appears to contribute to youth's accelerated effort to assimilate.

In the handful of cases of rapidly culturally assimilated students I observed, the most vulnerable youth within the immigrant generation were those who had been born in Mexico or Latin America, but who had lived most of their lives and had been schooled in the United States. These teens, among whom Elvia is a striking example, more closely resemble their U.S.-born peers than their immigrant counterparts and are referred to in the literature as "1.5 generation" youth (Vigil, 1997). Though revealing the importance of prior schooling experiences, the preceding discussion also highlights the interplay between subtractive cultural assimilation and student disaffection.

From a critical perspective on biculturalism (Darder, 1991, 1995), students' "choices" in identity, however constrained, are optimally premised on an affirmation of the new identity that effectively expands one's cultural and linguistic repertoire. "Choices" based on a disaffirmation of self—that is, one's original identity—is hardly a choice at all because this set of options pits one culture against the other. As with regular-track, U.S.-born youth, Elvia's case reveals the alienating consequences of schools' failure to be additive—a failure to confirm the language, history, and experiences of the cultural "other." If some immigrant youth are susceptible to the messages that demean their worth, how much more vulnerable are U.S.-born youth—whose Mexican identities are less firm—to such messages?

Teacher Perceptions

The view that students do not really care about school stems from several sources, including social and cultural distance in student-adult relationships and the school culture itself. Most of the school's staff neither live nor participate in their students' predominantly Mexican community. The non-Latino teachers who constitute the majority (81 percent non-Latino and 19 percent Latino) are doubtful and even defensive about the suggestion that more Latino teachers would make a difference in school climate. Seguín's high attrition rate—particularly among the newer staff—further exacerbates social distance and increases the difficulty of developing an explicit ethic of caring.

Some schools have consciously articulated an ethic of authentic caring (e.g., see Danin's [1994] ethnography of an elementary school), but no such effort has ever been deliberately undertaken at Seguín. Except for a minority of teachers for whom aesthetic and authentic caring are not mutually exclusive, a more general pattern of aesthetic caring prevails among those who teach the "middle majority" of regular-track youth.

In my conversations with teachers, only a few indicated that they knew many of their students in a personal way, and very few students said that they thought that their teachers knew them or that they would be willing to go to their teachers for help with a personal problem. This is not surprising. Despite perceiving themselves as caring, many teachers unconsciously communicate a different message—to their colleagues as well as to their students. Committed teachers who invest their time in students are chided for their efforts, with the reminder that working hard is not worth the effort "since these kids aren't going anywhere anyway." The subtext is more damning still: Seguín students "don't go anywhere" because they don't, can't, or won't "try."

Teachers sometimes make this view explicit. Consider the case of Mr. Johnson, an English teacher and self-proclaimed student advocate. Mr. Johnson is openly critical of the counselors and the administration for their sustained incompetence in handling students' course schedules. No doubt, Mr. Johnson does rescue some students from bureaucratic harm, but his good deeds are nullified by his abrasive and overbearing behavior in the classroom. As the following description of his teaching style illustrates, his apparent need to feel and be powerful cuts him off from the very individuals he seems to believe he is helping—or trying to help.

> One sunny day in April when I am observing in Mr. Johnson's ninth-grade English classroom, I hear him say to his class—yet somehow I know his comments are for my benefit—in a loud, deep, Southern drawl, "The main problem with these kids is their attitude. They're immature and they challenge authority. Look at them; they're not going anywhere. I can tell you right now, a full quarter of these students will drop out of school come May."
>
> One of the girls sitting right in front of Mr. Johnson smiles awkwardly and rolls her eyes in apparent disgust. Most students simply pretend not to hear him, though a few glance at me and chuckle nervously in embarrassment. The teacher sounds like he is joking, but the students do not find him funny.
>
> "See what I mean?" Mr. Johnson says. "They think they can get by in life without having to take orders from anyone."
>
> A student slumped in his chair with his chin and arms on his desk peers up, then lifts his head, responding in a mumble, "Aw, Mr. Johnson, you don't . . . you're just. . . ."
>
> Mr. Johnson interrupts, "Joel, stop thinking, you know it might hurt you, cause you some damage upstairs."
>
> Joel smiles wryly and sinks back into his chair.

As extreme as Mr. Johnson's behavior may seem, teachers at Seguín often engage in such verbal abuse. He communicates—perhaps more vividly than most—a sentiment shared by teachers and other school personnel, namely that Mexican students are immature, unambitious, and defiant of authority, and that teachers have no power to change the situation because it is the students' fault. The school's obvious systemic problems, most evident in its astronomical dropout rate, are brushed aside, and the burden of responsibility and the struggle for change is understood as rightfully residing first with the students, their families, and the community. A lack of urgency about the school's academic crisis itself is a sign of dangerously low expectations on the part of Seguín teachers and administrators.

During this entire interaction, students were passively sitting in their seats instead of working on the *Romeo and Juliet* writing assignment scribbled boldly on the chalkboard. So Mr. Johnson was accurate in one respect: they were challenging his ability to make them learn under abusive conditions. However, Mr. Johnson and other teachers conveniently overlooked the fact that they do have some sway in the classroom. In this case, for instance, no student showed outright anger, despite the tension in the air. Students were clearly deferring to his authority, thus demonstrating, ironically, the fallacy in the teacher's view. More importantly, they exhibited extraordinary self-control, hardly what one would expect from youth who are inherently "immature" and "defiant." That the students were, in fact, restraining themselves was made dramatically clear to me later when I spoke with Joel outside the classroom. Summing up his feelings toward his English teacher, Joel exploded, "Johnson's full of shit! . . . He's always got an attitude."

Students who say and act like they do not care about school mystify teachers; the latter profess great difficulty understanding such attitudes. The possibility that an uncaring attitude might be a coping strategy or a simple facade has little currency among Seguín teachers. My interactions and conversations with students, however, suggest that youth who maintain that they do not care about school often may really mean something else. For example, there are many students like Susana, a young woman with a fragile academic self-concept who takes comfort in the thought that she does not really care about learning in school. She protects herself from the pain of possibly failing to do well by choosing to do poorly. My investigation of Susana's withdrawn attitude (described below) supports, albeit negatively, the caring literature's hypothesized relationship between the teacher's apprehension of the student and the sense of academic competence and mastery that should ensue.

Mrs. Hutchins, a ninth-grade English teacher, asked me to talk to Susana to find out why she refused to answer when called upon in the classroom. I can only guess that Ms. Hutchins enlisted my assistance because she perceived my ethnicity as a possible route into Susana's world. "She always makes faces when I call on her," Mrs. Hutchins said, explaining her request. Then, she offered a theory about the reasons for Susana's behavior. "She doesn't want to be in my class. She may even resent me somehow." Mrs. Hutchins had introduced problem-solving techniques into her teaching, but she said that certain students still seemed beyond reach. After two years of teaching, she felt she had to get to the bottom of the problem of mentally absent students.

I approached Susana as she was settling into her desk just before the bell sounded on the following day. I complimented her on the length and beauty of her jet-black, braided hair and told her I was a researcher studying what students think about school. Susana briefly let down her guard. We exchanged a few words about what researchers do, and she told me that when she had seen me the day before she couldn't tell whether I was a teacher or a student.

I told her that I noticed many students who did not participate in classroom discussions when teachers asked them to, and I wanted to know what she thought about that. She took a deep breath and said, seriously, "You kinda' have to seem like you don't care because if you say something, and it comes out sounding stupid, then everybody will say you're dumb. And even the teacher will think you're dumb, when they didn't think that before." While Susana may sound unusually protective of her ego, her thinking is quite logical, inverting the relation of authentic caring and academic competence: a dearth of authentic relations with teachers subtracts, or minimizes, the opportunities youth have to develop and enjoy a sense of competence and mastery of the curriculum.

My discussion with Susana further revealed that her comportment toward her history teacher was a generalized response to schooling based on several past negative experiences with teachers. Susana's withdrawn, defensive posture was most fully revealed in the following statement, which ended our conversation:

> Once this bad science teacher asked me in front of everybody to stop raising my hand so much in class. And all the students laughed at me. I was trying to learn and he was a new teacher . . . hard to understand. I felt so stupid . . . so yeah, that and other things. . . . Teachers say that they want to talk to you, but I notice that they really don't. I used to get mad about it, but now it's like, "What's the use?" Not gonna change nuthin'. If I can just make it through the day without no problems. . . . So now if something bad happens, I know that I didn't cause it cuz I'm just here mindin' my business.

Teachers' repeated threats to Susana's academic self-concept have made her lower her expectations about the likelihood of forming productive relationships with teachers. As she was open with me, my guess is that Susana is not yet entirely lost because she hasn't quite given up. Later, when I shared what I had learned about Susana with Mrs. Hutchins, the teacher expressed a mixture of frustration, annoyance, and grief over the thought of having to deal with the consequences of Susana's previous teachers' mistakes and insensitivities.

> "As if teaching were not enough to preoccupy myself with," she sighed, and then continued in a more defensive tone, "It's overwhelming to think that this is the level we're dealing at, and frankly, neither was I trained nor am I paid to be a social worker."
>
> "Well, at least you know more of what you're up against in this situation," I offered.
>
> "Yeah, I suspected this would be the case, and it's uncomfortable for me to deal with someone who is hard set with the idea that teachers are the enemy."

Clearly, in this case both student and teacher resist a caring relationship. The effects of this mutual resistance are not equally balanced, however. Mrs. Hutchins may have to continue to put up with the distraction of funny faces rather than the positive classroom participation she would like, but Susana's adjustment will be much more costly. As her sense of alienation gets reinforced, her willingness to remain even marginally mentally engaged will steadily erode.

The individual histories that students and teachers bring to their classroom encounters necessarily influence the chances for successful relationship building. Still, in most cases, there is likely to be some room to maneuver—that is, if the situation is approached literally "with care." Notwithstanding her expressed desire to get at the root of Susana's problem, Mrs. Hutchins's rather self-absorbed, emotional response reveals the limitations of her aesthetic framework. In a contradictory fashion, she is angry with Susana's previous teachers' mistakes at the same time that she resists pursuing a possible solution arising directly out of my discussions with her student.

The Structure of Teacher Bias

The bias most mainstream teachers have toward the majority of Seguín students arises from many sources. Mainly White and middle-class, these adults' more privileged backgrounds inevitably set them up for disappointment in youth whose life circumstances differ so radically from their own. Students' failure to meet their teachers' expectations is further complicated by a generational divide. Like most adults, teachers misremember the past as a golden era; they recall a time when everyone was "honest," when old and young alike "worked hard," when school was "important" and students were "respectful." Some days, the teachers' lounge easily could be confused with the set of a daytime TV episode, as teachers exchange comments like, "My father was poor and he worked hard for everything he earned . . ."; "When I was young, things were different . . ."; "Where I grew up, if you raised your voice . . ."; and "I never even thought once that I shouldn't go to class. . . ." Without exception, the school's most dedicated teachers avoid the lounge altogether, fearing the disabling potential of their colleagues' negativity. Contemporary students, in failing to conform to this misty, mythical image of their historical counterparts, seem deficient, so teachers find it hard to see them in an appreciative, culture-affirming way.

Moreover, teachers see the differences in culture and language between themselves and their students from a culturally chauvinistic perspective that permits them to dismiss the possibility of a more culturally relevant approach in dealing with this population. For instance, teachers and counselors more often lament their students' linguistic limitations than they do their own. An affirming stance toward Mexican culture is deemed unnecessary because, as one teacher on Seguín's Shared Decision-Making Committee explained to me, "the school is already 'all-Mexican.' "

The interrelationship between the tendency to objectify students and the rejection of a nurturing view of education is clear in everyday classroom experiences at Seguín. An algebra teacher who appears to have little success in maintaining an orderly atmosphere in her class perceives rowdiness as evidence that many youth are not in school to learn. She complained to me one day, "I'm not here to baby-sit, and I'm certainly not their parent. . . . I finally told them, 'Listen, you don't have to be here if you don't want to be here. No one's forcing you.' " Teachers often give students the option of remaining in or leaving the classroom. Typically, they justify their actions by saying that they are trying to inculcate a sense of adult responsibility in these teenage boys and girls. When uttered in the absence of authentic caring, such language objectifies students as dispensable, non-essential parts of the school machinery.

Another dismissive expression that has prompted repeated complaints from Parent-Teacher Association (PTA) members involves teachers unilaterally rejecting students who have been assigned to already overcrowded classrooms at the beginning of each semester. Chaos always characterizes the first several weeks of each new year. The school's 10 to 12 counselors have the demonstrably impossible task of processing over a thousand new entrants, entering from the feeder middle schools, from other area high schools, and from outside the state or country. If the sheer size of this incoming tide were not enough to ensure the counselors' failure, the additional fact that they do not begin processing *any* students' fall schedules until the week before school opens would settle the matter. With so little time to process so many students, the counselors resort to simply over-assigning them to classes. This deliberate mis-scheduling is, predictably, purely bureaucratic: This is the easiest way to get students "into the system" so that they may be counted as enrolled.

In a "good" year, counselors "level off" these classes by the third week of school, when most students' schedules are finally "fixed"—that is, when students are assigned to the classes they should have been enrolled in from the first day of school. As might be expected, the first few weeks are extremely stressful. Massively long class rosters, teachers' and students' conflictual relations with counselors, extraordinarily large class sizes despite absent and disappearing bodies, insufficient numbers of desks, books, and teaching materials, and a lack of space, combine with students' displeasure over schooling to make for a state of high tension and intense normlessness.

In the fall 1995 semester, several Latino and White teachers grew so disgusted with the counselors that they appropriated a sense of leadership that they did not see operating within the school's administration by usurping the student assignment process from the counselors, superseding the principal's authority. Their actions created even greater havoc. The assignment process turned out not to be as simple as it seemed, and relations between teachers and counselors were polarized for a while. Fortunately, a cadre of Seguín parents and community activists mobilized to make Seguín accountable for the chaos that had developed. With community members participating, working groups formed, and by the seventh week of the semester, a modicum of equanimity evolved.

Among the handful of teacher leaders in this revolt, what became apparent was how their own sense of authentic caring markedly contrasted with their view of the counselors' penchant for aesthetic caring. Accordingly, one teacher leader said to me, "Yes, things got confused, but we wanted to do what was right for our kids. We're the ones who have to experience the effects of their [counselors'] actions." These teachers' moral authority came from their status as effective classroom teachers, as well as from their personal involvement on the school's central committees. Not surprisingly, one was also the Social Studies teacher who empowered her students with the skills and understandings they needed to successfully carry out a peaceful and non-violent walkout in October 1989. Hence, despite the confusion their actions created, the constructive dialogue and decisions that resulted would probably not have occurred had matters not indeed grown worse.

Personnel changes in Seguín's administration have made it difficult for principals and assistant principals to make any sustainable progress in improving the efficiency with which the school is run. Nor have they been able to alter the school's culture. Assistant Principal Ana Luera, who by her third year at Seguín had become significantly involved in working toward changing the school's culture, maintains that changing counselors' and teachers' practices is a long process that requires both patience and perseverance. Most importantly, she notes that no change can occur in the absence of mutual respect and trust:

> You can't do anything with them [teachers and counselors] your first couple of years because you have to gain their trust. They're just like kids. You have to show you love them. . . . Now, by the third year . . . you don't know *how many* teachers I called in to tell them to show more respect to the students, to not do certain things. Now that I got their trust, I can tell them. Sometimes they deny what they do or they admit it and say that they won't do it again. I respect them and I give them due process. You have to do that. . . . This year, we're going to do some cultural sensitivity training. . . . Students' schedules were also fixed this time at the end of the school year. . . . You just can't do anything as a new principal the first couple of years.

Luera at once confirms the problematic of teacher caring and the teachers' need to feel cared for. As Noblit (1994) similarly found in his case study of a caring school principal, principals can assert their leadership by authentically caring for teachers and also by promoting honest dialogue on how to authentically care for students. The brief tenure of principals is a widespread problem in HISD. In addition to "burnout," the district loses principals by adhering to an accountability scheme that makes the tenure of a principal's assignment contingent on raising students' test scores on a statewide exam within a three-year period. One unintended consequence of this "revolving door" approach to posting principals is that it reinforces counselors' and teachers' sense of autonomy and increases their power. In a system where they are the "old hands," they must be continually "won over" by top administrators, whose jobs may be hostage to their subordinates' willingness to cooperate.

The intransigence of teacher and counselor culture at Seguín has other consequences besides potentially undermining the efforts of a new principal. Parents, PTA members, and community advocates, whose appeals to Seguín staff are routinely dismissed without serious consideration, frequently resort to bypassing the school and carrying their concerns directly to the district superintendent or the school board. According to one PTA leader, the highly predictable surplus of students enrolling each semester relative to spaces available is tolerated because school staff knows "that the students will drop out anyway by the fifth or sixth week of classes." Enrollments of between 3,000 and 3,400 each semester in a physical facility capable of housing no more than 2,600 students lent credence to this claim. And not surprisingly, the numbers do substantially trim down in a five- to six-week time frame. A small, nearby alternative high school serving approximately 150 students annually—itself a remnant of a momentous district-wide 1970 school boycott (see Valenzuela,

1999)—rejects an average of 7 students per day who are attempting to re-enroll in school after having "dropped out." Unfortunately, Seguín does not keep tabs on such students' whereabouts.

Teachers occupy an uncomfortable middle ground. They are both victims of and collaborators with a system that structurally neglects Latino youth. Armed with limited classroom materials and often outdated equipment and resources, and facing large classes overflowing with average, at-risk, and underachieving youth, teachers frequently opt for efficiency and the "hard line" over a more humanistic approach. The district's emphasis on quantitative measures and "accountability" to evaluate students' commitment to school streamlines some aspects of teaching, but at the same time alienates scores of marginalized students. As the distance between teachers and their students widens, any possibility of an alliance between them evaporates. Isolated from and unhappy with one another, neither party finds much to call rewarding about a typical day at Seguín High School.

Fine (1991) provided reasons for the technical, aesthetic focus of schools that resonate with this study. Fine's investigation of dropouts, undertaken in a comprehensive, inner-city school similar to Seguín, led her to conclude that teachers are committed to an institutional "fetish" that views academics as the school's exclusive domain. This fetish supports the status quo by preserving the existing boundaries between the ostensibly "public" school and the "private" matters of family and community. Such reasoning is persuasive only if one first accepts as real—and right—the hypothesized public-private dichotomy in the realm of education.

When real-life concerns are thrust into the classroom, many teachers find themselves in uncomfortable and disorienting positions. They may be called on not only to impart their expert knowledge, but also to deal with barriers to students' learning, of which they may not be fully aware nor trained to recognize. If and when they do become aware of these contingencies, time and skill constraints remain. When teaching effectiveness gets reduced to methodological considerations and when no explicit culture of caring is in place, teachers lose the capacity to respond to their students as whole human beings and schools become uncaring places (Bartolomé, 1994; Prillaman & Eaker, 1994). Rather than address the enormity of the issues before them, teachers and administrators take solace in either sterile and mechanistic approaches to schooling or blanket judgments about ethnicity and "deficit" cultures too impoverished to value education.

These kinds of explanations are often embedded in a larger framework that co-identifies underachievement and students' dress, demeanor, and friendship choices. The tendency to place the onus of students' underachievement on the students themselves has been amply observed in other ethnographic research of youth in urban schools (Fine, 1991; McQuillan, 1998; Olsen, 1997; Orenstein, 1994; Peshkin, 1991; Yeo, 1997). Collective problems are regularly cast in individual terms, as if asymmetrical relations of power were irrelevant. Not weighed against individual students' proclivities are the larger structural features of schooling that subtract resources from youth, preempting a fair rendering of the parameters of low educational mobility. This absence of a self-critical discourse unwittingly promotes condescending views toward students, their parents, and the community they are supposedly there to serve.

"Not Caring" as Student Resistance

What looks to teachers and administrators like opposition and lack of caring feels to students like powerlessness and alienation. With their experiences of psychic and emotional withdrawal within the regular track, these teenagers demand with their voices and bodies, even more strongly than do their immigrant peers, a more humane vision of schooling. Some students' clear perception of the weakness of their position politicizes them into deliberately conveying an uncaring attitude as a form of resistance not to education, but to the irrelevant, uncaring, and controlling aspects of schooling (Callahan, 1962; LeCompte & Dworkin, 1991). Moreover, teachers' definition of caring, which involves a commitment to a predetermined set of ideas—is equivalent to cultural genocide. Success in school means consenting to the school's project of cultural disparagement and de-identification. Take, for example, Tisa, an astute, U.S.-born female whom I met in the course of my group interviews. When I asked Tisa whether a college education was necessary in order to have a nice house and car, and to live in a nice neighborhood, she provided the following response:

> You can make good money dealing drugs, but all the dealers—even if they drive great cars—they still spend their lives in the 'hood. Not to knock the 'hood at all. . . . If only us *Raza* [the Mexican American people] could find a way to have all three, money . . . *clean* money, education, and the 'hood.

In a very diplomatic way, she took issue with the way I framed the question. Rather than setting up two mutually compatible options of being successful and remaining in one's home community, Tisa interpreted my question in either/or terms, which in her mind unfairly juxtaposed success to living in the 'hood. That I myself failed to anticipate its potentially subtractive logic caused me to reflect on the power of the dominant narrative of mobility in U.S.-society—an "out-of-the-*barrio*" motif, as it were (Chavez, 1991; but also see Suro, 1998). These findings bring to mind the ethos that Ladson-Billings (1994) identified as central to culturally relevant pedagogy for African American youth. Specifically, effective teachers of African American children see their role as one of "giving back to the community."

A senior male, Rodrigo's approach is an even clearer example of how some students use "not caring" as a strategy of resistance. Though capable of excelling in honors' classes, he chooses to remain in the regular curriculum to which he had automatically been assigned after transferring to Seguín from a specialized academic program in another area school. Besides being an avid reader, Rodrigo has been writing poetry and prose for much of his young life. Wellsprings of inner strength emanate, in great part, from his role in his family's protracted struggle with his mother's long-standing comatose condition. "The last time I saw my mother was in kindergarten," he reminisces, referring to the last time he saw his mother as a whole, healthy person. After seeing Rodrigo off to school one day, she went to the hospital for a routine hysterectomy. During the operation, human error resulted in oxygen loss to her brain, causing extensive brain damage. Despite a decent monetary settlement and the passage of more than a decade, neither Rodrigo's father nor his two older half-sisters and half-brother have fully recovered from this catastrophe.

Rodrigo's breadth of knowledge of Chicana and Chicano literature easily rivals that of any college graduate specializing in this field. Not only does he have detailed knowledge of poetry and fiction, poets, and authors, he also knows which publishers are the most progressive on questions of multiculturalism. He has an expansive portfolio of written works, parts of which he takes to high schools and community gatherings where he has been invited to read. Gifts of books from publishers, professors, and other donors stand on shelves alongside those he purchases, filling a large space that he refers to as his "library" in his backyard garage.

Rodrigo laces his conversation with lines of poetry from various works, including his own. A memorable verse from one of his poems, titled "Woman," brought tears to my eyes as it flowed sweetly from his mouth: "I have touched Mexican women, but not as much as they have touched me." Personal tragedy, coupled with his literary expeditions, has made Rodrigo the feminist he is today.

When he and I first met, Rodrigo was involved in preparations to teach a multicultural literature class after school to at least 10 fellow students who had already expressed interest. Although he did secure the principal's permission to teach the class, in the end, Rodrigo's plans came to nothing. The principal was unable to come up with the funds needed to cover the cost of the text Rodrigo wanted to use. The process of preparing the class was an education in itself. When he came into contact with teachers at the high school who had not met him before, they wondered where this remarkable young man had come from. Some wondered, as well, whether he might be half White because of the lightness of his complexion. Rodrigo was insulted by the implication that a dark-skinned Mexican could not be either as gifted or as accomplished as he. One of the aims of his course was to combat just that kind of stereotyping, as well as other negative images teachers held toward his fellow students in the general curriculum track:

> They have this image of kids, that we are just messed up in the head. That's not really true because many students here—I think their intellectual ability is just too high for them to be in regular classes, but they don't enter honors classes. There are people out there who just think that we are into sex and drugs. That's not true. I can't say that I'm just one exception because there are many exceptions. At this school, there are many students, but some teachers at this school. . . . I'll start saying this because it's true. Certain teachers say, "No, let's not read this. This is too hard for these kids. No, let's not read John Keats. No, Shakespeare's Hamlet. Let's show the movie or let's not learn about Excalibur. Let's not read it, but let's watch the film." That's something that I see, always some other kind of source that they turn to that is some kind of a secondary source, something that is not on level, but a little bit more basic.

Rodrigo later enrolled as an undergraduate student at Kenyon College, a prestigious liberal arts college in the Midwest. He found out about the college from an information brochure he plucked out of the wastebasket in a Seguín counselor's office. The school looked beyond the "objective" data of grades and raw scores and admitted Rodrigo on the basis of his vast and creative intellect.

Rodrigo's words and experiences summarize students' experiences, generally, of profound alienation from, and hostility toward, uncaring bureaucracies. There is little reason to bother aspiring to higher education if the price of admission must be prepaid in yearly installments of humiliation and alienation. Making schools and schooling affirmative, truly educational experiences for all students requires implementing changes that reach deep into the structure of the educational system. Using daily life at Seguín as a guide, the first and arguably the most important step is to introduce a culture of authentic caring that incorporates all members of the school community as valued and respected partners in education.

Mexico- and U.S.-born youth have historically straddled Ogbu's immigrant and involuntary minority typology, respectively. While this helps explain the pro-school orientation and higher achievement that Mexican immigrant youth frequently share with other groups (Gibson, 1997), the imprecision of these categories begs for deeper analysis. At the macro level, Blauner (1987) resolved this tension by arguing that Mexican immigrant youth also should be considered involuntary minorities because they inherit the legacy of prejudice, exclusion, and discrimination historically faced by their U.S.-born counterparts. Blauner's contention acquires added significance when one considers that at Seguín, teacher-student relations entail a collective "othering" of students, as Rodrigo's and the other cases reveal.

At the micro level, Ogbu's typology provides a lens through which to evaluate a core notion within caring theory that all individuals need to be recognized and addressed as whole beings. All people share a basic need to be understood, appreciated, and respected. Among far too many immigrant and Mexican American youth in one school community in Houston, Texas, however, these basic needs go unmet during the hours they are in school. For the U.S.-born, their culturally assimilated status only exacerbates the problems inherent in an institutional relationship that defines them as in need of continuing socialization. That is, regardless of how much they assimilate, they rarely ever reach an end-state of being "fixed" or fully assimilated.

My findings show that American urban youth culture, filtered through a Mexican American ethnic minority experience, is at odds with adults' tastes and preferences in dress and self-representation. This generational divide combines with a subtractive schooling experience to heighten students' sense of disconnectedness from school and also to remind them of their lack of power. Rodrigo conveys teens' sense of powerlessness at school in his observation that "Kids have good arguments, but they have absolutely no argument skills." Unable to articulate their frustration and alienation effectively, and inexperienced with the idea of collective action, most regular-track students settle for individual-level acts of resistance. The few students who *are* adept articulators, like Rodrigo, condemn schooling, not education.

As Elvia's case demonstrates, the maladaptive consequences of subtractive schooling are magnified among immigrant youth who try to acculturate very rapidly. Her account suggests that schools should help youth sort out their cultural issues as they undergo change. Spindler and Spindler (1994) suggested that culturally appropriate training might allow teachers to help students better understand themselves and thus make it possible for youth to learn "with less rancor and resistance" (p. xiv).

Conclusion

By examining misunderstandings of caring, a fundamental source of students' alienation and resistance becomes apparent. Schools like Seguín not only fail to validate their students' culture, they also subtract cultural and linguistic resources from youth to their academic and social detriment. As mentioned in the first section above, the division between immigrant and U.S.-born youth manifests as differences in academically productive social capital. This is consequential to both groups. That is, regular-track, U.S.-born youth get deprived of the opportunity to have relations with those among them who exhibit an esprit-de-corps, pro-school ethos. Immigrant youth are similarly deprived of knowledge about the experiences and histories of their ethnic minority counterparts. This not only fosters inter-group divisions; it also frequently makes the assimilation process a haphazard, if not dangerous, journey.

To make schools truly caring institutions for members of historically oppressed, subordinate groups like Mexican Americans, *authentic caring, as currently described in the literature, is necessary but not sufficient.* As Ogbu's (1991) writings suggested, understanding U.S. minority youth requires knowing about how they adapt to their social and historical location, with school-based adults deliberately bringing issues of race, difference, and power into central focus. This approach necessitates abandoning the notion of a color-blind curriculum and a neutral assimilation process. A more profound and involved understanding of the socioeconomic, linguistic, sociocultural, and structural barriers that obstruct the mobility of U.S.-Mexican, as well as other minority, youth needs to inform all caring relationships (Delgado-Gaitan & Trueba, 1991; Phelan, Davidson, & Yu, 1993; Stanton-Salazar, 1997). Ogbu's theorizing therefore must be wedded to caring theory via the concept of politically aware, authentic caring. This is a more culturally relevant and comprehensive form of caring than exists in prior conceptualizations. It is one that is imbued with, and motivated by, political clarity (Bartolomé, 1994).

The finding that students oppose schooling rather than education expands current explanations for oppositional or reactive subcultures that characterize many urban, U.S.-born youth in inner-city schools. Rather than signifying an anti-achievement ethos, oppositional elements constitute a response to a Eurocentric, middle-class "culture of power" (see Delpit, 1995, for a similar argument with respect to African-American underachievement). This culture individualizes the problem of underachievement through its adherence to a power-neutral or power-blind conception of the world (Frankenberg, 1993; McIntyre, 1997; Twine, 1996). So deeply rooted and poorly apprehended is this culture of power that a 50–75 percent dropout rate at Seguín is systematically rationalized—year after year—as an individual-level problem.

Noddings (1992) rightly argued that the current crisis of meaning, direction, and purpose among youth in public schools derives from a poor ordering of priorities. The current emphasis on standardized testing and other narrow definitions of achievement lead many youth to conclude that adults do not care about them. Noddings further acknowledged that her call for a re-ordering of priorities to promote dedication to full human growth necessarily means that not all youth would be given exactly the same kind of education. Indeed, as the logic of politically aware, authentic caring dictates, a complete apprehension of the "other" means that the material, physical, psychological, cultural, and spiritual needs of youth will guide the educational process. Our youth deserve no less.

ACKNOWLEDGMENT

NOTES

*   This chapter is draws heavily from and provides an Ogbuan reframing of Chapters 1 and 3 in *Subtractive schooling: U.S.-Mexican youth and the politics of caring* (Albany: State University of New York Press, 1999). The author also wishes to acknowledge Linda Prieto for her reading a draft of this revised chapter.
1   All names used herein are pseudonyms.
2   I use the term "Mexican," a common self-referent, to refer to all persons of Mexican heritage when no distinction based on nativity or heritage is necessary.
3   The TEA's measurement of dropout statistics is the subject of much debate in Texas with critics maintaining that state data severely underestimate the true numbers (for example, see Intercultural Development Research Association, n.d.; Johnson, 2002). In a similar vein, see McNeil and Valenzuela (2002) and McNeil (2000) who speak to the flawed design of the state accountability.
4   My extensive observations of Seguín's CTE program have led me to conclude that the acquisition of work skills is compatible with students' college-going aspirations because it reinforces the academic curriculum. The CTE program is effective because its teachers enjoy higher salaries, small class sizes, access to career counselors, and, in the higher-level courses, the ability to select their students.
5   I administered a questionnaire to all 3,000 students in November 1992. It included questions about students' family background, English and Spanish language ability, generational status, school climate, teacher caring, and academic achievement. With a 75 percent response rate, a sample of 2,281 students for analysis resulted.
6   The comparable figures for Mexicans in California and the nation are 11.1 and 10.4 years of schooling completed and dropout rates of 39 and 48 percent, respectively. Mexicans from Texas are thus faring even more poorly than their underachieving counterparts nationwide (Chapa, 1988).
7   Survey data show that among immigrant youth located in Seguín's regular

track, each additional level of schooling attained in Mexico results in a corresponding increase in self-reported grades. This variable of prior schooling attained in Mexico also consistently held up as an independent, positive predictor of students' grades, even after the quality of such schooling was controlled for (data available upon request from author). Macías's research (1990, 1992) based on studies of classrooms in the Mexican state of Jalisco is suggestive. He posited that Mexico's challenging national curriculum at the *primaria* (elementary) level helps students learn the curriculum because it provides for greater uniformity in the instructional process across the land. My findings on immigrant youth also resonate with the sociolinguistic literature (Collier, 1995; Cummins, 1981) that holds that the academic competence of youth is maximized whenever they are schooled in their native tongue.

8   Gibson (1997) addressed the limitations of Ogbu's voluntary and involuntary minority typology. She noted a host of factors that may result in the construction of these statuses, including familiarity with the host language, contextual factors in the receiving country, whether migrants are economic or political refugees, and whether minorities attend schools that are minority-run.

REFERENCES

Axtman, K. (2005). When tests' cheaters are the teachers: Probe of Texas scores on high-stakes tests is the latest case in series of cheating incidents. *The Christian Science Monitor.* Retrieved on December 9, 2005, from <www.csmonitor.com/2005/0111/p01s03-ussc.html>.

Bartolomé, L. I. (1994). Beyond the methods fetish: Toward a humanizing pedagogy. *Harvard Educational Review, 64*, 173–194.

Blauner, R. (1987). Colonized and immigrant minorities. In R. Takaki (Ed.), *From different shores: Perspectives on race and ethnicity in America* (pp. 149–160). New York: Oxford University Press.

Buriel, R. (1984). Integration with traditional Mexican-American culture and sociocultural adjustment. In J. L. Martínez Jr. & R. Mendoza (Eds.), *Chicano Psychology*, 2d ed. (pp. 95–130). Orlando, FL: Academic Press.

Buriel, R., & Cardoza, D. (1988). Sociocultural correlates of achievement among three generations of Mexican American high school seniors. *American Educational Research Journal, 25*, 177–192.

Callahan, R. E. (1962). *Education and the cult of efficiency.* Chicago: University of Chicago Press.

Chapa, J. (1988). The question of Mexican American assimilation: Socioeconomic parity or underclass formation? *Public Affairs Comment, 35*(1), 1–14.

Chavez, L. (1991). *Out of the barrio: Toward a new politics of Hispanic assimilation.* New York: Basic Books.

Coleman, J. S. (1988). Social capital in the creation of human capital. *American Journal of Sociology, 94*, 95–120.

Coleman, J. S. (1990). *Foundations of social theory.* Cambridge, MA: Harvard University Press.

Collier, V. P. (1995). Acquiring a second language for school. *Directions in Language and Education, 1*(4), 2–14.

Cummins, J. (1981). The role of primary language development in promoting educational success for language minority students. In *Schooling and language minority students: A theoretical framework*. California State Department of Education. Los Angeles: Evaluation, Dissemination, and Assessment Center, California State University.

Danin, S. T. (1994). Contradictions and conflicts in caring. In A. R. Prillman, D. J. Eaker, & D. M. Kendrick (Eds.), *The tapestry of caring: Education as nurturance* (pp. 51–65). Norwood, NJ: Albex.

Darder, A. (1991). *Culture and power in the classroom: A critical foundation for bicultural education*. New York: Bergin and Garvey.

Darder, A. (1995). Buscando America. In C. E. Sleeter & P. L. McLaren (Eds.), *Multicultural education, critical pedagogy, and the politics of difference* (pp. 319–347). Albany, NY: State University of New York Press.

Delgado-Gaitan, C., & Trueba, H. (1991). *Crossing cultural borders: Education for immigrant families in America*. New York: Falmer Press.

Delpit, L. (1995). *Other people's children*. New York: The New Press.

Fine, M. (1991). *Framing dropouts: Notes on the politics of an urban public high school*. Albany, NY: State University of New York Press.

Fisher, B., & Tronto, J. (1990). Toward a feminist theory of caring. In E. K. Able & M. K. Nelson (Eds.), *Circles of care: Work and identity in women's lives* (pp. 35–62). Albany, NY: State University of New York Press.

Frankenberg, R. (1993). *White women, race matters: The social construction of whiteness*. Minneapolis: University of Minnesota Press.

Fry, R. (2005). *The higher drop-out rate of foreign-born teens: The role of schooling abroad*. Washington, DC: Pew Hispanic Center.

Gibson, M. (1997). Complicating the immigrant/involuntary minority typology. *Anthropology and Education Quarterly, 28*(3), 431–454.

Gilligan, C. (1982). *In a different voice*. Cambridge, MA: Harvard University Press.

Intercultural Development Research Association (n.d.). Policy update. Retrieved December 9, 2005, from <www.idra.org/alerts/policyupdates/schoolhp.htm>.

Johnson, R. L. (2002). Texas Schools Have Weak Holding Power: Texas Public School Attrition Study: 2001–02. *Intercultural Development Research Association Newsletter*. Retrieved October 23, 2005, from <www.idra.org/Newslttr/2004/Oct/Roy.htm>.

Kimball, R. (2004, November 9). HISD reports new dropout rate of less than 1%: Miracle or myth? *EducationNews.Org*. Retrieved October 23, 2005, from <www.educationnews.org/hisd-reports-new-dropout-rate-of.htm>.

Ladson-Billings, G. (1994). *The dreamkeepers: Successful teachers of African American children*. San Francisco: Jossey-Bass Publishers.

LeCompte, M., & Dworkin, A. (1991). *Giving up on school: Student dropouts and teacher burnouts*. Newbury Park, CA: Corwin Press.

Macías, J. (1990). Scholastic antecedents of immigrant students: Schooling in a Mexican immigrant-sending community. *Anthropology and Education Quarterly, 21*, 291–318.

Macías, J. (1992). The social nature of Instruction in a Mexican school: Implications for U.S. classroom practice. *The Journal of Educational Issues of Language Minority Students, 10,* 13–25.

Matute-Bianchi, M. E. (1991). Situational ethnicity and patterns of school performance among immigrant and nonimmigrant Mexican-descent students. In M. A. Gibson & J. U. Ogbu (Eds.), *Minority status and schooling: A comparative study of immigrant and involuntary minorities* (pp. 205–247). New York: Garland Publishing.

McIntyre, A. (1997). *Making meaning of whiteness: Exploring racial identity with white teachers.* Albany, NY: State University of New York Press.

McNeil, L. M. (2000). *Contradictions of school reform: Educational Costs of stardardized testing.* New York: Routledge.

McNeil, L. M., & Valenzuela, A. (2001). The harmful effects of the TAAS system of testing: Beneath the accountability rhetoric. In G. Orfield & M. Kornhaber (Eds.), *Raising standards or raising barriers? Inequality and high-stakes testing in public schooling* (pp. 127–150). New York: The Century Press.

McQuillan, P. J. (1998). *Educational opportunity in an urban American high school: A cultural analysis.* Albany, NY: State University of New York Press.

Noblit, G. W. (1994). The principal as caregiver. In R. Prillaman, D. J. Eaker, & D. M. Kendrick (Eds.), *The tapestry of caring: Education as nurturance* (pp. 67–85). Norwood, NJ: Ablex.

Noddings, N. (1984). *Caring: A feminine approach to ethics and moral education.* Berkeley: University of California Press.

Noddings, N. (1992). *The challenge to care in schools: An alternative approach to education.* New York: Teachers College Press.

Ogbu, J. U. (1974). *The next generation: An ethnography of education in an urban neighborhood.* Orlando, FL: Academic Press.

Ogbu, J. U. (1978). *Minority education and caste: The American system in cross-cultural perspective.* Orlando, FL: Academic Press.

Ogbu, J. U. (1991). Immigrant and involuntary minorities in comparative perspective. In *Minority status and Schooling: A Comparative Study of immigrant and involuntary minorities,* edited by M. A. Gibson & J. U. Ogbu. New York: Garland Publishing.

Olsen, L. (1997). *Made in America: Immigrant students in our public schools.* New York: The New Press.

Orenstein, P. (1994). *School girls: Young women, self-esteem, and the confidence gap.* New York: Anchor.

Patthey-Chavez, G. G. (1993). High school as an arena for cultural conflict and acculturation for Angelinos. *Anthropology and Education Quarterly, 24*(1), 33–60.

Peshkin, A. (1991). *The color of strangers, the color of friends: The play of ethnicity in school and community.* Chicago: University of Chicago Press.

Phelan, P., Davidson, A. L., & Yu, Hahn C. (1993). Students' multiple worlds: Navigating the borders of family, peer, and school cultures. In P. Phelan & A. L. Davidson. *Renegotiating cultural diversity in American schools* (pp. 52–88). New York: Teachers College.

Prillaman, A. R., & Eaker, D. J. (1994). The weave and the weaver: A tapestry begun. In A. R. Prillaman, D. J. Eaker, and D. M. Kendrick (Eds.), *The tapestry of caring: Education as nurturance* (1–11). Norwood, NJ: Ablex.

Putnam, R. D. (1993). The prosperous community: Social capital and public life. *American Prospect, 13*(spring), 35–42.

Putnam, R. D. (1995). Bowling alone: America's declining social capital. *Journal of Democracy, 6*(1), 65–78.

Reed, D., Hill, L. E., Jepsen, C., & Johnson, H. P. (2005). *Educational progress across immigrant generations in California.* San Francisco: Public Policy Institute of California.

Spencer, J. (2005, January 8). Teacher tried to report test cheating, union says: HISD allegedly wouldn't grant her immunity; now an office on oversight is being created. *Houston Chronicle,* 1A.

Spindler, G., & Spindler, L. (Eds.) (1994). *Pathways to cultural awareness: Cultural therapy with teachers and students.* Thousand Oaks, CA: Corwin Press.

Stanton-Salazar, R. (1997). A social capital framework for understanding the socialization of ethnic minority children and youths. *Harvard Educational Review, 67,* 1–39.

Suárez-Orozco, M. M. (1991). Hispanic immigrant adaptation to schooling: A Hispanic case. In M. A. Gibson & J. U. Ogbu (Eds.), *Minority status and schooling: A comparative study of immigrant and involuntary minorities* (pp. 37–61). New York: Garland Publishing.

Suro, R. (1998). *Strangers among us: How Latino immigration is transforming America.* New York: Alfred A. Knopf.

Texas Education Agency (2001). Academic Excellence Indicator System. Retrieved on November 4, 2005, from <www.tea.state.tx.us/>.

Texas Education Agency (2002). Academic Excellence Indicator System. Retrieved on November 4, 2005, from <www.tea.state.tx.us/>.

Texas Education Agency (2003). Academic Excellence Indicator System. Retrieved on November 4, 2005, from : <www.tea.state.tx.us/>.

Texas Education Agency (2004). Academic Excellence Indicator System. Retrieved on November 4, 2005, from <www.tea.state.tx.us/>.

Twine, F. W. (1996). Brown skinned white girls: Class, culture and the construction of white identity in suburban communities. *Gender, Place and Culture: A Journal of Feminist Geography, 3*(1), 205–224.

Urrieta, L., Jr. (2004). Dis-connections in "American" citizenship and the post/ neo-colonial: People of Mexican descent and whitestream pedagogy and curriculum. *Theory of Research in Social Education, 32*(4), 433–458.

Valenzuela, A. (1998). Subtractive schooling: U.S.-Mexican youth and the politics of caring. *Reflexiones 1998: New directions in Mexican American studies.* Center for Mexican American Studies, University of Texas.

Valenzuela, A. (1999). *Subtractive schooling: U.S.-Mexican youth and the politics of caring.* Albany, NY: State University of New York Press.

Valenzuela, A. (2004). *Leaving children behind: How "Texas-style" accountability fails Latino youth.* Albany, NY: State University of New York Press.

Vigil, D. (1997). *Personas Mexicanas: Chicano high schoolers in a changing Los Angeles.* Fort Worth, TX: Harcourt Brace College Publishers.

Yeo, F. L. (1997). *Inner-city schools, multiculturalism, and teacher education: A professional journey.* New York: Garland Publishing.

Part V

Model Programs and Applications

Chapter 22

Forming Academic Identities

Accommodation without Assimilation among Involuntary Minorities*

Hugh Mehan, Lea Hubbard, and Irene Villanueva

Students from linguistic and ethnic-minority backgrounds and low-income families do poorly in school in comparison with their majority and well-to-do contemporaries. They drop out at a higher rate. They score lower on tests. Their grades are lower (Coleman et al., 1966; Haycock & Navarro, 1988; Jencks et al., 1972). And most importantly for the topic of this chapter, they do not attend college as often (Carter & Wilson, 1991; Center for Education Statistics, 1986).

Students from linguistic- and ethnic-minority backgrounds are expected to compose an increasing percentage of the U.S. population through the early years of the 21st century (Carter & Wilson, 1991; Pelavin & Kane, 1990). Jobs that require higher education are expected to increase in number (CSAW, 1990; NCEE, 1990). The current census data, however, show that students from linguistic- and ethnic-minority backgrounds are not enrolling in college in sufficient numbers to qualify for the increasing number of jobs that will require baccalaureate degrees. If the enrollment of students from underrepresented backgrounds in colleges and universities does not increase and if these same students do not obtain college degrees, then the nation will not have achieved the educational, economic, and social equity that it has sought. It will not have the skilled workforce it needs to ensure a healthy and competitive economy, nor will it have the well-educated and thoughtful citizenry it needs for a vibrant and energetic democracy. Indeed, if the current college enrollment trends continue, then the social and economic gaps that exist between ethnic groups in the United States will widen.

We have been studying an "untracking" program in San Diego that is closing one of the educational gaps between minority and majority, low-income and upper-income students: college enrollment. The San Diego untracking experiment places students from low-income ethnic- and linguistic-minority backgrounds in college prep classes along with their high-achieving peers. In addition to placing high- and previously low-achieving students in the same heterogenously grouped courses, this program provides the students with a special elective class that emphasizes collaborative instruction, writing, and problem solving.

In a previous report (Mehan et al., 1992), we described the commendable college-enrollment record of the graduates of this program, compared to San Diego and national averages. As we conducted interviews of the untracked students and observed them in their classrooms and out of school, we discovered additional social consequences of this untracking effort that extend beyond its manifest educational consequences.

The African American and Latino students in the untracking program formed academically oriented peer groups and developed strategies for managing an academic identity at school and a neighborhood identity among friends at home. From these new voluntary associations, new ideologies developed. The students' belief statements displayed a healthy disrespect for the romantic tenets of achievement ideology and an affirmation of cultural identities, and they acknowledged the necessity of academic achievement for occupational success. Gibson called this ideology, and the course of action that flows from it, "accommodation without assimilation" (1988). This is a unique ideology, one not usually expressed by low-income Latino and African American youth. Gibson found it operating among *voluntary minorities* (such as Sikhs, Japanese, and Chinese) but not *involuntary minorities* (such as Latinos and African Americans).

In this chapter, we present the contours of the accommodationist ideology that we found among the Latino and African American youth in this untracking program. Then we describe some of the cultural processes and organizational practices that seem to have nurtured its development. Before doing so, we place this discussion in the context of the debate attempting to explain the educational inequities that break out along class, ethnic, and gender lines in the United States.

EXPLAINING EDUCATIONAL INEQUALITY

Why are students from minority and working-class backgrounds not as successful in school as their middle- and upper-income contemporaries? Why is there a strong tendency for working-class children to end up in working-class jobs? One of the most persuasive explanations of the inequality in educational outcomes is *reproduction theory*, which suggests that inequality is the consequence of capitalist structures and forces that constrain the mobility of lower-class youth.

The Reproduction of Inequality by Economic and Cultural Means

Bowles and Gintis posited a correspondence between the organization of work and the organization of schooling, which trained elites to accept their place at the top of the class economy and trained workers to accept their lower places at the bottom of the class economy (1976). The sons and daughters of workers, placed into ability groups or tracks that encourage docility and conformity to external rules and authority, learn the skills associated with manual work. By contrast, the sons and daughters of the elite are placed into tracks that encourage them to work at their own pace without supervision, to make intelligent choices among alternatives, and to internalize rather than externally follow constraining norms.

Bourdieu and Passeron provide us with a more subtle account of inequality, by proposing cultural elements that mediate the relationship between economic structures and people's lives (1977; cf. Bourdieu, 1986). Distinctive cultural knowledge is transmitted by the families of each social class. As a consequence, children of the dominant class inherit substantially different cultural knowledge, skills, manners, norms, dress, styles of interaction, and linguistic facilities than do the sons and daughters of lower-class origin. Students from the dominant class, by virtue of a certain linguistic and cultural competence acquired through family socialization, are provided the means of appropriating success in school. Children who read good books, visit museums, attend concerts, and go to the theatre acquire an ease, a familiarity with the dominant culture that the educational system implicitly requires of its students for academic attainment. Schools and other symbolic institutions contribute to the reproduction of inequality by devising a curriculum that rewards the *cultural capital* of the dominant classes and systematically devalues that of the lower classes.

Bourdieu and Passeron's more nuanced view (1977) overcomes some of the problems in Bowles and Gintis's economic formulation (1976), but the representation of the cause of inequality contained in cultural reproduction theory, while powerful, still suffers from an overly deterministic worldview. It emphasizes structural constraints while virtually ignoring the social organization of school practices and individuals' actions (Mehan, 1992). Students are treated mainly as bearers of cultural capital—a bundle of abilities, knowledge, and attitudes furnished by parents (Apple, 1983; Giroux, 1983; MacLeod, 1987). As a result, we second the motion made by Giroux and Simon (1989) and MacLeod (1987), who call for a reflexive relationship between social agency and social constraints.

Resistant and Oppositional Behavior: Students' Contributions to Their School Failure

A series of articulate ethnographies has begun to establish a balance between structural determinants and social agency in explaining inequality. While acknowledging that structural constraints inhibit mobility and that school practices contribute to inequality, they focus on students' own contributions to their difficulties. In these ethnographies, students from lower-income, ethnic- and linguistic-minority backgrounds have been represented as having a belief system that is different from the mainstream. While mainstream students are characterized as believing in the value of hard work and individual effort (oftentimes called the *achievement ideology*), low-income and minority students either directly challenge or disengage from the prevailing ideology of American society. Either they do not buy into, or they have given up on, the belief in hard work and individual effort. If they have beliefs at all, they are said to be anti-establishment. If not anti-intellectual, they are at least anti-academic because these students see little reason for their coursework and cannot envision how schooling will help them achieve their goals (LeCompte & Dworkin, 1991).

Willis's 1977 study of disaffected White working-class males in a British secondary school is the hallmark study in this so-called resistance tradition. He found the "lads," a group of high-school dropouts who rejected achievement ideology, subverted teacher and administrator authority, and disrupted classes. Willis said that the lads' rejection of the school is partly the result of their deep insights into the economic condition of their social class under capitalism. But their cultural outlook limited their options; equating manual labor with success and mental labor with failure prevented them from seeing that their actions led to dead-end, lower-paying jobs. Blind to the connection between schooling and mobility, they *choose* to join their brothers and fathers on the shop floor, a choice apparently made happily and freely from coercion. Thus, what begins as a potential insight into the social relations of production is transformed into a surprisingly uncritical affirmation of class domination. This identification of manual labor with masculinity ensures the lads' acceptance of their subordinate economic fate and the successful reproduction of the class structure.

Following in Willis's path, MacLeod (1987) and Foley (1990) invited us to listen to the anti-establishment ideology of the working class. Like the lads in England, the sons of the working class in the United States have developed a critique of the capitalist system that rationalizes their lack of academic and economic success. The "Hallway Hangers" in Boston and the "vatos" in South Texas realize that, no matter how hard they work, they will still be relegated to low-paying jobs or, worse, no jobs at all. These words are translated into deeds; they withdraw from academic pursuits, act up in class, ignore assignments and homework, and cut classes. Their critique, like that of the "lads," is somewhat short-sighted, however, because their ideology leads to actions that contribute to their stagnant position in the status hierarchy.

Ogbu's research into the folk models of schooling associated with voluntary minorities and involuntary minorities sharpened the oppositional and resistant representation of minority and working-class youth (1978, 1987). Voluntary minorities (such as Japanese, Koreans, and Chinese) accept school norms, work hard, and alternate their academic identity at school with a nonacademic identity with friends. Ogbu stated that African Americans and Latinos have a different folk model of schooling that encourages different patterns of behavior. These involuntary minorities tend to equate schooling with assimilation into the dominant group, a course of action that they actively resist. As a result, they do not try to achieve academically; instead, they engage in collective actions of resistance against school and societal norms.

Ogbu implied that the ideology that African Americans, Latinos, and other encapsulated minority groups have developed contributes to their relatively poor academic and economic success. Because it is collectivist and oppositional, the ideology of involuntary or encapsulated minorities has led them to adopt strategies that scorn the idea of individual achievement that is so important in American society, in favor of collective strategies that blame failure on racial discrimination and other structural forces.

Labov reported that low-income Black students formed a group identity based on in-group linguistic codes, Black English Vernacular (BEV), for example (1982). While these communication patterns help maintain group cohesion, they also have alienating effects. BEV use, like Rap and reggae, distinctive dress, and demeanor, is a source of distinction and pride (from the low-income, Black student's point of view), but is a sign of opposition and irritation (from the White teacher's point of view). In Labov's study, the folk model within the low-income Black peer culture required speech that was markedly different from the "good English" expected in school. Students who spoke "school English" and did well in school marked themselves as different and risked rejection by their peers. Because they valued peer praise, these students opted out of academic pursuits and into oppositional pursuits, which meant they spent more time resisting authority and being confrontational and much less time and effort in their schoolwork (1982).

Fordham and Ogbu (1986) expanded Labov's argument. Because involuntary immigrant groups still experience prejudice, they have come to believe that social and economic success is only possible by adopting the cultural and linguistic patterns of the majority culture. This puts high-achieving Blacks in a bind, because they must choose between maintaining their ethnic identity or striving for high achievement, which their ethnic peers regard as acting superior, or "acting White." To resolve this dilemma, many Blacks reject academic life in favor of an oppositional lifestyle.

In short, poor Black and Latino students are said to have an ideology and a course of action that directly challenges conventional American wisdom about the relationship between academic performance and occupational success. When Black high school students rebuke their Black peers for "acting White," they are actively resisting White structure and domination (Fordham & Ogbu, 1986). Likewise, when Black college students go through the routine of schooling but exert little effort in their study, they are resisting an education that they see as "only second best" to that available to Whites (Weis, 1985). So too, when West Indians in Toronto form separatist groups, refuse to follow school rules, and play sports to the exclusion of their schoolwork, they are creating a "lived culture" that contributes to their own school difficulties (Solomon, 1992). The ideology and practice of resistance contribute to the lowly position of Blacks and Latinos in the occupational structure, according to "resistance" theorists, because working-class students refuse to develop the skills, attitudes, manners and speech that are necessary for the achievement of success in capitalist societies.

The agency attributed to students, then, distinguishes these ethnographic accounts from the theorizing of either Bowles and Gintis or Bourdieu and Passeron. Unlike the students in Bowles and Gintis's rendition who passively internalize mainstream values of individual achievement or the students in Bourdieu and Passeron's theory who simply carry cultural capital on their backs or in their heads, these working-class, linguistic- and ethnic-minority students make real choices in their everyday lives. While at first glance, the working-class students' rebellious behavior, their low academic achievement, and their high dropout rate seem to stem from dullness, laziness, inability to project themselves into the future, and lack of self-discipline, their actual causes are quite different. Their unwillingness to participate comes from their assessment of the costs and benefits of playing the game. It is not that schooling will not propel them up the ladder of success; it is that chances are too slim to warrant the attempt. Given this logic, the oppositional behavior of MacLeod's Hallway Hangers; Foley's vatos, Willis's lads, and the others is a form of resistance to an institution that cannot deliver on its promise of upward mobility for all students.

Adding the notion of resistance to the lexicon employed to understand inequality in schools, then, reveals the contributions that social actors make to their own plight. As Ogbu (1991) phrased it, this line of research shows how victims contribute to their own victimization.

INSTITUTIONAL ARRANGEMENTS MEDIATING THE RELATIONS BETWEEN SOCIAL CONSTRAINTS AND EDUCATIONAL OUTCOMES

We encountered a set of institutional arrangements in which the sons and daughters of the working poor develop a very different ideology and adopt a very different course of action than has been previously described. Poor African American, Latino and European American high school students who have participated in an untracking program express a belief in their own efficacy and a belief in the power of schooling to improve their lives and the lives of others. They translate belief into action by participating actively in school. Yet they do not adopt a romantic or naive commitment to achievement ideology. They are all too aware of the barriers erected in front of them by the history of racism and discrimination. To handle the complexities of the world that they confront, they adopt strategies that many researchers have attributed to recent immigrants to the United States (Cummins, 1986; Gibson, 1988; Gibson & Ogbu, 1991; Ogbu, 1978, 1987; Suarez-Orozco, 1989), but not to encapsulated minorities: they maintain their ethnic identity while actively engaging in schooling.

The AVID Untracking Program

These students who accommodate to the norms of school and society without assimilating or compromising their ethnic identity participate in an "untracking" program in San Diego high schools, called AVID, an acronym that stands for Advancement Via Individual Determination. The idea of untracking low-achieving students was introduced to San Diego in 1980 at Claremont High School, a predominantly White school, by Mary Catherine Swanson, then a member of the English department, as a way to educate minority students bused to that school from predominantly ethnic-minority schools in Southeast San Diego under a court's desegregation order. Unwilling to segregate African American and Latino students into a separate, compensatory curriculum, Swanson and the Claremont faculty placed the bused students in regular "college prep" classes.

The expressed goals of the AVID untracking program are to motivate and prepare underachieving students from underrepresented linguistic- and ethnic-minority groups to perform well in high school and to seek a college education. Since 1991, 14 other "city schools," 50 high schools in San Diego County, and 84 high schools outside the county have introduced AVID programs.

AVID coordinators select students for the untracking program. Low-income, ethnic- and linguistic-minority students in the eighth or ninth grade who have average-to-high achievement test scores but low junior high school grades are eligible for AVID. Once teachers identify these high-potential/low-performance students, their parents are advised. Those parents who agree to support their children's participation in the academic program sign contracts to have their children participate in AVID as soon as they enroll in high school.

Once selected, students take a special elective class as part of their course load. This class emphasizes writing, inquiry, and collaboration (Swanson, n.d.). Writing is seen as a tool of learning. Students are taught a special form of note taking, the Cornell system, in which they are to jot detailed notes from their academic classes in a wide right-hand margin and, as homework, develop questions based on the notes, in a narrow left-hand column. The questions students develop as homework are supposed to be used the following day in the AVID class. In addition to note taking, the students are supposed to keep learning logs and practice "quick writes" to facilitate their learning (Swanson, n.d.).

Inquiry refers to the instructional strategy that teachers and tutors are to employ with the students in the elective AVID class. The program provides tutors (usually students recruited from local colleges, some of whom participated in AVID while they were in high school) to assist AVID students. Tutors are trained to lead study groups in specific subjects, such as math or English, based on the students' notes and questions. Tutors are not to give answers: they are to help the AVID students clarify their thoughts based on their questions. AVID encourages the use of the inquiry method so that the AVID class does not become a glorified study hall or homework session (Swanson, n.d.).

Collaboration is the instructional strategy that organizes students to work together to achieve instructional goals. Collaborative groups or study teams enable students to serve as sources of information for each other. Collaboration, AVID asserts, shifts the responsibility for learning from the teacher who directs lessons, to the students who participate in them (Swanson, n.d.).

The AVID central office suggests a basic plan for the weekly instructional activities within AVID classrooms. Two school days are designated tutorial days. On these days students are to work in small groups with the assistance of a tutor. On the other two days, writing as a tool for learning is emphasized. On these days, students engage in a variety of writing activities, including essays for their English classes and essays for college applications. One day a week, usually Fridays, is a "motivational day." Guest speakers are invited to address the class, and field trips to colleges are scheduled on these days.

The Academic Consequences of Untracking

This untracking program has been successful in preparing its students for college. In 1990 and 1991, 253 students who had participated in the AVID untracking experiment for three years graduated from 14 high schools in the San Diego City Schools (SDCS) system. In those years an additional 288 students started the program but left after completing one year or less. We interviewed 144 of the "graduates" and 72 of the students who left the program within one year (Mehan et al., 1992).

Of the 144 students who graduated from AVID, 72 (50 percent) reported attending four-year colleges, 60 (42 percent) reported attending two-year or junior colleges, and the remaining 12 students (8 percent) said they are working or doing other things. The 50 percent four-year college enrollment rate for students who were "untracked" compares favorably with the SDCS's average of 37 percent and the national average of 39 percent. It also compares favorably with the college enrollment rate of students who started but did not complete the untracking program; 31 percent of them enrolled in four-year colleges within a year of graduating from high school.

Furthermore, the untracking experiment assists students from low-income families and the two major ethnic groups that are under-represented in college. African Americans and Latinos from AVID enroll in college in numbers that exceed local and national averages. Of the Latino students who participated in AVID for three years, 44 percent enrolled in four-year colleges. This figure compares favorably to the SDCS's average of 25 percent and the national average of 29 percent. African American students who participated in AVID for three years also enrolled in college at rates higher than the local and national averages: 54 percent of Black students in AVID enrolled in four-year colleges, compared to 35 percent from the SDCS and the national average of 33 percent.

AVID students from the lowest income strata (parents' median income below $19,999) enrolled in four-year colleges in equal or higher proportion to students from higher income strata (parents' median income between $20,000 and $65,000). Furthermore, AVID students from families in which their parents do not have a college education enrolled in four-year colleges more often than students from families with parents who have a college education.

Students who completed three years of AVID enrolled in college in greater proportion than students who completed a year or less of AVID, regardless of the family's income level: 60 percent of three-year AVID students from families who earned less than $20,000 enrolled in college, compared to 29 percent of one-year AVID students whose families were in this income bracket; 44 percent of three-year AVID students from families in the $20,000 to $39,000 income range enrolled in college versus 30 percent of one-year AVID students whose families were in this range; 59 percent of three-year AVID students whose families were in the $40,000 to $59,000 range and 43 percent of the one-year AVID students whose families were in this income range enrolled in college.

The Social Consequences of Untracking

Improving the college enrollment of students from underrepresented linguistic- and ethnic-minority backgrounds is the expressed purpose of the AVID untracking program. And our research shows that the program is successful in this regard.

As we conducted interviews of the AVID students and observed them in their classrooms and out of school, we discovered additional social consequences of this untracking effort that extend beyond its manifest educational consequences. The African American and Latino students in AVID developed a reflective system of beliefs, a critical consciousness if you will, about the limits and possibilities of the actions they take and the limitations and constraints they face in life.

After we describe our research methods, we present the contours of the accommodationist ideology that we found among the Latino and African American youth in this untracking program. Then we describe some of the cultural processes and organizational practices that seem to have nurtured its development.

Data and Methods

We used materials from many sources in this study: official school records, interviews of students, teachers, parents, and school officials, as well as observations in classrooms. The San Diego City Schools (SDCS) kindly supplied us with the Cumulative School Records (CSRs) of AVID students in the classes of 1990 and 1991. We used information from the CSRs to determine students' ethnicity and to calculate their academic record in high school (AVID classes taken, Comprehensive Test of Basic Skills (CTBS) scores, college-prep courses taken and completed, etc.).

Of the 1,053 students enrolled in AVID in 1990 and 1991, we found 253 students in 14 high schools who had completed three years of AVID during their high school careers when they graduated. We also identified 188 students who had entered AVID in the same academic year as the "untracked" group but did not complete three years of the program. Instead, they left after one semester or one year.

In order to determine students' activities since they had graduated from high school, we attempted to interview the 253 graduates of the classes of 1990 and 1991 and the 188 students who started but did not complete

AVID. We were able to interview 144 of the program grads and 72 of the AVID comparison group. We asked both groups of students about their activities since they graduated from high school, that is, whether they had enrolled in four- or two-year colleges, were working, or were doing other things. In order to place students' college enrollment and work information in context, we asked students about their family background (e.g., parents' education, languages spoken in the home). We also discussed their high school and AVID experiences with them. This information helped us answer the question: Does untracking work?

We recognized that, in order to answer the question of how untracking works, we needed to go beyond correlational data and examine school practices and cultural processes. To do so, we conducted case studies of four of the San Diego high schools that are participating in this untracking experiment. We chose the four schools—Churchill, Monrovia, Pimlico, and Saratoga (all pseudonyms)—based on their ethnic enrollments, their college enrollment rate, and of course, their willingness to participate in the study. From October 1991 to August 1992, we observed in AVID classrooms, and Hubbard and Villanueva interviewed AVID teachers, students, and their parents from these four schools. In some cases we also observed in the academic classes that AVID students take and interviewed the parents of AVID students.

THE DEVELOPMENT OF A REFLECTIVE ACHIEVEMENT IDEOLOGY

The involuntary-minority students in AVID have developed an interesting set of beliefs about the relationship between school and success. They do not have a naive belief in the connection between academic performance and occupational success. While they voice enthusiastic support for the power of their own agency, their statements also display a critical awareness of structures of inequality and strategies for overcoming discrimination in society.

Belief in Individual Effort, Motivation, and Opportunity

AVID teaches a version of achievement ideology, telling students they can be successful (which AVID defines as going to college) if they are motivated and study hard. The AVID coordinator at Saratoga High School stated this philosophy succinctly when greeting her incoming freshman class:

The responsibility for your success is with you. AVID is here to help.

> Your goal should be to go to a four-year college. There is lots of work to be done, but you will have more help, support, and love than you will ever need.

Interviews with AVID students suggest that they internalize this ideology, articulating success in a way that reflects the message that AVID teaches. The following students highlight the value of motivation in providing equal opportunity:

> Before AVID I was unsure about college. I was always changing my mind. AVID teaches you that you have the same opportunity to get to college as anybody if you just stay motivated.

> I am more motivated to go to college because AVID made me want to go. Before I got into AVID, I didn't think I had many opportunities. I thought I couldn't afford it and that I couldn't get good-enough grades. Mrs. Lincoln says we can get financial aid. And well, now my grades are really good.

These students assert that their opportunity to achieve success is the result of their individual effort:

> I have a better opportunity than others because I am really striving for it. AVID helps me know what to do. I try hard; so I have to say I have the opportunity because of who I am. I have my own individual identity and not the identity of a group of people.

Students also echo the sentiments of the AVID program when they claim that they have the same opportunity to achieve as anyone else, regardless of their racial or ethnic background. An African American male at Saratoga maintains that he has an opportunity to succeed because "the key to success is your own body, your own self."

Experience with Prejudice and Discrimination

AVID students believe in individual effort, motivation, and opportunity. But these students also recognize that the world out there is full of discrimination, prejudice, and racism.

Many AVID students have personally experienced prejudice. In a group discussion Lea Hubbard had with African American AVID students at Saratoga, David and Rocky, two Saratoga seniors, said that they had stopped at a traffic light and that a White man in the car next to them got out of his car and pulled a gun on them for no reason. They took off "like fast." AVID students have experienced scrutiny and harassment from the police in ways that resonate with the tales told by Anderson (1991, pp. 190–206). Here are some incidents that these students rattled off to Hubbard during that discussion, which suggest that the police define their social-control work as keeping middle-income White neighborhoods "safe" from low-income Blacks:

> Rocky and two other friends were walking home from a school dance behind some White guys. A police patrol stopped and harassed them, but never stopped the White guys.

> Kam was at home one night when cops just burst into his home without reason and left without explanation.

When Lea Hubbard said to them, "It sounds like you are getting a bum deal," the boys agreed. But they were not resigned to these conditions; they believed they could overcome them: "If you work hard, you will succeed."

Dora, a Black female student at Saratoga, relayed similar experiences to Lea Hubbard in an interview:

> I'm gonna tell you something—I don't care if I should—but there's a whole lot of racism. My friend and I were alternates on the flag team . . . and when they needed to replace some permanent members, they got two new White girls and not my friend and I.

Khalada, another African American female student at Saratoga, also expressed an awareness of discrimination. She said her mother told her that she had to watch out. She might be friends with Whites now, but when it came to the business world later, they would let you down.

Experience with prejudice and discrimination is not confined to Black and Latino students. John Sing, a junior in AVID at Saratoga, is an ethnic Chinese born in Vietnam. Although he is doing well academically (carrying a 3.3 GPA), he confided to Lea Hubbard that he is afraid of the verbal portion of the Scholastic Aptitude Test (SAT) because he considers it a racist test. He is also afraid that his chances of going to college will be hampered by a quota system, which limits the number of Asian students, and that "there are lots of Asians smarter than me."

Strategies for Dealing with Discrimination

AVID students are not only aware of these structures of discrimination, but they have developed strategies for dealing with them. When Hubbard asked Dora about what happened after the flag-team incident (reported above), she said:

> My mom raised heck. [But] teachers don't care. They just think they
> are here to teach: "You've got to get yourself through." Except for
> three teachers. Mrs. Lincoln is one of them. Teachers don't say you are
> capable. No one really cares.

Later in this interview, she reinforced her earlier statement that individual
motivation overcomes racism:

> Most Blacks in the community are faced with prejudice and will be held
> back, not me.

Tipoli, a Saratoga junior, recognized there are barriers erected in her path
and in the path of African American students generally:

> I think teachers expect more out of us [Blacks]. Colleges recruit
> Blacks because of sports, but they don't get an education. That's dumb.
> There's lots of hurt and prejudice. People need to learn about differ-
> ent cultures and read about black people. They always look at us when
> we study about slaves as if we were slaves.

In addition to her general appeal for more culturally sensitive curricula,
her more personal strategy for dealing with prejudice is to "go to college.
I want to be there. It's the only way to get a job."

This opinion was reinforced by David, an African American student,
who says he does not have an equal opportunity to succeed because of
his race:

> There is more pressure because we are black and we are athletes.
> They are always looking to us to do the right thing, and if we do
> anything wrong, we're nobody.

Before he became involved with AVID, David said that his athletic prowess would lead him to success. Since he has been in AVID, his strategy for
dealing with the prejudice he has experienced has changed; now he plans
to get good grades and not rely on athletics as his ticket to success.

Several African American males reported tales of systematic discrimination at the hands of a particular counselor at Saratoga. In a group interview with Lea Hubbard, they reported that this counselor repeatedly
tells African American males that they "won't make it to a big time
college." One student reported asking for information about a four-year
college and being told, "What for? It's just a waste of your time and
mine. You won't make it anyway." The counselor then gave him only
information about two-year colleges and vocational schools. Even though
the students say they have protested the counselor's ill treatment of them,

he is unwilling to help them. When one male student tried to add a chemistry course to his schedule, this same counselor said no and that "he didn't need that for what he was going to do after graduation. Only college-bound kids need academics." To deal with this prejudicial situation, the AVID students have devised ways to avoid this counselor. Instead of going to him for advice, they rely on the AVID teacher to counsel them about college. They also advise each other and make it clear to new AVID students that they should avoid this counselor.

Students report incidents at Monrovia that suggest they are victims of backlash from their academic teachers. It appears as though some teachers think that AVID students are only in advanced classes because they are AVID students. This "sorting privilege" can operate against AVID students. One Monrovia student commented that her advanced-English teacher told her on her first day that "she wouldn't make it in her class." Her AVID teacher intervened on her behalf the next day, telling the English teacher that "the student would make it because she was getting extra help from AVID." The student finished the semester with a grade of B. Hubbard asked the student why she felt she was able to succeed. She said:

> I knew if I tried, I could, and I really wanted to show her I could do it. [The AVID coordinator] told me to work with the tutor. But boy was I hurt that [the advanced-English teacher] thought I couldn't do it. I know it was because I was a minority student. She didn't even know my ability.

Some African American males in AVID talk about their race strategically. In doing so, they sound like the "Brothers" in MacLeod's (1987) ethnography of urban youth. The Brothers said they thought they had more opportunity to succeed than their parents because of the influence of governmental civil rights laws. Darius, a Black male from Saratoga High School, is typical of many African American males in AVID in this respect. He feels he has a better opportunity because of his race. Colleges, especially those in California, are trying to meet affirmative-action goals, he says. Therefore, they recruit African American males such as himself to meet quotas. That is, in a civil rights climate, his race gives him an advantage, a fact that he can use strategically.

Discrimination can cut two ways. Darcey, one of a minority of White students in AVID, indexed what would be called reverse discrimination. He says that he does not have an equal opportunity because of his race: colleges are accepting Asians over White kids.

Accommodation without Assimilation

AVID students recognize that academic performance is necessary for occupational success, but they have not bought the naive proposition that their individual effort will automatically breed their success. The Latino and African American students in AVID (whom Ogbu would call "involuntary minorities") have also developed provocative beliefs and practices about culture contact. They affirm their cultural identities while at the same time recognizing the need to develop certain cultural practices, notably achieving academically, that are acceptable to the mainstream. Following Gibson (1988), we talk about this aspect of their ideology as "accommodation without assimilation."

Marta Garcia represents many Latino students in AVID who affirm their cultural identity while achieving academically. Marta confided to Lea Hubbard that her Latino cultural background is very important to her. In fact, when she was in third grade, she pledged to become perfectly bilingual, maintaining her native Spanish while developing acceptable English and academic skills. She has fulfilled this promise to herself and entered the University of Ihao Americana, Tijuana, Mexico in the fall of 1992.

When Lea Hubbard and Irene Villanueva interviewed Marta's Spanish-speaking parents, it was clear that Marta's identification with her Mexican heritage has been kept actively alive by her intense involvement with her parents. Spanish is the predominant language in the home; the family takes frequent trips to Mexico; and religious and cultural symbols are prevalent in the home. Marta's parents respect her bicultural moves. On the one hand, they are pleased that Marta and her friends are respectful of their background. On the other hand, they encourage the academic path their children are taking. It is perhaps symbolic of the way the parents are juggling these two worlds that Marta's older brother, also an excellent student, will be attending college with Marta.

Marta has two close friends, Serena and Maria, both of whom are in AVID. These girls reinforce each other's love of their cultural heritage and desire to succeed. They often discuss college plans and share their concerns and excitement in Spanish, a sure sign of their cultural accommodation.

Another sign of Serena's accommodation is found in her interactions with her mother about college. Serena's mother is a widow who speaks very little English and works as a domestic and food-services worker at the University of San Diego. Serena interacts with her mother in Spanish at home but seldom about academic matters, apparently. Mrs. Castro told Irene Villanueva that she provided Serena with general moral support (*apoyo morao*) but felt ill-equipped to provide the detailed technical skills Serena needed in school. Mrs. Castro always supported Serena's plans to go to college, although she did not want her to leave the San Diego area in order to pursue this goal. She is pleased, therefore, that Serena will attend the University of California at San Diego. When Irene asked Mrs. Castro about Serena's financial aid, Mrs. Castro laughed in an embarrassed way because she was completely unaware of what Serena would be receiving, what her fees are, or how they would be paid. Serena has assumed all the responsibilities associated with college matriculation and, in the process, simultaneously maintained her family life with her mother and her school life with her friends.

Managing Dual Identities

The space AVID has created is productive because it helps AVID students foster academic identities. But this same space also creates problems for AVID students, because they must deal with their friends who are academically oriented and their friends who are not academically oriented. AVID students develop a variety of strategies for balancing or managing this dilemma.

Gándara found that college-bound Latino students used "denial" as a strategy to keep up their grades while still keeping up their friendships (in press). One Latino student told her, "I didn't let on that I was studying or working hard. I mean you were cool if you didn't study."

While some AVID students submerged their academic identity entirely, most students maintained dual identities, one at school and one in the neighborhood. Because they were segregated by classes at school, it was not difficult to keep the two peer groups separate. At school, they were free to compete academically; at home in the afternoon, they would assume a different posture.

Laura is a Latina who lives in what she described as "the ghetto":

> You don't know how awful it is there. They don't give a damn about themselves. My mom doesn't have any education. My friends in the neighborhood think I am really stupid for staying in school. They tell me that, since I have enough credits to graduate, I ought to quit school and get a job. They think the most important thing is to get married and have babies.

Laura wants to be a lawyer, and she knows the only way to achieve that goal is to "put forth the effort and go to college." But she also wants to keep her friends. So she is active in AVID during school hours and continues to date boys from her neighborhood and go to the movies with her girlfriends who live on her street.

An African American male from Monrovia said in so many words that he lives two lives. Chris said he really wants to go to college and that

AVID provides him a place where his academic pursuits are encouraged and where he has academically oriented peers. But he has street friends, too. While he feels they are "wasting their lives" because "they are into being bad," he still hangs out with them. Chris also spends some of his free time as a peer counselor for Saratoga's African American students. His counseling activities bridge the two different worlds that he occupies.

The story of Hazzard, an African American male who attended Pimlico High School, exemplifies a third strategy for managing dual identities. He brought his nonacademic friends with him into academic settings. Hazzard was a member of a gang when he was selected into AVID. He retained his gang friends, while simultaneously developing new acquaintances in AVID. Like other AVID students, he wanted to go to college. He was, in fact, accepted at the University of California at Berkeley, San Diego State University, and a local junior college. Instead of enrolling at the Berkeley campus, he said he chose to attend the college closer to his home so that he could stay with his friends. Indeed, he brought them to classes with him. Hazzard was doing what he needed to do to pass academically, while retaining his membership in his peer group.

These "border crossing" strategies (Delgado-Gaitan & Trueba, 1991; Giroux, 1992; Rose, 1989) have special utility for minority students because, by the time they graduate, they will have had experience in moving between two cultures. They will have interacted with high-achieving Anglos and still be comfortable in the company of friends who would never leave the fields or the barrios or go to college (cf. Gándara, 1994).

GROUP FORMATION AND THE CONSTRUCTION OF ACADEMIC IDENTITIES

The African American and Latino students who participated in the AVID untracking program for three years developed strategies for managing dual identities and developed new ideologies. Importantly, these ideologies were neither conformist nor assimilationist. Instead, their belief statements displayed a healthy disrespect for the romantic tenets of achievement ideology and affirmed their cultural identities, while acknowledging the necessity of academic achievement for occupational success.

In the next few pages, we describe the institutional arrangements and cultural processes that contributed to the formation of academic identities and the development of a reflective achievement ideology.

Isolation of Group Members

In order to transform raw recruits into fighting men, the military isolates them from other, potentially conflicting social forces. Religious orders and gangs operate in a similar manner, shielding their recruits from competing interests and groups (Goffman, 1964; Jankowski, 1991).

Whether intentionally or not, AVID has adopted this principle. AVID selects promising students and isolates them in special classes that meet once a day, every day of the school year. Once students are in these classes, AVID provides them social supports that assist them through the transition from low-track to academic-track status. These scaffolds include explicit instruction in a special method of note taking, test-taking strategies, and general study tips. The note-taking technique stresses compiling and abstracting main ideas and generating questions to guide students' reading. Students are expected to apply these techniques in notebooks that they keep for their academic courses.

Test-taking skills were taught in all AVID classrooms, albeit differentially emphasized. At a minimum, students were given drill and practice on vocabulary items likely to appear on the Scholastic Aptitude Test (SAT). When a more extensive approach to test preparation was taken, students were provided explicit instruction in ways to eliminate distracting answers on multiple choice questions, strategies for approximating answers, and probabilities about the success of guessing. One AVID teacher devoted two successive weeks to SAT preparation, including practice with vocabulary items, administering practice tests, reviewing wrong answers, and teaching strategies for taking tests. This teacher reviewed the kinds of analogies typically found on the SAT with her students so that they could practice the kinds of problems they would encounter on their tests. This teacher also sent her students to an expert math teacher for assistance on math test items. She reinforced this teaching by explaining that she was teaching them the same academic tricks found in the expensive Princeton Review SAT preparation class.

While note-taking skills, test-taking strategies, and study tips were taught routinely, by far the most prevalent activity in the four AVID programs we studied during the 1991–92 school year revolved around the college-application process. Procedures for filing applications, meeting deadlines for SAT tests, and requesting financial aid and scholarships dominated discussion. At Pimlico High, for instance, students must complete a weekly AVID assignment in which students do writing and/or reading tasks directly related to college. The junior class at Saratoga received a handout, 'Choosing Your College', containing a checklist of information typically found in college catalogs. Students were instructed to fill in the information for that college according to the assigned checklist. This task presumably made them more familiar with college catalogs and would help them choose a college to fit their personal needs.

By dispensing these academic tricks, AVID is giving students explicit instruction in the hidden curriculum of the school. That is, AVID teaches explicitly in school what middle-income students learn implicitly at home. In Bourdieu's terms (1986), AVID gives low-income students some of the cultural capital at school that is similar to the cultural capital that more economically advantaged parents give to their children at home.

Public Markers of Group Identity

In addition to isolating students and providing them with social supports, AVID marks their group identity in a public manner. The special class set aside for their exclusive use is one such marker. Instead of going to shop or driver's education for their elective class period, they go to the AVID room, a classroom identified by signs and banners. Students often return to the AVID room at lunchtime or after school to do homework or socialize, actions that further mark their distinctive group membership.

AVID students are given special notebooks, emblazoned with the AVID logo, to take AVID-style class notes. These notebooks signal their membership in this special group. Some schools have designed distinctive ribbons and badges that AVID students wear on their clothes. Others have adorned their graduation gowns or mortarboards with AVID ribbons. Still other AVID classes publish a newspaper that reports the accomplishments of AVID students. All of these actions further distinguish AVID students as members of a special, academically oriented group.

These markers influence teachers as well as students. Teachers report that, when they saw AVID students with notebooks, taking notes in class and turning in neat assignments on time, it indicated to them that AVID students were serious.

Formation of Voluntary Associations

Special classrooms, badges of distinction—these are physical, material markers that define the space for AVID students to develop an academically oriented identity. Within this space, AVID students develop new academically oriented friends or join academic friends who were already in AVID.

Several Saratoga students told us that they really did not know anyone in AVID when they joined, but after a few years almost all their friends were from AVID. These friendships developed because they were together in classes throughout the day and worked together in study groups. Coordinators encouraged these friendships by minimizing competition.

The AVID coordinator at Monrovia High School, for example, told her students that they should think of themselves on "parallel ladders with each other. There should be no competition between students, but rather an opportunity to share notes and to help one another."

Some AVID students did join AVID to be with their friends. Cynthia, a Latina from Monrovia High School, said her friends were already in AVID, and because they were doing well, she wanted to be with them. Now all her friends are in AVID. Thomas, an African American male at Saratoga, said that he told his two good friends from elementary school that "they had to get into AVID because it would really help with their grades." He even called one of his friend's mother to convince her that AVID was good for her son. These three boys have remained good friends for their four AVID years and always study together.

AVID encourages the development of academically oriented associations among students through formally organized activities such as college visits. AVID coordinators take their students to such colleges as San Diego State University (SDSU), the University of California at San Diego (UCSD), the University of California at Los Angeles (UCLA), and the University of Southern California (USC). Of particular note, the AVID coordinator at Pimlico High takes her AVID students on a two-week trip to traditionally Black colleges and universities in Washington, DC. and Atlanta every other year. In addition to the usual college tours and dorm sleepovers, the current generation of AVID high school students meets AVID students who enrolled in these schools in previous years.

Less formal activities also do this work of developing academically oriented associations. Students in AVID classrooms often talk among themselves and discuss matters relevant to their adolescence. Students use this period of time to bounce their values and troubles off one another, to test their principles and ideas, and to react to others. In those schools where African American and Latino students are bused in, the AVID classroom may be the only time minority students see each other during school hours. In those classes in which older and younger AVID students mix, the younger students observe older students' behavior and how teachers interact with them.

The longer students are in the program, the more ties seem to intensify. A Latina who attends Monrovia articulated these sentiments. AVID provides a different environment for her. "At home they expect me to get married. Here they expect me to go to college." Because of the pressures she receives from home, Maria attributes much of her academic success to the girlfriends she has cultivated in AVID. She studies together with her two friends and:

> [we] chat a lot about college and what we want out of life. Our study group really opens up a lot of issues. Everyone is really motivated to go

to college. It really helps to be around others that want to go. It makes you want it more.

We thought the highly visible markers of AVID (the notebooks required to be carried to classes, the special class periods established for them, the college visits arranged for them, the newspapers they publish) would stigmatize AVID students in the eyes of their peers. But this marking process has had the opposite effect. AVID students reported that their friends who were not in AVID were jealous. They wanted to be in AVID for the camaraderie to be sure, but also because they wanted to take advantage of the resources that AVID made available to its students, such as information about scholarships, college-entrance exams, and visits to colleges.

Many Monrovia AVID students told us in interviews that their non-AVID friends were jealous and "wanted into" the program. One Latina student stated that her friends, who were mostly White, felt racially threatened by the advantages given to AVID students: "They don't like AVID because they feel racially threatened. They don't really know what it is. They are jealous and think AVID is unfair." Another Latina student, Maria, expressed a similar view:

> Many are really jealous of the help that AVID gives me. One friend told me that it wasn't fair that [the AVID coordinator] helped me with my composition. [But] they forget that I don't have a mother to proofread my papers like they do. I can't get any help from my parents.

Ngoc, a Vietnamese student who attended Monrovia High School, suggested that this jealousy can take on overtones of reverse discrimination; his friends think that the only reason he got into USCD was because he was in AVID. "They think that AVID can get you in," he said. While these peer attitudes lead Maria and Ngoc to feel defensive about their participation in this untracking program, such attitudes also seem to fuel an increased commitment and loyalty. Pressure from outside the group creates a bond inside the group. Many students felt they were lucky to be "chosen" for the program and know that they were chosen because they need help academically.

Conclusions

The actions that working-class African American and Latino youths take against limitations in the capitalist system have been blamed for their poor academic performance. The sons and daughters of the poor withdraw from academic pursuits because they realize that their access to high-paying jobs is limited. Their critique is limited and ironic, however, because their unwillingness to play the academic game ensures that they will stay in lowly economic positions.

Ogbu maintained that the status that African Americans, Latinos, and other involuntary immigrant groups, have in the power structure contributes to this condition. While voluntary minorities accept achievement ideology, involuntary minorities tend to equate schooling with assimilation into the dominant group, an equation they detest. As a result, they do not try to achieve academically: Instead, they engage in collective actions of resistance against school and societal norms. Ogbu implies that the collectivist and oppositional ideology that Blacks, Latinos, and other involuntary minority groups have developed contributes to their relatively poor academic and economic success. They fail in school because they blame failure on racial discrimination and other structural forces and do not take personal responsibility for their own actions and individual initiative, a course of action that Ogbu felt is fundamental for success in American society.

We did not find an oppositional ideology or pattern of resistance among the Black and Latino students who participated in the AVID untracking program. Instead, we found that AVID kids formed an academic identity and developed a reflective and critical ideology. Strictly speaking, their ideology was neither conformist nor assimilationist. Instead, it included a critique of many tenets of achievement ideology, an affirmation of cultural identity, while acknowledging the necessity of academic achievement for occupational success.

By isolating students for significant portions of the school day, marking them as members of a special group, and providing them social supports, AVID fostered the academic identity of its students. This newly acquired academic identity posed problems for AVID students who had many nonacademic friends, however. AVID students resolved this dilemma by managing dual identities, an academic identity with academic friends at school, and a nonacademic identity with friends after school. This border-crossing strategy is useful for minority students, because it provides them with experience in moving between two cultures: a high-achieving academic culture and a supportive community culture.

AVID students face discrimination and racism, to be sure. But these antagonisms do not result in the acts of cultural inversion suggested by Willis, MacLeod, Foley, and Ogbu. In fact, AVID students invite us to reexamine the typology Ogbu constructed that designates separate and distinct ideologies for voluntary and involuntary immigrant groups. The Blacks and Latinos who participate in AVID do not fit the typology proposed by Ogbu. While many African American students in AVID describe a system that is not sympathetic to students in general and discriminatory to Blacks in particular, they speak of their own opportunity in terms of their own individual hard work. One Black male from Saratoga summarizes this argument for us:

> We know that the teacher is not doing what's right. He is a real racist jerk, but if you work hard, you will succeed. If you get good grades, he can't hurt you.

The ethnic and linguistic minority students in this untracking project seem to have developed an ideology, a consciousness if you will, that is neither oppositional nor conformist. Instead, it combines a belief in achievement with a cultural affirmation, becoming more critical than conformist.

The ideology of AVID students, which is simultaneously culturally and academically affirming, puts a new twist on the traditional connection between academic achievement and economic success. Black and Latino AVID students sense the need to develop culturally appropriate linguistic styles, social behavior, and academic skills. And they develop these skills, but without erasing the cultural identity of theirs that is nurtured and displayed at home and in the neighborhood.

Furthermore, these students' ideology provides an interesting counterpoint to the ideology of resistance. Here we encounter circumstances in which members of ethnic- and linguistic-minority groups eschew oppositional ideologies in favor of the "accommodation without assimilation" belief system (Gibson, 1988), which is presumably reserved for members of voluntary immigrant groups (Cummins, 1986; Gibson & Ogbu, 1991; Ogbu, 1978; Suárez-Orozco, 1989).

In a sense, AVID students (who are successful by anyone's standards) have developed the ideology that Fine seemed to think was reserved for the rejects of the educational system (1991). She found that high school dropouts had developed a much more sophisticated critique of class, gender, and ethnic politics than high school graduates, who naively accepted the connection between hard work and academic success. It is important to note that AVID produces minority students who are successful in school and who have developed a critical consciousness. This means that a critical consciousness is not reserved only for the students rejected by the system. We have uncovered at least one set of social circumstances in which a critical consciousness develops among students who are academically successful.

In closing, we want to make a final comment about the concept of resistance that resides in many parts of reproduction theory. Our study shows that the expressive and behavioral repertoire of Latino and African American students is much more extensive than is portrayed in reproduction theory. The actions of Latino and African American students in AVID were not limited to opposing or resisting structures of constraints;

they took positive courses of action to achieve socially accepted goals and attempted to break down constraining barriers. The students in our study did not passively respond to structural forces; rather they shaped and defined those forces in creative ways.

Circumscribing students' actions as only negative or oppositional produces a limited portrait of their social agency. Having witnessed a wide and diverse range of students' actions, it is clear to us that we need a more subtle and inclusive conception of social agency in order to understand how the inequality between rich and poor, "majority" and "minority," is sustained generation after generation. This more comprehensive sense of agency to which we have alluded in this study attempts to capture the processes by which people give meaning to their lives through complex cultural and political processes while appreciating the power of the constraints under which they labor (cf. Giroux & Simon, 1989, p. 147).

ACKNOWLEDGMENTS

This research was funded by grants from the Linguistic Minority Research Institute of the University of California and the Office of Educational Research and Improvement, U.S. Department of Education. Our thanks to the San Diego City Schools, especially John Griffith and Peter Bell, for encouraging this research. We especially appreciate the support and cooperation of Mary Catherine Swanson and the AVID coordinators, teachers, and students at the four high schools.

NOTE

* Portions of this article were presented by Mehan to the Ethnography and Education Forum, the University of Pennsylvania, March 1993, and by Hubbard to the Linguistic Minority Research Institute, the University of California, Santa Barbara, May 1993.

REFERENCES

Anderson, E. (1991). *Streetwise: Race, class and change in an urban community.* Chicago: University of Chicago Press.

Apple, M. W. (1983). *Education and power.* Boston: Routledge and Kegan Paul.

Bourdieu, P. (1986). The forms of capital. In J. G. Richardson (Ed.), *Handbook of theory and research for the sociology of education* (pp. 241–258). New York: Greenwood Press.

Bourdieu, P., & Passeron, C. (1977). *Reproduction in education, society and culture.* Los Angeles: Sage.

Bowles, S., & Gintis, H. I. (1976). *Schooling in capitalist America*. New York: Basic Books.

Carter, D. J., & Wilson, R. (1991). *Minorities in higher education: Ninth annual status report*. Washington, DC: American Council on Education.

Center for Education Statistics. (1986). *The condition of education: A statistical report*. Washington, DC: U.S. Department of Education.

Coleman, J. S., Campbell, E. R., Hobson, C. J., McPartland, J., Mood, A. M., Wernfield, F. D., & York, R. I. (1966). *Inequality of educational opportunity*. Washington, DC: U.S. Government Printing Office.

CSAW (Commission on the Skills of the American Workforce). (1990). *America's choice: High skills or low wages!* Rochester, NY: National Center on Education and the Economy.

Cummins, J. (1986). Empowering minority students: A framework for intervention. *Harvard Educational Review, 56*(1), 18–36.

Delgado-Gaitan, C., & Trueba, H. (1991). *Crossing cultural borders*. New York: Falmer Press.

Fine, M. (1991). *Framing dropouts: Notes on the politics of an urban public high school*. Albany, NY: State University of New York Press.

Foley, D. (1990). *Learning capitalist culture: Deep in the heart of Texas*. Philadelphia: University of Pennsylvania Press.

Fordham, S., & Ogbu, J. U. (1986). Black students' school success: Coping with the burden of "acting White." *The Urban Review, 18*(3), 1–31.

Gándara, P. (in press). Choosing higher education: Antecedents to successful educational outcomes for low income Mexican American students.

Gibson, M. (1988). *Accommodation without assimilation: Sikh immigrants in an American high school*. New York: Cornell University Press.

Gibson, M., & Ogbu, J. U. (Eds.) (1991). *Minority status and schooling: A comparative study of immigrant and involuntary minorities*. New York: Garland.

Giroux, H. (1983). *Theory and resistance in education*. London: Heinemann Education Books.

Giroux, H. (1992). *Border crossing: Cultural workers and the politics of education*. London: Routledge & Kegan Paul.

Giroux, H., & Simon, R. (1989). Popular culture and critical pedagogy. In H. Giroux & P. MacLaren (Eds.), *Critical pedagogy, the state and cultural struggle*. Albany: State University of New York Press

Goffman, E. (1964). *Asylums*. New York: Doubleday.

Haycock, K., & Navarro, S. (1988). *Unfinished business*. Oakland, CA: The Achievement Council.

Jankowski, M. S. (1991). *Islands in the street: Gangs and American urban society*. Berkeley: University of California Press.

Jencks, C., Smith, M., Acland, H., Bane, M. J., Cohen, D., Gantis, H., Heyns, B., & Michelson, S. (1972). *Inequality: A reassessment of the effect of family and schooling in America*. New York: Basic Books.

Labov, W. (1982). Competing value systems in the inner city schools. In P. Gilmore & A. Glathom (Eds.), *Children in and out of school: Ethnography and education* (pp. 148–171). Washington, DC: Center for Applied Linguistics.

LeCompte, M., & Dworkin, A. (1991). *Giving up on school: Student dropouts and teacher burnouts*. Newberry Park, CA: Corwin Press.

MacLeod, J. (1987). *Ain't no makin' it: Leveled aspirations in a low-income neighborhood*. Boulder, CO: Westview Press.

Mehan, H. (1992). Understanding inequality in schools: The contribution of interpretive studies. *The Sociology of Education, 65*(1), 1–20.

Mehan, H., Datnow, A., Bratton, E., Tellez, C., Friedlaender, D., & Ngo, T. (1992). Untracking and college enrollment. Research Report 4. Santa Cruz, CA: *National Center for Research on Cultural Diversity and Second Language Learning*.

NCEE (National Center for Education and the Economy) (1990). *America's choice: High skills or low wages?* Washington, DC: NCEE.

Ogbu, J. U. (1978). *Minority education and caste: The American system in cross-cultural perspective*. New York: Academic Press.

Ogbu, J. U. (1987). Variability in minority school performance: A problem in search of an explanation. *Anthropology & Education Quarterly, 18*(4), 312–334.

Ogbu, J. U. (1991). Immigrant and involuntary minorities in comparative perspective. In M. Gibson & J. Ogbu (Eds.), *Minority status and schooling* (pp. 3–37). New York: Garland Publishing.

Pelavin, S. H., & Kane, M. (1990). *Changing the odds: Factors increasing access to college*. New York: College Entrance Examination Board.

Rose, M. (1989). *Lives on the boundary*. New York: The Free Press.

Solomon, R. P. (1992). *Black resistance in school: Forging a separatist culture*. Albany: State University of New York Press.

Suárez-Orozco, M. M. (1989). *Central American refugees and U.S. high schools: A psychosocial study of motivation and achievement*. Stanford, CA: Stanford University Press.

Swanson, M. C. (n.d.). *AVID: A college preparatory program for underrepresented students*. San Diego: San Diego County Office of Education.

Weis, L. (1985). *Between two worlds: Black students in an urban community college*. Boston: Routledge & Kegan Paul.

Willis, P. (1977). *Learning to labor*. New York: Columbia Teachers College Press.

Chapter 23

The Minority Achievement Committee

Students Leading Students to Greater Success in School

Mary Lynne McGovern, Astrid Davis and John U. Ogbu

One of the most puzzling issues in education is the persistent gap in academic achievement between Black and White students. In Shaker Heights and elsewhere in the nation, the Black community, school authorities, education policymakers, and researchers continue to explore ways to improve Black students' academic achievement. In this chapter, we review one effort, the Minority Achievement Committee (MAC) Program in Shaker Heights, Ohio, which has aimed to address African American students' persistent underachievement.

PREVIOUS EFFORTS TO CLOSE THE ACHIEVEMENT GAP

Nationwide, many approaches have been proposed and tried to close the achievement gap, but they have had very limited success. These approaches generally fall into three broad categories: (a) choice and market strategies; (b) cooperative learning; and (c) culturally responsive pedagogy. Common to these approaches is an assumption that Black students are academically unsuccessful because of conventional public school policies and practices.

Choice and Market Strategies

Choice and market strategies have gained currency as approaches that could improve the achievement gap. Strategies associated with these two approaches include vouchers, charter schools, contracting with for-profit entities to run schools, performance contracts, and merit pay (Good & Braden, 2000; see also Contreras, 1995; Cuban & Tyack, 2000; Fuller & Elmore, 1992; Gramlich & Koshelo, 1975; Johnson, 1984; Murnane & Cohen, 1986; Pederson, 2000; Ruenzel, 1995; Wells, 1998). The underlying argument by proponents of these approaches is that conventional structures and processes of the public school system must be changed or modified in order to increase the academic performance of Blacks and similar minorities, as well as poor students in general. Proponents argue that improvements in academic achievement can be achieved by offering parental choice and by operating schools like businesses. Parental choice uses education vouchers and charter schools within the public school system so that parents can choose where to send their children to school. Market strategies include contracting with private corporations to run public schools for profit and/or paying teachers based on their performance, as measured by students' test scores. The outcomes of the choice and market strategies have been mixed, and there are on-going debates about their effectiveness in regards to Black students' academic achievement.

The Cooperative Learning Approach

Cooperative learning consists of programs that emphasize cooperation and collaboration among schools, teachers, the minority community, and students. The cooperative learning approach is based on an assumption that black and similar minority cultures in the United States value cooperation and use collaboration to solve problems and that cooperation is an important feature of the learning styles in minority cultures. Examples of programs using this approach include Corner's School Development Program (Comer, Haynes, Joyer, & Ben-Avie, 1996), Levin's Accelerated Elementary School Education for Disadvantaged Students (Hopfenberg, Levin, & Associates, 1993), and AVID (see Chapter 22, this volume). These programs have been adopted by many school districts, including Shaker Heights. For example, as part of its school reform effort, Mercer Elementary School in Shaker Heights adopted the Accelerated Schools Model program to promote "the academic acceleration of all students. The goal would be achieved by integrating instructional/curricular practices, and active community involvement" (Project Achieve, 1997, p. 14). The programs are generally reported to be successful by their proponents, but independently evaluated results have been mixed (Cook, Habib, Phillips, Setterston, Shagle, & Degirmencioglu, 1998; Cook, Hunt, & Murphy, 1998). Our impression is that although the programs using a cooperative learning approach help improve the school performance of some Black students, they have not led to an overall increase in Black students' academic achievement because they do not take community dynamics into account.

Culturally Responsive Education

Culturally responsive education is the term we use to describe the third major approach to improving minority students' academic achievement.

562 Mary Lynne McGovern, Astrid Davis and John Ogbu

Culturally responsive education includes African-centered pedagogy, Afrocentric education, African immersion academies, rites of passage, cultural diversity, culturally responsive pedagogy, and multicultural education (Asante, 1992; Dei, 1994; Gay, 2000; Lee, 1995; Ogbu, 1992). Proponents of culturally responsive pedagogies argue that Black students and other students of color are failing in public schools because conventional classroom processes are based on European-American (or Eurocentric) cultural practices, while teaching and learning styles vary from culture to culture. The argument goes that because minority children have been socialized into different styles before entering the public school, they encounter discontinuities between their own styles and school practices. For example, during classroom lessons in Eurocentric cultures, teachers expect "protocols of attentiveness [with] emphasis placed on them" (Gay, 2000, p. 22); such protocols may conflict with minority students' learning styles. Proponents of culturally responsive education contend that minority students' academic achievement will improve "if schools and teachers are changed so that they reflect and draw on [the] cultural and language strengths of the minorities" (Banks, 2000, p. ix). This view has been supported by experiments by Allen and Boykin (1991, 1992), which have shown that Black students learn more when they are taught in a Black cultural style than in the conventional public school style.

Some Black students may benefit from culturally responsive pedagogies, Afro-centric education, African-centered pedagogies, and the like, but these approaches are a limited solution to academic disengagement and poor performance. Such approaches also raise two sets of issues: first, why are some minorities more academically successful in public schools than Black students, even though they are also culturally different, with different pedagogic traditions? Why do African American students need a pedagogic style unique to their own culture in order to do well in school? The second is a policy issue: given that most school systems that Black children attend have many other minorities, how feasible is it to provide Black students with culturally relevant pedagogy in the same classrooms with students from several other cultural groups? Our conclusion is that the culturally responsive strategy, although well meaning, is not practical because, after all, most Black children will continue to be educated in public schools with White and other minority children, rather than in African-immersion academies and other such institutions.

In sum, there is very little convincing evidence that choice, cooperative learning, and culturally responsive education are more effective than conventional public school practices for increasing Black students' academic achievement. Although they may help improve the school performance of some, they are not likely to lead to an overall reduction in the achievement gap between Black and White students because they do not address the many factors, including the community forces that influence academic engagement.

Attempts to reduce the achievement gap between Black and White students must address both the structural issues in education and community forces. The Minority Achievement Program (MAC) in Shaker Heights is such an attempt. Next, we describe the MAC program and its potential for promoting academic engagement.

THE SHAKER HEIGHTS COMMUNITY

Shaker Heights is a relatively affluent community in Ohio. Residents of Shaker Heights pride themselves on their diversity. Shaker Heights is a progressive community that has made deliberate efforts to integrate since the 1960s. Not only has Shaker Heights been integrated historically, but current residents also promote diversity within the community. From an early age, children learn and take pride in this image and strive to maintain it. Even at the high school, a group called Student Group on Race Relations (SGORR) was developed to promote understanding and tolerance. The group, which is student-run, addresses racial issues in the school. Outsiders probably would describe Shaker Heights as a model community to be replicated elsewhere because of its conscious and stated ideal of racial tolerance. Although the community actively promotes tolerance, it still faces many of the issues that define race relations in the United States. One such issue is the achievement gap between Black and White students.

THE ACHIEVEMENT OF BLACK AND WHITE STUDENTS ON SELECTED INDICATORS

In general, there was a considerable gap on every academic performance indicator between Black and White students in Shaker Heights. Based on the 1995–1996 school year data, differences between Black and White students in proficiency tests were evident at all grade levels. For example, among eighth graders, White students scored 92 percent in mathematics, 100 percent in reading, 93 percent in writing, and 91 percent in science; the comparable scores for black students were 37 percent, 83 percent, 77 percent, and 48 percent, respectively. On the Scholastic Aptitude Tests (SATs), Blacks scored an average of 485 on the verbal portion and 598 in math (Whittington, 1996). Another indicator, grade point average (GPA) also finds Black students achieving less than their White counterparts. The average GPA of Black students for the graduating classes of

1992–1996 was 2.2, compared to 3.34 for Whites. Few blacks enrolled in Honors classes or graduated with honors. The gap was also wider for Black males. About 79 percent of Black females and 69 percent of Black males proceeded to college.

THE MINORITY ACHIEVEMENT PROGRAM (MAC)

This gap in achievement is a major concern for the school district, families, and students in Shaker Heights. Consequently, Shaker Heights, like many school districts, has initiated programs to help all students improve their academic achievement, including staff development, tutoring centers, all-day kindergarten, school reforms, accelerated schools, Comer's program, the Minority Achievement Committee Program (MAC), special education services, programs for low-and-underachieving students, an English-as-a-second-language program, Learning-to-Learn project, mathematics labs, Proficiency Review of Basic Essentials, and so on. From our observations, discussions with school authorities, and a review of evaluations of these programs, we were impressed by the school district's efforts to find solutions for the low academic achievement of its students, especially Black students. Here, we will focus on the MAC program because of its relevance to Ogbu's Cultural Ecological Model (CEM).

The MAC Program was created by Mary Lynne McGovern, a student advisor at Shaker Heights High School; Hubert McIntyre, a co-advisor; and members of the Faculty Achievement Committee (FAC). In the mid 1980s, 15 faculty members formed the FAC out of a concern about the persistent underachievement of minority students, especially Black males. In spring 1990, the FAC invited several high-achieving Black students to a meeting to help them understand the causes of underachievement. These students, referred to as consultants, were selected from the ninth, tenth, eleventh, and twelfth grades. They met several times with the FAC to gain insights into the causes of minority underachievement. To a degree, the students acknowledged some role in their own academic performance. Peer pressure also emerged as a factor having a negative impact on their achievement. In addition, students cited parental roles and expectations as strong indicators of achievement, as well as teacher expectations.

Participation and Structure of the MAC Program

After the MAC program's inception, the Scholars/consultants suggested that one way to reverse the cycle of underachievement would be for high-achieving students to work with low/underachieving students. The MAC Program is made up of three categories of students, each with a different degree of academic success. The first group consists of high-achieving students who are the MAC Scholars. They include eleventh and twelfth graders whose averages are a high C or above and who are enrolled in Honors and Advanced Placement classes. The minimum academic requirement to become a MAC Scholar is currently a 2.7 grade point average, though most Scholars have well into the 3.0 and above range. Initially, a 2.5 GPA was considered adequate, but the Scholars voted to raise the standard to 2.7. The second group, the Potential Scholars, includes students in the ninth and tenth grades who are not high achieving and generally have less than a 2.0 GPA. The third group, the Emerging Scholars, is composed of tenth graders who have shown some improvement, but have not yet achieved the necessary academic growth to become Scholars.

Though the first group of MAC Scholars was selected by the faculty, all future Scholars have been selected through an interview process conducted by established Scholars. Each candidate must qualify for an interview by earning a recommendation from another Scholar or faculty member. The process begins with the Academic Advisor, who notifies each eligible student by written invitation delivered through the student's classroom teacher. The recommended students are asked to meet with the Academic Advisor for a preliminary interview. Following these interviews, the Academic Advisor turns over the list of candidates to the Scholars for a group interview. Following the interview process the Scholars deliberate, sometimes for over 2 hours, over who will be selected as MAC Scholars. Often the process involves lobbying for their individual choices as they point out specific observations they have made about a specific candidate that others may have overlooked. In addition to academic performance, several criteria are used to select the new Scholars. Candidates must have integrity, willingness to dedicate time and energy to the program and an interest in helping others succeed. Candidates who are not chosen as Scholars are invited to become MAC Mentors to individual ninth grade Potential Scholars.

When selections are finalized, the Academic Advisor informs faculty members and provides a list of newly selected MAC Scholars. The MAC program works with faculty (1) to enable students to attend meetings and, (2) to encourage monitoring of Scholars and Potential Scholars and reporting their progress to the Academic Advisor.

Although they may receive support from the Academic Advisor, the FAC, and some teachers, the MAC Scholars Program is student-run. The program has instituted some organizational structures, including meeting schedules, format, and content. The Scholars have written a pledge which is recited at every meeting. They have also developed five precepts: mutual respect between Scholars and Potential Scholars; pride in one's success; honesty related to one's academic status; sensitivity toward students who are working to achieve; and confidence in one's own and in other's ability to achieve.

Essentially, the MAC program enables high-achieving Black male students (the Scholars) to work with Potential and Emerging Scholars. The interventions include meetings (groups and one-on-one), mentoring, and modeling. The Scholars also work as coaches and provide academic support to struggling students. For example, the Scholars meet with the Potential Scholars after report cards and progress reports are distributed. The Scholars discuss the individual report cards with the Potential Scholars and an agreement is reached on a plan of action.

AN EVALUATION OF THE MAC PROGRAM

The results reported here are based on an evaluation of the first six years of the MAC program (1991–1996). More recent data on the program are not available. It is also important to note that the program was not set up as a research project, and thus this evaluation is not based on a stringent methodology with random sampling, a large sample, or any effort to reduce bias. Data were not tested for significance. Participation was voluntary and the sample was small.

A total of 161 students, in four cohorts, participated in the program. The results for each cohort are shown in Tables 23.1, 23.2, 23.3, 23.4 and 23.5. Fifty-six students did not participate and were used as the control. Of the total participants, 47 percent passed the proficiency exam for their grade, as compared with 21 percent for the control group.

There were also differences in GPAs between program participants and the control group. Among the MAC participants, 61 percent of the participants showed improvements in their GPA, while 50 percent of the

Table 23.1 One year of high school (1994–1995)

		MAC students	Control group
Proficiency	Passed	9	3
Proficiency	Exempt	4	3
Proficiency	Failed	36	6
GPA	Improved	27	4
GPA	Declined	13	2
GPA	Insufficient data	9	6
Enrollment	Enrolled	45	11
Enrollment	Withdrew	4	1
TOTAL		49	12

Data source: *MAC Resource Guide*

Table 23.2 Two years of high school (1993–1995)

		MAC students	Control group
Proficiency	Passed	18	2
Proficiency	Exempt	6	7
Proficiency	Failed	20	8
GPA	Improved	16	4
GPA	Declined	19	6
GPA	Insufficient data	9	7
Enrollment	Enrolled	37	11
Enrollment	Withdrew	7	6
TOTAL		44	17

Data source: *MAC Resource Guide*

Table 23.3 Three years of high school (1992–1995)

		MAC students	Control group
Proficiency	Passed	18	4
Proficiency	Exempt	6	9
Proficiency	Failed	5	6
GPA	Improved	12	1
GPA	Declined	8	1
GPA	Insufficient data	9	17
Enrollment	Enrolled	25	13
Enrollment	Withdrew	4	6
TOTAL		29	19

Data source: *MAC Resource Guide*

Table 23.4 Four years of high school (1991–1995)

		MAC students	Control group
Proficiency	Passed	31	3
Proficiency	Exempt	3	3
Proficiency	Failed	5	2
GPA	Improved	22	1
GPA	Declined	10	1
GPA	Insufficient data	7	6
Enrollment	Enrolled	26	3
Enrollment	Withdrew	13	5
TOTAL		39	8

Data source: *MAC Resource Guide*

Table 23.5 Summary of MAC students' performance

		MAC students	Control group
Proficiency	Passed	76	12
Proficiency	Exempt	19	22
Proficiency	Failed	66	22
GPA	Improved	77	10
GPA	Declined	50	10
GPA	Insufficient data	34	36
Enrollment	Enrolled	133	38
Enrollment	Withdrew	28	18
TOTAL		161	56

Data source: *MAC Resource Guide*

students in the control group improved their GPAs. Enrollment rates of
the two groups also were compared. About 17 percent of MAC participants withdrew from school, compared to 32 percent of the control
group. Graduation rates also were examined. Here again, after four
years of high school, the graduation rate for the MAC Scholars was 67
percent, almost double the control group's rate of 38 percent (*The MAC
Resource Guide*).

These results reveal that the MAC Scholars had a higher rate of passing
proficiency tests, a lower rate of withdrawal from school, and a greater
likelihood of improving their GPAs than the control group. If the MAC
program is evaluated with a purely quantitative measure, such as GPA, it
is easy to dismiss the results as inconclusive or unimpressive. However, if
we use other, non-tangible but important indicators for school engagement, such as effort, attitudes toward school and learning, personal investment in learning, and the belief that such an investment will lead to
higher achievement, then the MAC program clearly has been successful.
As described in the MAC curriculum;

> Although, as noted, some of the changes are not dramatic, the MAC
> program has been successful on many other subjective measures.
> Evidence abounds that the program is successful in seizing the atten-
> tion of underachieving ninth grade black males and changing many
> of their attitudes related to school and how they view themselves as
> learners. Written evaluations by the Potential Scholars reveal their
> sense of belonging to a group they feel aligned with and whose pur-
> pose is to help them become successful students. They express admir-
> ation for the Scholars and many acknowledge that they would like to
> "be like them."

Also noted is the fact that Potential Scholars are more willing to attend teacher conferences, work directly with the Scholars to improve their grades, get tutoring when needed, and become conscious of their classroom behaviors. For the Scholars, there is an added benefit: the development of leadership, mentoring, and communication skills. These skills also lead Scholars to develop greater confidence. Therefore, even though these attitudes and new skill sets may not automatically translate into GPA improvements, they lay the groundwork for future academic engagement. Hence the contribution of the MAC program is better appreciated if we look at changes in skills sets and attitudes, as well as students' potential for future academic achievement.

INCORPORATING COMMUNITY FORCES INTO THE MAC PROGRAM

Although many aspects of the MAC program have contributed to its success, we have chosen to highlight three positive features of the community forces we identified in our Shaker Heights study: collective identity, peer pressure, and educational strategies.

Collective Identity

The MAC program integrates Black collective identity with academic identity, and thus many MAC participants have come to believe that there is no conflict between their collective identity and being academically engaged. This is clearly illustrated by the MAC pledge:

> I am an African American and I pledge to uphold the name and image of the African American man. I will do so by striving for academic excellence, conducting myself with dignity and respecting others as if they were my brothers and sisters.

During our study at Shaker Heights, students noted that some high-achieving Black students were often not popular among their peers. The MAC consultants expressed a similar belief while the program was being formed, which is why the MAC Scholars may have decided that helping weaker students was the best way to reverse the cycle. The MAC pledge is therefore an initiation into a community of scholars with a collective identity, marked with various symbols, such as a handshake and a dress code. MAC Scholars are now known and respected by other students as role models. For example, as a group they enjoy popularity, not just among Potential Scholars, but also among non-participants. In interviews, other students identified MAC Scholars as a popular group that they would be willing to join. The Scholars demonstrate that academic achievement is possible even for those who are still struggling.

Positive Peer Pressures

The second feature is the development of positive peer pressure: Among the MAC Scholars, Emerging Scholars, and Potential Scholars, peer pressures are directed toward academic engagement because of the supportive environment that the MAC Program provides. MAC Scholars are recognized and even have gained popularity through the program. Some students noted that they were able to resist pressures toward academic disengagement.

One of the many precepts of the MAC Scholars is that they should show pride in their own school success. This precept is reinforced by various recognition ceremonies. The names of Scholars who have made improvements, or who have made the Honor Roll, are announced at the MAC meetings. In addition to the meetings, there is also an awards ceremony at which students are publicly recognized and congratulated. The awards ceremony serves three important functions for MAC participants: recognition, visibility, and credibility.

One issue that emerged from interviews with the first groups of Scholars was that of visibility. These students felt that virtually no Blacks were represented in areas that celebrated academic success, such as the Honor Roll. Hence they suggested having three academic rolls: Honor Roll for GPAs 3.5 and above; Merit Roll for 3.0 to 3.49; and Recognition Roll for 2.5 to 2.99. This led to a more inclusive Honor Roll. Representation is important because of the many functions it serves for students. Black students now see themselves represented and visible as high achievers. The Roll change provides students with opportunities to aspire to the higher, traditional Honor Roll. As the MAC curriculum notes:

> The Scholars' recommendation was put into place the following year and continues to date with striking results. Students crowd the area while the three academic rolls are being posted. Black students are now well represented, openly express pride when they see their names, challenge each other to move up to the next higher roll or, if their names are not listed, vow they will make it next time. The Scholars' idea was the catalyst for making black achievers visible at Shaker Heights High School.

The change in the Honor Roll categories also has the important effect of changing the view of people who may not view Blacks as achievers. And equally important is the fact that both potential participants and those not interested in the program have come to recognize the MAC program as important.

The awards ceremony is important in highlighting the program. It acknowledges and celebrates the Scholars' success and welcomes the new Scholars. Scholars who have graduated return as guest speakers. This motivates students, giving them concrete examples of how high achievement in school leads to future success. One of the problems for students who are not achieving is centered on not being able to connect their school performance with the role it will play in their future success. The awards ceremony illustrates that connection and makes learning relevant.

School administrators and community groups are invited to the award ceremonies. Their participation is important to the MAC program's success and credibility. The awards ceremony gives the Black community an opportunity to share in its students' success. Too often, negative attention is paid to underachieving students. By highlighting successes instead of failures, a new standard of excellence can be set. Achievers are not looked on as aberrations or rarities, but as normal students.

Educational Strategies

The third positive feature is the inclusion of educational strategies. Our study revealed several factors that interfered with Black students' academic efforts. Although students verbalized attitudes, skills, and behaviors that are conducive to making good grades, they did not practice them.

During our study, we observed that the MAC program included strategies for school success. Standard agenda items for the group meetings addressed numerous important topics, including: the connection between school and the future, dealing with negative attitudes about school, goal setting, developing good study habits, where and how to get help in school, approaching teachers, learning to advocate for one's self, developing self-discipline, confronting behavior/discipline issues, and dealing with barriers to school achievement. There were also discussions of study habits, taking notes during lessons, preparing for examinations, time budgeting, and the like. Scholars also tutored Potential Scholars and counseled students individually who were having behavioral problems in the classroom. The MAC program thus provides effective socialization for academic achievement and/or acquisition of the norms for maximum academic effort.

Conclusion

Our findings suggest that any attempt to increase Black students' academic engagement would require changes in the system, as well as changes in community forces. Most interventions have focused exclusively on the school system: curricula, teachers, and so on, but MAC went beyond this. It represents an attempt to address the other half of the achievement equation: the students themselves.

The MAC program has effectively raised Black students' academic engagement and popularity among students. One of the most important contributions of the MAC program to Black students' academic engagement has been the creation of a community of students/scholars where academic identity is valued, supported, and sought after. Whether by design or by accident, the MAC program addresses a number of issues that contribute to poor academic engagement. Through the recognition and participation of former students, Potential Scholars learn the connection between their schooling or their present academic effort and their adult futures. Students also internalize a belief in their own intelligence. We believe that the program's effectiveness and popularity can be further enhanced by formally incorporating some of our research findings into its routine activities (Ogbu, 2003).

REFERENCES

Allen, B. A., & Boykin, W. A. (1991). The influence of contextual factors on African American and Euro-American children's performance: Effect of movement opportunity and music. *International Journal of Psychology, 26*(3), 373–386.

Allen, B. A., & Boykin, W. A. (1992). African American children and the educational process: Alleviating cultural discontinuity through prescriptive pedagogy. *School Psychology Review, 21*(4), 586–598.

Asante, M. (1991–1992). Afrocentric curriculum. *Education Leadership, 49*(4), 28–31.

Banks, J. A. (2000). Series forward. In G. Gay (Ed.), *Cultural responsive teaching: Theory, research and practice* (p. ix). New York: Teachers Press.

Comer, J. P., Haynes, N. M., Joyer, E. T., & Ben-Avie, M. (1996). *Rallying the whole village: The Comer process for reforming education.* Thousand Oaks, CA: Corwin Press.

Contreras, A. R. (1995). The charter school movement in California and elsewhere. *Education and Urban Society, 27*(2), 213–228.

Cook, T. D., Habib, F. N., Phillips, M., Setterston, R. A., Shagle, S. C., & Degirmencioglu, S. M. (1998). *Comer's school development program in Prince George's County, Maryland: A theory-based evaluation.* Evanston, IL: Northwestern University, Institute for Policy Research.

Cook, T. D., Hunt, H. D., & Murphy, R. F. (1998). *Comer's school development program in Chicago: A theory-based evaluation.* Evanston, IL: Northwestern University, Institute for Policy Research.

Cuban, L., & Tyack, D. B. (2000). Lessons from history. *Rethinking Schools, 14*(3), 11.

Dei, G. J. S. (1994). Afrocentricity: A cornerstone of pedagogy. *Anthropology and Education Quarterly, 25*(1), 3–25.

Fuller, B., & Elmore, R. F. (Eds.) (1992). *Who chooses? Culture, institutions and the unequal effects of school choice.* New York: Teachers College Press.

Gay, G. (2000). *Cultural responsive teaching: Theory, research and practice.* New York: Teachers College Press.

Good T. L., & Braden, J. S. (2000). *The great school debate: Choice, vouchers, and charters.* Mahwah, NJ: Lawrence Erlbaum.

Gramlich, E. M., & Koshelo, P. P. (1975). *Education performance contracting: An evaluation of an experiment.* Washington, DC: The Brookings Institute.

Hopfenberg, W., Levin, H. M., & Associates (1993). *The accelerated schools resource guide.* Menlo Park, CA: Jossey-Bass.

Johnson, S. M. (1984). Merit pay for teachers: A prescription for reform. *Harvard Educational Review, 54,* 175–185.

Lee, C. (1995). African-centered pedagogy: Complexities and possibilities. In M. J. Shujaa (Ed.), *Too much schooling, too little education: A paradox of Black life in White societies* (pp. 295–318). Trenton, NJ: African World.

Murnane, R., & Cohen, D. (1986). Merit pay and the evaluation problem: Why most merit pay plans fail and a few survive. *Harvard Education Review, 56,* 1–17.

Ogbu, J. U. (2003). *Black Americans in an affluent suburb: A study in academic disengagement.* Mahwah, NJ: Lawrence Erlbaum.

Ogbu, J. U. (1992). Understanding cultural diversity and learning. *Educational Researcher, 21*(8), 4–14.

Pederson, B. (2000). Merit: To pay or not to pay? Teachers grapple with yet another marketplace reform. *Rethinking Schools, 14*(3), 9–11.

Project Achieve (1997). *Report.* Unpublished document, Shaker Heights School District, Shaker Heights, OH.

Ruenzel, D. (1995, September 27). A choice in the matter. *Education Week, 4,* 22–27.

The Minority Achievement Committee (1998). *Students leading students to greater success in school: Resource guide.* Shaker Heights, OH.

Wells, A. S. (1998). *Beyond the rhetoric of charter school reform: A study of ten California school districts.* Unpublished manuscript, University of California, Los Angeles.

Whittington, D. (1996). *Analyses of under-achievement.* Unpublished document, Shaker Heights School District, Shaker Heights, OH.

Part VI

Conclusion

Chapter 24

Forward-Looking Criticism
Critiques and Enhancements for the Next Generation of the Cultural-Ecological Model

Kevin Michael Foster

I open the concluding section of this volume with a rhetorical question I have asked elsewhere regarding John Ogbu's work: "Of the many wonderful scholars who have conducted education research, how many have produced grand assessments that have remained relevant and worthy of discussion thirty years after their initial formulation?" (Foster, 2005b, p. 559). This is, of course, a framing question, one that assumes—and perhaps demands—our acknowledgment that whether we agree or disagree with Ogbu's cultural-ecological model of minority academic achievement, his ideas were powerful, resonant with large numbers and groups of people, and have had a tremendous influence on the last three decades of educational research.

In this closing chapter, I would like to address two interlocking questions: Where should "we"—educational researchers interested in minority student achievement—stand in relation to the cultural-ecological model (CEM)? And where should we go from here? To do this, I will offer an assessment of what I see as the strengths and weaknesses of Ogbu's overall work and then suggest theoretical interventions that, if incorporated, stand to ensure the future usefulness of the CEM. My argument is threefold: that (a) Ogbu's general framework is strong and potentially useful; but that (b) it was undermined by specific and correctable problems in his analysis of contemporary and historic data; and finally that (c) the continued relevance of the CEM will be secured by considering and including recent theoretical innovations in cultural anthropology, including reflexivity and more nuanced understandings of culture and cultural process.

Most of the ideas in this chapter are reproduced from my earlier writings (especially Foster, 2004, 2005b, 2005d) that specifically addressed Ogbu's CEM, as well as another work (Foster, 2005c) that examined academic motivation among high-achieving Black college students, including voluntary and involuntary minorities. Before commenting upon Ogbu's ideas, however, I will offer some comments regarding collegiality in the field. At first glance this may seem a tangent, but I include this section because the varied receptions—not just to Ogbu's work, but to Ogbu himself—speak to our ability to communicate with one another across differences of opinion and hence, to our ability to advance knowledge through a process that includes both fieldwork and mutual, collegial, critical engagement.

Ogbu's work incited strong reactions, was read in divergent ways by different readers from within and beyond the academy, and occasionally divided classrooms and conference sessions into those who were sympathetic to his ideas and those who were not. Given this, our ability to step back, take stock of the ongoing debates, and push our understanding of minority student achievement forward (regardless of whether we agree or disagree with Ogbu's work) is a measure of our development as progressive, rigorous, and grounded scholars who should be less concerned with *being seen as right at all costs*, and more concerned that we are always *working to get it right at all costs*—even when that means gaining insights from those with whom we generally disagree.

COLLEGIALITY IN THE FIELD

In the few years since John Ogbu's 2003 passing, I have been impressed with educational researchers' ongoing consideration of his work. First, the quality of the engagements—the understanding of Ogbu's work; the seriousness with which his work has been tested, contested, and followed up; and the conclusions drawn with regards to the CEM's continued efficacy—have been exemplary. In addition to works reprinted for this volume, special issues of *Qualitative Studies in Education* (Foster, 2005a) and *Intercultural Education* (Foster & Gobbo, 2004) have continued discussions about the ongoing relevance of Ogbu's work. Several particularly exciting works have gone beyond the intricacies of the CEM to address more personal and difficult issues, including professional relationships among scholars, how scholars receive one another and one another's works, and how our writings can be differently read among scholars, public officials, and others who all come to our works by different means and read our works through different lenses.

Two educational anthropologists who have addressed larger issues of reception and consideration of Ogbu's work are Doug Foley (2005) and Ted Hamann (2004). In "Elusive Prey: John Ogbu and the search for a grand theory of minority academic disengagement," Foley expressed admiration for Ogbu and wrestled with the mutual hurt feelings that resulted from his failed intellectual engagement with him. In "Lessons from the interpretation/misinterpretation of John Ogbu's scholarship," Hamann discussed the implications connected to the appropriations of Ogbu's work by those within and beyond the academy. A third piece that addressed relational issues that surpass ideas and texts is Signithia Fordham's wonderful (2004) piece, " 'Signithia, you can do better than that': John Ogbu (and me) and the nine lives peoples" (reprinted as Chapter 6, this volume). Fordham considered the ongoing association of two people—joined together first as student and mentor, and then by the production of an influential work (the widely cited 1986 *Urban Review* piece on "acting White" [Fordham & Ogbu, 1996])—as well as the relational strains and difficulties associated with a professional relationship that spanned decades.

Even beyond texts like those by Foley, Fordham, and Hamann, which invite author and reader reflexivity and include an implicit acknowledgment of the humanity behind scholars and scholarship, the tone of the posthumous debate around Ogbu's work has been exemplary. The debate has been characterized by collegiality, seriousness, and a lack of animosity that I believe takes all of us to a new level in terms of our ability to engage one another seriously on the controversial topic of minority student achievement.

This stands in contrast to the strongly worded, negative responses to Ogbu's work at academic conferences in the past. Several colleagues have attested to instances of Ogbu's defensiveness and dismissiveness, as well as his subsequent difficulty engaging in scholarly debate without feeling personally attacked (Foley, 2005). Yet other colleagues have offered that in settings of collegiality and trust, Ogbu took criticism well. A year or two before John Ogbu's passing, I asked a mentor and (now) colleague, Angela Valenzuela, about how and whether to try and engage him in a critical dialogue. She had met Ogbu while she was a student at Stanford University, and he had strongly supported her work. Her words echoed those Doug Foley heard about Ogbu from Signithia Fordham in another conversation. "Oh, don't worry about John," Angela more or less told me, "He's a big boy; I think you guys can have a good dialogue."

I did converse and correspond with Ogbu in 2002 and 2003, and we agreed to come together, but the dialogue was cut off before it truly began. While I wish that there had been more dialogues while Ogbu was alive, I am at least pleased that such a wide range of scholars as has been included in this volume are able to engage Ogbu's work, and one another, now. I keep in mind that our deepest mission is to serve students through our work. The animosity, mutual hurt feelings, and bitterness that has sometimes characterized past debates dishonor and undermine our ultimate goals. Thus, the recent work around Ogbu's research has been especially noteworthy because it serves students, families, communities, and schools by providing deep, rich, insightful conversations, and analyses that facilitate reforms in teaching and learning settings, honor strengths in those same settings, and provide new insights into the many and complex facets of education.

Finally, it is worth noting the obvious—that the ongoing engagement of Ogbu's work has included both considerable praise and considerable criticism. Since Ogbu's passing, he has not been honored with universal agreement with everything he had to say, but rather with engagement from many intellectual quarters, including popular commentators and the U.S. press (Goleman, 1988; Page, 2003; Rothstein, 2000; Tough, 2004). In the scholarly context, this is much more profound and meaningful than effusive praise, and a much greater honor. In the spirit of forthright critical analysis, the remainder of this chapter will engage key tenets of the CEM, pointing to strengths and weaknesses and to theoretical interventions that will ensure its future relevance.

FORWARD-LOOKING CRITICISM OF THE CULTURAL-ECOLOGICAL MODEL

Ogbu's CEM includes four important layers: (a) the general idea that students' academic success is impacted by community and system forces; (b) distinctions among voluntary, involuntary, and autonomous minorities; (c) the recognition of universal, primary, and secondary discontinuities between students and the schools they attend; and (d) the idea that involuntary minorities have developed survival strategies—some that facilitate academic success and others that hinder it—including clientship/Uncle Tomming, collective struggle, hustling, emulation of Whites, and camouflage, while voluntary minorities have developed instrumental approaches to schooling and have proven more adept at successfully negotiating schools in order to realize academic success. The fact that Ogbu repeated these ideas in numerous publications has been greeted with consternation by some, but also has ensured that his ideas have been disseminated to a broad range of academic audiences and that we have a stable and unambiguous record of his thinking.

The sheer number of articles that comment upon, build upon, rely upon, or refute the CEM attests to its importance. The CEM established for countless educational researchers a framework for thinking about minority approaches to schooling. Some insights stand out. For instance, it was the CEM that most succinctly articulated that the historical circumstances in which a group of people comes to its minority status is critical to understanding its approaches to schooling. In addition, the distinction of layers of cultural difference between groups and schools (universal, primary, and secondary) offers one way for researchers to distinguish between cultural traits that students bring with them to school and those that they actively reproduce.

Even as several researchers have applied tenets of the CEM to their own work, many have resisted or refuted Ogbu's analyses, particularly his characterizations of involuntary minorities' norms and behaviors. I contend that while critics correctly have found fault with many of Ogbu's analyses, the problems are not with his model as much as with his applications of the framework he developed. I turn now to examples of shortcomings in Ogbu's findings and analyses, before offering theoretical interventions that will account for these shortcomings and that will enrich the CEM and broaden its applications and usefulness.

Few have challenged the usefulness of thinking about involuntary and voluntary minorities, although some have presented circumstances in which the situation ultimately proved more complicated than that initial conception (Hermans, 2004; Kalekin-Fishman, 2004). Rather, challenges to Ogbu's analyses have addressed such issues as his unintended slippage into culture-of-poverty arguments (Gould, 1999), his failure to recognize the range of normative and status-earning behaviors within the groups of minorities he identified (Chapter 8, this volume; Flores-Gonzalez, 1999; Foster, 2001; Zou & Trueba, 1998), and a body of research and writing that is "overwhelmingly preoccupied with explaining the academic failure of . . . marginal populations" (O'Conner, 1997, p. 597). Others have complicated the meaning and implications of "acting White" (Chapter 10, this volume) or have offered cases in which involuntary minority oppositional culture does not undermine academic success as predicted in Ogbu's writings (Chapters 9 and 14, this volume).

To those general challenges and complications, I would add five problems with Ogbu's use of the CEM that we would be well advised to account for if we are to move the model forward in the future. Just as Ogbu's analyses most frequently relied upon examples from Blacks in the United States, these challenges to his analyses do so as well:

1 Ogbu's writings do not account for African Americans' behaviors that are conducive to school success that routinely manifest among large groups of African Americans;

2 Ogbu's understanding of African Americans' responses to schooling relies upon a consistent misreading of African American cultural history;

3 Ogbu's use of data depends upon a myopic reading of *contemporary* data;

4 Ogbu's analysis of voluntary minority approaches to schooling fails to account for important facets of their response to schooling, especially the frequent reliance upon looking down upon involuntary minorities as maladapted and deficient;

5 Ogbu's work relies upon a vision of culture that lacks nuance and complexity, especially given his anthropological training.

These challenges are related not to Ogbu's CEM as a whole, but to his use of data to support the ideas he developed within that framework. In other words, while there are significant problems that need to be rooted out before we can make best use of the CEM, these are problems of data collection and analysis, not of the framework itself. Challenge 5 does point to the need for enhancing the framework conceptually, but even here we are talking about introducing nuance, not questioning the frame itself. Below is an elaboration of these five challenges.

1. Ogbu's writings do not account for behaviors that are both conducive to school success and routinely manifest among large groups of African Americans, past and present (Chapters 9 and 14, this volume). This is important because African Americans are the minority group that Ogbu most often used as an example of the typical norms, values, and behaviors of involuntary minorities. Examples Ogbu missed include race-conscious, African American high achievers, today and in the past, who tie their success to and are driven by a sense of responsibility to their race. To the extent that such individuals, student organizations, and community organizations are noticed (as in the passing awareness of the MAC program documented in the Shaker Heights study [Ogbu, 2003]), they are treated as novel and anomalous instead of manifestations of deeply rooted aspects of Black cultural and intellectual history.

Throughout Ogbu's work, in fact, there is little room for the existence of involuntary minority high-achievers whose motivations to strive and succeed are rooted in their inculcation and embodiment of norms, values, and practices that were developed within and organic to their involuntary minority community. As an engaged, activist educational anthropologist, I am most concerned with promoting academic success, which means not only examining failure, but also taking just as hard a look at success. Thus, Ogbu's inability to recognize organically rooted paths to academic success among involuntary minorities is frustrating. Nowhere in his analysis, for instance, is there adequate recognition of racial uplift, a talented tenth, or racial responsibility as community-based concepts that facilitate academic success among African Americans, even though these are deeply rooted forces in the African American community (Banks, 1996; Foster, 1997; Gaines, 1996; Perry, 2003). Therefore, the challenge is not to the conception of the involuntary minority—the moniker applies quite aptly to African Americans. Rather, somehow in his data gathering and analysis, Ogbu missed key aspects of African Americans' experience and reality as an involuntary minority group.

2. Ogbu's understanding of African American responses to schooling likewise relies upon an analysis of African American cultural history that is selective, contestable, and occasionally inaccurate. For example, we can point to his contention that in order to experience success, African Americans have avoided "White domains" and instead have focused on areas that were not White dominated (Fordham & Ogbu,

1986, pp. 181–183; Ogbu 1982, p. 302). This characterization lacks nuance and ignores not just individual counter-examples, but modes of conduct for entire groups of African Americans throughout American history. For instance, two decades ago, Henry Louis Gates (1987) ably analyzed enslaved and recently freed Africans' efforts to reclaim their humanity by writing down their life stories in narrative form. In the case of these freedom narratives, enslaved and recently freed Africans participated in the so-called White domain of literate culture so as to demonstrate their humanity and equal worth. Acknowledgment or consideration of such engagement with dominant domains is not included in Ogbu's analysis of involuntary minority responses to discrimination. Other such examples of a misreading of cultural history include discussions of Black participation in sports, discussions of Black settlement patterns, and a failure to seriously engage the rhetorical traditions and cultural intellectual institutions associated with racial uplift and the talented tenth.

With regards to the sports example, to show how African Americans have entered what he called non-White domains in order to experience success, Ogbu (1982, p. 302) offered sports participation as an "obvious example" of how African Americans historically have chosen to excel in non-White domains. Whereas in the case of Black literacy in historical perspective Ogbu was (apparently) unaware of this important aspect of American cultural history, in the case of his comments regarding African American historic sports participation he was simply wrong. A well-established literature supports the fact that historically, African Americans have promoted Black engagement in the White American sports establishment for a number of reasons, most of which had to do with an understanding of sports as domains where Blacks could compete against Whites on the equal footing of shared, articulated, and equally applied rules, and with the idea that sports offered an arena where African Americans could stand side by side with other (White) Americans to represent the nation in international arenas and thus prove their worth of citizenship (Harris, 1998; McRae 2003; Miller, 1995). So when the Brown Bomber (boxer Joe Louis) or the Say Hey Kid (baseball player Willie Mays) competed successfully against Whites, they stood in for all African Americans in a demonstration of Blacks' equality with Whites. (Further, this work and impulse came not in the context of a popular mythology of Black athletic superiority—which is more a product of the contemporary popular imagination than is generally understood—but rather in the context of a popular American mythology that described Blacks as both mentally *and physically* inferior.) Likewise, when the Brown Bomber fought the Nazi Stooge, Max Schmeling (who was a German, but not actually a Nazi), and when Jesse Owens won four gold medals in the 1936 Olympics in front of Adolf Hitler, these men were seen as making statements about African Americans as patriots and contributors to the nation's life and defense, and again, as worthy of full rights of citizenship. Of course, these are no longer among the prominent reasons for Black youths' sports participation. I agree with Hoberman's (1997) analysis that sports are a tremendous distraction to many Black youths today. But today is not yesterday, and here as elsewhere Ogbu projected a contemporary circumstance into his ideas about the past.

3. An additional challenge to Ogbu's use of data relates to a myopic reading of *contemporary* data generated during his fieldwork. There are several examples to draw upon, including some that influenced his reading of minority student coping strategies, and others that influenced his conception of the basis for African Americans' oppositional behaviors. An example of the former is Ogbu's discussion of the minority survival strategy of "tomming." Here, as elsewhere, the CEM holds, but the details of his analysis, and the subsequent category he creates, do not. His discussions of tomming did not include observational data of tomming in action (see Ogbu, 1983, 1990, 1991). Rather, he offered Black students generic descriptions of tomming as something that *other* Blacks do. Ogbu's data seemed to point to the possibility that tomming may exist less as an identified and practiced strategy for self, and more of a strategy that is attributed to others. Since tomming is generally cast pejoratively, the ascription of tomming behaviors to others in a given community of Black students raises intriguing questions about what critical race theorist Regina Austin (1995) called policing for solidarity among African Americans. Perhaps the use, or threat of use, of this pejorative category to describe some Black students encourages all to avoid whatever behaviors would earn the moniker "Uncle Tom." Addressing this issue of self-acknowledged identity versus identity as ascribed by others would greatly improve many cultural-ecological analyses.

In other cases, the myopic reading of contemporary data resulted from Ogbu's insistence on focusing more on community forces than on system forces. As will be developed later in this chapter, Ogbu's insistence on privileging community forces in his analyses led him to miss important insights regarding the system forces in action, and regarding the dynamic interaction between system forces and community forces.

4. Ogbu's analysis of voluntary minorities' approaches to schooling is incomplete, failing to account for important facets of their response to schooling. Most notably, along with an instrumental approach to schools, many voluntary minorities construct themselves as distinct from, or even opposite to, involuntary minorities. Divergent backgrounds are collapsed into new categories that serve to distinguish voluntary minorities from involuntary minorities and to facilitate this distancing from involuntary minorities. In the United States, Black involuntary minorities often become the foil against which Black voluntary minorities construct themselves as

high achievers. Waters (1994) reported similar findings in her work with West Indian Blacks in the United States.

In my work with African immigrants and international students attending U.S. universities, the conception of the voluntary minority holds up well, although the group is more fluid and has much more porous boundaries for inclusion than Ogbu recognized. Differences among Africans of different ethnicities and nationalities were downplayed in a process of inscription and ascription that brought these Black students together under the voluntary minority identity of "African." Other Black immigrants and international students similarly came together under the multinational identity of Caribbean or West Indian. Ogbu's descriptions of the success orientation of African voluntary immigrants to the United States concurred with my fieldwork findings, and with my ongoing interactions with this "kind" of student, to the extent that most have been highly motivated and have adopted an instrumental approach to their teachers and to the educational resources that have been available to them. What Ogbu did not notice, but which has come up repeatedly in my experiences, is the extent to which voluntary minorities actively construct themselves in opposition to involuntary minorities when they construct themselves as high achievers.

The African students in the United States that I have interviewed and observed often possess an active and actively reproduced willingness to look down upon involuntary minorities with pity—as maladjusted and systematic underachievers—but they also draw upon that same group as a resource for providing social and other extracurricular outlets that help them maintain their mental health as they proceed through high school or college. Thus, the success of voluntary minorities sometimes is linked to how they imagine and interact with involuntary minorities. This is an important feature of voluntary minority community forces that Ogbu never noticed.

In terms of his understanding of voluntary minority's circumstances, Ogbu did not account for immigrant minorities' wide range of class, status, and wealth backgrounds. In contrast to Ogbu's assertion that immigrant minorities generally enter a host society to improve their status, some already hold high status and wealth when they come to another country. Entrance into a country like the United States to pursue advanced degrees and launch careers is often a reflection of privilege, as well as a means by which privilege is more deeply entrenched.

5. Finally, as will be more fully discussed in the next section, Ogbu's work relied upon a vision of culture that lacked nuance and complexity, especially given his anthropological training. As the discipline of anthropology has progressed—undergoing what Fischer (2004) called a theoretical and methodological retooling in the 1980s and 1990s—Ogbu's analyses retained a view of culture as singular, bounded, and linearly

produced. To be sure, Ogbu's analyses are much more sophisticated than those of McWhorter (2001) or D'Souza (1998), but the assessment (such as that of Shanafelt [2004]) that Ogbu's use of culture was complex and adequately accounted for dynamic interactions among systemic, community, and individual variables, is generous to a fault.

In attempting to come to terms with the shortcomings above, I have identified several areas where the CEM can be further developed such that as a theoretical lens it is more attuned to aspects of social and cultural processes and analyses are less likely to be inaccurate. Two are developed in the following pages. As scholars apply the CEM to minority students' circumstances in different contexts, we would do well to ensure that we operate with a complex and dynamic notion of culture, both within and among groups, and notice the ongoing and dynamic interplay between community and system forces. An additional consideration would include recognizing the fluidity between such categories as involuntary and voluntary minorities because individual identities are malleable and because some individuals maintain a voluntary minority identity despite being involuntary minorities, and vice versa. A final improvement would be greater researcher reflexivity, acknowledgment of subject positioning, and a wrestling with the ways in which a researcher's subject positioning influences data collection and analysis. In Ogbu's case, during his 30 years of work, he begged the question as to how his status as an involuntary minority in a host country impacted what he saw and how he saw it.

ENHANCEMENT #1: OPERATING WITH A MORE COMPLEX NOTION OF CULTURE

The CEM emphasizes how historical and contemporary circumstances and contexts influence the norms, values, and behaviors of a group of similarly situated individuals. Thus, it can quite comfortably accommodate a notion of culture as dynamic, constantly negotiated, and shifting over time—in other words, the important notion that culture is always in process. To this extent, the CEM is well positioned to incorporate recent developments in cultural anthropology (Fischer, 2004).

In the many instances in which Ogbu listed the traits of various involuntary or voluntary minority groups, he described culture in terms of bounded and static units of analysis instead of as dynamic, relational, and constantly negotiated and contested. To his credit, Ogbu was true to the concept of what Fischer (2004, p. 3) called the distinct anthropological voice—the aspiration for a cross-culturally comparative, socially grounded, linguistically and culturally attentive perspective. At the same time, his comparisons reduced groups to several characteristics, which he imbedded in a linear description of different cultural groups' development and resultant socio-material circumstances. As the late educational anthropologist Henry Trueba (1987) noted years ago, one of the problems with Ogbu's analyses is that they did not account for the shifting identities of individuals that he classified as involuntary or voluntary minorities—especially those individuals whose affiliations, genealogies, and loyalties made it difficult to place them neatly into one category or another (pp. 9–10). Nor did Ogbu explain how (much less acknowledge that) attitudes, norms, values, and behaviors shift over time among cultural actors.

Fischer (1994) may as well have been writing against Ogbu when he described some scientists' use of culture as a "fixed variable" and when he argued against such use as "precisely the sort of thing to which anthropological notions of culture cannot be reduced and that lead to the promotion of stereotype thinking and invidious forms of comparative research" (p. 7). To Fischer,

> Culture is not a variable; culture is relational, it is elsewhere, it is in passage, it is where meaning is woven and renewed, often through gaps and silences, and forces beyond the conscious control of individuals, and yet the space where individual and institutional social responsibility and ethical struggle take place.
>
> (p. 7)

Moreover, while culture is "configured historically," it is an ongoing and interactive process that is forged in context. Culture (or the culture of an ideal type group like the voluntary minority) is not a singular entity that, once formed, never changes. Rather, to understand culture and cultural process, we must consider what Weber (1992 [1930], p. 49) referred to as a complex interaction of innumerable different historical factors. Culture is also thoroughly contested and constantly negotiated, from within and without, through inscription and ascription, and in conscious responses and involuntary reactions (Foster, 2003). Thus, it is precisely "the coming into form, the work of maintenance, and the processes of decay, the dynamics of the weaving," that is the anthropologist's special purview and interest (Fischer, 2004, p. 8).

Such a dynamic, complex, and even dizzying understanding of culture (and cultural process) disallows the possibility of viewing culture as a fixed variable in analysis. It also allows for the possibility of interesting norm and value permutations, such as those arising from ongoing interactions between voluntary and involuntary minorities. Adopting this approach to culture would reorient and greatly enhance the CEM, as theorists would be less likely to be satisfied with lists of traits to describe this or that minority group and more likely to notice the constant and never resolved negotiations over which traits will accurately characterize one group or another. Finally, from the standpoint of activist researchers, examining ongoing cultural production provides space for effecting dynamic and responsive interventions in ways that are not available when one group is labeled as adaptive to school success and another group is labeled less adaptive because of their supposed traits.

ENHANCEMENT #2: NOTICING THE DYNAMIC INTERPLAY BETWEEN SYSTEM AND COMMUNITY FORCES

Ogbu's stated opinion about community and system forces was consistent; he argued that both were important to understanding minority responses to schooling, but that community forces were systematically understudied. Thus, he devoted his time to understanding community forces. A problem that arose is that in his desire to bring attention to community forces, he went too far in that direction, overemphasizing them, overemphasizing their negative impacts, and undermining his contention that both sets of forces were important. In his many books, articles, and book chapters, Ogbu's mentioning of community and system forces as equally important became a *pro forma* act. He typically mentioned them in one or two introductory sentences to articles that repeated his assessments about involuntary minorities' roles in their own academic failure. This problem is one of emphasis and impression, but nonetheless it is important because Ogbu's work increasingly has been used to bolster the culture-of-poverty arguments that he actually saw himself as arguing against (Hamann, 2004).

Another problem with Ogbu's discussion of community and system forces reflects a need for deeper engagement with anthropological and sociological theory. In the case of any dichotomy, or any set of ideal types, it is important to remember that these are constructions. They help researchers think about problems, but must be used carefully, and with an understanding that categories and types are generally more fluid and unpredictable than the concepts actually allow. One understudied aspect of system and community forces is the extent to which they exist interdependently and constantly influence each other. In Ogbu's (1978) work, the initial conception that a job ceiling, along with other forms of discrimination, led to certain responses by involuntary minorities is a case in which system forces facilitated a set of communal responses that became instituted strongly enough and shared widely enough to become community forces. But the impact of one set of forces upon another does not only occur during a formative period to produce an everlasting result. The system changes, and the community changes, and they continually impact one another. An enhanced CEM would be much stronger with this recognition.

Especially in terms of accounting for and minimizing those community forces that Ogbu identified as undermining academic success, it is worth paying special attention to how individuals perceive specific system forces, and how the system incorporates and accounts for actions generated by community members. To an extent, Ogbu's (2003) Shaker Heights work, *Black American Students in an Affluent Suburb* began to address this complex task. Even there, however, he underplayed or did not provide an analysis for data that seemed to shed light on how system forces impacted students' responses to schooling, as well as how system forces impacted their academic achievement, placement, and outcomes. Examples occurred throughout the text, but are especially noticeable on pages 112, 117, and 237. In these places, Ogbu recorded comments by students, parents, and teachers that could have been used to shed light on system forces as involuntary minorities perceived them. Especially in those instances in which community members commented on system forces, Ogbu missed an opportunity to analyze how system forces interact with, inform, and are challenged by community forces.

In sum, while the point that community forces have not received enough attention is well taken, in any schooling situation, it remains important to maintain balance and perspective, to examine how both community forces and system forces impact students' academic outcomes and also to look at the two as they interrelate, reinforce, or undermine one another. As a final repetition of this chapter's mantra, greater focus on these areas will not compromise the basic tenets of the CEM, but enhance it by facilitating our understanding of the factors that influence minority responses to schooling, as well as how they operate.

CONCLUSION

In earlier work (Foster, 2004), I outlined Ogbu's CEM so as to facilitate wider understanding and more nuanced use or criticism of his work. In the opening chapters of this volume, Ogbu likewise reiterated his key ideas, including additional consideration of the "acting White" hypothesis that he developed with Signithia Fordham. Between these works, the chapters in this volume, and additional works that did not find their way into this volume, we come away with a definitive sense of Ogbu's ideas, and with important criticisms of his opus. We thus are well equipped to move forward. For my part, I have tried to use the concluding piece of this volume to frame and state my critique in such a way as to allow future researchers to utilize the CEM, refine it, build upon its strengths, and correct its shortcomings. I also have ventured into the delicate and seldom written about politics of reception that often surround prolific scholars, and that certainly surrounded Ogbu's work.

The criticisms here—especially those related to static notions of culture, poorly founded readings of cultural history, and underdeveloped notions of cultural process—are, in my view, the most essential to correct if we are to make the most use of the CEM in the future. Actively incorporating more sophisticated, processual considerations around culture will ultimately further, rather than destabilize or undermine, Ogbu's important ideas about minority responses to schooling. Forthrightly laying out a body of theory, and then allowing for and engaging in its criticism—as has been accomplished in this volume—not only secures John Ogbu's legacy, but also encourages a dynamic approach to ideas, where we see a seminal body of work not as the final answer to a question or set of questions, but rather as an important and lasting contribution to ongoing and vitally important discussions.

REFERENCES

Austin, R. (1995). The black community: Its lawbreakers and a politics of identification. In R. Delgado (Ed.), *Critical race theory: The cutting edge* (pp. 293–304). Philadelphia: Temple University Press.

Banks, W. (1996). *Black intellectuals*. New York: W.W. Norton and Company.

D'Souza, D. (1998). *Illiberal education: The politics of race and sex on campus*. New York: Free Press.

Fischer, M. (2004). *Emergent forms of life and the anthropological voice*. Durham, NC: Duke University Press.

Flores-Gonzalez N. (1999). Puerto Rican high-achievers: An example of ethnic and academic identity compatibility. *Anthropology and Education Quarterly*, *30*(3), 344–362.

Foley, D. (2005). Elusive prey: John Ogbu and the search for a grand theory of minority academic disengagement. *Qualitative Studies in Education*, *18*(5), 643–657.

Fordham, S. (2004). "Signithia, you can do better than that": John Ogbu (and me) and the nine lives peoples. *Anthropology & Education Quarterly*, *35*(1), 149–161.

Fordham, S., & Ogbu, J. (1986). Black students' school success: Coping with the burden of "acting White." *The Urban Review*, *18*, 176–206.

Foster, K. (1997). Vindicationist politics: A foundation and point of departure for an African Diaspora studies paradigm. *Transforming Anthropology*, *6*(1/2), 2–9.

Foster, K. (2001). *Success on whose terms? Academic achievement and status production among Black students on a predominantly White university campus*. University of Texas: Dissertation.

Foster, K. (2003). The contours of community: The formation and maintenance of a Black student community on a predominantly White campus. *Race, Ethnicity and Education, 6*(3), 265–282.

Foster, K. (2004). Coming to terms: A discussion of John Ogbu's cultural-ecological theory of minority academic achievement. *Intercultural Education, 15*(4), 369–384.

Foster, K. (ed.). (2005a). (Ogbu Special Issue.) *International Qualitative Studies in Education, 18*(5).

Foster, K. (2005b). How do you ensure the fair consideration of a complex ancestor? Multiple approaches to assessing the work and legacy of John Ogbu. *International Journal of Qualitative Studies in Education, 18*(5), 559–564.

Foster, K. (2005c). Gods or vermin: Alternative readings of the African American experience among African and African American college students. *Transforming Anthropology, 13*(1), 34–46.

Foster, K. (2005d). Narratives of the social scientist: Understanding the work of John Ogbu. *International Journal of Qualitative Studies in Education, 18*(5), 565–580.

Foster, K., & Gobbo, F. (Eds.) (2004). (Ogbu Special Issue). *Intercultural Education, 15*(4).

Gaines, K. (1996). *Uplifting the race.* Chapel Hill: University of North Carolina Press.

Gates, H. (1987). *The classic slave narratives.* New York: Penguin.

Goleman, D. (1988, August 10). An emerging theory on blacks' I.Q. scores. *The New York Times*; Final Edition, Section 12, p. 22.

Gould, M. (1999). Race and theory: Culture, poverty and adaptation to discrimination in Wilson and Ogbu. *Sociological Theory, 17*(2), 171–200.

Hamann, T. (2004). Lessons from the interpretation/misinterpretation of John Ogbu's scholarship. *Intercultural Education, 15*(4), 399–412.

Harris, O. (1998). The role of sports in the Black community. In G. Sailes (Ed.), *African Americans in sport* (pp.3–13). Brunswick and London: Transaction Publishers.

Hermans, P. (2004). Applying Ogbu's theory of minority academic achievement to the situation of Moroccans in the low countries. *Intercultural Education, 15*(4), 430–439.

Hoberman, J. (1997). *Darwin's athletes.* New York: Houghton-Mifflin Company.

Kalekin-Fishman, D. (2004). Diagnosing inequalities in schooling: Ogbu's orientation and wider implications. *Intercultural Education, 15*(4), 413–430.

O'Conner, C. (1997). Dispositions toward collective struggle and educational resilience in the inner city: A case analysis of six African American high school students. *American Educational Research Journal, 34*(4), 593–629.

McRae, D. (2003). *Heroes without a country: America's betrayal of Joe Louis and Jesse Owens.* New York: Harperville.

McWhorter, J. (2001). *Losing the race: Self-sabotage in Black America.* New York: Simon Schuster.

Miller, P. (1995). To bring the race along rapidly: Sport, student culture, and the educational mission at historically black colleges during the interwar years. *History of Education Quarterly, 35*(2), 111–133.

Ogbu, J. (1978). *Minority education and caste: The American system in cross-cultural perspective.* New York: Academic Press.

Ogbu, J. (1982). Cultural discontinuities and schooling. *Anthropology and Education Quarterly*, *13*(4), 290–307.

Ogbu, J. (1983). Minority status and schooling in plural societies. *Comparative Education Review*, *27*(2), 168–190.

Ogbu, J. (1990). Minority education in comparative perspective. *Journal of Negro Education*, *59*(1), 45–57.

Ogbu, J. (1991). Minority coping responses and school experience. *Journal of Psychohistory*, *18*(4), 433–456.

Ogbu, J. (2003). *Black students in an affluent suburb: A study of academic disengagement*. Mahwah, NJ: Lawrence Erlbaum.

Page, C. (2003, September 9). Lessons from an anthropologist, *Jewish World Review*. Retrieved from <www.jewishworldreview.com/0903/page090903.asp>.

Perry, T. (2003). Up from parched earth: Towards a theory of African American achievement. In T. Perry, C. Steele, & A. Hilliard (Eds.), *Young, gifted, and Black* (pp. 1–108). Boston: Beacon Press.

Rothstein, R. (2000, October 11). Lessons: On culture and learning. *The New York Times*, Late Edition—Final, Section B, p. 10.

Shanafelt, R. (2004). Conservative critiques of African American culture. *Anthropology Theory*, *4*(1), 89–118.

Tough, P. (2004, December 12). The 4th annual: Year in ideas; "acting White" myth. *The New York Times*. Retrieved from <www.nytimes.com>.

Trueba E. (1987). *Success or failure: Learning and the language minority student*. Cambridge: Newbury House.

Waters, M. (1994). Ethnic and racial identities of second-generation black immigrants in New York City. *International Migration Review*, *28*(4), 401–444.

Weber, M. (1992[1930]). *The Protestant ethic and spirit of capitalism*. London: Routledge.

Zou, Y., & Trueba, E. (Eds.) (1998). Introduction. In Y. Zou & E. Trueba (Eds.), *Ethnic identity and power: Cultural contexts of political action in school and society* (pp. 1–25). Albany, NY: State University of New York Press.

Appendix

Black Students' School Success

Coping with the "Burden of 'Acting White'" *

Signithia Fordham and John U. Ogbu

The following vignettes point to the central problem addressed in this paper. The first is from Dorothy Gilliam's column in the *Washington Post* of February 15, 1982, entitled "Success":

> My friend was talking to her son, who is 20, when he blurted out a secret half as old as he. It was the explanation for his ambivalence toward success. It began, he said, in his early school years, when a fifth-grade teacher questioned whether he had really written the outstanding essay he'd turned in about the life of squirrels. It ended when the teacher gave him a grade that clearly showed that she did not believe the boy's outraged denial of plagiarism.
>
> Because the young man is Black and the teacher is White, and because such incidents had happened before, he arrived at a youthful solution: "I never tried again," he recently told his mother, who had suffered misery as her son's grades had plummeted and his interest in school had waned. He had sold himself short because he was humiliated.
>
> Today he reads the classics but has only a high school diploma; today he can finally articulate his feelings. Today he feels he was manipulated by society not to achieve, and feels he has been tricked into lowering his performance. He is furious that he blocked his own talents.
>
> As my distraught friend recounted this disturbing episode, we looked at each other and grimaced. Each of us knows people of her son's generation, and of our own, who are ambivalent about success.
>
> (p. B1)

Gilliam goes on to recount how the existing ecological conditions have led Black parents unwittingly to teach their children a double message: "You must be twice as good to go half as far," and "Don't get the big head, don't blow your own horn." Generations of Black children have

learned this lesson so well that what appears to have emerged in some
segments of the Black community is a kind of cultural orientation that
defines academic learning in school as "acting White," and academic
success as the prerogative of White Americans. This orientation embodies
both social pressures against striving for academic success and fear of
striving for academic success. The following passage from Abdul-Jabbar's
autobiography illustrates a part of this *evolved cultural orientation
toward schooling*:

> I got there [Holy Providence School in Cornwall Heights, right out-
> side of Philadelphia] and immediately found I could read better than
> anyone in the school. My father's example and my mother's training
> had made that come easy; I could pick up a book, read it out loud,
> pronounce the words with proper inflections and actually know what
> they meant. When the nuns found this out they paid me a lot of
> attention, once even asking me, a fourth grader, to read to the seventh
> grade. When the kids found this out I became a target . . .
>
> It was my first time away from home, my first experience in an all-
> Black situation, and I found myself being punished for doing every-
> thing I'd ever been taught was right. I got all As and was hated for it;
> I spoke correctly and was called a punk. I had to learn a new lan-
> guage simply to be able to deal with the threads. I had good manners
> and was a good little boy and paid for it with my hide.
>
> (Abdul-Jabbar, 1983, p. 16)

Our main point in this paper is that *one major reason* Black students do
poorly in school is that they experience inordinate ambivalence and affective dissonance in regard to academic effort and success. This problem
arose partly because White Americans traditionally refused to acknowledge that Black Americans are capable of intellectual achievement, and
partly because Black Americans subsequently began to doubt their own
intellectual ability, began to define academic success as White people's
prerogative, and began to discourage their peers, perhaps unconsciously,
from emulating White people in academic striving, i.e., from "acting
White." Because of the ambivalence, affective dissonance, and social
pressures, many Black students who are academically able do not put
forth the necessary effort and perseverance in their schoolwork and, consequently, do poorly in school. Even Black students who do not fail generally perform well below their potential for the same reasons. We will
illustrate this phenomenon with data from a recent ethnographic study of
both successful and unsuccessful students in a predominantly Black high
school in Washington, DC.

We will begin with a conceptual background and framework. This will
be followed by a presentation of the case study from Washington, DC. In
the third section we will show that the phenomenon exists in other parts

of the United States and probably can be found among other, similar minority groups in the United States and other societies. We will discuss the implications of our paper for policy and programs designed to increase minority school performance in the last, concluding section of the paper.

BACKGROUND AND CONCEPTUAL FRAMEWORK

Cultural-Ecological Influences on Schooling

It is well known that some minority groups are academically successful in school, while other minority groups are not (Coleman et al., 1966). The differences in the school performance of the various minority groups exist even when the minority groups face similar language, cultural, and educational barriers in school as well as barriers in the opportunity structure (e.g., job discrimination) in adult life (see Ogbu, 1984; Ogbu & Matute-Bianchi, 1986). In order to account for this variability, we have suggested that minority groups should be classified into three types: *autonomous minorities*, who are minorities primarily in a numerical sense; *immigrant minorities*, who came to America more or less *voluntarily* with the expectation of improving their economic, political, and social status; and *subordinate* or *castelike minorities*, who were *involuntarily and permanently* incorporated into American society through slavery or conquest. Black Americans are an example par excellence of castelike minorities because they were brought to America as slaves and after emancipation were relegated to menial status through legal and extralegal devices (Berreman, 1960; Myrdal, 1944). American Indians, Mexican Americans, and Native Hawaiians share, to some extent, features of castelike minorities. American Indians, the original owners of the land, were conquered and sent to live on reservations (Spicer, 1962). Mexican Americans in the Southwest were also conquered and displaced from power; and Mexicans who later immigrated from Mexico were given the status of the conquered group and treated in the same manner (Acuna, 1972; Ogbu, 1978; Schmidt, 1970).

We initially explained the disproportionate and persistent high rates of school failure of subordinate minorities from a cultural-ecological perspective because this perspective allowed us to examine the school performance of the minorities in the context of historical, structural, and cultural forces which affect the schooling of such groups (Ogbu, 1978, 1981). In the case of Black Americans we suggested that the disproportionately high rate of low school performance is a kind of adaptation to their limited social and economic opportunities in adult life. That is, the low school performance is an adaptive response to the requirements of cultural imperatives within their ecological structure.

Within their ecological structure, Black Americans traditionally have been provided with substandard schooling, based on White Americans' perceptions of the educational needs of Black Americans; and White Americans have controlled Black Americans' education. Another feature of their ecological structure is that Black Americans have faced a job ceiling, so that even when they achieved in school in the past, i.e., had good educational credentials, they were not necessarily given access to jobs, wages, and other benefits commensurate with their academic accomplishments. The third component of the ecological structure is that in response to substandard schooling and barriers in the adult opportunity structure, Black Americans developed several "survival strategies" and other coping mechanisms.

We suggested how these ecological factors might enter into the schooling of Black children and adversely affect their academic performance. The job ceiling, for example, tends to give rise to disillusionment about the real value of schooling, especially among older children, and thereby discourages them from working hard in school (Hunter, 1980; Ogbu, 1974). Frustrations over the job ceiling and substandard schooling create conflicts and distrust between Black Americans and the public schools, making it more difficult for Black Americans than for White Americans to believe what the schools say and to behave according to school norms. Survival strategies, such as collective struggle, Uncle Tomming, and hustling, may encourage Black Americans to develop attitudes, perceptions, behaviors, and competencies that are not necessarily congruent with those required to do well in school. The job ceiling and other discriminatory treatment engender among Black Americans a feeling of impotence and a lack of self-confidence that they can compete successfully with Whites *in matters considered traditionally as White people's domain*, such as good jobs and academic tasks. Finally, the experience of slavery with its attendant "compulsory ignorance" has meant that Black Americans have had a limited development of academic tradition.

Under these circumstances, attitudes and behaviors of Black students, though different from those of White students, are not deviant or pathological, but should be considered as a mode of adaptation necessitated by the ecological structure or effective environment of the Black community. That is, the attitudes and behaviors which Black children learn in this community as they grow up and which they bring to school are those required by and appropriate for the niche Black Americans have traditionally occupied in the American corporate economy and racial stratification system. In sum, the low school performance of Black children stems from the following factors: first, White people provide them with inferior schooling and treat them differently in school; second, by imposing a job ceiling, White people fail to reward them adequately for their educational accomplishments in adult life; and third, Black Americans develop coping devices which, in turn, further limit their striving for academic success.

A concept which allows one to comprehend more fully the academic attitudes and behaviors of Black Americans under this circumstance is that of *status mobility system* (LeVine, 1967; Ogbu, 1978). A status mobility system is the socially or culturally approved strategy for getting ahead within a given population or a given society. It is the people's *folk theory of making it* or getting ahead, however the particular population defines getting ahead. A central premise of the concept is that a given status mobility system generates its own ideal personality types, distinguished by those orientations, qualities, and competencies which one needs to get ahead in the particular population. Furthermore, the way members of a population, including a subordinate population, prepare their children for adulthood, through child rearing as well as formal schooling, is influenced by their ideal images and characteristics of successful members of the population, living or dead; these images are incorporated into the value systems of parents and others responsible for the upbringing of children. As the children get older and begin to understand the status mobility system of their group, they themselves tend to play an active role in learning how to get ahead in the manner prescribed by their culture.

In a given population the orientations, qualities, competencies, and behaviors fostered by the system of status mobility will reflect the social and economic realities of its members. Thus, people's way of bringing up children, through which they inculcate those orientations, qualities, competencies, and behaviors they consider essential for competence in adulthood, is not divorced from their social and economic realities. In the case of subordinate minorities like Black Americans, the schooling offered to them by the dominant group usually reflects the dominant group members' perceptions of the place of the minorities in the opportunity structure; equally important, however, are the responses of the minorities, which reflect their perceptions of their social and economic realities, their strategies for getting ahead.

The cultural-ecological explanation has undergone modifications because the original formulation did not explain differences in school success among Black students. Why, for example, are some Black children academically successful even though as a group Black Americans face a limited adult opportunity structure and are given substandard education? The original formulation has also been criticized for focusing on Black school failure while ignoring possible explanations for Black school success (Fordham, 1981). But in fairness to the theory, it should be pointed out that it was initially proposed as a response to earlier theories that attributed disproportionately high rates of Black school failure to genetic factors (Jensen, 1969) or to cultural deprivation (Bloom, Davis, & Hess, 1965).

Collective Identity, Cultural Frame, and Schooling

Since 1980 (Ogbu, 1980, 1982) the recognition of the above weakness, as well as the need to explain better the academic success of some other minority groups, has led the authors to modify the cultural-ecological explanation. The modification has involved going beyond factors of instrumental exploitation (limitations in opportunity structure, such "job ceilings") and instrumental responses, to examine the expressive dimension of the relationship between the dominant group and the minorities. Specifically, in studying the expressive dimension of minority-majority group relations, we have isolated two additional factors we believe make the relationship between Blacks and Whites in American qualitatively different from the relationship between White Americans and other types of minorities, especially the immigrants. These additional factors also shed some light on the intragroup differences or individual differences within the Black population. The two factors are an *oppositional collective* or *social identity* and *oppositional cultural frame of reference* (Fordham, 1981, 1982a; Ogbu, 1980, 1981, 1984).

Our clue to the twin phenomena comes from reviewing cross-cultural studies of minorities. We have found the work of Spicer (1966, 1971), DeVos (1967, 1984), Castile and Kushner (1981), Green (1981), and others particularly helpful in this regard. These scholars have analyzed conflicts and oppositional processes between minority groups and dominant groups in both traditional societies and contemporary urban industrial societies, and they have concluded that the conflicts and opposition often cause the minorities to form oppositional social identities and oppositional cultural frames of reference (Ogbu, 1986a). A close analysis of the relationship between subordinate minorities and the dominant White Americans reveals these same kinds of conflicts and oppositional processes.

Subordinate minorities like Black Americans develop a sense of collective identity or sense of peoplehood in opposition to the social identity of White Americans because of the way White Americans treat them in economic, political, social, and psychological domains, including White exclusion of these groups from true assimilation. The oppositional identity of the minority evolves also because they perceive and experience the treatment by Whites as collective and enduring oppression. They realize and believe that, regardless of their individual ability and training or education, and regardless of their place of origin (e.g., in Africa) or residence in America, regardless of their individual economic status or physical appearance, they cannot expect to be treated like White Americans, their "fellow citizens"; nor can they easily escape from their more or less birth-ascribed membership in a subordinate and disparaged group by "passing" or by returning to "a homeland" (Green, 1981).

Along with the formation of an oppositional social identity, subordinate minorities also develop an oppositional cultural frame of reference that includes devices for protecting their identity and for maintaining boundaries between them and white Americans. Thus subordinate minorities regard certain forms of behavior and certain activities or events, symbols, and meanings as *not appropriate* for them because those behaviors, events, symbols, and meanings are characteristic of White Americans. At the same time, they emphasize other forms of behavior and other events, symbols, and meanings as more appropriate for them because these are *not* a part of White Americans' way of life. To behave in the manner defined as falling within a White cultural frame of reference is to "act White" and is negatively sanctioned.

The cultural frame of reference of subordinate minorities is emotionally charged because it is closely tied to their sense of collective identity and security. Therefore individuals who try to behave like White Americans or try to cross cultural boundaries or to "act White" in *forbidden domains* face opposition from their peers and probably from other members of the minority community. Their peers often construe such behaviors as trying to join the enemy (DeVos, 1967). Individuals trying to cross cultural boundaries or pass culturally may also experience internal stress, what DeVos (1967) calls "affective dissonance." The reason for the affective dissonance is that such individuals share their minority-group's sense of collective oppositional identity, a belief that may cause them to feel that they are, indeed, betraying their group and its cause. The individuals may also experience psychological stress because they are uncertain that White Americans will accept them if they succeed in learning to "act White" (Fordham, 1985; Ogbu, 1986b). Indeed, DeVos (1984) argues that in a situation involving an oppositional process, subordinate-group members may automatically or unconsciously perceive learning some aspects of the culture of their "oppressors" as harmful to their identity. That is, learning itself may arouse a sense of "impending conflict over one's future identity." Of course, not every member of the minority group feels this way. Some do not identify with the oppositional identity and oppositional cultural frame of reference of their group. Some identify only marginally; and some even repudiate their group's social identity and cultural frame of reference (Fordham, 1985).

An oppositional cultural frame of reference is applied by the minorities selectively. The target areas appear to be those traditionally defined as prerogatives of White Americans, both by White people themselves and by the minorities. These are areas in which it was long believed that only Whites could perform well and in which few minorities traditionally were given the opportunity to try or were rewarded if they tried and succeeded. They are areas where criteria of performance have been established by Whites and competence in performance is judged by Whites or their representatives, and where rewards for performance are determined by White people according to White criteria. Academic tasks represent one such area, as was noted in our comment in the vignettes presented earlier.

How do the oppositional identity and oppositional cultural frame of reference enter into the process of subordinate minorities' schooling? The oppositional identity and oppositional cultural frame of reference enter into the process of minority schooling through the minorities' perceptions and interpretations of schooling as learning the White American cultural frame of reference which they have come to assume to have adverse effects on their own cultural and identity integrity. Learning school curriculum and learning to follow the standard academic practices of the school are often equated by the minorities with learning to "act White" or as actually "acting White" while simultaneously giving up acting like a minority person. School learning is therefore consciously or unconsciously perceived *as a subtractive process*: a minority person who learns successfully in school or who follows the standard practices of the school is perceived as becoming acculturated into the White American cultural frame of reference at the expense of the minorities' cultural frame of reference and collective welfare. *It is important to point out that, even though the perceptions and behavioral responses are manifested by students, as peer groups and individuals, the perceptions and interpretations are a part of a cultural orientation toward schooling which exists within the minority community and which evolved during many generations when White Americans insisted that minorities were incapable of academic success, denied them the opportunity to succeed academically, and did not reward them adequately when they succeeded.*

The perception of schooling as a subtractive process causes subordinate minorities to "oppose" or "resist" academic striving, both socially and psychologically. At the social level, peer groups discourage their members from putting forth the time and effort required to do well in school and from adopting the attitudes and standard practices that enhance academic success. They oppose adopting appropriate academic attitudes and behaviors because they are considered "White." Peer group pressures against academic striving take many forms, including labeling (e.g., "brainiac" for students who receive good grades in their courses), exclusion from peer activities or ostracism, and physical assault. Individuals "resist" striving to do well academically partly out of fear of peer responses and partly to avoid affective dissonance. Because they also share their group's sense of collective identity and cultural frame of reference, individuals may not want to behave in a manner they themselves define as "acting White."

Fictive Kinship and Schooling

In our study of the twin phenomena of oppositional social identity and oppositional cultural frame of reference among Black Americans, we have found the concept of fictive kinship (see Fordham 1981, 1985) an appropriate one to convey their meanings. In anthropology, fictive kinship refers to a kinship-like relationship between persons not related by blood or marriage in a society, but who have some reciprocal social or economic relationship. There is usually a native term for it, or a number of native terms expressing or indicating its presence (Brain, 1971; Freed, 1973; Norbeck & Befu, 1958; Pitt-Rivers, 1968). Fictive kinship in the anthropological sense also exists among Black Americans. Sometimes Black people refer to persons in that kind of relationship as "play-kin" (Shimkin, Shimkin, & Frate, 1978).

But there is a much wider meaning of fictive kinship among Black Americans. In this latter sense the term conveys the idea of "brotherhood" and "sisterhood" of all Black Americans. This sense of peoplehood or collective social identity is evident in numerous kinship and pseudo-kinship terms that Black Americans use to refer to one another. The following are examples of the kinship and pseudo-kinship terms most commonly used by adolescents and adults: "brother," "sister," "soul brother," "soul sister," "blood," "bleed," "folk," "members," "the people," "my people" (see Folb, 1980; Liebow, 1967; Sargent, 1985; Stack, 1974). In this paper we are using the term fictive kinship in the second, wider sense; that is, fictive kinship is used to denote a cultural symbol of collective identity of Black Americans.

More specifically, fictive kinship is used to describe the particular mind set, i.e., the specific world view of those persons who are appropriately labeled "Black." Since "blackness" is more than a skin color, fictive kinship is the concept used to denote the moral judgment the group makes on its members (see Brain, 1972). Essentially, the concept suggests that the mere possession of African features and/or being of African descent does not automatically make one a Black person, nor does it suggest that one is a member in good standing of the group. One can be Black in color, but choose not to seek membership in the fictive kinship system, and/or be denied membership by the group because one's behavior, activities, and lack of manifest loyalty are at variance with those thought to be appropriate and group-specific.

The Black American fictive kinship system probably developed from their responses to two types of treatment they received from White Americans. One is the economic and other instrumental exploitation by Whites both during and after slavery (Anderson, 1975; Bullock, 1970; Drake & Cayton, 1970; Myrdal, 1944; Spivey, 1978). The other kind of treatment is the tendency of White Americans historically to treat Blacks as an undifferentiated mass of people, ascribing to them indiscriminately certain inherent strengths and weaknesses. It appears that Blacks have sometimes responded by inverting the negative stereotypes and assumptions of Whites into positive and functional attributes (Fordham, 1982a; Holt, 1972; Ogbu, 1983). Thus, Blacks may have transformed White assumptions of black homogeneity into a collective identity system and a coping strategy.

An example of collective treatment by White Americans which may have promoted the formation of Black people's sense of collective identity *in opposition* to White identity *and* expressed the oppositional identity in the idiom of fictive kinship occurred following Nat Turner's "insurrection" in Southampton, Virginia, in 1831. After that incident, Whites restricted the movement of Blacks as well as Black contact amongst themselves, regardless of their place of residence or personal involvement in the insurrection (Haley, 1976; Styron, 1966). Even Black children in Washington, DC were forbidden by Whites from attending Sunday school with White children after the incident, although local Whites knew that Black children in Washington, DC had no part in the insurrection. What was well understood by Blacks in Southampton, Virginia, in Washington, DC and elsewhere in the country was that the *onus* for Turner's behavior was extended to all Black Americans solely on the basis of their being Black. Numerous arbitrary treatments of this kind, coupled with a knowledge that they were denied true assimilation into the mainstream of American life, encouraged Blacks to develop what DeVos (1967) calls "ethnic consolidation," a sense of peoplehood (Green, 1981) expressed in fictive kinship feelings and language.

Because fictive kinship symbolizes a Black American sense of peoplehood in opposition to White American social identity, we suggest that it is closely tied to their various boundary-maintaining behaviors and attitudes towards Whites. An example is the tendency for Black Americans to emphasize *group loyalty* in situations involving conflict or competition with Whites. Furthermore, Black people have a tendency to negatively sanction behaviors and attitudes they consider to be at variance with their group identity symbols and criteria of membership. We also note that, since only Black Americans are involved in the evaluation of group members' eligibility for membership in the fictive kinship system, they control the criteria used to judge one's worthiness for membership, and the criteria are totally group-specific. That is, the determination and control of the criteria for membership in the fictive kinship system are in contrast to the determination and control of the criteria for earning grades in school or promotion in the mainstream workplace by White people. Fictive kinship means a lot to Black people because they regard it as the ideal by which members of the group are judged; it is also the medium through which Blacks distinguish "real" from "spurious" members (M. Williams, 1981).

Black children learn the meaning of fictive kinship from their parents and peers while they are growing up. And it appears that the children learn it early and well enough so that they more or less unconsciously but strongly tend to associate their life chances and "success" potential with those of their peers and members of their community. Group membership is important in Black peer relations; as a result, when it comes to dealing with Whites and White institutions, the unexpressed assumption guiding behavior seems to be that "my brother is my brother regardless of what he does or has done" (Haskins, 1976; Sargent, 1985). In the next section we will illustrate how the fictive kinship phenomenon enters into and affects the schooling of Black children in one local community, Washington, DC.

"ACTING WHITE" AT CAPITAL HIGH

The setting of the study, Capital High School[1] and its surrounding community, has been described in detail elsewhere (Fordham, 1982b, 1984, 1985). Suffice it here to say that Capital High is a predominantly Black high school (some 99 percent Black—1,868 out of 1,886 students at the start of the research effort in 1982). It is located in a historically Black section of Washington, DC, in a relatively low-income area.

The influence of fictive kinship is extensive among the students at Capital High. It shows up not only in conflicts between Blacks and Whites and between Black students and Black teachers, who are often perceived to be "functionaries" of the dominant society, but also in the students' constant need to reassure one another of Black loyalty and identity. They appear to achieve this group loyalty by defining certain attitudes and behaviors as "White" and therefore unacceptable, and then employing numerous devices to discourage one another from engaging in those behaviors and attitudes, i.e., from "acting White."

Among the attitudes and behaviors that Black students at Capital High identify as "acting White" and therefore unacceptable are: (1) speaking Standard English; (2) listening to White music and White radio stations; (3) going to the opera or ballet; (4) spending a lot of time in the library studying; (5) working hard to get good grades in school; (6) getting good grades in school (those who get good grades are labeled "brainiacs"); (7) going to the Smithsonian; (8) going to a Rolling Stones concert at the Capital Center; (9) doing volunteer work; (10) going camping, hiking, or mountain climbing; (11) having cocktails or a cocktail party; (12) going to a symphony orchestra concert; (13) having a party with no music; (14) listening to classical music; (15) being on time; (16) reading and writing poetry; and (17) putting on "airs," and so forth. This list is not exhaustive, but indicates the kind of attitudes and behaviors likely to be negatively sanctioned and therefore avoided by a large number of students.

As operationally defined in this paper, the idea of "coping with the burden of 'acting White' " suggests the various strategies that Black students at Capital High use to resolve, successfully or unsuccessfully, the tension between students desiring to do well academically and meet the expectations of school authorities on the one hand and the demands of peers for conformity to group-sanctioned attitudes and behaviors that validate Black identity and cultural frame on the other. Black students at Capital High who choose to pursue academic success are perceived by their peers as "being kind of white" (Weis, 1985, p. 101) and therefore not truly Black. This gives rise to the tension between those who want to succeed (i.e., who in the eyes of their peers want to "act White") and others insisting on highlighting group-sanctioned attitudes and behaviors. Under the circumstance, students who want to do well in school must find some strategy to resolve the tension. This tension, along with the extra responsibility it places on students who choose to pursue academic success in spite of it, and its effects on the performance of those who resolve the tension successfully and those who do not, constitute "the burden of 'acting White'." The few high-achieving students, as we will show, have learned how to cope successfully with the burden of acting White; the many underachieving students have not succeeded in a manner that enhances academic success. It is this tension and its effects on Black students' academic efforts and outcomes that are explored in the case study of Capital High students.

Ethnographic data in the study were collected over a period of more than one year. During the study some 33 students in the eleventh grade were studied intensively, and our examples are drawn from this sample. Below we describe 8 cases, 4 males and 4 females. Two of the males and 2 of the females are underachievers, while 2 of the males and 2 of the females are high achievers.

Underachieving Students

Underachieving Black students in the sample appear to have the ability to do well in school, at least better than their present records show. But they have apparently decided, consciously or unconsciously, to avoid "acting White." That is, they choose to avoid adopting attitudes and putting in enough time and effort in their schoolwork because their peers (and they themselves) would interpret their behaviors as "White." Their main strategy for coping with the burden of acting white tends, therefore, to be *avoidance*.

Our first example of an underachieving male is *Sidney*. Like most students in the sample, Sidney took the Preliminary Scholastic Aptitude Test (PSAT) and did fairly well, scoring at the 67th percentile on the math section of the test and at the 54th percentile on the verbal section. His scores on the Comprehensive Test of Basic Skills (CTBS) in the ninth grade indicate that he was performing well above grade level: his composite score in reading was 12.2; he scored at the college level on the language component (13.6); on the math component he scored just above eleventh grade (11.3), making his total battery on these three components 11.8. He scored above college level in the reference skills, science, and social studies sections. On the whole, his performance on standardized tests is far higher than that of many high-achieving males in our sample.

In spite of this relatively good performance on standardized tests, his grade point average is only C. Sidney is surprised and disgusted with his inability to earn grades comparable to those he earned in elementary and junior high school. While he takes most of the courses available to eleventh graders from the Advanced Placement sequence, he is not making the As and Bs at Capital High that he consistently made during his earlier schooling.

Sidney is an outstanding football player who appears to be encapsulated in the very forces that he maintains are largely responsible for the lack of upward mobility in the local Black community. He is very much aware of the need to earn good grades in school in order to take advantage of the few opportunities he thinks are available to Black Americans. However, he appears unable to control his life and act in opposition to the forces he identifies as detrimental to his academic progress.

His friends are primarily football players and other athletes. He is able to mix and mingle easily with them despite the fact that, unlike most of them, he takes advanced courses; he claims that this is because of his status as an athlete. His friends are aware of his decision to take these advanced courses, and they jokingly refer to him as "Mr. Advanced Placement."

Sidney readily admits that he could do a lot better in school, but says that he, like many of his friends, does not value what he is asked to learn in school. He also reluctantly admits that the fear of being called a "brainiac" prevents him from putting more time and effort into his schoolwork. According to him, the term "brainiac" is used in a disparaging manner at Capital High for students who do well in their courses:

ANTHROPOLOGIST: Have you heard the word "brainiac" used here?

SIDNEY: Yes. [When referring to students who take the Advanced Placement courses here.] That's a term for the smartest person in class. Brainiac—jerk—you know, those terms. If you're smart, you're a jerk, you're a brainiac.

ANTHRO: Are all those words synonyms?

SIDNEY: Yes.

ANTHRO: So it's not a positive [term]?

SIDNEY: No, it's a negative [term], as far as brilliant academic students are concerned.

> ANTHRO: Why is that?
> SIDNEY: That's just the way the school population is.

Although Sidney takes the Advanced Placement courses, he is not making much effort to get good grades; instead, he spends his time and effort developing a persona that will nullify any claims that he is a brainiac, as can be seen in the following interview excerpt:

> ANTHROPOLOGIST: Has anyone ever called you a [brainiac]?
> SIDNEY: Brainiac? No.
> ANTHRO: Why not?
> SIDNEY: Well, I haven't given them a reason to. And, too, well, I don't excel in all my classes like I *should* be—that's another reason . . . I couldn't blame it on the environment. I have come to blame it on myself—for partaking *in* the environment. But I *can* tell you that—going back to what we *were* talking about—another reason why they don't call me a "brainiac," because I'm an athlete.
> ANTHRO: So . . . if a kid is smart, for example, one of the ways to limit the negative reaction to him or her, and his or her brilliance, is . . .
> SIDNEY: Yeah, do something extracurricular in the school . . . [like] being an athlete, cheerleader squad, in the band—like that . . . Yeah, *something that's important* [emphasis added], that has something to do with—that represents your school.

Sidney admits that the fear of being known as a brainiac has negatively affected his academic effort a great deal. The fear of being discovered as an "imposter" among his friends leads him to choose carefully those persons with whom he will interact within the classroom; all of the males with whom he interacts who also take Advanced Placement courses are, like him, primarily concerned with "mak[ing] it over the hump."

He also attributes his lack of greater effort in school to his lack of will-power and time on task. And he thinks that his low performance is due to this greater emphasis on athletic achievement and his emerging manhood, and less emphasis on the core curriculum. He does not study. He spends very little time completing his homework assignments, usually 15 minutes before breakfast. On the whole, Sidney is not proud of his academic record. But he does not feel that he can change the direction of his school career because he does not want to be known as a brainiac.

The second example of an underachieving male student is *Max*. Max scored higher than many high-achieving males on the PSAT, scoring at the 58th percentile on the verbal and at the 52nd percentile on the math component. But his course grades, at all levels, have been mostly Cs with a few Bs and an occasional A. Since coming to Capital High, his grades have fallen even further from their earlier low in junior high. For example, during his first year at Capital High he earned two Fs, two Ds, one C, and one A.

Max, like Sidney, is a football player who "puts brakes," i.e., limitations, on his academic effort. He also takes most of his courses from the Advanced Placement courses for eleventh graders. However, unlike Sidney, who chose to come to Capital High because of the advanced courses, Max takes these courses only because his parents insist that he take them.

Listening to this student's responses to questions, or hearing him talk about his life experiences, one is struck by the tenacity of his desire to remain encapsulated in peer-group relations and norms. This is quite contrary to his mother's constant effort to "liberate" him from that encapsulation. Max is different from his friends because of his middle-class background. He knows that he is different, but values their friendship very much:

> We don't think the same, me and my friends. That's why I used to think that I wasn't—I used to think that I wasn't—I used to always put myself down, I wasn't good enough. Because I could—the things they'd want me to do, I didn't want to do because I knew it was wrong, and that I wouldn't get anything out of it. And, really, a cheap thrill isn't really all that much to me—really it isn't. It's just not worth it, you know. Why go through the trouble? So—that's just the way I think. I used to try and change it, but it didn't work . . . not for me, it didn't, anyways.

Because his friends are critically important to him and his sense of identity, Max not only holds on to them at the expense of his academic progress, but he also resorts to necessary role playing to ensure that he retains the integrity of his social identity. For him, role playing means underestimating his level of intelligence and insight. In fact, he argues that the role he has played over the years has become so much a part of him that he is forced at different junctures to say to himself that he must snap out of the socially constructed persona. This role—limiting his academic effort and performance—is so much a part of who he is seen to be, that Max claims it is "something like a split personality, kind, of, but it isn't."

What is the effort of these factors on Max's school career? He feels sad when he reflects on his school career thus far:

> You know, I just sacrificed a whole lot out of myself, what I could do, just to make my friends happy, you know. And it never—it just didn't work. They—you know, all of them didn't take advantage of me. They really didn't bother—it bothered me, but it wasn't that they were all trying just to take advantage of me, it was just that, you know, sometimes when I got my mind—you know, I just got—I'd get myself

psyched out, worrying about what other people thought of me. But it really doesn't matter all that much, anymore. Not as much as it did then. I guess that's just growing up.

Shelvy is our first example of the underachieving female students. Her performance on standardized tests supports her teachers' evaluation of her academic ability. On her eleventh grade CTBS, her composite score in the three major areas—reading, language, and mathematics—was the highest overall grade equivalent (OGE) possible, 13.6. Because she assumes that she will not be able to go to college (her parents are very poor), she did not see any value in trying to convince her parents to give her the five dollars needed to pay for the PSAT, and she opted not to take it.

In the elementary school her grades were "mostly VGs As, Bs and stuff like that." Despite the resistance to academic success by students in the two elementary and two junior high schools (all in the Capital community) she attended prior to coming to Capital High, she continued to obtain good grades. In fact, in the second junior high school she was placed in the only honors section of the ninth grade class. This made it much easier for her because everybody there had been identified as a potentially good student. As she puts it:

> I went to Garden [Junior High School]. That was *fairly* well, but in the eighth grade I had the problem of the same thing—everybody saying, "Well, she thinks she's smart," and all this. I had the same problem in the eighth grade. But in the ninth grade, they placed me in an all-academic section and, you know, everyone in there was smart, so it wasn't recognized—they recognized everybody as being a smart section, instead of an individual.

She made the Honor Roll during both her eighth and ninth grade years, and this pattern of academic success continued during her first year at Capital High when she earned two Bs, two As, and two Cs.

At the time of this study, however, things had changed for Shelvy. She is no longer enthusiastic about school and is not making any concerted effort to improve the level of her performance. The reason for this development is unclear. However, from her account of students' attitudes and behaviors in the school she attended and at Capital, we speculate that she finally submitted to peer pressures not to "act White." Therefore she has not resorted to the coping strategies that worked for her in earlier school years.

Speaking of her earlier school experiences, Shelvy says that her first contact with the notion of success as a risky task began in the elementary school, and probably came to full fruition during the sixth grade when, for the first time in her life, she heard the word "brainiac" used to refer to her. She says that ideally everybody wants to be a brainiac, but one is paralyzed with fear that if he or she performs well in school he or she will be discovered, and that would bring some added responsibilities and problems.

Perhaps more than any other underachieving female, Shelvy's academic performance reflects the pain and frustration associated with trying to camouflage one's abilities from peers. Having been a "good student" in elementary school, she knows firsthand how difficult it is to avoid encapsulation in anti-academic peer groups:

> In the sixth grade, it was me and these two girls, we used to hang together all the time. They used to say we was brainiacs, and no one really liked us . . . It's not something—well, *it's something that you want to be, but you don't want your friends to know* [emphasis added] . . . Because once they find out you're a brainiac, then the first thing they'll say is, "Well, she thinks she's cute, and she thinks she's smart, she thinks she's better than anyone else." So what most brainiacs do, they sit back and they know an answer, and they won't answer it . . . 'Cause, see, first thing everybody say, "Well, they're trying to show off." So they really don't—they might answer once in a while, but . . . Because if you let . . . all your friends know how smart you are, then when you take a test or something, then they're going to know you know the answer and they're going to want the answers. And if you don't give them to them, then they're going to get upset with you.

When asked how their being upset would be manifested, Shelvy replied, "Well, they might start rumors about you, might give you a bad name or something like that."

Shelvy's analysis of the dilemma of the brainiac clearly suggests that the academically successful Black student's life is fraught with conflicts and ambivalence. The fear of being differentiated and labeled as a brainiac often leads to social isolation and a social self which is hurt by negative perceptions. Essentially Shelvy claims that a student who is identified as a brainiac is more vulnerable to "social death" than one who is not.

Shelvy is more aware than many of her peers concerning why she is not performing as well academically as she could and perhaps should. As she explains it, she is keenly aware of her peers' concurrent "embracement and rejection" of school norms and behaviors. In that sense she realizes that seeking school success at Capital High is immersed in boundary-maintaining devices. It is the boundary-maintaining tendencies of her peers, which negatively sanction behaviors associated with the label "brainiac," that are negatively affecting her school performance. Her fear of being labeled a "brainiac" and burdened with all the expectations attendant thereto, as well as her negative perception of the opportunity structure, has led her to resort to lowering her effort in school. Her fear of academic excellence is readily apparent when observed in the classroom context. When she is called upon by teachers, she responds quickly and correctly; however, having learned from negative experiences associated with academic success in the elementary and junior high schools, she "puts brakes" on her academic effort to minimize bringing attention to herself.

Kaela is our second example of an underachieving female student. Kaela did not take the PSAT in the eleventh grade, so it is not one of the available measures of her academic ability. Nor did she take the CTBS. She did, however, take the Life Skills Examination, a standardized test required of all eleventh graders by the DC Public School System. In fact, she had a perfect score on that exam.

Kaela's teachers say that she not only has the ability to do the work required in their courses, but she is also more capable than most other students taking their courses. Yet, Kaela failed nearly all her major courses during her first semester at Capital High. The primary reason for her failure is her unwillingness to come to school regularly, i.e., her repeated absence from her assigned classes. For example, her English teacher was pleased with her performance, but could not give her a passing grade, because of poor attendance. Her history teacher was "forced" to give her a failing grade because of excessive absenteeism, although she scored 88 percent on the semester examination.

Kaela attended Catholic elementary and junior high schools in the Washington, DC area, and her academic records from those schools show that she was a good student and a high achiever. For example, during her ninth grade year, she earned high honors and received a full scholarship. She apparently attended school regularly before coming to Capital High. When questioned directly about her repeated absence at Capital High, Kaela says that she does not know why she and other students are absent:

> I don't really know why. I don't even know why I don't come, when I know I should come. It's just that we [Black students] don't have that much support. We don't get—I know we know that we should do things, but it's—you know, you know something pushing you. And when you don't have that, sometimes you feel like nobody cares, so why should *you* care? It gets like that sometimes. But then other times, I don't know why. Sometimes I don't want to come if I haven't done my homework. And then—I don't understand. I don't know why. I think we're scared to take responsibility and stuff. And that's because the people we keep company with, you know. And it's just—I don't know—people—when we see people, you know, and they're like role models. But they don't necessarily have to be *good* role models. And then we just settle for that. And we—I know that I don't

want to settle for that, but it's just something *in* me that won't let me do more. So I settle. I know I could make the Honor Roll here . . .

An examination of Kaela's schooling history shows that her problem probably began to develop back in Catholic schools when she started to develop a sense of collective identity. She says that she began to lose interest in her schoolwork after she found that the parochial school administrators were treating her differently from the way they treated other Black students, as if she were special. Since she, too, is a Black person, she began to seriously limit her school effort and could not be persuaded by her teachers or parents to believe that she was unlike the other Black students. Thus, while her teachers insist on treating her as an individual, Kaela sees herself first and foremost as a Black person, and it is her growing sense of identity as a Black person which has negatively affected her school performance. She appears convinced that opportunities for Black Americans are small and her personal future very limited because (a) she is Black, (b) her family is very poor and cannot pay for her college education, and (c) the competition for highly valued positions in school and the workplace is too keen for her. Therefore she decided to "put brakes" on her academic effort in order to reduce the frustration from being overqualified for the low-status jobs she thinks she will get eventually.

Kaela attributes the behaviors and low academic achievement of other black Americans at Capital High to the same factors as those operating in her situation. She says that students perceive an opportunity structure in which they are judged primarily on the basis of their race. This discourages students from persevering in their schoolwork and from academic success. As Kaela was being interviewed at a time when students were selecting their classes for the next year, she used the event to point out the effect of students' perceptions of dismal futures on their course selections:

> [The students at Capital High would try harder to make good grades in school if they thought they had a real chance.] I *know* that. Because I've heard a lot of people say, "Well, I don't know why I'm taking all these hard classes. I ain't never going to see this stuff again in my life! Why am I going to sit up here and make my record look bad, trying to take all these hard classes and get bad grades? I ain't going to need this stuff. I'm just going to take what I need to get my diploma. Forget all that other stuff. And, you know, *I thought like that for a while, too* [emphasis added]. But it's not the right way. I mean, we should try to better ourselves in any possible way. But a lot of people don't think that way.

Kaela's views of Black Americans' opportunity structure as being racially biased have contributed to her diminishing interest and effort in school.

Her refusal to put forth the necessary effort to do well in school also stems from her growing identification with the problems and concerns of Black people. Her growing racial awareness is thus inversely related to her school effort and achievement. It seems that Kaela's absence from school is one way she tries to cope with the "burden of 'acting White.' "

High-Achieving Students

Students at Capital High who are relatively successful academically also face the problem of coping with the "burden of 'acting White.' " But they have usually adopted strategies that enable them to succeed. These students decide more or less consciously (a) to pursue academic success and (b) to use specific strategies to cope with the burden of acting white.

Martin is our first example of a high-achieving male student. His scores on the standardized tests, PSAT and CTBS, are unfortunately not available to help us assess his ability. But he has a relatively good academic record. He graduated tenth in his junior high school class; and in the tenth grade at Capital High, he earned three Bs, one A–, and a D. He is a member of the school's chapter of the National Honor Society. Although Martin is still uncertain about his overall academic ability because of absence of reliable scores on standardized tests, he gets good grades in class, attends school regularly, has a positive attitude about school, and receives good evaluations from teachers.

Martin is fully aware of peer pressures to discourage male students at Capital High from striving toward academic success. The most discouraging factor, in his view, is the fear of being labeled a "brainiac" or, worse, a "pervert brainiac." To be known as a brainiac is bad enough, but to be known as a pervert brainiac is tantamount to receiving a kiss of death. For a male student to be known as a brainiac, according to Martin, is to question his manhood; to be known as a pervert brainiac leaves little doubt. He claims that there are persistent rumors that some male students taking all or a large number of the Advanced Placement courses are homosexuals; this is far less the case for male students who do not take the advanced courses. Also it is believed at Capital High that males who do *not* make good grades are less likely to be gay.

Martin says that the best strategy for a male student making good grades or wanting to succeed academically and yet escape the label of brainiac is for him to handle his school persona carefully and to cloak it in other activities that minimize hostility against academically successful students. One such "cloaking activity" is "lunching": that is, to avoid being called a brainiac and thereby bringing one's manhood into question, a male student who desires good grades will often resort to behaviors suggesting that he is a clown, comedian, or does not work very hard to earn the grades he receives.

MARTIN: Okay. Lunching is like when you be acting crazy, you know, having fun with women, you know. Okay, you still be going to class, but you—like me, okay, they call *me* crazy, 'cause I'll be having fun . . .

ANTHROPOLOGIST: Do they say you're "lunching"?

MARTIN: Yeah. Go ask [my girlfriend]. She be saying I'm lunching. 'cause I be—'cause I be doin' my homework, and I be playin' at the same time, and I get it done. I don't know how I do that.

ANTHRO: So It's important to be a clown, too—I mean, to be a comedian?

MARTIN: Yeah. Yeah, a comedian, because you—yeah.

ANTHRO: A comedian is a male? There's no doubt that a comedian is a male?

MARTIN: A male, uh-huh! 'Cause if you be all about [concerned only about] your schoolwork, right? And you know a lot of your *friends* not about it, if you don't act like a clown, your friends gonna start calling you a brainiac.

ANTHRO: And it's not good to be called a brainiac?

MARTIN: Yeah, it's—I don't want nobody to be calling *me* one, 'cause I know I ain't no brainiac. But if they call you one, you might seem odd to them. 'Cause they'll always be joning on you. See? Wen I was at Kaplan [Junior High school], that's what they called me—"brainiac," 'cause I made straight As and Bs, that's all in the First Advisory. So that's why . . .

The interview with Martin left us with the impression that he does not put forth as much effort and time as he might have were he not shackled with the burden of worrying about his peers' perceptions of him as a brainiac. Therefore, although he comes to school every day (he missed only one day during the tenth grade) and completes most of his homework, he does not do more than the officially required academic tasks.

Norris is another high-achieving male student who has developed specific strategies for coping with the burden of acting White. His performance on the verbal and math sections of the PSAT was at the 85th and 96th percentile, respectively. His scores on the CTBS are similarly impressive. His overall grade equivalent in every section—reading, language, math, reference skills, science, and social studies, as well as in every subsection—is at the college level (13.6 OGE—overall grade equivalent).

He has maintained an outstanding academic record since elementary school, where he was recommended to skip the fifth grade. He graduated from Garden Junior High as the Valedictorian of his class. He also received several ancillary awards, including "the most improved student," "the most likely to succeed," etc. He earned all As in his first semester at Capital High, taking Advanced Placement courses. His cumulative grade average is A.

How does Norris do so well in school and still cope with the burden of acting White? Norris says that he has faced the problem of coping with the burden of acting White since his elementary school days, when he discovered that he was academically ahead of other students, and that they did not like anyone doing well academically like himself. He says that what has been critically important in his acceptance by his peers, even though he is a good student, is his appearance of not putting forth much academic effort. At the elementary and junior high schools, where his peers thought that he got good grades without studying, they attributed his academic success to his "natural talent" or special gift. Therefore they did not view him as a pervert brainiac.

The public elementary school he attended was "filled with hoodlums, thugs, and the dregs of society," in his words. Fighting was a frequent pastime among the students. Under this circumstance Norris' strategy was to choose friends who would protect him in exchange for his helping them with homework assignments, tests, etc. He explains the strategy as follows:

> I didn't want to—you know, be with anybody that was like me, 'cause I didn't want to get beat up. The school I went to, Berkeley, was really rough, see? It was really tough, you know. Lived in the projects and everything, and known tough and everything. So I used to hang with them. If anybody ever came in my face and wanted to pick on me, they'd always be there to help me. So I always made sure I had at least two or three bullies to be my friends. Even though if it does mean I had to give up answers in class . . . I was willing to give up a little to get a lot. So I did that for elementary school. Then, by the time I got to junior high school, I said, "Forget it. If people don't tend to accept me the way I am, that's too bad. I don't need any friends, I have myself."

His alliance with "bullies" and "hoodlums" worked at the elementary school. At the junior high level, he had a second factor in his favor, namely, his growing athletic prowess. This helped to lessen the image of him as a pervert brainiac. But he also deliberately employed another strategy, this time acting as a clown or comedian. He explains it this way:

> In junior high school] I had to act crazy then . . . you know, nutty, kind of loony, they say . . . [the students would then say], "He's crazy"—not a *class* clown, to get on the teachers' nerves, I never did that to the— around *them*. I'd be crazy. As soon as I hit that class, it was serious business . . . Only the people who knew me knew my crazy side, when they found out I was smart, they wouldn't believe it. And the people that knew that I was smart, wouldn't believe it if they were told that I was crazy. So I went through that. I'm still like that *now*, though.

Norris continues his comedian strategy at Capital High. He says that it is important for him to employ this strategy because he wants to do well in order to go to college on scholarships.

High-achieving females use certain gender-specific strategies to cope with the burden of acting White. But, like the males, they camouflage to avoid being perceived as brainiacs. More than the males, they camouflage to avoid being perceived as brainiacs. More than the males, the female high achievers work to maintain low profiles in school. Katrina and Rita will serve as examples.

Katrina's performance on the math component of the PSAT was at the 95th percentile. Only one other student, Norris, scored higher and another student had a comparable score. Katrina's score on the verbal component was not as high, being at the 75th percentile. But her overall score far surpassed those of most other students. Her performance on the CTBS was equally impressive, with an overall grade equivalent of 13.6, or college level, in every section—math, reading, and language, and in every subsection, as well as in the ancillary sections, namely, reference skills, social studies, and science. She also performed well on the Life Skills examination, which measures students' ability to process information in nine different areas. Katrina scored 100 percent in each of the nine areas.

In the classroom her performance has been equally outstanding. She had As in all subjects except handwriting in the elementary school. Her final grades in the ninth grade (i.e., junior high school) were all As; and in the tenth grade, her first year at Capital High, her final grades were all As.

Katrina has heard of the term "brainiac" not only at Capital High, but as far back as at the elementary and junior high school levels. And she is very much aware of the nuances associated with the term. She explains:

> When they [other students] call someone a "brainiac," they mean he's always in the books. But he probably isn't always in the books. Straight A, maybe—you know, or As and Bs. A Goody-Two-Shoes with the teacher, maybe—you know, the teacher always calling on them, and they're always the leaders in the class or something.

She acknowledges that she is often referred to as a brainiac, but that she always denies it because she does not want her peers to see her that way. To treat her as a brainiac "blows her cover" and exposes her to the very forces she has sought so hard to avoid: alienation, ridicule, physical harm, and the inability to live up to the name.

How does Katrina avoid being called a brainiac and treated with hostility while at the same time managing to keep up her outstanding academic performance? Katrina admits that she has had to "put brakes" on her academic performance in order to minimize the stress she experiences. She says that she is much better at handling subject matter than at handling her peers. To solve the peer problem, she tries not to be conspicuous. As she puts it:

> Junior high, I didn't have much problem. I mean, I didn't have—there were always a lot of people in the classroom who did the work, so I wasn't like, the only one who did this assignment. So—I mean, I might do better at it, but I wasn't the only one. And so a lot of times, I'd let other kids answer—I mean, not *let* them, but . . . All right, I *let* them answer questions [laughter], and I'd hold back. So I never really got into any arguments, you know, about school and my grades or anything.

She is extremely fearful of peer reactions if she were identified as acting White. Since she wants to continue doing well in school, she chooses to "go underground," that is, not to bring attention to herself. Her reluctance to participate in Capital High's "It's Academic" Club, a TV competition program, illustrates her desire to maintain a low profile. "It's Academic" is perhaps the most "intellectual" extracurricular activity at the school. To participate in the three-person team, a student must take a test prepared by the faculty sponsoring it. The three top scorers are eligible to represent the school in the TV competition. Katrina reluctantly took the test at the suggestion of her physics teacher, the club sponsor. However, she had a prior agreement that she would not be selected to participate on the team *even if she had the top score.* She was one of the three top scorers, but because of the prior agreement was made only an alternate member of the team.

Rita, our second high-achieving female, had one of the best performances on the standardized tests given at Capital High. She had the highest score on the verbal component of the PSAT, at the 96th percentile. Her math score was not as high, being at the 62nd percentile. As a result of her high performance on the PSAT, Rita was one of only five students from Capital High nominated for the National Merit Scholarship for Outstanding Black Students. Her performance on the CTBS was equally outstanding: she scored almost at grade level, 11.8. On the Life Skills Examination, she scored higher on each of the nine areas than the minimum required.

Rita makes fairly good grades in school, although her effort and her performance are not consistent. She switches from being a good student to an average or near-average student. For example, during her first year at Capital High, she received four Cs, two Ds, and one B. But in the second year she got three As, three Bs, and one C.

The inconsistency in Rita's performance appears to be due to one of the strategies she claims to have adopted to cope with the burden of acting White, namely, irregular class attendance as a way of maintaining a low profile. She readily admits that she strategically cuts classes and makes deliberate plans for achieving her goal of getting the most in return for as little effort as possible in all her classes.

Rita's current main strategy is, however, comedic. She is seen as a clown and is often described by friends, peers and classmates as "that crazy Rita." This is true even though they know that her academic performance is among the best at the school. But her main impression on people is that she is "crazy," because of the way she interacts with peers, classmates, and even with her teachers. Rita believes that this comedic behavior enables her to cope with pressures of schoolwork and pressure from peers. The comedic strategy is unusual among the female students at Capital High; but it works for Rita just as it works for Norris: it thwarts latent hostility of peers, while allowing her to do well on some measures of school success.

To summarize, all the high-achieving students wrestle with the conflict inherent in the unique relationship of Black people with the dominant institution: the struggle to achieve success while retaining group support and approval. In school, the immediate issue is how to obtain good grades and meet the expectation of school authorities without being rejected by peers for acting White. Our examples show that successful students at Capital High generally adopt specific strategies to solve this problem.

THE BURDEN OF ACTING WHITE IN COMPARATIVE PERSPECTIVE

The burden of acting White, how Black adolescents cope with it, and its effects on their academic careers have not been generally recognized, let alone systematically studied. Nevertheless, there are references here and there suggesting that similar problems are faced by Black students in other schools and in other parts of the United States. One example from Philadelphia, that of Abdul-Jabbar, has already been cited. Another is that of E. Sargent, a journalist with the *Washington Post*, who attended public schools in Washington, DC.

Sargent describes, in a column in the *Washington Post* (Feb. 10, 1985), how he used his emerging sense of Black identity to minimize the conflicts associated with academic success among Black students. He attributes his ability to deal with the burden of acting White to his broader sense of Black American history, which he acquired *outside* the public schools. As he puts it:

> While I had always been a good student, I became a better one as a result of my sense of Black history. I began to notice that my public-school teachers very rarely mentioned Black contributions to the sciences, math, and other areas of study . . . They never talked about

ways Blacks could collectively use their education to solve the great economic and social problems facing the race.

My mind was undergoing a metamorphosis that made the world change its texture. Everything became relevant because I knew Blacks had made an impact on all facets of life. *I felt a part of things that most Blacks thought only White people had a claim to* [our emphasis]. Knowing that there is a serious speculation that Beethoven was black—a mullato [*sic*]—made me enjoy classical music. "Man, why do you listen to that junk? That's White music," my friends would say. "Wrong. Beethoven was a brother." I was now bicultural, a distinction most Americans could not claim. I could switch from boogie to rock, from funk to jazz and from rhythm-and-blues to Beethoven and Bach . . . I moved from thinking of myself as disadvantaged to realizing that I was actually "super-advantaged."

(pp. D1, D4)

Black students in desegregated and integrated schools also face the burden of acting White. A study by Petroni and Hirsch (1970) shows how the phenomenon operates in a midwestern city. They present several examples of academically successful students at Plains High School and the problems confronting them, as well as the strategies they adopt to cope with the burden of acting White. Take the case of Pat, an academically successful Black female whole dilemma they describe. Pat appears to be different from other Black students in the school, and she seems to be subjected to different kinds of pressures from Black and White students. However, she indicates that the more difficult pressures come from Black students:

I [feel] the greatest pressure from members of my own race. I'm an all A student; I'm always on the Honor Roll; I'm in Madrigals, and so on. Because of these small accomplishments, there's a tendency for the [Blacks] to think that I'm better than they are. They think I'm boasting. Take Nancy—Nancy ran for office, and I've heard other [Black students] say, "She thinks she's so good." I don't think of it this way. These small accomplishments that I've achieved aren't just for me, but they're to help the Black cause. I do things for my race, not just for myself. Most of the time, though, I don't pay too much attention to these kids. It's just a small percentage of [Blacks] anyway, who're the troublemakers, and they resent the fact that I'm dong something, and they aren't.

(Petroni & Hirsch, 1970, p. 20)

The burden of acting White becomes heavier when academically able Black students face both pressures from Blacks peers to conform, and doubts from Whites about their ability, as the following cases show. The former is described in a series of articles on adolescents' school behavior in a predominantly White suburban school system near Washington, DC, by Elsa Walsh (1984). Her account highlights the problems of high-achieving Black students in integrated schools, especially the paralyzing effects of coping with the burden of acting White.

Our first case is that of "K," who Walsh identifies as a 13-year-old, academically gifted, female, Black student. Walsh describes K's feeling of loneliness and isolation in the predominantly White honors courses to which she was assigned. She also points out that Black students at the school reject K and often accuse her of being "stuck up" and thinking she is "too good for them." At the same time, K's White classmates doubt that she actually has the ability to do the work in the honors courses. All of these factors erode K's confidence.

An example of a similar dilemma is Gray's (1985) description of the futility of her efforts to minimize her "blackness" through academic excellence in a predominantly White school and community:

> No matter how refined my speech, or how well educated or assimi-lated [sic] I become, I fear I will always be an outsider. I'm almost like a naturalized alien—in this place but not of it . . . During my pompous period, I dealt with my insecurities by wearing a veil of superiority. Except around my family and neighbors, I played the role—the un-Black.
>
> To Whites I tried to appear perfect—I earned good grades and spoke impeccable English, was well-mannered and well-groomed. Poor whites, however, made me nervous. They seldom concealed their concept for blacks, especially "uppity" ones like myself . . . To blacks, I was all of the above and extremely stuck up. I pretended not to see them on the street, spoke to them only when spoken to and cringed in the presence of blacks being loud in front of the whites. The more integrated my Catholic grammar school became, the more uncomfortable I was there. I had heard white parents on TV, grum-bling about blacks ruining their schools; I didn't want anyone to think that I, too, might bring down Sacred Heart Academy. So I behaved, hoping that no one would associated [sic] me with "them."
>
> (Gray, 1985, pp. E1, E5)

In summary, Black students elsewhere, like those at Capital High, in predominantly Black schools as well as in integrated schools, appear to face the burden of acting White. Under this circumstance, students who are clever enough to use certain deliberate strategies succeed in "making it." In predominantly Black schools, they succeed in protecting them-selves from the antagonisms of Black peers who define their academic striving negatively as acting White. In integrated schools, their problem is further complicated by the negative and often implicit assumptions of Whites about the intellectual ability of Black people. In such schools, White Americans' doubts may erode the academic confidence of Black students who are taking "White courses."

Other Minority Groups

Other subordinate minorities in the United States and elsewhere also appear to face a similar problem. There are indications, for instance, that American Indians and Mexican Americans perceive the public schools as an agent of assimilation into the White American or Anglo cultural frame of reference; and that these minorities consider such assimilation or linear acculturation to be detrimental to the integrity of their cultures, languages, and identities (Virgil, 1980; Ogbu & Matute-Bianchi, 1986). Some Mexican-American students have been reported to say that school learning is "doing the anglo thing" and to appear to resist learning what is taught in the school context (Ogbu & Matute-Bianchi, 1986; Matute-Bianchi, 1986).

The problem of coping with the burden of acting White has also been reported for some American Indian students. Studies by Erickson and Mohatt (1982) among Odawa Indian students, and by Philips (1983) among Warm Springs Reservation Indian students suggest that older elementary school students are already affected by it. These children come to the classroom "resisting" school rules and standard practices. That is, they enter the classroom with a sort of cultural convention that dictates that they should not adopt the rules of behavior and standard practices expected of children in the public schools taught by the White teachers. This indicates that for them perhaps the rules and practices are considered White.

Outside the United States, there are also subordinate minorities who perceive the learning of the formal school curriculum as a *subtractive process*, i.e., as one-way acculturation into the cultural frame of reference of the dominant group members of their society. Among these subordinate minorities are Australian Aborigines (Bourke, 1983), the Buraku Outcastes in Japan (DeVos & Wagatsuma, 1967), some Indians of South American (Varese, 1985), and the Maoris of New Zealand (Smith, 1983). Good ethnographic studies of actual school and classroom attitudes and behaviors of these minorities are needed to determine the strategies of the students for coping with the burden of acting like the dominant group.

SUMMARY AND IMPLICATIONS

We have suggested in this paper that Black students' academic efforts are hampered by both external factors and within-group factors. We have tried to show that Black students who are academically successful in the face of these factors have usually adopted specific strategies to avoid them. Although we recognize and have described elsewhere in detail the external, including school, factors which adversely affect Black adolescents' school performance (Forham, 1982a, 1985; Ogbu, 1974, 1978), our focus in this paper is on the within-group factors, especially on how Black students respond to other Black students who are trying to "make it" academically.

We began by noting that the instrumental factors postulated in our earlier cultural-ecological explanation of minority school performance, namely, inferior schooling, limited opportunity structure, and such peoples' own perceptions of and responses to schooling, are important, but that there are additional factors involved. We identified the additional factors as an oppositional collective or social identity and an oppositional cultural frame of reference, both symbolized, in the case of Black Americans, by a fictive kinship system.

Fictive kinship is, then, not only a symbol of social identity for Black Americans, it is also a medium of boundary maintenance vis-à-vis White Americans. The school experience of Black children is implicated because, under the circumstance, schooling is perceived by Blacks, especially by Black adolescents, as learning to act White, as acting White, or as trying to cross cultural boundaries. And, importantly, school learning is viewed as a subtractive process. In our view, then, the academic learning and performance problems of Black children arise not only from a limited opportunity structure and Black people's responses to it, but also from the way Black people attempt to cope with the "burden of 'acting White.' " The sources of their school difficulties—perceptions of and responses to the limited opportunity structure and the burden of acting White—are particularly important during the adolescent period in the children's school careers.

We chose to focus our analysis on the burden of acting White and its effects on the academic effort and performance of Black children because it seems to us to be a very important but as yet widely unrecognized dilemma of Black students, particularly Black adolescents. In other words, while we fully recognize the role of external forces—societal and school forces—in creating academic problems for the students, *we also argue that how Black students respond to other Black students who are trying to make it is also important in determining the outcome of their education.*

In the case study of Capital High School in Washington, DC, we showed that coping with the burden of acting White affects the academic performance of both underachieving and high-achieving students. Black students who are encapsulated in the fictive kinship system or oppositional process experience greater difficulty in crossing cultural boundaries; i.e., in accepting standard academic attitudes and practices of the school and in investing sufficient time and effort in pursuing their educational goals. Some of the high-achieving students do not identify with the fictive kinship system; others more or less deliberately adopt sex-specific strategies to camouflage their academic pursuits and achievements.

The strategies of the academically successful students include engaging in activities that mute perceptions of their being preoccupied with academic excellence leading eventually to individual success outside the group, i.e., eventual upward mobility. Among them are athletic activities (which are regarded as "Black activities") and other "team"-oriented activities, for male students. Other high-achieving students camouflage their academic effort by clowning. Still others do well in school by acquiring the protection of "bullies" and "hoodlums" in return for assisting the latter in their schoolwork and homework. In general, academically successful Black students at Capital High (and probably elsewhere) are careful not to brag about their achievements or otherwise bring too much attention to themselves. We conclude, however, from this study of high-achieving students at Capital High, that they would do much better if they did not have to divert time and effort into strategies designed to camouflage their academic pursuit.

There are several implications of our analysis, and the implications are at different levels. As this analysis clearly demonstrates, the first and critically important change must occur in the existing opportunity structure, through an elimination of the job ceiling and related barriers. Changes in the opportunity structure are a prerequisite to changes in the behaviors and expectations of Black adolescents for two salient reasons: (1) to change the students' perceptions of what is available to them as adult workers in the labor force and (2) to minimize the exacerbation of the extant achievement problem of Black adolescents who are expected to master the technical skills taught and condoned in the school context but who are, nonetheless, unable to find employment in areas where they demonstrate exemplary expertise. Barring changes in the opportunity structure, the perceptions, behaviors, and academic effort of Black adolescents are unlikely to change to the extent necessary to have a significant effect on the existing boundary-maintaining mechanisms in the community. Therefore, until the perceptions of the nature and configuration of the opportunity structure change (see J. Williams, 1985), the response of Black students in the school context is likely to continue to be one which suggests that school achievement is a kind of risk that necessitates strategies enabling them to cope with the "burden of acting White." Second, educational barriers, both the gross and subtle mechanisms by which schools differentiate the academic careers of Black and White children, should be eliminated.

Third, and particularly important in terms of our analysis, *the unique academic learning and performance problems created by the burden of acting White should be recognized and made a target of educational policies and remediation effort.* Both the schools and the Black community have important roles to play in this regard. School personnel should try to understand the influence of the fictive kinship system in the students' perceptions of learning and the standard academic attitudes and practices or behaviors expected. The schools should then develop programs, including appropriate counseling, to help the students learn to divorce academic pursuit from the idea of acting White. The schools should also reinforce Black identity in a manner compatible with academic pursuits, as in the case of Sargent (1985).

The Black community has an important part to play in changing the situation. The community should develop programs to teach Black children that academic pursuit is not synonymous with one-way acculturation into a White cultural frame of reference or acting White. To do this effectively, however, the Black community must reexamine its own perceptions and interpretations of school learning. Apparently, Black children's general perception that academic pursuit is "acting White" is learned in the Black community. The ideology of the community in regard to the cultural meaning of schooling is, therefore, implicated and needs to be reexamined. Another thing the Black community can do is to provide visible and concrete evidence for Black youths that the community appreciates and encourages academic effort and success. Cultural or public recognition of those who are academically successful should be made a frequent event, as is generally done in the case of those who succeed in the fields of sports and entertainment.

ACKNOWLEDGMENTS

The research and preparation of the paper were made possible by grants from the National Institute of Education (NIE-G-82 0037) and the Spencer Foundation, by a Dissertation Research Grant from The American University, Washington, DC, and by the Faculty Research Fund, University of California, Berkeley. We wish to thank the District of Columbia Public School System and the faculty, staff, and students at Capital High (a pseudonym), without whose cooperation and assistance this study would not have been possible. We are grateful to Dr. John L. Johnson of the University of the District of Columbia for his characterization of the research effort as one which centers around how Black adolescents struggle with the "burden of 'acting White.' " An earlier version of the paper was presented by Fordham at the 84th Annual Meeting of the American Anthropological Association, Washington, DC, December 5, 1985.

NOTES

*   This paper is based on Fordham's two-year ethnographic study as part of doctoral dissertation requirements.
1   Capital High and all other proper names are pseudonyms.

REFERENCES

Abdul-Jabbar, K., & Knobles, P. (1983). *Giant steps: The autobiography of Kareem Abdul-Jabbar*. New York: Bantam Books.
Acuna, R. (1972). *Occupied America: The Chicano's struggle toward liberation*. San Francisco: Canfield Press.
Anderson, J. D. (1975). Education and the manipulation of black workers. In W. Feinberg & H. Rosemont, Jr. (Eds.), *Work, technology, and education: Dissenting essays in the intellectual foundations of American foundation*. Chicago: University of Illinois Press.
Berreman, G. D. (1960). Caste in India and the United States. *The American Journal of Sociology, 66*, 120–127.
Bloom, B. S., Davis, A., & Hess, R. (1965). *Compensatory education for cultural deprivation*. New York: Holt.
Bourke, C. J. (1983). Reactions to these concepts from aboriginal Australia. In OECD (ed.), *The education of minority groups: An enquiry into problems and practices of fifteen countries* (pp. 317–335). Paris: OECD, Center for Educational Research and Innovation.
Brain, J. J. (1972). Kinship terms. *Man, 7*(1), 137–138.
Bullock, H. A. (1970). *A history of Negro education in the South: From 1619 to the present*. New York: Praeger.
Castile, G. P., & Kushner, G. (Eds.) (1981). *Persistent peoples: Cultural enclaves in perspective*. Tucson: University of Arizona Press.
Coleman, J. S., Campbell, E. R., Hobson, C. J., McPartland, J., Mood, A. M., Wernfield, F. D., & York, R. I. (1966). *Equality of educational opportunity*. Washington, DC: U.S. Government Printing Office.
DeVos, G. A. (1984). *Ethnic Persistence and Role Degradation: An Illustration from Japan*. Prepared for the American-Soviet Symposium on Contemporary Ethnic Processes in the USA and the USSR, New Orleans, April 14–16. Unpublished ms.
DeVos, G. A. (1967). Essential elements of caste: psychological determinants in structural theory. In G. A. DeVos & H. Wagatsuma (Eds.), *Japan's invisible race: Caste in culture and personality* (pp. 332–384). Berkeley: University of California Press.
DeVos, G. A., & Wagatsuma, H. (Eds.) (1967). *Japan's invisible race: Caste in culture and personality*. Berkeley: University of California Press.

Drake, S. C., & Cayton, H. (1970). *Black metropolis*. New York: Harcourt, Brace.

Erickson, F., & Mohatt, J. (1982). Cultural organization of participant structure in two classrooms of Indian students. In G. D. Spindler (Ed.), *Doing the ethnography of schooling: Educational anthropology in action* (pp. 132–175). New York: Holt.

Folb, E. A. (1980). *Runnin' down some lines: The language and culture of Black teenagers*. Cambridge, MA: Harvard University Press.

Fordham, S. (1985). *Black student school success as related to fictive kinship*. Final Report. The National Institute of Education, Washington, DC.

Fordham, S. (1984). *Ethnography in a Black high school: Learning not to be a native*. A paper presented at the 83rd Annual Meeting, American Anthropological Association, Denver, Nov. 14–18.

Fordham, S. (1982a). *Black student school success as related to fictive kinship: an ethnographic study in the Washington, DC public school system*. A research proposal submitted to the National Institute of Education.

Fordham, S. (1982b). *Cultural inversion and Black children's school performance*. Paper presented at the 81st Annual Meeting, American Anthropological Association, Washington, DC, Dec. 3–7.

Fordham, S. (1981). *Black student school success as related to fictive kinship: A study in the Washington, DC public school system*. A dissertation proposal submitted to the Department of Anthropology, The American University.

Freed, S. A. (1973). Fictive kinship in a Northern Indian village. *Ethnology*, 11(1), 86–103.

Gray, J. (1985, March 17). A Black American princess: New game, new rules. *The Washington Post*, pp. E1, E5.

Green, V. (1981). Blacks in the United States: The creation of an enduring people? In G. P. Castile & G. Kushner (Eds.), *Persistent peoples: Cultural enclaves in perspective* (pp. 69–77). Tucson: University of Arizona Press.

Haley, A. (1976). *Roots: The saga of an American family*. Garden City, NY: Doubleday.

Haskins, K. (1976). You have no right to put a kid out of school. *The Urban Review*, 8(4), 273–287.

Holt, G. S. (1972). "Inversion" in Black communication. In T. Kochman (Ed.), *Rappin' and stylin' out: Communication in urban Black America*. Chicago: University of Illinois Press.

Hunter, D. (1980, August 18). Ducks vs. hard rocks. *Newsweek*, pp. 14–15.

Jensen, A. R. (1969). How much can we boost IQ and scholastic achievement? *Harvard Educational Review*, 39, 1–123.

LeVine, R. A. (1967). *Dreams and deeds: Achievement motivation in Nigeria*. Chicago: University of Chicago Press.

Liebow, E. (1967). *Tally's corner*. Boston: Little, Brown.

Matute-Bianchi, M. D. (1986). *Variations in patterns of school performance among Mexican, Chicano and Japanese youth*. Santa Cruz, CA: Merrill College, University of California. Unpublished ms.

Myrdal, G. (1944). *An American dilemma: The Negro problem and modern democracy*. New York: Harper.

Norbeck, E., & Befu, H. (1958). Informal fictive kinship in Japan. *American Anthropologist*, 60, 102–117.

Ogbu, J. U. (1987). Variability in minority responses to schooling: non-immigrants vs. immigrants. In G. D. Spindler (Ed.), *Education and cultural process*.

Ogbu, J. U. (1986a). Class stratification, racial stratification and schooling. In L. Weis (Ed.), *Race, class and schooling. Special studies in comparative education*, #17, pp. 6–35. Comparative Education Center, State University of New York at Buffalo.

Ogbu, J. U. (1986b). *Cross-cultural study of minority education: contributions from Stockton research*. 23rd Annual J. William Harris Lecture, School of Education, University of the Pacific, Stockton, Calif.

Ogbu, J. U. (1984). *Understanding community forces affecting minority students' academic effort*. Paper prepared for the Achievement Council, Oakland, Calif.

Ogbu, J. U. (1983). Minority status and schooling in plural societies. *Comparative Education Review*, 27(2), 168–190.

Ogbu, J. U. (1982). Cultural discontinuities and schooling. *Anthropology and Education Quarterly*, 13(4), 290–307.

Ogbu, J. U. (1981). *Schooling in the ghetto: An ecological perspective on community and home influences*. Prepared for NIE Conference on Follow Through, Philadelphia, Feb. 10–11.

Ogbu, J. U. (1980). *Cultural differences vs. alternative cultures: A critique of "cultural discontinuity" hypothesis in classroom ethnographies*. A paper presented at the 79th Annual Meeting, American Anthropological Association, Washington, DC.

Ogbu, J. U. (1978). *Minority education and Caste: The American system in cross-cultural perspective*. New York: Academic Press.

Ogbu, J. U. (1974). *The next generation: An ethnography of education in an urban neighborhood*. New York: Academic Press.

Ogbu, J. U., & Matute-Bianchi, M. E. (1986). Understanding sociocultural factors in education: knowledge, identity, and adjustment. In *Beyond language: Sociocultural factors in schooling, language, and minority students*. California State Department of Education. Los Angeles: Education Dissemination and Assessment center, California State University, Los Angeles, pp. 71–143.

Petroni, F. A., & Hirsch, E. A. (1970). *Two, four, six, eight, when you gonna integrate?* New York: Behavioral Publications.

Philips, S. U. (1983). *The invisible culture: Communication in classroom and community on the Warm Springs Indian Reservation*. New York: Longman.

Pitt-Rivers, J. (1968). Pseudo-kinship. In D. L. Sills (Ed.), *The International encyclopedia of social science*. New York: Macmillan.

Sargent, E. (1985). Freeing myself: discoveries that unshackle the mind. *The Washington Post*, Feb. 10.

Schmidt, F. H. (1970). *Spanish surname American employment in the Southwest*. Washington, DC: U.S. Government Printing Office.

Shimkin, D. B., Shimkin, E. M., & Frate, D. A. (Eds.) (1978). *The extended family in Black societies*. The Hague: Mouton.

Smith, A. F. (1983). A response for the Maori population of New Zealand. In *The education of minority groups: An enquiry into problems and practices of fifteen countries* (pp. 293–315). Paris: OECD, Center for Educational Research and Innovation.

Spicer, E. H. (1971). Persistent cultural systems: a comparative study of identity systems that can adapt to contrasting environments. *Science, 174,* 795–800.

Spicer, E. H. (1966). The process of cultural enclavement in Middle America. Proceedings, *36th Congreso Internacional de Americanistas,* Vol. 3, pp. 267–279. Seville.

Spicer, E. H. (1962). *Cycles of conquest: The impact of Spain, Mexico and the United States on the Indians of the Southwest, 1533–1960.* Tucson: University of Arizona Press.

Spivey, D. (1978). *Schooling for the new slavery: Black industrial education, 1868–1915.* Westport, CT: Greenwood Press.

Stack, C. (1974). *All our kin: Strategies for survival in a Black community.* New York: Harper & Row.

Styron, W. (1966). *The confessions of Nat Turner.* New York: Random House.

Varese, S. (1985). Cultural development in ethnic groups: anthropological explorations in education. *International Social Science Journal, 37*(2), 201–216.

Virgil, J. D. (1980). *From Indians to Chicanos: A sociocultural history.* St. Louis: C. V. Mosby.

Walsh, E. (1984). Trouble at thirteen: Being Black poses special problems. *The Washington Post,* April 24, pp. A1, A6.

Weis, L. (1985). *Between two worlds: Black students in an urban community college.* Boston: Routledge & Kegan Paul.

Williams, J. (1985). The vast gap between black and white visions of reality. *The Washington Post* (March 31), pp. K1, K4.

Williams, M. D. (1981). *On the street where I lived.* New York: Holt, Rinehart & Winston.

Contributors

Antwi Akom is Assistant Professor of Urban Sociology and Africana Studies and Co-Director of Educational Equity at the Cesar Chavez Institute, San Francisco State University. He received his undergraduate degree at University of California at Berkeley, his Masters in Education and teaching credential from Stanford University, and Ph.D. in sociology from the University of Pennsylvania in 2004. His research interests include: racial identity formation, youth culture, poverty, sociology of education, and African Diaspora. He is winner of the 2002 AERA minority dissertation award and has served as a state-sponsored consultant examining educational inequality in high poverty low achieving schools. Dr. Akom's articles have appeared in numerous journals and publications, including *Sociology of Education*, the *International Journal of Qualitative Studies in Education*, as well as popular magazines such as *Blaze* and *The Nation*.

David A. Bergin is Associate Professor of Educational Psychology at the University of Missouri-Columbia. He was also a visiting research assistant professor at the University of Illinois Urbana-Champaign for one year and taught at the University of Toledo for 13 years. His research focuses on the study of motivation for learning in various settings and manifestations, including studies of kindergartners using computers, special programs for students of color, the influence of achievement goals on college students, and the development of hands-on engineering activities for high school students.

Philip J. Cook is ITT/Sanford Professor of Public Policy, and Professor of Economics and Sociology, at Duke University. He served as director and chair of Duke's Sanford Institute of Public Policy in 1985–89, and again in 1997–99. He has served in a variety of capacities with the National Academy of Sciences, including membership on expert panels dealing with alcohol-abuse prevention, with violence, with school rampage shootings, and with prevention of underage drinking. He also served on the NRC's Committee on Law and Justice, and is currently a member of the Division Committee for the Behavioral and Social Sciences and Education. He has co-authored two other books: with Charles Clotfelter on the state lotteries (*Selling Hope: State Lotteries in America*, Harvard University Press, 1989), and with Robert H. Frank on the causes and consequences of the growing inequality of earnings (*The Winner-Take-All Society*, The Free Press, 1995), which was named a "Notable Book of the Year, 1995" by the *New York Times Book Review*. He is a member of the Institute of Medicine of the National Academy of Sciences.

Helen C. Cooks is Associate Professor of Social Foundations, College of Education, Assistant Vice President of EXCELLENCE Programs (TOLEDO EXCEL, PREP/TECH, GEAR UP, TRIO Upward Bound and TRIO Student Support Services) at the University of Toledo, in Toledo, Ohio. Her experience includes fifteen years teaching in the College of Education, fifteen years directing TOLEDO EXCEL, six years as Assistant Director of Student Development at the University, and a year as Director of Talent Search at Bowling Green State University. She holds an earned doctorate in Social Foundations of Education from the University of Toledo, and has published and presented research papers on various educational/cultural issues affecting minority student achievement, her area of continuing research.

Linwood H. Cousins is Associate Professor and Chair of the Department of Social Work and Communications Disorder at Longwood University, Virginia. He is a social worker and cultural anthropologist with a variety of research and practice interests. He teaches social work practice courses that focus on families and communities, research, human diversity, and human development. His research centers on how race, ethnicity, and social class, as sociocultural processes, influence the engagement of African Americans and other ethnic groups in education, schooling and community life. He is co-author of *African Americans in Michigan*.

Astrid Davis graduated from the University of California at Berkeley with a degree in Anthropology. She conducted fieldwork with Professor John Ogbu in Shaker Heights, Ohio and contributed to the publication *Black American Students in an Affluent Suburb: A study of Academic Disengagement*. Astrid currently works for a minority owned business that focuses on the development of affordable housing projects in urban communities.

Donna Deyhle is a Professor in the Department of Educational Studies and the Ethnic Studies Program, and past Co-Director of the American Indian Resource Center, at the University of Utah. Her major professional interests are anthropology and education, cultural conflict, racism, critical race theory, the education of American Indians, and Navajos. Her research and field work has focused on educational issues in cross-cultural settings of Brazil, Peru, Australia, and various American Indian reservations in the United States. She has taught on-site teacher training programs on the Navajo reservation and at Laguna, Acoma, and Zuni Pueblos. Her publications include "Navajo Youth and Anglo Racism: Cultural Integrity and Resistance" in *Harvard Educational Review* (1995), "Culture and Child Development: Navajo Youth and the Middle School" (with M. LeCompte), in *Theory into Practice* (1994), which earned an award for the Educational Press Association of America. Most recently she co-edited a special issue on Critical Race Theory and Education (with L. Parker, S. Villenas, and K. Nebeker) in the *International Journal of Qualitative Studies in Education* (1998), and (with Parker and Villenas) *Race Is, Race Isn't: Critical Race Theory and Qualitative Studies in Education* (1999). In 2002 she was awarded the George and Louise Spindler Award from the Council of Anthropology and Education, American Anthropology Association, for a distinguished career in Education and Anthropology.

Douglas B. Downey is Associate Professor of Sociology at the Ohio State University. His research addresses issues of stratification with an emphasis on education and family. Currently, he is developing a conceptual model to explain gender differences in school performance (with Anastasia Vogt-Yuan), testing theories of gendered behavior by comparing parenting behavior and children's outcomes in single-mother and single-father households (with Mikaela J. Dufur and James W. Ainsworth), exploring the role of schooling in shaping inequality by making seasonal comparisons (with Beckett Broh), estimating the effect of siblings on interpersonal skills across the life course (with Dennis J. Condron), and studying the consequences of delayed entry into kindergarten for stratification (with Lisa N. Hickman).

George Farkas is Professor of Sociology, Demography, and Education at the Pennsylvania State University. His research focuses on schooling inequality and how it can be reduced. His tutoring program, Reading One-to-One, helped invent President Clinton's America Reads initiative. His most recent book was *Human Capital or Cultural Capital? Ethnicity and Poverty Groups in an Urban School District* (Aldine de Gruyter, 1996). His articles have appeared in the *American Sociological Review*, the *American Journal of Sociology*, the *American Educational Research Journal*, *Brookings Papers on Educational Policy*, *The Annual Review of Sociology*, and other journals. From 1996 to 1999, he was the editor of the *Rose Monograph Series of the American Sociological Association*.

Signithia Fordham is Associate Professor and Susan B. Anthony Professor of Gender and Women's Studies at the University of Rochester, NY. She was a Visiting Fellow in African & African-American Studies at Yale University in 1988–1989, the first Presidential Fellow in the Afro-American Studies Program at Princeton University in 1991–1992 and also taught at Rutgers, UMBC and UCONN. She conducted field research in 1981–1984 in a public high school in Washington, DC supported by grants from the Spencer Foundation, NSF, and the OERI (formerly the NIE). Her publications include her ethnography *Blacked Out: Dilemmas of Race, Identity and Success at Capital High* (University of Chicago Press, 1996); "Black Students' success: Coping with the Burden of Acting White" (with John Ogbu [1986]); "Why Can't Sonya (and Kwame) Fail Math" (2000); "Speaking Standard English from Nine to Three: Language Usage as Guerrilla Warfare at Capital High" (1998); and "Those Loud Black Girls: (Black) Women, Silence, and Gender 'Passing' in the Academy" (1993). Race, gender and identity politics are among her research interests and current projects include *Passin' for Black: Performing Kinship, Race and Identity in the Imagined Black Community* (on race); *Help!! My Girl Friends Are My Enemies: On Relational Aggression and the PO MO (Post Modern [Black]) Girl's Academic Performance)* (gender); and "*Acting White after Capital High*", a longitudinal study of the achievements and failures of the key informants at Capital High.

Kevin Michael Foster is Assistant Professor of the Department of Curriculum and Instruction, and Cultural Studies in Education at the University of Texas at Austin. He is an educational anthropologist whose work includes three interrelated interests. First, he looks at the social, cultural and structural factors affecting African Americans students' educational outcomes. Second, he looks at the intersection of race and sports in education settings. Third, he considers the potential and actual impact of the black racial uplift tradition among African American students. His ultimate goals are (1) to identify the norms and values that facilitate student success as well as the structural barriers that hinder success, and (2) to turn those findings into concrete programs and policies that positively impact students' educational attainment.

Vinay Harpalani is currently a 2nd year law student at New York University School of Law. He earned his Masters of Science in Education, Masters of Bioethics and Ph.D in Education, all from University of Pennsylvania.

Lea Hubbard is Associate Professor in the foundation area of Learning and Teaching Program in the School of Education at University of

California, San Diego. She has written and co-authored a number of articles and books on education reform and school success.

Cynthia Hudley is Professor of Education at University of California, Santa Barbara Gervirtz Graduate School of Education. Her research interest is children's social perception and social behavior in school and community settings. She has written extensively and conducted research on peer interactions and social determinants of children's achievement motivation. She has been Principal Investigator on a variety of research projects, including a CDC implementation and evaluation of the BrainPower curriculum.

Miles Anthony Irving is Assistant Professor of Education Psychology and Special Education at Georgia State University. Prior to earning his doctorate, he taught high school in Oakland, California. His research focuses on the investigation of the impact of cultural and social variables on human agency and cognition. He is specifically interested in the relationship between identity, achievement, and self-efficacy.

Jens Ludwig is Professor of Public Policy and Associate Dean for Public Policy Admissions at Georgetown University, and is also a Faculty Research Fellow at the National Bureau of Economic Research. He has been a visiting scholar at both the Northwestern University/University of Chicago Joint Center for Poverty Research and the Brookings Institution, and a National Academy of Education/Spencer Foundation Postdoctoral Fellow. Ludwig currently serves on the Policy Council (board of directors) of the Association for Public Policy Analysis and Management, and on the editorial boards of the *Journal of Policy Analysis and Management* and the *Journal of Quantitative Criminology*. His research on gun violence and gun control has been published in leading scholarly and scientific journals, presented to state legislatures and committees in California, Kansas and Minnesota, and featured in articles and reports by major media outlets.

Hugh Mehan is Professor of Teacher Education and Director of the Center for Research on Educational Equity, Access, and Teaching Excellence (CREATE) at UCSD. He has studied classroom organization, educational testing, tracking and untracking, computer use in schools and the construction of identities such as the "competent student." He has worked closely with K-12 educators to insure that excellent educational opportunities are available to all children. He has authored and co-edited several books, including *Extending School Reform: From One School to Many* (with Amanda Datnow and Lea Hubbard); *The Reality of Ethnomethodology, Learning Lessons, Handicapping the Handicapped, and Constructing School Success* and *Language Use and School Performance, The Write Help, The Social*

Organization of Intellectual Behavior. He is a member of the National Academy of Education and the recipient of a number of awards for outstanding teaching at UCSD, including the Muir College "Most Valuable Professor" (MVP) award in 2001.

Mary Lynne McGovern is Academic Advisor of Shaker Heights High School in Ohio where she helps develop projects and programs to address the achievement gap between Black and White students. She has been the co-advisor, along with fellow faculty member Hubert McIntyre, for the Minority Achievement Committee (MAC) scholars since its inception in 1990. McGovern and McIntyre have made presentations on the MAC program at national professional meetings and have advised many school districts on creating similar programs. McGovern was a teacher at Shaker Heights High School prior to becoming an Academic Advisor.

Roslyn Arlin Mickelson is Professor of Sociology at the University of North Carolina at Charlotte. Her research focuses upon the political economy of schooling and school reform, particularly the relationships among race, ethnicity, gender, class, and educational processes and outcomes. With support from the National Science Foundation and the Ford Foundation, she examined the equity effects of market-oriented educational reforms on students from low-income and ethnic minority families. Currently, she is investigating the effects of segregation, including racially-identifiable tracking, on academic outcomes. Her book, *Children on the Streets of the Americas: Globalization, Homelessness, and Education in the United States, Brazil, and Cuba* (2000) is published by Routledge.

Suzette L. Speight is Associate Professor of Counseling Psychology in the Department of Leadership, Foundations, and Counseling Psychology at Loyola University Chicago where she has been since 1991. She teaches courses such as Multicultural Counseling, Ethics and Legal Issues in Counseling Psychology, Identity and Pluralism, Psychology of Oppression, and Professional Issues for Counselors. Her research and scholarly interests include the psychology of oppression, identity development, multicultural counseling, and suicide in the African American community.

Margaret Beale Spencer is a GSE Board of Overseers at the University of Pennsylvania. She is Professor of Education and Psychology, Director of Interdisciplinary Studies in Human Development, CHANGES and W.E.B. Du Bois Collective Research Institute. Dr. Spencer has published numerous books, articles and chapters since 1973, and received more than two dozen proposals funded by several foundations and federal agencies (e.g., the National Institute of Mental Health [NIMH], the

National Science Foundation [NSF], and the Office of Educational Research Improvement [OERI]). She serves on several editorial boards, national committees, and as a trustee on Boards for the Foundation for Child Development (FCD) and National 4 H Council. She is the recipient of numerous awards, including Fellow status of Divisions 7, 15, and 45 of the American Psychological Association and most recently, International Fellow in Applied Developmental Science at the Eliot-Pearson Department of Child Development at Tufts University (February 2002) and the International Fellows Award in Applied Developmental Science by Tufts University, endowed by the Bergstrom family (2001) and the Janet Helms Award for Mentoring and Scholarship in Psychology and Education by the Columbia University Teachers College Winter Roundtable (March 2000, NYC).

April Taylor is Assistant Professor, Child and Adolescent Development at California State University Northridge. Her research interests lie in the general domain of the development of motivation and more specifically concern motivation for academic achievement among urban minority youth. Her research examines social, cultural, and social-psychological influences on achievement motivation, and the identification of theory guided motivation-enhancing practices. She is currently examining how oppositional identity may moderate the interaction between students' gender and ethnicity and their value for academic achievement, achievement outcomes, and peer perceptions. In addition, she is qualitatively examining African American and Latino middle school students' concept of success—what they think it means to be successful among members of their ethnic group.

Anita Jones Thomas is Assistant Professor of Psychology at Loyola University, Chicago. She is also a counseling Psychologist with specialization in multicultural counseling and family therapy. Her research interests include racial identity, racial socialization, and parenting issues for African Americans. She has also conducted training seminar and workshops on multicultural issues. She is associate professor at Northeastern Illinois University, where she teaches courses in multicultural issues, family therapy, professional identity, and ethics. Her research interests include racial identity, racial socialization, and parenting issues for African Americans. She has also conducted training seminars and workshops on multicultural issues for state and national professional organizations in counseling and psychology, hospitals and corporations, as well as served as a consultant for human service organizations.

Angela Valenzuela is Associate Professor in Education and Mexican American Studies at the University of Texas at Austin. Her book,

Subtractive Schooling: U.S.–Mexican Youth and the Politics of Caring recently won the American Educational Research Association's Outstanding Book Award. At this time, she is involved in a research project studying the concept of additive schooling with a focus on effective teaching practices with respect to Latino youth located in reform-oriented, inner-city Houston schools. As the recipient of the University of Houston's Center for Mexican American Studies Visiting Scholars' award for 1998–99, she is currently working on a study called, "Becoming Additive." This study evaluates the history and process of whole-school reform in two inner-city schools which have recently received awards from the Houston Annenberg Challenge Foundation to enable further their reformist agendas. Both schools feature dual language programs which have enhanced the achievement of Latino youth in these schools.

Irene Villanueva is a researcher and co-author of *Constructing School Success: The consequences of untracking low achievement students.*

Lois Weis is SUNY Distinguished Professor in the Department of Educational Leadership and Policy at the University of Buffalo Graduate School of Education, New York and is the author or co-author of numerous books and articles pertaining to social class, race, gender and schooling in the United States. Her most recent books include *Silenced Voices and Extraordinary Conversations: Re-Imagining Schools* (Teachers College Press, 2003, with Michelle Fine); *The Unknown City: The Lives of Poor and Working Class Young Adults* (Beacon Press, 1998, with Michelle Fine); *Speed Bumps: A Student Friendly Guide to Qualitative Research* (Teachers College Press, 2000, with Michelle Fine); and *Beyond Black and White: New Faces and Voices in US Schools* (State University of New York Press, 1997, with Maxine Seller). She sits on numerous editorial boards and is the editor of the Power, Social Identity and Education book series with SUNY Press.

Karen McCurtis Witherspoon is Associate Professor of Psychology at Chicago State University (CSU). She teaches courses in counseling. Her research interests are in identity, mental health and cognitive self-appraisal. She has received funding from the National Institute of Mental Health to study the role of oppression in mental health issues for African Americans. As a licensed psychologist, she maintains her clinical expertise through part-time consulting with various public schools and social service agencies.

Index

Please note that references to Notes will have the letter "n" following the note. Any page references to non-textual information such as Figures will be in *italic* print.

net stress engagement 231
net vulnerability level 230
The New Negro 41
The New York Times 136
The Next Generation (Ogbu) xxviii
NFI (normed fit index) 383
NHS (Navajo High School) 434,
452, 461
Nigrescence framework (Cross) 21,
50, 223, 228–9, 232, 259
"The Nine Lives People's Book" *see*
*Persistent People's Cultural
Enclaves in Perspective* (Castile
and Kushner)
Noddings, N. 504
normed fit index (NFI) 383

Oakland, California: academic
success and group membership
103; coping with social sanctions
or peer pressures 103–7;
ethnographic research 77;
methodological research
approaches 67, 68; peer pressures
in 19, 54, 55, 58, 102–7; school
engagement and peer pressures
102–3; site of study, reasons for
78; size of city 112–13; *see also*
Howard community, Oakland
Obama, Barack xv, xix
observations, searching for concepts
to capture 8
OCF (oppositional cultural
framework) 349, 352, 354, 358,
363, 366, 368
O'Connor, Carla xvi
Ogbu, Ada (John's wife) xviii, xix,
xx, xxvii–xxx
Ogbu, John xxii, xxi; as
anthropologist 313; caring theory
503–4; on community forces *see*
community forces; critics xix,
577–90; on cultural inversion *see*
inversion; cultural-ecological
model *see* cultural-ecological
model of collective identity
(Ogbu); death of xviii, xxvii, 137,
223; and Fordham xvii, 130–9;
health problems xvii–xviii;
minority hypothesis, voluntary and
involuntary 503–5; on Navajo
community 472; oppositional

identity model 388; publications
by xviii, xxviii; tragedy of career
xvi; university education 7; *see
also* Fordham-Ogbu thesis
Ogbu, Marcellina Ada *see* Ogbu, Ada
(John's wife)
Olneck, Michael 248
oppositional collective identity xxiv;
Black community, contemporary
45–56; dialect frames 48–9; frames
of reference, oppositional 47–8;
"White" culture, interpretations of
adoption of 48–9; *see also*
oppositional identity, African
American males
oppositional cultural framework
(OCF) 349, 352, 354, 358, 363,
366, 368
oppositional culture theory: attitude-
behavior inconsistency, myth
303–5; believing Blacks' reports
303–7; Blacks' attitudes, problems
with 305–7; Blacks' reports 300–7;
confirming 298–309; and cultural-
ecological model 29; dismissal of
Blacks' reports 301–3; individual
vs. group opportunities,
perceptions 307; quantitative
studies *see* quantitative studies,
oppositional culture; school racial
context, effects on culture 322;
student reports, peer-group
oppositional culture 325–6
oppositional identity, African
American males 374–91; academic
achievement and oppositional
identity 389; alternatives to
oppositional identity 376;
assessing oppositional identity
377–8; cultural-ecological model
of collective identity (Ogbu) 375;
instruments 379–81; limitations,
implications and future studies
390–1; research methodology
378–81; Socio-Economic Status
381, 386, 389–90; variability in
identity 376–7; *see also*
oppositional identity, African
American/Latino students
oppositional identity, African
American/Latino students:
attitudes towards school 487;